Georges van Vrekhem is a Flemish speaking Belgian. He became quite well-known in his country as a poet and playwright. For some time he was the artistic manager of a professional theatre company, "Het Nederlands Toneel" at Gent.

He was first acquainted with the works of Sri Aurobindo and the Mother in 1964. In 1970 he joined the Sri Aurobindo Ashram in Pondicherry and in 1978 he became a member of Auroville, which he has made his home since. He has translated several books of Sri Aurobindo, the Mother and Satprem, as well as selected writings from the Ramayana and the Mahabharata into Dutch.

After a thirty-year study of the source material, some of which has never been presented before as a whole by other authors, he has worked for six years on this impressive book. *Beyond Man* was published in the Netherlands in 1995, where it was widely and unanimously acclaimed. The English version, published in India in 1997, was hailed by specialists as a standard text and a fount of information on the life and work of Sri Aurobindo and the Mother, ranking with the best that have been written on them. The American and Russian editions of *Beyond Man* were published during the summer of 1998. The French and German translations are under preparation.

PRAISE FOR *BEYOND MAN*

The book is so informative and thought-provoking that its length feels rather like a bonus than an ordeal ... The inclusion of interesting historical, philosophical and spiritual vistas drawn from other sources has resulted in a richly embroidered tapestry as a background to the exceptional life of the Two-in-One, 'the double-poled Avatar of the Supermind' as Van Vrekhem calls Sri Aurobindo and the Mother ... *Beyond Man* is a standard text and a fount of information on the life and work of Sri Aurobindo and the Mother.
— Carel Thieme, *Mother India*

I think this is one of the best books on the subject. It is simply written and the author's command over the source material is admirable. I don't think that anybody else has used the vast body of source material as effectively as he has.
— M.V. Nadkarni, Secunderabad

I think your book ranks with the best books .... written on Sri Aurobindo and the Mother.
— K. .... disciple, ... he author

It is an impressive account, written with great profundity, erudition and knowledge of the hard to describe life and work of Sri Aurobindo and the Mother ... The person who is looking for a penetrating knowledge of the life of both of them cannot do without this standard work.

— Jenno Sijtsma, *De Zwolse Courant*

A better or more fitting tribute than this book to the Master's life and thought can scarcely be found. It contains an astonishing volume of information and analysis interwoven into the gripping narrative ... [The book] is likely to be an authoritative source of reference and interpretation in the growing international family of the followers and admirers of Sri Aurobindo, and in the wider reading public ... What makes the book special is that it manages to speak to both the general and the specialist reader. This, especially with a subject like Sri Aurobindo and the Mother, is extremely difficult, if not impossible to accomplish. Van Vrekhem's book, however, can be read as a basic exposition of the yoga of Sri Aurobindo and the Mother; it can also be read by initiates as a sophisticated and revealing account on topics hitherto little discussed or known.

— Makarand Paranjape, *Biblio*

This book is a fitting ode to one of the greatest spiritual thinkers of our times. What makes it extremely valuable is the fact that it assembles documents which have never been presented before as a whole by other authors.

— 'Short takes', *Sunday*

This book has gripped and deeply moved me from the first to the last page ... Van Vrekhem is a first-class writer. He tries in ordinary language to bring a complex whole of experiences within the reach of the reader. He has fully succeeded in this effort ... 'Beyond Man' is an important, encouraging book which stimulates and activates the reader ...

— Lambert de Kwant, *Tattwa Bulletin*

Van Vrekhem has tried in 'human language' to bring a very complex whole of experiences within the reader's reach. Besides, the book is based on documents never before presented as a whole by others and shows the history of this century in a new light ... Van Vrekhem makes a very interesting effort to formulate an occult process in words, also because he does not recoil from interpreting developments in recent history and discoveries in the field of quantum mechanics, significative of great changes on the Earth ... This is, for those interested, an extremely remarkable and dauntless book, in which the author succeeds in formulating experiments and ideas with relation to the present human evolution.

— Simon Vinkenoog, *Bres*

A splendid book, richly documented and beautifully presented.

— Marcel Messing, *Prana*

Beyond Man

Life and Work of Sri Aurobindo and the Mother

GEORGES VAN VREKHEM

Rupa & Co

First published in Dutch in 1995 by
Stichting Aurofonds

Published 2007 by
Rupa & Co
7/16, Ansari Road, Daryaganj,
New Delhi 110 002

Sales Centres:

Allahabad Bangalore Chandigarh
Chennai Hyderabad Jaipur Kathmandu
Kolkata Mumbai Pune

Typeset by
Nikita Overseas Pvt Ltd
1410 Chiranjiv Tower,
43 Nehru Place
New Delhi 110 019

Printed in India by
Gopsons Papers Ltd.
A-14 Sector 60
Noida 201 301

For Sudha

The author wishes to thank the Dutch Foundations 'Aurofonds' and 'De Zaaier' and the American 'Foundation for World Education' for their financial and moral support towards the preparation and writing of this book. He also thanks Mr Carel Thieme, who has helped him throughout and who has been instrumental in the publication of this book.

CONTENTS

Part Three:
THE MOTHER ALONE

The changes we see in the world today are intellectual, moral, physical in their ideal and intention: the spiritual revolution waits for its hour and throws up meanwhile its waves here and there. Until it comes the sense of the others cannot be understood and till then all interpretations of present happenings and forecast of man's future are vain things. For its nature, power, event are that which will determine the next cycle of our humanity.

—Sri Aurobindo

Sri Aurobindo has come to announce to the world the beauty of the future that will be realised. He has come to bring not a hope but the certainty of the splendour towards which the world is moving. The world is not an unfortunate accident: it is a miracle moving towards its expression.

—The Mother

PROLOGUE

History very seldom records the things that were decisive but took place behind the veil; it records the show in front of the curtain.[1]*

—Sri Aurobindo

IT LOOKED as if the advance of the German armies was unstoppable in those days of August 1914, and the fate of Paris and the whole of France seemed sealed. The Germans had followed the von Schlieffen Plan to the letter and with spectacular success. Their right flank, fast advancing parallel to the Channel coast, still had to march in a southerly direction for a couple of days and then turn left to encircle what remained of the apparently defeated French and British troops. They would then march triumphantly into Paris, the capital and symbol of Western civilization. The French government had fled to Bordeaux under cover of darkness. The weak Paris garrison, commanded by General Joseph Galliéni, expected that it would be exterminated along with the city.

It was then that Madame Richard, née Mirra Alfassa, thirty-six years of age, was sitting in meditation near the window of a house in Dupleix Street in Pondicherry, a small French port with some surrounding territory on the Coromandel coast in South India. The Parisian Madame Richard, was an accomplished occultist and advanced in spirituality. She had accompanied her second husband, Paul

---

* The numbers in superscript refer to the list of references at the back of this book.

Richard, to Pondicherry in order to meet Aurobindo Ghose, the revolutionary extremist politician from Bengal, who had sought refuge in that sleepy French town to escape the grip of the British and work out his still more revolutionary yoga. Their meetings had been up to Mirra's highest expectations and she now sat near that window with a view of the house where Aurobindo Ghose resided.

All at once, immersed in deep concentration but with her eyes open, she saw Kali, the naked, black goddess of battle and destruction, wearing a garland of skulls around her neck, entering the room through the door. 'She executed her dance, a really wild dance. And she said to me: "Paris is taken! Paris will be destroyed!" We had no news at all [about the war situation] ... I was in meditation. I turned towards her and said: "No, Paris will not be taken, Paris will be saved," quietly, without raising my voice, but with a certain emphasis.'[2] That was how Mirra Alfassa told the incident to the children of the Ashram many years later, when everybody called her the Mother.

The extreme German right wing was under the command of General von Kluck, the very model of the Prussian military man. So thoroughly convinced was he of a debacle in the enemy ranks, that he deemed it unnecessary to follow von Schlieffen's strategic plan any longer. Instead of marching on towards the south and then moving left, straight towards Paris, he intended to execute the left turn at once in order to cut off the withdrawing, exhausted enemy, and to deal with Paris afterwards. German headquarters, informed too late about von Kluck's intentions, approved of the plan — a blunder which would cost the Germans victory and eventually the war, as vividly narrated in Barbara Tuchman's book, *The Guns of August*. What nobody had thought possible happened: the physical and moral resources of the French were still sufficient to reorganize their battered armies; for once the British cooperated with them readily; and the garrison of Paris, reinforced in the meantime, attacked the Germans in their virtually unprotected right flank. The situation developed into the Battle of the Marne and the war of the quick marches became a war of the trenches. Paris was not taken, Paris was saved.

Another crucial historical event. In May 1940, the Germans, this time led by their Führer, Adolf Hitler, again looked unstoppable. Their tanks rumbled through the low countries and through the Ardennes towards the French Channel ports. By this manoeuvre they would, again, try to cut off the withdrawing French forces and the British Expeditionary Force. The Blitzkrieg would then be over in less than no time, and Hitler would reign as the supreme lord and master of the greatest part of Europe and maybe of the world.

However, 'That evening [of 24 May] four Panzer divisions were stopped at the Aa Canal. The tank crews were astounded. No fire was coming from the opposite shore! Beyond, they could make out the peaceful spires of Dunkirk. Had Operations gone crazy? The division commanders were even more amazed. They knew they could take Dunkirk with little trouble since the British were still heavily engaged near Lille. Why weren't they allowed to seize the last escape route to England?'[3] Thus writes John Toland in his standard biography of Adolf Hitler. The hesitation would eventually cost the Germans dearly: it would cost them the war. Goering had requested from Hitler the honour and the pleasure of being allowed to smash with his Luftwaffe the enemy troops, densely and helplessly packed on the beaches of Dunkirk; for reasons as yet incomprehensible, Hitler had given his consent. 'But fog came to the rescue of the British. Not only was Dunkirk itself enshrouded but all the Luftwaffe fields were blanketed by low clouds which grounded their three thousand bombers.'[4] In the meantime an unbelievable ragtag fleet of about 900 ships and boats of all shapes and sizes carried 338,226 British and Allied troops across the Channel between 24 May and 4 June. 'Oddly, the continuing evacuation did not seem to perturb Hitler,' remarks Toland, and his prey had escaped before he realized what was going on.

In Pondicherry, Aurobindo Ghose, now called Sri Aurobindo, sat in the company of a few disciples for their daily conversation in his apartment, which he had not left since 1926. He had already pointed to the fact that the surrender of Belgium meant that the harbours of Dunkirk and Calais would fall to the Germans. 'There is no hope for them [the Allies] unless Dunkirk can hold on or if they can rush through a gap in the French line.'⁵ Remarkable strategic insight from a yogi who lived in apparent retirement but followed the war step by step with utmost attention. Nirodbaran noted down in his *Talks With Sri Aurobindo* what Sri Aurobindo had said on the evening of 31 May: 'So, they are getting away from Dunkirk!' A disciple had answered: 'Yes. It seems the fog helped the evacuation.' To which Sri Aurobindo had added: 'Yes. Fog is rather unusual at this time.' And Nirodbaran comments: 'By saying this, it seemed Sri Aurobindo wanted to hint that the Mother and he had made this fog to help the Allies.'⁶ The war events are discussed in the conversations throughout the book, and Sri Aurobindo twice confirms explicitly that Great Britain and her allies were saved 'by divine intervention'. Afterwards he wrote in a letter (about himself although in the third person): 'In his retirement Sri Aurobindo kept a close watch on all that was happening in the world and in India and actively intervened whenever necessary, but solely with a spiritual force and silent spiritual action ... Inwardly, he put his spiritual force behind the Allies from the moment of Dunkirk when everybody was expecting the immediate fall of England and the definite triumph of Hitler, and he had the satisfaction of seeing the rush of German victory almost immediately arrested and the tide of war begin to turn in the opposite direction.'⁷

These are but two of the many times Sri Aurobindo and the Mother intervened in the history of the twentieth century, as related by themselves and as documented in the literature which they have left behind. Never did they flaunt these actions; they mentioned their interventions most of the time casually in confidential conversations that were made public long afterwards. Putting all the facts together, one gets the impression that the historical unfolding of the twentieth century happened, as it were, in interaction with their spiritual endeavour. While this may sound nonsensical or grossly exaggerated, there can be no doubt about the consistency and the sincerity of their sayings.

There is a vast and rich literature in connection with this subject. The collected works of Sri Aurobindo comprise more than thirty volumes, many of them quite substantial; up to now, eighteen volumes of the collected works of the Mother have been published, consisting for the most part of tape-recorded conversations afterwards written out and approved by her; the *Agenda* containing her conversations with Satprem is published in thirteen volumes; there is also their correspondence, countless conversations noted down by Nirodbaran Talukdar, A.B. Purani and others; and also reminiscences, collections of anecdotes, newly discovered and deciphered texts published by the Archives of the Sri Aurobindo Ashram, material in the commentaries of diverse authors, and so on. It is probably the most extensive literature available in connection with any spiritual personality.

The Life Divine, Sri Aurobindo's philosophical magnum opus, was praised by Aldous Huxley and his epic poems *Savitri* and *Ilion* by Herbert Read. The latter wrote: 'Sri Aurobindo's *Ilion* is a remarkable achievement by any standard and I am full of amazement that someone not of English origin should have such a wonderful command not only of our English language as such, but of its skillful elaboration in poetic diction of such high quality.'[8] Golconde, a guest house for visitors of the Ashram, planned by the Mother in the Thirties and built under her direct supervision, was lauded by the great architect Charles Correa as 'the finest example of modern functional architecture built in India in the pre-Independence period.'[9] The Swedish academy was examining Sri Aurobindo's candidature for the Nobel Prize for literature in 1950, the year he expired; his nomination had been seconded by Gabriela Mistral* and Pearl S. Buck. In December 1972 *Newsweek* magazine published in its international edition an article on the Mother under the heading, *The Next Great Religion?*

Yet, Sri Aurobindo and the Mother are but little known and if

---

* Gabriela Mistral wrote of Sri Aurobindo: 'Six foreign languages have given the Master of Pondicherry a gift of co-ordination, a clarity free from gaudiness, and a charm that borders on the magical ... These are indeed 'glad tidings' that come to us: to know that there is a place in the world where culture has reached its tone of dignity by uniting in one man a supernatural life with a consummate literary style, thus making use of his beautifully austere and classical prose to serve as the handmaid of the spirit.' (Quoted in D.K. Roy, *Sri Aurobindo Came to Me*.)

known, usually misunderstood. Upon what did they base their claims of their occult influence on the historical processes which have carried the world to the threshold of a new millennium? What was the deeper meaning of the collaboration between a freedom fighter and yogi from Bengal and a Parisian occultist, who had been living in the city of her birth for ten years among the impressionist and post-impressionist crowd of writers, painters and sculptors? If so much of their literary, philosophical and practical accomplishments have been appreciated by knowlegeable persons, could it be that what they considered their real Work was nothing but a delusion?

I have based this book on all available documents; these documents had, for various reasons, not yet been treated as a whole by previous authors. The truthfulness of the authentic writings, conversations and sayings of Sri Aurobindo and the Mother is not in question. The result of the convergence of these documents is important to all of us and may provide some insight into the things that were decisive but took place behind the veil. It is an insight that will enable us to comprehend the present planetary crisis and to cast a glance into the next century, into the new millennium.

Avatar

Is there a possible foundation for the presumption that the history of our planet, during one of its most dramatic crises or whenever, has taken place 'in interaction' with one or two individuals? The rashly judging rationalist will at once dismiss the question as utter nonsense, but the age-old wisdom of Hinduism, that huge body of knowledge, answers it in the affirmative. In its vision of the world the figure of the Avatar plays a central role known to all Hindus and accepted by them as a matter of course. Day after day, somewhere in India, there will be some graceful, thoroughly trained Bharatnatyam dancer performing the tale of the 'Ten Avatars', a tale familiar to the people in her audience since their childhood.

The ten Avatars are: the Fish, the Tortoise, the Boar, the Man-Lion, the Dwarf, Parasurama alias Rama-with-the-axe, Rama (with the bow), Krishna, the Buddha and finally Kalki, who according to tradition is still to come. The succession, even at first sight, shows a continuity. 'The Hindu procession of the ten Avatars is itself, as it were, a parable of evolution,' writes Sri Aurobindo, 'the progression is striking and unmistakable.'[10]

The fish was the first vertebrate in the womb of the ocean. Then comes the tortoise, an amphibian, then the boar, a mammal. The man-lion represents the transitional beings between animal and man. Then follows *homo faber* as Rama-with-the-axe, followed by Rama-with-the-bow, i.e., *homo sapiens,* the species we all belong to and which is now present in great numbers on this planet. In mentally conscious humanity an opening is possible toward the supramental realms thanks to Krishna, and the nirvanic state can be consciously attained by following the path of the Buddha. Kalki, finally, will bring about the great revolution which will result in the superhuman and the Kingdom of God no longer in an ethereal, hypothetical hereafter, but on a transformed Earth. Thus will come about the realization of the dream cherished since its origin by the toiling, suffering, unsatisfied human species.

The evolutionary line represented by the Avatars is no doubt remarkable considering that the Hindu tradition is thousands of years old while *The Origin of Species* was not published until 1859. The Avatar is clearly connected with evolution and even seems to play a central role in it.

The word 'avatar' means 'descent' in Sanskrit. 'It is a coming down of the Divine below the line which divides the divine from the human world or status.'[11] In other words, the Avatar is an embodiment of the Divine in a materialized living form, a direct divine incarnation on earth.

It becomes clear at once that the avatar concept is actually well-known in the West, for Jesus Christ was an avatar according to this definition. This is why the theological disputation concerning his avatarhood or the preponderance of either his divine or his human nature has its parallels in the literature of the Hindus. And this is why Sri Aurobindo, in his *Essays on the Gita*, mentions time and again the names of Christ, Krishna and the Buddha in the chapters about avatarhood.

However, while the East recognizes the full evolutionary line of the ten (and in certain enumerations more) Avatars, the Christianized West recognizes only one. The importance of the Christ-avatar is generally accepted, but the evolutionary and historical development of the Earth and of mankind is put into a warped perspective by affirming him as the one and only avatar, a belief which makes the mission of Christ appear arbitrary and unreal. The cause of this attitude was probably the religious and cultural 'monadism' of the West — the unconscious or sometimes very conscious egocentric attitude, the imperialistic hedgehog position, the psychological igloo.

The following story is culled from old Indian texts.

There is the One that IS. That is everything and that still would be wholly itself without all that exists. And next to that One there is nothing, because it is everything.

That One has names in all languages, but no name can define it. It is That. It is That that IS. Without bounds, without flaws, without suffering, without needs. Therefore the wise say that the One is not only Being and Consciousness but also Joy, absolute Bliss.

And it beholds itself, it sees itself. And what it sees in itself, exists. For its Consciousness is absolute and instantly effective power — Omnipotence.

This means that the endless joy of its self-seeing, of its self-scanning, is at the same time an endless creation, a formation of what was, is, and will be, potentially present in the One in all eternity.

Out of the creative joy of its self-seeing grew the spectrum of the worlds, each one different from the others, the work of an artist with an inexhaustible power of self-discovery and intense creativity.

One of this multitude of worlds is ours, an evolutionary world. In our world the One of Light has created Night; the absolute Consciousness has donned the cloak of the darkest Unconsciousness to hide from itself and so to create the possibility of experiencing the joy of self-rediscovery.

It is a long and arduous journey, this rediscovery, this quest of the Self for itself in us. But the darker the Night, the more ecstatic will be the Dawn when the Light breaks through again. The journey back home takes place step by patient, time-consuming step: out of the Inconscient evolved Matter, out of Matter evolved Life and out of Life evolved Mental Consciousness — everything in accordance with the design which the One had self-seen and by seeing established for our evolutionary world.

But Man, the being which is the embodiment of mental consciousness, is still far from the rediscovery by the One of itself in him — just as, looking back, he is already far off from the darkness of total Inconscience. The transitional being, which is Man, finds himself somewhere in between these two extremes, stretched out like on a cross.

Man carries all that has grown in the past in himself. He consists of matter, and of life, and of mental consciousness by which he looks back to yesterday and ahead to tomorrow, and by which he sees himself in the act of doing things. And he contains in himself a particle of the One, a spark of the light, which is his inmost self, his soul.

The grand design as seen by the One forbids that beings of a certain order in the evolving hierarchy should reach out beyond their boundaries. A fish cannot wander about on dry land of its own volition, a primate cannot ponder the writing of a letter. For a change of that magnitude the One has to accord its fiat by intervening itself in its creation (which is a self-manifestation) and, lest there be chaos, by building the necessary steps for every new range of evolution. Such is the law it has preordained for this, our universe.

That is why at the moment of each great transition, the One, time and again, has to descend and do its work, a task exceeding the possibilities of evolutionary beings. Time and again, at the crucial moments of evolution, the One has to incarnate itself on Earth as an Avatar.

Divine omnipotence has no limitations. That is the very reason why it can limit itself, which is a miracle of omnipotence. The worlds manifested by it have some built-in processes to support their structures. As Sri Aurobindo wrote in this connection: 'All is possible, but all is not licit — except by a recognizable process ...'[12] Certain conditions have been established for the game',[13] for the Cosmic play, the *Lila* of the Divine manifestation.

In the 'game' or process by which our universe is functioning the Avatar plays the leading role. He appears on the cosmic stage to intervene in periods of transition, at times of crisis when a new, higher rung is being inserted into the ladder of evolution. Every such crisis is part of the Great Design; it indicates that at these moments cosmic evolution is ripe for a new phase of its unfolding. The manifestation, its crises included, expresses only what exists within the One, within the Divine, in all eternity.

'The Avatar is one who comes to open the Way for humanity to a higher consciousness'[14] (Sri Aurobindo) — in the evolutionary stage of the Earth in which humankind has been present, that is, for previously Avatars have also helped in creating higher forms of animal life, as may be concluded from the procession of the Avatars. In order to work out a new evolutionary phase the Avatar has to take into himself and assimilate everything that has been worked out before; it is by this act of concrete and factual representation that he acquires his true evolutionary meaning and function. 'He who would save the world must be one with the world.'[15]

According to Sri Aurobindo and the Mother, the human being is not the highest being on Earth, the lord of creation, 'the masterpiece of masterpieces'. Not so very long ago, an assertion of this kind might have led to the pyre, but in this century of science fiction, mutants and extra terrestrials it sounds almost like commonsense. Moreover, isn't man much too imperfect to be considered God's masterpiece? As the Dutch poet Gerbrand A. Bredero said, we only have 'to take a look inside ourselves'. Shouldn't God be capable of something better?

But then, who or what might succeed man on this planet? Who or what might reap the fruits of his labour, of his suffering and misery throughout the centuries? A robot free from fault or failure? A Nietzschean superman? Sri Aurobindo and the Mother propose a different answer, surprising and apparently impossible. But they had come to make that impossibility possible, as Avatars.

Who would expect an Avatar now, at this point in time? Hasn't everything of spiritual or essential importance happened, once and for all, in times past? But then times past also once were times present.

'I have said, "Follow my path, the way I have discovered for you through my own efforts and example. Transform your nature from the animal to the spiritual, grow into a higher divine consciousness. All this you can do by your own aspiration aided by the force of the Divine Shakti." That, if you please, is not the utterance of a madman or an imbecile. I have said, "I have opened the way; now you with the Divine help can follow it." '[16] These are the words of Sri Aurobindo, addressed to a disciple who is still alive at the time this book is being written. And in the same correspondence Sri Aurobindo speaks about 'the Path I have opened, as Christ, Krishna, Buddha, Chaitanya, etc., opened theirs.'[17]

The task of the Avatar cannot be executed by ordinary earthly beings; that is why the Divine has to come to do the job Himself. Such a mission would be meaningless if the Avatar, to show the way or the Path did not take upon himself the burden of man, helplessly stretched between the two extremes of their possibilities. 'Anyone who wants to change earth-nature must first accept it in order to change it,'[18] unconditionally and fully, making the evolution meaningful by his acceptance. But man does not know that, for he does not perceive it. It is too lofty for him and his brain cannot reach there. The animal still stirs in him and slashes the helping, uplifting hand. Gethsemane and Golgotha are the rewards of the Avatar.

> God must be born on earth and be as man
> That man being human may grow even as God.[19]
>
> —*Savitri*

If Sri Aurobindo and the Mother were Avatars, what were their Gethsemane and Golgotha?

Part One

Aurobindo Ghose
and Mirra Alfassa

Chapter One

A PERFECT GENTLEMAN

SRI AUROBINDO wrote to one of his first biographers: 'I see you have persisted in giving a biography — is it really necessary or useful? The attempt is bound to be a failure, because neither you nor anyone else knows anything at all of my life; it has not been on the surface for men to see.'[1]

It is not the intention to include in this book an extensive biography of Sri Aurobindo and the Mother, not even a concise one, but it seems indispensable to narrate some of the principal facts and events in their lives, for otherwise much of our story of their work might be difficult to follow. Besides, a brief glimpse of their lives will provide readers who have no idea of who they were with some points of reference.

Aurobindo Akroyd Ghose, the third son of a medical doctor, Kristo Dhan Ghose, was born in Calcutta on 15 August 1872. (Afterwards the family would be expanded by a girl and another boy.) His father, 'a thoroughly anglicized Bengali,' demanded that English be exclusively spoken in his house and not a word in Bengali, the local Indian language. Consequently, Aurobindo grew up speaking English as his mother tongue.

Let us glance back at that period for a moment. A considerable part of India, 'the jewel in the crown,' was a British colony ruled with gusto by the subjects of Her Majesty, Queen Victoria. They were the masters not only of the territories they had conquered, but indirectly also of the 635 kingdoms, big and small, ruled by colourful rajahs and maharajahs. The latter, absolute despots, could act out to their heart's content their sometimes enlightened but often obscure fancies and desires as long as they did not displease the British authorities. A relatively small British Army, and especially a well-trained body of able functionaries, kept the colony under their thumb. After the revolt of 1857 the Indian populace had accepted the situation practically without exception, continuing their traditional way of living under the watchful eye of the haughty white masters.

Dr K.D. Ghose had done his medical studies in England; he was 'a terrible atheist' and a fervent admirer of all things British. It was his ambition that his children would become the best of the best, 'beacons to the world'. Only one career would do for them, the Indian Civil Service (ICS), that exemplary body of colonial civil servants, accessible to Indians too on condition of their passing an entrance examination. This was only practicable for those who had been studying in Great Britain. And so it came to pass, in 1879, that Dr Ghose took his three eldest sons to Manchester, then the most populous city in the United Kingdom. The boys were put into the care of the Reverend William H. Drewett, with the explicit order that they must be kept away from anything or anybody even remotely connected with India. 'Aurobindo spent his formative years totally cut off from the culture of his birth,'[2] writes his biographer Peter Heehs.

Drewett and his wife personally looked after Aurobindo's education. He seemed to have a gift for languages. He absorbed English automatically from his environment and made remarkable progress in Latin. Recently his first published poem, *Light*, has been found; it was written inspired by Shelley's *The Cloud*, and published in a local magazine when he was ten years old.

He was so advanced in Latin that he was allowed to skip the first class at St Paul's secondary school in London. Along with the normal curriculum, by following which he made rapid progress in Latin, Greek and French, he also taught himself Italian, German and Spanish to read Dante, Goethe and Cervantes in the original. As to English literature, he showed much interest in the Elizabethan theatre and for the great romantic poetry, particularly that of Keats, Shelley and Byron. He was also fascinated by Jeanne d'Arc, Mazzini and other heroes from history who had fought for the liberation of their motherland. As later told by him, he felt the urge to work for the freedom of India already at that time.

Aurobindo passed the entrance examination for the ICS brilliantly, his marks for Latin and Greek being the highest ever. To become a member of the ICS he now had to study for two years at a university. This was a well-nigh insurmountable problem, for his father could no longer send any money and Aurobindo and his brothers were living in poverty. Their daily sustenance consisted of 'a slice or two of sandwich bread and butter and a cup of tea in the morning and in the evening a penny saveloy [sausage]',[3] and there was no money to buy new clothes. Aurobindo decided to try and obtain a scholarship offered by King's College of Cambridge University. He sat for the examination in December 1889 and came out first. Oscar Browning, then a renowned linguist and writer, confided later to Aurobindo that his papers for Greek and Latin had been the best submitted to him as an examiner in thirteen years.

In his recently published *Sri Aurobindo: A Brief Biography*, Peter Heehs writes: 'King's College, founded in 1441, is among the older foundations of Cambridge University. As a classical scholar, Aurobindo was participating in an educational system whose traditions went back to the Renaissance. To master Greek and Latin, to read Homer and Sophocles, Virgil and Horace, to absorb the culture of classical Greece and Rome — these were considered the proper training of an English gentleman. And what one learned in the classroom and lecture hall was only a part, and not the most important part, of the Cambridge experience. The university's atmosphere took hold of those who entered it and wrought a comprehensive change.'[4]

Aurobindo Ghose became an exceptional classical scholar and was soon also generally known as a master of the English language. An Englishman in later years travelling in India asked: 'Do you know where Ghose is now, the classical scholar of Cambridge, who has come away to India to waste his future?'[5] All his life, Sri Aurobindo would refer back to the knowledge he had acquired during his youth. At the end, when his eyes had become too weak to continue writing himself, he dictated a series of articles to Nirodbaran. 'As he was dictating,' remembers Nirodbaran, 'I marvelled at so much knowledge of Ancient Greece and Ancient India stored up somewhere in his superconscious memory and now pouring down at his command in a smooth flow. No notes were consulted, no books were needed, yet after a lapse of so many decades everything was fresh, spontaneous and recalled in vivid detail!'[6]

Sri Aurobindo's unfinished epic, *Ilion*, about the last day of the siege of Troy, is a monument of classical knowledge. There is his drama, *Perseus the Deliverer*. There is *Heraclitus*, an essay on the pre-Socratic philosopher, which reads fluently even after seventy years and would still be accorded a place of honour in any philosophical publication. There is his essay on quantitative hexametres in the English language, his book, *The Future Poetry*, still undiscovered by the contemporary poets and theorists of poetry, and his writings on 'overhead poetry' — on the 'overmental' poetical sources. There is his abundant correspondence about poetry with his disciples — for it looked as if he had made his Ashram into a breeding-ground of poets. There are his poems such as *Rose of God, A God's Labour* and *Musa Spiritus*, belonging to the highest range of mystical poetry. And above all there is his epic, *Savitri*. All this would, by itself, suffice to justify the efforts of a lifetime — a lifetime of a scholar in the Western classical languages and of a poet in the English language.

But Aurobindo Ghose did not become an ICS officer. The call to serve his mother country had grown more insistent, and he had developed an aversion of colonial officialdom however highly esteemed. Ranked among the best in his class, he would have had no difficulty in bringing his training to a satisfactory end — he had won the awards for classical poetry at the end of each academic year — but he failed because he did not show up for the decisive horse riding test. I say, a gentleman should be able to ride on horseback! But the nearest connection Aurobindo ever had with sports was his (non-playing) membership of the cricket club at Baroda* — and at the first

---

* When practising his yoga, he would subject his body to an incredibly harsh discipline.

riding test for the ICS he had fallen from the horse. Nevertheless,
he was called three more times to prove he was an able horseman,
but he preferred to roam about in the streets of London instead.
Those who knew him thought his eventual rejection of the ICS a
scandalous waste. But the Maharajah of Baroda, Sayaji Gaekwad, was
in luck; he found himself in London precisely at that moment and
so got the chance to hire a young man with the capabilities of
Aurobindo Ghose, an ICS trainee, for 200 rupees per month.

Swami Vivekananda, the great disciple of Ramakrishna
Paramahansa, travelled to the West in 1893; in the beginning of the
same year, Aurobindo Ghose sailed on the *SS Carthage* back to his
motherland after an absence of thirteen years. His father had expected him on the *SS Roumania* and died of grief after being told
that this ship had perished in a storm before the coast of Portugal.
Two days after his arrival on Indian soil, at the Apollo Bunder in
Bombay, Aurobindo had to report for service in Baroda.

Chapter Two

THE MOST DANGEROUS MAN
IN INDIA

*My life has been a battle from its early
years and is still a battle.*[1]
— Sri Aurobindo

IN BARODA, Aurobindo was at first given the tasks of
a lowly functionary at the office of revenue stamps and other government agencies. After about a year, the Maharaja found a way to
make better use of Aurobindo's talents, appointing him as his unof-
ficial private secretary and calling him to the palace whenever an
important document had to be composed in English. Aurobindo also
began to teach part-time at the University of Baroda in 1897; a year
later he was nominated professor of English and lecturer of French.
He would eventually become vice-principal of the College. If such
had been his ambition, he would easily have been able to obtain a
top post in the state with all the honours, comforts and financial
benefits thereof; for the Maharaja continued to call for his services
as a private secretary, and it would not have been that difficult for
Aurobindo to influence the prince to his own advantage.

However, such possibilities did not interest Aurobindo in the least,
not even after his marriage in 1901 to the fourteen-year-old Mrinalini
Bose. After five years of marriage, he wrote to his father-in-law: 'I
am afraid I shall never be good for much in the way of domestic

virtues. I have tried, very ineffectively, to do some part of my duty as a son, a brother and a husband, but there is something too strong in me which forces me to subordinate everything else to it.'[2] This 'something' was Mother India.

'I entered into political action and continued it from 1903 to 1910 with one aim and one alone, to get into the mind of the people a settled will for freedom and the necessity of a struggle to achieve it in place of the futile ambling Congress methods till then in vogue,'[3] wrote Sri Aurobindo. The Congress, founded in 1885 on the initiative of an Englishman, was at that time still the sole political party. Aurobindo's aim meant no less than a complete reorientation of its political strivings — a daunting task for a young man who did not even speak his mother tongue.

Barely four months after his arrival in India he had already written a series of articles, in sonorous English of course, for the daily *Indu Prakash*, titled *New Lamps for Old*, in which he criticized the subservient attitude of the Congress towards the British rulers without mincing his words. These words sounded so bold that he was asked to tone them down. Aurobindo was not willing to do so and preferred to remain silent for the time being. Those articles are unmistakable proof of the early maturity of his political thought, of which the main elements must already have been present at the time he stepped ashore in Bombay.

When he entered politics, the idea of an independent India 'was regarded ... by the vast majority of Indians as unpractical and impossible, an almost insane chimera,'[4] wrote Sri Aurobindo later; and again in the third person he wrote about himself: 'He has always stood for India's complete independence which he was the first to advocate publicly and without compromise as the only ideal worthy of a self-respecting nation.'[5]

During his last years in Baroda, his political activity grew more and more intense. He met with like-minded people and sounded out the possibility of an openly waged freedom struggle. The collaboration with his younger brother, Barindrakumar or Barin for short, grew more frequent, and he used his holidays in Bengal for revolutionary purposes.

The partition of Bengal by Lord Curzon in 1905 caused general public indignation — an atmosphere conducive to the spread of the spirit of revolution. In Calcutta, the National University of Bengal was founded for students who had participated in political manifestations and who were for that reason expelled from the other educational institutions. Aurobindo accepted the invitation to be the first vice-principal of the new university, which opened its doors on 15 August 1906, his birthday. The Baroda interlude now belonged to the past.

An incredibly busy time started for Aurobindo, for he soon became one of the leaders of the nationalists, often called 'extremists', who strove single-mindedly for India's unconditional and total independence. Because of his contributions to the newly founded weekly *Bande Mataram* ('Hail the Mother', a title that was to become the rallying cry everywhere in the country), he had acquired the stature of a nationally known political personality. It was of *Bande Mataram* that S.K. Ratcliffe, Chief Editor of *The Statesman*, wrote that it was 'full of leading and special articles written in English with brilliance and pungency not hitherto attained in the Indian Press ... the most effective voice of what we then called nationalist extremism.'[6] That English flowed out of the pen of Aurobindo Ghose, who became after a short while himself the unnamed Chief Editor of the weekly.

He also supervised the ideological contents of another weekly, *Yugantar*. This was the organ of the youthful revolutionaries who clustered around Aurobindo's younger brother Barin; impatient, they preferred acting instead of talking and wanted to accelerate the realization of their holiest aim, the liberation of Mother India, through terrorism. They were naïve and inexperienced, committing one blunder after another, but they made the British nervous. Around this time Aurobindo fell seriously ill, though he still found time to write plays.

In 1907, he was prosecuted for the first time for 'activities against the state' and acquitted. He made no secret of his demand for unconditional independence, neither in his articles nor in his speeches at public or private meetings (teeming with police spies), but he always knew how to formulate his words without crossing the red line of illegality.

Within the Congress, he worked together with other extremists like Bal Gangadhar Tilak and Bipin Chandra Pal for the acceptance of a radical programme. It was tough going for the young idealists to take a stand against the established and highly respected political stalwarts, most of whom had had their share in the founding of the party. 'I used to practise what you may call voluntary self-effacement or self-denial, and I liked to keep myself behind,'⁷ said Sri Aurobindo many years later. He wrote about himself: 'He preferred to remain and act and even to lead from behind the scenes without his name being known in public.'⁸ But his prosecution in 1907 had ended his anonymity; no longer was he a hero only in Bengal, he had become a national celebrity.

Such was the situation in 1907 when the Bengal leaders of the Congress travelled in a chartered train to Surat, a town on the west coast of the Indian subcontinent. 'The whole thousand-mile route from Kharagpur to Surat was a triumphal journey of lights, crowds, and continued cheering,' wrote Barin, who had accompanied his brother. 'Aurobindo, the new idol of the nation, was hardly known then by his face, and at every small and big station a frantic crowd rushed about in the station platforms looking for him in the first and second class carriages, while all the time Aurobindo sat unobserved in a third class compartment.'⁹

It was in Surat that the Congress split into a conservative and an extremist wing. Historians had all along supposed that Tilak was responsible for the break-up, although he had time and again denied it himself. A letter of Sri Aurobindo's was published in 1954, written twenty years before, in which the truth finally surfaced: 'History very seldom registers the things that were decisive but took place behind the veil; it records the show in front of the curtain. Very few people know that it was I (without consulting Tilak) who gave the order that led to the breaking of the Congress ...'¹⁰

After the indescribable confusion on the day of the schism, Aurobindo presided over two meetings of the extremists in which all efforts at reconciliation were rejected. The Congress would be re-united only in 1917. It was Aurobindo's aim 'to imprint in the spirit of the people the will for freedom'. Because of his decisive interventions in Surat, this would henceforth be an integral part of the political programme, ultimately leading to India's independence.

Barin and his young terrorists committed one of their blunders when they killed two English ladies in Muzaffarpur with a primitive bomb destined for an English Magistrate. This time the British authorities retaliated mercilessly. At the top of their list was written the name of Aurobindo Ghose. He was arrested on 5 May 1908 and locked up in the prison of Alipore, a suburb of Calcutta, together with more than twenty other suspects, under the charge of 'waging war against the king,' the British-Indian equivalent of high treason. 'The Alipore Bomb Trial, as it became known, was "the first state trial of any magnitude in India."'[11] The judge was C.P. Beachcroft, ICS, a classmate of Aurobindo's at Cambridge. (In the entrance examination of their ICS class, Beachcroft had come second to Aurobindo in Greek; ironically, in the final examination, Beachcroft had done better than Aurobindo in Bengali.)

After some early experiences, Aurobindo's spiritual path had broadened considerably, and he paid but scant attention to the proceedings in the courtroom and the goings-on in jail. His inner voice had told him that he would be acquitted for lack of evidence and so it happened.

In his peroration, an inspired C.R. Das, Aurobindo's lawyer, had spoken the following words about his client: 'Long after this controversy is hushed in silence, long after this turmoil, this agitation ceases, long after he is dead and gone, he will be looked upon as the poet of patriotism, as the prophet of nationalism and the lover of humanity. Long after he is dead and gone his words will be echoed and re-echoed not only in India, but across distant seas and lands. Therefore I say that the man in his position is not only standing before the bar of this Court but before the bar of the High Court of History.'[12]

Aurobindo was free again, but he stood alone in a desolate political landscape. The other extremist leaders were in exile or doing long prison sentences, and the publication of their daily newspapers and weekly magazines had been forbidden. Barin and Ullaskar Dutt were condemned to death by hanging, but their sentence was later commuted to lifelong exile in the infamous prison of Port Blair, on the Andaman Islands, now a national monument. (Only in 1920 would Barin return to his motherland.)

In the course of the trial the British prosecution had already remarked that 'Aurobindo was treated with the reverence of a king wherever he had gone,' and that he 'in fact was considered not only as the leader of Bengal but of the whole country.' His fame had spread even more because of the Alipore Trial and the British authorities regretted that they had let him go scot-free once more. Letters of that time prove that the highest circles had examined the possibility of doing away once and for all with 'the famous Aurobindo.' The First Secretary of the Bengal government described him as 'the most dangerous of our adversaries now at large.' The same epithet was used by the Lieutenant-Governors of Bengal and Eastern Bengal and Assam, and afterwards by the Viceroy of India, who called him 'the most dangerous man we have to deal with at present.'[13]

In the beginning of 1910 Aurobindo was warned by Sister Nivedita, an English disciple of Swami Vivekananda, that the trap set for him could be sprung at any moment. It was time for him to leave the scene. As a farewell, he penned an article in which he expressed his ideals openly. This article, his political testament, he published in the *Karmayogin* — the weekly he had started after being acquitted and which after his departure was kept going for a while by the nationalistic activist, Sister Nivedita. His inner Voice gave him his 'marching orders'. 'When thou hast the command, care only to fulfil it,'[14] reads one of his aphorisms. Less than half an hour after the warning, he was on the Ganges in a rowing boat that took him to Chandernagore, a French enclave a few miles to the north of Calcutta. Then, after more than a month spent in absolute seclusion, he travelled, under the name of Jitendranath Mitra and in the company of a young revolutionary, on the *SS Dupleix* from Calcutta to Pondicherry. He arrived there on 4 April 1910 and was received and housed by the local freedom fighters.

The political period in Aurobindo Ghose's life had come to an end. The numerous articles and other writings he left behind are there to show that he was the first to discern and to define the essential objects of the freedom struggle: unconditional independence; the use of indigenous goods and materials; boycott of all things British; political disobedience of the colonial authority; a new educational system suitable to the Indian nature and character; and, perhaps of all his ideas to be later on the most distorted, non-violence as a political weapon.

As Sri Aurobindo has written about himself: 'The part Sri Aurobindo took publicly in Indian politics was of brief duration, for he turned aside from it in 1910 and withdrew to Pondicherry; much of his programme lapsed in his absence, but enough had been done to change the whole face of Indian politics and the whole spirit of the Indian people to make independence its aim and non-cooperation and resistance its method, and even an imperfect application of this policy heightening into sporadic periods of revolt has been sufficient to bring about the victory. The course of subsequent events followed largely the line of Sri Aurobindo's idea. The Congress was finally captured by the Nationalist Party, declared independence its aim, organised itself for action ... and eventually formed the first national, though not as yet independent, Government in India and secured from Britain acceptance of independence for India.'[15]

Each time *Doordarshan*, the Indian national television, reports the daily parliamentary proceedings in New Delhi, it shows first a picture of the parliament building, then a statue of Mahatma Gandhi, then a statue of Dr Ambedkar, a defender of the backward classes, and then a bust of Sri Aurobindo.

Chapter Three

A BACKDOOR TO SPIRITUALITY

THE INDIA in which he arrived from Great Britain must have looked like a cultural desert to Aurobindo Ghose. The literature of the regional languages was still in its infancy (except in Bengal) and the literary production in English was of poor quality. Far away now were the lush cultural pastures of Cambridge and London, where Aurobindo's eldest brother, the poet Manmohan, had befriended Laurence Binyon, Stephen Philips and Oscar Wilde, the last calling him 'an Indian panther in evening brown.' Small wonder that Aurobindo spent a substantial part of his salary on crates of English books ordered from Bombay and which, wherever he settled down, occupied the main part of his living space.

He learned several Indian languages: Gujarati, the local language in Baroda; Marathi, spoken in the Bombay Presidency; Hindi, a direct offspring of Sanskrit and then, as now, the main language of India except for the deep Dravidian South. He also learned Bengali, which should have been his mother tongue, as he began needing it for his political activities; before long, he would be able to write articles and deliver speeches in Bengali. And he learned Sanskrit, the language that gave him access to the *Mahabharata* and the *Ramayana*, to the plays of Kalidasa, to the *Upanishads* and the *Bhagavat Gita* — to the age-old wisdom of India and its *sanatana dharma*, the 'eternal religion'.

Up until then, Aurobindo had been an indifferent agnostic and he had not followed up on the few rationally inexplicable inner experiences he had known. Sanskrit literature, however, opened up for him unexpected vistas — and did the yogis not claim they possessed extraordinary powers? If the wise were indeed wise, would it not be worthwhile to take a closer look at what they had found so interesting? On one occasion he himself had witnessed how a wandering *sadhu* (monk) had cured his brother Barin's fever by muttering some words, drawing with a knife a crosswise figure in a glass of water and making his brother drink it. He had met the great yogi Swami Brahmananda of the Ganga Math in Chandod and he had been impressed. In England he had already been familiar with the writings of Ramakrishna Paramhamsa and Vivekananda. Maybe he would find in yoga some resource to help realize his political ideals? 'I wanted Yoga to help me in my political work, for inspiration and power and capacity. I didn't want to give up my activities for the sake of Yoga.'[1]

He dreamed the most daring dreams but he was at the same time an arch-realist and a headstrong, undaunted perseverer — something one would not have expected from this apparently reticent, formally polite and almost timid man. While still in Baroda, he took up *pranayama*, a yogic breathing technique; daily he devoted six hours of his time to it, but the only effect was an abundant flow of poetic inspiration, resulting among others in his long poem *Love and Death,* all of which was written in a very short time. But *pranayama* without expert guidance is dangerous, and when he stopped practising it in Calcutta, he nearly paid with his life.

Shortly after the Surat conference, Aurobindo went to Baroda to meet some of his former friends and acquaintances and to reconnoitre the political lay of the land. There he met, through Barin, the tantric yogi Vishnu Bhaskar Lele, and they withdrew to the attic of the house where Aurobindo was staying. Lele was astounded to see that Aurobindo obtained in three days one of the mightiest realizations yoga can give, the realization of the passive Brahman. '[Lele] said: "Sit still and try to make your mind quiet and empty of thoughts. You will see that all your thoughts come from outside. As you perceive them, simply throw them away before they can enter in you." I tried and did it. In three days my mind became entirely quiet and vacant, without any thoughts at all, and it was in that condition of Nirvanic Silence that I went first to Poona and then to Bombay. Everything seemed to me unreal, I was absorbed in the One Reality.'[2] This mental silence would never leave him anymore. In three days he had a realization attempted and not always obtained by great yogis in a lifetime. A certain predisposition must have lain dormant in him.

From then on, he only trusted the One Divine, present in the heart of all human beings; he surrendered himself to it unconditionally and in all things. This surrender would be the cornerstone of his yoga. The *Upanishads*, and in prison the *Bhagavad Gita*, became his guides and source of inspiration. Who could have imagined that this radical politician, considered a very dangerous man and so involved in that busy life of his, was continuously absorbed in inner concentration?

In Alipore jail, he had his second important realization — this time of the omnipresent Brahman, the One within whom everything exists, and of the cosmic consciousness. 'I looked at the jail that secluded me from man and it was no longer by its high walls that I was imprisoned; no, it was Vasudeva who surrounded me. I walked under the branches of the tree in front of my cell but it was not the tree, I knew it was Vasudeva, it was Sri Krishna whom I saw standing there and holding over me his shade. I looked at the bars of my cell, the very grating that did duty for a door, and again I saw Vasudeva.' Vasudeva is one of the many names of Sri Krishna, and Sri Krishna, the former Avatar, is a personification of the One Divine. 'I looked at the prisoners in the jail, the thieves, the murderers, the swindlers, and as I looked at them I saw Vasudeva ... I looked and it was not the Magistrate whom I saw, it was Vasudeva, it was Narayana who was sitting there on the bench.'[3]

Everyday reality had become a spiritual reality for him, wherever and whenever, whether he sat in concentration, ate, wrote, moved among the people, or gave a speech at a political meeting — something he had to do quite often as he had become the top leader of the extremists.

In Pondicherry, he was able to devote his full attention to his spiritual life. He had thought his withdrawal there — which he called his 'cave of tapasya' — would be of short duration, a couple of years at the most. But 'the two years extended to four, then ten, then twenty. Never during this period did he abandon his intention of returning to the field of action; but his idea of the relation between action and yoga underwent a fundamental change.'⁴ He had taken up yoga to find power and support for his political action. Gradually, by following with sincere surrender the unknown and the novel path that was being shown to him, step by step, he had acquired cosmic consciousness. His quest would lead him to 'the one thing needful,' namely That, the One. Once That is found, all is found, the whole cosmos and more — for That holds the cosmos in the palm of its hand, with all that the cosmos contains, also this Earth, also India and everything India stands for, including at that time her political liberation. The road of his exploration had widened steadfastly, 'for the country, for the world, finally for the Divine.'⁵ Through the backdoor of politics, he had arrived at the great Realization.

Who had been guiding him on his way? 'Sri Aurobindo never took any formal initiation from anyone; he started his sadhana on his own account by the practice of *pranayama* and never asked for help except from Lele,'⁶ he wrote of himself. This does not mean that he did not receive help from other, most often non-material sources. One of these, as mentioned in Sri Aurobindo's personal notes, was Ramakrishna Paramhamsa, who had died in 1886, and another was Vivekananda. '[Vivekananda] visited me for fifteen days in Alipore Jail and, until I could grasp the whole thing, he went on teaching me and impressed upon my mind the working of the Higher Consciousness ... He would not leave me until he had put it all into my head,'⁷ Sri Aurobindo later confided to some of his disciples. Swami Vivekananda, that pillar of strength and the spiritual crown-prince of Ramakrishna Paramhamsa, had died in 1902, six years ago.

However, Aurobindo's highest mentors, his true and abiding instructors, were Sri Krishna and, ultimately, the Great Mother. Once put upon the path with the help of Lele, his intense and unusually fast development led him from one surprising discovery to the other, and he soon realized that, after his unconditional surrender at the beginning, as a human being he hardly had any part in his own spiritual unfolding. Higher powers in him had taken up the reins of his destiny; out of Aurobindo A. Ghose was growing Sri Aurobindo.

After his arrival in Pondicherry, Sri Krishna sketched out for him the lines of his further growth, 'the map of my spiritual progress'. Between 1912 and 1920 Sri Aurobindo kept a detailed diary of his *sadhana* (spiritual discipline). He noted everything down in a series of notebooks; after he left his body, it had always been known that those notebooks were there among the other documents of his estate, but they have only recently been deciphered and published by the researchers of the Sri Aurobindo Archives. It looks as if the significance of their contents still has not been fully fathomed, perhaps because these hundreds of pages with cryptic abbreviations in several languages are no easy reading matter. The *Record of Yoga*, as these have been named, 'provides a first-hand account of the day-to-day growth of the spiritual faculties of an advanced yogi.'[8] These experiences would lead him to his great spiritual discoveries, which afterwards he found confirmed in the *Vedas* and the *Upanishads*, and which would change the destiny of the world. What had started as a struggle for the liberation of India, became a struggle for the liberation of the human species from the shackles of its nature.

Chapter Four

OF PAINTERS AND OCCULTISTS

MATHILDE ISMALOUN was born in Alexandria, at one time the crossroads of the world, and her husband, Maurice Alfassa, came from Adrianople, now the Turkish town of Edirne. 'He had the skin of the people of the Middle-East, just like mine,' the Mother would say. As the story goes, the nonconformist Mathilde once refused to bow to the Khedive in the manner exacted by protocol and as a consequence was banished from Egypt. The young household, with its son Mattéo still less than a year old, went to live in Paris in 1877. They were somewhat familiar with their new surroundings, thanks to Mathilde's mother, Mira Ismaloun, for her time a remarkably cosmopolitan woman, as much at home in Paris, Geneva and Nice as she was in Cairo, and who had many famous friends like Ferdinand de Lesseps, the engineer who dug the Suez Canal, and the composer Gioacchino Rossini.

And so it happened that Mathilde's third child — her first, a son, had died from a vaccination when he was six months old — was born in Paris on the 21st of February 1878, at 41 Boulevard Haussmann. It was a girl, and she was named Blanche Rachel Mirra. Everybody called her Mirra. Only in 1890, twelve years after Mirra's birth, was Maurice Alfassa to become a naturalized Frenchman.

Mathilde wanted, just like Dr K.D. Ghose, that her children would grow up to be the best in the world. Long after she was known as the Mother, Mirra Alfassa once characterized Mathilde as 'an ascetic, stoical mother, like an iron rod.' Although Mathilde was a confirmed atheist, she adored her son and treated Mattéo as if he were her god, till she had to let go of him when he married. Her daughter, on the contrary, could seldom come to her with her problems and questions, for time and again she got scolded or repulsed without any reason. And 'all the time I was told that I would be good for nothing ...'

Mirra's parents lived separate lives. Her father, an exceptionally strong man with a gift for languages and mathematics, had his own bedroom, where he told his children stories with himself as the hero and where he let his canaries and other pet birds fly around freely. He loved going to the circus and took his children with him. He took them also to Buffalo Bill's *Great Wild West Show* in 1889, the year of the Paris World Exhibition and of the erection of the Eiffel Tower.

Mattéo and Mirra were bosom friends, although Mattéo had such a violent temper that, in his outbursts of fury, he more than once gave his sister a near fatal blow. He studied at the École Polytechnique and at the École Normale Superieure, at the time and afterwards, together with the Sorbonne the most highly reputed educationl institution in France. He would build up a successful career and rise to become governor of French Equatorial Africa. At the end, he could look back on a life of exemplary, unselfish and totally dedicated service.

Perhaps it was as a reaction against the rigorous way in which Mathilde ruled her household that Mirra plunged into the world of painters and artists. At the age of sixteen or thereabouts, she began following the classes of the Académie Julian, a painting school, and later on she studied at the prestigious École des Beaux Arts. The quality of her paintings was good enough for them to be exhibited at the highly esteemed *Salon* (exhibition) of the Société Nationale des Beaux Arts in 1903, 1904 and 1905. 'I have been living among the artists for ten years ... I met all great painters of that time and I was the Benjamin among them. That was at the end of the last century and the beginning of the present one, with the World Exhibition of 1900 and all those who by then had made a name for themselves in the arts.' In the same conversation of 1962, she assessed herself as 'a very mediocre painter'.

The high tide of Impressionism, as described by Jean Jacques Crespelle in his *La vie quotidienne des Impressionistes* (the daily life of the Impressionists), ran from 1863 to 1883. 'Their oeuvre was not finished by then, far from it, but the movement, as it had come to the fore after 1863, did not exist any longer.'[2] If we suppose that Mirra's formative years as a painter started somewhere in 1894, then at that time even postimpressionism (Cézanne, Seurat, Van Gogh, Gauguin) belonged already to the past as a movement; neo-impressionism was the order of the day, and Fauvism (Matisse, Vlaminck), with its countless twentieth century epigones, was on the verge of making its appearance.

This explosive moment in the history of the Western arts is tellingly illustrated by an anecdote related much later by Mirra, then called the Mother, to the children of the Ashram. It was about a painter 'who was a pupil of Gustave Moreau. He really was an excellent artist, he knew his art through and through, but ... he went hungry and did not know how to make both ends meet.' (Mirra herself lived in rather straitened circumstances at the time, for she had to varnish her shoes before she went out, so that nobody would notice the creases.) One day, when a dealer in paintings deigned to visit his studio, the talented painter showed him all his best work but the dealer did not seem impressed. Till somewhere in a corner he found a canvas on which the painter had been living out his fancy with the paint scrapings of his palette. "This is it! My friend, you are a genius! This is miraculous! You must show this to the world! Just look at the richness of these shades of colour, at this inventiveness of forms! What an imagination!" "But sir," said the poor painter, "these are the scrapings of my palette!" The dealer took hold of him: "You foolish man, don't say that! Give these paintings to me, give me as many as you can produce, I'll see to it that they are sold. Ten, twenty, thirty a month, I'll sell them all and make you famous."[3]

And famous he has become! For all indications point to the fact that the painter in question was Henri Matisse: he was well known to Mirra; he had been a pupil of Gustave Moreau; the incident occurred 'around the time of the World Exhibition in 1900', and Fauvism made its appearance in 1898 and had its first formal exhibition in 1905; and 'if I would tell you his name, all of you would know him.'

Another of her friends was the then aged sculptor Auguste Rodin. 'He looked magnificent. He had the head of a faun, a Greek faun. He was of small stature, very sturdy, stoutly built, with shrewd little eyes. He was exceedingly ironical and even somewhat [sarcastic?]' And it was to Mirra that he came to unburden his heart and to ask for advice regarding his sentimental vicissitudes.

It was the time of one of the great culminations of European art with the music of Berlioz, Franck, Saint-Saëns, the poetry of Baudelaire, Verlaine, Rimbaud and Mallarmé, the novels of Zola, the operas of Massenet, the recitals of Eugène Ysaÿe, a Belgian violinist of genius, of the *bals* (dancing halls), the *Moulin Rouge* and the *Grand Guignol* ... all that in the cultural capital of the world, Paris. That was where Mirra lived.

When she was nineteen she married a painter, Henri Morisset, also a pupil of Gustave Moreau. A year later their son André was born. Henri Morisset was a talented painter, but not talented enough to have his name mentioned in the *Petit Larousse* or for one of his canvasses to be hung up in the museum of the Quai d'Orsay. Little is known about him. And little did Mirra realize at the time that a completely different future was awaiting her.

Tlemcen

> *To know these [occult] things and to bring their truths and forces into the life of humanity is a necessary part of its evolution ... It may even be found that a supraphysical knowledge is necessary for the completion of physical knowledge, because the processes of physical Nature have behind them a supraphysical factor, a power and action mental, vital or spiritual which is not tangible to any outer means of knowledge.[4]*
>
> — Sri Aurobindo

The fact that there is a more profound knowledge and power present behind the surface of what in the various cultures has been (and is being) accepted as the dominant form of knowledge, was known even in Europe since the earliest times. The search for this hidden knowledge and the application of it is called occultism. All religions have their occult practices, many going back to a so-called pagan period by which every religion is preceded. The formulation of our rational-positivistic science has for the most part been a reaction against the hollow claims of an immature Western occultism, which has in many circles been the cause of the denigration of all occultism. Yet this denigration has not been able to prevent popular occultism from taking on enormous proportions even in the present so-called techno-scientific world. The credulous and the desperate pay vast amounts of money for the services of often unskilled practitioners of occultism, giving in to the ineradicable need to be shown a glimmer of light in the darkness of existence, to find protection against the countless invisible dangers threatening them from the cradle to the grave, or to obtain a modicum of power in a world in which the human being is one of the most helpless of creatures.

The lack of skill and knowledge or the false pretensions of the practitioners of occultism cannot be a valid argument against the existence of the occult. Were it so, the same argument could be used, for instance, against medical science. Among the occultists in prescientific times were some of the greatest savants, e.g., among the true alchemists, who as an acknowledgment of their lifelong labour now get a tiny footnote in the history of science because they discovered some chemical element or process. But their endeavour, their search for knowledge had a much higher aim: they were looking for an understanding of man and of the universe in which man lives, and they tried to transcend the limits of the human species. The true alchemists did not value 'the philosopher's stone' and 'the elixir of life' as material gains, but as the fulfilment of the promise, given to man at the commencement of his long journey through the centuries, that one day he would be even as God. Let us not forget that Isaac Newton, one of the most prominent names in the pantheon of modern science, has written more about alchemy and other occult matters of interest than about his fundamental scientific discoveries, and so has Johannes Kepler.

'Over the last 25 or so years there has been an occult boom, a "magical explosion", of a sort not experienced since the later years of the Roman Empire,' write Francis King and Isabel Sutherland in *The Rebirth of Magic*, published in 1982.[5] The works of the occult 'masters' of the last one hundred years and even of the Renaissance and the Middle Ages are now generally available in the bookshops — treatises by Eliphas Lévi, Stanislas de Guaita, Papus, Fulcanelli, Eugène Canseliet, Armand Barbault, or by John Dee, MacGregor Mathers, Alister Crowley ('the wickedest man in the world'), Dion Fortune, Alice A. Bailey, Arthur Machen, etc. One of the foremost poets of this century, W.B. Yeats, was a member of the Hermetic Order of the Golden Dawn. Freemasonry, a collective name for a variety of occult sects, counts thousands of prominent personalities among its members.

Taking all this into consideration, it is amazing that perhaps the two greatest occultists from the end of the previous century and the beginning of the present one, commanding a knowledge and a power few others have ever equalled, would have remained unknown if Mirra Alfassa had not crossed their path.

The real name of Max Théon, who also called himself Aia Aziz, was Louis Bimstein and he was born in 1847, the son of a rabbi.* Little is known about the years of his life before he met Mirra Alfassa. It seems he had spent some time in India, for he knew Sanskrit and the Vedas. He is also said to have been a collaborator of Madame Blavatsky in Egypt. It was in this country that he got acquainted with the French occultist Charles Barlet, who brought him into contact with France. After Théon had left Egypt for some obscure reason, we find him again in London, where he married Mary Christine Woodroffe Ware, alias Alma. They went to live on the outskirts of Tlemcen, an Algerian town at the foot of the Atlas Mountains.

Théon was a multifaceted personality. He spoke several languages, was well read, could draw from a rich experience, had an artistic sense and knew how to use his hands. He usually wore a kind of

---

* Some recently discovered biographical data mentioned in this chapter were found in the book by Sujata Nahar, *Mirra the Occultist.*

white or brown robe, tightened around his middle with a red cord. He was a smooth talker and rolled, with nimble fingers, one cigarette after the other.

Alma, three years younger than her husband according to the marriage document, was of a small and chubby build. She had lost an eye in an occult battle. She was usually in trance, but she had trained her body in such a way that, even while in trance, it allowed her to go about her normal daily occupations. For hours on end, she scribbled down her inexhaustible occult experiences and has left over twelve thousand pages. 'Madame Théon was an extraordinary occultist. She possessed exceptional abilities, that woman, exceptional!'[6] said the Mother, who was not lacking in such abilities herself. For Alma it was a simple matter to make her slippers come shoving towards her all by themselves, to make the gong sound from a distance, to have the table jump up without touching it, or to dematerialize a bunch of flowers and rematerialize it on Mirra's pillow in her locked bedroom.

It was Alma who had the occult experiences and who communicated her knowledge to Théon. Théon, according to the Mother, 'had a great deal of knowledge', and she talked about his stupendous powers, for instance how she had witnessed with her own eyes how he struck a bolt of lightning out of its course. 'Théon had terrible power ... Once, while there was a thunderstorm, he climbed on top of the terrace on the roof, above the drawing-room ... I went with him. He started pronouncing some formulas, and I clearly saw how a bolt of lightning came straight towards us and how he caused it to deviate. People will say that this is impossible, but I have seen it with my own eyes. The lightning has hit a tree a little further on.' Yes, Théon was 'a formidable fighter, and this is a matter of course, for he was an incarnation of an Asura.' *Asuras* are titans, the dark opponents of the gods. The significance of these words of the Mother will become clear to us later on. 'He was terrible, that man, he had terrible power. But outwardly you wouldn't have suspected a thing.'[7]*

---

* All quotations from the Mother originally spoken by her in French have been translated by the author. Some of the Mother's quotations were originally written in English, as the context will make clear. They have been quoted literally, of course, also where her phrasing or spelling might not agree with the standard language.

Théon had founded a periodical, the *Revue cosmique* (cosmic review), which was published in France under the editorship of Charles Barlet. The first issue had come out in January 1902. A certain Georges Thémanlys, a disciple of Théon, was responsible for the printing and the publishing of the review, and Thémanlys was acquainted with Mirra's brother Mattéo. This is how Mirra came to know about the *Groupe cosmique*, the group inspired by Théon and Alma. At last she found an explanation for the numerous inner experiences she had had without expecting or knowing anything and about which she had never been able to talk in Mathilde's harshly positivistic household. She had tried once, years ago, and Mathilde had taken her without ado to the family doctor, convinced that her daughter suffered from some sort of brain disease. Thanks to the articles and symbolical stories in the *Revue cosmique,* Mirra found an explanation for her experiences and knew that she did not have a brain disease.

Thémanlys was an easy-going person, and before long the full burden of publishing the *Revue cosmique* came to rest on Mirra's shoulders. She found a new printer, corrected the proofs, kept the accounts and even rewrote the articles sent to her from Tlemcen. These articles had been translated from Alma's English into French by Theresa, the English secretary who would assist the Théons for the rest of their life, and who thought so highly of her poor knowledge of French that she found it unnecessary to use a dictionary. In 1905 Théon was in Paris; he met with Mirra Alfassa, sensed her capacities as an occultist and invited her to Tlemcen.

It was Mirra's first long journey, in 1906, by way of Marseille and Oran. 'It was the first time in my life that I was travelling by myself and the first time I crossed the sea. Then followed a rather long journey by train from Oran to Tlemcen. Anyhow, I managed to get by. I arrived at my destination. He was waiting for me at the railway station. He took me to his house in his car, for it was some distance away. Then we arrived at his estate: a splendour! One first reached the foot of the hill — for the property covered a whole hill and looked out over the valley — and then one climbed through broad avenues up to the house on top ... We still had to walk a short distance on foot, and suddenly he stops, without any apparent reason. He turns around, comes and stands in front of me, and says: "You are now in my power. Aren't you afraid?" Just like that. I looked at him, smiled and told him: "I am never afraid. I have the Divine here".[8] The Mother pointed to her heart. 'And believe me,' she added, smiling at the remembrance, 'he grew pale.' It was in Théon's very own *Revue cosmique* that Mirra had learned how to discover the Divine in her heart. She never found theory interesting except when it could be turned into practice.

The Mother has often reminisced about the fantastic occult world of Tlemcen. However interesting those anecdotes or those countless occult miracles may be, the broad picture behind them is much more important. Alma and Théon had immediately felt who Mirra essentially was and they gave her an intense occult training, in 1906 and 1907, both times from July to October. Mirra's unusual capacities made her a student who quickly equalled her teachers. Like Alma she was able to leave her gross material body, then the subtle body, then the next still more subtle body, and so on — twelve times one after the other, because each successive body consisted of the ever subtler substance of the twelve worlds gradually ascending from our material world up to the highest, outer limit of manifestation. But always there is the silver cord or thread of life which has to keep connecting the subtle bodies with their material base on earth, for if it snaps one dies in the material world. Once, during a working session, Théon had a terrible outburst of anger, thus cutting off Mirra's silver thread; happily both of them were sufficiently knowledgeable to connect it again with her material body (after she had been dead for a short while!). Why had Théon become so angry? Because he knew that Mirra in her state of exteriorization had found, somewhere in another world, the mantra of life, the formula which can give and take life, and because she had refused to tell him that mantra, knowing who he was and what he might do with it. Afterwards she confided the mantra to Sri Aurobindo.

No, Théon and Alma were not after small things. They were the inheritors of a tradition going back to times before the Chaldeans and the Vedas in which have been laid the foundations of both. They had a profound knowledge of the forces in and behind the universe, of the meaning of evolution and the destiny of man. They knew that man is an evolutionary being somewhere halfway in cosmic development, and that for him the time has come to be transmuted into a new being, called by some 'superman' for lack of a better word; the body of this new being would wholly consist of the divine matter which is now on the verge of taking shape on our planet.

'Théon knew that he was not meant to succeed but had only come to prepare the way to a certain extent for others to come and perfect it ... It was [Alma] who had been supporting Théon with her knowledge and powers; without her he was nothing and naturally after her death the entire project suffered shipwreck.'⁹ (Sri Aurobindo)

One has the impression that Alma withdrew from life of her own will. After she and Théon had spent the summer of 1908 in France with Georges and Claire Thémanlys, she wanted, in the beginning of September, to visit the British Channel Islands. (She herself had been born in the Isle of Wight.) Before the departure of the ferryboat from the harbour of Côteret, there was some time left for a stroll along a rather dangerous path between rocks protruding over the sea. Eyewitnesses say that she slipped, probably in trance as usual, and fell into the cold waters. She did not want to postpone her outing but became very ill during the crossing. On her arrival in the port of Gorey, on the island of Jersey, she was taken to a hotel, where she died that very day, 10 September.

Théon never got over Alma's death. The *Revue cosmique* ceased to appear in December of the same year, 1908. Afterwards he himself lived as a recluse in Tlemcen, so much so that Mirra, like most others, thought he had died somewhere in 1913, the year he had met with a serious car accident. He died much later, however, in 1927, with the faithful Theresa at his side. She would survive him less than a year.

Théon's death, like that of Alma, got but a few lines in a local newspaper. They, who had probably been the greatest occultists of their time, died even less known than when alive. Nevertheless, as precursors to the New Age they had not been working in vain, for their occult knowledge lived on in Mirra Alfassa, who would always remember them in gratitude. 'Théon has taught me occultism really well, I was really very good at it.' Their qualities, because of which Mirra had had to become their pupil, were a comprehensive knowledge, the synthesis of the occult schools from very ancient times but always checked out by personal experience, and their fundamental sincerity.

'Occultism in the West could be thus easily pushed aside because it never reached its majority, never acquired ripeness and a philosophic or sound systematic foundation. It indulged too freely in the romance of the supernatural or made the mistake of concentrating its major effort on the discovery of formulas and effective modes for using supernatural powers. It deviated into magic, white and black, or into romantic or thaumaturgic paraphernalia of occult mysticism and the exaggeration of what was after all a limited and scanty knowledge. These tendencies and this insecurity of a mental foundation made it difficult to defend and easy to discredit, a target facile and vulnerable. In Egypt and the East this line of knowledge arrived at a greater and more comprehensive endeavour,'[10] writes Sri Aurobindo in *The Life Divine*.

To build up their worldwide synthesis, Aurobindo Ghose would test out on his own person everything the hidden Eastern knowledge had to offer, and Mirra Alfassa would contribute the best of what the West had discovered and what Max Théon and Alma, better than anybody else, had represented.

And so the Mother could say, when looking back in the last years of her earthly life: 'Isn't it strange, Théon and Sri Aurobindo did not know each other, they had never met each other ... Without knowing each other they have followed the same lines, they have reached the same conclusion ... **And I have** known both of them.'[11]

Chapter Five

TWELVE PEARLS

*The eternal Goddess moved in her cosmic house
Sporting with God as a Mother with her child ...* [1]
— *Savitri*

THE MOTHER has said more than once that she had chosen her parents. 'I have chosen my parents to have a solid physical base, for I knew the work I had to do was very, very difficult and needed a solid base.'[2] She also said that for her start in life no better training was imaginable than the no-nonsense attitude of the materialistic Mathilde with her constant hammering on the necessity of perfection. Not an easy environment for a child, but 'a wonderful education' for someone who had come to do a great and difficult work.

All her inner experiences had occurred totally unexpectedly, which according to the Mother is the necessary condition for them so as not to be falsified. Expectation limits the experience and distorts it. Often expectation even creates the experience which then adapts itself to the artificial, imaginary world of the subject which no longer has any relation with reality. Little then remains of the experience except illusion.

From her early years Mirra was aware of something she could neither name nor describe. 'There was a kind of inner light, a Presence. I was born with that.' She went and sat in a little chair, especially made for her, to feel that Presence, which probably exerted a light, rather pleasant pressure on her brain; out of this Presence she then regarded the disconcerting world around her, which lacked so much in comprehension and sympathy, and which was full of lies, anger and friction, of enmity, nastiness and ignorance. The little human children, not yet hardened by life, are so often hurt by the 'affectionate' grown-ups around them, who are unaware of the hidden aggressiveness of their words and actions. And in Mirra the Beauty from which she had come remained totally alive. 'Even in her childish movements could be felt / The nearness of a light still kept from earth.'[3] (*Savitri*).

'When I was a child of about thirteen, for nearly a year, every night as soon as I had gone to bed it seemed to me that I went out of my body and rose straight up above the house, then above the city [Paris], very high above. Then I used to see myself clad in a magnificent golden robe, much longer than myself; and as I rose higher, the robe would stretch, spreading out in a circle around me to form a kind of immense roof over the city. Then I would see men, women, children, old men, the sick, the unfortunate coming out from every side; they would gather under the outspread robe, begging for help, telling of their miseries, their sufferings, their hardships. In reply, the robe, supple and alive, would extend towards each one of them individually, and as soon as they had touched it, they were comforted and healed, and went back into their bodies happier and stronger than when they had come out of them. Nothing seemed more beautiful to me, nothing could make me happier; and all the activities of the day seemed dull and colourless and without any real life, beside this activity of the night which was the true life for me.'[4] Thus wrote Mirra in her spiritual diary *Prières et Méditations* (Prayers and Meditations).

There are many stories about her, such as how, as a demonstration for her friends, she jumped from one corner to another of a twelve-meter wide drawing-room, only once touching the floor in the middle with the tip of one foot. Or how when playing in the forest of Fontainebleau, and perhaps chased by her brother, she ran as fast as she could without noticing the high bank of a road cutting through the forest; suddenly she felt projected into emptiness, but something caught hold of her and she descended on the flints of the road as softly as a feather. Or how, during a formal family dinner, she became so spellbound by something in the aura of her nephew that she forgot herself and remained motionless for minutes with her fork in the air. The Mother has told it all herself, so there is no need to weave a web of legends around her. Undoubtedly much more has happened than what she has confided from time to time to the people around her.

Most interesting, however, was the great Presence in that lightly bronzed girl, whom all of us probably would have passed by without noticing anything at all, as we are wont to do. 'Between 11 and 13 a series of psychic and spiritual experiences revealed to me not only the existence of God but man's possibility of uniting with Him, of realizing Him integrally in consciousness and action, of manifesting Him upon Earth in a life divine. This, along with a practical discipline for its accomplishment, was given to me during my body's sleep by several teachers, some of whom I met afterwards on the physical plane.'[5]

The self-discovery, the self-realization had taken place gradually. We have already seen how Mirra had found the inner Divine, thanks to the teachings of Alma and Théon in the *Revue cosmique*. After her two sojourns in Tlemcen and after the review had ceased to appear, she became actively interested in all kinds of occult circles and unorthodox and progressive groups in Paris. It was at that time that she met an Indian who gave her a French translation of the *Bhagavad Gita* to read.* About the same time Mirra got a copy of Vivekananda's *Raja Yoga*. She was overjoyed that the many questions which had occupied her mind were explained in these texts and that moreover they presented her with a method of spiritual realization. She had always taken up every task with a total dedication — which she did this time too. Her inner growth progressed from one realization to the next.

But who was she actually? Who was this young Parisian woman

This Indian was Jnanendra Nath Chakravarti, later vice-chancellor of Lucknow University and husband of Monika Devi, who under the name Yashodama would become the guru of the English yogi Krishnaprem. Krishaprem, by his encounters and correspondence with Dilip Kumar Roy, one of Sri Aurobindo's disciples, developed a personal contact with Sri Aurobindo himself. A circle was closed.

who had such extraordinary experiences, who was probably the greatest occultist of her time without anybody knowing it, and who by the Presence in her heart had been told that she had to accomplish something special?

Alma, half-blind but clairvoyant, had known who Mirra was. 'Madame Théon had recognized me because I had the twelve pearls in the correct sequence above my head. She said to me: "You are That, because you have that. Only That has that." It was far from anything I might have imagined, happily!'[6]

Twelve is the number of Mahashakti, the Universal Mother. The twelve pearls are her crown.

There is the One that exists beyond time, in all eternity. It has no beginning and no end, it IS. And in the bliss of its being, it wants to see itself externalized. And what it wants, by the fact that it wants it, exists: a manifestation of its endless qualities unfolding before its creating eye in worlds without number, in an endless, inexhaustible act of creation.

It is as if the One divides into two: into something which remains the essence having the joy of the creative self-contemplation and into something that makes this contemplation possible. This division into two is, on the one hand, a very real fact as we can deduce from the existence of our world, but it is, on the other hand, only a Play because the One never really can be divided.

Thus arose in the One the creative impulse, the fiat at the origin of all things manifested, and at the same time arose the consciousness force by which that impulse is rendered into reality. This consciousness force is called the Great Mother — she who holds the worlds in the palm of her hand, in whom they originate and dissolve, and to whom a grain of sand or a shell on the beach are as important a creation as a cluster of galaxies.

In God's supreme withdrawn and timeless hush,
A seeing Self and potent Energy met;
The Silence knew itself and thought took form:
Self-made from the dual power creation rose.[7]

— *Savitri*

The Mother is the consciousness force of the Divine. The opening words of the Gospel of St John, directly influenced by the Chaldean tradition, are well known: 'In the beginning was the Word, and the Word was with God, and the Word was God.' The *Kathaka Upanishad* says the same: '*Prajapati* [the Father of all beings] was then the whole Universe. *Vak* [the Word] had come forth from him. He united with her and she became pregnant. She went out from him and made all these worlds, and she went back to him.'[8] The Word is Sound; Sound is Vibration; Vibration is the potent concretization in the unbounded All. The basis of creation consists in all eternity of the primal *mantra*, the Word. And this Word is the Great Mother, worshipped by the children of man under a thousand names. Alma Théon had recognized Mirra as 'the human image of the deathless Word.'[9]

After Tlemcen, Mirra was no longer the Parisian painter, her horizon had widened. We hear one last time of Henri Morisset when he came to Tlemcen to join his wife and got involved in a vehement quarrel with Théon about the name of the exact shade of the colour of his robe. After returning from her second stay in Tlemcen, Mirra decided to live alone.

Earlier, she had once founded a small group of seekers under the name *Idéa*. She now started another one, *L'union des pensées féminines* (the union of feminist thought). Her feminist views were in fact the logical outcome of her general way of thinking — trying to find the fundamental truth in all things and therefore going almost automatically against the grain of all conventions, distorted truths and therefore lies. And is not the suppression of woman by man one of the most unreasonable conventions in the history of mankind?

We have already seen that Mirra concentrated on an intense inner development guided by the *Bhagavad Gita* and Vivekananda's *Raja Yoga*. In her social life, she tried to contact persons who represented some aspect or other of her newly discovered values. She became acquainted with Abd ol-Baha, who had succeeded his father Baha Ullah as the head of Bahaism. Inayat Khan, the prophet of Sufism in the West, gave a talk in her house. She also visited occult *séances* and addressed various circles. And there was Alexandra David-Néel, the modern prophetess of Buddhism and fearless explorer, who would be the first non-Tibetan woman to enter Lhasa in disguise. For a time they met every day and went for walks in the Bois de Boulogne, where the first airplanes, 'like giant grasshoppers', with sputtering engines contrived to stay a few seconds in the air.

The legal divorce from Henri Morisset took place in 1908. In that same year Mirra met Paul Richard, who too was very interested in occultism and had come into contact with Théon and Alma by reading the *Revue cosmique*. Paul Richard had received theological training, and had been a minister of the Reformed Church of France in Lille for about ten years. He had felt ever more attracted to politics and occultism. Because of politics he had taken up the study of law, and his interest in occultism had led to his contact with the Théons. Richard was awarded his law degree in 1908 and shortly afterwards became a barrister at the Paris Court of Appeals.

In 1910, Richard journeyed to Pondicherry to campaign in the elections there for the French House of Representatives. Pondicherry (*Pondichéry*) was French territory and had two elected representatives in Paris. Richard had probably been sent there by the Radical and Radical-Socialist League for the Republican Defense and Propagation, 'a party that combined a leftist ideology with a conservative financial programme (and a strong Masonic influence)'.[10] Richard was a freemason, and it was his mission to support the election campaign of a certain Bluysen.

However, Richard was also interested in meeting an authentic Indian yogi. He was in luck, for he was told that a very great yogi had just arrived from Bengal and that his name was Aurobindo Ghose. In 1910 Aurobindo consented to receive him. Richard was very impressed by the encounter, so much so that later, in a talk in Japan, he would declare: 'The hour is coming of great things, of great events, and also of great men, the divine men of Asia. All my life I have searched for them across the world, for all my life I have felt they must exist somewhere in the world, that this world would die if they did not live. For they are its light, its heat, its life. It is in Asia that I have found the greatest among them — the leader, the hero of tomorrow. His name is Aurobindo Ghose.'[11]

Four years later, Richard travelled again to Pondicherry, this time to try and have himself elected. He was accompanied by Mirra, who for pragmatic reasons had married him in 1911. After his first trip to Pondicherry, the enthusiastic Richard had shown her a photo of Aurobindo Ghose, but strange to say, Mirra had not seen him for who he essentially was; she had only seen the politician in him.

It may be recalled how between her eleventh and thirteenth year she had met several seers in her sleep. 'Later on, as the interior and exterior development proceeded, the spiritual and psychic relation with one of these beings became more and more clear and frequent; and although I knew little of the Indian philosophies and religions at that time I was led to call him Krishna, and henceforth I was aware that it was with him (whom I knew I should meet on earth one day) that the divine work was to be done ... As soon as I saw Sri Aurobindo I recognized in him the well-known being whom I used to call Krishna.'[12]

She wanted to meet him alone, that first time on 29 March 1914. And there he stood at the top of the staircase waiting for her, exactly as the 'Krishna' she had seen in her visions. The next day she wrote in her diary: 'It matters little that there are thousands of beings plunged in the densest ignorance, He whom we saw yesterday is on earth; his presence is enough to prove that a day will come when darkness shall be transformed into light, and Thy reign shall be indeed established upon earth.'[13] This time it was not Aurobindo Ghose but Sri Aurobindo whom she had perceived.

The Avatar is an earthly incarnation of the Divine. It is as if a part of the divine Self separates from the whole and descends to accomplish a special task in creation. That is why one can say that every human being in a sense is an Avatar, for man carries in him a growing 'psychic being', the core of which is a 'divine spark'. (A child once asked the Mother: 'Mother, are you God?' She answered: 'Yes, my child, and so are you.') But the soul in man has taken up the adventure in the night of the Inconscient and regains only gradually, in life after life, the remembrance of its origin. The Avatar, on the contrary, remains constantly conscious of what he is, namely that One. All the same, when he takes on an earthly body, the incarnating divine personality has to undergo a process of becoming conscious by which it progressively realizes its innermost Self, till the divine nature takes possession of the incarnation directly and fully.

At first Aurobindo Ghose and Mirra Alfassa were not at all aware of their avatarhood; at one time both of them had even been convinced atheists. Mirra had been taken aback when Madame Théon told her who she was in the essence of her being, because 'That alone has that', the crown of the twelve pearls. It is not known when exactly Aurobindo had become the conscious Avatar Sri Aurobindo — probably during the first year of his withdrawal in Pondicherry and surely before his first meeting with Mirra Richard, as her diary note on 30 March 1914 confirms. (The name Sri Aurobindo was publicly used only from 1926 onwards. Before that everybody in Pondicherry called him 'AG' after his initials. It was also from 1926 that Mirra was called 'the Mother'.)

But we know when Mirra became 'the Mother'. Sri Aurobindo had confirmed the correctness of Alma's vision, and he had said to Mirra: 'You are She', meaning the Great Mother. He repeated his confirmation several times in later years, mostly in answer to questions of Indian disciples who had problems in accepting an Avatar who was not only a woman, but a twice-married Parisian woman to boot! 'It was in 1914 that the identification with the Universal Mother took place, the identification of the physical consciousness with Her. Of course, I knew before that I was the Mother, but the complete identification has taken place only in 1914.'[14] — 'The great World-Mother now in her arose.'[15] (*Savitri*) — In her *Prayers and Meditations* we read on 13 September 1914: 'With fervour I hail Thee, O divine Mother, and in deep affection identify myself with Thee. United with our divine Mother I turn, O Lord, to Thee, and bow to Thee in mute adoration and in an ardent aspiration identify myself with Thee.'[16] (In mystical texts the Divine is often experienced in such intimate terms that He is addressed in the most affectionate form, the Mother here in the original French using *Tu* and *Toi*.) In the same diary we find already on 31 August: 'Mother, sweet Mother who I am ...' and then again on 14 October: 'Mother divine, Thou art with us; every day thou givest me the assurance and, closely united in an identity that grows more and more total, more and more constant, we turn to the Lord of the Universe and to That which is beyond in a great aspiration towards the new Light. All the earth is in our arms like a sick child who must be cured and for whom one has a special affection because of his very weakness.'

Sick she was, the earth, for a month earlier the First World War had erupted.

It is at this point that the important historical event took place, mentioned at the very beginning of this book and called by Barbara Tuchman 'von Kluck's Turn'. In 1970 the Mother again referred to it. She told once more how Kali had entered her room dancing and had cried out, 'Paris is being taken! Paris is being destroyed!' But this time she narrates how the Great Mother herself, the Mahashakti with whom she had identified, came into the room behind Kali and said no, very simply but irrevocably. Now we have a somewhat better idea of the power by which an intervention of this kind was made possible.

Without the world knowing, Sri Aurobindo and the Mother, the Two who were One, had found themselves and each other. The earth shook with the fury of the war; maybe it was her way of reacting to the incarnated promise of a new era.

Chapter Six

THE ARYA

AT THE end of 1911 Alexandra David-Néel was travelling in India. She seized the opportunity to take the train to Pondicherry and visit Aurobindo Ghose 'of whom friends of mine have had such a good opinion'. These friends obviously were Mirra and Paul Richard. About her visit she wrote the next day to her husband: 'I spent two wonderful hours reviewing the ancient philosophical ideas of India with a man of rare intelligence. He belongs to that uncommon category that I so much admire, the reasonable mystic. I am truly grateful to the friends who advised me to visit this man. He thinks with such clarity, there is such lucidness in his reasoning, such lustre in his eyes, that he leaves one with the impression of having contemplated the genius of India such as one dreams it to be after reading the noblest pages of Hindu philosophy.'[1]

But her visit had not gone unnoticed. When her train pulled into the station of Madras, the head of the Criminal Investigation Department, was waiting for her in person. 'He asked me — very civilly and politely, I must say — what I had been doing in Pondicherry in the house of this suspicious character.' Madame David-Néel had a whole collection of letters of recommendation by the British government in her handbag, and the suspicions of the chief of police were soon put to rest. '[Aurobindo] certainly is a very remarkable scholar,' he then said, 'but he is a dangerous man. We hold him responsible for the recent assassination of Mr. Ashe, a British official.' Madam David-Néel replied that she thought it improbable that a learned man, who had spoken to her so penetratingly on philosophical topics, was an assassin. 'He certainly did not kill Mr. Ashe himself,' replied the chief of police, 'he had him killed.'

So the British colonial authorities had not forgotten Aurobindo Ghose. On the contrary, he still was a thorn in their side. Lord Minto, the Viceroy of India, said that he would not rest till he had crushed Aurobindo Ghose.[2] Aurobindo's house was under surveillance night and day, and the young Bengalis who were living with him were shadowed wherever they went, as were his friends and acquaintances. To this end quite a substantial contingent of British police were engaged and permission obtained of the French government in Pondicherry, to keep an eye on Aurobindo Ghose and other revolutionaries on the run. Nolini Kanta Gupta, one of Aurobindo's first four companions, writes in his *Reminiscences:* 'The British Indian police set up a regular station there, in a rented house with several permanent men. They were of course plainclothes men, for they had no right to wear uniform within French territory. They kept watch both on our visitors and guests. Soon they got into the habit of sitting on the pavement round the corner next to our house in groups of three or four. They chatted away the whole day and only now and again took down something in their notebooks ... The police gave reports all based on pure fancy, they made up all sorts of stories at their sweet will. As they found it difficult to gather correct and precise information, they would just fabricate the news.'[3]

The British tried their best to make the French extradite Aurobindo Ghose. Incriminating and false documents were hidden in a well in the house of V.V.S. Aiyar, but they were found by a maidservant. A police spy was smuggled into Aurobindo's house as attendant of an invalid guest. Rumors were afloat that Aurobindo would be kidnapped, and his young associates kept watch night and day armed with bottles of acid. Paid informers had accused Aurobindo in court of all kinds of subversive activities, but when a French examining magistrate (*juge d'instruction*) on a domiciliary visit saw his Greek and Latin books, he annulled the prosecution on the spot. An Indian who read Homer and Virgil in the original language! No, this could not be the sinister conspirator depicted to him.

Pondicherry was — and is — a small port on the Coromandel Coast, one hundred and sixty kilometers south of Madras. Visiting ships had to weigh anchor. With its carefully kept sea front and park it is one of the most attractive towns in India, but at that time it seemed a place out of a *Three Penny Opera*. It was divided into the 'white town' near to the sea, with the spacious houses of the French colonists, and the 'black town' more inland, with the small houses in local style and the hutments of the Tamil population. The two parts of the town were separated by a straight 'canal', actually the smelly main drain of the town. Out of reach of the British, Pondicherry was a French free port and a den of smugglers of weapons, liquor and all kinds of Western produce greatly in demand, of gangs employed by totally unscrupulous politicians, of police spies and professional informers, and of numerous fugitives, idealistic freedom fighters as well as common criminals. After a visit in 1921 A.B. Purani wrote: 'Pondicherry as a city was lethargic, with a colonial atmosphere — an exhibition of the worst elements of European and Indian culture. The market was dirty and stinking and the people had no idea of sanitation. The sea-beach was made filthy by them. Smuggling was the main business.'[4]

After the beginning of the First World War the British exerted strong pressure on the French governor to expel all fugitive revolutionaries from the Pondicherrian enclave to Africa, more specifically to Algeria or Djibouti. Strange to say, most of the freedom fighters, including the poet Subramania Bharati, found that a good idea, maybe under the delusion that in Africa they would have total freedom of movement, but without realizing that the aim of their life would lose its meaning in a place so far away from their motherland. At a meeting called to decide about the voluntary exile, Aurobindo Ghose refused categorically 'to budge one inch'. Madame Richard exerted her influence on the French governor of Pondicherry, and her brother Mattéo managed to hush up the affair at the Ministry of the Colonies in Paris. The British authorities would continue keeping an eye on Sri Aurobindo till 1936.

In June 1914, Sri Aurobindo and Paul and Mirra Richard decided to publish a periodical to spread Sri Aurobindo's ideas. It is difficult to find out who convinced whom of doing so. Sri Aurobindo wrote in a letter at the time: 'So far as my share is concerned, it will be the intellectual side of my work for the world.'⁵ In the four years of his stay in Pondicherry, he had filled many notebooks with brief annotations and essays on the Vedas and Upanishads, comparative linguistics and a lot of other subjects — all the while involved in the intensive yoga which he was practising constantly. In a couple of months he managed to compose a prospectus for enlisting subscribers, and to write a series of articles which would become his major works. He also translated Richard's contributions, a collection of apothegms about *The Wherefore of the Worlds* and quotations of sages from all parts of the world, entitled *The Eternal Wisdom*. Mirra, as she had done for the *Revue cosmique*, took on the administration of the review and helped Richard translating Sri Aurobindo's texts, for the periodical would be published in English and in French. The first English issue of *Arya*, as the monthly was called, came out on 15 August 1914, Sri Aurobindo's forty-second birthday.

An Aryan is 'whoever cultivates the field that the Supreme Spirit has made for him, his earth of plenty within and without', and who 'does not leave it barren or allows it to run to seed, but labours to exact from it its full yield'. The word Aryan in the original Sanskrit is not tainted with the racist connotations it later developed in Germany and Austria, and of which Sri Aurobindo was of course aware. Basing himself on his extensive linguistic studies, he gave in the second issue of the review the following definition: 'The Aryan is he who strives and overcomes all outside him and within him that stand opposed to human advance ... Self-perfection is the aim of his self-conquest. Therefore what he conquers, he does not destroy, but ennobles and fulfils. He knows that the body, life and mind are given him in order to attain something higher than they; therefore they must be transcended and overcome, their limitations denied, the absorption of their gratifications rejected ... The Aryan is a worker and warrior. He spares himself no labour of mind or body whether to seek the Highest or to serve it. He avoids no difficulty, he accepts no cessation from fatigue. Always he fights for the coming of that kingdom within himself and in the world.'⁶

The periodical, with the title in Devanagari characters on the front-page, was 'a philosophical review' and intended to contribute to the presence on earth of the noble, perfect man, who in fact would be a new species beyond the existing imperfect, transitory human race. Sri Aurobindo's very first contribution, which would later be chapter one of his magnum opus *The Life Divine*, opens with the following splendid paragraph, once called a 'living entity' by Nolini Kanta Gupta: 'The earliest preoccupation of man in his awakened thoughts and, as it seems, his inevitable and ultimate preoccupation — for it survives the longest periods of skepticism and returns after every banishment — is also the highest which his thought can envisage. It manifests itself in the divination of the Godhead, the impulse towards perfection, the search after pure Truth and unmixed Bliss, the sense of a secret immortality. The ancient dawns of human knowledge have left us their witness to this constant aspiration; today we see a humanity satiated but not satisfied by victorious analysis of the externalities of Nature preparing to return to its primeval longings. The earliest formula of Wisdom promises to be its last — God, Light, Freedom, Immortality.' (*Arya*, first volume, first issue, page 1.)

That is how it resounded, this voice, but to the world it was at first drowned by the thunder of the guns. The monthly, though no easy reading matter, never was in the red during the seven years of its publication, but the French edition, under the name *Arya - Revue de grande synthèse philosophique*, had to be discontinued because Paul Richard had been called up for military service.

All of Sri Aurobindo's important works, with the exception of his poetry and *The Supramental Manifestation*, have been serialised in the *Arya*. At the present time, eighty years after their first appearance, they still have not been accorded a generally recognized place in the cultural heritage of humanity. This may have its advantages, for they were not destined for the general public but for the few for whom the world, as it is, is no longer livable and who, from the bottom of their heart, long for something else, something more worthwhile.

The Life Divine has been found by some to be the philosophical masterpiece of the century. In *The Synthesis of Yoga*, Sri Aurobindo describes in detail the synthetic yogic method, worked out by him in the course of the previous years to reach the threshold of a supramental manifestation. *The Secret of the Veda* gives a reinterpretation of the Vedas, which no longer seems to be a kind of very old folkloristic sayings but are the most meaningful revelations ever received by mankind. Month after month Sri Aurobindo published in the *Arya* his translations from the Vedas, to be later collected under the title, *Hymns to the Mystic Fire*, as well as articles about a future mantric poetry which were published as *The Future Poetry*. In *Essays on the Gita* he wrote down his interpretation of the *Bhagavad Gita* which, at one time, was one of the principal sources of his inspiration. And there are perhaps the least understood or appreciated political and social writings, *The Human Cycle* and *The Ideal of Human Unity*, which contain the key to the destiny of man as a social being and the conditions which may lead to a world of general development, harmony and unity.

All this was composed in the organ mode of Sri Aurobindo's English. And in spite of such an impressive contribution he said he was no philosopher! 'And philosophy! Let me tell you in confidence that I never, never, never was a philosopher,'[7] he wrote in a letter. And he explained: 'My philosophy was formed first by the study of the Upanishads and the Gita; the Vedas came later. They were the basis of my first practice of Yoga; I tried to realize what I read in my spiritual experience and succeeded; in fact I was never satisfied till experience came and it was on this experience that later on I founded my philosophy, not on ideas by themselves. I owed nothing in my philosophy to intellectual abstractions, ratiocination or dialectics; when I have used these means it was simply to explain my philosophy and justify it to the intellect of others. The other source of my philosophy was the knowledge that flowed from above when I sat in meditation, especially from the plane of the Higher Mind when I reached that level. They [the ideas of the Higher Mind] came down in a mighty flood which swelled into a sea of direct Knowledge always translating itself into experience, or they were intuitions starting from an experience and leading to other intuitions and a corresponding experience. This source was exceedingly catholic and many-sided and all sorts of ideas came in which might have belonged to conflicting philosophies but they were here reconciled in a large synthetic whole.'[8]

This is typical of Sri Aurobindo: a 'crystal-clear vision' (said the Mother) which integrates everything, even the smallest details, in a large synthetic whole. That is why he could say: 'There is very little argument in my philosophy — the elaborate metaphysical reasoning full of abstract words with which the metaphysician tries to establish his conclusions is not there. What is there is a harmonizing of the different parts of a many-sided knowledge so that all unites logically together. But it is not by force of logical argument that it is done, but by a clear vision of the relations and sequences of the Knowledge.'[9]

This enormous 'mental' activity, which we can witness for almost seven full years thanks to the *Arya*, used as its instruments a completely inactive brain (since the realization with Lele in Baroda) and fingers that typed directly on a prehistoric Remington what was inspired into them, including the corrections. In summer it is dreadfully warm in Pondicherry, but Sri Aurobindo, in yogic detachment, was totally oblivious to its effect on his health and remained concentrated on his work, though according to eye-witnesses he was perspiring so much that his sweat dripped on the floor.

Looking back on the first year of the *Arya's* publication, he opened the second as follows: 'Our Review has been conceived neither as a mirror of the fleeting interests and surface thoughts of the period we live in, nor as the mouthpiece of a sect, school or already organized way of thinking. Its object is to feel out for the thought of the future, to help in shaping its foundations and to link it to the best and most vital thought of the past.'[10]

In the July issue of 1918 he concluded the fourth year with the words: 'We start from the idea that humanity is moving to a great change in its life which will even lead to a new life of the race — in all countries where men think, there is now in various forms that idea and that hope — and our aim has been to search for the spiritual, religious and other truth which can enlighten and guide the race in this movement and endeavour. The spiritual experience and the general truths on which such an attempt could be based, were already present in us, otherwise we should have had no right to make the endeavour at all; but the complete intellectual statement of them and their results and issues had to be found. This meant a continuous thinking, a high and subtle and difficult thinking on several lines, and this strain, which we had to impose on ourselves, we were obliged to impose also on our readers. This too is the reason why we have adopted the serial form which in a subject like philosophy has its very obvious disadvantages, but was the only one possible.'[11] Sri Aurobindo simultaneously wrote eight books of his profoundest experiences in monthly instalments, an example of mental power seldom equalled. But it is true that this was not exactly what we know as 'mental power'.

A synthetic, non-linear way of thinking or seeing is very complex and difficult to formulate in human language, especially when, like Sri Aurobindo, one wants to express oneself adequately and completely throughout. This is one of the reasons why some people find that Sri Aurobindo's works are difficult reading, as is the fact that to follow him in his philosophical texts, a certain degree of intellectual perception is perhaps necessary. But Sri Aurobindo's books are inspired works and like all inspired works, when reading them for the first time one is confronted, as it were, with a closed, forbidding gate; one pushes against the gate with the full intensity of one's aspiration and all at once, unexpectedly, one finds it ajar; one goes on pushing, perhaps reading a certain book once again after several years, and suddenly the gate swings open and for the first time one puts a step into the garden beyond the printed characters — a garden extending far, far ahead, as it is a whole new world.

Satprem has phrased it beautifully: 'I tell you that *every sentence* of Sri Aurobindo's is the expression or the translation of an exact experience, and that it not only contains as it were a whole world in a few words, but that it contains the *vibration* of the experience, almost the quality of light of the particular world it touches, and that through the words without much difficulty one can come into contact with the experience ... Sri Aurobindo has never written one word too many.'[12]

Paul Richard, a lamb among the wolves of Pondicherrian politics, had miserably failed in his political ambitions; of the four candidates for the French House of Representatives he had got the lowest number of votes. More important for posterity however was the role he played in founding the *Arya,* on the cover of which his name remains printed forever next to the names of Sri Aurobindo and Mirra Alfassa. Sri Aurobindo would continue mentioning him as an editor, even when he could not contribute to the review any longer.

Richard was not in the good books of the British because of 'his intimate contacts with the extremists,' and they used all possible means to have him expelled from Pondicherry. He was called up for military duty in the beginning of August 1914, but life in the trenches had but little attraction for him. Eventually the British pressure became too strong and he was unable, even with the best legal advice, to fight the expulsion order of January 1915. The Richards left Pondicherry on 22 February, the day following Mirra's birthday, which she probably had wanted to spend near Sri Aurobindo. From now on the burden of writing, printing, publishing and administering the *Arya* rested solely on Sri Aurobindo's shoulders. He would carry on dutifully till January 1921.

For Mirra the separation was especially painful. She knew that her place was with Sri Aurobindo, but she had promised herself that she would convert Paul Richard who, like Max Théon, was the incarnation of a great *Asura*; this was particularly important in these times of transition and it was the true reason for her marriage with Richard. The moment of her full collaboration with Sri Aurobindo had not yet arrived. 'I had left my psychic being with [Sri Aurobindo]. How much he was present all the time that I was not with him, and how much he has guided my sojourn in Japan!'

Separating your body from your psychic being is a risky enterprise, even for an experienced occultist, and in the south of France, where the Richards were staying for a time, Mirra fell seriously ill — an illness which attacked all the nerves of the body and was extremely painful.

Aboard the *Kama Maru*, the Japanese ship on which she and Richard had sailed from Colombo to Europe, she had noted in her diary: 'Solitude, a harsh, intense solitude, and always this strong impression of having been flung headlong into a hell of darkness!

Never at any moment of my life, have I felt myself living in surroundings so entirely opposite to all that I am conscious of as true, so contrary to all that is the essence of my life.'[13] Having recovered, she went to Lunel to help and take care of the wounded soldiers transported by the trainload to the south of France. The frenetic dance of the dark powers on earth seemed unstoppable and Mirra received her share of the suffering. In the meantime the spiritual experience and the invisible work kept going on in her. She may not have known — or she may have — that the dark night and the suffering in Lunel were only a foretaste of what was to await her in the years to come.

Paul Richard got exempted from military service. In March 1916, the Richards managed to sail from London and arrived in Japan in June. They would stay in that country for four years, mainly in Tokyo and Kyoto. The Mother would often talk about Japan — about the splendour of the gardens, the landscapes and the buildings, about the cleanliness and politeness but also the mental rigidity of the people, about her encounters with persons of all kinds, Rabindranath Tagore and the son of Leo Tolstoy among them. But she was silent about her intimate but fierce struggle with the *Asura* who was her companion, except that at the end of those four years she had not won the battle and therefore had been unable to fulfil her promise. When one day she had to face the fact, the Supreme appeared to her in a vision 'more beautiful than in the Gita'. He took her in his arms like a newborn child and turned with her towards the West, towards India, where Sri Aurobindo was awaiting her.

The Richards travelled back to India via China. The definitive meeting of the Mother and Sri Aurobindo took place on 24 April 1920. 'An hour began, the matrix of new time.'[14] Richard finally gave up his resistance and disappeared from the scene. The Mother never left Pondicherry again.

Many years later two of her Indian devotees met with Dr. O. Okawa in Japan. He had lodged the Richards in his house for some time. 'You would like to know, my young friends, what struck me about your Mother?' he asked. 'She had a will that moved mountains and an intellect sharp as the edge of a sword. Her thought was clarity itself and her resolve stronger than the roots of a giant oak. Her mystic depths were deeper than the ocean. But her intellect was a plummet that could sound her deepest depths. An artist, she could paint pictures of an unearthly loveliness. A musician, she enchanted my soul when she played on an organ or guitar. A scientist, she could formulate a new heaven and earth, a new cosmogony. I do not know what Mirra had not become or was not capable of becoming. But to me she was a sister and a comrade in spirit. That is how I know her.'[15]

Chapter Seven

SRI AUROBINDO'S VISION

*It is an enormous spiritual revolution
rehabilitating matter and the creation.*[1]
— The Mother

AUROBINDO GHOSE and Mirra Alfassa, whom henceforth we will only call Sri Aurobindo* and the Mother, had from very different backgrounds arrived at the same experiences and the same vision. 'There is no difference between the Mother's path and mine; we have and have always had the same path, the path that leads to the supramental change and the divine realization; not only at the end, but from the beginning they have been the same,'[2] wrote Sri Aurobindo. Truth is one in all its gradations, and they had come to work out a new gradation of it, 'a truer Truth', on Earth. Yet, because those experiences and that vision have been formulated mainly by Sri Aurobindo, with the *Arya* as his instrument, we call it Sri Aurobindo's vision for the sake of simplicity. This vision has been developed progressively, always with spiritual experience as its foundation and touchstone. At no time has it been the intention of Sri Aurobindo and the Mother to stop somewhere on the way, to review their gained knowledge at that point and to mould it into a system.

---

* The prefix 'Sri', traditionally used as a mark of respect or worship, in this case forms an integral part of the name (pronounced: Shri AuroBINdo). It is important to keep this in mind because *all* names have mantric power.

Theirs was an open vision, and they have employed everything in their power to build up, literally every minute of their life, as much as possible of a new world on Earth.

The starting point of Sri Aurobindo's thoughts is known in India as Vedanta, with the idea of the Brahman at its centre. 'Brahman is the Alpha and the Omega. Brahman is the One besides whom there is nothing else existent.'³ 'Brahman' is a densely vibrating Sanskrit word denoting what in the West is called the One or the Absolute. It is of some importance to use at first a neuter word for the beginning, middle and end of all things, because otherwise we get stuck from the start with a male-female dichotomy which taints and distorts the manner in which the supreme Reality is perceived. 'It is our first premise that the Absolute is the supreme Reality' (Sri Aurobindo). From this first premise, and from the fact of the existence of the world as experienced by us, follows everything else. We are continually confronted with the world, it is visible and tangible to us; the first premise is not so self-evident, because the Absolute cannot be known and still less defined by the human intellect — it is a fact of experience directly perceived by the great in spirit of all times and climes, and confirmed by others after them over and over again. One can live the Absolute but one cannot name, describe or define it. 'The only way of knowing the Divine is by identifying oneself with Him'⁴ (the Mother).

All is Brahman. There is nothing that is not Brahman, for outside Brahman nothing exists — because all is Brahman. 'Thou art man and woman, boy and girl; old and worn out, thou walkest bent over a staff; thou art the blue bird and the green and the scarlet-eyed ...' sings the *Swetaswatara Upanishad* (IV.3, 4). 'If it is true that only the Self exists, then it must also be true that everything is the Self.' (Sri Aurobindo). As simple as that, but fundamental. The Mother said it still more categorically: 'There is only That. Only That exists. That, what? — Only That exists!' And That is the one 'all containing, everywhere present point without dimensions.'

The concept of the absolute one Reality which is all, though confirmed by Western mystics too, is not generally current in the West. The reason, called by the Mother 'the error at the origin', is a supposed rift, probably first thought of in Chaldea, between God on the one hand and Creation on the other. 'There is no separation between that what you call God and that what you call creation ... It is through the whole of this creation, little by little, step by step, that [the Divine] rediscovers himself, that he unites with himself, that he realizes himself, that he expresses himself ... It is not at all something that he has willed in an arbitrary way or that he has done in an autocratic way: it is the growing expression, developing ever more, of a consciousness which objectifies itself to itself.'[5] From the Chaldean world-view derived the Jewish, and from the Jewish, the Christian. And God remains seated on his throne above the clouds, and the human goes on fighting the good fight in the earthly valley of tears hoping for a heavenly reward, and the devil keeps stoking his eternal fires in an eternal hell.

Many have rebelled against this sort of world-view, which after all was intended to form the background and justification of their life — as did the Mother in her youth. 'Up to my twenty-fifth year, or thereabouts, I knew only the God of the religions, the God as men have made him, and I did not want anything of it, nothing at all!' (Then, as we know, she discovered the *Revue cosmique* with its teaching of the immanent God, the Presence in the heart of man.) A God who has placed the ignorant, helpless human being in a world like the present one, she found a monster and our kind of life a hell — a very understandable point of view despite all theological arguments to the contrary. 'If God exists, then he is a veritable scoundrel! He is a villain, and I do not want a God like the one who has created us,' she wrote at the time. 'You know, the idea of the God who is quietly seated in his heaven, who then makes the world and takes pleasure in watching it, and who then says: "How well it is made!" No! I said by myself: "I do not want anything to do with that monster." '[6]

All her life the Mother had felt uncomfortable about the use of the word 'God'. 'I do not like using the word "God" because the religions have made it into the name of an omnipotent being who differs from his creation and stands outside of it, which is not true.' She found it 'a dangerously hollow word,' associated with a supra-earthly tyrant. Therefore she, like Sri Aurobindo, usually called the supreme Being 'the Divine' (*le Divin*) instead of 'God'. Or she named the Unnamable simply 'That', or 'the Lord', or 'the Supreme,' etc., 'because anyhow one has to use a word,' for otherwise one cannot talk.

Brahman, says the Vedanta, exists in itself, outside and beyond all manifestation. Its three highest attributes are *Sat* = Being, *Chit* = Consciousness and *Ananda* = Bliss. Consequently, *Satchitananda*, in Sanskrit spelled *Sachchidananda*, is one of the names of Brahman. These three attributes are absolute and unlimited, for limitations would have to be imposed from the outside, which is impossible as outside the Brahman there is nothing. 'For we cannot suppose that the sole Entity is compelled by something outside or other than Itself, since no such thing exists.'[7] This also means that there is no Nothing, since all that is, is That; if there were a Nothing, it too would have to be That and therefore could not be Nothing.

Absolute Consciousness also means absolute power, Omnipotence, something the human imaginative faculty cannot grasp, because in man consciousness is separated from the power of realization. It is through its Omnipotence that the limitless Brahman is able to limit *itself* in forms, by which it can as it were unfold itself to its own view. 'Its self-limitation is itself an act of omnipotence.' That is how the great Play of manifestation originated, the Play of *Ananda*, a Play called *Lila* in Sanskrit. 'The transcendent God is playing his material Play in Himself, by Himself and with Himself.'

This unfolding, this self-manifestation of the Brahman is infinite just like the Brahman itself, and like the Brahman it has neither beginning nor end. According to the terminology descended from the Chaldeans we usually talk about a 'creation', as a 'Creator' is supposed to have brought forth everything out of nothing, which is considered a proof of his omnipotence. But there being no nothing, 'nothing' cannot possibly be the origin of things existent. The sole source is That, the Brahman that is everything. 'The Infinite does not create, it manifests what is present in itself'(Sri Aurobindo). The act of omnipotence, in all eternity and at each moment, consists of the fact that the Brahman, to manifest itself, concretizes itself, thereby limiting itself. The Infinite causes itself, seemingly, to become finite. Conversely, all things finite remain, essentially, infinite, otherwise they could not be. 'All finites are in their spiritual essence the Infinite,' says Sri Aurobindo.

As a consequence, in the manifestation also there is nothing but Brahman. Which means that there can only be *Ananda* in all the worlds throughout the scale of manifestation. In the manifestation of Brahman, logically speaking, the presence of suffering, need, fear or any feeling of incompleteness is an impossibility, and death can only be a meaningful and joyful metamorphosis. In the scale of manifestation there are material, vital, mental and supramental worlds, and worlds with beings partaking of the highest attributes of the Brahman, up to the borderline where the finest, subtlest forms of materialization dim in the immaterial, absolute, self-existing Being of the Godhead — 'the Absolute, the Perfect, the Alone.'

> He is the Maker and the world he made,
> He is the vision and he is the seer;
> He is himself the actor and the act,
> He is himself the knower and the known,
> He is himself the dreamer and the dream.[8]

> — *Savitri*

Climbing down from those high abstractions* with so many capital letters, we cannot but ask the pertinent question: 'If everything is the Brahman, this, our world, must be the Brahman too. Then how comes that here undeniably there is suffering, fear and death?'

Vedanta has an answer to this question: as in the infinity of the Brahman the number of possibilities is infinite, necessarily its own

---

* Because of the way the human beings are inserted into the world, everything which to them looks qualitatively or evolutionarily *more* also seems to be *higher*. The religions have turned this 'verticalized' way of feeling into a thought habit formalized in the language. One could as well consider the Godhead or the Brahman to be deeper inside oneself. For the Godhead is 'a circle whose centre is everywhere.'

negation must have been one of the possibilities. In a state of absolute Consciousness, which is Omnipotence, to 'see' a possibility means to realize it. Therefore the Brahman, in one of its manifestations, has as it were plunged into its opposites which is how Being became Inertia, Light became Night, consciousness became ignorance, and Bliss became blind dullness.

But like all manifestation this too is a Play, by which the Brahman, so to speak, hides itself from its own view so that it may rediscover itself, in which it has plunged into the Night to experience the ecstasy, the glory of Dawn. For, remember, the Brahman can only be itself, and nothing, not even the negation of itself, can exist outside it.

The rediscovery takes place by a process which we call 'evolution'. In the night is present the light, by us unmarked, in every atom, in every molecule shaped in the course of the evolution. In every elementary particle the Godhead is present in his full potential. The Godhead grows in his creation; he reveals himself gradually more and more to his own perception till the moment that he will also objectively be what he has always subjectively been and experience that which is the stake of the whole Play: pure, divine Love.

We are the growing Godhead. 'Brahman, sir, is the name given by Indian philosophy since the beginning of time to the one Reality, eternal and infinite, which is the Self, the Divine, the All, the more than All ... In fact, sir, you are Brahman,'[9] wrote Sri Aurobindo in meaningful jest to Nirodbaran. The Godhead is present in every part of our material, vital and mental body. He is especially present, wholly himself, in our heart which we feel as the location of our soul. What we call the soul is purely That. At the origin, where the Spirit plunged into Time, it was we ourselves, souls in all eternity existing in That, who have undertaken the great adventure because we must have felt it worth its while.

Evolution is the growth process, also in us, of the materialized Godhead towards his manifested completeness. The world is an unfolding miracle, but the unfolding takes time, and at every rebirth we drop so heavily on our head, said the Mother, that we forget where we have come from. 'We are the Godhead who has forgotten himself.' Humanity had also forgotten where it came from, namely from the womb of Mother Earth, but recently it has found this out again, though it is not yet aware where it is going to; neither does it realize that if there have been so many evolutionary steps before it, logically speaking there should or could also follow some after it. Having read the morning paper or looked at oneself in the mirror, it is rather difficult for man to keep contending that mankind has reached the summit of perfection or that man is 'the masterpiece of masterpieces.'

But here we are no longer following Vedanta, at least not as interpreted by most Indian sages who, like the rest of us, found life on Earth such a mess that they declared it to be a bad dream, a chimera, an illusion, advising us to get out of it as soon as possible. Following their line of reasoning, these sages did not seem to be aware that they were pulling the carpet if not from under the feet of the Brahman, then surely from under the structure of their own logic. How in the omniscient, omnipotent and all-blissful Brahman could there possibly be a world — for instance a spinning, bluish globe with little humans on it — that is so worthless that one has to get out of it as soon as possible? Has the Omniscient made a blunder? Has the Omnipotent lacked in power? And the All-Blissful, has he taken pleasure in the miserable lives of creatures with a veiled consciousness?

Yet many religions in the East and the West essentially agree with this interpretation of Vedanta: somewhere something has gone wrong (maybe by the magic intervention of a Black Demiurge?); the Earth is no more than a necessary evil (as, once born on it, our incarnation cannot be helped); and we can only try to get in the Hereafter by the shortest possible way (hopefully in the enjoyable regions of it) or to get rid of the nightmare once and for all (in Nirvana). Some say that we get out of the ordeal after this absurdly short life, others that we have to come back hundreds or thousands of times. Whatever the truth, the escapist solution is the same for most religions.

But that is not how Sri Aurobindo saw things. He did not avoid the logical conclusions from the Vedantic line of thinking. If absolute Being-Consciousness-Bliss is the essence of all existence, also of existence in evolution, then evolution must inevitably contain these attributes in itself too and should manifest them sooner or later. Besides, such is the promise given to mankind according to all great occult traditions — the promise of the establishment of the Kingdom of God on the earth.

'Evolution is not finished; reason is not the last word nor the reasoning animal the supreme figure of Nature. As man emerged out of the animal, so out of man the superman emerges,'[10] reads one of Sri Aurobindo's aphorisms. And in the first pages of *The Life Divine* he writes: 'The animal is a living laboratory in which Nature has, it is said, worked out man. Man himself may well be a thinking and living laboratory in whom and with whose conscious cooperation she wills to work out the superman, the god.'[11] To him this was not only a possibility, it was a certainty because it was 'inevitable', resulting from the essence and process of evolution when seen in the correct perspective. 'The supramental change is a thing decreed and inevitable in the evolution of the earth-consciousness; for its upward ascent is not ended and mind is not the last summit.'[12]

Evolution and Involution

'The word evolution carries with it in its intrinsic sense, in the idea at its root, the necessity of a previous involution,'[13] writes Sri Aurobindo. For 'nothing can evolve out of Matter which is not already therein contained.'[14] 'Evolution of life in matter supposes a previous involution of it there, unless we suppose it to be a new creation magically and unaccountably introduced into Nature.'[15] 'The evolution of consciousness and knowledge cannot be accounted for unless there is already a concealed consciousness in things with its inherent and native powers emerging little by little.'[16] In other words: what is not contained in the evolving stuff cannot come out of it, and as it has come out of it, it must have been contained in it, in the basic evolutionary material.

The process of creation, the model of our evolutionary world, can therefore be metaphorically represented by a stair of worlds manifested by the Godhead first to descend into its manifestation from the highest consciousness to the lowest, total unconsciousness, and by which, objectively incarnated in ever higher evolutionary forms, it now climbs back to his absolute perfection. One might suppose that at this juncture it is, in man, somewhere halfway in its climb back up.

The lowest steps of the stairs are clearly discernible for anyone not wearing the dark glasses of dogmatic materialism: at the bottom there is matter (the minerals), then life (plants and lower animals), then mental consciousness (higher animals and man). Each of these levels has grown out of the levels underneath and contains all their elements in itself. An original thinker like the economist E.F. Schumacher, author of *Small is Beautiful*, explained this evolutionary stratification in a conversation with Fritjof Capra, who writes: 'Schumacher expressed his belief in a fundamental hierarchical order consisting of four characteristic elements — mineral, plant, animal, and human — with four others — matter, life, consciousness, and self-awareness — which are manifest in such a way that each level possesses not only its own characteristic element but also those of all lower levels. This, of course, was the ancient idea of the Great Chain of Being, which Schumacher presented in modern language and with considerable subtlety. However, he maintained that the four elements are irreducible mysteries that cannot be explained, and that the differences between them represent fundamental jumps in the vertical dimension, "ontological discontinuities," as he put it. "This is why physics cannot have any philosophical impact," he repeated. "It cannot deal with the whole; it deals only with the lowest level," the level of matter.'[17] (*Uncommon Wisdom*).

Schumacher's words are remarkable because he had managed to break through the boundaries of the generally dominant scientific reductionism and to perceive reality with an unprejudiced eye. The laws of science are indeed exclusively, and only partially, the laws of the material level of existence, occupying the outer layer of the Globe of Being. This is why, out of necessity, they must remain incomplete till science can get out of its vicious circle asserting that everything is matter because there is nothing but matter.

Above these levels there are still others also experienced by us, though much less concretely perceptible, such as the level of our inspirations and intuitions, or above it the world of the great beings whom man calls gods, angels or beings of light. Considering the diversity of cultures and the abundance of their creations throughout the centuries, and the role played by religion in the world of men, it would be absurd to deny the existence of these levels surpassing our ordinary mental consciousness. Surely, all that had to emerge from somewhere. And is there one important scientific discovery or invention that was not the result of an inspiration, of a sudden 'insight' or 'illumination'?

According to Sri Aurobindo, all the afore-mentioned levels belong to the lower half of the evolutionary stair, to the lower hemisphere of the Globe of Being — perhaps a better term than 'Chain of Being', which remains associated with a linear mode of thinking. Part of the higher hemisphere are the worlds of the attributes of the Godhead, of Being, Consciousness and Bliss, held by the seers to be the highest qualities of existence. When one thinks of Zeus and his Olympic court, of the Hindu pantheon, or of Yahweh and his hosts of angels, it becomes obvious that Brahman with its attributes must be higher, or deeper, or more inclusive. The worlds of the gods are manifested worlds, while Being is the manifesting source beyond all names and manifestations.

In spiritual experience there is a division between the worlds of the divine attributes and the worlds of the gods, a separation which the ancient Indian writings call 'a golden lid'; it is this separation which is the rationale behind the supposed 'gap' between God and his creation as taught by the religions of the Chaldean family. This golden lid is a gate, as it were, which man in his present state is not allowed to pass, for the Vedas say that he who goes through 'the gate of the Sun' cannot come back.

Sri Aurobindo and the Mother have passed through it — and they have come back, because they were the first beings destined for this adventure. They have explored the divine solar world between the uppermost levels of *Sat-Chit-Ananda* and the ones our world and we ourselves consist of. They have found that the lower hemisphere of existence originates from and is supported by the higher. Some seers had already viewed this sun-world, among them the Vedic rishis, but for them the time had not yet come to insert it into the ascending stair of evolution. Sri Aurobindo, using a technical, neutral term, has called the sun-world 'the Supramental,' because it is far above the mental consciousness, even above its highest reaches.

The Supramental — itself a resplendent prism of worlds — is essentially a principle of Unity, to us unimaginable. For in our world everything is divided, separated into I, you, he and she, in things on a cosmic, human or atomic scale; we are bumping into everyone and everything, and we are not certain about what is going on behind the eyes of a cat, of our own child or of our beloved. A great Western philosopher has even said that everything exists in itself and that it is impossible to know something that is not oneself. In the Supramental, on the contrary, everything is consciously and constantly present in everything else at the same time; there life is shadowless bliss (the divine *Ananda*) and immortal. 'Light is [there] one with Force, the vibrations of knowledge with the rhythm of the will and both are one, perfectly and without seeking, groping or effort, with the assured result.'[18] The Supramental 'has the knowledge of the One, but it is able to draw out of the One its hidden multitudes; it manifests the Many, but does not lose itself in their differentiations.'[19]

The Supramental, being the directly manifested Godhead and therefore possessing the intrinsic unity of the Godhead, is present everywhere and in everything, even now, in the paper on which these words are printed and in the iris of the eye that reads them as well as in the ice of the comets beyond Pluto and in the burning core of the quasars. Without the Supramental nothing could possibly exist. It will be remembered that God is not only 'higher' but also deeper, more inward, and it is from the 'inside' that, by his supramental creation, he keeps up our darkened world. But indeed, how is it that our world has been 'darkened'? How is it that we are living in such a troublesome world of division, separation and ignorance? Because the golden sunrays of the Consciousness of Unity have been filtered, so to speak, by the lid between the hemispheres, thus being dimmed and turned into what we call the mental consciousness, or 'the mental' for short. The mental is an instrument of knowledge able to see only from a certain standpoint and never from all possible standpoints at the same time like the supramental Consciousness of Unity; therefore it can only perceive aspects, aspects that are parts, flakes or chips of the One Reality. This is why Sri Aurobindo called man 'the mental being', halfway on the ascending ladder of evolution, between the dark abyss of the Inconscient and the radiant summit of the all-seeing, all-knowing and all-powerful Being.

Thus evolution actually means the rebuilding in Matter of the stair, or the supercosmic column, or the tower of worlds, up to the point where the manifestation will become the fully conscious incarnation of its Maker. Mother Nature, an aspect of the Great Mother, takes an endless time for the work, at least when measured against our brief human lifespan, and she seems to revel in the modelling of a wonderful variety of creatures, having surpassed the most beautiful inventions of the modern artists millions of years ago in works of art that are alive, that swim, run and fly. A new step of the stair, we have seen, is made out of the already existing materials of the previous steps — man carrying in him the complete preceding evolution — plus something more that, thanks to the involution, lay waiting in them. When one step, or one species, in the material evolution has reached its upper limit and in its completeness keeps pushing against this ceiling, then the evolutionary impulse to further development acts as a call for the realization of the following step, for a new, higher species.

'Involution' is another word for the full scale of manifested but, to our eye, hidden worlds; these are non-evolutionary 'typal' worlds, in other words, worlds in which the beings do not change or evolve as they are fully satisfied with their way of being and with their type, a satisfaction which is the expression of the fundamental omnipresent *Ananda* or Bliss. These worlds represent the complete consciousness scale from the highest *Ananda* to the lowest vital level. From the 'column' of typal worlds — which is the manifestation of the Godhead, a 'slice' or gradation (i.e., a world with its laws and beings) has to be inserted at each higher step in the material evolution; this happens in answer to the impulse from below, to the pressure against the temporary evolutionary ceiling. The coordination of both forces, of the impulse from below and the answer from above, results in the material manifestation of a new, higher species. This has happened time and again when the lower and higher life-forms made their appearance on planet Earth, followed by the ever more mentalized animals and then by the full-grown, typical mental being, the human.

All this implies that somewhere in the typal manifestation there must have existed a mental world belonging to mental beings like the human aeons before he became materially incarnated on Earth. The Mother formulates it as follows: 'Man does not belong to the Earth only: man is essentially a universal being, but he has a special manifestation on Earth.'[20] In Sri Aurobindo's words: '[Man] expresses, under the conditions of the terrestrial world he inhabits, the mental power of the universal existence.'[21] And he wrote to a disciple: 'You speak as if the evolution were the sole creation; the creation or manifestation is very vast and contains many planes and worlds that existed before the evolution, all different in character and with different kinds of beings.'[22]

Seen in this way, the divine manifestation, including earthly evolution, is not the result or the scene of a dictatorial divine fancy. The omnipotent Godhead has limited himself in his creation by building laws into it, thus providing it with a supporting structure. This is the reason why evolution has to follow certain processes. One of these laws exacts the insertion of ever higher universal levels of consciousness into the ascending material stair of evolution as an answer to the evolutionary impulse when the previous, lower level has reached its ceiling. Another necessary process is the intervention of the Godhead itself in its evolving creation to make the insertion of a new gradation possible. To this end the Godhead incarnates on Earth as an Avatar.

According to Sri Aurobindo and the Mother, the existing human species, at present, has reached its ceiling after a long-lasting development of which only the most recent phase is known to us, the period in time which we call history. The vision of the evolutionary saltus, of the evolutionary quantum leap was given to them because they had come to execute it in their own person. The Kingdom of God on Earth was promised to humankind at its origin and the moment of its fulfilment has now arrived, they say. The human being is inwardly mutating into a new, higher, divine being which as yet has no name, though it is sometimes called 'superman'. Out of the mental being, whether it knows it or not, whether it consciously wants it or not, evolves NOW the supramental being. The Pioneers have already formed the archetype of the new species in themselves and prepared the Earth for its appearance, as we shall see further on in this book. The future on the threshold of the new millennium is not sombre or catastrophic: on Earth, the Earth of unified human-kind, the Kingdom of God is being built.

All this does not mean that the world of mankind on Earth has been an enviable one, now or in former times. Somewhere something occurred that has turned our planet into a place of abomination. There are traditions that tell about a moral fall, others about a cosmic accident. Let us conclude this brief introductory note to Sri Aurobindo's vision with a story told by the Mother more than once, with small variations. She mentioned that she had the story from a hoary occult tradition and that it carries a profound meaning. Al-though symbolic, it is a true story.

When the Supreme decided to externalize himself in order to contemplate himself, he first formed within himself the Knowledge and Power of manifestation. This Knowledge-Power or Conscious-ness-Force is the Great Mother. (Every power and every force is a vibration; every vibration is a consciousness; and every consciousness is a personal being — without exception.) The Supreme had decided that Joy and Freedom would form the foundation of his manifesta-tion, the two qualities without which a divine expression of *Ananda* is impossible — and the Mother, the great Creatrix, of course ex-ecuted his decision.

After the formation of the fundamental divine Joy and Freedom, the Mother created four Beings. Because from these Four there had to evolve everything else of the exteriorization, they were the incar-nation of the divine attributes, the original fountainheads and pillars of creation: 1. Consciousness that is Light; 2. Life; 3. Bliss that is Love; and 4. Truth. They were magnificent and exceedingly powerful beings, for each of them, being the incarnation of a divine attribute, resembled the Godhead almost totally. They possessed the full free-dom to enjoy their essential divinity. And it happened that these first Four splendid beings, almost totally resembling the Godhead, became as it were intoxicated by their joy and their freedom, so much so that they began imagining they were equal to the Godhead, nay, that they were the Supreme himself.

As we know, the Supreme is also the One in whom division is impossible. But because in the Four the delusion had arisen by which each one of them imagined he was the Supreme, the delusion of division also arose in the whole creation. In their consciousness the Four separated from each other and from their Origin, and as a consequence they became the opposite of what they had been at first. The Being of Consciousness and Light became the Lord of Darkness; the Being of Bliss and Love became the Lord of Suffering; the Being of Truth became the Lord of Falsehood; the Being of Life became the Lord of Death. This is how, because of them, the world became as we know it.

When the Great Mother saw the damage her children had done, she turned towards the Supreme and beseeched him for a means to reverse the disaster.

He then commanded her to pour out her Consciousness of Light into that inconscience, her Truth into that falsehood and her Love into that suffering. And the Great Mother did so, with an even greater intensity than when she had created the first Four. She plunged into the terror of the Night of the Inconscient and again awoke in it Consciousness, Love and Truth to activate the salvation which would carry the universe back to its Origin of everlasting Bliss. The gradual realization of this salvation we call evolution.

We have now arrived at the point where evolution has reached the threshold of a supramental, divine world. The realization of this divine world will not happen at the blink of an eye, but the foun-dations have been laid. And after this, there will occur many other and higher developments on Earth, till the Supreme will fully become himself again. But by then ignorance, darkness, death, suffering and falsehood will long have disappeared, because the Four will have been reintegrated into their Origin.

Chapter Eight

HOMO SUM ...

*Man is Nature's great term of
transition in which she grows
conscious of her aim; in him she looks
up from the animal with open eyes
towards the divine ideal.*[1]
— Sri Aurobindo

'A STORY has neither a beginning nor an end: arbitrarily one chooses that moment of experience from which to look back or from which to look ahead.' These are the opening words of Graham Greene's novel *The End of the Affair*. The story of man has neither a beginning nor an end. It moves between two infinities: behind man his origin, ahead of him his destiny. And both are the same, 'a consciousness ... against which the universe seems to stand out like a petty picture against an immeasurable background'[2] (Sri Aurobindo).

Man carries in him all that has preceded him in the manifestation. He carries the Godhead in him that he essentially still is and has to become again fully. He carries in him the features of the big Four who where his primordial progenitors in the creation; because of them his Earth has been perverted and become susceptible to darkness, suffering, falsehood and death. And he carries in him everything that has emerged before in the evolution, not only matter and life but also mental consciousness, which is why he is able to think, to reason and even to 'see' a little. Although his true nature is that of an incarnated mental consciousness in matter and life, the lower evolutionary gradations still prevail in him to such a degree that he may still be considered to be animal man, not the mental being in its pure form which in times to come may take shape as a higher species on Earth.

He is great, he is little. He is terribly vulnerable though in essence immortal. He is ignorant but has the omniscience in him and therefore at every moment does exactly the action that is required for the destiny of himself and of the Whole. He is a dwarf, a worm, a speck of dust on the sleeve of the universe, and he is the child of the Great Mother, the princely child of the Queen with the crown of twelve pearls. It is true, 'man as he is cannot be the last term of the evolution: he is too imperfect an expression of the Spirit'.[3] (Sri Aurobindo). It is also true that 'we are the first possible instruments to begin and make the world progress.'[4] 'It is man who will do the job. He is the one who will change. He is the one who will transform his Earth'[5] (The Mother). 'For man is precisely that term and symbol of a higher Existence descended into the material world in which it is possible for the lower to transfigure itself and put on the nature of the higher and the higher to reveal itself in the forms of the lower'[6] (Sri Aurobindo). Man is the crux, the big X. He stands at the intersection of the universal lines of force, he is the cross and the crucified, impotent in his concealed omnipotence, flogged and crowned with thorns as the grotesque and yet true king of Creation.

And he is the child of Mother Earth. 'Heaven is his father, the Earth his mother,' says Hermes Trismegistos in the *Tabula Smaragdina*. According to the present scientific model, planet Earth is a small ball in space as there are probably millions more. Nothing much in fact, and if life-forms have appeared on it, it can only have been by accident. But on this point too science is revising its opinion, and some cosmologists now dare to suggest that Earth as the bearer of life might be unique. The recently introduced weak and strong anthropic principles prove how even the sober men of science are in need of an explanation of the improbable chain of coincidences that leads up to their own existence.

The view of Sri Aurobindo and the Mother, referring to the great traditions and based on their own occult experience, differs radically from the generally accepted scientific model. 'In the whole creation the earth has a place of distinction, because unlike any other planet it is evolutionary with a psychic entity at its centre,'[7] wrote the Mother. To the children of the Ashram she said: 'The Earth is a sort of symbolical crystallization of universal life, a reduction, a concentration, to facilitate the work of evolution and to participate in it.'[8] Sri Aurobindo wrote: 'Our attention must be fixed on the earth because our work is here. Besides, the earth is a concentration of all the other worlds and one can touch them by touching something corresponding in the earth-atmosphere.'[9] By this he does not mean the physical atmosphere, but the extremely complex invisible body of Earth, the living entity, her physical body being to our senses the perceptible exteriorization of it.

Seen in this way, the Earth is no longer some little globe spinning in space, one out of a probably countless number — as one so often reads: a small satellite of an average sun somewhere in the outer end of one of the arms of a common galaxy. It is again awarded a central position in the material cosmos, even *the* central position from the standpoint of evolution and of everything that is of vital importance to us. 'The Earth has been formed in a special way by a direct intervention, without anything intermediary, of the supreme Consciousness [the Great Mother] in the Inconscient [after the fall of the four original Beings] ... I have taken great pains to tell you that it was a symbolical creation and that every action on this special point [the Earth] radiates in the whole universe. Don't forget this and don't go about telling that the Earth has been formed from something ejected by the sun,'[10] the Mother said to the children of the Ashram.

After the complete development of their occult capacities, Sri Aurobindo and the Mother had access to all manifested worlds. Sri Aurobindo has described the whole range of them in detail in his epic poem *Savitri*, a revelation with a lasting place in the occult and spiritual world literature. For him and for the Mother it was not difficult to visit in their subtle body the planets of our own solar system, and they have done so. But it soon became clear to them that those planetary worlds were of secondary importance to their work when compared to Earth and its central place in the cosmic order. 'The evolution takes place on the earth and the earth is therefore the right field of progress,' wrote Sri Aurobindo, and also: 'I am concerned with the earth, not with worlds beyond for their own sake.' All cosmic elements being present in the Earth, everything that happens here transmits its vibrations to similar elements elsewhere in the cosmos. As the nucleus of a cell determines the functioning of the whole of the cell, so too Earth determines the life and development of the cosmos.

We who have been living under the nuclear threat of the Cold War receive from Sri Aurobindo and the Mother an unexpected reassurance. 'The Earth has been built with a certain purpose and it will not disappear before the things have been accomplished,'[11] said the Mother in 1960. She repeated this emphatically eleven years later, when many feared that humanity, together with its planet, would volatilize in nuclear radiation before the end of the century. 'The Earth will not be destroyed,' not before it has accomplished the purpose for which it was built. This does not mean that it might not be subject to changes of great moment at the present time or in times to come.

Indeed, some pronouncements by Sri Aurobindo and the Mother are based on a cosmology completely different from the one generally accepted today, which after all is quite recent and exclusively constructed on what is materially perceptible (though physics, with its neutron stars, quasars and black holes, has grown much more occult than it likes to acknowledge). How to interpret for instance the following aphorism of Sri Aurobindo: 'To the senses it is always true that the sun moves round the earth; this is false for reason. To the reason it is always true that the earth moves round the sun; this is false to the supreme vision. Neither earth moves nor the sun; there is only a change in the relation of sun-consciousness and earth-consciousness'?[12] One feels that here a fundamental, albeit for us still incomprehensible, truth has been formulated.

Or let us quote the following paragraph by Sri Aurobindo, expressing a view parallel to the scientific one: 'Necessarily, by terrestrial we do not mean this one earth and its period of duration, but use earth in the wider root-sense of the Vedantic prithwi, the earth-principle creating habitations of physical form for the soul.'[13] This is the earth-principle that together with the principles of water, fire, air and ether constitutes the five elements of which things consist.*

We have been told that the divine manifestation has neither beginning nor end. From this we might deduce that the drama of evolution, that is the incarnation of the Divine Consciousness in a material, 'Earthly' environment, must have taken place countless times before, in a 'habitation' — a planet or a world — where the Self in its variety of selves (souls) has taken on physical forms. We find this supposition confirmed in the following paragraph of Sri Aurobindo: 'The experiment of human life on an earth is not now for the first time enacted. It has been conducted a million times before and the long drama will again a million times be repeated. In all that we do now, our dreams, our discoveries, our swift or difficult attainments, we profit subconsciously by the experience of innumerable precursors and our labour will be fecund in planets unknown to us and in worlds yet uncreated. The plan, the peripeties, the denouement differ continually, yet are always governed by the conventions of an eternal Art. God, Man, Nature are the three perpetual symbols.'[14] This still virtually unknown text of Sri Aurobindo, written in the late Twenties or the early Thirties and for the first time published in 1982 by the *Sri Aurobindo Archives and Research*, is the logical, staggering consequence of his general outlook.

And he also wrote: 'Then he [the Creator] creates out of this solar body of Vishnu the planets, each of which successively becomes the Bhumi [Earth] or place of manifestation for Manu, the mental being, who is the nodus of manifest life-existence and the link between the life and the spirit. The present earth in its turn appears as the scene of life, Mars being its last theatre.'[15] These words are from an essay

---

* The ether has a real existence, according to Sri Aurobindo, too subtle to be measured even by the present-day scientific instruments though the fields of quantum mechanics, which form the basis of matter, resemble it more and more. Maybe we will live to see the ether rehabilitated by modern science.

written by Sri Aurobindo in 1914 under the title *The Evolutionary Scale*. Might this be the reason why we are still so fascinated by Mars?

Sri Aurobindo and the Mother have seldom given much attention to speculations about other planets and stellar systems. There are beings anywhere in the manifestation, they say, but materialized beings are found exclusively on Earth. It is too easy to indulge in all kinds of romantic fantasies as long as we do not fully know and master ourselves, as long as we have not found a solution to the problems of existence confronting us here.

'The world in which we live is not a meaningless accident that has unaccountably taken place in the void of Space; it is the scene of an evolution in which an eternal Truth has been embodied, hidden in a form of things, and is secretly in process of unfoldment through the ages. There is a meaning in our existence, a purpose in our birth and death and travail, a consummation of all our labour. All are parts of a single plan; nothing has been idly made in the universe; nothing is vain in our life'[16] (Sri Aurobindo).

Some not totally disinterested promoters of space travel, which according to the Mother is 'a game for grown-up children,' give as an important reason for its further development that we might find somewhere in the universe the explanation of our being and our existence. However, this explanation is not to be found in matter as such, here or elsewhere, but in That which has brought matter forth and by which it exists. Besides, it seems somewhat improbable that on the other side of the universe should be found what is not present here; on the contrary, the Earth, as we have seen, is a symbolic condensation of the universe, with all its shades of light and darkness. Man carries the fundamental problems in himself, be it in jeans or in a space suit.

The evolution of our universe, seen in a broad perspective, is a concatenation of miracles, of improbabilities which all the same have happened in one way or another, and about which science has a lot of suppositions and theories but no explanations. Science actually has only models, i.e. mathematical descriptions of processes, but not a single fundamental explanation whatsoever. For to explain one single phenomenon, however simple, one has to know everything, as everything is inseparably, intrinsically connected. 'The universe as a whole explains every single thing at any moment.'[17] 'The tree does not explain the seed, nor the seed the tree; cosmos explains both and God explains cosmos.'[18]

There is no scientific explanation of the Big Bang, which, precisely because of its uniqueness, is called a 'singularity'. Neither is there a scientific explanation of the phenomenon Earth, 'a habitable planet in an inhabitable system' (Sri Aurobindo). And there is no scientific explanation of the 'ontological discontinuities', called 'irreducible mysteries' by E.F. Schumacher, namely the hierarchically ordered forms of existence that have appeared on Earth: matter, life, lower and higher mental consciousness.

Let there be no misunderstanding: the origin of life on Earth has not yet been scientifically accounted for. In this matter, as in many others, official science gives in to wishful thinking. It refers for example to the experiments of Urey and Miller, who are supposed to have proven the life-producing possibilities of a hypothetical prebiotic soup, and even to a modern version of 'panspermia', which holds that life was brought to the Earth somewhere from the universe by comets or other carriers. Even if it were true that life has originated in some other place in the universe, this would not bring us one step nearer to an explanation of it.

All seven present theories of the origin of life have been examined by Robert Shapiro, an expert in the research on DNA, in his book *Origins: A Skeptic's Guide to the Creation of Life on Earth*. He arrives at the conclusion that, these theories notwithstanding, life on our planet still seems to be a *generatio spontanea* as it was in former times. 'The improbability involved in generating even one bacterium is so large that it reduces all considerations of time and space to nothingness' (p. 128).

If life on Earth indeed has come into existence by an ontological discontinuity or 'quantum leap', then its gestation and its essence cannot but remain out of reach of materialistic science; for then it is something wholly other than an epiphenomenon of material processes — in the supposition that these processes could exist by themselves — and then the cell, like every living organism, is much more than a machine (cf. 'The cell is indeed a machine,' Jacques Monod in *Le Hasard et la Nécessité*, p. 145). Life has its own laws and processes that are yet to be discovered by the true, comprehensive science of the future.

The same reasoning is valid, and in still greater measure, in theories concerning mental consciousness. To us the processes of life can still be directly experienced, most intimately in our beating heart, but the mental processes are a lot more impalpable and intangible, so much so that they are frequently mistaken for spiritual phenomena, both ranges of existence then being covered by what is called 'spirit' or by similar terms.

The great confusion, with regrettable consequences, in every discussion about 'body' and 'spirit' has been caused by a philosopher who is generally thought of as the very epitome of clear thinking, René Descartes. To him man is a body, which is a machine composed of measurable substances, and 'spirit'; what man thinks with, as well as the higher domains determining his thinking and what is supposedly spiritual or divine, is abstract, unmeasurable and therefore insubstantial. Secondly, science must consider only the measurable. The result of both premises, however, was that science declared itself to be an abstraction, an epiphenomenon of matter, with the absurd consequence that science was and is being practised by something it has declared an abstraction. For the scientist's awareness of his own life experiences, including his reflections and thus his scientific thinking, is according to his own assumptions something unmeasurable and therefore scientifically unreal. Science too, the standard bearer of matter and of the concrete, has declared the human experience and consequently the experienced world to be an illusion!

Material and Spiritual Evolution

It may seem amazing how near E.F. Schumacher brings the higher animal to man. Sri Aurobindo and the Mother go still further in this. 'Man and the animal are both mentally conscious beings ...'[19] In the animal the human intellect is being prepared, 'for the animal too thinks'[20] (Sri Aurobindo). Studying their line of thinking one concludes that the deep gap assumed by man between himself and the animal is actually the expression of a kind of self-defense; he tries to distance himself from his own animality by elevating himself as high as possible above it. No ardent self-contemplation is needed to realize our external similarities with, let us say, the primates, and all human history testifies to our inner similarities with the animal, so much so that comparisons often turn out to the advantage of it.

How has man originated? The human species has come about in accordance with the evolutionary mechanisms that have already been described. On the one hand there were the primates who had reached their ceiling, in whom evolution had worked out the possibility of a higher form of consciousness and in whom it now called for the descent of this higher form; on the other hand there was the answer from above by which a higher mental world, the world of the 'typal' man, was inserted into the evolutionary ladder, thus enabling the incarnation of a species on a higher rung of the ladder, earthman.

When approximately did this take place? Paleontologists say that the human being made its appearance on Earth between one and three million years ago, and according to the Mother a million years had already elapsed between the descent of the mental principle on Earth and the first material incarnation of the human being. 'After the mental had descended on earth, between the time of the manifestation of the mental in the atmosphere and the time of the appearance of the first man, something like a million years has gone by.'[21] The mental consciousness as incarnated in the human being, with the reason, the reflective consciousness, the awareness of space and time and the inception of the capacity of a higher 'seeing', should consequently have descended into the earth-atmosphere between two and four million years ago. The Mother also said: 'There have most certainly been intermediaries or parallel forms between the ape and man.'[22] It is now common knowledge that the fossil remains of several intermediary beings have been found and classified by paleontologists.

The Mother confirms the teachings of the ancient traditions and also what is stated in the Bible: that beings from a higher world first came on the Earth in their pure form, but that later on they united

with the higher animals, which resulted in a long transition of probably very bizarre corporeal forms, of which the human being finally
was the harmonious outcome. 'It was only when man was made, that
the gods were satisfied ... and cried, "Man indeed is well and
wonderfully made; the higher evolution can now begin!" He is like
God, the sum of all other creatures from the animal to the god,
infinitely variable where they are fixed, dynamic where they, even
the highest are static, and therefore, although in the present and in
his attainment a little lower than the angels, yet in the eventuality
and in his culmination considerably higher than the gods'[23] (Sri
Aurobindo).

Evolution on Earth is a development, a growth of consciousness
in material forms, which becomes ever more refined and complex
as the growth proceeds. 'The evolution has always had a spiritual
significance and the physical change was only instrumental'[24] (Sri
Aurobindo). It is consciousness which, by the described non-material
processes, irresistibly drives evolution onwards and upwards, and
works out every gradation of it. The origin and the goal of evolution
on Earth are spiritual; the mechanisms of evolution are procedures
of the spirit in matter, and its results are ever higher gradations of
material forms.

'A theory of spiritual evolution is not identical with a scientific
theory of form-evolution and physical life-evolution; it must stand
on its own inherent justification: it may accept the scientific account
of physical evolution as a support or an element, but the support is
not indispensable. The scientific theory is concerned only with the
outward and visible machinery and process, with the details of
Nature's execution, with the physical development of things in
Matter and the law of development of Life and Mind in Matter; its
account of the process may have to be considerably changed or may
be dropped altogether in the light of new discovery, but that will not
affect the self-evident fact of a spiritual evolution, an evolution of
Consciousness, a progression of the soul's manifestation in material
existence' (*The Life Divine*, p. 835).

Seen from the standpoint of the Spirit, 'the material universe is
only the facade of an immense building which has other structures

behind it, and it is only if one knows the whole that one can have some knowledge of the truth of the material universe'[25] (Sri Aurobindo). Science sees things exactly the other way around, because for science it is not the Spirit but Matter that is primordial and even the sole existent. As for evolution, science seems to be very much assured of its knowledge. Paul Davies, for instance, writes: 'The basic principles and mechanisms of evolution are no longer seriously in doubt.'[26] And in *Le hasard et la nécessité*, which some years ago was a French best-seller by Nobel Prize winner and champion of materialistic positivism Jacques Monod, we read: 'Today one can say that the elementary mechanisms of evolution are not only understood in principle but identified with precision.'[27] Is that so?

While talking about the appearance of life on Earth, we have already mentioned Robert Shapiro's book *Origins*, first published in 1986, in which is clearly shown that *not one* theory of life comes even near to explaining the origin of a living, self-reproducing organism on our planet. The papers of the 1993 congress in Barcelona on the same subject contain masses of data and a lot of hopeful surmises, but they have not taken us a step nearer to the explanation of life.

The truth is that science knows little about the mechanisms of evolution, and that all declarations to the contrary are self-delusions and often a form of demagogy practised by the creed of materialism, not to say an untruth consciously kept alive. Francis Hitching puts it as follows: 'In three crucial areas where neo-Darwinism [at present still the generally recognized evolutionary 'school'] can be tested, it has failed: 1. The fossil records reveal a pattern of evolutionary leaps rather than gradual change. 2. Genes are a powerful stabilizing mechanism whose main function is to prevent new forms evolving. 3. Random step-by-step mutations at the molecular level cannot explain the organized and growing complexity of life.'[28]

In other words, the theory of gradualism (i.e., the gradual apparition of evolutionary changes during very long periods of time), to be unconditionally accepted at the cost of ridicule by the scientific community, does not seem to hold water; the genes are not the fundamental evolutionary factors as molecular biology continues to teach; evolution is not a matter of random mutations and mutants, for these result almost exclusively in non-viable deformations and consequently cannot be the building elements in the grandiose and extremely complex order of evolution as a whole and of each of its gradations in particular. This means, briefly summarized, that the three pillars of neo-Darwinism, and accordingly of the generally accepted theory of evolution at present, are without foundation.

Equally important is the fact that the famous 'missing links', the untraceable transitory forms between the species, remain missing. Most paleontologists now admit that they do not exist. 'It is not even possible to make a caricature [i.e., a resemblance] of evolution out of palaeobiological facts. The fossil material is now so complete that the lack of transitional series cannot be explained by the scarcity of the material. The deficiencies are real, they will never be filled.'[29] These are the words of N. Heribert-Nilsson, professor at the University of Lund, after forty years of study of the subject. 'There are missing links that remain always missing,'[30] wrote an ironical Sri Aurobindo in *The Life Divine*. We now know the explanation: the evolutionary leaps take place in Consciousness, the essence, carrier and developing factor of all manifestation, and the material life forms are what the processes in Consciousness have fixed in Matter because they proved to be viable organisms.

It is important to give some consideration to this topic. For questions about humankind and its origins arise in everybody's mind, and explanations provided by religion are, for the most part, so unreasonable that they invariably lose out against the arguments of science, which make the scientific view look irrefutable.

Sri Aurobindo's vision is a rational elaboration of the fundamentals of everyday experience as well as of a higher experience in which the cosmic events and the smallest common details are provided with a justified and meaningful place, for he wanted his view 'to agree with all the facts of existence.' To the relation between science and spirituality we will come back later, and in the next chapter we will take a look at the apparent lack of concreteness of things 'spiritual'. Sri Aurobindo always kept 'a healthy grip on the facts' and favoured a 'spiritual positivism'. His aim was 'the widest, the most flexible, the most catholic affirmation possible.'[31] 'As in science, so in metaphysical thought, that general and ultimate solution is likely to be the best which includes and accounts for all so that each truth of experience takes its place in the whole.'[32]

'The touch of Earth is always reinvigorating to the son of Earth, even when he seeks a supraphysical Knowledge. It may even be said that the supraphysical can only be really mastered in its fullness — to its heights we can always reach — when we keep our feet firmly on the physical. "Earth is his footing," says the Upanishad whenever it images the Self that manifests in the universe. And it is certainly a fact that the wider we extend and the surer we make our knowledge of the physical world, the wider and surer becomes our foundation of the higher knowledge, even for the highest, even for the *Brahmavidya* [the knowledge of Brahman]' (*The Life Divine*, p. 11).

> Earth is the chosen place of mightiest souls;
> Earth is the heroic spirit's battlefield,
> The forge where the Arch-mason shapes his works.
> Thy servitudes on earth are greater, king,
> Than all the glorious liberties of heaven.[33]
>
> — *Savitri*

Chapter Nine

FROM MAN TO SUPERMAN

[Present] man is but the shadow of
Man; Man is but the shadow of God.[1]
Inscription deciphered
on a bas-relief in a
Babylonian temple.

TO MOST of us, anything related to the spirit seems airy, insubstantial, unreal and on the whole fictitious. We have been cheated too many times by the so-called representatives of the spirit vaunting their abilities to describe to us the intangible and invisible, and to formulate the inaudible. Their contact with the spirit was the only true contact, they claimed, and had to be accepted at face value under the penalty of eternal damnation of our soul. They imprinted in our mind the belief that we ourselves could not directly contact the truth they held up to us because we were unworthy to do so. Even in the present day there is no shortage of usurpers and swindlers of the spirit, and the emptiness within us is so deep, the human distress so exasperating, that the 'men of God' always find an eager audience and a flourishing trade.

Sri Aurobindo and the Mother never made any effort to recruit disciples or devotees. We quote Sri Aurobindo's well-known letter, perhaps addressed to a too zealous disciple: 'I don't believe in advertisement except for books etc., and in propaganda except for politics and patent medicines. But for serious work it is a poison. It means either a stunt or a boom — and stunts and booms exhaust the thing they carry on their crest and leave it lifeless and broken high and dry on the shores of nowhere — or it means a movement. A movement in the case of a work like mine means the founding of a school or a sect or some other damned* nonsense. It means that hundreds or thousands of useless people join in and corrupt the work or reduce it to a pompous farce from which the Truth that was coming down recedes into secrecy and silence. This is what happened to the "religions" and it is the reason of their failure.'[2] And he added: 'I prefer to do solid work,' and that, if the work got accomplished, it would spread by itself. 'If that work gets done, then it will propagate itself so far as propagation is necessary — if it were not to get done, propagation would be useless.'

'I have a profound aversion to publicity,' said the Mother. And she had as strong an aversion to sectarianism in all its forms — the contorted self-righteousness of egocentric opinionatedness and narrow, stunted thinking.

Sri Aurobindo and the Mother were aware that their fully elaborated and forceful vision of the superman and supermanhood could easily lead to the growing self-assertion of fanatic sectarians. The Mother therefore warned: 'Truth is not a dogma that one can learn once and for all and impose as a rule. Truth is infinite like the supreme Lord himself and it manifests at every moment in those who are sincere and attentive.'[3] And she wrote to their own disciples: 'I repeat that in connection with Sri Aurobindo it is impos-

---

* Sri Aurobindo and the Mother had an innate sense of humour. 'Luckily Sri Aurobindo and I have met at this point', the Mother would say afterwards. One of his aphorisms goes as follows: 'To listen to some devout people, one would imagine that God never laughs; Heine was nearer the mark when he found in Him the divine Aristophanes.' For reasons unknown to Nirodbaran — 'Let it have no name,' wrote Sri Aurobindo — Sri Aurobindo in his correspondence with him one day, started writing in a humorous vein, something he and the Mother could rarely take the liberty of doing because their disciples would have taken their jest seriously and as a consequence interpreted their words in the wrong way. Like in the passage quoted here, Sri Aurobindo sometimes even used strong language to make a point. 'There is no law that wisdom should be something rigidly solemn and without a smile', he wrote, and also: 'Sense of humour? It is the salt of existence.'

sible to talk of a teaching or even of a revelation: his is a direct Action by the Lord, and thereon no religion can be founded ... Spiritual life can only exist in its purity when it is free of all forms of mental dogma.'[4]

Sometimes she saw the distortion, the narrowing and the hardening of Sri Aurobindo's synthetic and flexible thought take place before her very eyes, in the writings of a disciple or in his brain, more easily accessible to her than an open book. 'One must at any price prevent this from becoming a new religion. For as soon as it would be formulated in an elegant, impressive and somewhat forceful way, it would be finished.'[5] Sri Aurobindo had written: 'I may say that it is far from my purpose to propagate any religion, new or old, for humanity in the future. A way to be opened that is still blocked, not a religion to be founded, is my conception of the matter.'[6] The Mother also said: 'I have told you these things because it is necessary for you to hear them. But do not make an absolute dogma of it, for that would completely deprive them of their truth.'[7] And she wrote it down on paper: 'Do not take my words for a teaching. Always they are a force in action, uttered with a definite purpose, and they lose their true power when separated from that purpose.'[8] This warning is printed at the beginning of every volume of the English edition of her collected works and often quoted — especially by people who act exactly to the contrary.

The human being longs for the heights, but time and again is pulled downwards by the weight of the past it carries in him, by the darkness, the ignorance and the burden of the subconscious, by the weight of matter and the irrationality of the lower vital — all the invisible but very real forces affecting his thinking, usually a bobbing cork on the restless inner waves. Sri Aurobindo called this 'the downward gravitation'. Moreover, the mental consciousness of the human cannot actually know reality. We have seen that of reality, which is a whole, it can only know fragments, aspects, flints — the pieces of a puzzle of which it feels that it exists as a whole but which it can never know because it is unable to perceive it as a whole. True knowledge is only possible by identification, something human thought is incapable of doing.

In the human being only the lowest three steps of the stair of Existence have been realized. Higher on, there are many more 'spiritual' steps. As the word 'spirit' is often misleading, when using it and its derivations we will keep in mind the difference between the ordinary mental consciousness and the gradations above it; 'spiritual' is henceforth used exclusively in relation to these higher gradations.

All things spiritual seem airy, insubstantial and unreal to humans because of the downward gravitation in them, because of the fact that their material senses can only perceive material objects, and because of the slipping grip of their intellect on reality. These limitations cause humans to see the spiritual worlds as an unreal fiction. And this is why, after centuries of contradictory accounts and descriptions by those who claimed to have access to these worlds, humankind has resolutely put both feet on the solid ground of matter and declared this to be its true domain.

Still, humans know little of the spiritual worlds. They sometimes sense them so intensely that their familiar world is turned upside down. One can only sense what one has in oneself, for otherwise the sensory capacity would not be there, and one can only make contact with what is already in some way present in oneself.

According to Sri Aurobindo and the Mother, who follow the ancient yogic tradition in this, the human body in the manifestation of the human being on Earth consists of several 'sheaths' (of the soul). The material, visible sheath, made out of what we call tangible matter, is only our most outward or 'gross' body. This material sheath is surrounded by or embedded in a vital sheath consisting of substance of the vital plane. It is in this vital body that we go in search of adventure in our vital dreams and that we leave our material or gross body for good at the time of death. Both bodies are in their turn surrounded by or embedded in a mental sheath, made of the still more subtle substance of the mental worlds. If our mental body is sufficiently developed we can roam about in it through mental dream worlds, and after death we spend some time in it, after having left the vital worlds by discarding our vital body. Then there still is a more subtle sheath, sometimes called the 'causal body', in which we may enter the supramental worlds once that body has completely been formed.

Seen in this way, the human being is, just like the Earth, a condensation or representation of the cosmos. This is why it was called
a microcosm in the occult mysteries and by the alchemists. 'Man, the
microcosm, has all these planes in his own being, ranged from his
subconscient to his superconscient existence,'[9] wrote Sri Aurobindo
referring to the sheaths described above. 'All things are potentially
present in the substance out of which man has been formed ... In
an essential way, every human being contains in himself all universal
potentialities,'[10] said the Mother; and she wrote to a disciple: 'If we
did not carry in ourselves something corresponding to all that exists
in the universe, the universe wouldn't exist for us.'[11]

Although the spiritual ranges seem to us airy, insubstantial and
unreal, we relate to them because we partially consist of them. This
is the reason why we continue thinking about them — and also why
the mountebanks of spirituality can have such an influence on us, the
naïve and the credulous. For we would like so fervently that all that
is pure, elevated, beautiful and good in us might also exist here and
now, because we feel it existing 'somewhere.'

'As we ascend, a finer but far stronger and more truly and spiritually concrete substance emerges, a greater luminosity and potent
stuff of consciousness, a subtler, sweeter, purer and more powerfully
ecstatic energy of delight,'[12] wrote Sri Aurobindo. And about the
gradations of existence he said: 'The more subtle is also the more
powerful — one might say the more truly concrete; it is less bound
than the gross, it has a greater permanence in its being along with
a greater potentiality, plasticity and range in its becoming. Each
plateau of the hill of being gives to our widening experience a higher
plane of our consciousness and a richer world of our existence.'[13]

'Consciousness is a fundamental thing, the fundamental thing in
existence'[14] (Sri Aurobindo). Of this we actually have no idea because
we are not conscious of our consciousness. We are conscious of so
little. Existence to us is like a fallow ground with a frail flower here
and there, an illuminating thought or a moment of coherent reflective
thinking after having made an intense effort. But if consciousness is
the fundamental fact, then it is the foundation of all planes of
existence including ours. It is present in the atom, the cell, the body

organ, the nervous system and the vital sheath. We are a (mainly unconscious) fantastically complex phenomenon of consciousness, and what we in ordinary parlance mean by consciousness is little more than a thin peel on the surface of an onion.

'Consciousness is usually identified with mind, but mental consciousness is only the human range which no more exhausts all the possible ranges of consciousness than human sight exhausts all the gradations of colour or human hearing all the gradations of sound,'[15] wrote Sri Aurobindo. In the endless scale of vibrations of consciousness, our consciousness covers only a few degrees somewhere in the middle range.

'Consciousness is not something abstract, it is like existence itself or *ananda* or mind or *prana*, something very concrete. If one becomes aware of the inner consciousness, one can do all sorts of things with it, send it out as a stream of force, erect a circle or wall of consciousness around oneself, direct an idea so that it shall enter somebody's head in America, etc., etc.'[16] As the yogis of all ages have said, one can learn how to manipulate consciousness. Sri Aurobindo has in the course of many years tested out all these possibilities 'more scrupulously than any scientist his theory or his method on the physical plane.'[17] Of the Mother we know that already in Tlemcen she was able to climb the twelve steps of the universal scale of consciousness upto the border where the manifested worlds fade out at the gates of the eternal white silence.

In letter after letter from some disciples, Sri Aurobindo had to read how unreal, cold, distant, abstract, monotonous, unreachable and scarcely desirable Consciousness, the Godhead and all things spiritual appeared to them. Most of them, like the other children of men, still remained buried upto their chin in the subconscious quicksand of matter, and of the open spaces of the spirit, they knew only from hearsay one can breathe freely. Sri Aurobindo encouraged them in their arduous upward effort by sometimes telling them an experience of his own. 'When the peace of God descends on you, when the Divine Presence is there within you, when the Ananda rushes on you like a sea, when you are driven like a leaf before the wind by the breath of the Divine Force, when Love flowers out from you on all creation, when Divine Knowledge floods you with a Light which illumines and transforms in a moment all that was before dark, sorrowful and obscure, when all that is becomes part of the One Reality, when the Reality is all around you, you feel at once by the spiritual contact, by the inner vision, by the illumined and seeing thought, by the vital sensation and even by the very physical sense, everywhere you see, hear, touch only the Divine. Then you can much less doubt it or deny it than you can doubt or deny daylight or air or the sun in heaven — for of these physical things you cannot be sure but they are what your senses represent them to be; but in the concrete experiences of the Divine, doubt is impossible.'[18]

Sri Aurobindo has related quite a few of his experiences (he said, just like the Mother: 'I can only base myself on what I have experienced myself'), most extensively in *Savitri*. His philosophical works and letters are also full of them if one can read behind the printed word. Mystical experience is abstract only if one knows about it from hearsay; as direct experience — and all mystics agree about this — it is more concrete than the rock one stumbles on. 'And what is the end of the whole matter? As if honey could taste itself and all its drops could taste each other and each the whole honeycomb as itself, so should the end be with God and the soul of man and the universe.'[19] The Mother said that this is a realistic description of the highest *ananda* experience. And one is reminded of the words of the Flemish mystic Jan van Ruusbroec addressing the Divine: 'Thou tastest sweeter to me than the honeycomb.'

Humans, illiterate, literate or highly learned, talk and talk about so much that surpasses them. 'That prattles, and that prattles, and it does not even know what it is saying,' the parrot keeps croaking about the humans surrounding it in Raymond Queneau's *Zazie dans le metro* — about soccer, the latest automobiles and film stars, and tomato soup with little meat balls, about themselves and others, about life and death, God and maybe the soul, about spirituality and mysticism ... 'If mankind only caught a glimpse of what infinite enjoyments, what perfect forces, what luminous reaches of spontaneous knowledge, what wide calms of our being lie waiting for us in the tracts which our animal evolution has not yet conquered, they would leave all and never rest till they had gained these treasures. But the way is narrow, the doors are hard to force, and fear, distrust and scepticism are there, sentinels of Nature, to forbid the turning away of our feet from her ordinary pastures'[20] (Sri Aurobindo).

The Soul

The soul in man is greater than his fate.[21]

— Sri Aurobindo

'When thou hast the instrument that can show thee man's soul as thou seest a picture, then thou wilt smile at the wonders of physical Science as the playthings of babies,'[22] reads one of Sri Aurobindo's aphorisms. But to us the soul, said to be our true self, our innermost core, source of power or the higher I — 'the Daemon, the Godhead within'[23] — seems to be as airy, unreal and insubstantial as everything else that is spiritual. It is said that the soul is created by God at the moment of our birth and breathed into us, and that it continues existing in all eternity, in heaven or in hell. Sometimes it is pictured as a tiny, naked being, a miniature of the living person, escaping out of the body at the time of death and then going through all kinds of vicissitudes in scary places in the underworld. Or it is presented as a butterfly, a ghost, or in an animal form. Or it sings in harmony with the choirs of angels the eternal praise of God. All these seem rather childish if the soul really is a part, a 'spark' of the Godhead itself.

According to Eastern wisdom it is so indeed, in all its infinite greatness. 'The soul, representative of the central being, is a spark of the Divine supporting all individual existence in Nature,'[24] (Sri Aurobindo). Being literally the Divine himself, it exists in all eternity, having no end and therefore no beginning. For that which has an infinite future must of necessity have had an infinite past. In the soul the adventure of evolution has been chosen before it started; in the soul it will find its fulfilment.

We know that the Divine is one, perfect and absolute, without the necessity of a manifestation. But it pleases him to contemplate his infinite potentialities in a play of worlds without number, which are the mirrorings of his potentialities. In all other worlds this exteriorization happens directly and without any problem; we call those worlds 'typal' because their laws do not change but always conform to their original type, and their beings are fully satisfied within the gradation of the *ananda* of which they are the incarnations.

However, there is one world (as far as we know) which is not typal but evolutionary: the world created with *ananda* and freedom as its principle. We have seen how the first four incarnations of this world, which is ours, misused the freedom bestowed on them as it were, and how this error caused their 'fall' into darkness, suffering, falsehood and death. To compensate for the catastrophe of the fall, the Great Mother poured out the divine essence of Love in the dark Inconscient 'with a greater intensity than at the time of the creation of the four original beings.' This Love is the essence of the Divine, the essence of the Self, of the All-Soul in our world.

Because of the presence of the divine Love, the Inconscient could no longer remain stagnant in its inertia, in its endless sleep. Love was the catalyst by which the degenerated manifestation would be led back towards the origin which had become its goal in a movement we call evolution. In the black Inconscient a hierarchy of forms — material, vital, mental — gradually took shape, ever more complex materializations of the Love that is the essence of the one Self, of the primordial Soul. All these gradual materializations are, within their limits and like all other created beings, reflections of the potentialities present in the Self of the Divine. As this world evolves, their limitations are progressively widened till the divine potentialities at the end of the adventure, manifested in their full glory, will again have become what they were at the origin and what essentially they will have remained all along.

Earth is the symbol or condensation of our universe; our universe evolves in and through the earth; what happens on earth has its repercussions in all whirling, flaming and radiating, or in the dark, condensed and spun-out matter of our universe. It is here that the involution of love-matter, which is soul-matter, has taken place. By its presence the evolution has commenced; because of its presence the evolution cannot rest before it has reached its aim.

There is nothing on Earth that does *not* have the divine Presence in itself. The Presence is there in the atom, in the crystal, the brick and the beech, in the watch, the airplane and the particle accelerator, in plants and animals — ever more complex according to the ever higher evolutionary gradations. Plants and animals, not yet individualized or self-reflecting, have a group-soul. In the animals this group-soul is as it were concentrated in and radiating through the whole species from their 'archetype' or 'king', known to us from legends and fairy tales.

In the human being, child of the Earth, evolution attains a crucial phase; the soul has grown sufficiently throughout its earthly embodiments to function as an individuality and to become conscious of itself within the material manifestation. Of this individually functioning soul, all the time an integral part of the All-Soul, one can say: 'The soul is something that belongs specifically to mankind, it exists only in man.'[25]

'All knowledge in all traditions, wherever on earth, says that the formation of the psychic* is an earthly formation and that the growth of the psychic being is something that takes place on earth,'[26] said the Mother. For 'it is only *on the Earth* — I do not even mean the material universe — only on the Earth that this descent of divine Love, at the origin of the divine Presence in the heart of matter, has taken place.'[27] That is why only human beings — the human beings of the evolution, children of an earthly creation — 'have a psychic being.'[28] By this they are superior to all other creatures, even to the gods, who have to take on an earthly body if they want to evolve further.

The *Katha Upanishad* says that the soul is 'no larger than a man's thumb'; the *Swetaswatara Upanishad* says it is 'smaller than the hundredth part of the tip of a hair.' Actually, these figurative descriptions mean to say that the soul has no dimensions in our tridimensional world. It belongs to a dimension behind the three

---

* Sri Aurobindo and the Mother used the words 'psyche' and 'psychic' exclusively for the true soul, the living Godhead in us, and not in the derived and sometimes very confusing meanings both words have acquired in present-day usage, as well as in parapsychology and other scientific research in occult phenomena.

outward dimensions familiar to us, and the point where it touches our material body is situated behind the heart, in the *chakra* of the heart. 'Is the psychic being located in the heart?' the Mother was asked by a little girl, and she answered: 'Not in the physical heart, not in the heart muscle. It is in a fourth dimension, an internal dimension. But it is somewhere thereabouts, somewhere behind the solar plexus; that is where one finds it most easily. The psychic being is in a fourth dimension outside our physical being.'[29] It is felt by us as if it were in the heart, and this is how it is spoken about metaphorically: 'The true secret soul in us burns in the temple of the inmost heart,' writes Sri Aurobindo; there is 'the light in the hidden crypt of the heart's innermost sanctuary', 'a secluded King in a secret chamber,' 'a hidden king behind rich tapestries in his secret room.' (*Savitri*)

> "Cross and Christians, end to end, I examined. He was not on the cross. I went to the Hindu temple, to the ancient pagoda. In none of them was there any sign. To the uplands of Herat I went, and to Kandahar. I looked. He was not on the heights or in the lowlands. Resolutely, I went to the summit of the mountain of Kaf. There only was the dwelling of the Anqa bird. I went to the Kaaba of Mecca. He was not there. I asked about him from Avicenna the philosopher. He was beyond the range of Avicenna ... I looked into my own heart. In that place, I saw him. He was in no other place."[30]
> (Jalal ud-Din-ar-Rumi)

Rebirth

We can deduce from all this that the soul plays a prominent role in evolution, which essentially is a continuous evolution of Consciousness and only on the outside a saltatory evolution of material embodiments of Consciousness. If the soul is a part of the Godhead it must be infinite, for each part of the infinite is infinite too. In other words, the soul is immortal, and it is in the evolutionary process the ever present and growing force which makes evolution possible: it is the evolving element.

This automatically raises the question of reincarnation or rebirth. Reincarnation is for many Westerners a stumbling block in their approach of Eastern spirituality because the concept has been stigmatized as heresy by Christian orthodoxy and Western thought is permeated by Christianity. Not many know that the young Christian movement, like its twin Gnosticism, accepted reincarnation. Joe Fisher writes in *The Case for Reincarnation*: 'The fact remains that before Christianity became a vehicle for the imperial ambitions of Roman emperors, rebirth was widely accepted among the persecuted faithful.'[31] He quotes the church father Origenes (c. 185-254): 'Every soul ... comes into this world strengthened by the victories or weakened by the defeats of its previous life. Its place in this world as a vessel appointed to honor or dishonor, is determined by its previous merits or demerits. Its work in this world determines its place in the world which is to follow this.' The definitive formulation of the Catholic dogma concerning rebirth followed a long and complicated succession of changing positions, definitions and condemnations, from the Council of Nicea in AD 325 to the Second Council of Constantinople in AD 553, when the official tenet of the Church concerning 'the supposedly continued existence of the souls' was decreed once and for all. This is not the place for a detailed review of the arguments in favour of rebirth, and only one or two of the most relevant points should be borne in mind.

Notable Westerners have believed in reincarnation: Pythagoras, Plato, Leonardo da Vinci, Leibniz, Benjamin Franklin, Goethe, Shelley, Victor Hugo, Balzac, Richard Wagner, Walt Whitman, Nietzsche, Thomas Edison, Henry Ford, Gauguin, Strindberg, Mondrian, Jung, H.G. Wells. It was the great composer and director Gustave Mahler who wrote: 'We all return; it is this certainty that gives meaning to life and it does not make the slightest difference whether in a later incarnation we remember the former life. What counts is not the individual and his well-being, but the great aspiration towards the Perfect and the Pure which goes on in each incarnation.'[32] And is it not amazing that, in spite of the deeply imprinted psychological condemnation of rebirth, there still are a great many who believe in it? 'In 1982, the Gallup poll organization announced that very nearly one American in four believed in reincarnation. Three years earlier, a *Sunday Telegraph* poll had reported the same belief was held by twenty-eight per cent of all British adults — an increase of ten per cent in ten years. And in 1980, twenty-nine per cent of 1,314 people responding to a questionnaire in the ultra-conservative *Times* attested to a belief in reincarnation.'[33] 'The theory of rebirth is almost as ancient as thought itself and its origin is unknown,' wrote Sri Aurobindo in the *Arya*. 'We may according to our prepossessions accept it as the fruit of ancient psychological experience always renewable and verifiable and therefore true or dismiss it as a philosophical dogma and ingenious speculation; but in either case the doctrine, even as it is in all appearances well-nigh as old as human thought itself, is likely to endure as long as human beings continue to think.'[34]

Reincarnation is often mistaken for transmigration, which is an ill-considered popular belief. Transmigration holds that the soul rather haphazardly comes back in all sorts of animal bodies and even in plants, but most often in the last species of animal the dying person has set eyes on before his death. According to Sri Aurobindo and the Mother, the growth of the soul, in its various evolutionary stages, is the development of a spiritual consciousness at all times directed, meaningful and irreversible. And so Sri Aurobindo wrote: 'We have to ask whether the soul, having once arrived at humanity, can go back to the animal life and body, a retrogression which the old popular theories of transmigration have supposed to be an ordinary movement. It seems impossible that it should so go back with any entirety, and for this reason that the transit from the animal to human life means a decisive conversion of the vital consciousness, quite as decisive as the conversion of the vital consciousness of the plant into the mental consciousness of the animal. It is surely impossible that a conversion so decisive made by Nature should be reversed by the soul and the decision of the spirit within her come, as it were, to naught' (*The Life Divine*, p. 762).

Sri Aurobindo goes on to say that a regression to a lower level may still be possible in the border areas just before reaching the threshold of humanity, but not after this threshold has been crossed.

It is also possible, he writes, that parts of the vital composition of the personality may drop back, so that for instance a violent, unsatiated sexual desire may be integrated into an animal, but this of course is something very different from a falling back of the soul. 'The soul does not go back to the animal condition; but a part of the vital personality may disjoin itself and join an animal birth to work out its animal propensities there.'[35]

Another misunderstanding that may hinder a right understanding of reincarnation is what the Mother called the 'three-penny romances' often woven around it, the cheap and for the most part totally imaginary romanticization of putative former lives. How many reincarnations of Cleopatra, Napoleon, Alexander the Great, or of some mysterious Egyptian or Babylonian priests or priestesses have dwelt unnoticed among ordinary mortals! Sri Aurobindo warned his disciples: 'Seriously, these historical identifications are a perilous game and open a hundred doors to the play of imagination'[36] — a perilous play for those who want to know and master themselves integrally.

A frequent error concerning reincarnation is that the soul moving from body to body is an unalterable entity. 'You must avoid a common popular blunder about reincarnation,' Sri Aurobindo noted in a letter. 'The popular idea is that Titus Balbus is reborn again as John Smith, a man with the same personality, character, attainments as he had in a former life with the sole difference that he wears coat and trousers instead of a toga and speaks in cockney English instead of popular Latin. That is not the case. What would be the earthly use of repeating the same personality or character a million times from the beginning of time till its end? The soul comes into birth for experience, for growth, for evolution till it can bring the Divine into Matter.'[37]

A strong argument in favour of reincarnation is the blatant injustice of the one and only life, so short and so precarious, that is measured out to us. Is a human being really so intelligent and of a stature so high as to commit sins against God — supposing that one *could* sin against God — sins of such a nature that his soul would have to burn eternally in hell? What understanding has man of God, sin, hell and eternity? Are his psychological and physiological shortcomings not too much of a disadvantage in his struggle for virtuous perfection and spiritual indemnity? And what use are the few years accorded him in a contest with God and eternity for the salvation of his soul? The answers to these questions provided by religion, however threatening and severe, remain unsatisfactory.

Sri Aurobindo wrote in the *Arya*: 'There is too the difficulty that this soul inherits a past for which it is in no way responsible, or is burdened with mastering propensities imposed on it not by its own act, and is yet responsible for its future which is treated as if it were in no way determined by that often deplorable inheritance, *damnosa hereditas*, of that unfair creation, and were entirely of its own making. We are made helplessly what we are and are yet responsible for what we are, or at least for what we shall be hereafter, which is inevitably determined to a large extent by what we are originally. And we have only this one chance. Plato and the Hottentot, the fortunate child of saints or Rishis and the born and trained criminal plunged from beginning to end in the lowest fetid corruption of a great modern city have equally to create by the action or belief of this one unequal life all their eternal future.' And he concluded: 'This is a paradox which offends both the soul and the reason, the ethical sense and the spiritual intuition.'[38]

'Note that the idea of rebirth and the circumstances of the new life as a reward or punishment ... is a crude human idea of "justice" which is quite unphilosophical and unspiritual and distorts the true intention of life. Life here is an evolution and the soul grows by experience, working out by it this or that in the nature, and if there is suffering, it is for the purpose of that working out, not as a judgment inflicted by God or Cosmic Law on the errors or stumblings which are inevitable in the Ignorance' (*Letters on Yoga*, p. 441).

Rebirth or reincarnation is the process of the growth of the soul in a material evolution. The soul necessarily takes on body after body because material bodies are not supple enough to adapt to the soul's development. The soul always remains essentially what it is in all eternity, but it has taken up the adventure of evolution, plunging into the Night of its opposite. By the intervention of the Great Mother the way back to the Light has become possible; this is an evolutionary process in which the soul is the active agent and in which it plays the central role.

In the Night arose Matter, in Matter arose Life, and in Life Mental Consciousness, because the Soul, the bearer of Consciousness, Love and Light, has developed in ever more complex forms of Matter, Life and Mental Consciousness. To Sri Aurobindo and the Mother, reincarnation is the mechanism of the growth of the soul, which is the presence of the Divine in his evolving creation. Reincarnation is the indispensable spiritual mechanism of the growth of the soul, this growth being the cause of the otherwise unexplainable material mechanism of the development of material forms.

The soul has taken up the adventure of forgetting itself so that it may experience the joy of rediscovering itself in the evolution. This happens gradually, first as the slowly differentiating Earth-soul in the material forms, then as a group-soul in plants and animals, till it has sufficiently matured to become an individualized soul in man. Once that far, it extracts or filters, as it were, out of each life the experiences or elements required for its further growth and which are the reasons why it has chosen this particular life and no other. To use another metaphor: the soul chooses the necessary experiences in life after life, and each experience is like the cut of a chisel to sculpt the divine figure it essentially is and has wanted to become anew in the material manifestation.

Most of our life is a subconscious routine. But every now and then something happens to which the soul is really present because it needs this happening for its self-becoming. These kinds of happenings are intensely charged, unforgettable instants in our life, the moments when we are fully present to an event and which remain etched indelibly in our memory. The soul harbours those moments forever — moments of highest courage or lowest cowardice, of unbearable suffering or intense joy, of terror or rapture. For all this was and is needed to become who we are. The world is not an unfortunate accident; it is the mould of the living divine golden figure which we are already carrying in us and which in the future will also exist and act on Earth.

From our numerous previous lives we can only remember the events in which our soul has participated when inwardly we are grown enough to become aware of those remembrances, i.e. when they may be meaningful for our spiritual development. They contain the essence of our existence in time; they are the stuff of our eternal existence. These constructive remembrances can only be gathered by an individualized soul, a soul of a human being. In animal life there is not yet enough soul-stuff to produce a remembrance, remaining beyond death and rebirth.

Between two lives the soul goes and rests in an internatal, harmonious psychic world where it assimilates its experiences from the former life. When it has taken all that into itself, it is ready to descend once more into the manifestation and to carry on its adventure. (Ancient texts say that at that moment it begins to perspire.) It chooses the earthly scene of its next experience and when it sees the light that calls for it, it takes on a new body in evolution. The programme of the experiences the soul is destined to have has been drawn up by its essential Omniscience. It is the soul which governs the life of man and which determines all his experiences even before he is born.

This means that we should not put the blame for being here on anyone else: we have willed and picked everything ourselves, and the adversities we may be cursing are unconsciously a source of the intense joy of becoming. 'When the Soul came into the manifestation, it was not that God threw it down into earth by force, but the Soul willingly chose to come down. There was no compulsion of the Divine,'[39] said Sri Aurobindo in a conversation. And when a disciple for the umpteenth time complained about his difficulties, Sri Aurobindo wrote to him: 'In the beginning it was you (not the human you who is now complaining but the central being) who accepted or even invited the adventure of the Ignorance. Sorrow and struggle are a necessary consequence of the plunge into the Inconscience and the evolutionary emergence out of it. The explanation is that it had an object, the eventual play of the Divine Consciousness and Ananda not in its original transcendence but under conditions for which the plunge into the Inconscience was necessary.'[40]

O mortal who complainst of death and fate,
Accuse none of the harms thyself hast called;
This troubled world thou hast chosen for thy home,
Thou art thyself the author of thy pain.[41]

— *Savitri*

The soul or psyche thus exists in different aspects: 1. It is an eternal part of the Godhead in his one transcendent multiplicity (the *jivatman* of the Hindus); 2. It is the projection of that eternal part into the manifestation because the Great Mother has brought the divine Self as Love into this manifestation; the soul is the divine Presence, the divine 'spark' in all that exists in the manifestation (the *antaratman*); 3. It is the growing Godhead in man, sculpting its original being in life after life, but now in a materially manifested form. This growing Godhead in man, as it were the growing body of the essential 'spark-soul', was called 'the psychic being' by Sri Aurobindo and the Mother. The psychic being is 'the true evolving individual in our nature.' These three aspects of the soul are the three forms of the one, very concrete reality which is the truth and foundation of our life and through which we belong to the All-Soul, to the Great Self.

A stone I died and rose again a plant,
A plant I died and rose again an animal;
I died an animal and was born a man.
Why should I fear? When was I less by dying?[42]

— Jalal ud-Din ar-Rumi

Our true self is in the manifestation of our growing soul. Whatever we do can only increase the growth of our self and the human being can only become itself by surpassing itself. This means that it is not man who becomes the superman; he is the link between the animal and the god, the laboratory in which the material and spiritual conditions for the formation of the superman are worked out, but not the superman as such. 'The hiatus between the animal and the human is so great in consciousness, however physically small, that the scientists' alleged cousinship of monkey and man looks psychologically almost incredible. And yet the difference between vital animal and mental man is as nothing to that which will be between man's mind and the superman's vaster consciousness and richer powers. That past step will be to this new one as the snail's slow march in the grass to a Titan's sudden thousand league stride from continent to continent.'[43] (Sri Aurobindo).

We may suppose that the transitional process from man to superman takes place in a way analogous to what has happened everytime a higher species appeared on Earth: the human species has reached its ceiling; because of the irresistible evolutionary impulse in it, its soul has called for the manifestation on Earth of a higher consciousness in a new material form; this higher consciousness, in this case the supramental Unity-consciousness, has answered from its own typal world where it is already a part of the infinite Self-manifestation; and to render the transition possible, something the human species is not able to accomplish by itself, the Supreme has incarnated on Earth as an Avatar.

The transition, thanks to the complete, two-bodied Avatar Sri Aurobindo and the Mother, who have made it possible by their superhuman yoga, is happening now, as we will learn further on. This time the aim is not a new evolutionary step or gradation in the lower hemisphere of being. The aim this time is a mutation from the lower to the higher hemisphere, from the mental consciousness to the supramental consciousness, from our divisive, partial, impotent consciousness to a global, omnipotent, divine Unity-consciousness. All our misery and impotence derives from our divided consciousness; the new being, yet without a name, will constantly live in the essential divine Unity with its highest attributes of Being, Consciousness and Bliss. Therefore the present moment in the evolution of the Earth, which is the spiritual growth of the Earth, is its most important turning point. The foundations of the Kingdom of God have been dug and built. Its establishment is assured. The promise given to mankind at its origin is now being fulfilled. And all our suffering will not have been in vain.

Chapter Ten

THE TWO-IN-ONE

... the deathless Two-in-One,
a single being in two bodies clasped ...[1]
— *Savitri*

'I HAD met Sri Aurobindo before, but it only began clearly in 1920.' *It*, the Great Work they had to undertake together, 'an alchemic transmutation of all the inner and outer existence,'[2] (Sri Aurobindo). It was to be a transmutation that would produce the body of a higher species, but this time not within the scope of the lower hemisphere of Existence and not with a gradual change which perhaps might have led to a Nietzschean superman. This new species would possess a supramental, divine consciousness of the higher hemisphere, and accordingly a supramental, divine body.

In a new act of the drama of the world
The united Two began a greater age.[3]
— *Savitri*

They knew that their reunification — which would prove to be definitive — meant that the promise given to mankind at its origin would now at last be fulfilled, thanks to them.

Her return to Pondicherry was 'the tangible sign of the Victory over the hostile forces,' the Mother would later write about herself. She has not expanded on the meaning of these words, but Paul

Richard, an incarnation of the *Asura* of Falsehood, whom she had been unable to convert despite her promise, certainly had something to do with it. The few times she has mentioned in passing their stay in Japan and their last months together in Pondicherry leave one with the impression that it must have been a 'diabolical' period. It could be that Sri Aurobindo had not deemed his yoga sufficiently developed in 1915 to commence the Great Work together with her at that time. 'In 1914 I had to go away. He did not keep me, what could I do? I had to go. But I left my psychic being with him.'⁴ This brought her to the brink of death: 'The doctors had given me up.'

Her return in 1920 effected drastic changes in Sri Aurobindo's outer way of life which until then was rather spartan. His four young companions of the first hour who shared these circumstances in Pondicherry deserve to be mentioned by name: Bejoy Nag, one of the co-defendants in the Alipore Bomb Case and who had accompanied Sri Aurobindo on the adventurous journey to Pondicherry; Suresh Chakravarty, known as Moni, who had been sent ahead by Sri Aurobindo to prepare for his arrival and housing by the freedom fighters living in Pondicherry; Saurin Bose, who had joined the small group in October 1914 and who was a cousin of Sri Aurobindo's wife Mrinalini; and Nolini Kanta Gupta, who had arrived in November of the same year and who too had been a defendant in the Alipore case. The financial situation of the group was usually so desperate that Sri Aurobindo once wrote in a letter to a friend: 'The situation just now is that we have Rs. 1½ or so in hand ... No doubt, God will provide, but He has contracted a bad habit of waiting till the last moment.'⁵

In his *Reminiscences* Nolini tells about this period: 'Each of us possessed a mat, and this mat had to serve as our bedstead, mattress, coverlet and pillow; this was all our furniture. And mosquito curtains? That was a luxury we could not even dream of. If there were too many mosquitoes, we would carry the mats out on the terrace for a little air, assuming, that is, that there was any. Only for Sri Aurobindo we had somehow managed a chair and a table and a camp cot. We lived a real camp life.'⁶ They also had a couple of rickety chairs for visitors, and at one time *one* candle for the personal use of Sri Aurobindo. He took his daily bath under the tap in the courtyard just like the others, but usually he was the last person to do so, using the only towel the household possessed.

Besides his yogic discipline, his study of the Vedas and other subjects, e.g., comparative linguistics, and the writing of plays, essays and articles (during the *Arya* period sixty-four pages a month), Sri Aurobindo still found time to instruct those of his companions who were eager to learn. Foremost among them were Nolini and Moni, who had had to stop their college studies because of their revolutionary activities. He taught them French, Greek, Latin and Italian, *L'Avare*, *Medea*, *Antigone*, Vergil and Dante. Both Nolini and Moni would gain fame as writers in Bengali.

They had to eat too. 'We did the cooking ourselves and each of us developed a specialty,' narrates Nolini. 'I did the rice, perhaps because that was the easiest. Moni took charge of *dal* (pulses), and Bejoy being the expert had the vegetables and the curry.' Saurin looked after the visitors who came from the four corners of India and were mostly unwelcome, so much so that Sri Aurobindo had to have a letter published in a Madras newspaper confirming that he had retired from political life and requesting that he not be disturbed in his spiritual work. Money was often lacking to buy the spices of which Indians are so fond, and sometimes they also had to go barefoot out of sheer necessity.

In Pondicherry, the young Bengalis were highly rated as football players. (The three professional football teams of Calcutta are even now the foremost in the country.) Spiritual life was the least of their concerns. 'We had hitherto known [Sri Aurobindo] as a dear friend and a close companion, and although in our mind and heart he had the position of a Guru, in our outward relations we seemed to behave as if he were just like one of ourselves. He too had been averse to the use of the words "Guru" and "Ashram".'[7]

The return in 1920 of the Mother, whom most of them already knew from her first stay, caused a thorough change in the life of the small group, which at that time was about twice its original size. 'The house had undergone a great change. There was a clean garden in the open courtyard, every room had simple and decent furniture — a mat, a chair, and a small table. There was an air of tidiness and order. This was, no doubt, the effect of the Mother's presence.'[8] Not only did the housekeeping become a lot less problematical, but by her own attitude towards Sri Aurobindo she showed his young companions who he actually was. She must have done this very tactfully, for they knew her as Madame Richard, and although Sri Aurobindo had made them understand that she was far advanced in occultism and spirituality, to them she was nevertheless a twice-married woman. As K.D. Sethna writes: 'Even in regard to the Mother a group of *sadhaks* in the twenties, when she returned to India for permanent stay near Sri Aurobindo, was averse to accept her as an incarnation of the Divine — merely because she was from the West and a woman besides, while all the Avatars of tradition had been Indians and, furthermore, exclusively of the masculine gender.'[9] The resistance against her Western origin will in future make itself felt sharply from time to time with the more traditionally-minded disciples.

Sri Aurobindo had repeatedly made known and even written in the newspapers that he had distanced himself from all political activity, but in 1920 his fame as a politician was still very much alive in the minds of his countrymen. In this year he was offered the editorship of the organ of a new party of which Bal Gangadhar Tilak was one of the co-founders. Yet more important was the offer to be the president of the Congress, 'the greatest honour the national movement could award.' As on previous occasions, this time too Sri Aurobindo sent his thanks politely saying that at present he did not want to take political office, his interest now being exclusively concentrated on his inner development.

In 1920, in a letter to his brother Barin, then recently released from prison, Sri Aurobindo wrote in Bengali: 'The indwelling Guru of the world indicated my path to me completely, its full theory, the ten limbs of the body of the yoga. These ten years he has been making me develop it in experience; it is not yet finished. It may take another two years. And so long as it is not finished, I probably will not be able to return to Bengal.'[10] This shows clearly that it was not Sri Aurobindo's intention to remain in seclusion in his Pondicherrian 'cave of tapasya'. He would in future confirm this several times, as late as in 1943 to Dilip K. Roy and even — most astonishingly — in 1950, the year of his passing, to K.M. Munshi.

Many who did not know or understand the true reason of Sri Aurobindo's withdrawal from the freedom movement were very disillusioned and made no bones about it. Among them was the Gaekwad of Baroda, his former employer, who said: 'Mister Ghose is now an extinct volcano: he has become a yogi!' In 1908 Rabindranath Tagore had published in *Bande Mataram* his poem, still well known in India, beginning with the lines: 'Rabindranath, O Aurobindo, bows to thee! / O friend, my country's friend, O voice incarnate, free, / of India's soul! ...' Now he complained to Dilip K. Roy: 'But he is lost to us, Dilip, soaring in the cloudland of mysticism, he won't return to lead the country again.'[11]* And in Peter Heehs' biography we read: 'Among the disillusioned was Jawaharlal Nehru, who wrote in 1962: "When Gandhiji started his non-cooperation movement and convulsed India, we expected Sri Aurobindo to emerge from his retirement and join the great struggle. We were disappointed at his not doing so." '[12] This lack of understanding was one of the reasons why, in 1942, Mohandas K. Gandhi refused to listen when Sri Aurobindo insisted that the Cripps offer of dominion status for India be accepted; had it been, the division of the country into India and Pakistan might have been prevented.

---

* Tagore would revise his opinion after an exceptionally cordial meeting with Sri Aurobindo in 1928, about which he wrote for the *Modern Review*: 'His face was radiant with an inner light ... I felt the utterance of the ancient Rishi spoke from him of that equanimity which gives the human soul its freedom of entrance into the All. I said to him: "You have the word and we are waiting to accept it from you. India will speak through your voice to the world." ... Years ago I saw Sri Aurobindo in the atmosphere of his earlier heroic youth and I sang to him: "Aurobindo, accept the salutation of Rabindranath." Today I saw him in a deeper atmosphere of reticent richness of wisdom and again sang to him in silence: "Aurobindo, accept the salutation of Rabindranath".'

In her he found a vastness like his own ...
In her he met his own eternity.[13]

— *Savitri*

The Avatar is a direct embodiment of the Godhead. 'An Avatar, roughly speaking, is one who is conscious of the presence and the power of the Divine born in him or descended into him and governing from within his will and life and action; he feels identified inwardly with the divine power and presence,'[14] (Sri Aurobindo). Being the Son of Man he is also literally the Son of God. To human comprehension this remains an enigma, because the common human contact with the Avatar is, during his lifetime, through the senses or the thinking, and an advanced psychic development is needed to be able to perceive the inner divinity of the Avatar. However, the metaphysical definition of the Avatar and the function of his incarnation in evolution are not difficult to understand according to the traditional formulation.

Less evident is the role of the Great Mother as a divine incarnation, as an Avatar. We have already seen that some traditionalistic, conservative followers of Sri Aurobindo had difficulties understanding it and to accept 'that French woman,' freely moving among them, as the Embodied Godhead. This went on even after Sri Aurobindo had pronounced on the matter and used his authority to declare her an Avatar: 'The Mother is the consciousness and force of the Supreme.'[15] 'The Mother was inwardly above the human even in childhood ... It is so that you should regard her as the Divine Shakti ... She is that in the body, but in her whole consciousness she is also identified with all the other aspects of the Divine.'[16] When some of his beautiful letters about the Mother had been collected and published as a booklet, the then still very young disciple Nagin Doshi asked him straight out: 'Do you not refer to the Mother (our Mother) in your book "The Mother"?' Sri Aurobindo answered laconically: 'Yes.'

The difficulty of accepting the Mother on a par with the masculine Avatar had several reasons. One of these was, as already mentioned, that the divine incarnations in all traditions have always been men; moreover those men, once they came to the fore as a divine incarnation, did not keep a feminine 'complement' by their side, not even when they had been married. The reason why a very long era, now coming to an end, has been an era of undisputed male supremacy has not yet been satisfactorily explained. Some ancient cultures are known in which a goddess or goddesses were worshipped, but in practically all cases they have been replaced by male-dominated cultures and religions, and the worship of the mother-goddess has generally been vilified as orgiastic or evil. In India everybody knows that a god has a wife who is a goddess; she is his *shakti*, i.e. his force, power or strength, but she is, all the same, always pictured as smaller in size. And in everyday life the husband is literally the god, the lord of the married woman, whom she does not address by his name but calls him 'the Lord of my house', and whom she worships with ceremonial *pujas* just like the statues of the gods in the house.

A second reason for lower respect shown to the Mother-force is the comparison with the Supreme, generally considered as masculine: she is his force, his *shakti*, having come forth from him and as a consequence of secondary importance. But this is the human interpretation of a metaphysical fact that is inexpressible in words and that is therefore in the ancient texts told by the great seers as a humanized story. One will remember the words from the Upanishad: '*Prajapati* [the Father of all creatures] then was this Universe. *Vak* [the Word] was second to him. He united with her and she became pregnant. She went out from him and produced all the creation and again re-entered him.' However, the Power, the Force or the Potency of the Absolute One IS the Absolute One is its totality and in all eternity.

The primordial masculine element is often named *Purusha* in the ancient Hindu writings and the feminine element *Prakriti*. When a child, in one of the Mother's weekly French evening classes, asked for a clarification of the *Purusha-Prakriti* relationship, she abruptly turned towards Nolini, who with some other adults also attended the classes: 'Nolini, you will have to explain this ... I don't understand a thing of it. It does not correspond with an inner experience as far as I am concerned. I have never had this kind of experience, therefore I cannot talk about it ... To make a division like that and to name the one Purusha, masculine, and the other Prakriti, feminine, is something I simply won't do ... To me it is something resulting from — if you will excuse me — a somewhat degenerated masculine mentality ... IT IS NOT CORRECT ... At the very top there is not the slightest notion of "masculine" and "feminine" ... This is a concept that has come from below ...'[17]

We now understand Sri Aurobindo's fundamental pronouncements: 'The Mother's consciousness and mine are the same, the one Divine Consciousness in two, because that is necessary for the play.'[18] 'The Mother and I are one but in two bodies.'[19] 'The Mother and myself stand for the same Power in two forms.'[20] The Mother from her side said: 'Sri Aurobindo and I are always one and the same consciousness, one and the same person.'[21] Like the 'masculine' Avatar the 'feminine' Avatar represents the whole Godhead: both are ONE. Therefore a *mantra* given by Sri Aurobindo in Sanskrit was translated by the Mother as follows: 'OM — She the Ananda, She the Consciousness, She the Truth, She the Supreme' (17.11.63). And the Mother once wrote their names as 'MOTHERSRIAUROBINDO' to demonstrate their essential unity.

The indivisible unity of the Divine, his manifesting Power and his manifestation are not only of theoretical importance, there are also very important practical consequences. One of these is that the soul, as part of the sexless Divine, is sexless too. In human beings it has to take on a sexual body out of necessity, in its first human incarnations frequently changing from one sex to the other, but keeping one sexual gender, the one of its choice, once it has acquired or is acquiring its maturity. As it is intrinsically sexless, however, in the species beyond man it will manifest in a sexless supramental body.

The sexes are a phenomenon of the lower hemisphere of Existence from the gods down to the lower vital creatures. 'The concept that has come from below,' as the Mother said, has therefore been projected from the lower hemisphere of division on the higher hemisphere of divine Unity. 'It is a concept that is useful psychologically, but that is all.'[22] It is not to be denied, of course, that there is a masculine and a feminine sex in the lower hemisphere. The origin of the two complementary sexes obviously has its origin in the functional differentiation between *Purusha* and *Prakriti*, the One and its *Shakti*, its *Maya*.*

It is little known that the relation *Purusha-Prakriti* created a problem to the manifested two-poled Avatar, Sri Aurobindo and the Mother. For it has always been, 'almost for eternities,' the aspiration of the creative Power to unite with the Creator in a total and unconditional surrender, 'so that the whole Being might exist' in the manifestation. Practically speaking, this meant that the Mother in her attitude of surrender always put Sri Aurobindo above her, which was the reason why she usually sat down at his feet on the floor or on a small stool. But Sri Aurobindo's yogic development had revealed the Divine Mother to him, and he on his part had surrendered totally and unconditionally to her. This revelation and his surrender he has expressed in the canto of *Savitri* called *The Adoration of the Divine Mother*:

> She is the golden bridge, the wonderful fire.
> The luminous heart of the Unknown is she,
> A power of silence in the depths of God;
> She is the Force, the inevitable Word,
> The magnet of our difficult ascent,
> The sun from which we kindle all our suns,
> The light that leans from the unrealised Vasts,
> The joy that beckons from the impossible,
> The Might of all that never yet came down ...
> Once seen, his heart acknowledged only her.[23]

---

* 'Maya' is a word that only since the illusionism of the *Mayavada* has been charged with a negative significance. Originally it signified the transcendent Mother in her measuring, limiting Power-aspect of the divine Omnipotence, in other words the Power who has manifested the worlds, the Creatrix.

The practical consequence, for himself as well as for his disciples was, as he wrote in a letter: 'It is not our force but the Shakti of God who is the sole *sadhika* [practitioner] of this yoga.' This follows logically from the fact that the evolution is a development back to the Divine Origin and that it is the Divine Mother who has enabled and worked out this development. (This means, besides, that all human beings, as living elements of the evolution, participate in the evolutionary yoga, whether they want it or not.) 'The whole of life is the Yoga of Nature.'[24] 'All life is yoga. It is therefore impossible to live without practising the supreme yoga.'[25]

The play of the relations between the Godhead and his manifesting *Shakti*, who is the Great Mother, is sublimely illustrated in the images of the Mother of God with her radiant Child on her lap — the Child who is her Origin and Lord but of whose embodied existence she is the mother. It is no coincidence that we find this image, well-known from the Roman Catholic iconography, also in *Savitri*, as already quoted elsewhere in this book.

How then to situate the incarnated *Prakriti*, the Mother, in relation to the incarnated *Purusha*, Sri Aurobindo? This is a question of primary importance to the subject of this book; without a clear insight into their two-in-oneness, their Work and its results cannot be understood. The Mother was of course not Sri Aurobindo's wife, as stated in a couple of guide books for travellers which have probably obtained their information from Pondicherrian tea shop customers. (And neither was she the wife of the French governor of Pondicherry as asserted in an edition of the French *Guide du routard*.) In most writings and books by their disciples, one reads that the Mother was the 'collaborator' of Sri Aurobindo, and some even say his 'disciple and collaborator'. The rationale of the matter is now known to us, namely that she was an incarnation of the Divine Consciousness and as such the Divine itself. As Sri Aurobindo wrote: 'Either she is that ... or she is not and then no one need to stay here,'[26] meaning in the Ashram.

The Mother cannot be called a disciple, devotee or follower of Sri Aurobindo. An opinion like this not only stems from the fact that some regarded her less highly because she was a woman and a Westerner, but also because of a wrong interpretation of Sri Aurobindo's words concerning her exceptional complete surrender when she first met him in 1914. 'The first time Sri Aurobindo described her qualities, he said he had never seen anywhere a self-surrender so absolute and unreserved,'[27] wrote Nolini in his *Reminiscences*. Amrita too, a Tamil from Pondicherry who had been one of the first to join the small group of Bengalis, is quoted as a source in this connection. 'He told me,' writes K.D. Sethna, 'that after the Mother's arrival in Pondicherry Sri Aurobindo declared to the young men with him at the time, of whom Amrita was one: "I never knew the meaning of 'surrender' until Mirra surrendered herself to me." '[28] It is not possible to question these statements by two prominent disciples, but they cover only one side of the relationship and leave out Sri Aurobindo's reciprocal surrender to the Mother. 'A vast surrender was his only strength.'[29] Moreover, Sri Aurobindo himself has written explicitly, probably to straighten out some distorted opinions among his disciples: 'The Mother is not a disciple of Sri Aurobindo. She has had the same realisation and experience as myself.'[30]

'The Mother stands on an equal and exactly complementary footing with Sri Aurobindo,'[31] writes K.D. Sethna, the most reliable authority of the Ashram. And he goes on: 'Side by side though Sri Aurobindo and the Mother stood, she often took the position of a "disciple" and spoke of carrying out a work allotted to her and of promulgating his message to the world. On the other hand, he never tired of declaring her to be not only equal to him but also indispensable for his mission and even suggested that if she were not there as his counterpart he would be incomplete.'[32]

It is no easy matter to define the exact relationship between Sri Aurobindo and the Mother, as some events during their life and some sectarian developments after their passing have amply demonstrated.

Immortal rhythms swayed in her time-born steps...[33]

— *Savitri*

It is significant in the light of the above that several authors have written about the human side of the divine incarnation who was the Mother whereas one seldom reads about the human side of Sri Aurobindo, although there are plenty of letters, for instance in his correspondence with Nirodbaran, to illustrate how 'human' Sri Aurobindo was too. That the so-called human side of the Mother is so often mentioned can partially be explained by the fact that she moved day after day among the members of the Ashram, whereas Sri Aurobindo never left his apartment after 24 November 1926. But sometimes there is also a suspicion of the more human and more reassuring quality attributed to the Mother along with her supposed discipleship.

We find traces of this attitude towards the Mother in some of the most prominent authors. Nirodbaran writes in *Twelve Years With Sri Aurobindo*: 'Though Divine, her human motherly instinct could not be forgotten.'[34] The following words are from M.P. Pandit: 'She was supremely divine but equally intensely human.'[35] Satprem writes in the second volume of his trilogy about the Mother: 'She was so human too, this Mother, let there be no mistake; her consciousness was not like ours, her energies were not like ours, but her body consisted of our matter, the same suffering matter.'[36] In the same vein we could cull dozens of quotations by other writers or from reminiscences by disciples.

At first sight such sayings seem to be reasonable, and the accentuation of the superhuman aspect of the Avatar, while omitting or glossing over the human side, might look like an act of devotional narrow-mindedness, not to say devotional bigotry. And didn't Sri Aurobindo write: 'The Divine has to put on humanity in order that the human being may rise to be divine,'[37] and: 'The Divine when he takes on the burden of terrestrial nature, takes it fully, sincerely and without any conjuring tricks or pretense'?[38] The question of the prevalence of either the divine or the human aspect of the Avatar has, throughout history, caused endless disputation and sectarian attitudes — about Christ in Gnosticism and early Christendom in all its varieties, as well as about the Avatars of the Hindus in their philosophical disputations. It is necessary to consider this question in some detail, for it is a matter of importance to our subject, as we will see in the third part of this book.

First some statements by Sri Aurobindo.

About the Avatar in general: 'The Divine puts on an appearance of humanity, assumes the outward human nature in order to tread the path and show it to human beings, but does not cease to be the Divine.'[39]

About the contacts of the Mother with others, in particular the disciples: 'You must remember that for her a physical contact of this kind with others is not a mere social or domestic meeting with a few superficial movements which make no great difference one way or the other. It means for her an interchange, a pouring out of her forces and a receiving of things good, bad and mixed from them which often involves a great labour of adjustment and elimination and in many cases, though not in all, a severe strain on the body.'[40]

About the relations between the disciples and the Mother: 'But why do you want to meet her as a "human" Mother? If you can see the Divine Mother in a human body that should be enough and a more fruitful attitude. Those who approach her as a human Mother often get into trouble by their conception making all sorts of mistakes in their approach to her.'[41]

And in *Savitri* he wrote: 'Even when she bent to meet earth's intimacies / Her spirit kept the stature of the gods.'[42]

We also give some pronouncements of the Mother on this subject.

About the Avatar in general: 'They may be sure to misjudge the Divine if they stick to the superficial aspect of his [or her] actions, for they will never understand that what seems to resemble a human way of acting is nevertheless completely different and arises from a source which is not human ... The [incarnated] Divine seems to act like other people, but this is only an appearance.'[43]

About the everyday contact of the disciples with her physical being: 'They have very little real contact with what my body really is, and with the formidable accumulation of conscious energy it represents.'[44]

The Mother had always liked to play tennis and she kept playing till she was eighty. In this context she said: 'You have here this extraordinary opportunity of being able to play a game and to take exercise in an atmosphere filled with Divine Consciousness, Light and Power in such a way that each of your movements is, so to say, permeated by the consciousness and the light and the power which is in itself an intensive yoga; and your ignorant unconsciousness, your blindness and your lack of sensitiveness is such that you believe you are giving a game or even helping a good old lady to play for whom you feel a little gratefulness and some kind of affection.'[45]

About her physical body: 'Each point of the body is symbolical of an inner movement; there is there a world of subtle correspondences.'[46] This is a truth applicable to all bodies, but each point in hers was conscious.

These statements by Sri Aurobindo and the Mother from various periods and sources speak for themselves and leave no room for relativism or toned down interpretations. Either they were That or they were not That (and if they were That, they still are That). This is not a matter of devotion or bigotry but a question of spiritual fact which one accepts or does not accept. Sri Aurobindo and the Mother have never imposed their views on anybody, but it is not possible to understand or explain their Work without clearly defining the basic principles and the outline of it. 'Humanizing' their personalities and activities has been catastrophic for the spiritual development of many of their disciples who lacked insight, were doubting or too self-willed; it might also distort the subject of this book. This subject may appear fantastic and unbelievable to the unprepared and surprising and not immediately comprehensible to the interested or like-minded, but in itself it is coherent, meaningful and, with acceptance of the basic principles, logical and irrefutable.

After their complete identification with their Divine Origin, everything Sri Aurobindo and the Mother did, even the most ordinary everyday actions, had a higher intensity and a higher sense. This is exactly the basis of the divine transformation of all things human which they wanted to bring about. We can therefore conclude with K.D. Sethna: 'All actions of the Divine incarnate have, whether the outer mind is allowed to know it or not, a truth-impulsion,'[47] — an impulse of the Truth-Consciousness that is an essential quality of the Divine, also of the Incarnated Divine.

Disciples

I do not very readily accept disciples as this path of Yoga is a difficult one and it can be followed only if there is a special call.[48]
— Sri Aurobindo

After 1920, more disciples arrived, people who felt the urge to dedicate their life to the work of Sri Aurobindo and the Mother. Some of them would not prove up to the severe demands of this integral path and would leave, sometimes after many years; others would become the pillars of the work. There are names that have become well-known for a variety of reasons: Dyuman, Champaklal, Barin, Purani, Dilip Kumar Roy, Pavitra, Pujalal, Nirodbaran, K.D. Sethna (of his Ashram name Amal Kiran), etc. Others, and not necessarily less notable, have given their best in anonymity. In 1925 there were about fifteen of them, according to Pavitra; a year later, when the small group around Sri Aurobindo and the Mother officially became an ashram, called the Sri Aurobindo Ashram, there were already twenty-four. We have some idea about the life of some members of the group like Nolini, Bejoy and Barin, because it coincided for the most part with the political life of Sri Aurobindo. By way of illustration, we are giving here a brief sketch of the well-documented lives of two other disciples with very dissimilar backgrounds and whom we will meet again further on.

Let us first take the above-mentioned Pavitra. He was a Frenchman, called Philippe B. Saint-Hilaire before Sri Aurobindo gave him his Sanskrit name signifying 'the Pure'. He had an engineering diploma from the renowned *École polytechnique* in Paris. Immediately after finishing his studies — 'in 1914 I was exactly twenty' — he was enlisted for the war as an artillery officer. Even during the war he got more and more interested in occultism and read the books of the French occultists. His preoccupation with occultism stemmed, however, from a deep attraction to spirituality. After surviving the war, and having been employed as an engineer with the Ministry of Transport and Communications — 'I had a whole section of the Seine, mostly in Paris, under my direction' — he left for Japan in 1920 to study Zen Buddhism. 'I knew ... yes, *I knew,* for it was a certainty to me — that my life would be a life of spiritual realization, that nothing else counted for me, and that somewhere on earth, and I mean effectively on earth, there had to be someone who could give me ... who could lead me towards the light.'*

Paul and Mirra Richard had left Japan a few months before Pavitra arrived there. 'I heard about them. We had common friends. What I heard about them interested me very, very much and I decided to write to her.' But.he got no answer, not even to a second letter. In the following four years he got involved in 'many experiences, the study of Buddhism, especially Zen Buddhism, life in the temples and, at night in my home, the continuation of my studies of Indian, Japanese and Chinese spirituality.' He went through 'alternations of light and darkness, of advance and standstill — all kinds of difficulties met with by those who are searching for the light, and who search for it alone, or apparently alone.'

Pavitra, as an engineer and chemist, was a true scientist. The editor of *Conversations avec Pavitra*, the annotation of Pavitra's conversations with Sri Aurobindo, writes in his preface the following intriguing paragraph: 'In a brief monologue, part of a theatre play, Pavitra represented a chemist (like himself) who in the course of his experiments accidentally finds a very simple method to liberate nuclear energy from common metals (not only from rare metals like thorium and uranium) by a chemical process — a way which would have brought enormous powers within the reach of whomever — and who destroys his discovery. We strongly suspect that he was relating his own experiences in the laboratories of Japan, before he went on his way to the monasteries of the lamas in Mongolia and afterwards to India.'

The journey to Mongolia, in the company of a Mongolian lama who taught him his language, took place in 1924. 'And so I left [Japan]. We had to cross northern China to reach the monastery where only Tibetan lamas were living.' He was there for nine months,

---

* All Pavitra's quotations are from the story of his life as told by him to the students of the school of the Sri Aurobindo Ashram and printed as an introduction to *Conversations avec Pavitra*.

passing the severe winter 'well protected and completely cut off from all contacts.'

Years earlier he had chanced on an issue of the French edition of the *Arya*. He had found it interesting, 'but, to tell the truth, it had not touched me more than the rest.' Now he felt compelled to travel to India. 'To the others — my family and friends — I said: "I am coming back to Europe by way of India," but inwardly I knew that I would stay in India.'

'At that time [in 1925], Sri Aurobindo still talked with his disciples. He was so kind to me. I explained to him the way I had followed and what I was looking for ... The first day it was I who did the talking.' That night, he was received by the Mother. 'Of the Mother I especially remember her eyes, her eyes of light.' The next day, he again had a meeting with Sri Aurobindo, who this time did the talking himself.

'He then told me that what I was searching for could be given to me by several persons in India, but that it was not easy to approach them, especially not for a European. And he went on that he himself was of the opinion that what I was looking for — the identification with God, the realization of the Brahman — was, as it were, the first step, a necessary phase. But this was not everything, for there was a second phase: the descent of the power of the Divine in the human consciousness to transform it, and that *this* was what he, Sri Aurobindo, was trying to do. And he said to me: "If you want to try this, then you can stay here." I threw myself at his feet, and that was that.'

This is how Pavitra recounted how he had reached the destination of his pilgrimage to the children of the Ashram school forty years later, when already for many years he had been one of the closest collaborators of the Mother and the head of the very same school. And he concluded: 'There was not yet an ashram then. There were only a few houses belonging to Sri Aurobindo, and the Mother mainly looked after Sri Aurobindo — also a little after the disciples, but they were more or less left to themselves. So I have had the enormous privilege to meet Sri Aurobindo every day, to listen to him, to hear him answer daily the questions we put to him.'

These daily conversations of Sri Aurobindo with his disciples have been partly noted down by some of those present, among others by V. Chidanandam and especially by A.B. Purani, who has collected his notes in the book *Evening Talks With Sri Aurobindo*. In his introduction Purani writes: '[Sri Aurobindo] came dressed as usual in *dhoti*, part of which was used by him to cover the upper part of his body ... How much these sittings were dependent on him may be gathered from the fact that there were days when more than three-fourths of the time passed in complete silence without any outer suggestion from him, or there was only an abrupt yes or no to all attempts at drawing him out in conversation. Even when he participated in the talk one always felt that his voice was that of one who does not let his whole being flow into his words; there was a reserve and what was left unsaid was perhaps more than what was spoken. What was spoken was what he felt necessary to speak.

'Very often some news item in the daily newspaper, town-gossip, or some interesting letter received either by him or by a disciple, or a question from one of the gathering, occasionally some remark or query from himself would set the ball rolling for the talk. The whole thing was so informal that one could never predict the turn the conversation would take. The whole house therefore was in a mood to enjoy the freshness and the delight of meeting the unexpected. There were peals of laughter and light talk, jokes and criticism which might be called personal — there was seriousness and earnestness in abundance.'[49]

Dilip Kumar Roy was born in 'one of the most aristocratic Brahmin families of Bengal.' His father was a poet and playwright, and Dilip when still young, made a name for himself as a singer, mainly of religious songs, after having studied mathematics and music in Cambridge. He spoke several Indian languages besides English, French and German. Among his acquaintances were Mohandas K. Gandhi, Rabindranath Tagore, Romain Rolland, Bertrand Russell, Georges Duhamel and Subhas Chandra Bose. He would become the author of not less than seventy-five books in Bengali and twenty-six in English.

It was Ronald Nixon, a former British war pilot and professor in

English at the University of Lucknow, who, in 1923, had first drawn Dilip's attention to Sri Aurobindo's *Essays on the Gita* saying that never before had he read such a masterly exegesis of the *Bhagavad Gita*. Nixon was an ardent devotee of Krishna, so much so that shortly afterwards he gave up his career as a professor and withdrew, under the name Krishnaprem, in Almora, accepting as his guru Yashodama, a very cultivated woman, who was the wife of the vice-chancellor of the University of Lucknow.*

His appreciation of the *Essays on the Gita* led Dilip to read other works of Sri Aurobindo and eventually to meet the *Mahayogi* (great yogi) himself, which he did for the first time in 1924. He has written down in detail the two conversations he then had with Sri Aurobindo. 'A deep aura of peace encircled him, an ineffable yet concrete peace that drew you almost at once into its magic orbit. But it was the eyes that fascinated me most — shining like beacons. His torso was bare except for a scarf thrown across.'*

So deep was Sri Aurobindo's impression on Dilip that he asked to be accepted as his disciple. Sri Aurobindo, however, thought the time was not yet ripe, and the disillusioned aspirant-yogi left Pondicherry under the impression that he had been refused. All the same his spiritual aspirations did not prevent him from leading an extremely active social life, with song recitals, lectures and meetings of all kinds, for the most part in the higher social circles. He described his temperament as 'pre-eminently social' and he enjoyed 'exulting in the sunlit soil of travel, music, laughter and robust optimism.' 'I became popular and made friends, numerous friends — thanks to my patrimony, musical gifts, social qualities and lastly the pathetic awe and esteem that people feel when you can talk glibly about continental culture in continental languages.'

But Sri Aurobindo's refusal kept nagging him. Sri Aurobindo had

---

* The reader may remember that it was her husband, Jnanendra Nath Chakravarti, who, in 1908, had given the *Bhagavad Gita* to read to Mirra Alfassa in Paris.

* The quotations from Dilip Kumar Roy are taken from the section about Sri Aurobindo in his book *Among the Great*.

said: 'I can accept only those with whom yoga has become such a necessity that nothing else seems worthwhile. In your case it hasn't yet become so urgent. Your seeking is for some sort of partial elucidation of life's mysteries. This is at best an intellectual seeking — not an urgent need of the central being.'

Having gone back to Calcutta, Dilip sought acceptance as a disciple from Swami Abhedananda, a direct disciple of Ramakrishna Paramhamsa. 'But a friend of mine, a quondam disciple of Sri Aurobindo, intervened at the psychological moment and took me to consult a friend of his, a Yogi with remarkable occult powers. It was in a far-off village where we had to be his guests for the night.' Dilip told the yogi 'how desperate was his need of a Guru'. The yogi said nothing but: 'Sit down and close your eyes.' Dilip was not accustomed to being talked to in such an abrupt way, but he obeyed all the same, 'a little nettled'. 'I don't know how long we sat there with closed eyes, for a deepening peace had made me lose count of the passage of time.'

His friend gave him a nudge and he opened his eyes. The yogi said: 'But why are you hunting for a guru now that Sri Aurobindo himself has accepted you?' Dilip could not believe what he heard and asked for some explication. 'But it is simplicity itself,' said the yogi. '[Sri Aurobindo] just appeared there — yes, just behind you — and told me to advise you to wait. He asked me to tell you that he would draw you to him as soon as you were ready. Is that explicit enough?'

'His eyes twinkled in irony,' writes Dilip. '"Look here," he chimed in his forthright way, "shall I tell you something more convincing still?" He seemed to deliberate a moment before he added: "Tell me: do you happen to have some ailment in your left abdomen?" I stared at him in blank surprise. "But how did you know?" "I didn't — that is, not before he told me." "T—told you?" I stammered. "B—but who?" "Who else but your Guru — who has come here to tell you that you already had been advised by him to wait till the ailment was cured before you practised yoga ... But what is it?" "It's hernia. A tug-of-war caused the rupture." "That explains it. For yoga will mean pressure on these parts, the vitals. Maybe that's why he asked you to wait till it healed up."'

In March 1927, Dilip was invited to make a series of recordings for Edison's Gramophone Company in New York, but for some reason or other he never got farther than Europe. A lecture-demonstration of his music in the house of a Countess in Nice, was probably attended by an acquaintance of Paul Richard, who went to see Dilip the next day in his hotel. Dilip knew him from hearsay, mostly from Rabindranath Tagore who had met the Richards in Japan and had spoken in great praise of Paul Richard. To Dilip's amazement, Paul Richard confessed 'in the revealing stillness of midnight' that he often thought of committing suicide. He never got over the fact that he had not been able to accept Sri Aurobindo for what he really was, 'the one man to whom I have bowed down in my life as to a superior ... and the only seer who has truly fortified my faith in a Divine Purpose ... He and no one else has the key of the world to be, and my tragedy is that my love of self-will forced me to leave his aegis and choose the alternative of living a pointless life away from the *one* man whose society I rate over that of all the others put together.'

The meeting with Richard, 'a wreck of a brilliant man so many had admired,' strengthened Dilip's need to put himself under Sri Aurobindo's 'aegis'. 'I decided to return home, but not before an operation I had undergone so that my hernia might not stand in the way of my being accepted. Also I saw [Bertrand] Russell in his Cornwall home, gave a few lectures here and there and booked a passage home in November, 1927.' After a short stay in Bengal, he arrived for the second time in Pondicherry in August 1928.

'I was a little crestfallen to learn that Sri Aurobindo had in the meanwhile gone into seclusion.' He had an interview with the Mother, who told him that Sri Aurobindo had said to her that he was now ready to practise his yoga. 'I was accepted and came finally to follow their lead three months later ... dedicating all I had to what I have learned to love more and more as the holiest cause to which I could possibly consecrate my life.'

His *sadhana* had some encouraging ups but also many downs of despair, doubt and revolt. As Sri Aurobindo and the Mother have said repeatedly: 'Everybody here represents an impossibility that has to be made possible.' Nobody came to them without a reason and they possessed the knowledge to discern each person's past and future, his difficulties and his potential. During one of Dilip's dark nights, Sri Aurobindo would even write to him: 'I have cherished you like a friend and a son,'[50] and: 'It is a strong and lasting personal relation that I have felt with you ever since we met ... Even before I met you for the first time, I knew of you and felt at once the contact of one with whom I had that relation which declares itself constantly through many lives and followed your career ... with a close sympathy and interest. It is a feeling which is never mistaken and gives the impression of one not only close to one but a part of one's existence ... It was the same inward recognition (apart even from the deepest spiritual connection) that brought you here.'[51]

Dilip Kumar Roy always held his guru in high respect, but he never fully understood who Sri Aurobindo actually was nor the mission he had come to execute on Earth. The Mother he never accepted inwardly, and in the second edition of his book *Sri Aurobindo Came to Me* he even deleted all references to her. After Sri Aurobindo's passing, he left the Ashram without further ado to start, together with Indira Devi, the Hari Krishna Mandir in Poona. A permanent fruit of his *sadhana* and of Sri Aurobindo's inexhaustible compassion and comprehension are the four thousand highly illuminating letters Sri Aurobindo wrote to him on various topics. Many of those letters have been included in Sri Aurobindo's collected correspondence; they have their place side by side with Nirodbaran's correspondence with Sri Aurobindo and Satprem's talks with the Mother.

Chapter Eleven

ALL LIFE IS YOGA

*In the right view both of life and of
Yoga all life is either consciously or
subconsciously a Yoga.*[1]
— Sri Aurobindo

IN OUR story we have now arrived at 1926, the year
Sri Aurobindo withdrew in seclusion for the rest of his life and put
the Mother in charge of the corporeally present guidance of the
disciples; by this fact the small group around them became an *ashram,*
a spiritual community. To fully understand the importance of this
milestone in the life of Sri Aurobindo and the Mother, it is necessary
to take a closer look at the effort at transformation they had made
up to then.

A.B. Purani tells us how the consequences of that effort had
become visible: 'The greatest surprise of my visit in 1921 was the
"darshan" of Sri Aurobindo. During the interval of two years his body
had undergone a transformation which could only be described as
miraculous. In 1918 the colour of the body was like that of an
ordinary Bengali — rather dark — though there was a lustre on the
face and the gaze was penetrating. On going upstairs to see him ...
I found his cheeks wore an apple-pink colour and the whole body
glowed with a soft creamy white light. So great and unexpected was
the change that I could not help exclaiming, "What has happened
to you?" Instead of giving a direct reply he parried the question, as

I have grown a beard: "And what has happened to you?" But afterwards in the course of the talk he explained to me that when the Higher Consciousness, after descending to the mental level, comes down to the vital and even below the vital, then a transformation takes place in the nervous system and even in the physical being. He asked me to join the meditation in the afternoon and also the evening sittings. This time I saw the Mother for the first time. She was standing near the staircase when Sri Aurobindo was going up after lunch. Such unearthly beauty I had never seen — she appeared to be about 20 whereas she was more than 37 years old.'[2] In fact, she was then forty-three years old.

The parallels between the ways followed by Sri Aurobindo and the Mother are striking. The parents of both wanted their children to be the best of the best. Their parents were atheists, and in their youth Sri Aurobindo and the Mother themselves had been atheists (the Mother: 'I was a convinced atheist') The yoga of Aurobindo Ghose began with an intensive practice of *pranayama* in Baroda, in 1905; about the same time Mirra Alfassa stumbled upon the *Revue cosmique* which put her into contact with Théon's teachings and the Divine within. After a period of spiritual stagnation and 'inner dryness', Aurobindo met with the yogi Vishnu Bhaskar Lele at the end of 1907; Mirra's yoga, properly speaking, began immediately afterwards ('I began my true yoga in 1908'). The *Bhagavad Gita* played an important role in the initial development of both. Both were guided by incorporeal instructors for some time. Sri Aurobindo started his annotations in his *Record of Yoga* when the Mother began writing her *Prières et Méditations*, her spiritual diary, which in its present form comprises only a fraction of the original entries. As young Aurobindo had journeyed from East to West to receive a thorough Western education, so Mirra later travelled from West to East; their union and collaboration resulted in an intimate global synthesis. And the path both followed led them to the discovery of the Supramental.

And so the Mother could say, when commenting on an early text of hers: 'This was the complete programme of what Sri Aurobindo has done and the way to perform the work on earth, and I had foreseen all that in 1912. I have met Sri Aurobindo for the first time in 1914, two years later, and I had already worked out the complete programme,'[3] a programme that was the outcome of an inner realization. 'And I have arrived here in that state, with a world of experiences and already the conscious union with the Divine above and within — everything consciously realized, noted down, and so on — when I came to Sri Aurobindo.'[4] We are reminded of Sri Aurobindo's words: 'There is no difference between the Mother's path and mine; we have and have always had the same path, the path that leads to the supramental change and the divine realisation; not only at the end, but from the beginning they were the same.' In 1938 he said, as noted down by Nirodbaran: 'All my realisations — Nirvana and others — would have remained theoretical, as it were, as far as the outward world is concerned. It is the Mother who showed the way to a practical form. Without her, no organised manifestation would have been possible. She has been doing this kind of sadhana and work from her very childhood.'[5]

The Traditional Yogas

The process of Yoga is a turning of the human soul from the egoistic state of consciousness absorbed in the outward appearances and attractions of things to a higher state ...[6]
— Sri Aurobindo

The word 'yoga', now familiar to most people, remains associated for many in the West with bizarre, exotic Indian practices, with fakirs besmeared with ashes, with leprous beggars and holy cows, and trying to see God by standing on the head. It is true that various yogic disciplines have been developed in India and practised on a scale and with a naturalness as has never been the case in the West; but yoga — the seeking for God and the union with God — is, just like the concept of the Avatar, much more widespread in the West than most people would suspect. As Sri Aurobindo wrote: 'These things have been experienced, it is true, by a small minority of the human race, but still there has been a host of independent witnesses to them in all times, climes and conditions, and numbered among them are some of the greatest intelligences of the past, some of the world's most remarkable figures.'[7] The Mother said: 'The experience of all of them is the same. When they have touched the Thing, it is for all of them the same thing. The proof that they have touched That is precisely the fact that it is the same for everybody ... And to That you can give the names you like, it does not matter.'[8]

By way of illustration: 'Seek ye first the kingdom of God, and his righteousness,' said Christ, 'and all these things shall be added unto you.' So is to know God 'the one thing needful' of Sri Aurobindo, from which ensues all else. Without knowledge and the unification with God, all else is nothing but 'vanity of vanities' while mankind keeps plodding around in its mental circle. 'Yoga is not a thing of ideas but of inner spiritual experience. Merely to be attracted to any set of religious or spiritual ideas does not bring with it any realization. Yoga means a change of consciousness; a mere mental activity will not bring a change of consciousness, it can only bring a change of mind,'[9] Sri Aurobindo wrote tersely, and also, 'Yoga is not a field for intellectual argument or dissertation. It is not by the exercise of the logical or debating mind that one can arrive at a true understanding of yoga and follow it.'[10]

Above the entrance of the Apollo temple in Delphi was written: 'Know yourself'. Nowadays, this adage is generally understood in the humanistic, psychological sense, but it was the key word from the core of the secret Greek mysteries: know your Self and you will know the world and God, because your Self *is* the world and God. That concise Greek formula contains also, for instance, the whole message of the realized soul that was Ramana Maharshi, a contemporary of Sri Aurobindo. And Christ said: 'The Kingdom of God is within you.'

Does not *The Imitation of Christ* by Thomas à Kempis provide the soul with a method, a discipline to experience the revelation of its Beloved and to enjoy the resplendence of his Presence? Is not the Jesus prayer of the Orthodox Church a *japa*, a repetition of words charged with power and condensed in a *mantra* (formula) so that the soul, by the power of the word, may transcend everyday reality and emerge in a higher reality? Have not the repetition of the Lord's prayer or the Ave Maria, or some phrases from the Psalms, the same function and effect, even unconsciously? Is not the Rule of St Benedict, for instance, essentially a discipline of God-realization contained in the practical regulation of a monastic community? And there are the spiritual paths of so many saints and mystics who have been the fine flower of their age and culture.

This is why Anne Bancroft could write in *The Luminous Vision*, her book about six medieval mystics: 'The three essential beliefs of mysticism, that the beingness of oneself is also that of the God-ground, or timeless Reality; that to find this unconditioned beingness we have to let go our dependence on conditioned things; and that actually to do this reveals to us the nature of our true life as a human being — these three beliefs are not only those of Dionysius and the Christian mystics who followed him but also the basic beliefs of all religions, particularly Buddhism — indeed the Four Noble Truths are echoed time and again in medieval words'(p. 6). Those 'essential beliefs' are also the main pillars of Sufism and of the traditional Yogas.*

All this allows us to conclude that yoga has indeed been very well known in the West, albeit in another garb or under other names, long before various schools of Eastern spirituality induced its conscious revival in the course of the present century. The need for a direct individual contact with the Godhead, or with the true Self, has in the course of the past centuries grown ever more urgent because of the authoritarianism of the Christian Churches, for they have put themselves between the soul and its God who is its Self, and they have appropriated the exclusive right of mediation and intercession with God on the basis of dubious religious claims. No formal

---

* 'The experiences of the mediaeval European *bhakta* or mystic are precisely the same in substance, however differing in names, forms, religious colouring, etc., as those of the mediaeval Indian *bhakta* or mystic — yet these people were not corresponding with one another or aware of each other's experiences and results ... That would seem to show that there is something there identical, universal and presumably true — however the colour of translation may differ because of the difference of mental language.' (Sri Aurobindo, *Letters on Yoga*, p. 190)

grouping of men has up to now succeeded in keeping alive the teachings of an authentic, missioned or realized Founder. What in the beginning was intended as a religious apostolate has time and again been formalized into an Earth-bound community of interests, motivated by the urge for power, social esteem and material possession. The Churches have played an irreplaceable role historically and culturally, but their main victim has been the living soul of the faithful. The Eastern 'sects' which are now attracting so many people in the West can only fulfil their true mission if they know how to escape the snares of human nature in group formation, and if they keep pointing, beyond themselves, to 'the one thing needful' of which every soul is a part and grows into the living image, and that eventually must lead to the foundation of the Kingdom of God on Earth.

'Yoga is nothing but practical psychology,' wrote Sri Aurobindo in *The Synthesis of Yoga*, the literary formulation of his experiments, experiences and realizations from 1912 till 1921, cryptically noted down in his *Record of Yoga*. 'Essentially, Yoga is a generic name for the processes and the results of processes by which we transcend or shred off our present modes of being and rise to a new, a higher, a wider mode of consciousness which is not that of the ordinary animal and intellectual man.'[11] These processes are based on the general psychological characteristics of the human being, and have been found to be realizable and repeatable by others as tried out by generations of practitioners in India.

For man the active being there is the yoga of the will or of works, *karmayoga*; for man the emotional being there is the yoga of devotion or love, *bhaktiyoga*; for man the thinking, reflective being there is the yoga of knowledge, *jnanayoga*. These are the three main procedures by which the human being can use its fundamental qualities to rise above its ordinary state and to find access to the Above. But it is also embodied in several 'sheaths': the visible material sheath and the invisible vital and mental sheaths. The totality of this complex embodiment — called the *adhara* in India and much more complex than the commonly supposed single material body — also has its possibility of perfection through *hathayoga*, which in the West is practically synonymous with yoga in general. *Hathayoga*, however, is the most limited and least spiritual form of yoga because it exclusively aims at the perfection of the *adhara;* to touch higher realities, it has to borrow elements from other yogic disciplines. There is also *rajayoga*, probably the most practised method of yoga in India, which has organically integrated elements of the other yogas into an effective whole and is accessible to the greatest diversity of spiritual aspirants. A wide range of literature is now available about all these systems of yoga.

Like all existing forms of spirituality and all religions, the methods of yoga too have only one goal: to escape from this nightmarish world, this valley of tears, this prison, this place of banishment, into higher, more agreeable worlds or states of being, or into a state of non-being. On the one hand, there is this impossible world in which the soul for some reason or other has been plunged or has plunged of its own choosing; on the other hand, there is the hereafter, mostly the positive projection of our negative experience of the world — and in between there is nothing. It is therefore a matter of some urgency to get away from here as soon as possible and never come back, if possible, for instance by disappearing forever into the Godhead or into Nirvana. But in Nirvana there is nobody left to congratulate oneself on the liberation. 'Sri Aurobindo often said: the people who choose to get out of [the manifestation] forget that, at the same time, they will lose the consciousness with which they might congratulate themselves on their choice'[12] (the Mother). Moreover, if God is the perfect being he is supposed to be, why has he made this hell-like world and us in it?

One school of yoga has tackled this problem courageously, the *tantrayoga*. Although its final aim too is to attain *mukti*, liberation, it does not turn its back on the creation; on the contrary, it utilizes the difficulties in the creation as possibilities. While all Vedantic yogas (the ones mentioned earlier) turn towards the hidden Supreme Being that is the *Purusha*, the *tantrayoga* worships the creative Power, the *Shakti*, the World-Mother, and it worships her works because of her. One who has read the previous chapter will find here something of Sri Aurobindo's relation with the Great Mother, accentuated by his confirmation in principle that the Creation too is the

Godhead — because the Godhead is everything and nothing can exist outside it. (Because of these two reasons — the recognition of the role of the Great Mother and the positive evaluation of her creation — Sri Aurobindo's yoga could in fact be considered as a kind of super-tantra.)

Sri Aurobindo's Integral Yoga

'Sri Aurobindo has always told that his yoga begins where the others' end,' said the Mother, 'and that to be able to realize his yoga, one first has to attain the extreme limit of what the other yogas have realized.'[13] This is no small prerequisite. But the Work the double-poled Avatar had come to do was no small work either.

Sri Aurobindo and the Mother have mastered, if not all the details, all the essence of the traditional yogas. 'Will, knowledge and love are the three divine powers in human nature and the life of man, and they point to the three paths by which the human soul rises to the Divine. Their integrality, the union of man with God in all the three, must therefore ... be the foundation of an integral Yoga.'[14] 'In this yoga all sides of the Truth are taken up, not in the systematic forms given them formerly but in their essence, and carried to the fullest and highest significance.'[15] 'As for the Mother and myself, we have had to try all ways, follow all methods, to surmount mountains of difficulties, a far heavier burden to bear than you or anybody else in the Ashram or outside, far more difficult conditions, battles to fight, wounds to endure, ways to cleave through impenetrable morass and desert and forest, hostile masses to conquer — a work such as, I am certain, none else had to do before us. For the Leader of the Way in a work like ours has not only to bring down and represent and embody the Divine, but to represent too the ascending element in humanity and to bear the burden of humanity to the full and experience, not in a mere play or Lila but in grim earnest, all the obstruction, difficulty, opposition, baffled and hampered and only slowly victorious labour which are possible on the Path.'[16] Their discovery of the New World was the consequence of an integral knowledge and experience of the old one. They could only build on an integral synthesis of what existed to work out the profound significance of the evolution in themselves and in others.

Their attitude towards the traditional paths of yoga and spirituality has, of course, never been denigrating. Isn't it yoga and spirituality which, 'in all times, climes and circumstances,' have gifted mankind with its greatest exponents? Wouldn't humanity be a sorry mess if it had not produced those beacons of light? Sri Aurobindo once put one of his disciples in his place: 'One can and ought to believe and follow one's own path without condemning or looking down on others for having beliefs different from those one thinks or sees to be the best or the largest in truth. The spiritual field is many-sided and full of complexities and there is room for an immense variety of experiences. Besides, all mental egoism — and spiritual egoism — has to be surmounted and this sense of superiority should therefore not be cherished.'[17]

In the course of their personal evolution, it had become clear to Sri Aurobindo and the Mother that they, as Avatars, had been sent to build the foundations of the material realization of a new species on Earth. This time the issue was not the embodiment of a higher being within the mental range, but of a divine being in the literal sense of the word. Their own yoga, work or development — whatever one wants to call it — therefore consisted of the following: (i) the complete identification with their divine nature; (ii) the realization in themselves of their divine consciousness in a dynamic way (a yoga beyond the existing yogas), to render that consciousness active in the world; and (iii) to progressively embody that divine consciousness themselves, first on the mental, then on the vital and finally on the material level. The result of all that should be that a divine species, as the successor of the present human being, would inhabit the Earth and that the Kingdom of God would no longer be a promise or a dream, but a reality beyond our highest expectations. 'Then all the long labour of Nature will end in a crowning justification.'[18]

Evidently, a yoga to turn such a fantastic ambition into reality — the coming of the Golden Age — required other means than those available in the traditional yogas, however much tested and practised, for the practitioners of those yogas do not intend a divine creation here on Earth but try, without exception, to escape as soon as possible from hell on Earth.

Sri Aurobindo's new method was unbelievably simple and at the same time very daring. If that new something was so new, if it was the intention of the Supreme and his manifesting power to embody in evolution something superhuman, a divine species succeeding the existing human species, then the only way to collaborate was to open inadequate human nature totally and unconditionally to the new Divine Action, to *surrender* to it. 'Surrender', the total giving of oneself, is *the* keyword in Sri Aurobindo and the Mother's yoga — also called the Integral Yoga, the *Purna* [complete] Yoga or the Supramental Yoga. If the comprehension as well as the power and the effects of the totally new Event on Earth surpass the human being, and if the human being wants to collaborate on the coming of a New World, then it can only try and open itself to the Divine Action in the hope that this Action will permeate and transform its physical, vital and mental limitations.

'The first word of the supramental Yoga is surrender; its last word also is surrender,'[19] wrote Sri Aurobindo in a recently discovered note of his. Surrender had been the beginning and the foundation of his own journey of discovery. About his meeting with Lele, he narrates: 'In my own case I owe the first decisive turn of my inner life to one who was infinitely inferior to me in intellect, education and capacity and by no means spiritually perfect or supreme; but, having seen a Power behind him and decided to turn there for help, I gave myself entirely into his hands and followed with an automatic passivity the guidance. He himself was astonished and said to others that he had never met anyone before who could surrender himself so absolutely and without reserve or question to the guidance of the helper [i.e., Lele].'[20] This reminds one, of course, of Sri Aurobindo's own pronouncement about the surrender of the Mother.

'Before parting I told Lele: "Now that we shall not be together I should like you to give me instructions about Sadhana [his spiritual discipline]." In the meantime I told him of a Mantra that had arisen in my heart. He was giving me instructions when he suddenly stopped and asked me if I could rely absolutely on Him who had given me the Mantra. I said I could always do it. Then Lele said there was no need for instructions ... Some months later, he came to Calcutta. He asked me if I meditated in the morning and in the evening. I said, no. Then he thought that some devil had taken possession of me.'[21]

This extract is from a conversation noted down by A.B. Purani in 1923. Fifteen years later, Sri Aurobindo, answering a question on this subject, said: 'I [then] said to myself: "You have handed me over to the Divine and if as a result of that the Devil catches hold of me, I will say that the Divine has sent the Devil and I will follow him."'[22] Sri Aurobindo was still more radical in the spiritual revolution he had brought about than he was as the ideologist of the political extremists.

This radicality, this unconditionality we find also in the first lines of the first chapter of *The Synthesis of Yoga*, the greatest book about yoga ever written, where as a kind of programmatic declaration one reads: 'The supreme Shastra [scripture] of the integral Yoga is the eternal Veda [knowledge] in the heart of every thinking and living being.'[23] Further on in the same book, he writes: 'If we are to be free in the Spirit, if we are to be subject only to the supreme Truth, we must discard the idea that our mental or moral laws are binding on the Infinite or that there can be anything sacrosanct, absolute or eternal even in the highest of our existing standards of conduct.'[24] 'For the Sadhaka [practitioner] of the integral Yoga it is necessary to remember that no written Shastra, however great its authority or however large its spirit, can be more than a partial expression of the eternal Knowledge. He will use, but never bind himself even by the greatest Scripture ... He must live in his own soul beyond the written Truth ... He is a Sadhaka of the infinite.'[25] 'Either the Shastra grows obsolete and has to be progressively changed or finally cast away or else it stands as a rigid barrier to the self-development of the individual and the race. The Shastra erects a collective and external standard; it ignores the inner nature of the individual, the indeterminable elements of a secret spiritual force within him. But the nature of the individual will not be ignored; its demand is inexorable.'[26] 'The decision lies between God and our self ... It is altogether from within that must come the knowledge of the work that has to be done.'[27]

This does not mean that Sri Aurobindo wanted to wipe the past off the map. As we have already seen, he and the Mother had completely assimilated the existing yogic disciplines, and we know that they, as Avatars, had to take into them the whole pre-existence of humanity to work out the inner meaning of the evolution and to manifest a higher gradation of it. 'I had my past and the world's past to assimilate and overpass before I could find and found the future.'[28] (Sri Aurobindo) But the transformation of the human in a divine species demanded a radically new approach. They were the pioneers of a new creation on the Earth who at first were the only ones to know about it and who had to built the foundations of it in themselves before they could involve other, selected representatives of the existing human species. This was a task which by far surpassed the potentialities of the human nature in which they had incarnated and which therefore required the unconditional surrender to the Divine and his Executrix, the Great Mother. 'This surrender is the indispensable means of the supramental change,'[29] wrote Sri Aurobindo, and more personally in *Savitri*: 'A vast surrender was his only strength.'[30]

Of that supramental change they were the forerunners, the founders, the avant-gardists. As with all Avatars, it was also their job to clear a path in the unknown, this time to make real the utopia of all utopias. Sri Aurobindo called himself 'a path-finder hewing his way through a virgin forest.'[31] This is a metaphor the Mother, when alone, burdened with the task after Sri Aurobindo's passing, would use time and again, for instance in 1961: 'I am really hewing a road in a virgin forest ... What is the road? Is there a road? Is there a procedure? Probably not.' The old yogas, roads on the established map of spirituality, were already far behind them. They had ventured into the unknown, into the impossible. 'Let all men jeer at me if they will or all Hell fall upon me if it will for my presumption — I go on till I conquer or perish. This is the spirit in which I seek the Supermind, no hunting for greatness for myself or others,'[32] asserted Sri Aurobindo emphatically. The Mother said with as much emphasis to the youth of the Ashram, among whom were present some of the elect: 'It looks like foolishness, but everything new has always seemed foolish before it became reality ... And as we are all here for reasons probably unknown to most of you, but which are very conscious reasons, we can choose the fulfilment of that foolishness as our aim. It will at least be worthwhile to participate in the experience.'[33]

'The traditions of the past are very great in their own place, in the past, but I do not see why we should merely repeat them and not go farther. In the spiritual development of the consciousness upon earth the great past ought to be followed by a greater future.'[34] There is no gainsaying this. However, human nature is distrustful and conservative. 'They admit and jealously defend the changes compelled by the progressive mind in the past, but combat with equal zeal the changes that are being made by it in the present,'[35] Sri Aurobindo wrote ironically. And then in his inimitable humorous vein to a more ignorant than sceptical Nirodbaran: 'What a wonderful argument! Since it has not been done, it cannot be done! At that rate the whole history of the earth must have stopped long before the protoplasm. When it was a mass of gases, no life had been born, ergo, life could not be born — when only life was there, mind was not born, so mind could not be born. Since mind is there but nothing beyond, as there is no supermind manifested in anybody, so supermind can never be born. Sobhanallah! [Glory to God!] Glory, glory, glory to the human reason!! Luckily the Divine or the Cosmic Spirit or Nature or whoever is there cares a damn for the human reason. He or she or it does what he or she or it has to do, whether it can or cannot be done.'[36]

In what way does Sri Aurobindo's yoga differ from the traditional yogas? He has clearly explained this in one of his letters:

It is new as compared with the old yogas:

'1. Because it aims not at a departure out of world and life into Heaven or Nirvana, but at a change of life and existence, not as something subordinate or incidental, but as a distinct and central object. If there is a descent in other yogas, yet it is only an incident on the way or resulting from the ascent — the ascent is the real thing. Here the ascent is the first step, but it is a means for the descent. It is the descent of the new consciousness attained by the ascent that is the stamp and seal of the sadhana.

Even the Tantra and Vaishavism end in the release from life; here the object is the divine fulfilment of life.

'2. Because the object sought after is not an individual achievement of divine realisation for the sake of the individual, but something to be gained for the earth-consciousness here, a cosmic, not solely a supra-cosmic achievement. The thing to be gained also is the bringing in of a Power of Consciousness (the supramental) not yet organised or active directly in earth-nature, even in the spiritual life, but yet to be organised and made directly active.

'3. Because a method has been recognized for achieving this purpose which is as total and integral as the aim set before it, viz., the total and integral change of the consciousness and nature, taking up old methods but only as a part action and present aid to others that are distinctive. I have not found this method (as a whole) or anything like it professed or realised in the old yogas. If I had, I should not have wasted my time in hewing out a road and in thirty years of search and inner creation when I could have hastened home safely to my goal in an easy canter over paths already blazed out, laid down, perfectly mapped, macadamised, made secure and public. Our yoga is not a retreading of old walks, but a spiritual adventure.'[37]

It was an incredible load Sri Aurobindo and the Mother had taken on their shoulders, a load all but invisible to others. They had to take evolution a gigantic leap forward; they had to take everything into them in order to transform it; to be able to activate the divine supramental power in the earth-substance, they not only had to have it at their own command, but they also had to be able to manifest it on every level of their personality in accordance with the particular conditions of that level; and nothing of the existing reality could remain outside the scope of their work, for the Supramental is a Truth-Consciousness that is a Unity-Consciousness, and anything not taken up into the transforming movement, however small or apparently unimportant, would frustrate it. 'Nothing is actually done as long as everything is not done.' 'If everything does not change, nothing will change' (the Mother).

'In this Yoga nothing is too small not to be utilised and nothing too big not to be tried out,' wrote Sri Aurobindo. He and the Mother were, like all Avatars, accelerators of the evolution. Yoga is always a condensation, a densification, a telescoping of the evolution, which under normal circumstances is the work of Mother Nature, and she amuses herself with her magic of producing new forms and takes her time of it. 'Yoga is a rapid and concentrated conscious evolution of the being ... It may effect in a single life what in an instrumental Nature might take centuries and millenniums or many hundreds of lives.'[38] The Avatar turns evolution into revolution. This is the reason why so few can understand him or even believe in the certainty of his vision of Light.

Sri Aurobindo wanted to fix the base of a manifested supramental world for all future time. '[He] cast his deeds like bronze to front the years.'[39] Ever the revolutionary and radical extremist, he wrote that it was his wish that the supramental victory, manifestation and transformation should be for now. His followers, like all human beings eager for the miraculous, interpreted such words in their naïve way: they forgot that the work of the Avatar, however quick and powerful — and in itself a miracle — had to take into account the evolutionary mechanisms built into her creation by the Creatrix. 'The whole *samskara* [the established habits] of the whole universe' is against his efforts. Nirodbaran too was of the opinion that the work of his gurus — 'the most difficult imaginable' (Sri Aurobindo) — went rather slowly; therefore Sri Aurobindo asked him: 'What would have satisfied your rational mind — 3 years? 3 months? 3 weeks? Considering that by ordinary evolution it could not have been done even at Nature's express speed in less than 3000 years, and would ordinarily have taken anything from 30,000 to 300,000, the transit of 30 years is perhaps not too slow.'[40] Sri Aurobindo wrote this in 1936, when after about thirty years of *sadhana* he thought the manifestation of the supramental was imminent. (The manifestation, however, would take place twenty years later and after a whole series of dramatic events. So many expectations of Sri Aurobindo and the Mother have time and again been postponed by the opposition of the hostile forces who tenaciously resist every inch of progress. This uncertainty in the battle of cosmic dimensions they had to fight and the unimaginable suffering that went with it is, as it were, the seal of authenticity on their work.)

To execute the total, global Work in which nothing was too small or too big, they had to include the whole world in their embrace. 'The thing to be done is as large as human life, and therefore the individuals who lead the way will take all human life for their province. These pioneers will consider nothing as alien to them, nothing as outside their scope. For every part of human life has to be taken up by the spiritual — not only the intellectual, the aesthetic, the ethical, but the dynamic, the vital, the physical; therefore for none of these things or the activities that spring from them will they have contempt or aversion, however they may insist on a change of the spirit and a transmutation of the form.'[41]

What Sri Aurobindo describes here as the indispensable attitude of those who want to collaborate on the great work, was the attitude he and the Mother themselves had found necessary for their Work. 'All life is Yoga' is the motto of Sri Aurobindo's *Synthesis*. 'Sri Aurobindo took the difficulties like this,' said the Mother, opening her arms to embrace all, 'and then he worked on it so that there be no difficulties anymore.'[42] And that was what she did too, she pressed the whole world on her bosom.

At his first meeting with Lele, Sri Aurobindo, to his own and Lele's surprise, had had the realization of the passive Brahman. (A spiritual experience is, generally speaking, an unexpected but relatively brief event; a realization causes a permanent change or acquisition in the personality.) After the following intensive practice of the yoga and guided by the Master of the yoga in his heart, Sri Aurobindo had had the realization of the Omnipresent Divine and of the Cosmic Consciousness in the prison at Alipore. One of those two realizations is for the greatest yogis, in most cases, the fruit of a lifelong *sadhana*.

The date of Sri Aurobindo's third realization cannot be fixed accurately. The letter in which he mentions it has been printed in the *Supplement* to his Collected Works and is dated as from 1913 with a question mark. He writes: '15th August [his birthday] is usually a turning point or a notable day for me personally either in Sadhana or life, — indirectly only for others. This time it has been very important for me. My subjective Sadhana may be said to have received its final seal and something like its consummation by a prolonged realisation and dwelling in the Parabrahman [at once the passive and the active Brahman, the Supreme Godhead] for many hours. Since then, egoism is dead for all in me except the Annamaya Atma, — the physical self which awaits one farther realisation before it is entirely liberated from occasional visitings or external touches of the old separated existence.'[43] Sri Aurobindo was at that moment a fully realized Yogi, completely at one with the Divine, except for certain states in which the material body was still experienced as something personal. The meaning of this, we, ordinary mortals, cannot even attempt to understand.

Peter Heehs writes in connection with this third great realization: 'Sri Aurobindo's resumption of action after having entered the silence of the Brahman was, in our opinion, the principal turning-point in his life. A yogin who realizes Brahman has no need to proceed further.'[44] K.D. Sethna probably supposes that Sri Aurobindo's realization of the Parabrahman must have happened some time earlier, for he writes: 'This means that by 1910 — the year in which he [Sri Aurobindo] came to Pondicherry, he could have rested on his laurels, for, in matters of God-realisation as traditionally envisaged he had nothing more to achieve.'[45] Whatever the correct date may be, the opinion of both writers converges on the same fact: that Sri Aurobindo after having reached the supreme individual *siddhi* (yogic realization) turned back towards the Earth and mankind to continue the work for which he had been born: 'My mission in life is to bring down the Supermind into Mind, Life and Body.'[46] 'I have no intention of achieving the Supermind for myself only — I am not doing anything for myself, as I have no personal need of anything, neither of salvation (*moksha*) nor supramentalisation. If I am seeking after supramentalisation, it is because it is a thing that has to be done for the earth-consciousness and if it is not done in myself, it cannot be done in others ... My *sadhana* was not done for myself but for the earth-consciousness.'[47]

As always, he has been working at his proposed aim without respite, even during the years he wrote the *Arya,* as witnessed in his *Record of Yoga.* This is why the Mother could say: 'When I returned in 1920, he was bringing the Supramental in the mental consciousness', i.e. in the highest of the three elements humans are made of. In Purani's report about his meeting with Sri Aurobindo in 1921, we read that Sri Aurobindo and the Mother were already bringing down the Supramental into the vital, which is the domain of the life-forces — the very reason why they were looking so different and, as it were, rejuvenated. (We know that spiritual force is more concrete and mightier than material force, and that consciousness literally is a concrete entity; otherwise spirituality and yoga would only be a fiction and the transformation of the body a chimera.) 'Something strange happened; when we were in the vital: all at once my body became young again just like I was eighteen!' told the Mother. 'There was a young man named Pearson, a disciple of Tagore, who had been in Japan [at the same time as us] and who had come back to India, and he came to visit me. When he saw me, he was stupefied. He said: "But what has happened to you?" He did not recognize me. It has not lasted very long, only a few months. At that time I received some old photographs from France and Sri Aurobindo saw a photo of mine from the time I was eighteen. He said: "See here! This is how you are now!" My hair was dressed differently, but I had become eighteen again!'[48]

Since then five, six more years had gone by — years of intensive, now combined *sadhana* for Sri Aurobindo and the Mother. Their dedication was total, their effort an act of every moment, night and day, and their capabilities the highest which embodied beings on Earth had ever acquired. And this is how we arrive at a new milestone in their work which we will relate in the next chapter.

The Concept of the 'Superman'

The higher, divine being that will succeed man has as yet no name. Sri Aurobindo called it the gnostic or supramental being, or more often the *superman*. However, the word 'superman'* can easily be

---

* It is difficult to replace 'superman' by a 'gender inclusive' word, as 'superman' has been the word used throughout by Sri Aurobindo and by the other writers of his time. Wherever possible, the term 'supramental being' will be used in this book.

misunderstood because it actually means a human being with greater quantitative and/or qualitative human capacities than at present. This is one of the reasons why it immediately brings to mind Nietzsche's *Übermensch*, while Sri Aurobindo meant by it a 'supraman', i.e. a being spiritually and physically of a totally different and higher order from the humans, just like the supramental is a higher and totally different consciousness compared with the mental.

It is practically impossible to find a reference book which gives an undistorted outline of Sri Aurobindo's ideas, and he is often represented as an epigone of Friedrich Nietzsche. At the time he gave in the *Arya* a philosophical shape to his inner experiences and coined the terminology for them, he was of course aware of the possible association with Nietzsche, if only because of the word 'superman' and its connotations. This is why in one of the first issues of the review he published an article to define unequivocally Nietzsche's conception of the superman and his own. The difference is not a matter of nuances, it is poles apart. But later experience has shown that few writers have been so badly, or so partially, or so superficially read and understood as Sri Aurobindo; this is the reason why time and again he has been wrongly labelled as a philosopher and as a spiritual innovator.

Sri Aurobindo held Nietzsche in high esteem. He called him 'the most vivid, concrete and suggestive of modern thinkers'[48] and he regretted 'the misapplication by Treitschke of the teachings of Nietzsche to national and international uses which would have profoundly disgusted the philosopher himself.'[50] One should keep in mind that the *Arya* was written for the most part during the first World War, when Nietzsche's sister too was turning his (sometimes falsified) writings into propaganda material of the *Herrenvolk*, the master race. 'Two books belonged to the standard equipment of the German soldier in the first World War: *Also Sprach Zarathustra* and the *Gospel of St John*. It is difficult to say which of both authors thereby was most misused'(Bernal Maguus).

Sri Aurobindo writes in *The Human Cycle*: 'Nietzsche's idea that to develop the superman out of our present very unsatisfactory manhood is our real business, is in itself an absolutely sound teaching.

His formulation of our aim, "to become ourselves," "to exceed ourselves," implying, as it does, that man has not yet found his true self, his true nature by which he can successfully and spontaneously live, could not be bettered. But then the question of questions is there, what is our self, and what is our real nature? What is that which is growing in us, but into which we have not yet grown?'[51]

We are now familiar with Sri Aurobindo's answer. The human being is a transitional being that is the embodiment of an eternal, divine soul. It is the evolution of this divine soul which causes and supports the material evolution from the deepest Inertia back to its divine Origin. As before man there has been a whole gradation of evolutionary steps, so after him there will be still more steps, for at present he does not come close to incarnating the divine potential contained in his soul. The most important means of transition to the following species, the species of the Aurobindonian supramental being, is a complete surrender to the Evolving Power by which, after the example of the double-poled, complete Avatar, Sri Aurobindo and the Mother, the present human qualities and way of being will be supramentalized. We have heard Sri Aurobindo say that only the Divine *Shakti* can accomplish the integral yoga of this transformation. He consequently also said: 'It is a great mistake to suppose that one can "do" the Purna Yoga [the complete or integral Yoga] ... No human being can do that.'[52] No species can break through its own ceiling all by itself. The Unity-Consciousness, which will be the essence of the supramental being, surpasses man as much 'as a lizard differs from a man.' 'As man is removed from the animal, so would be the Superman from man.'[53] (*Evening Talks*)

The differences with Nietzsche's philosophy are evident. For instance, Nietzsche believed in an endless succession of cycles, not in an evolution with a beginning and an end (which does not exclude a cyclical development, but then as it were in a spiral, the cycles being repeated on an ever higher level and directed towards a goal). His superman was the product of a *Wille-zur-Macht*, an attitude of superiority and hunger for power and the will by which he had to rise above all moral norms to become the master, driven by an inspiration of which the source is difficult to define. The higher characteristics of this superman are not the (by us still unrealized) spiritual qualities of Light, Love, Harmony and Unity-Consciousness, but the aggrandized, 'colossalized' (Sri Aurobindo's word) human capacities as known to us in our present state. When Nietzsche talks about the soul, he means something quite different — usually a concentration of life-forces — from the presence of the Supreme in us. In short, Friedrich Nietzsche was a strongly inspired seer and poet, much more than a philosopher, whose brain almost literally burst because of the pressure of the awareness that the time of the incarnation of a higher species on Earth was imminent. Imprisoned by mental limitations he had suffered like few others, but being born too early and too much to the West was unable to escape from the mental prison and had dashed himself to insanity against its glass walls.

As an evaluation of Friedrich Nietzsche, we may conclude with the following words of Sri Aurobindo: 'Nietzsche first cast it, the mystic of Will-worship, the troubled, profound, half-luminous Hellenising Slav with his strange clarities, his violent half-ideas, his rare gleaming intuitions that came marked with the stamp of an absolute truth and sovereignty of light. But Nietzsche was an apostle who never entirely understood his own message. His prophetic style was like that of the Delphic oracles, which spoke constantly the word of the Truth but turned it into untruth in the mind of the hearer. Not always indeed; for sometimes he rose beyond his personal temperament and individual mind, his European inheritance and environment, his revolt against the Christ-idea, his war against current moral values and spoke out the Word as he had heard it, the Truth as he had seen it, bare, luminous, impersonal and therefore flawless and imperishable. But for the most part this message that had come to his inner hearing, vibrating out of a distant Infinite like a strain caught from the lyre of far-off Gods, did get, in his effort to appropriate and make it near to him, mixed up with a somewhat turbulent surge of collateral ideas that drowned much of the pure original note.' (*Arya*, first volume, p. 571).

Friedrich Nietzsche too, who like few others sensed that a New Age was at hand, was a veritable precursor.

Part Two

**Sri Aurobindo
and the Mother**

Chapter Twelve

KRISHNA AND THE WORLD
OF THE GODS

IN 1926, Sri Aurobindo and the Mother had, as we have seen, the supramental realization in the parts of their personality which we might call, using Sri Aurobindo's terminology, the mental and the vital. This means nothing less than that in these parts of their evolution embodied *adhara* they were the manifested Divine, not theoretically but factually and practically. That they chose not to proclaim this fact does not diminish the grandeur of it, but as a consequence of its unimaginability, few disciples have been aware of the high degree and the concrete results the efforts of Sri Aurobindo and the Mother had obtained at that moment. In naïve expectation and without having any notion of the enormous dimensions of the Work, most disciples were looking forward to a sudden physical transformation of Sri Aurobindo and the Mother and the day they would, in a glorified supramental body, turn their faithful into an identical glorious state, hopefully in the twinkling of an eye. But first a lot remained to be done and it was very difficult work indeed. In this work, 24 November 1926 was one of the milestones.

In the course of that year, Sri Aurobindo began talking quite often about the Gods and their world, called by him the 'Overmind'. In the first days of November, he had said, as noted by A.B. Purani: 'I spoke about the world of the Gods [in a previous conversation] because not to speak of it would be dangerous. I spoke of it so that the mind may understand the thing if it comes down. I am trying to bring it down into the physical as it can no longer be delayed and then things may happen. Formerly, to speak of it would have been undesirable but now not to speak of it might be dangerous.'[1] It is clear that he expected an important event involving the Gods, which might have a confusing and even bewildering effect on his entourage if they were not prepared.

We remember that, in the scheme of things, the world of the Gods occupies the highest level of the lower hemisphere, there where the divine Unity is no longer one but for the first time divided in a process that finally leads up to the general Ignorance and Darkness. The One Force was divided into the great cosmic forces and that division resulted ultimately in a material manifestation. Every force is a consciousness and every consciousness a being. The positive cosmic forces are the cosmic Beings called 'Gods'. 'They are the various facets of Something that exists in itself. Those beings are endowed with different aspects according to the countries and civilisations,' said the Mother. The cosmic forces are evidently the same in the whole cosmos, but in the conceptual world of the humans they are called Demeter, Mars, the archangel Gabriel, Anubis or Krishna.

> The Spirit's truths take form as living Gods
> And each can build a world in its own right.[2]
> — *Savitri*

'The Gods ... are in origin and essence permanent Emanations of the Divine put forth from the Supreme by the Transcendent Mother,'[3] writes Sri Aurobindo. 'Men can build forms [of the Gods] which they will accept, but these forms too are inspired into men's mind from the planes to which the Gods belong. All creation has two sides, the formed and the formless; the Gods too are formless and yet have forms, but a Godhead can take many forms, here Maheshwari, there Pallas Athene. Maheshwari herself has many forms in her lesser manifestations, Durga, Uma, Parvati, Chandi, etc. The Gods are not limited to human forms — man also has not always seen them in human forms only.'[4] They were and are often seen as light or as a play of lights.

The world of the Gods is called the 'Overmind' in Sri Aurobindo's terminology. In the history of mankind, this world is often considered as the highest form of existence — the one of the high, not terrestrial beings and sometimes of the Supreme Being. 'That Overmind has ruled the world by means of all the religions,'[5] said the Mother. Man has tried to represent its dimensions symbolically in his temples and cathedrals.

According to the order of things as seen by Sri Aurobindo and the Mother, the Overmind, however high above the world of our experience, is 'nothing but the highest gradation of the lower hemisphere'; this gradation is separated from the higher hemisphere of divine Unity by a 'golden lid' — the gate human beings cannot pass through without casting off their material body. It is as if by that lid the Light of Unity is filtered into rays of (apparent) division — a division which is subdivided endlessly into our mental consciousness which can no longer conceive of total unity, and ultimately into the so-called elementary particles of matter, into the fields which constitute matter, and into their mysterious basis. 'It is the line of the soul's turning away from the complete and indivisible knowledge and its descent towards the Ignorance,'[6] wrote Sri Aurobindo.

> The line that parts and joins the hemispheres
> Closes in on the labour of the Gods
> Fencing Eternity from the toil of Time.[7]
>
> — *Savitri*

'Although [the Overmind] draws from the Truth, it is here that begins the separation of aspects of the Truth, the forces and their working out as if they were independent truths and this is a process that ends, as one descends to ordinary Mind, Life and Matter, in a complete division, fragmentation, separation from the indivisible Truth above,'[8] writes Sri Aurobindo in a letter. In *The Life Divine*, about the Gods and the Overmind he says: 'If we regard the Powers of the Reality as so many Godheads, we can say that the Overmind releases a million Godheads into action, each empowered to create its own world, each world capable of relation, communication and interplay

with the others. In the Vedas there are different formulations of the
nature of the Gods: it is said they are all one Existence to which the
sages give different names; yet each God is worshipped as if he by
himself is that Existence, one who is all the other Gods together or
contains them in his being; and yet again each is a separate deity
acting sometimes in unison with companion deities, sometimes separately, sometimes even in apparent opposition to other Godheads of
the same Existence. In the Supermind all this would be held together
as a harmonised play of the one Existence; in the Overmind each
of these three conditions could be a separate action or basis of action
and have its own principle of development and consequences and yet
each keep the power to combine with the others in a more composite
harmony.'9

24 November 1926

'From [the beginning of] 1926, the Mother began to assume more
and more of Sri Aurobindo's responsibilities for the spiritual guidance
of the *sadhaks* [disciples], as if giving him the needed relief so that
he might attend to his more important work,' writes K.R. Srinivasa
Iyengar in his biography of Sri Aurobindo. 'An air of intensity began
building up slowly, an air of expectancy; and the *sadhaks* had the
feeling that they were on the threshold of new developments. After
Sri Aurobindo's birthday [15 August], the evening talks took on a new
fervour and potency ... In the evenings, the group meditation started
later and later, not at half-past four as formerly, but at six or seven
or eight, and once well past midnight.'10

For what happened on 24 November 1926, our best source is A.B.
Purani, an eyewitness, in his classical report.

'From the beginning of November 1926 the pressure of the Higher
Power began to be unbearable. Then at last the great day ... arrived
on 24 November. The sun had almost set, and everyone was occupied
with his own activity — some had gone out to the seaside for a
walk — when the Mother sent word to all the disciples to assemble
as soon as possible in the verandah where the usual meditation was
held. It did not take long for the message to go round to all. By

then most of the disciples had gathered. It was becoming dark. In the verandah on the wall near Sri Aurobindo's door, just behind his chair, a black silk curtain with gold lace work representing three Chinese dragons was hung. The three dragons were so represented that the tail of one reached up to the mouth of the other and the three of them covered the curtain from end to end. We came to know afterwards that there is a prophecy in China that the Truth will manifest itself on earth when the three dragons (the dragons of the earth, of the mind region and of the sky) meet. Today on 24 November the Truth was descending and the hanging of the curtain was significant.

'There was a deep silence in the atmosphere after the disciples had gathered there. Many saw an oceanic flood of light rushing down from above. Everyone present felt a kind of pressure above his head. The whole atmosphere was surcharged with some electrical energy. In that silence, in that atmosphere full of concentrated expectation and aspiration, in the electrically charged atmosphere, the usual, yet on this day quite unusual, tick was heard behind the door of the entrance. Expectation rose in a flood. Sri Aurobindo and the Mother could be seen through the half-opened door. The Mother with a gesture of her eyes requested Sri Aurobindo to step out first. Sri Aurobindo with a similar gesture suggested to her to do the same. With a slow dignified step the Mother came out first, followed by Sri Aurobindo with his majestic gait. The small table that used to be in front of Sri Aurobindo's chair was removed this day. The Mother sat on a small stool to his right.

'Silence absolute, living silence — not merely living but overflowing with divinity. The meditation lasted about forty-five minutes. After that one by one the disciples bowed to the Mother.

'She and Sri Aurobindo gave blessings to them. Whenever a disciple bowed to the Mother, Sri Aurobindo's right hand came forward behind the Mother's as if blessing him through the Mother. After the blessings, in the same silence there was a short meditation ...

'Sri Aurobindo and the Mother went inside. Immediately Datta was inspired. In that silence she spoke: "The Lord has descended into the physical today".'

And Purani goes on naming all twenty-four disciples present. (A.B. Purani, *Life of Sri Aurobindo*, p. 125 ff.)

There are different versions of Datta's words. Rajani Palit writes: 'Now Datta came out, inspired, and declared: "The Master has conquered death, decay, hunger and sleep!"' According to Nolini Kanta Gupta, it went as follows: 'Datta ... suddenly exclaimed at the top of her voice, as though an inspired Prophetess of the old mysteries, "The Lord has descended. He has conquered death and sorrow. He has brought down immortality".'[11]

In Nirodbaran's *Correspondence With Sri Aurobindo* — a correspondence unique in spiritual literature — we read:

'Nirodbaran: Today I shall request you to "stand and deliver" on a different subject. What exactly is the significance of the 24th of November? Different people have different ideas about it. Some say that the Avatar of the Supermind descended in you.

'Sri Aurobindo: Rubbish! Whose imagination was that?

'Nirodbaran: Others say that you were through and through overmentalised.

'Sri Aurobindo: Well, it is not quite the truth, but nearer to the mark.

'Nirodbaran: I myself understood that on that day you achieved the Supermind.

'Sri Aurobindo: There was never any mention of that from our side.

'Nirodbaran: If you did not achieve the Supermind at that time, how was it possible for you to talk about it or know anything about it?

'Sri Aurobindo: Well, I am hanged. You can't know anything about a thing before you have "achieved" it? Because I have seen it and am in contact with it, O logical baby that you are! But achieving it is another business.

'Nirodbaran: Didn't you say that some things were getting supramentalised in parts?

'Sri Aurobindo: Getting supramentalised is one thing and the achieved supramental is another.

'Nirodbaran: You have unnerved many people by the statement that you haven't achieved the Supermind.

'Sri Aurobindo: Good Lord! And what do those people think I meant when I was saying persistently that I was trying to get the supermind down into the material? If I had achieved it on Nov. 24, 1926, it would have been there already for the last nine years, isn't it?

'Nirodbaran: Datta seems to have declared on that day that you had conquered sleep, food, disease and death. On what authority did she proclaim it then?

'Sri Aurobindo: I am not aware of this gorgeous proclamation. What was said was that the Divine (Krishna or the Divine Presence or whatever you like) had come down into the material. It was also proclaimed that I was retiring — obviously to work things out. If all that was achieved on the 24th [November 1926], what on earth remained to work out, and if the Supramental was there, for what blazing purpose did I need to retire? Besides, are these things achieved in a single day?' (*Correspondence With Sri Aurobindo*, p. 293 ff.).

This conversation took place nine years after the event, and Nirodbaran was not the only one to whom the significance of the 'Siddhi Day'* remained a riddle. Dyuman, for instance, one of the eldest and most respected of the Ashramites, was uncertain about its significance even in 1988, as we shall see later.

In 1961, the Mother made the following declaration: 'In 1926 ... I had started a sort of creation of the Overmind, which means that I had made the Overmind descend into matter, on earth, and I began to prepare all that. (There began to be miracles and all kinds of things.) And so I asked those Gods to incarnate, to identify themselves with a body. There were some who refused categorically. But I have seen with my own eyes how Krishna, who was always in contact with Sri Aurobindo, consented to come into his body. It happened on a 24 November. It was the beginning of "Mother"' — when Sri Aurobindo put Mirra Alfassa in charge of the disciples, which implied

---

* In the Ashram, 24 November 1926 is commemorated every year as the Siddhi Day, the day of the great yogic realization or fulfilment.

the foundation of the Sri Aurobindo Ashram, and she was called 'the Mother' from then onwards. 'It was Krishna who consented to descend in the body of Sri Aurobindo, to establish himself in it, you understand?'[12]

In 1926, Sri Aurobindo and the Mother had already realized the Supermind in the mental and vital parts of their embodied personality. To bring the Supermind in the material part — the crucial and by far the most difficult step in the process — their material substance and the material substance of the whole Earth first had to be prepared. To this end, it was necessary to bring into matter, concretely, actively and dynamically, all levels above the mental, especially the so-called Overmind. Because of the preparatory work done by Sri Aurobindo and the Mother, Krishna, one of the greater Forces or Gods of the Overmind, had consented, at their request, to descend and establish himself in matter — in Sri Aurobindo's material body, purified by years of intense and advanced yoga. This means, *mirabile dictu*, that from 24 November 1926 onwards that body housed two great beings!

In the same conversation, the Mother mentions the exact meaning of Datta's inspired words — an inspiration which probably was not received in its pure form or only partially understood or remembered by those present. 'When I went back inside together with Sri Aurobindo, she started talking. She said that she felt Sri Aurobindo speaking within her. She explained everything: that it was Krishna who had incarnated, and that from that moment onwards Sri Aurobindo was going to do an intensive *sadhana* for the descent of the Supramental [in matter]. That it was an adhesion, as it were, of Krishna to the descent of the Supramental on earth, and that, as Sri Aurobindo would be busy and would not be able to look after the people [the disciples], he had put me in charge, and that I was going to do all the work. And that was that.'[13] It was as if, from above, Krishna had put the seal of approval on the Work of Sri Aurobindo and the Mother that would lead to the realization of the Supramental in terrestrial matter. The Siddhi Day was the day of the definitive certainty that their work would be brought to a good end.

Sri Aurobindo had a very close relation with Krishna. We already know that Krishna had played an important role in his yoga, among other things by dictating him 'the ten limbs' of it. Sri Aurobindo himself spoke about 'the prominent and dominant role' played by Krishna in his *sadhana,* which he had worked out 'with the help of Krishna and the Divine Shakti.' 'I always saw [Krishna] near Sri Aurobindo,' said the Mother. We remember that Krishna was one of the Ten Avatars, more specifically, the Avatar of the Overmind. 'It was a descent of the Supreme ... who consented to participate in the new manifestation,' said the Mother, and she added: 'For Sri Aurobindo personally, it made no difference: it was a formation from the past which accepted to participate in the present creation, this is all — nothing else.'[14] In the simplest of words, the Mother opens here a perspective on the past in which the Great Being, now called Sri Aurobindo and the Avatar of the Supermind present on Earth had already been on Earth as Sri Krishna (and very probably as other divine incarnations before).

A disciple asked a question: 'We believe that you and the Mother are Avatars. But is it only in this life that both of you have shown your divinity? It is said that you and she have been on the earth constantly since its creation. What were you doing during the previous lives?' Sri Aurobindo's unforgettable answer: 'Carrying on the evolution.'[15]

Few disciples were aware that Sri Aurobindo literally was Krishna, firstly as the same aspect of the Central Divine that also had manifested in the Krishna Avatar, and secondly because Krishna was permanently present in Sri Aurobindo's body which, since that 24 November, he had made his own. The Mother has said more than once that the Buddha is still present in the atmosphere of the Earth and goes on working to keep his promise, given out of compassion when he was about to enter Nirvana, that he would assist humanity all along on the road of its complete liberation. It is one of the surprising discoveries in the study of the life and work of Sri Aurobindo and the Mother that another Avatar, Krishna, has been present and embodied on Earth from 1926 to 1950 in the body, in the *adhara* of Sri Aurobindo.

In *Champaklal Speaks,* a book in which Champaklal, the faithful and great yogi who had served Sri Aurobindo and the Mother all his life, narrates his experiences, he says the following: 'When I came here to stay, Mahesh came with me. Ostensibly we both came for the same purpose. But I found a difference in Sri Aurobindo's way of dealing with us. To me he was speaking and showing practices of *sadhāna*. But to Mahesh he was speaking of worship and *upasana* [devotion] of Krishna. Later I found out that Mahesh had a strong attraction to Krishna and his way was different from mine. One day, however, when he expressed to Sri Aurobindo his difficulty in reconciling his adoration of Krishna with his devotion to Sri Aurobindo, Sri Aurobindo told him: 'There is no difference between me and Krishna.'[16]

To Dilip Kumar Roy, who had till the end struggled with a similar problem of divided loyalties, Sri Aurobindo wrote: 'Krishna is here in the Ashram and it is his work that is being done here,' and to another *sadhak:* 'If you can give yourself to him, you can give yourself to me.'[17] Sri Aurobindo's light is the same as the light of 'the blue God' Krishna: 'Whitish blue is Sri Aurobindo's light or Krishna's light,'[18] he wrote himself. (The Mother's light is the pure white diamond light.)

Among the gods who had been unwilling to take up a terrestrial body was Shiva. As the Mother later told: 'Shiva refused. Shiva said: "No. I will come when you have finished your work, not in a world like it is now. But I am quite willing to help." It was the day that he was present in my room, and he was so tall that his head touched the ceiling, with that particular light of him that is a mixture of gold and red — tremendous, a tremendous being!'[19] The Mother is the mother of the whole manifested universe and everything it contains — a fact of which her greatest offspring, the positive forces called gods, are the most conscious, as are also the negative forces, the whole fiendish and devilish brood: *Asuras, rakshasas* and *pishachas.*

One generally assumes that Sri Aurobindo withdrew in seclusion on that very day of 24 November 1926, but this does not agree with Purani's testimony in the *Evening Talks:* 'The evening sittings used to be after meditation at 4 or 4.30 p.m.' In Pondicherry nightfall is always after six o'clock in winter and seven o'clock in summer. 'Around

November 24, 1926, the sitting began to be later and later till the limit of one o'clock at night was reached. Then the curtain fell. Sri Aurobindo retired completely after December 1926 and the evening sittings came to a close.'[20]

The Word of Creation

As the Mother was now put in charge of the disciples, the six most carefree years of her life belonged to the past. In 1926, there were only twenty-four disciples, but the number would increase rapidly. In 1927, there were thirty-six and in the following year already eighty-five. The material side of the work demanded by the organization, housing, feeding and financing of the constantly increasing group was by itself enormous, especially in the India of that time. As for the spiritual side, there is no more difficult occupation than that of the *true* spiritual leader, the guru, for he takes the destiny of his disciples on himself, inclusive of all their difficulties, especially the psychological and therefore least perceptible ones. 'I carried all of them in my consciousness as in an egg,' the Mother would say later. It was she who was actually doing their yoga, so much so that Sri Aurobindo had to enlighten the disciples: 'The Mother in order to do her work had to take all the Sadhaks inside her personal being and consciousness; thus personally (not merely impersonally) taken inside, all the disturbances and difficulties in them including illnesses could throw themselves upon her in a way that could not have happened if she had not renounced the self-protection of separateness. Not only illnesses of others could translate themselves into attacks on her body — these she could generally throw off as soon as she knew from what quarter and why they came — but their inner difficulties, revolts, outbursts of anger and hatred against her could have the same and a worse effect.'[21]

The feeling that she was 'nothing but a Western woman' who had come to live in India only a few years before, was still very much present in the minds of some Indian disciples. It even surfaces repeatedly in the literature, e.g., in K.R. Srinivasa Iyengar's biography of the Mother: 'There was no question about her managerial ability, her unfailing friendliness and her personal spiritual eminence. And yet ... the 'Mother' of the Ashram? ... With complete authority to direct its affairs and ordain the destinies of the inmates? After all, some of the sadhaks — so they felt — had been doing quite well in their sadhana under the old dispensation. Why, then, this drastic change? Was it sanctified by Indian tradition? Would it work after all? The new dispensation with the Mother at the head of the Ashram meant, first, an unquestioning acceptance of her as the spiritual Mother, second, a total surrender to her of one's whole life, and third, a ready and happy submission to the discipline laid down by her for the smooth and efficient functioning of the Ashram.'[22]

Sri Aurobindo himself wrote about this problem in 1934: 'The opposition between the Mother's consciousness and my conscious-ness was an invention of the old days ... and emerged at a time when the Mother was not fully recognised or accepted by some of those who were here at the beginning. Even after they had recognised her they persisted in this meaningless opposition and did great harm to them and others.' And here follows the well-known declaration: 'The Mother's consciousness and mine are the same, the one Divine Consciousness in two, because that is necessary for the play ... If anybody really feels her consciousness, he should know that I am there behind it and if he feels me it is the same with hers.'[23]

The Mother embarked on the work, as always, with the force of the full commitment of her immense occult and spiritual knowledge and her supernatural powers. As she herself sometimes said jokingly, she always worked 'at a gallop', 'with the force of a cyclone' or 'at the speed of a jet plane'. 'I have not wasted my time,' she said. She being an embodiment of the Great Mother, Maheshwari, Mahakali and Durga with their mighty divine capacities were three of her many emanations, and she held in herself the Power which creates the worlds. 'Mother's pressure for a change is always strong — even when she doesn't put it as a force,' wrote Sri Aurobindo. 'It is there by the very nature of the Divine Energy in her,'[24] the Divine *Shakti*.

The Overmind in the person of Krishna having established itself in matter, the Mother now started to work out its possibilities without delay. As she herself relates: 'Sri Aurobindo had put me in charge of the external work because he wanted to withdraw in concentration to hasten the manifestation of the supramental Consciousness, and he had announced to the ones who were there [on 24 November 1926] that he confided to me the task of helping and guiding them; that I would remain in contact with him, of course; and that he would do the work through me. Things suddenly, immediately took a certain form: a very brilliant creation was being worked out with extraordinary precision, wonderful experiences, contacts with divine beings, and all sorts of manifestations which are considered to be miraculous. Experiences followed upon experiences. In brief, it developed in a completely brilliant way which was ... I must say extremely interesting.'[25]

'I had started a kind of "overmental creation", to make each God come down in a [human] being,'[26] she said. The Mother, as Mother of the Gods and with her exceptional occult powers, had started materializing the Overmind, the world of the Gods, on the Earth. She was in possession of the Word of Creation, the Word that becomes Reality when uttered. K.D. Sethna says: 'I vividly remember the substance of her account of it to me in an interview. She said she had come to possess the Word of Creation. When I looked a little puzzled she added: "You know that Brahma* is said to create by his Word. In the same way whatever I would express could take place. I had willed to express a whole new world of superhuman reality. Everything was prepared in subtle dimensions and was waiting to be precipitated upon earth." '[27]

Elsewhere, the same author writes: 'The nine or ten months after the Overmind's descent were a history of spectacular spiritual events. All who were present have testified that miracles were the order of the day ... Those which were common occurences in those ten months were most strikingly miraculous and, if they had continued, a new religion could have been established with the whole world's eyes focussed in wonder on Pondicherry.'[28]

---

* The Hindu Trinity consists of Brahma, the creator, Vishnu, the preserver and according to tradition the Divine aspect incarnating in the succession of Avatars, and Shiva, the destroyer. One should not confound Brahma with the Brahman.

A God was embodied in each *sadhak* — the God he represented in his inmost being. For all of us have a part of the One Godhead in us, and this part belongs necessarily to the divine manifestation. At the origin stands the Great Mother; out of her issued the cosmic Forces who are the Gods; out of them issued the forces which, for the most part, still remain unrealized in us. Sri Aurobindo said that 'the inner being of every man is born in the *ansha* [a substantial part] of one Devata [God] or the other.' To fathom this gives a deep insight into the glorious destination awaiting each of us and which is the aim of the evolutionary adventure we have undertaken of our own free will and choice.

Regrettably, the aspirants of the newly formed Ashram were not yet ready for that stupendous transformation which would have made them into overmental beings on Earth. About these days, Narayan Prasad has related the following: 'Between the end of 1926 and the end of 1927, the Mother was trying to bring down the Overmind gods into our beings. But the *adharas* were not ready to bear them; on the contrary there were violent reactions though some had good experiences. There was a sadhak whose consciousness was so open that he could know what the Mother and the Master were talking about. One sadhak would get up while meditating and touch the centre of obstruction in someone else's body. There were others who thought that the Supermind had descended into them. One or two got mentally unbalanced because of the inability to stand the pressure.'[29]

We go back to the narrative of the Mother. 'One day, I went as usual to relate to Sri Aurobindo what had happened [in the course of the day]. We had arrived at something really very interesting and I may have shown some enthusiasm in my relation of what had happened. Sri Aurobindo then looked at me and said ... : "Yes, it is a creation of the Overmind. It is very interesting, it is very well done. You will work miracles which will make you famous throughout the world, you will be able to turn the events of the earth upside down, in a word ..." And he smiled and said: "It will be a *big* success. But it is a creation of the Overmind. And what we want is not success: we want to establish the Supermind on the Earth. One must be capable of renouncing an immediate success to create the new world, the supramental world in its integrality." With my inner consciousness I understood immediately — a few hours later, the creation did not exist anymore ... And from that moment onwards, we have started again on different bases.'[30]

Later, the Mother once more looked back on that incredible moment in the history of mankind when the greatest religion the world has ever known might have been born. 'He has textually told me: "Yes, it is an overmental creation, but it is not the truth we want. It is not the truth, *the highest truth*,"[*] he said. I said nothing, not a word. In half an hour I have undone everything. I have undone everything, really undone everything — cut the connection between the Gods and the human beings, and destroyed everything, everything. For I knew that as long as it was there, it was so attractive, you know — one saw amazing things all the time — that one might have been tempted to go on with it, thinking: "We will adjust what is necessary afterwards," but that was impossible. And so I have remained quiet half an hour, sitting down, and I have undone everything. We had to start something else. But I did not tell it, I told it to nobody except him. Nobody knew it at that time, for they would have been completely discouraged.'[31]

In 1939, when after the fracture of his thigh Sri Aurobindo again conversed with some of his disciples, he himself would look back on those fantastic months. He said in answer to a question by A.B. Purani: 'At the time you speak of we were in the vital.' By this, he meant that he and the Mother by then had brought the Supramental Consciousness down into the vital. '[It was] the brilliant period of the Ashram. People were having brilliant experiences, big push, energy, etc. If our Yoga had taken that line, we could have ended by establishing a great religion, bringing about a great creation, etc., but our real work is different, so we had to come down into the physical. And working on the physical is like digging the ground; the physical is absolutely inert, dead like stone.... You have to go on working and

---

* In English in the text.

working year after year, point after point, till you come to a central point in the subconscious which has to be conquered and it is the crux of the whole problem, hence exceedingly difficult ... This point in the subconscient is the seed and it goes on sprouting and sprouting till you have cut out the seed.'[32]

The limits of their Work were shifted again and again, every time beyond the horizon of the possible, of their expectation. After that brief brilliancy of the miraculous world of the Gods on the earth, Sri Aurobindo and the Mother descended in the black pit of Matter and of the Inconscient supporting Matter. Only when the Hell of the Night was conquered and exterminated in the underground caves of our world could the Heavens of the One Godhead be founded on earth. *That* was what they had come for, the Two-in-One — not for a realization somewhere halfway, however glorious. The Mother had effaced the greatest, most miraculous creation in the history of the world in less than an hour. 'The greatest power in any hands during human history was set aside as if it were a trifle,'[33] writes K.D. Sethna, and also: 'This was without any doubt the mightiest deed of renunciation in spiritual history.'[34] And nobody knew about it.

Chapter Thirteen

SRI AUROBINDO AND THE 'LABORATORY'

*The Divine does not need to suffer or
struggle for himself; if he takes on these
things it is in order to bear the world-
burden and help the world and men;
and if the sufferings and struggles are
to be of any help, they must be real ...
They must be as real as the struggles
and sufferings of men themselves —
the Divine bears them and at the same
time shows the way out of them.*[1]
— Sri Aurobindo

'THEREFORE WE had to descend into the physical,' said
Sri Aurobindo looking back. They had to descend into the mine shafts
of Matter — no, they had to dig those shafts themselves, in a physical
substance 'dead as stone'. But Matter is an already highly organized
and conscious mode of existence compared to its base: the
Subconscient and, all the way down, the Inconscient.

The Inconscient is the state of absolute Inertia, the endless, starless
Night — 'darkness wrapped in darkness' (*Rig Veda*) — the primeval
stuff out of which evolution would successively create its forms, ever
more complex and conscious, to mould from the substance of the

Black Dragon the radiant body of the Godhead. 'The black dragon of the Inconscience sustains with its vast wings and its back of darkness the whole structure of the material universe.'[2] (*The Life Divine*) Nevertheless, the Supreme is also present in that utter Inconscience and in the Subconscient, for nothing can exist outside of him. 'The Inconscient is the sleep of the Superconscient,' wrote Sri Aurobindo in *Savitri*, and he named the Inconscient also 'a masked Gnosis', as such infinite.

'We had tried to do it [the descent of the Supramental] from above through the mind and the higher vital,' as we have seen in the previous chapter, 'but it could not be because the Sadhaks were not ready to follow — their lower vital and physical refused to share in what was coming down or else misused it and became full of exaggerated and violent reactions. Since then the Sadhana as a whole has come down along with us into the physical consciousness. Many have followed ... The total descent into the physical is a very troublesome affair — it means a long and trying pressure of difficulties, for the physical is normally obscure, inert, impervious to the Light. It is a thing of habits, very largely a slave of the subconscient and its mechanical reactions ... We would have preferred to do all the hard work ourselves there and called others down when an easier movement was established, but it did not prove possible.'[3] (Sri Aurobindo)

One should fully realize the significance of these words. Here it is clearly said that the decisive evolutionary step, deemed impossible in the whole of the previous history of mankind by all the Great-of-soul, has been consciously and willingly taken by Sri Aurobindo and the Mother sometime in 1927. Matter is the first-born of the Inconscient and Subconscient and completely impregnated by them, also in the human body. As a result of which the transformation of this body, in other words the heightening of its consciousness and its eventual divinization, were held by one and all to be unachievable. For to transform and immortalize the material body — an indispensable condition for a truly divine life on Earth — its material substance and hence the basis of that substance had to be transformed too. This is to say that the Subconscient and ultimately the universal Inconscient had to be transformed, an enterprise nobody had dared to undertake upto then. Sri Aurobindo and the Mother have taken this gigantic step because they had come to take it. A new phase of evolution began in which the Unity-Consciousness would be established in their body, therefore in the body of humanity, therefore in the mother-body of the Earth, and therefore in the evolutionary cosmos of which the Earth is the symbolical condensation and representation.

A point of increasing importance seems to be the role of the 'others' in the process of transformation. As later told by the Mother: 'This exactly is the problem which confronted Sri Aurobindo here and myself in France: does one have to delimit one's way, first reach the goal and then take up the rest to begin the work of the integral transformation, or does one have to advance progressively, leaving nothing aside and eliminating nothing from the way, taking up all possibilities at the same time and progressing on all points at the same time? In other words, does one have to withdraw from life and action till one has reached one's goal, becoming conscious of the Supramental and realising it oneself, or does one have to embrace all creation and progressively advance together with all creation towards the Supramental?'[4]

The question was of vital importance. The answer would decide on the choice of one out of two totally opposite ways to go about their work, on the inner as well as on the outer level. In the one case they would personally work out the supramental transformation for themselves and take up the burden of the mass of humanity only after their own body had been transformed, in the other theirs would be an action on all fronts simultaneously. They themselves did not know beforehand which was the right solution to the problem, for up to then nobody had tried to solve it, nobody had preceded them on that road. 'This was the first question that arose when I met Sri Aurobindo,' remembers the Mother. 'Should we do an intensive sadhana withdrawing from the world, that is to say having no contact with others any more, arrive at the goal and thereafter deal with the others? Or should we allow all those others to come who had the same aspiration, let the group form itself naturally and spontaneously, and march all together towards the goal? The two possibilities were there. The decision was not a mental choice, not at all. Quite naturally, spontaneously the group formed and asserted itself as an imperative necessity. No choice had to be made.'⁵ We have seen how some of the very first 'others' had come to Sri Aurobindo, how since November 1926 the already existing group was formally called Sri Aurobindo Ashram, and how Sri Aurobindo and the Mother were doing their yoga of divine transformation in this more and more expanding and representative body they called the 'laboratory'.

This draws our attention to that highly intimate collaboration between Sri Aurobindo and the Mother, which was often not sufficiently realized or forgotten because of what we might call their 'division of tasks' and because their physical presence in the Ashram differed. But their work was complementary and their division of tasks rooted in the One, in the inner core of those Great Beings behind their visible personality. Sri Aurobindo as the 'masculine' *Purusha* or *Ishwara* [Lord] kept himself in the background and worked from there, while the Mother as the 'feminine' *Prakriti*, *Shakti* or Creatrix converted his spiritual acquisitions into practical facts of change and growth. But they always were *one* divine Consciousness and therefore acted on a plane far above, behind and within the physically perceptible.

'I already had all my experiences,' said the Mother in 1962, 'but in the thirty years I have lived with Sri Aurobindo (a little more than thirty years) I lived in an absoluteness, and this absoluteness was an absoluteness of security, a feeling of total security, even physical security, even the most material — a feeling of total security because Sri Aurobindo was there. And that supported me, you know, like this [Mother makes a gesture as if she was carried]. In those thirty years, that has not left me for one minute ... I did my work on that basis, you know — a basis of absoluteness, of eternity.'⁶

In their division of tasks, Sri Aurobindo had taken up the 'inner' labour, and the Mother left that completely to him even with regard to the transformation of her own body 'because I knew he was looking after it.' For 'all realizations he had, I had too, automatically.' And everything she received in this way, she transferred as much as possible to the group she had accepted as the laboratory and in her consciousness 'as in an egg.' She guided and organized all that. The Mother converted Sri Aurobindo's realizations into a concrete, material form for the Earth.

'All upon earth is based on the Inconscient as it is called, though it is not really inconscient at all, but rather a complete subconscience in which there is everything but nothing formulated or expressed. The subconscient of which I speak lies in between the Inconscient and conscious mind, life and body. It contains all the reactions to life which struggle out as a slowly evolving and self-formulating consciousness, but it contains them not as ideas or perceptions or conscious reactions but as the blind substance of these things. Also all that is consciously experienced sinks down into the subconscient not as experience but as obscure but obstinate impressions of experience and can come up at any time as dreams, as mechanical repetitions of past thought, feeling, action, etc., as "complexes" exploding into action and event, etc. The subconscient is the main cause why all things repeat themselves and nothing ever gets changed except in appearance. It is the cause why, people say, character cannot be changed, also of the constant return of things one hoped to have got rid of. All seeds are there and all the *sanskaras* of the mind and vital and body — it is the main support of death and disease and the last fortress (seemingly impregnable) of Ignorance. All that is suppressed without being wholly got rid of sinks down there and remains in seed ready to surge up or sprout up at any moment.'[7] This is how Sri Aurobindo described the action of the Subconscient at the time he was labouring in it.

It is an endless, repugnant labour of which one gets an idea only later on in the conversations of the Mother with Satprem. As the latter noticed, the Mother got tears in her eyes when from the hell she was living in she could deduce what Sri Aurobindo must have suffered. But he never showed anything of that suffering, not even to her. All the same, he writes about it in one or two biographical poems and in *Savitri*. It is no exaggeration to maintain that practically all poetry of Sri Aurobindo's written after his first great experiences was autobiographical. In it he conveyed his experiences on the higher planes, among them those from where the poets in general, often without actually realizing it, draw their inspiration — and he formulated those experiences in the highest poetic expression of the irreplaceable word.

Two months after the above quoted passage about the subconscious, Sri Aurobindo wrote the deeply moving poem, *A God's Labour*. In this poem we read:

> My gaping wounds are a thousand and one
> And the Titan kings assail,
> But I cannot rest till my task is done
> And wrought the eternal will ...
>
> A voice cried, "Go where none have gone!
> Dig deeper, deeper yet
> Till thou reach the grim foundation stone
> And knock at the keyless gate."
>
> I saw that a falsehood was planted deep
> At the very root of things
> Where the gray Sphinx guards God's riddle sleep
> On the Dragon's outspread wings.
>
> I left the surface gods of mind
> And life's unsatisfied seas
> And plunged through the body's alleys blind
> To the nether mysteries.
>
> I have delved through the dumb Earth's dreadful heart
> And heard her black mass' bell.
> I have seen the source whence her agonies part
> And the inner reason of hell.[8]

Expressed in an almost freely floating, singing rhythm, the words ring through with the ominous, conjuring force of the experiences undergone by Sri Aurobindo. To those who are not familiar with the work Sri Aurobindo and the Mother have performed for the Earth, these lines will probably be not much more than bizarre fiction, but when one has got some insight in their pioneering work, they provide a profound understanding of their action. Here no word is fictitious, superfluous or poetically overstated. The poem gives a condensed impression of their descent into matter and into the Subconscient and the Inconscient, which influence and even determine most of our human condition. That was the place where the battle had to be fought and the victory won — at the root of things — if Sri Aurobindo and the Mother wanted to lay bare the mystery of our evolutionary world and transform existence. The source of evil, falsehood, suffering and death had to be drained or transformed into the Divine Realities which that source essentially had always contained, even in spite of their distortion.

The Hostile Forces

This may be a good occasion to bring the 'hostile forces' on the scene, including the 'Titan kings' and a numerous brood of lesser rank, so active in the wings of the visible world and of our inner theatre, and so powerful outside the fluctuating limitations of our tridimensional world that they can play with human beings as with marionettes.

'As there are Powers of Knowledge and Forces of the Light [e.g., the Gods], so there are Powers of Ignorance and tenebrous Forces of Darkness whose work is to prolong the reign of Ignorance and Inconscience,'[9] wrote Sri Aurobindo in *The Life Divine*. In his correspondence he wrote: 'Behind visible events in the world there is always a mass of invisible forces at work unknown to the outward minds of men.'[10] He cautioned an anonymous disciple: 'The hostile forces exist and have been known to yogic experience ever since the days of the Veda and Zoroaster in Asia (and the mysteries of Egypt and the Cabbala) and in Europe also from old times.'[11] And he warned Nirodbaran: 'Man, don't talk lightly like that of the devil. He is too active to be trifled with in that way.'[12]

The origin of the hostile forces is known to us. The four primordial Powers of Light, Truth, Life and Bliss (Lucifer and his three companions) started imagining that they were, each by himself, the Supreme. This is how they separated from the One in their consciousness and thereby became, as it were, its counter forces as the Lords of Darkness, Falsehood, Suffering and Death. It was the great 'Fall' in the beginning, from which originated our universe fundamentally based on the principles of Freedom and *Ananda* (Bliss) — precisely the freedom and enjoyment by which the four great Lords had been able to fancy that they were the Divine. In India, these four Lords are called *Asuras*. Further on we will hear more of them. Like all higher beings, they had the power to produce lesser entities of themselves, emanations existing by themselves and able to act independently, but essentially remaining the being who put them forth. The big Four have brought forth cascades of lesser beings, so to speak, who are intensely active on the lower levels of creation. 'There are only a few big ones and then countless emanations.' (the Mother)

The four *Asuras* were *les premiers émanés*, the very first four emanated by the Divine out of Himself. The Gods, then, are *les seconds émanés*, emanated by the Divine at the request of the Great Mother after the fall of the first four. The Gods work for the fulfilment of the divine Plan in the evolutionary creation; the *Asuras* work obstinately and mercilessly for the obstruction or the abolition of the Plan. One can read about this never-ending battle between the Gods and the anti-Gods in the traditional texts of all great civilizations.

However, the four big *Asuras* are not the only progenitors of hostile forces. We know that the One ceaselessly manifests 'typal' worlds out of himself which are the concretizations of his inherent qualities, from the highest — Existence, Consciousness, Bliss — down to the lowest, i.e. the lower vital worlds. All those worlds exist in their own gradation of substance, but the (gross) substance we know of and are made of, and which we call 'matter', is a product of the Inconscient and therefore exists exclusively in our evolutionary world. (It is as if our world originated in a shadow cast by the Supreme and is, provisionally, the dark spot in the limitless garden of worlds which is his ecstatic, prolific manifestation.) We have also seen that by the process of evolution time after time a higher gradation, or world, of the hierarchy of typal worlds is inserted in our evolving universe. The beings of the typal worlds are immortal and on their level fully satisfied with their existence, this according to the basic principle of the omnipresent divine *Ananda* or Bliss. So too are the beings of the lower vital worlds, who for the most part are vicious little mischief-makers; their nasty games and tricks are a source of inexhaustible fun for themselves, but they are very bothersome for us, humans, when we are the butt of their fun. They have no motive to collaborate in any way whatsoever and they only pursue the satisfaction of their petty desires.

In India, the hostile forces are broadly divided in three categories. At the top are the *Asuras*, (a word usually written with a capital letter by Sri Aurobindo) already known to us, and their nearest emanations still big enough also to be called 'Asura'. They belong to the mental and the higher vital levels. All *Asuras* are radically *against* the work of the divine evolution and do everything possible to thwart it, on the one hand out of pure self-complacency which has no urge or aspiration for anything more elevated, and on the other hand because the material embodiment on the earth of divine beings, like the future supramental beings, would bring the mastery they are now exerting here to an end. (We will meet with a example of this in one of the following chapters.)

Far below the *Asuras* are the *Rakshasas*, beings of the lower vital and often a kind of ogres, especially in the occult way. To satisfy their insatiable hunger, they prey on all possible kinds of embodied and unembodied forces and feed on them. They are ugly folk but can take on the most seductive shapes and even appear as divinities, and they mainly roam about in the dark. At the bottom of the hierarchy are the *Pishachas*, the little gruesome people, finding their vicious pleasure in the annoying little tricks they can pester themselves and the humans with, making our lives into an uninterrupted affair of unease, dissatisfaction and restlessness. (Those who are familiar with Tolkien's 'Middle World' will have been reminded of many of these kinds of beings in it.)

> To all half-conscious worlds they extend their reign.
> Here too these godlings drive our human hearts,
> Our nature's twilight is their lurking place.[13]
>
> — *Savitri*

All those beings, like all beings not embodied in (gross) matter, are immortal — like the Titan from Greek mythology (a *rakshasa*) who, when slain, became alive again through each contact with the life-force of the Earth and continued fighting. The only medium that can bring to an end their manifested existence is the divine White Light, by which they are dissolved into their Origin. This White Light is the light of the Mother. 'There is only one Force in the world that can destroy them categorically, without any hope of return, and this is a force belonging to the supreme creative Power. It is a force from beyond the supramental world and therefore not at everybody's disposal. It is a luminous force, of a dazzling whiteness, so brilliant that ordinary eyes would be blinded if they looked into it. It suffices that a being of the vital world be touched by this light to make it dissolve instantly — it liquefies, like the snails that turn into water when you put some salt on them,'[14] said the Mother herself.

Nevertheless, the hostile forces too have their significance and their role in the great Plan. The Mother wrote: 'In the occult world, or rather if you look at the world from the occult point of view, those adverse forces are very real, their action is very real, completely concrete, and their attitude towards the divine realisation is positively hostile. But as soon as you pass beyond this domain and enter in the spiritual world where there is nothing other than the Divine, who is everything, and where there is nothing that is not divine, these "adverse forces" become a part of the total play and they can no longer be called adverse forces. It is only a posture that they have taken; to speak more exactly, it is only a posture that the Divine has taken in his play.'[15] (We always return to our first premise: there is nothing but That.) All the same, it may be a play from the viewpoint of the Divine, but to the beings incarnated on the Earth, including the humans, that play is in dire earnest, even when having been promised a more enjoyable future.

Sri Aurobindo and the Mother, the centre of the accelerated evolution on Earth, were also the focus of the resistance and attacks of hostile forces of every breed. As early as 1924, Sri Aurobindo had already told some disciples in passing: 'You do not know how strong they are. I alone know it, you have only a glimpse of it.'[16] The figure of speech, becoming a gentleman, is as a rule, rather an understatement than an exaggeration. He also wrote: 'Wherever Yoga or Yajna [offering] is done, there the hostile forces gather together to stop it by any means.'[17] (This should be a warning for anyone who feels attracted to seriously taking up yoga.) To the hostile forces this was no inoffensive yoga, for it was clearly the intention of the Two-in-One to terminate the dominance of those forces on the Earth by bringing the divine Light into the twilight of the Subconscient and into the pitch darkness of the Inconscient, in order to make the transformation of matter and the formation of the supramental body possible.

At the end of 1926, Sri Aurobindo had withdrawn in seclusion 'to work things out' and devote himself totally to 'a dynamic meditation'. 'Dynamic' is another of his keywords; he always uses it in the sense of an active spiritual practice aimed at the improvement of the Earth, in contrast with the usual static aspiration to escape from the Earth and to leave it unaltered under the pretext that it is unalterable anyway — which, to Sri Aurobindo and the Mother, is 'a supreme act of egoism.'

After his withdrawal, Sri Aurobindo wrote in a letter: 'All has been for long slow, difficult, almost sterile in appearance, and now it is again becoming possible to go forward. But for the advance to be anything like general or swift in its process, the attitude of the Sadhaks, not of a few only, must change.'[18] All those years, Sri Aurobindo had laboured, struggled and suffered in a material 'dead like stone' and with his unique capabilities, and only now, was he able to report a shift of the front-line. Personally, he and the Mother would have shot forwards like tracer bullets in the night, but the *sadhaks,* representing humanity and the Earth as a whole, had to be dragged along. This had been preordained, and to act otherwise had not been possible, as we have seen.

The Tail of the Whale

He drew the energies that transmute an age.[19]

— *Savitri*

In Sri Aurobindo's correspondence with Nirodbaran we can follow his Herculean effort better than anywhere else. On 26 March 1935

Sri Aurobindo writes: 'I am too busy trying to get things done to spend time in getting them written.' A few days later: 'Just now I am fighting all day and night — can't stop fighting to write.' Again some days later: 'Never has there been such an uprush of mud and brimstone as during the past few months ... It was not inevitable — if the sadhaks had been a less neurotic company, it could have been done quietly. As it is there is the Revolt of the Subconscient.' And we get a look back: '[The Supermind] was coming down before Nov. 34, but afterwards all the damned mud arose and it stopped.'[20] It was a dirty, nauseating job Sri Aurobindo had to do day and night, an uninterrupted nightmare of the kind horror films are made of, but experienced as stark reality and without the anticipation that the lights would be switched on after one and a half hours.

And suddenly came the breakthrough! On 16 August 1935 (the day following his birthday) we read: 'I am travelling forward like a flash of lightning, that is to say zigzag but fairly fast ... Like a very Einstein I have got the mathematical formula of the whole affair (unintelligible as in his case to anybody but myself) and I am working it out figure by figure.' A mysterious but apparently very important announcement. One week later: 'There is always an adverse movement after the darshan, the *revanche* of the lower forces. I had a stoppage myself, but I am off again, riding on the back of my Einsteinian formula.' Shortly afterwards he declared having got a hold of the tail of the supramental whale (!) and in November of the same year he reported: 'My formula is working out rapidly ... The tail of the supermind is descending, descending, descending.'

In their correspondence, Sri Aurobindo and Nirodbaran went on using the comparison of the Supermind with a gigantic whale and the first indications of the descent of the Supermind into matter with the hanging-down or descending tail of that whale. On 17 May 1936 Nirodbaran asks: 'Is the Tail in view?' Sri Aurobindo answers: 'Of course. Coming down as fast as you fellows will allow.' And he states a year later: 'Tail is there — but no use without the head,' and once again: 'Too busy trying to get the supramental Light down to waste time on that [i.e. correspondence on a certain subject].'

From all this information phrased in the most simple and even playful way, we can deduce without any doubt that Sri Aurobindo had covered an enormous distance on the road, despite all possible resistance of the hostile forces, and that a decisive achievement could be expected. But then came November 1938. The adversary was never to be underestimated.

The Correspondence

Nirodbaran's 1,200 printed pages of correspondence are only a small part of the letters Sri Aurobindo had been penning in those years, ten hours a day. In his biography of Sri Aurobindo, K.R. Srinivasa Iyengar calls the years from 1933 to 38 'the golden years of his yogic correspondence.' We are indebted to those years for the 4,000 letters to Dilip Kumar Roy, the three volumes of correspondence with Nagin Doshi and the ample exchange of letters with K.D. Sethna, as well as for the numerous letters to so many others. The *Letters on Yoga* in Sri Aurobindo's Collected Works comprise 1,774 pages.

This extensive written exchange between Master and disciples naturally had its reason. This was a Master the disciples could see only three times a year, on the *darshan* days, the 'see-days', of his birthday (15 August), the birthday of the Mother (21 February) and the anniversary of the founding of the Ashram (24 November). Moreover, these briefest of meetings, however spiritually important and intense according to the testimony of so many, took place in silence. The correspondence was a means of contact, explanation, illumination, teaching, and especially of self-discovery of the disciples.

One of them asked: 'You and the Mother are supposed to know what is going on in us, how and what we are aspiring for, how our nature is reacting to help and guidance. What is then the necessity of writing to you all that?' Sri Aurobindo answered: 'It is necessary for you to be conscious and to put your self-observation before us; it is on that that we can act. A mere action on our observation without any corresponding consciousness in that part of the Sadhak would lead to nothing.'[21] And to another disciple he wrote: 'It is an undoubted fact proved by hundreds of instances that for many the exact statement of their difficulties to us is the best and often, though not always, an immediate, even an instantaneous means of release.'[22]

But the daily correspondence was an occupation the proportions of which grew too time-consuming in the whole of Sri Aurobindo's work. In the correspondence with Nirodbaran, in which he expressed himself more freely than with others, we read time and again, especially from the beginning of 1936 onwards: 'A too damned thick stack of letters to write ...' 'My dear sir, if you saw me nowadays with my nose to paper from afternoon to morning, deciphering, deciphering, writing, writing, writing, even the rocky heart of a disciple would be touched and you would not talk about typescripts and hibernation. [Nirodbaran had asked if his typed poems, sent to Sri Aurobindo for correction and commentary, perhaps were hibernating.] I have given up (for the present at least) the attempt to minimise the cataract of correspondence; I accept my fate ... but at least don't add anguish to annihilation by talking about typescripts.'[23] 'Light went off, in my rooms only, mark — tried candle power, no go. The Age of Candles is evidently over. So "requests, beseeches, entreats" [Nirodbaran's words] were all in vain. Not my fault. Blame Fate! However, I had a delightful time, 3 hours of undisturbed concentration on my real work — a luxury denied to me for ages.'[24]

Sri Aurobindo also gives his daily time schedule. 'From 4 p.m. to 6 p.m. afternoon correspondence, meal, newspapers. Evening correspondence from 7 or 7.30 to 9. From 9 to 10 concentration, 10 to 12 correspondence, 12 to 12.30 bath, meal, rest, 2.30 to 5 or 6 a.m. correspondence unless I am lucky. Where is the sufficient time for concentration?'[25] Indeed, where? 'When people write four letters a day in small hand closely running to some 10 pages without a gap anywhere and one gets 20 letters in the afternoon and forty at night (of course not all like that, but still!) it becomes a little too too.'[26]

His finely etched handwriting became more and more unreadable. Nirodbaran protested: 'Good Lord, your writing is exceeding all limits, Sir!' Sri Aurobindo: 'Transformation of handwriting. The self exceeds all limits, the handwriting should do so also.'[27] Sometimes this had comical consequences, for example when Nirodbaran deciphered 'neurasthenics' as 'nervous thieves'. Sri Aurobindo: 'It is altogether irrational to expect me to read my own handwriting — I write for others to read, not for myself.'

The truth was that he very often wrote in a state of trance. No matter how incredible it may sound, while he was penning those letters about all kinds of subjects imaginable, he was inwardly occupied with other things elsewhere in this world or in other worlds and probably often in the person or situation to whom or about whom he was writing. His handwriting is in many cases clearly a trance-handwriting, at the time decipherable by only a very few and best of all by Nolini, who had the privilege of distributing the 'heavenly mail' in the morning. Sri Aurobindo has written himself: 'It does not mean that I lose the higher consciousness while doing the work of correspondence. If I did that, I would not only not be supramental, but would be very far even from the full Yogic consciousness.'[28]

As mentioned earlier, many of Sri Aurobindo's letters have been gathered in three volumes of the Centenary Edition of his Collected Works under the title *Letters on Yoga*. According to Peter Heehs, this is 'a three-volume work that constitutes the most complete presentation of his yoga as given to others. It is remarkable, however, that nowhere in the two thousand pages of his published correspondence did he put forward a set method of practice. The "perfect technique" for a yoga that aimed not only at personal liberation, but also at a transformation of the nature of the individual and eventually of the world, was not, he wrote, 'one that takes a man by a little bit of him somewhere, attaches a hook, and pulls him up by a pulley into Nirvana or Paradise. The technique of a world-changing yoga has to be as multiform, sinuous, patient, all-including as the world itself.'[29]

It is logical that he who would lead others must have a better insight into their problems than the guided themselves. As Sri Aurobindo and the Mother intended a world-transformation, they themselves, as leaders and builders of men and women who represented the full spectrum of human psychological complexity, had to have the broadest possible experience. Disciples always put their master(s) on a pedestal of unapproachable reverence, and as few *sadhaks* in the Ashram had an idea of the details of the life of Sri Aurobindo and still less of the life of the Mother before Pondicherry, they deemed them so highly superior to the small problems of human existence that they were thought to have but a vague notion of them.

Sri Aurobindo found it necessary to clarify these matters more than once. 'No difficulty that can come on the Sadhak but has faced us on the path; against many we have had to struggle hundreds of times (in fact, that is an understatement) before we could overcome; many still remain protesting that they have a right until the perfect perfection is there. But we have never consented to admit their inevitable necessity for others. It is, in fact, to ensure an easier path to others hereafter that we have borne that burden.'[30] 'I have borne every attack which human beings have borne, otherwise I would be unable to assure anybody "This too can be conquered". At least I would have no right to say so ... The Divine, when he takes on the burden of terrestrial nature, takes it fully, sincerely and without any conjuring tricks or pretense. If he has something behind him which emerges always out of the coverings, it is the same thing in essence, even if greater in degree, that there is behind others — and it is to awaken that that he is there.'[31] Thus spoke the Avatar.

'I think I know as much about the dualities, weaknesses, ignorance of human nature as you do and a great deal more,' he wrote to a disciple. 'The idea that the Mother or I are spiritually great but ignorant of everything practical seems to be common in the Ashram. It is an error to suppose that to be on a high spiritual plane makes one ignorant or unobservant of the world or of human nature. If I know nothing of human nature or do not consider it, I am obviously unfit to be anybody's guide in the work of transformation, for nobody can transform human nature if he does not know what human nature is, does not see its workings or even if he sees, does not take them into consideration at all. If I think that the human plane is like the plane or planes of infinite Light, Power, Ananda, infallible Will Force, then I must be either a stark lunatic or a gibbering imbecile or a fool so abysmally idiotic as to be worth keeping in a museum as an exhibit.'[32]

A Hotbed of Poets

It is remarkable that Sri Aurobindo, besides all the work he was doing, still found the time and the interest to make the Ashram into a hotbed of poets. To him, however, culture was not a superficial layer of varnish; it was the product of a dimension, or of dimensions, without which the human being is not fully human. And poetry, to him, was not an irrational fancy of characters who cannot manage reality: it was a direct contact with the 'overhead' regions between our ordinary mental consciousness and the Supramental. To Sri Aurobindo, writing poetry was not a fanciful flight of the imagination, but a means of access to higher worlds and therefore a form of spirituality if practised with the right inner attitude. The great poets have never doubted the reality of their inspiration or the concreteness of what they saw and where they saw. Here now was somebody with a knowledgeable, practical, everyday involvement with those worlds, for whom poetry was a higher form of experience of great importance, and who helped his disciples with sufficient capacities or interest in their efforts to express those overhead worlds in words, to become aware by means of the word, as part of their *sadhana*.

'To us poetry is a revel of intellect and fancy, imagination a plaything and caterer for our amusement, our entertainer, the nautch-girl of the mind. But to the men of old the poet was a seer, a revealer of hidden truths, imagination no dancing courtesan, but a priestess in God's house commissioned not to spin fictions but to imagine difficult and hidden truths; even the metaphor or simile in the Vedic style is used with a serious purpose and expected to convey a reality, not to suggest a pleasing artifice or thought. The image was to these seers a revelative symbol of the unrevealed and it was used because it could hint luminously to the mind what the precise intellectual word, apt only for logical or practical thought or to express the physical and superficial, could not at all hope to manifest.'[33]

The best known Ashram poets were: Dilip Kumar Roy, as a poet characterized by Rabindranath Tagore as 'the cripple who threw away his crutches and started running' since he wrote under Sri Aurobindo's guidance and inspiration; Arjava, the Sanskrit name of the British mathematician John Chadwick; Amal Kiran (K.D. Sethna), according to Sri Aurobindo a poet of international stature, whose collected poems have been published in 1993 under the title *The Secret Splendour*; Jyotirmoyee, Harindranath Chattopadyaya and Nishikanto Roychaudhuri, who gained fame as poets in Bengali; Pujalal, who wrote in Gujarati, etc. And there was the phenomenal Nirodbaran, worth some special consideration.

Nirodbaran had obtained his medical certificate in Great Britain from the University of Edinburgh. He heard for the first time of Sri Aurobindo and the Mother in a meeting with Dilip Kumar Roy in Paris. In 1930, he visited Pondicherry and had an interview with the Mother. After two or three disappointing years as a physician in Burma, he was accepted as a member of the Sri Aurobindo Ashram. He became the Ashram doctor, as abundantly illustrated in his *Correspondence With Sri Aurobindo*; in this correspondence, Sri Aurobindo, generally considered grave and unapproachable, showed a scintillating sense of humour and suddenly started writing in an unusual confidential tone to the amazement of his correspondent.

Nirodbaran, probably awed by D.K. Roy, K.D. Sethna and others, developed literary and more specifically poetical ambitions. But he was, in Sri Aurobindo's words, 'not a born poet', and his literary English was old-fashioned and stilted. Under Sri Aurobindo's influence, however, he began writing, after a couple of years, exceptionally good poems in a surrealistic vein of which he himself did not understand a thing, as little as he did of the contents of his poems and of their poetic qualities. His poem *Bright Mystery of Earth* was evaluated by Sri Aurobindo as: 'Quite awfully fine. *Gaudeamus igitur.*' When *Sleep of Light* was sent to Sri Aurobindo, Nirodbaran himself found it only a little sprat, but Sri Aurobindo said it was a goldfish! And so on. Only in the period from March to August 1938, Nirodbaran wrote not less than 136 poems, 15 of which Sri Aurobindo judged to be 'exceptionally fine'. Later on, he published the volumes *Sunblossoms* and *50 Poems of Nirodbaran* with Sri Aurobindo's corrections and comments. He remained as nonplussed as ever about the way it all had come about. (Nirodbaran: 'Last night

I tried to compose a poem. It was a failure, I fell asleep over its first two lines.' Sri Aurobindo: 'You call it a failure — when you have discovered a new soporific.')

And then to think that the Gaekwad of Baroda, Mohandas K. Gandhi, Jawaharlal Nehru and so many others were of the opinion that Aurobindo Ghose had withdrawn in a mystical cloud-world. A mystic he was, Sri Aurobindo, and one of a very high order, but not of the nebulous, unearthly type. 'My gaping wounds are a thousand and one ...' His yoga was a battle, in which no quarter was given, against the allied hostile forces and for the growth of humanity. His correspondence was a means of direct contact with and a transmission of forces to the human elements who had felt the call to participate in that battle; without the spiritual force accompanying the letters, the written word would have been but of little use. In the meantime, Sri Aurobindo worked with his yogic powers on the events and personalities on the Earth, on everything that fulfilled a key-role on this momentous turning point of the evolution.

To Sri Aurobindo, power was not a forbidden fruit of yoga; power was its legitimate and desirable result if it was used for the divine Cause and not for selfish aims. In his *Record of Yoga*, we read on so many pages how he practised influencing humans and even other kinds of living beings invisibly. The yogic force is a real, concrete force. Sri Aurobindo and the Mother could not possibly do their work without acquiring that force and without the ability to use or apply it. For they had come to transform the Earth — a labour which would be successful only if they had at their disposal a greater force than that of the invisible masters of the ruling order and so end their sovereignty.

I look across the world and no horizon walls my gaze;
I see Paris and Tokyo and New York,
I see the bombs bursting in Barcelona and on Canton
streets ... [34]

Sri Aurobindo wrote these lines in September 1938. The unifying world suffered the labour pains of the birth of a new era — from the beginning of the century, actually. A.B. Purani has noted down Sri Aurobindo's words spoken to a few confidants: 'It would look ridiculous and also arrogant if I were to say that I worked for the success of the Russian revolution for three years. Yet I was one of the influences that worked to make it a success. I also worked for Turkey.' In December 1938, Sri Aurobindo once more talked about his work in the world to the handful of disciples gathering every evening in his room. His assessment, as somewhat roughly noted down by Purani: '[When] I have tried to work in the world, results have been varied. In Spain I was splendidly successful [at that time]. General Miaca [i.e., Miaja, the defender of Madrid] was an admirable instrument to work on. [The] working of the Force depends on the instrument. [The] Basque [Provinces were] an utter failure. [The] Negus was a good instrument but [the] people around him, though good warriors, were too ill organised and ill occupied. Egypt was not successful. Ireland and Turkey were a tremendous success. In Ireland, I have done exactly what I wanted to do in Bengal.'[36]

'I have never had a strong and persistent will for anything to happen in the world — I am not speaking of personal things — which did not eventually happen even after delay, defeat or even disaster,'[37] wrote Sri Aurobindo. The Mother once gave the following message: 'What Sri Aurobindo represents in the world's history is not a teaching, not even a revelation; it is a decisive action direct from the Supreme,'[38] and she signed her words with that winged signature of hers. Much later, she said confidentially about herself to Satprem: 'I don't know if I ever told you, but there has always been an identification of the consciousness of this [her] body with all revolutionary movements. I have always known and guided them even before I heard of them: in Russia, in Italy, in Spain and elsewhere — always, everywhere. And it always was essentially that same Force which wants to hasten the coming of the future — always — but which has to adapt its means of action to the state in which is the mass.'[39]

About their work in history, we will soon hear more. In the meantime, Sri Aurobindo's constant effort to make the Supermind descend into matter had reached a critical phase. We have already seen how he complained sometimes about the fact that the daily torrent of correspondence prevented him from doing his 'real work'. In November 1937, Nirodbaran wrote to him: 'Guru, I dare to disturb you, as daring has become a necessity. I feel utterly blank and am in need of some support, I can't write poetry by myself, without your help. Have you stopped the correspondence because of your eye-trouble or for concentration? In either case, then, I don't insist on your seeing my poems. You will understand that I don't write for the sake of writing, but for a support from you. Please give me a line in reply, after which I won't bother you any more.' Sri Aurobindo replied: 'Apart from the eye question, I have stopped because there are certain things I have positively to get done before I can take up any regular correspondence work again. If I start again now, I shall probably have to stop again soon for a long, long time. Better get things finished now — that's the idea. You must hold on somehow for the present.'[40] Yet, a couple of months later he started writing again, probably out of Aurobindonian compassion (as the Mother has named a little flower). But 'the golden years of correspondence' neared their sudden end, and nobody saw it coming.

Chapter Fourteen

THE MOTHER AND THE 'LABORATORY'

> People [in the Ashram] are an epitome
> of the world. Each one represents a
> type of humanity. If he is changed, it
> means a victory for all who belong to
> his type and thus a great achievement
> for our work.[1]
>
> — Sri Aurobindo

THE MOTHER too had gone down into hell, without the slightest hesitation, along 'the downward road on which I started the descent together with Sri Aurobindo. And there is no end to the labour there ...' 'O my Lord, my sweet Master, for the accomplishment of Thy work I have sunk down in the unfathomable depths of Matter, I have touched with my finger the horror and the falsehood and the inconscience, I have reached the seat of oblivion and a supreme obscurity,'[2] she wrote in one of her last *Prayers and Meditations*. With an unconditional dedication she had taken up her material task, namely the building of a livable place where the souls who had incarnated as human beings to answer the Call could live in a community in order to contribute, through an increasing self-denial, their effort to the supramental transformation, to the divinization of the Earth. This community was in actual fact a psychological and physical prolongation of the embodied personalities of Sri Aurobindo and the Mother. Through this community, which consisted of typical characters representing the whole of humanity, they would take in the human race in their work; through those personalities living around and *in* them, they would work on humanity as a whole. 'The Earth is a symbolical representation of the universe, and the group is a symbolical representation of the Earth.'[3] (the Mother)

The group now had a name, 'Sri Aurobindo Ashram', but this was 'a conventional name' according to Sri Aurobindo. For the word 'ashram' evokes a kind of exotic monastery where Indian monks or ascetics live in isolation and self-abnegation at the feet of a guru, in order to obtain as soon as possible the liberation of their soul and escape from the cycle of rebirths. However, here the perfection of the soul of the *sadhaks* was no more than the first step; it had to be followed by the perfection of their character and body, and through them by the transformation of the physical body of Mother Earth. Sri Aurobindo had never felt much for the title of guru, and neither had the Mother. 'I don't trust the old profession of guru,' she said, 'I am not eager to be the guru of anyone.' What did she want to be, then? 'It is more spontaneously natural for me to be the universal Mother and to act in silence through love.'[4] She therefore declared simply that the *sadhaks* and *sadhikas* of the spiritual community she was building up were not her disciples but her children. This meant much more than mere words. As Sri Aurobindo wrote: 'It is true of every soul on earth that it is a portion of the Divine Mother passing through the experiences of the Ignorance in order to arrive at the truth of its being and be the instrument of a Divine Manifestation and work here.'[5] He also wrote: 'The soul goes to the Mother-Soul in all its desires and troubles,'[6] and: 'It is a far greater relation than that of the physical mother to her child.'[7]

To enlighten the *sadhaks* about the true nature of the one whom he and they called 'the Mother', in charge of the organization of their daily life and the transformation of their being, Sri Aurobindo wrote some letters, which were afterwards collected and published under the title *The Mother*. In this booklet he says: 'There are three ways of being of the Mother of which you can become aware when you enter into touch of oneness with the Conscious Force that upholds us and the universe. Transcendent, the original supreme Shakti, she stands above the worlds and links the creation to the ever unmanifest mystery of the Supreme. Universal, the cosmic Mahashakti, she creates all these beings and contains and enters, supports and conducts all these million processes and forces. Individual, she embodies the power of these two vaster ways of her existence, makes them living and near to us and mediates between the human personality and the divine Nature.'[8]

The Mother as Maheshwari is the personification of the supreme power and wisdom, as Mahalakshmi of harmony and beauty, as Mahakali of the combative force which destroys with Love in order to build up what is greater, and as Mahasaraswati she is the omnipotent but meticulous power who organizes the cosmos and the molecule.

The Family of the Aspiration

The Mother was present everywhere simultaneously, in worlds with beings of which we do not even suspect the existence because we cannot possibly imagine them, in the events on the unifying planet Earth, and visibly in that fast growing community in Pondicherry, 'the cradle of the new world.'[9] No, this was not an ashram in the ordinary meaning of the word which she was building: it was a testing ground, an experiment in accelerated evolution, a laboratory to work out the species of the future, beyond man. In this laboratory, each guinea pig represented 'an impossibility' from the evolutionary past which had to be transformed into a possibility of the divinized future of the Earth. 'Everybody represents at the same time a possibility and a special difficulty which has to be resolved. I have even said, I think, that everybody here is an impossibility.'[10] (the Mother) The transformation of all this was only achievable, as we have seen, by eradicating the impossibility, the falsehood, at its roots in the subconscient and inconscient, or to transform it into Truth. But the evolutionary past with its 'downward gravitation', its magnetic down-pulling force, was present in each atom of the body of Sri Aurobindo and the Mother as it was in each atom of the body of their disciples and in each psychological movement of their character, in most cases darkening the flame of the soul.

Every *sadhak* and every *sadhika*, as the representatives of a certain type of man or woman on earth, were special and had their particular psychological structure with its possibilities and impossibilities. It was the maturity of their soul which had made them into *sadhaks* and *sadhikas*, ready to participate in the great adventure. Their preparedness had proved so irresistible that it had driven them to Sri Aurobindo and the Mother, and that they, perhaps unconsciously but by the 'instinct' of their soul, had recognized in them the Masters directing the work for which they had been born on earth as participants. 'We know that certain groups of people reunite time and again, since the beginning of human history, to collectively express a certain state of the soul,'[11] said the Mother. It was 'the family of the aspiration, the family of the spiritual tendency.'[12] 'It is evident that all those who are born now and are here now, are here because they have asked to participate and have prepared themselves in former lives.'[13]

This is why the Mother told her children: 'We have all been together in former lives; otherwise we would never have been able to meet in this life. We all belong to the same family and we have been working together throughout the centuries for the victory of the Divine and his manifestation on the earth.'[14] Deeply moving were her words to that wide-eyed youth of the Ashram school on one of the evenings she was supposedly teaching them French under the starry tropical sky: 'There are great families of beings who work for the same cause, who have met each other in greater or lesser numbers and who come down in a kind of group. It is as if at certain moments [in the past] a kind of awakening took place in the psychic world, as if a lot of sleeping little children were woken up: "It is time! Quick, quick! Go down!" And they scurried. Sometimes they did not come down on the same spot, they were scattered here and there. In such cases there is inwardly something that bothers them, that impels them; for one reason or another they feel attracted to something, and that is how they are brought together again.'[15] This time, in the present, they had been and were being brought together on the coast of the Bay of Bengal, in Pondicherry.

The Avatar never comes alone. Together with him descend the souls who want to share in the Great Work, 'the pioneers of the new creation,' 'the great dynamic souls,' 'the rare souls that are mature.'[16]

> I saw the Omnipotent's flaming pioneers
> Over the heavenly verge which turns towards life
> Come crowding down the amber stairs of birth;
> Forerunners of a divine multitude,
> Out of the paths of the morning star they came
> Into the little room of mortal life.[17]
>
> — *Savitri*

'Mature' is the psychic being that has gone through the full trajectory of its evolutionary development. 'Afterwards, it is no longer bound by the necessity to come down on earth; it has finished its development and can freely choose either to consecrate itself to the Divine Work or to go and roam about elsewhere, in higher worlds,' said the Mother. 'But generally, once arrived at that stage, it remembers everything it had to go through and it becomes aware of the great necessity to come and help those who are still struggling and in difficulty. The psychic beings of this kind consecrate their existence to the Divine Work. This is neither absolute nor inevitable, they have a free choice, but they do so ninety times out of one hundred.'[18] Sri Aurobindo therefore wrote: 'Some psychic beings have come here who are ready to join with the great lines of consciousness above ... and are therefore specially fitted to join with the Mother intimately in the great work that has to be done. These have all a special relation with the Mother which adds to the past one.'[19]

The Mother has at times revealed to the *sadhaks* some of their past lives in cases where this knowledge could contribute to their spiritual growth; she also told some of them at which moment in a former life they had chosen to collaborate on the future supramental transformation, usually in a past when they had been together with her or near her. A documented case is that of the Frenchman Satprem, one of those to whom she had promised in Ancient Egypt that they would again be together with her on Earth at the decisive time. (The Mother herself has said that she had been, among others, Queen Hatshepsut and Queen Tiy, the mother of the revolutionary Pharaoh Akhenaton.) 'There is a certain number to whom I have given the promise, not all in the same period, in different periods.'[20]

Another verified case* is that of Nata, an Italian *sadhak*. When on one of his birthdays he was received by the Mother in the room she then no longer left, she asked him whether he had a special wish on the occasion of that day. Nata said that in future lives he always wanted to be together with her on Earth, and the Mother consented. After he had left her room, she turned with a smile towards one of the persons present and said: 'He does not remember that we have always been together since Egypt.'

All this does not mean that all members of the Ashram were *sadhaks* or *sadhikas* in the true sense of the word, i.e. practitioners of the yoga. They were so in the beginning, practically without exception; but as the group grew, more and more persons were accepted because they represented typical problems of the world and who completed that 'world in miniature' by their presence without therefore taking up the yoga unconditionally. And besides both these categories, there were birds of different feathers, like the ones who had fallen asleep in their yoga or who considered the Ashram as a kind of hospitable halfway house on the road to other destinations in life, and so on. In later years, the Mother would say that not even half of the Ashramites were practising or even trying to practice the yoga.

Nor does it mean that the specially descended souls — the 'free-born' or *les bien nés*, the 'well-born' — no longer had to struggle with problems because theirs was a mature soul. Nobody was more well-born than Sri Aurobindo and the Mother, and in the course of their yoga they had to confront enormous problems, as we have heard

---

* Personal communication to the author.

from themselves. As incarnated earthlings, the *sadhaks,* by the fact of their birth, took on the existing 'impossibilities' of the current stage of the earthly evolution. Few of them were totally conscious of their true being. Their meeting with Sri Aurobindo and the Mother had awakened the soul in some of them, to be sure, while others had felt the irresistible impulse to join in the yoga because of some unforeseen and sometimes improbable or seemingly unimportant event — in the case of K.D. Sethna the reading of an article about the Ashram in a piece of newspaper wrapped around a newly purchased pair of shoes — but this did not mean that they did not have to make a concentrated and long-lasting yogic effort.

The past of each *sadhak,* just like that of every other human being, was different. 'Every individual is a special manifestation in the universe, consequently his true way must be absolutely unique,'[21] said the Mother. She also said: 'This is precisely the motive of the creation of the universe, namely that all are one, that all are one in their origin; but everything, every element, every being has the mission to reveal a part of that unity to itself, and it is this singularity that has to be cultivated in each and everybody, while at the same time awakening the sense of the original unity.'[22]

These almost abstract words mean that in fact there is no general path, no 'royal road', not even for a special group as a whole. The way of each one is personal, 'each one carries his truth in himself, and this is a unique truth, belonging to each one personally and to be expressed by him in his life.'[23] (the Mother) Each disciple of the Ashram, being a representative of a type of humanity in the process of general transformation, had to be guided in a personal way. This actually was the one and only rule the Mother recognized. 'No rules! By all means no rules!' she once exclaimed. 'For me there are no rules, no regulations and no principles. For me each one is an exceptional case, to be dealt with in a special way. No two cases are similar.'[24] This was, of course, completely in accordance with the view of Sri Aurobindo, who wrote: 'If there is no freedom, there can be no change — there could only be a routine practice of conformity to the Yogic ideal without the reality.'[25] And he therefore wrote to a *sadhak:* 'What the Mother wants is for people to have their full chance for their souls, be the method short and swift or long and tortuous. Each she must treat according to his nature.'[26]

This is the reason, as pointed out by Peter Heehs, why in Sri Aurobindo's voluminous correspondence one cannot find a cut and dried method of the Integral Yoga. The three established main yogas were the path of love (*bhaktiyoga*), the path of knowledge (*jnanayoga*) and the path of works or action (*karmayoga*). Those three methods of yoga are clearly based on the three fundamental qualities every human being has in himself: feeling, thinking and acting. Everybody must be allowed to proceed on the road towards divine perfection to the extent that these three principal qualities are developed in him, which is always in an unequal measure. The more he develops one of the three qualities, the more the other two will also blossom in due time, till all three are fully developed and the *sadhak* is ready for the Integral Yoga. For we know that the Integral Yoga begins where the traditional paths end. In this way, the fully developed soul reaching the threshold of the Integral Yoga has at its command all necessary means to follow the new way discovered and cleared by Sri Aurobindo and the Mother. It is by their labour that the Integral Yoga has become a possibility at this critical juncture of the terrestrial evolution. The promise in times past given to many by the Mother, and also by Sri Aurobindo, was destined to be fulfilled now. The great Change is happening NOW.

It becomes clear why Sri Aurobindo's yoga is only for those who feel attracted to it and how only they can be guided by him and by the Mother, whatever be the way by which they have come to this yoga. The pioneers who have opened a new path for humanity always keep helping it to follow that path. (One is reminded of the example of the Buddha who out of compassion turned back on the threshold of Nirvana to keep helping humanity on the road to its goal.) This general truth is also valid in the case of Sri Aurobindo and the Mother now that they have left their body.

Still there are those seekers who get acquainted with the work of Sri Aurobindo and feel uneasy because of the lack of a method with fixed rules in his yoga. It may therefore be suitable to quote here the following words of his from 1938, noted down in *Talks With Sri*

Aurobindo: 'I believe in a certain amount of freedom, freedom to find out things for oneself in one's own way, freedom to commit blunders even. Nature leads us through various errors and eccentricities. When Nature created the human being with all his possibilities for good and ill, she knew very well what she was about. Freedom for experiment in human life is a great thing. Without freedom to take risks and commit mistakes, there can be no progress.'[27]

The Relation with the *Sadhaks*

The Mother, with her profound occult knowledge of human nature, must certainly have been aware of the scope of the task she took on her shoulders, or rather in her heart, from the beginning. This included the petty side of the human character which becomes most readily perceptible where people live closely together. Moreover, the growth in the yogic *sadhana* is 'from within outwards', as Sri Aurobindo has so often reminded his correspondents; this means that persons inwardly advanced in yoga may outwardly still show very pusillanimous characteristics. The outer transformation comes last, as Sri Aurobindo has so often repeated, and this needs to be kept in mind when we follow the transformation of the Mother further on.

About the communal life, Sri Aurobindo wrote: 'Wherever human beings are obliged to associate closely, what I saw described the other day as "the astonishing meannesses and caddishnesses inherent in human nature" come quickly out. I have seen that in the Ashram, in political work, in social attempts at united living, everywhere in fact where it gets a chance. But when one tries to do Yoga, one cannot fail to see that in oneself and not only, as most people do, see it in others, and once seen, then? Is it to be got rid of or to be kept? Most people here seem to want to keep it. Or they say it is too strong for them, they can't help it!'[28]

He therefore found it necessary to make clear what things in the Ashram were about. 'There are only two possible foundations for the material life here. One is that one is a member of an Ashram founded on the principle of self-giving and surrender. One belongs to the

Divine and all one has belongs to the Divine; in giving one gives not what is one's own but what already belongs to the Divine. There is no question of payment or return, no bargain, no room for demand and desire. The Mother is in sole charge and arranges things as best they can be arranged within the means at her disposal and the capacities of her instruments. She is under no obligation to act according to mental standards or vital desires and claims of the *Sadhaks;* she is not obliged to use a democratic equality in her dealings with them. She is free to deal with each according to what she sees to be his true need or what is best for him in his spiritual progress. No one can be her judge or impose on her his own rule and standard; she alone can make rules, and she can depart from them too if she thinks it fit, but no one can demand that she shall do so ... This is the spiritual discipline of which the one who represents or embodies the Divine Truth is the centre. Either she is that and all this is the plain common sense of the matter; or she is not and then no one need stay here. Each can go his own way and there is no Ashram and no Yoga.'[29]

Telling words indeed, addressed to the right person at the right moment. The Mother had to bear it all: the resistance of the *sadhaks,* their revolt, their hatred, their dissatisfaction, discouragement, despair, misunderstanding, dullness and malevolence. They projected everything on her and she had to deal with it as if it were her own condition; she had to bring it into the Light and transform it. For they were living *in* her, those *sadhaks,* every minute of the twenty-four hours of her day. There were periods when she did not sleep more than two hours a day. And her 'sleep' could hardly be called so because when resting she did not sink down in the subconscious like we all do, but went on working consciously as the Universal Mother in this universe and in others, and as the embodied Mother where her presence was required on Earth, especially in those whom she had accepted as her disciples and instruments. 'Seen from the outside, you may say that there are people in the world who are much superior to you, and I will not contradict it. But from the occult point of view, this is a selection,' she said one evening to the Ashram youth. 'One can say without being mistaken that the majority of the young ones who are here have come because it had been told to them that they would be present at the time of the Realisation. But they don't remember.'[30] And she smiled. At the moment of birth, it is as if one drops on one's head, she said, and because of the blow one forgets everything that has preceded one's birth.

How have the disciples of Christ been behaving, how those of the Buddha? If one knew the unadorned truth about them, it probably would be a very human chronicle despite the fact of their now being venerated as superhuman saints. What had they understood, let alone realised, of the message of their Masters, both Avatars? Not so very much, considering the words passed down of those Masters themselves. Still those were the souls with a mission then, at the initial turning point of their era, of lasting importance for the whole of humanity.

'A perfect yoga requires perfect balance,'[31] Sri Aurobindo had said to his very first followers. Time and again the *sadhaks* had to be reminded of this primordial condition of their inner work, throughout all their idiosyncrasies and the often bizarre imaginings and distortions which the inner exploration can bring with it. There is no Master who has not been cautioning that spiritual commitment is like fire, which one had better refrain from touching if one is not sufficiently purified.

About the Integral Yoga, Sri Aurobindo had warned in a chapter in his *Synthesis of Yoga* that, 'This is not a Yoga in which abnormality of any kind, even if it be an exalted abnormality, can be admitted as a way to self-fulfilment or spiritual realisation. Even when one enters into supernormal and suprarational experience, there should be no disturbance of the poise which must be kept firm from the summit of the consciousness to its base ... A sane grasp on facts and a high spiritualised positivism must always be there. It is not by becoming irrational or infrarational that one can go beyond ordinary nature into supernature; it should be done by passing through reason to a greater light of superreason.'[32] 'One needs a very solid base,' said the Mother. 'Who wants to transform grim reality should not withdraw from it, neither in physical nor in psychological seclusion but come to grips with it like a wrestler with his opponent. Reality being very strong and sturdy and without any intention of letting itself being floored, the wrestler has to be as strong and sturdy if he wants to remain upright, and stronger if he wants to conquer it.'

Integral Yoga, as one can gather from many sayings of Sri Aurobindo and the Mother, is not a path for people soft of mind or constitution; it is a yoga requiring the temperament of the heroic warrior. 'Without heroism man cannot grow into the Godhead. Courage, energy and strength are among the very first principles of the divine nature in action,'[33] wrote Sri Aurobindo. The Mother wrote after his passing away: 'To follow Sri Aurobindo in the great adventure of his Integral Yoga, one needed always to be a warrior; now that he has left us physically, one needs to be a hero.'[34] We have not come for Peace but for Victory, because in a world ruled by the hostile forces Victory has to precede Peace. No, this is not a yoga of *ahimsa* and no sinecure somewhere in the rarefied air of high hills; it is a battle with very real, implacable, strong and extremely intelligent forces mostly fought in the dingy basement of our own personality. 'Our yoga is not for cowards; if you have no courage, better leave it.'[35] (the Mother)

The Growth of the Ashram

There is nothing that is impossible to her who is the conscious Power and universal Goddess all-creative from eternity and armed with the Spirit's omnipotence. All knowledge, all strengths, all triumph and victory, all skill and works are in her hands.[36]

— Sri Aurobindo

The Ashram grew steadily: 24 members in 1926, 80 to 85 in 1929, 150 in 1936, between 170 and 200 in 1938. In letters to her son André, whom she had not met since 1916, the Mother reported about its material expansion: 'five cars, twelve bicycles, four sewing machines, a dozen typewriters ... an automobile repair workshop ... a library and reading-room ...'[37] It was becoming an enormous undertaking, especially considering the circumstances in India and

Pondicherry, at a time when practically everything had to be imported, mostly from France, and at a place where the local conditions were not exactly favourable for material organization. Everything was done on the Mother's initiative, with her help and encouragement, under her supervision. The various departments and services of the Ashram took shape: the bakery, laundry, tailoring department, kitchen and dining room, nursing home and pharmacy, a printing press (to become one of the best in India), a dairy, and two farms outside the town.

She also wrote to André: 'I would like to show you our establishment. [He would not come to Pondicherry until 1949.] It has just acquired four houses which I bought in my name to simplify the legal technicalities, but it goes without saying that *I do not own them* ... The Ashram with all its real estate and movable property belongs to Sri Aurobindo ... You will readily understand why I am telling you all this; it is so that you can bear it in mind just in case.'[38] Here André was made to understand that he could not lay any legal claims to property belonging to the Ashram.

It was also to her son that she wrote: 'At no time do I fall back into the inconscience which is the sign of ordinary sleep. But I give my body the rest it needs, that is, two or three hours of lying down in an absolute immobility, but in which the whole being, mental, psychic, vital and physical, enters into a complete rest made of perfect peace, absolute silence and total immobility, while the consciousness remains completely awake; or else I enter into an internal activity of one or more states of the being, an activity which constitutes the occult work and which, needless to say, is also perfectly conscious. So I can say, in all truth, that I never lose consciousness throughout the twenty-four hours which thus form an unbroken sequence, and that I no longer experience ordinary sleep, while yet giving my body the rest that it needs.'[39]

Her daily schedule changed in the course of the years, but generally speaking one can say that the Mother was occupied among and with the *sadhaks* from four o'clock in the morning till midnight, and sometimes even later, all the while supervising the activities related to the service of Sri Aurobindo. She did not even have a room of her own and often ate her meal on a cleared corner of a table here or there.

One of the most important Ashram activities was the daily *pranam* (salutation), when the *sadhaks* passed by her one after the other and received from her a meaningful flower and the inner support they needed. (The Mother has given names to most of the flowers that grow in South India, in relation with their essence and their true vibration. As was discovered afterwards, the meaning of those names agrees with the significance of the flowers in the old Indian traditions of religious devotion and herbal healing.) But the disciples created problems about the *pranam* too, just like of everything else. How had the Mother looked at them that day and what had they read in her eyes? And why had she smiled at this or that one yesterday but not today? And if she looked so seriously at that other one, he surely must have done something wrong or committed some mischief? The *pranam* keeps cropping up endlessly in the correspondence. The following is an example from the correspondence of Nirodbaran.

He writes on 28 July 1934: 'Mother,* there are days when I am awfully afraid to go to *pranam*, lest I should have the misfortune to see your grave face, with no smile at all. All my despair, melancholy, etc., is intensified after that, while your smile disperses all gloom.' To which Sri Aurobindo answers: 'All this about the Mother's smile and her gravity is simply a trick of the vital. Very often I notice people talk of the Mother's being grave, stern, displeased, angry at Pranam when there has been nothing of the kind — they have attributed to her something created by their own vital imagination. Apart from that the Mother's smiling or not smiling has nothing to do with the sadhak's merits or demerits, fitness or unfitness — it is not deliberately done as a reward or a punishment. The Mother smiles on all, without regard to these things. When she does not smile, it is because

---

* The daily correspondence, including Nirodbaran's, was actually addressed to the Mother, guide of the *sadhaks*. The letters, on loose sheets or in note-books, were first read by her, then discussed with Sri Aurobindo if necessary, and finally answered by the latter. The Mother wrote the answers only when Sri Aurobindo for some reason temporarily had to stop corresponding.

she is either in trance or absorbed, or concentrated on something within the sadhak that needs her attention — something that has to be done for him or brought down or looked at. It does not mean that there is anything bad or wrong in him. I have told this a hundred times to any number of sadhaks — but in many the vital does not want to accept that because it would lose its main source of grievance, revolt, abhiman [wounded pride], desire to go away or give up the Yoga, things which are very precious to it.'[40] The problem — a wrong interpretation of the facial expression, corporeal attitude or acts of the Mother — cropped up time after time, it being inspired by 'the Adversary' as Sri Aurobindo called him.

When Nirodbaran admits: 'I know from my own experience that we have abused the Pranam,' Sri Aurobindo replies without mincing words: 'That is that. The Pranam (like the soup the evening before) has been very badly misused. What is the Pranam for? That people might receive in the most direct and integral way — a way that includes the physical consciousness and makes it a channel — what the Mother could give them and they were ready for. Instead people sit as if at a court reception noting what the Mother does (and generally misobserving), making inferences, gossiping afterwards as to her attitude to this or that person, who is the more favoured, who is the less favoured — as if the Mother were doling out her favour or disfavour or appreciation or disapproval there, just as courtiers in a court might do ... The whole thing tends to become a routine, even where there are not these reactions. Some of course profit, those who can keep something of the right attitude. If there were the right attitude in all, well by this time things would have gone very far towards the spiritual goal.'[41]

We have taken a closer look at the *pranam* because this is an excellent example of the way in which the Mother dealt with the *sadhaks* and how her ways were perceived or interpreted by them. The *pranam*, just like the other Ashram activities, was never intended to be a kind of ceremony; it was an occasion on which the Mother could transmit her spiritual force and make it active in the *sadhaks*.

Sri Aurobindo's intriguing words about 'the soup in the evening' refer to an activity the Ashramites called 'the soup ceremony' and which was held till the day in 1931 when the Mother became seriously ill. 'It was a very important function every evening. It impressed one like a snatch of the Ancient Mysteries ... The atmosphere was as in some secret temple of Egyptian or Greek times,'[42] relates K.D. Sethna in a talk. And he writes: 'Every evening ... we used to sit in semi-darkness, meditating. The Mother would be in a chair in front of us. Champaklal would bring a big cauldron of hot soup and place it on a stool in front of her. He stood by while she went into trance. After some minutes, with her eyes still shut, she would spontaneously stretch out her arms, and her palms were poised over the cauldron. She was transmitting the power of Sri Aurobindo into the soup. After a while her eyes opened and she withdrew her hands. Then the distribution started. Each of us went to her, bent down on his knees and gave her his enamel cup. Then with a ladle she poured the soup from the cauldron into our cups. Before handing each cup back she would again withdraw inward with eyes half shut and take a sip ... The occult truth behind the ceremony was that she was putting something of her own spiritualised subtle-physical substance into the soup in our cups.'[43]

Be it noted that the Mother and Sri Aurobindo have never really been in 'trance', though Sri Aurobindo uses this word in a previous quotation. To go into trance means that one passes into another reality, thereby losing the awareness of the terrestrial reality and not remembering what has gone on in the other reality once one comes back to everyday circumstances. The Mother has said that she and Sri Aurobindo have always remained conscious on any level of reality and that they have always retained the complete awareness and memory of their experiences. A second noteworthy point in connection with the last quotation is that the force the Mother put into the soup, however difficult to name or to define, was clearly intended to work on the material body of the *sadhaks* and to stimulate its transformation or at least its receptivity by means of the nutritious drink they partook of and which via their digestive system penetrated into their cells. Although 'soup' may be a rather prosaic food or word, there is no reason to suppose that the water and its other components should be spiritually inferior to, let us say, wheat in the form of bread.

Over and above the collective activities, there were also personal meetings of the Mother with the *sadhaks,* conversations in their room or house, inspections of the various departments and services, and so on. A few *sadhaks* regularly met with her for some sort of symbolical games. And even on the way from one room to another in the central Ashram building, she was time and again held up by *sadhaks* with personal or organizational problems. For her nothing was too big and nothing too small or unimportant in a yoga which was meant to encompass all life.

As mentioned earlier, on 18 October 1931 the Mother fell seriously ill. The causes of her illness were undoubtedly complex and she has never disclosed them. Much later she once told that a 'titan', more specifically a powerful emanation of the Lord of Falsehood, was after her life since her birth and that he did not let one occasion go by to bring, if possible, her mission on Earth to a premature end. This may have been one of the causes of an illness serious enough for her to interrupt her activities temporarily. But another cause was certainly the lack of receptivity in the *sadhaks.*

Sri Aurobindo wrote on 12 November 1931 to one of them: 'The Mother has had a very severe attack and she must absolutely husband her forces in view of the strain the 24th November [*darshan* day] will mean for her. It is quite out of the question for her to begin seeing everybody and receiving them meanwhile — a single morning of that kind would exhaust her altogether.' Then follows the paragraph we have quoted in an earlier chapter: 'You must remember that for her a physical contact of this kind with others is not a mere social or domestic meeting with a few superficial movements ... It means for her an interchange, a pouring out of her forces and a receiving of things good, bad and mixed from them ...' And he continues: 'If it had been only a question of two or three people, it would have been a different matter; but there is the whole Ashram here ready to enforce each one his claim the moment she opens her doors. You surely do not want to put all that upon her before she has recovered her health and her strength! In the interest of the work itself — the Mother has never cared in the least for her body or her health for its own sake and that indifference has been one reason, though only an outward one, for the damage done — I must insist on her going slowly in the resumption of the work and doing only so much at first as her health can bear.'[44]

On that occasion, we read from Sri Aurobindo's pen about the significance of his and the Mother's work: 'I have not yet said anything about the Mother's illness because to do so would have needed a long consideration of what those who are at the centre of a work like this have to be, what they have to take upon themselves of human terrestrial nature and its limitations and how much they have to bear of the difficulties of transformation.'[45] Two years later, he would refer to this subject once more: 'The Mother by the very nature of her work had to identify herself with the Sadhaks, to support all their difficulties, to receive into herself all the poison in their nature, to take up besides all the difficulties of the universal earth-Nature, including the possibility of death and disease in order to fight them out. If she had not done that [and if he had not done that], not a single Sadhak would have been able to practise this Yoga. The Divine has to put on humanity in order that the human being may rise to the Divine. It is a simple truth, but nobody in the Ashram seems able to understand that the Divine can do that and yet remain different from them — can still remain the Divine.'[46] These words, put in their historical context, give us a profound insight into the work of Sri Aurobindo and the Mother. We will recall what Sri Aurobindo has written about fighting death and disease when in our story we come to the day that he himself will leave his body.

She resumed her daunting daily tasks as soon as possible. Where she was not corporeally present, her consciousness in one of its emanations was there. There was an emanation of her with everybody she had accepted as *sadhak* or *sadhika* and enclosed in her consciousness. Sri Aurobindo explained this: 'The Emanation is not a deputy, but the Mother herself. She is not bound to her body, but can put herself out (emanate) in any way she likes. What emanates, suits itself to the nature of the personal relation she has with the sadhak, which is different with each, but that does not prevent it from being herself. Its presence with the sadhak is not dependent on his consciousness of it. If everything were dependent on the surface consciousness of the sadhak, there would be no possibility of the divine action any-where; the human worm would remain the human worm and the human ass, the human ass, for ever and ever. For if the Divine could not be there behind the veil, how could either ever become conscious of anything but their wormhood and asshood even throughout the ages?'[47] This quotation is taken from his correspondence with Nirodbaran, of course.

By the fact that all were moving inside her consciousness, she knew everything concerning the most intimate details of their life — an indispensable condition to do their yoga for them. The embodied Mother had 'a knowledge by intimate contact with the truth of things and beings which is intuitive and born of a secret oneness.'[48] Her intuition was not what this word commonly means to us, to wit, a kind of irrational capacity of feeling things which may be surprisingly correct but also very unreliable. In Sri Aurobindo's scheme of the world, Intuition is one of the higher spiritual planes. When he wrote that the Mother knew by means of her intuition, he meant that she knew the things by a direct knowledge derived from the Unity-Consciousness where all is known in 'the three times,' past, present, future — a Unity-Consciousness that is the Divine Consciousness.

This too was a point which the intellect of many disciples could not fathom and which had to be clarified by Sri Aurobindo. Question: 'In what sense is the Mother everywhere? Does she know all happenings in the physical plane?' His answer: 'Including what Lloyd George* had for breakfast today or what Roosevelt** said to his wife about the servants? Why should the Mother "know" in the human way all happenings in the physical plane? Her business in her embodiment is to know the workings of the universal forces and use them for her works; for the rest she knows what she needs to know, sometimes with her inner self, sometimes with her physical mind. All knowledge is available in her universal self, but she brings

---

*   David Lloyd George (1863-1945), prominent British politician, prime minister from 1916 to 1922.

** Franklin Delano Roosevelt (1882-1945), president of the USA from 1933 to 1945.

forward only what is needed to be brought forward so that the working is done.'[49]

The Mother herself had more than once explained that the knowledge of events on the various levels of existence was, as it were, stored in the gradations of her consciousness which corresponded to those levels, and that for her embodied personality that passive knowledge could be made actively available if she concentrated on it. This was all the more true concerning the movements in the persons she had taken up in her consciousness and the events which were for her of special interest for one reason or another.

After her illness, the daily 'balcony *darshan*' started unintentionally, and it would go on till the day in 1962 when the Mother could no longer come out of her room. 'It was the Mother's habit soon after her return to active work to come out early in the morning to the north balcony adjoining Pavitra's room ... In course of time, a few sadhaks started assembling on the opposite pavement to have a glimpse of the Mother when she came out on the balcony. With the passage of a few weeks or months ... almost the entire Ashram would gather, the whole street would be packed with the expectant sadhaks, visitors and others,'[50] we read in Iyengar's biography of the Mother.

Just like the balcony *darshan*, no other Ashram activity of any importance had been planned in advance. A need arose for some spiritual reason connected to the Work and made itself felt spontaneously. Some of Sri Aurobindo's major writings had originated in the same way, casually as it were, in reaction to an article or book he read (*The Human Cycle, The Future Poetry, The Foundations of Indian Culture*) or to a text he started commenting upon (*The Life Divine, The Secret of the Veda*). Sri Aurobindo and the Mother never planned something beforehand, in order not to limit or distort it by a projection of the expectation. They followed their divine intuition and supramental knowledge in total surrender to That which guided their earthly work. 'There has never been, at any time, a mental plan or an organisation decided beforehand. The whole thing has taken birth, grown and developed as a living being by a movement of consciousness ... constantly maintained, increased and fortified.'[51] (Sri Aurobindo)

The Progress of the *Sadhaks*

It may be that some of the quotations put the members of the Ashram in an unfavourable light. Moreover, the Ashramites have often been attacked because of their external and internal shortcomings, particularly after the passing away of the Mother in 1973. As already mentioned in Sri Aurobindo's own words, it is mainly where human beings are living day after day closely together that the petty sides of their character become most clearly visible, most childish and even grotesque or embarrassing. All communities in all climes are witness to this phenomenon — be they religious, social, military, utopian or experimental. It is a sorry fact that humans for the greatest part of their surface personality are petty beings, and the habits and mental blindness of 'these small, pathetic, dwarfish creatures' deny them any clear discernment. 'People are exceedingly silly,' wrote Sri Aurobindo to Nirodbaran, 'but I suppose they cannot help themselves. The more I observe humanity, the more that forces itself upon me — the abyss of silliness of which the mind is capable.'[52] He did not come from another planet like the fictional little men of Mars, but he saw with a consciousness worlds above the ordinary human mind.

It would be rather easy to make a substantial compilation of the sayings by Sri Aurobindo and the Mother analogous with the following: 'The Mother and I have to give nine-tenths of our energy to smoothing down things, to keep the Sadhaks tolerably contented, etc. etc. etc. One-tenth and in the Mother's case not even that can go to the real work; it is not enough.'[53] However, quotations of this kind would present a wrong picture of the Ashram members as well as of Sri Aurobindo and the Mother's attitude towards them. For much more important are the letters in which they encourage their disciples, emphasize their positive capabilities and assure them of their everlasting love, support and protection. This is abundantly illustrated, for instance, in the Mother's letters to Huta, published in *White Roses* and other collections, in their correspondence with Nirodbaran and K.D. Sethna, and in many other letters. They knew full well what human nature consisted of and consequently what they had taken upon them in their collective yoga. They also knew that they could expect little in return from human beings, even from the *sadhaks* of their own yoga. Question: 'Mother, what can we expect from you?' The Mother: 'Everything.' Second question: 'Mother, what do you expect from us?' The Mother: 'Nothing.'

The Integral Yoga, to which the *sadhaks* had dedicated their life, was for that matter the most difficult endeavour a human being could take on. Its aim, as we know, was a complete transformation of the human into a divine nature and ultimately of the human body in a body that must be able to contain and express divinity. When somebody once asked him: 'You have said, Sir, in *The Life Divine* that only the absolute idealist can persist in this path. How then can ordinary mortals like us ...?' Sri Aurobindo broke off his question with a polite smile: 'It is not for ordinary mortals.'[54] And he wrote: 'This path of Yoga is a difficult one and it can be followed only when there is a special call.'[55]

It may be assumed that the aspirants accepted by Sri Aurobindo and the Mother had this special call. In other words, they may in most cases be assumed to have been 'mature souls' because no others were up to the trail-blazing work in collaboration with the Avatar and to the representation of their earthly brothers and sisters. They must belong to 'the number of souls sent to make that it will be for now,' as Sri Aurobindo said. Is there any confirmation to be found of this?

One reads in the *Agenda* how the Mother once told Satprem that Nolini (Kanta Gupta), one of the first companions of Sri Aurobindo whom we have already met in this story, inwardly could rise at will to the plane of Being-Consciousness-Bliss — that is to say to the highest level of the divine manifestation. After Nolini's demise, in 1984, several persons have published their remembrances of him. There we read that he had himself told that he was a reincarnation of the Latin poet Virgil, of the French poet Pierre de Ronsard, and of André Le Nôtre who designed the gardens of Versailles. The Mother significantly wrote in one of his birthday cards: 'Nolini *en route* towards the superman', and in 1973: 'With my love and blessings ... for the transformation.' Nirodbaran, who with the other doctors of the Ashram assisted Nolini at the end, narrates: 'A few days later, as he was lying in his bed, I asked him through Anima where his consciousness could be. He answered: "Why, with the Mother!" I wanted more precision. Then he answered: "In the Overmind." I was simply swept off my feet ... Later I learned from Anima that Nolini-da* had confided in her that he was mostly in the Overmind but at times a little beyond it.'[56] The Overmind is the world of the cosmic beings called Gods; a little higher begins the Supermind.

The same Nirodbaran wrote fifty years earlier to Sri Aurobindo: 'I sometimes wonder if anyone here is attaining anything at all; has anybody realised the Divine? Please don't ask me what I mean by the Divine. It is difficult to explain these things.' Sri Aurobindo answered: 'Why shouldn't I ask? If you mean the Vedantic realisation, several have had it. Bhakti realisation also. If I were to publish the letters on sadhana experiences that have come to me, people would marvel and think that the Ashram was packed full of great Yogis! Those who know something about Yoga would not mind about the dark periods, eclipses, hostile attacks, despairings, falls, for they know that these things happen to Yogis. Even the failures would have become Gurus, if I had allowed it, with circles of Shishyas [disciples]! B. did become one. Z. of course. But all that does not count here, because what is a full realisation outside, is here only a faint beginning of siddhi. Here the test is transformation of the nature, psychic, spiritual, finally supramental. That and nothing else is what makes it so difficult.'[57] The letters with these great realizations have never been published by the sadhaks concerned out of discretion.

Another time, Sri Aurobindo amended the observations of the same correspondent: 'The quality of the sadhaks is so low? I should say there is a considerable amount of ability and capacity in the Ashram. Only the standard demanded is higher than outside even in spiritual matters. There are half a dozen people here perhaps who live in the Brahman consciousness — outside they would make a big noise and be considered as great Yogis — here their condition is not known and in the Yoga it is regarded not as siddhi but only as a

---

* 'Da' in Bengali is a suffix added to the name of an elder brother and also of a respected but in some way familiar person.

beginning.'[58] (Nirodbaran: 'Could you whisper to me the names of those lucky fellows, those "half dozen people"?' Sri Aurobindo, in capital letters: 'NO, SIR.')

The last two quotations are from 1936. It may reasonably be presumed that the *sadhaks* Sri Aurobindo had in mind had made further progress afterwards and that some of them, like Nolini, reached a very high level indeed. They were nevertheless still far from the transformation of the physical body — the reason why the ordinary eye could discern very little or nothing in them. They are the unknown heroes from the first phase of the transformation of the Earth; maybe they are now resting 'somewhere' and waiting to continue or accomplish their work when terrestrial matter will be ready for it.

Finally, a remarkable tale on this subject. It is from Champaklal's memoirs as told in his simple style to another *sadhak*. Champaklal narrates an event from 1959. '[I] informed Mother in the morning of the passing away of Mritunjoy's elder sister. Mother said: "Yes, she was not keeping well for a long time. She was sick." When Mother had her breakfast after Balcony [the balcony *darshan*], she said that she had come to know a very interesting thing. She had seen on the forehead of Mritunjoy's elder sister (who had just passed away) the symbol of Sri Aurobindo. Mother said she was very much surprised and said to herself: "What? On this ...?" Then she heard Sri Aurobindo saying: "Henceforth whoever dies here, I will put my seal upon him and in any condition unconditional protection will be given."'[59] In the *Agenda*, we find this confirmed in the Mother's own words.

When the soul leaves the material body, it first stays for some time in the vital worlds in its vital sheath before it passes through the mental regions into the psychic world, to rest there and to assimilate the experiences from the recently concluded life. The lower vital worlds are inhabited by the malicious beings we have already met and who in the West are called devils. The temporary passage of the soul through those lower vital worlds is the rationale of the various types of hell in the religions. Far from being an eternal punishment with which to threaten the faithful, it is a transient experience of the soul, which nonetheless may be very frightening and sometimes even dangerous.

As the Mother said, it had been one of her tasks, from her very childhood, to look after the souls of the deceased and to guide them safely to the world of psychic rest. 'So many people come to her in the night for the passage to the other side,'[60] wrote Sri Aurobindo. To make that passage safe for all of them, the Mother has with her occult powers constructed a path of light which the vital beings would not venture to touch and where therefore they cannot bother the souls of the deceased any longer. In the Mother's own words: 'There are now what one might call "bridges", "protected passages" built in the vital world to traverse all those dangers.'[61] She also said that she had done this work at the beginning of the century and that she had been occupied with it for months on end. 'It must be part of the work for which I have come on Earth,' she remarked. So Sri Aurobindo could write: 'The one who dies here is assisted in his passage to the psychic world and helped in his future evolution towards the Divine.'[62] As a token thereof he placed his symbol on the forehead of everyone who died in the Ashram.

Golconde

There is no building, no room, no corner in the Ashram without an interesting story about it. It is no exaggeration to say that the Mother stood behind and next to everything, not as an authoritarian mother superior but to confer the inspiration, encouragement and realizing power required for the implementation of her work in the Ashram. Everything had its occult incentive, meaning and goal, for the Ashram stood for the world and therefore each action, even in everyday life, was charged with a far-reaching symbolical sense. From the many projects realized by the Mother from scratch, with meagre means and in difficult circumstances, we will briefly consider the 'guest house' which she named *Golconde*.

What the Mother intended with Golconde was typical of the significance of the Ashram as a whole. All sources indicate that she wanted a symbolical architectural achievement of the highest beauty and perfection, giving shape as perfectly as possible to a spiritual intention and power. (Later on, she must have intended the same but on a bigger scale with Auroville.)

Sri Aurobindo wrote in a letter: 'In Golconde Mother has worked out her own idea through Raymond, Sammer and others. First, Mother believes in beauty as a part of spirituality and divine living; secondly, she believes that physical things have the Divine Consciousness underlying them as much as living things; and thirdly that they have an individuality of their own and ought to be properly treated, used in the right way ... It is on this basis that she planned Golconde. First, she wanted a high architectural beauty, and in this she succeeded ... but also she wanted all objects in it, the rooms, the fitting, the furniture to be individually artistic and to form a harmonious whole.'[63]

To this end she invited the architect Antonin Raymond, a Czech, notwithstanding his typically French name. Raymond was a student of Frank Lloyd Wright, whom he had accompanied to Japan in 1923 to help in the rebuilding of Tokyo after the disastrous earthquake which had destroyed most of the city. That was where he met and befriended Philippe Barbier de Saint-Hilaire, later called Pavitra. In 1938, the year he was invited to design the plans for Golconde, Raymond had built up a successful firm of architects, two of whom would assist him in building Golconde. One was Franticêk Sammer, a student of Le Corbusier and also a Czech; he had assisted Le Corbusier in the building of a housing complex in Moscow, and afterwards he had travelled to Japan where he had met Raymond. The other was George Nakashima, an American born of Japanese parents.

About his work for Golconde, Raymond has written:* 'We lived as in a dream. No time, no money were stipulated in the contract. There was no contract. Here indeed was an ideal state of existence

---

* Most of this material in connection with Golconde is based on a series of articles by Shraddavan, published in the monthly magazine *Mother India* during 1989 and 1990.

in which the purpose of all activity was clearly a spiritual one. The purpose, as a matter of fact, of the dormitory [later used as a guest house] was not primarily the housing of the disciples; it was the creating of an activity, the materialisation of an idea, by which the disciples might learn, might experience, might develop, through contact with the erection of a fine building. Time and money were of secondary value. This situation was quite other than the usual one of being pinched between a client and a contractor. Here everything was done to free the architect completely so that he might give himself entirely to his art and science.

'And yet, simultaneously, on the job perfect order was maintained, every nail was counted. Among various disciples chosen to work on the building, this one engrossed in the business of testing the soil might have been a retired dentist; the one responsible for opening and closing the gate — he actually had been a banker — did his job with a consciousness impossible to obtain in a world where a man listens to the sound of the 5 o'clock whistle. There were engineers among the disciples [Pavitra, Chandulal and Udar]: everyone lent a hand.

'Under the invisible guidance of the leaders of the Ashram, whose presence was always felt, to whom daily all was reported, whose concern was the spiritual growth of each member of the community, I achieved the best architecture of my career. Golconde, the dormitory was called.'[64]

This name is the French version of 'Golconda', at that time a famous goldmine near Hyderabad, the town which, before India's independence, was the capital of the state of the same name ruled by an immensely wealthy Nizam. (Hyderabad is now the capital of the Union state of Andhra Pradesh.) It was this Mohammedan Nizam who, at the request of his *diwan* (chief minister), had donated one lakh rupees for the building of the guest house. A lakh is 100,000. Nowadays an average car costs three to four lakhs in India, but in 1938 a lakh of rupees was still a considerable sum. As Udar Pinto, one of the engineers, remembers: 'Today, one lakh does not seem much, but in those days it was indeed quite a large sum, as its buying power was over twenty times what it is now [in 1990], especially at

Pondicherry where things were remarkably cheap. A ton of cement, good Japanese cement, cost only around 25 rupees and steel about 200 rupees per ton. Pondicherry was then a free port and there were absolutely no customs or import charges or restrictions. And as we had then a good off-loading pier; shipments from Japan came directly to Pondicherry.'[65] Udar was responsible for the manufacturing of the tools, accessories and fittings in metal required for Golconde. Nearly all of these objects were custom-made, and to this end Udar had started a workshop with the sum of exactly 1 (one) rupee. The workshop was called *Harpagon* by the Mother, after the main character in the comedy *L'Avare* (The Miser) by Molière.

What were the qualities that made it Antonin Raymond's best architectural work? In the prologue we have already quoted Charles Correa's high opinion of it. At the congress *Solar World*, held in Perth, Australia, in 1983, the following was said about Golconde: 'In one of the most remote parts of India, one of the most advanced buildings in the world was constructed under the most demanding circumstances concerning material and craftsmen. This reinforced concrete structure was completed primarily by unskilled volunteers with the most uncertain supplies, and with virtually every fitting custom-fabricated. Yet this handsome building has world stature, both architecturally and in its bio-climatic response to a tropical climate, 13°N of the equator.'[66] An entrant in a photographic contest organized by the *International Asbestos-Cement Review* in 1959 noted: 'In Golconde, severity has melted into dream-delicacy; sensitive lines, varied yet harmonious surfaces and a simple distribution of simple masses have magically combined to create a visual poem in space ... a photographer's dream.'[67]

The work had started on 10 October 1937; it would take ten years for Golconde to be completed. The Second World War had loomed up on the horizon, but the trio of architects, obliged to return to their homeland, never lost contact with their work and with the Ashram. The plans were worked out under the supervision of the Ashram engineers, but the materials from other countries arrived with much delay or not at all, and the prices sky-rocketed. Still, no quarter was given as to the quality of the building. In a quiet neighbourhood of Pondicherry, a stone's throw away from the central Ashram building and about two hundred meters from the blue sea, Golconde still stands in all its originality and well-preserved beauty.

Chapter Fifteen

A NIGHT IN NOVEMBER

*For us, historical events sometimes
have reasons which reason does not
know, and the lines of force of history
may be as invisible but nonetheless as
real as the lines of force of a magnetic
field.*[1]

— Louis Pauwels

THE THREE *darshan* days were the highlights of the
year in the Ashram. All Ashramites looked forward to them because
once again they would see Sri Aurobindo for a couple of minutes,
with the Mother at his right side, both of them seated on a sofa in
a small enclosed room in his apartment from eight in the morning
till about three o'clock in the afternoon, with only one brief breathing
pause. One by one, the waiting Ashramites and a number of specially
admitted visitors then stood for a moment face to face with the
smiling embodied Presence who, with the blessing of the day, gave
to all what they needed for their inner well-being and progress.

On every occasion, the *darshans* were prepared by Sri Aurobindo
and the Mother on the occult plane. 'There is usually a descent, but
there is also a great opposition to the descent at these times[2] ... It
is true that attacks are frequent at that time.'[3] (Sri Aurobindo) The
resistance and the attacks of course came from the hostile forces, who
used all possible means to prevent each and every descent from the

Higher Power and who doggedly fought every spiritual step forward. Sri Aurobindo's concentration to ward off the attacks was so often required at these times that he put a temporary halt to the correspondence.

On that 23 November 1938, the expectations were once again keen ánd the air festive. Visitors had come from everywhere, including foreign countries. This time the centre of attention among them was Margaret Wilson, daughter of the American President Woodrow Wilson. She had read books by Sri Aurobindo in the New York Library and had started corresponding with him and the Mother. Sri Aurobindo, at her request, had given her a Sanskrit name, as always significant of the spiritual possibilities he saw in the person rather than an indication of already acquired capacities. Margaret Wilson was now called 'Nishta' in the Ashram, a name which, in Sri Aurobindo's words written to her, meant 'one-pointed, fixed and steady concentration, devotion and faith in the single aim — the Divine and the Divine Realisation.'

Sri Aurobindo had duly warned her before she undertook the long journey from the United States: 'We [i.e. he and the Mother] are doubtful about the advisability of your coming here next winter. Your illness [she had arthritis] and the fact that you suffer from the heat stand in the way ... Finally, you do not know perhaps that I am living at present in an entire retirement, not seeing or speaking with anyone, even the disciples in the Ashram, only coming out to give a silent blessing three times a year. The Mother also has no time to give free or frequent access to those who are here. You would therefore probably be disappointed if you came here with the idea of a personal contact with us to help you in your spiritual endeavour. The personal touch is there, but it is more of an inward closeness with only a few points of physical contact to support it. But the inner contact, inner help can very well be received at a distance.'[4]

In the silence of the tropical night preceding the busy *darshan* day, only one light was on — a lamp in Sri Aurobindo's room. The heaving, roaring breakers must have crashed against the sea-wall as usual. At that time of the year Orion rises in the night-sky. Then the unexpected happened.

'Between 2.20 and 2.30 the Mother rang the bell,' writes A.B. Purani, who was on voluntary night duty. 'I ran up the staircase to be told suddenly that an accident had happened to Sri Aurobindo's leg and that I should fetch the doctor.'[5] While going from his room to the bathroom, Sri Aurobindo had stumbled over a tiger skin, one of the many presented to him by followers and admirers and of which two or three can still be seen in his apartment. The first doctor called upon was Dr. Manilal. 'When we other doctors came up, we saw that Dr. Manilal was busy examining Sri Aurobindo's injured leg. The Mother was sitting by his side, fanning him gently,'[6] writes Nirodbaran.

It was clear from the unnatural position of the leg that it was broken. The fracture was more serious than thought at first. An orthopaedic surgeon and a radiologist from Madras were summoned as quickly as possible, with the required equipment to examine and treat Sri Aurobindo in his apartment. Their conclusion: a compound fracture of the right thigh bone. The leg was put in traction.

The news of Sri Aurobindo's accident caused consternation, commotion and disillusionment all over the Ashram. The *darshan* everyone had been looking forward to so expectantly would not take place. (Still, a smiling Mother alone gave *darshan* in the evening.) And in the mind of one and all the question must have arisen: how could Sri Aurobindo, the Mahayogi, the Avatar others were praying for protection, himself have become the victim of an accident? However quietly and with dignity they comported themselves outwardly, most of them were no doubt tremendously shaken.

Indeed, how had that accident been possible? Sri Aurobindo said shortly afterwards: 'The hostile forces have tried many times to prevent things like the darshan, but I have succeeded in warding off all their attacks. At the time the accident to my leg happened, I was more occupied with guarding the Mother and I forgot about myself. I didn't think the hostiles would attack me. That was my mistake.'[7] 'It was because I was unguarded and something forced its way into the subconscient. There is a stage in yogic advance when the least negligence would not do.'[8] And he also said: 'I didn't think they would dare.'

But dare they did, and they had chosen the best possible moment to hit the victim of their attack with a heavy physical blow and at the same time humiliate him in everybody's eyes. The Mother said about this: 'It was a formation (a hostile force) and he did not take enough precautions because that force was directed against both of us, more particularly against me. It had already tried a couple of times to break my head — things like that. Therefore [Sri Aurobindo] was under tension to prevent that it seriously might hit my body. And that's how it managed to approach him unnoticed and to break his leg. It was a shocking event.'[9]

Sri Aurobindo and the Mother were probably the only ones who could destroy a hostile being by dissolving it into its Origin. The reason why the Adversary had run the risk of an attack like this was that in 1938 Sri Aurobindo had reached a point in his yoga where the general manifestation* of the Supramental, the main objective of his effort, had become a distinct possibility. In an earlier chapter, we have followed his advance in the previous years and we have seen that he, 'riding on his Einsteinian formula', was progressing rapidly. According to several witnesses, the Great Event of the Supramental Manifestation could have taken place at any moment in 1938.

Sri Aurobindo himself announced at the time: '[The Supramental] is coming down against tremendous resistance.'[10] K.D. Sethna is more categorical: 'The Truth-Consciousness's manifestation on a world-wide scale was originally expected by the Mother as far back as that year [1938],'[11] a statement he repeats in several places in his writings. Nirodbaran writes in his *Twelve Years With Sri Aurobindo*: 'The Mother told a sadhak in 1935 that in ten years' time she would look as young as a girl of 16. To me also she narrated at length a similar vision of hers, the gist of which is that both of them [Sri Aurobindo and the Mother] had become young and exquisite, so much so that none of the sadhaks could recognise them. From Sri Aurobindo's

---

* A 'descent' in Sri Aurobindo and the Mother's terminology is a limited and mostly personal realization by which a higher force descends or is brought down in the terrestrial plane; a 'manifestation' is a more general descent, for humanity and for the earth as a whole.

letters too we had the intuition that the 'Supramental descent in the physical was imminent.'[12]

Many years later, the Mother declared: 'There was such constant tension for Sri Aurobindo and me that it interrupted the yoga completely during the whole war. And it was for that reason that the war had come: to stop the Work. For there was an extraordinary descent of the Supermind at that time, it came like this [massive gesture] — a descent ...! That was exactly in 1939. Then the war has come and has stopped everything, completely. For if we personally had gone on with the Work, we would not have been sure that we had the time to finish it before "the other one" had made a mess of the world, and the whole affair would have been postponed for centuries. That had to be stopped first of all: that action of the Lord of the Nations — the Lord of Falsehood.'[13]

With these words, the Mother put Sri Aurobindo's accident in perspective. The black forces were running amuck at the time. In 1936, Hitler's troops had entered the Rhineland, welcomed by priests honouring them with waving censers. The German rearmament programme was already in full swing. The *Anschluss* with Austria, approved by a plebiscite of more than ninety-nine per cent of the Austrian population, was effected on 12 March 1938. On 29 September of the same year, Hitler, Mussolini, Chamberlain and Daladier signed the Munich Pact, an agreement which was the death-blow to Czechoslovakia. The pogrom against the Jews in Germany started on 9 November with the infamous *Kristallnacht*. The crisis over Czechoslovakia, with a threat of general mobilization and war, became acute in those months. The Germans occupied the Sudetenland one week after Sri Aurobindo's accident, and they paraded in Prague three months later. Spain was in the grip of civil war; Benito Mussolini tried to live out his Caesarian fantasies; the Japanese aggressively enlarged their empire in Asia. The world was on fire.

One of the letters from the Mother to her son André is dated 22 October 1938. In this letter she wrote to him: 'Speaking of recent events, you ask me whether it was "a dangerous bluff" or whether we "narrowly escaped disaster." To assume both at the same time would be nearer to the truth. Hitler was certainly bluffing — if that is what you call being boisterous and proffering threats with the intention of intimidating those one is talking to, and obtaining as much as one can. Tactics and diplomacy were used, but on the other hand, behind every human will forces are acting whose origin is not human and who strive consciously for certain goals. The play of those forces is very complex and generally eludes the human consciousness. But for the sake of explanation and understanding, they can be divided into two main opposing tendencies: those who work for the fulfilment of the Divine Work upon earth and those who are opposed to this fulfilment ... Hitler is a choice instrument for the anti-divine forces who want violence, upheavals and war, for they know that these things delay and hinder the action of the divine forces. That is why disaster was very close although no human government consciously wanted it. But there was to be no war at any cost, and that is why war has been avoided ... for the time being.'[14]

These rather abstract sounding sentences tell us the following: 1. The dangerous international situation was the work of forces inimical to the Divine Work. 2. Hitler was an instrument of those forces. 3. War could have erupted at that moment but was provisionally prevented. The Divine Work was the effort of materializing a higher consciousness, the Supermind, in the terrestrial evolution. Sri Aurobindo and the Mother were the protagonists of this Work, which in 1938 had reached a critical phase and could have been accomplished any moment. The antidivine forces did everything possible to avert that accomplishment, for it would have put an end to their sovereignty over the earth. Hitler was their choice instrument. War was inevitable because of the occult all-or-nothing situation in the world, but it was provisionally averted by the divine protagonists for reasons known only to them though certainly related to the massive descent of the Supermind at the time. Nirodbaran asked Sri Aurobindo on 14 December 1938: 'Did you stop the war the last time there was a chance of it?' Sri Aurobindo answered: 'Yes — for many reasons war was not favourable at that time',[15] — shortly before the Munich Conference. The antidivine forces had then turned directly against Sri Aurobindo and taken revenge by causing the fall which broke his right thigh.

The reader will remember that in the beginning of this book the question was asked whether it is possible that the history of humanity unfolds in interaction with one or two individuals. In answer to this question, we have heard about the nature and the mission of the Avatar. We also have become acquainted with the personalities and the Work of the Avatar of our time, a double embodiment of the Divine on earth named Sri Aurobindo and the Mother. We have learned about their goal and their Work, that would consist in making possible the appearance of a new species on our planet and eventually in the long expected establishment of the Kingdom of God on earth. One can conclude from many statements by Sri Aurobindo and the Mother that they have played an active and even decisive role in world history.

We now come to the worldwide conflagration still imprinted with painful accuracy in the memory of humankind: the Second World War, called by Sri Aurobindo 'the Mother's war', and of which all explanations remain unsatisfactory. The wind of madness that blew over the earth in those years, the Order of the Death's Head, the *Endlösung* for which millions of human beings were killed like beasts, and the fatal fascination exerted by a rather trivial man — all that can hardly be explained by economic charts, population data, armament statistics, or psychological and sociological theories. The interpretation of the Second World War proposed here tállies with a lot more facts, psychological as well as material. Reality is always much more fantastic than the human mind can imagine, as Arthur C. Clarke and others have said. As the twentieth century is rushing towards its end, it is important that we finally understand what it has signified if we wish to be capable of looking ahead to the events of the coming era with some degree of understanding.

In their eye-opening book first published in 1956, *Le Matin des Magiciens*, Louis Pauwels and Jacques Bergier wrote about the Second World War: 'The judges of Nuremberg, spokesmen of the victorious civilization, did not realize that this war had been a spiritual war. The vision they had of their own world was not lofty enough. They only thought that Good had been victorious over Evil without having perceived the profundity of the vanquished evil and the height of the victorious good.'[16] We will look into that presently.

A Look in Sri Aurobindo's Rooms

Sri Aurobindo's way of living since 1926 had undergone thorough changes. During twelve years he had had near him only the Mother and Champaklal, that epitome of the faithful servant. Now a team of physicians and volunteers was formed to assist Sri Aurobindo in his physical ordeal. The physicians were Manilal, Satyendra, Becharlal and Nirodbaran, and the other volunteers were Champaklal, Purani and Mulsankar. Theirs was the privilege to be allowed to enter the holy of holies, to see and help Sri Aurobindo and to hear him talk.

To a few of them, we owe some information of the daily life in Sri Aurobindo's apartment and how he passed his days, outwardly that is. Our most important source once again is Nirodbaran, who has published four volumes of *Talks With Sri Aurobindo* which cover the period from 10 December 1938 to 28 September 1941. 'There was no subject that was not touched, not a mystery that he did not illumine, not a phenomenon that passed unnoticed, humorous or serious, superficial or profound, mundane or mystic. Reminiscences, stories, talks on art and culture, on world problems poured down in abundant streams from an otherwise silent and reticent vastness of knowledge and love and bliss. It was an unforgettable reward he accorded to us for our humble service.'[17]

Nirodbaran has also writtten his personal reminiscences of those years in *Twelve Years With Sri Aurobindo*. From that source we know how Sri Aurobindo was sitting and lying down (during those relaxed conversations often with his hands under his head), what he ate (he was still very fond of Bengali sweets), what kind of mouthwash he used (*Vademecum*) and that in his rooms imported Chinese spirals were burned to ward off mosquitoes. 'Be it eating, drinking, walking or talking — he did it always in a slow and measured rhythm, giving the impression that every moment was conscious and consecrated.'[18] Moreover, in this book the fantastic rumours that had been circulating about him for a long time were given the lie once and for all. He did not live in a subterranean cave, he did not float above the ground, and he did indeed take food and rest. Sri Aurobindo himself once said in jest: 'I shall have to write [my biography] just in order to contradict the biographers. I shall have to entitle the book: "What I did not do in my life." '[19]

'All that was visible to our naked eye was that he sat silently in his bed, afterwards in the capacious armchair, with his eyes wide open just as any other person would. Only he passed hours and hours thus, changing his position at times and making himself comfortable, the eyes moving a little, and though usually gazing at the wall in front, never fixed *tratak*-like* at any particular point. Sometimes the face would beam with a bright smile without apparent reason, much to our amusement, as a child smiles in sleep. Only it was a waking sleep, for as we passed across the room, there was a dim recognition of our shadow-like movements. Occasionally he would look towards the door. That was when he heard some sound which might indicate the Mother's coming. But his external consciousness would certainly not be obliterated. When he wanted something, his voice seemed to come from a distant cave; rarely would we find him plunged within, with his eyes closed.'[20] This is how Sri Aurobindo did his Work; this is how, in his subtle body, he moved in this world and in many worlds; this is how he fought the good fight.

In the Battle is the title of a sonnet from the remarkable series written by Sri Aurobindo in the year after his accident. These sonnets provide us with a multifaceted insight in what he was inwardly occupied with, while apparently sitting quietly in concentration — an inconspicuous attitude rendered possible by his complete yogic mastery. In the sonnet mentioned, we read:

> All around me now the Titan forces press;
> This world is theirs, they hold its days in fee;
> I am full of wounds and the fight merciless.[21]

These lines remind one straight away of the passage from *A God's Labour*, written in 1935 and quoted in an earlier chapter: 'My gaping

---

* *Tratak* is a yogic exercise of concentration on a flame or a point of light.

wounds are a thousand and one / and the Titan kings assail ...' Sri Aurobindo has written mostly about his struggles and sufferings and about his yogic realizations in his poetry — but who takes poems seriously? Still it is in his poems and in *Savitri* that we find most of the facts to build up an understanding of his work and realizations; he probably cast them in this form 'to front the years', just like his deeds, and to be conserved for posterity.

Also worth mentioning here is the informative case of Mridu. 'Mridu was a simple Bengali village widow,' writes Nirodbaran. 'She, like the other ladies, called Sri Aurobindo her father, and took great pride in cooking for him. Her "father" also liked very much her *luchis* [a kind of delicacy], she would boast, and these creations of hers have been immortalized by him in one of his letters to her. She was given to maniacal fits of threatening suicide, and Sri Aurobindo would console her with, "If you commit suicide, who will cook *luchis* for me?" '[22]

Strange to say: 'One regular interlude during his meal was the arrival of our rampaging luchi-maker, Mridu. I do not know how she obtained this exceptional privilege. She would come like an innocent lamb with incense and flowers, kneel down in front of the door and wait with folded hands for "her Father's blessings". On our drawing Sri Aurobindo's attention to her presence, he would stop eating and cast a quiet glance at her. Her boisterous, unruly nature would become humble for a while before Sri Aurobindo. Whenever it was reported that she had manifested her violent temper, she was threatened with the loss of this *Darshan*.'[23]

And stranger still, as one reads in the *Agenda*, the Mother later reported that the by then deceased Mridu was one of those she had met, after Sri Aurobindo's passing, in his permanent dwelling in the subtle worlds! Which shows that it is difficult, especially in spiritual matters, to judge from outward appearances.

Some weeks after his accident, Sri Aurobindo began to revise the text of *The Life Divine*, published more than twenty years before. His revision was so thorough that many new pages and even several chapters were added — according to Peter Heehs the greatest volume of prose Sri Aurobindo has written after terminating the publication of the *Arya* in January 1921. Nirodbaran observed Sri Aurobindo while he was working on the revision: 'There he was, then, sitting on the bed, with his right leg stretched out. I was watching his movements from behind the bed. No sooner had he begun than line followed after line as if everything was chalked out in the mind, or as he used to say, a tap was turned on and a stream poured down. Absorbed in perfect poise, gazing now and then in front, wiping the perspiration of his hands — for he perspired profusely — he would go on for about two hours.'[24] *The Life Divine* was published in two volumes, the first in July 1940. The first issue of the *Arya* had come out on 15 August 1914. It may be by chance that the preparation and the printing of both these important publications corresponded so closely with the beginning of the two world wars. C.G. Jung would have called this a synchronicity. This, for sure, was a very suggestive coincidence.

Chapter Sixteen

THE LORD OF THE NATIONS

> *It is well-known that the Nazi party proved itself to be anti-intellectual in a blunt and even boisterous manner, that it burned books and classified the theoretical physicists among its 'Judeo-Marxist' enemies. It is less well-known in favour of which explanations of the world it rejected the official Western sciences. And still less is known about the concept of man on which Nazism was based, at least in the minds of some of its leaders. When knowing this, it is easier to situate the last World War within the framework of the great spiritual conflicts; history regains the breath of the Legend of the Ages.*[1]
> — Louis Pauwels

The Medium Adolf Hitler

'Hitler is a choice instrument of the hostile forces,' the Mother wrote in a letter to her son André. Many would have agreed with her if they had read that letter. For instance, Dusty Sklar writes in her book *The Nazis and the Occult*: 'Hitler was abandoning himself to forces which were carrying him away — forces of dark and destructive violence. He imagined that he still had freedom of choice, but he had long been in bondage to a magic which might well have been described, not only in metaphor but in literal fact, as that of evil spirits.'[2] And Denis de Rougemont said of Hitler: 'Some people think, because of what they have experienced in his presence ... that he is possessed by a Dominion, a Throne or a Power, as Saint Paul typifies the spirits of the second order, who can take possession of any human body whatsoever and occupy it like a garrison. I have heard him deliver one of his great speeches. From where does he get that superhuman power he then emanates? One feels very well that an energy of this nature does not come from the person in question and that it could even manifest without that person being of any importance, for he is only the instrument of a power outside our psychological understanding. What I say here would be romanticism of the worst kind were it not that the work done by this man — and I do mean by that power through him — is a reality which stupefies the century.'[3]

The best known eye-witness account in this connection is that of Hermann Rauschning, former head of the government of Danzig: 'A member of his entourage has told me that Hitler wakes up in the night shouting impulsively. He calls for help, sitting on the edge of his bed, he is paralyzed as it were. He is in the grip of a panic which makes him tremble so violently that the bed shakes. He utters confused and incomprehensible vociferations. He gasps for breath as if he were going to choke. The same person has narrated to me one of those crises with details which I would refuse to believe, were it not that my source is absolutely trustworthy. Hitler was standing in his room, swaying, looking around him in bewilderment. "There he is! There he is! He has come here!" he groaned. His lips were pale. Sweat ran down in big drops. Suddenly he started pronouncing numbers without any meaning, then words, snippets of sentences. It was terrible. He used terms put together in bizarre ways, completely out of the ordinary. Then he became silent again but was still moving his lips. He was then given a massage and something to drink. But again, all at once, he screamed: "There! There! In the corner! He is there!" He stamped on the parquet floor and shouted ..."⁴ 'When we say that Hitler is possessed by a Vital Power, it is a statement of fact, not a moral judgment,'⁵ said Sri Aurobindo in January 1939.

Who was the 'spirit' or 'power' by whom Hitler was possessed? He is already known to us as the Lord of Falsehood, one of the four great *Asuras* from the drama at the beginning of time. 'He calls himself the Lord of the Nations. It is he who initiates all wars ... We talk to each other. Over and above all that we are in contact with each other ... After all, I am his mother!' the Mother told smilingly. 'He once told me: "I know that you will destroy me, but before being destroyed, I will cause as much damage as possible, be sure of that."'⁶

Being one of the first four great emanated Beings by the Creating Mother, he was and is her son. At one time he was the Incarnation of Truth, but after the fall he became the Lord of Falsehood who with his three brothers has held this world in his grip up to now. As one of the original *Asuras*, he was fully aware of the presence of Sri Aurobindo and the Mother on Earth, and of their effort to change Falsehood into Truth, Darkness into Light, Suffering into shadowless Bliss and Death into Immortality. In other words, this meant that it was their aim to put an end to the sovereignty over this creation of the Negative Forces, to whom was left the choice either to convert and become once again the brilliant great Beings they had been at the beginning, or to be dissolved into their Origin and thus annihilated as individual forms of existence.

As the Mother once told, the *Asura* of Darkness, who is the original incarnation of Light Lucifer, has been converted. In the years of her intense occult activity in the beginning of the century, he agreed that she would give him a vital body, and since then he has been cooperating for the general Transformation. The *Asura* of Suffering, on the contrary, has been dissolved into his Origin. (One should not forget, however, that the four *Asuras* have emanated 'cascades' of secondary beings who remain active independently and who may go on existing for a long time to come.) Max Théon, the teacher of Mirra Alfassa, was a humanly incarnated emanation of the *Asura* of Death and Paul Richard of the *Asura* of Falsehood. As Sri Aurobindo himself has said, Paul Richard has even written an unpublished book entitled

Le Seigneur des Nations (The Lord of the Nations) in which he accurately expounded the aim and methods of that Being. The Mother had done everything possible to convert Richard; this was the reason why she had married him and the cause of the hell their relation had been for her all along, also in Japan and during their last months together in Pondicherry. Richard knew very well who Mirra essentially was, and despite his appreciation of Sri Aurobindo, he himself wanted to be recognized by her as the Avatar! All this makes us understand better his depressions and suicidal thoughts which he confided in a nocturnal conversation to Dilip Kumar Roy in Nice.

However, an emanation is not the being itself in its fullness, and the *Asuras* of Death and Falsehood watchfully refrain from incarnating themselves in their essence, for by so doing they would be subjected to the laws of the evolution. Even the *Asura* who possessed Hitler was not the essential Lord of the Nations. It was 'not the Lord of the Nations in his origin but an emanation of him, a very powerful one.'[7]

'Hitler was a medium, a first rate medium.* He has become possessed during spiritistic seances. It is then that he became seized by crises which were thought to be epileptic. Actually they were not, they were crises of possession,' told the Mother to the youth of the Ashram in one of the conversations afterwards published as the series *Entretiens*. 'It was therefore that he had that kind of power, which in fact was not very great. But when he wanted to know something from that Power, he went to his castle** to "meditate", and there he addressed a very intense appeal to what he called his "god", his

---

* His birthplace, Braunau-am-Inn, was known in Austria as a cradle of mediums.
** The Mother no doubt means the *Berghof*, Hitler's villa in Obersalzberg. In his polemic poem about Hitler, *The Dwarf Napoleon*, Sri Aurobindo writes:

In his high villa on the fatal hill
Alone he listens to that sovereign Voice,
Dictator of his action's sudden choice.   (*Collected Poems*, p. 111)
John Toland too calls the *Berghof* 'Hitler's place of inspiration', where he went into retirement before his important and always unexpected decisions.

supreme god, who was the Lord of the Nations ... This was a being
... he was small, and he appeared to him in a silver armour, with
a silver helmet and a golden aigrette. He looked magnificent. And
he appeared in such a blinding light that the eyes hardly could look
at him and bear the brilliance. He did not appear physically, of course:
Hitler was a medium, he "saw". He had a certain clairvoyance. And
it was in those cases [when meeting the Lord of the Nations] that
he suffered his crises: he rolled about on the floor, he slavered, he
bit in the carpets — it was a terrible state he was in. The people
around him knew that.'[8] This is a confirmation of Rauschning's
testimony from a very different corner. It is worth mentioning that
a poster on the street walls of Munich at the time Hitler became
politically active there showed him in silver armour.

How had the Lord of the Nations been able to take hold of Hitler,
to possess him? August Kubizek, Hitler's friend and confidant during
the latter's years in Vienna, remembered after the war a strange experience he had had with him in 1906 after an evening at the Opera. The
two inseparable friends were regular visitors of the famous Opera
House. (Years later Hitler was still able to whistle faultlessly all of the
Meistersinger, and at one time he even had started writing an opera
himself.) It was after a performance of Wagner's *Rienzi* that something
happened which Kubizek never forgot: 'I was struck by something
strange, which I had never noticed before, even when he had talked
to me in moments of the greatest excitement. It was as if another being
spoke out of his body and moved him as much as it did me ... I rather
felt as though he himself listened with astonishment and emotion to
what burst forth from him with elementary force. I will not attempt
to interpret this phenomenon, but it was a state of complete ecstasy
and rapture, in which he transferred the character of Rienzi ... with
visionary power to the plane of his own ambitions.' Hitler evoked in
grandiose, inspired images his own future and that of his people.
'Hitherto I had been convinced that my friend wanted to become an
artist, a painter, or perhaps an architect. Now this was no longer the
case. Now he aspired to something higher, which I could not yet fully
grasp.'[9] As this was a one-time experience, it cannot be termed possession, but the fact that another being seemed to speak through Hitler

was typical of the medium he was. Some doors in him were clearly ajar. At that time, he was seventeen.

On the subject of possession of a person by an invisible being, the Mother said: 'There are cases in which people become very ill and come out of the illness totally different from what they were before.'[10] These words immediately call to mind an event in Hitler's life mentioned by all his biographers. After having been blinded in the First World War, during a gas attack near the Belgian town of Wervik, he was transported by train to a military hospital at Pasewalk, in Pomerania. It was there that he heard the news of the collapse of Germany and its unconditional surrender. He became a prey to unfathomable despair. In *Mein Kampf* he wrote about this crisis: 'I went back to the dormitory where I threw myself on my bed and buried my burning head under the bedcover and the cushion ... Terrible days and still more terrible nights followed ... In those sleepless nights, I felt growing in me the hatred against those guilty of this catastrophe. It was then that I became conscious of my life's true destiny ... As to me, I took the decision to become a politician.'

It is astonishing how much the (courageous) corporal-courier Adolf Hitler was protected throughout that war. Time after time he felt as if driven by an inner impulse to leave a certain place which promptly afterwards was hit by a shell. The historian John Toland calls it 'a series of narrow escapes verging on the miraculous.' Hitler himself told the British correspondent Ward Price how one day he was eating his dinner in a trench with several comrades. 'Suddenly a voice seemed to be saying to me, "Get up and go over there." It was so clear and insistent that I obeyed mechanically, as if it had been a military order. I rose at once to my feet and walked twenty yards along the trench, carrying my dinner in its tin-can with me. Then I sat down to go on eating, my mind being once more at rest. Hardly had I done so when a flash and deafening report came from the part of the trench I had just left. A stray shell had burst over the group in which I had been sitting, and every member of it was killed.'[11] This protection would never leave him till the day of his death.

The Mother has said that the possession took hold of him 'during spiritistic seances'. One does not have to search long to find out where and when this may have happened. During the years of Hitler's political schooling and rise in Munich, he was strongly influenced by two persons, both of whom had ties with Eastern occultism. The first was Dietrich Eckart, called by André Brissaud 'the great initiator' of Hitler. 'Until his death [in 1923] Dietrich Eckart will be the great mentor of Adolf Hitler. The future *Führer* of the Third *Reich* will owe him much, to begin with his "initiation" in the legend of Thule and the development of his mediumistic faculties. Eckart will contribute considerably to the development in Hitler of an unshakable self-confidence, founded on the certitude of being in possession of the most important secrets to dominate the world.'[12] These words certainly leave sufficient space for secret seances. Besides, shortly before his death Eckart will say to Karl Haushofer and Alfred Rosenberg: 'Follow Hitler. He will dance, but I am the one who has composed the tune. We have given him the means to communicate with Them ... Do not mourn for me: I will have influenced history more than any other German.'[13]

André Brissaud writes about the secret Thule society: 'It will be the life-source of National Socialism which was, we repeat, not only a movement aiming at success, supremacy and the exertion of political power, but also, and mainly, an instrument to develop a *Weltanschauung* [world-view] in its human totality; the political will-to-power went hand in hand with the firm determination to promote an ideology capable of assuring a decisive human transmutation, a metamorphosis integrally racist, biological, moral, social, economical, political, religious and philosophical. Those who discard this truth will never understand a thing about the Nazi phenomenon.'[14]

The other person who has left his mark on Hitler was the 'geo-politician' Karl Haushofer, a general in the First World War (Rudolf Hess was his adjutant) and a specialist in Eastern religions and mysticism. F. Sondern wrote in 1941: 'Dr. Haushofer and his men dominate Hitler's thinking ... It was Haushofer who taught the hysterical, planless agitator in a Munich jail to think in terms of continents and empires. Haushofer virtually dictated the famous Chapter XVI of *Mein Kampf* which outlined the foreign policy Hitler has since followed to the letter.'[15] He thought up Hitler's *Lebensraum* [living-space] theory. He also had a fundamental plan which we shall discuss shortly.

Haushofer's nefarious influence on Adolf Hitler has been dramatically confirmed by his son, Albrecht Haushofer. The latter was involved in the Stauffenberg plot leading to the failed attempt on Hitler's life on 20 July 1944. Albrecht was imprisoned in Moabit jail, in Berlin. He wrote a cycle of sonnets before his execution — that is to say in circumstances which usually warrant a complete sincerity. One of those sonnets is entitled *The Father* and in it he wrote: 'Once it was in the power of his will / To push the demon back into his cell. / My father held the seal and broke it. / He did not sense the breath of evil / And out into the world he let the devil.'[16]

Everything Sri Aurobindo and the Mother, with their extensive occult knowledge, have said about Hitler being possessed by the Demon could be confirmed by many more historical facts. But the so-called 'objective' historians do not have the necessary norms, knowledge or insight to appraise this sort of data. Therefore 'objective history' always produces a drab picture of what really happened and is not much more than documented highbrow journalism. And therefore 'objective' historians sometimes write such 'reasonable' but inane psychological dissections of personalities like Joan of Arc, Napoleon, Alexander the Great, Julius Caesar, and of ancient cultures — in brief, of everything that really mattered on the wearisome and tortuous road of the human pilgrimage. The norms of rationalistic historical writing are always too superficial to explain the forces behind the past event. The monstrosities committed by the Nazis could be inspired by nothing but a monstrous Power to which (or rather to whom) humans are dwarf-like, ant-like beings, though sometimes instruments temporarily inflated by the invisible powers they open themselves to in their ignorance — but afterwards Adolf Eichman again, functionary and civilian, in the dock of history.

The Hitlerian Man-god

Indeed, as Brissaud wrote: 'Those who discard this truth will never understand a thing about the Nazi phenomenon.' Neither will those who remain ignorant of the work of Sri Aurobindo and the Mother. The *Asura*, Lord of Falsehood, has definitively refused to be converted and sworn that he, before his own destruction of the Earth, would inflict the greatest possible damage. The Mother once said that all the wars of the twentieth century are actually episodes of one single war and that all have been his doing. The whole was one single war of the dark forces dominating the Earth against the White Force of the evolutionary yoga of the double Avatar. The aim of this war, as far as the dark forces are concerned, has always been the annihilation of civilization, of all progress gained by humanity, to plunge it again into the night of barbarism as illustrated by the Nazi regime in Germany and Stalinist communism in Russia.

The result the action of the *Asura* aimed at this time was ultimately the retardation and if possible the obstruction of the work of Sri Aurobindo and the Mother. We have already seen how in his anger and frustration he turned directly against Sri Aurobindo, in November 1938, when Sri Aurobindo was on the point of effecting the manifestation of the Supermind on Earth, to this end putting off the beginning of the imminent war. We have also heard the Mother say that their work was completely interrupted by the war, which demanded their full attention and occult intervention to avoid the clock of history once again, like so often in the past, being put back.

All these assertions become much more acceptable if one realizes that Hitler's design was, as it were, the shadow of the aim of Sri Aurobindo and the Mother. That 'infrarational mystic', as Sri Aurobindo called him, was driven by his vision of the *Übermensch*, a superman far superior to the one Friedrich Nietzsche had envisaged, a vision which could have been inspired into him only by the *Asura* (very probably via Eckart and Haushofer). In the words of Achilles Delmas: 'Hitler's aim is not the establishment of the master race, nor world conquest either; these are only the means of the great work dreamed of by him. His true objective is to perform a work of creation, a divine work, the aim of biological mutation. It will result in an ascension of humanity without equal up to now, in "the apparition of a humanity of heroes, of half-gods, of men-gods." '[17]

Hermann Rauschning quotes Hitler's own words: 'When Hitler turned to me, he tried to formulate his vocation as the harbinger of a new humanity in rational and concrete terms. He said: "Creation is not finished. It is clear that man has reached a phase of metamorphosis. The old human species has already entered a stage of perishment and survival. Humanity takes a step upwards every seven hundred years, and the stake of the struggle on a still longer term is the coming of the Sons of God. All creative force will be concentrated in a new species. The two varieties will evolve quickly while separating from each other. The one will disappear and the other will develop. It will surpass present man infinitely ... Do you now understand the profound meaning of our National Socialist movement? He who understands National Socialism as nothing but a political movement does not know much about it." '[18]

To the same Rauschning, Hitler cried out triumphantly: 'The new man lives among us! He is here! Is this enough for you? I shall tell you a secret: I have seen the new man. He is intrepid and cruel. I have been afraid in his presence.' 'When he spoke these words,' Rauschning adds, 'Hitler trembled with ecstatic fervour.'[19] Rauschning also reports a conversation Hitler had with Bernhard Förster, Nietzsche's brother-in-law: '[Hitler said he] would not reveal his unique mission until later. He permitted glimpses of it only to a few. When the time came, however, Hitler would bring the world a new religion ... The blessed consciousness of eternal life in union with the great universal life, and in membership of an immortal people — that was the message he would impart to the world when the time came. Hitler would be the first to achieve what Christianity was meant to have been, a joyous message that liberated men from the things that burdened their life. We should no longer have any fear of death and should lose the fear of a so-called bad conscience. Hitler would restore men to the self-confident divinity with which nature had endowed them. They would be able to trust their instincts, would no longer be citizens of two worlds, but would be rooted in the single, eternal life of this world.'[20] A vision of this kind Rauschning would not have been able to invent all by himself — and Hitler neither.

Hitler considered himself more and more as the prototype of his own idea of the man-god. This is clear from a paragraph in Toland's biography, in which one hears echoes of the last quotation from Rauschning: 'He had also come to regard himself as a man of destiny, superior to any other human being, whose genius and will power would conquer any enemy. Mesmerized by his political and military victories, he explained to one Nazi commander that he was the first and only mortal who had emerged into a "superhuman state." His nature was "more godlike than human," and therefore as the first of the new race of supermen he was "bound by none of the conventions of human morality" and stood "above the law." '[21] And after a law had been voted which gave Hitler full plenipotentiary powers, Toland writes: 'He was now officially above the law with the power of life and death. He had, in essence, appointed himself God's deputy and could do the Lord's work: wipe out the vermin and create a race of supermen.'[22] In the Third Reich, not a single important decision was taken without the knowledge and the permission of the Führer, 'a man who had cruelty in his blood' according to the phrase from January 1939 of Sri Aurobindo, who did not have to wait till the discovery of the extermination camps to see through Hitler.

From the beginning, Sri Aurobindo and the Mother knew exactly the kind of adversary they were dealing with and the human instruments he had sought out. When Sri Aurobindo saw a newspaper photo of Chamberlain and Hitler in Munich, he compared them respectively to a fly and a spider watching the fly from its web. He said that Hermann Goering and Joseph Goebbels, as well as Hitler, were possessed by 'forces from the vital world'. Gregor Strasser, a true idealist and one of Hitler's companions of the first hour who would soon disagree with him and pay for his idealism and disagreement with his life, warned a friend of his: 'I am a man marked by death ... Whatever happens, mark what I say: From now on Germany is in the hands of an Austrian, who is a congenital liar, a former officer [Goering], who is a pervert, and a clubfoot [Goebbels]. And I tell you the last is the worst of them all. This is Satan in human form.'[23]

It is worth noticing that almost all the main actors in the great Nazi drama came together in the right place, Munich, at the right time: Dietrich Eckart, Anton Drexler, founder of the DAP, Ernst Roehm, organizer of the SA, Karl Haushofer, Rudolf Hess, Alfred Rosenberg, Hans Frank, Julius Streicher, Heinrich Himmler, Hermann Goering, and others. One who has heard the Mother on the instinctive reunification of souls with specific tasks in the evolutionary occurrence cannot but conclude that there are also soul-families of the negative forces. One who would join the group several years later was Heinrich Heydrich; of him his closest collaborator, SS General Walter Schellenberg, would later personally tell André Brissaud: 'Heydrich was a cold-blooded animal. He had the look of a reptile. He made me freeze. His venom was mortal. I have never met a similar being. His power of fascination — in a completely different domain from that of Hitler — was demoniacal.'[24]

Nowadays, it is too often forgotten that at a certain moment in the twentieth century human beings possessed by devils and incarnated devils had, according to Sri Aurobindo's estimation, a fifty per cent chance of success in their designs. Moreover, it is convenient to forget how much Hitler and his consorts were initially lauded, by what masses of thousands of ordinary, 'decent' citizens they were enthusiastically cheered, how many literally took Hitler for a new Saviour, for the Christ of modern times. If history can teach one lesson — except the lesson that nobody learns anything from history, ever — it is perhaps the fact that human beings are not only petty and malicious, but also blind and ignorant, now as well as then. 'Nazism was one of those rare moments in the history of our civilization that a door opened on something other, in a clamorous and visible way. It is truly remarkable that the people behave as if they have seen or heard nothing, except the spectacle and the ordinary noises of the disorder of war and politics.'[25]

In part 21 of the deeply moving BBC serial about the Second World War, 'The World at War', Hitler's valet Heinz Linge was interviewed about the last days in the bunker in Berlin. He tells how the Fuehrer, before comitting suicide together with his wife Eva Braun, said good-bye to all those present. They had lined up for a last salute or handshake and Linge stood at the end of the line. After Hitler had told him that the last units of the German Army should break through the Russian lines in groups to try and reach the Western Allies, and that the personnel in the bunker should join one of such groups, Linge asked him, '*Mein Fuehrer*, for whom then shall we fight henceforward?' Hitler's answer (and these were his very last words), '*Fuer den kommenden Mann*' for the coming man. These words are only understandable in the light of the view explained in this chapter.

The Springing Tigers

Alas, discernment was lacking among the Ashramites too — not in all, but in many. As we know, a number of Sri Aurobindo's disciples had been ready to sacrifice their life for the liberation of India. These had remained very anti-British, and reasoning that the enemies of their enemies were their friends, they were pro-Hitler and sympathetic to everybody on his side. This was dangerous, for these 'misguided patriots' formed unwittingly a channel, an instrument by means of which the *Asura* could directly hit out at the heart of his true target. 'If this Asuric influence acting through Hitler is being cast on the Ashram too, it is dangerous,'[26] Sri Aurobindo cautioned. 'The Asura is more concerned with us than with anything else. He is inventing new situations so that we may fall into difficulty.'[27]

Another, younger sort of pro-Hitlerian Ashramites were the supporters of Subhash Chandra Bose, the Indian 'Führer' — which is the literal meaning of 'Netaji' as he was and is still called in India.

Subhash Chandra Bose, though born in the old Oriya town of Cuttack, was a Bengali. He had also, like Sri Aurobindo some thirty years earlier, studied at Cambridge University for the Indian Civil Service, but he had submitted his resignation before being enlisted. His mentor was Chittaranjan Das, the barrister who had defended Sri Aurobindo in the Alipore Bomb Affair. By now, C.R. Das himself had become a nationalistic politician of prominence. He was called 'Deshbandhu', Friend of the Nation, and had become, at the time Bose put himself under his aegis, the vice-chancellor of the National College in Calcutta which had opened its doors under the rectorate of Sri Aurobindo.

Against this background, somewhat familiar to us, the gifted and ambitious Bose quickly rose to the top. He became mayor of

Calcutta, and in 1927 general secretary of the Congress jointly with Jawaharlal Nehru. He was more than once put behind bars because of anti-British agitation; all the same, he obtained in 1937 from the British authorities permission to travel to Europe for medical treatment. There he became fascinated by the Fascist dictators, whom he met personally. (It was he, very probably, who gave books by Sri Aurobindo to Mussolini to read.) The aspiration of becoming a dictator himself grew in him. In 1938 he was elected national president of the Congress. His opinions, however, did no longer concur with the 'ahimsa' of that other authoritarian man, Mohandas K. Gandhi, and Bose founded, within the Congress, his Forward Block.

In 1941 he escaped the watchful eye of the British. He reached Germany after an adventurous journey via Peshawar, Kabul, Bokhara and Moscow. In Germany, he founded the Indian Legion, mainly with Indian prisoners of war who had fought in the British ranks. He chose as their flag the Indian tricolour — horizontal orange-white-green — with a springing tiger in the middle. This is how they became known as 'the Springing Tigers.' But Germany was very, very far from India and Hitler did not show any intention of marching towards it in order to satisfy Netaji's desires or demands.

However, marching on India were Hitler's allies, the Japanese. Bose therefore decided to try from the East what was denied him in the West. A German U-boat took him from Kiel to the south of Madagascar, where he transshipped at sea to a Japanese submarine. He reached Tokyo after a journey of eighteen weeks. The Japanese considered him potentially useful and gave him some of the assistance he asked for. He founded the Indian National Army, this time not only with Indian prisoners of war but also with Indian expatriates living in South-Asia. He also formed a Provisional Government of Free India with himself as head of state, prime minister and minister of war and foreign affairs. One of his biographers, Hugh Toye, writes: 'Everywhere Bose met adulation, near adoration, devotion which moved him so that sometimes, simply in answer to the popular mood, he would make claims and promises which his most sanguine admirers deplored. But his audience cheered the more. He toured the prisoner-of-war camps and won two thousand volunteers, he spoke to Indian meetings everywhere, he conferred constantly with the Japanese. In August he was at the Burmese Independence celebrations in Rangoon. There followed visits to Bangkok and Saigon. There were more speeches, interviews without number and long meetings with Japanese commanders and government officials.'[28]

On 19 March 1944, a Japanese army of 230,000 men crossed the Indian border. It was the beginning of the campaign spearheaded at Imphal, a small town in North-East India. Three thousand soldiers of Bose's Indian Army took part in it. That Imphal would fall, in spite of the dogged resistance by the British and the Indian troops loyal to the British Crown, was 'a foregone conclusion.' But the monsoon rains came suddenly, totally unexpected because it was more than a month early, and 'the Japanese chances of success were washed away.' It became, writes Hugh Toye, 'a military catastrophe of the first magnitude.'[29]

The Japanese, no more than the Germans, had never intended relinquishing any power over India to somebody else — supposing the country did fall into their hands — not even to the naïve Netaji. They had nothing but contempt for the Indian troops, who in their eyes were deserters and betrayers of their motherland. S.C. Bose died on 18 March 1944 on the island of Formosa (the present Taiwan) where, *en route* to Tokyo, he had been mortally wounded and burned in an airplane crash. In India, which shortly afterwards became independent without him, rumours kept circulating for a long time afterwards that he was wandering through the country as an anonymous monk. He is revered as a national hero, and in documentary films one still can see him smile, basking in the company of Hitler, von Ribbentrop or Tojo Hideki, without any of the viewers taking umbrage.

Hugh Toye says that Subhash Chandra Bose had only three friends in his life: his brother Sarat in the early years; Emilie Schenkl, a German girl who at first was his secretary, whom he later married, and who was left behind with their baby daughter in Vienna; and Dilip Kumar Roy, known to us and who brings us back again on the path of our story.

In 1933, Bose 'begged his friend Dilip Kumar Roy to leave his yogic cell because he needed someone he could trust' to present India to the world. That 'yogic cell' should be taken with a substantial grain of salt, for the Mother had put a full floor in a former colonial house at Roy's disposition and he lived there like a prince, in the midst of a circle of friends and admirers, with daily visits at tea-time and musical evenings starring himself and others. Roy, from his end, sometimes tried to convert Bose to Sri Aurobindo's yoga — something for which Sri Aurobindo showed little enthusiasm, as we read repeatedly in his correspondence with Nirodbaran. As a rule, 'great' men and women are but seldom detached, supple and receptive characters, and however great they may seem to the eye of the outside world, they might be the last to take up a life of yogic surrender and self-abnegation.

The Ashram in Difficulty

Everything we have seen corroborates the supposition that in the Ashram not only a pro-Hitler group of idealistic freedom fighters but also a pro-Hitler group of Bose-sympathizers must have been present — although Dilip Kumar Roy himself, enlightened by Sri Aurobindo, seems to have sided with the Allies. The former freedom fighters and the Bose-sympathizers together formed a considerable part of the Ashram population and the situation became very tense, more particularly after the shooting war started and Germany invaded the Low Countries. In *Talks With Sri Aurobindo* Nirodbaran says on 11 May 1940: 'In the Ashram the feelings are divided. Some are for the British and some for Hitler.' Sri Aurobindo asks: 'For Hitler?' Satyendra answers: 'Not exactly, but they are anti-British.' Sri Aurobindo's reply: 'Not a rational feeling. How can India, who wants freedom, take sides with somebody who takes away freedom from other nations?'

On 17 May, Sri Aurobindo himself starts the conversation: 'It seems it is not five or six of our people but more than half who are in sympathy with Hitler and want him to win.' Purani (laughing): 'Half?' Sri Aurobindo: 'No, it is not a matter to laugh at. It is a very serious matter. The [French] Government can dissolve the Ashram at any moment. In Indo-China all religious bodies have been dissolved. And here the whole of Pondicherry is against us. Only because Governor Bonvin is friendly towards us they can't do anything. But even he — if he hears that the people in the Ashram are pro-Hitler — will be compelled to take steps and at least expel those who are so. If these people want that the Ashram should be dissolved, they can come and tell me and I will dissolve it instead of the police doing it. They have no idea about the world and talk like little children. Hitler is the greatest menace the world has ever met. If Hitler wins, do they think that India has any chance of being free? It is a well-known fact that Hitler has an eye on India. He is openly talking of world-empire. He will turn towards the Balkans, crushing Italy on the way, which would be a matter of weeks, then Turkey and then Asia Minor. Asia Minor means ultimately India. If there he meets Stalin, then it is a question as to who wins and comes to India.'

Nirodbaran mentions in a note that in the morning of that same day, the Mother had said to Nolini: 'It is treachery against Sri Aurobindo to wish for Hitler's victory. Sri Aurobindo's cause is closely connected with that of the Allies and he is working night and day for it. It is because my nationality is French that the Ashram is allowed to exist. Otherwise it would have been dissolved long ago.'[30]

On 23 May, Sri Aurobindo said to Purani: 'The Ashram has been declared a nest of pro-Nazis and pro-Communists by your friend the Consul. He says he can even produce documents ... The movement against the Ashram is growing ... The danger is not only to the Allies but to us also.'[31]

On 19 September 1940, Sri Aurobindo and the Mother made a public stand in favour of the Allies by contributing, via the British Governor of Madras, one thousand rupees to the war fund of the Viceroy. In the accompanying letter, Sri Aurobindo wrote: 'We feel that not only is this a battle waged in just self-defence and in defence of the Nations threatened with the world-domination of Germany and the Nazi system of life, but that it is a defence of civilisation and its highest attained social, cultural and spiritual values and of the whole future of humanity.'[32]

Even in 1942 it was still necessary for Sri Aurobindo to explicitly formulate his standpoint in a letter to a disciple: 'You have said that you have begun to doubt whether it was the Mother's war and ask me to make you feel again that it is. I affirm again most strongly that this is the Mother's war. You should not think of it as a fight for certain nations against others or even for India; it is a struggle for an ideal that has to establish itself on earth in the life of humanity, for a Truth that has yet to realise itself fully and against a darkness and falsehood that are trying to overwhelm the earth and mankind in the immediate future. It is the forces behind the battle that have to be seen and not this or that superficial circumstance ... It is a struggle for the liberty of mankind to develop, for conditions in which men have freedom and room to think and act according to the light in them and grow in the Truth, grow in the Spirit. There cannot be the slightest doubt that if one side wins, there will be an end of all such freedom and hope of light and truth and the work that has to be done will be subjected to conditions which would make it humanly impossible; there will be a reign of falsehood and darkness, a cruel oppression and degradation for most of the human race such as people in this country do not dream of and cannot yet realise. If the other side that has declared itself for the free future of humanity triumphs, this terrible danger will have been averted and conditions will have been created in which there will be a chance for the Ideal to grow, for the Divine Work to be done, for the spiritual Truth for which we stand to establish itself on the earth. Those who fight for this cause are fighting for the Divine and against the threatened reign of the Asura.'[33]

Many have felt all this throughout the war, especially those whose lives were at stake, but few have understood or been able to formulate it intellectually, and almost all have forgotten about it by now. However, this was what the Second World War was all about and this is the cause of the hypnotic power it still exerts, even though for most people it is the hypnotic power of Evil.

Target India

The aim of the *Asura* consisted in counteracting the Work of Sri Aurobindo and the Mother; such was his nature and he fought for his survival. All the same, did Hitler (and Stalin) really intend to push through towards India, or was this a patriotic exaggeration of Sri Aurobindo's?

This ultimate target of the Lord of the Nations must surely have been present in the vision of his main human instruments. John Toland writes: 'On February 17 [1941] Hitler ordered the preparation of a drive to the heart of Britain's empire, India. This would be accompanied,' just as foretold by Sri Aurobindo, 'by seizure of the Near East in a pincer movement: on the left from Russia across Iran and on the right from North Africa toward the Suez Canal. While these grandiose plans were primarily designed to force Britain onto the side of Germany, they indicated the extent of Hitler's vaulting aspirations.'[34] The same author tells also how von Ribbentrop persistently tried to talk the Japanese into a massive attack on India. 'The Wehrmacht [the German armies],' he said, 'was about to invade the Caucasus and once that oil region was seized the road to Persia would be open. Then the Germans and Japanese could catch all the British Far East forces [including those in India] in a giant pincer movement.'[35] More and more people who knew Hitler from close by became convinced that the man had become insane; Toland quotes among others the opinion of Dr. Ferdinand Sauerbruch, who 'told friends that during a recent visit to the Führer he had heard an old and broken Hitler muttering such disjointed phrases as, "I must go to India." '[36] An obsession, yes — but disjointed?

A newspaper report from Moscow under the headline 'Hitler planned conquest of India, documents reveal' and dated 21 June 1986, was published the next day in the *Indian Express*. According to the documents on which this report is based, Germany, Italy and Japan had signed an agreement, in January 1942, on the division of the spheres. Hitler counted on a quick defeat of Russia to invade, in the spring of the same year, West Asia, which would then serve as a springboard for reaching India. But he had had to postpone his plans because of his defeat before Moscow and the unexpectedly strong resistance of the Russians. Nonetheless, he never left India definitively to the Japanese.

Another report from the Press Trust of India in the same newspaper and dated 22 April 1989 has the headline: 'Hitler had plans to invade India'. It reads as follows: 'Hitler saw India as part of his huge Nazi empire to be formed after Germany attained world domination, states a monograph by Soviet professor Carlo Tskitishvrili.

Called the "Rout of the Brown Monster", the monograph reveals some startling facts about the German command's plans to conquer West Asia and India, reports the Soviet news agency APN. Hitler signed Directive No. 41 which named a "breakthrough to the Caucasus" as one of the principal tasks in the war on April 5, 1942. The Hitlerite general staff saw the Caucasus and Transcaucasia as a support base for a subsequent invasion of West Asia and India, the monograph stated ... On April 7, 1941, a draft plan was drawn up by the German command for raising a 43-division group of land forces to operate in the tropics including India.'

All data point in the same direction and at the same target. Already in May 1940, Sri Aurobindo had said: 'It is a very simple thing to see that Hitler wants world domination and his next move will be towards India.'[37] He forewarned: 'Hitler doesn't bluff. He has done everything he has said, but at the time it suited him.'[38] When comparing the data concerning this subject, one finds that Sri Aurobindo's foresight about Hitler's ultimate intentions dated from a year before the historically documented facts.

A Suitable Person

In the prologue to this book, we have narrated Hitler's inexplicable and fatal hesitation at the time his tank divisions, in the beginning of the war, had been able to take prisoners or destroy the whole British Expeditionary Force at Dunkirk. We remember that Sri Aurobindo wrote of himself in the third person: 'Inwardly, he put his spiritual force behind the Allies from the moment of Dunkirk when everybody was expecting the immediate fall of England and the definite triumph of Hitler, and he had the satisfaction of seeing the rush of German victory almost immediately arrested and the tide of war begin to turn in the opposite direction.'

But the danger was far from averted. If Hitler had gone on with the invasion of Great Britain immediately after the surrender of France, nothing could have thwarted him anymore, according to Sri Aurobindo. 'Hitler had his chance after the fall of France. If he had at once attacked then, it would have been difficult for England to resist. Hitler really missed the bus.' '[The British] were saved by Divine Intervention during this War. They would have been smashed if Hitler had invaded England at the right time, after the fall of France.'[39] All the same, in October 1940 he still gave Hitler a fifty per cent chance of succeeding. 'It is only the British Navy that stands against Hitler's world domination ... He is practically master of Europe.'[40] 'Now only Hitler's death can save the situation ... I want him to be eliminated ... I don't care about the date. If he dies it is enough.'[41]

Sri Aurobindo and the Mother followed the war very closely, not only in the newspapers but also on the radio. At first, Pavitra and Pavita (the former secretary of the writer Paul Brunton) went every evening to the house of Udar Pinto who had a radio. Pavita noted down the news bulletin in shorthand, wrote it out in longhand at home and sent it to Sri Aurobindo's apartment. When this was no longer possible because Udar had to be absent for some time, the radio was installed in Pavitra's room and later on connected with a loudspeaker in Sri Aurobindo's apartment, allowing the latter to hear the news directly for himself.

The White Force, just like the Black Force, needs its human instruments to intervene actively in the affairs of the world. The *Asura* had his; Sri Aurobindo and the Mother were searching for theirs. Strong personalities were hardly available among the leaders of the Allies, as appears from their hesitant diplomatic manoeuvering before the outbreak of the hostilities. Politicians of the kind of Daladier and Chamberlain were no match for Hitler and Stalin. Their gullible, spineless and watered-down democratic idealism time and again lost out against the inspired, unscrupulous and daring cunning of their opponents. Sri Aurobindo at first thought he had found 'the man of destiny' in Hore-Belisha, the British Secretary of War from 1937 to 1940 who, in the spring of 1939, had introduced general conscription in Great Britain. But then Winston Chuchill rose to his true stature.

There is evidence that Winston Churchill has been directly inspired by Sri Aurobindo and the Mother. When A.B. Purani spoke with praise about Churchill's famous speech in which he had nothing to offer the British people but 'blood, hard work, tears and sweat,' Sri Aurobindo answered laconically: 'Yes, he was inspired,' surely not meaning some vague poetical inspiration. Maggi Lidchi-Grassi, who had free access to the Mother, writes in *The Light that Shone in the Deep Abyss*: 'The Mother told the author how Sri Aurobindo used to tell her of the words that he would put into the mouth of Churchill before the famous broadcasts, and certain passages were spoken by Churchill word for word* ... His secretary Nirodbaran had heard of this, and Dyumanbhai, at present managing trustee of the Ashram [1992], has confirmed it. He told me that certain passages in Churchill's speeches often were repetitions of words already spoken in Pondicherry. Anuben Purani tells me that her father A.B. Purani, one of the few people who saw Sri Aurobindo every day, told her the same thing.'[42]

Churchill himself declared openly in the British Lower House on 13 October 1942: 'I sometimes have a feeling — in fact I feel it very strongly — a feeling of interference. I want to stress that I have a feeling sometimes that some guiding hand has interfered. I have the feeling that we have a guardian because we serve a great cause, and that we shall have that guardian so long as we serve that cause faithfully.'[43] In January 1941, he had already pronounced: 'I have absolutely no doubt that we shall win a complete and decisive victory over the forces of evil, and that victory itself will be only a stimulus to further efforts to conquer ourselves.'[44] Unusual words from a politician, but he could not have put it better.

There is no doubt that Sri Aurobindo and the Mother have constantly intervened in the war events with their spiritual force. We already know about the 'miraculous' escape of the British Expeditionary Force at Dunkirk. Hitler had promised that a couple of months later, more exactly on 15 August 1940, he would address the world from Buckingham Palace. August 15 is the anniversary of Sri Aurobindo and Hitler's choice was probably not coincidental. ('I have not seen any other person who has followed, with such

---

* A typical Aurobindonian passage from the same 'blood and tears' speech: '... For without victory, there is no survival. Let that be realised; no survival for the British Empire, no survival for all that the British Empire has stood for, *no survival for the urge and impulse of the ages, that mankind will move forward towards its goal.*'

242 • *Beyond Man*

extraordinary fidelity, the Asura,'[45] said Sri Aurobindo.) But in the Battle of Britain on that day forty-four Germans airplanes were shot down, the highest number in one day so far.

A particularly interesting example of the intervention of Sri Aurobindo and the Mother in the war is Operation Barbarossa — the codename of Hitler's campaign against the USSR. Ideologically, Hitler could not but turn against communist Russia if he did not want to go against the grain of everything he had written and proclaimed very loudly. The Slavs to him were an inferior race, not much better than animals, and only fit to be led by the superior master race; they were governed by a scandalous Jewish regime; and the land inhabited by that race of *Untermenschen* (underlings) was needed by the German *Herrenvolk* for its *Lebensraum*. The Non-aggression Pact of 1939, cynically calculated, was signed by both parties for no other reason than to gain as much time as possible and meanwhile improve their respective positions.

In fact, Stalin was even more evil than Hitler. Hitler was human after all, and he therefore had a soul, albeit one possessed by an *Asura*; Stalin was a direct incarnation of a malevolent vital force — literally a titanic, power-hungry being without conscience or soul, whose deeds of monumental cruelty are written in history with letters of blood. 'There are some rare individuals who are born without a psychic being and who are exceptionally villainous,' said the Mother. And K.D. Sethna writes: 'In Stalin Sri Aurobindo and the Mother discerned a phenomenon not merely of possession but of incarnation, a vital being born in a human form and not just employing that form as its medium.'[46] Sri Aurobindo saw Stalin as a greater danger than Hitler.

'On the face of it, Stalin and Hitler were most unlikely allies. What could they possibly have in common?' asks John Toland. He gives the answer himself: 'In fact, there were a number of similarities. One admired Peter the Great while the other saw himself as the heir of Frederick the Great. Both were advocates of ruthless force and operated under ideologies that were not essentially different. Communists and Nazis alike were self-righteous and dogmatic; both were totalitarian and both believed that the end justified the means, sanctifying injustice, as it were, in the name of state and progress.'[47]

Already in March 1940, Sri Aurobindo declared: 'There is no chance for the world unless something happens in Germany or else Hitler and Stalin quarrel.' But the asuric protection of Hitler was so strong that it prevented or foiled all attempts on Hitler's life. (There have been more attempts than is usually remembered nowadays.) Then the Mother intervened personally.

She has narrated that intervention several times. The following is the version of 5 November 1961 from the *Agenda*: 'It was the Lord of the Nations, the being that appeared to Hitler ... And I knew when they were going to have their next meeting (for, after all, he is my son, that's what was so comical!). So, for once I took his place and became Hitler's god, and I advised him to attack Russia. Two days afterwards, he attacked Russia. But on leaving the meeting, I met the other one [the *Asura*] who came to his appointment! He was rather furious. He asked me why I had done such a thing. I answered: "That is none of your business — because it had to be done." Then he replied: "Wait and see. I know — I know! — that you will destroy me, but before being destroyed, I will cause as much damage as possible, you may be sure of it." Then I came back from my nocturnal outings and told everything to Sri Aurobindo. That kind of life! ... People do not know what is going on. They know nothing. Nothing.'[48]

Hitler had told field marshal von Brauchitsch as early as July 1940 that they 'should start thinking of the Russians'. It was in that summer that Hitler decided 'that the time had come for Lebensraum and the destruction of Bolshevism. He instructed the army to make preparations in this direction ... A surprise attack was to be launched on the Soviet Union as soon as possible — May 1941.'[49] The staff-officers whom General Jodl informed of Hitler's decision could not believe their ears. Germany was still fully involved in the war against England and... this was the two-front war which had defeated Germany in the First World War! 'Jodl cut short the debate with the words: "Gentlemen, it is not a question for discussion but a decision of the Führer." '[50]

The initial resistance of those experienced officers against Hitler's senseless decision must have been spontaneous and forceful. Nevertheless, this was not the moment the Mother took the place of the Lord of the Nations, for in an earlier version of her intervention she says that Hitler attacked Russia 'two days later,' [51] and in another version: 'Two days later we got the news of the attack.'[52] Her 'divine' intervention, most probably on 20 June 1941, must have tipped the scales for Hitler to issue the irrevocable order to launch Operation Barbarossa against all reasonable arguments and the advice of his planning staff. We find an argument in favour of this supposition in Hitler's *Tischgespräche* (table talk), secretly noted down by Heinrich Heim and Werner Köppen. In these talks, 'Hitler expounded on the spirit of decision, which consisted, he said, "in not hesitating when an inner conviction commands you." ' And he gave an example: 'The tremendous military operation now in progress, he said, had been widely criticized as impracticable. "I had to throw all my authority into the scales to force it through. I note in passing that a great part of our successes has originated in 'mistakes' we've had the audacity to commit." '[53] This time, however, the inspiration of the audacious 'mistake' came from another source than the usual. The German troops saw Moscow only from afar; Stalingrad became a German mass grave (*Stalingrad Massengrab*); against 'General Winter' no senseless audacity would do; and the two-front war caused once more the defeat of Germany.

Sri Aurobindo and the Mother have intervened in countless big and small events during the war, some known but most of them unknown. For instance, it was not the courageously fighting but vanquished British-Indian Army which inflicted on the Japanese their first 'military catastrophe of the first magnitude' in North-East India, but the completely unexpected, very premature and extraordinarily heavy monsoon rains, as we have seen in the life sketch of S.C. Bose — just like the British Expeditionary Force was saved from Goering's bombers by meteorologically unexplainable fog. Another instance: the only parts of Stalingrad still in Russian hands were three small enclaves on the bank of the Volga, but twenty-four German generals could not take them...

In 1914, the Mother had prevented the occupation of Paris, the metropolis said by Sri Aurobindo to be the symbol of Western civilization — representing everything this civilization had gained since the Renaissance in individual freedom and possibilities of progress for mankind, thereby opening the gates of the future. When in 1940 the Germans entered the city, Sri Aurobindo feared for a while that they, under the inspiration of the *Asura*, would level it to the ground. 'Paris has been the centre of human civilisation for three centuries. Now he [Hitler] will destroy it. That is the sign of the Asura ... Destruction of Paris means the destruction of modern European civilisation.'[54] How many know that, at that moment, Paris was saved for the second time by the Mother and protected by her throughout the war? 'From time to time there were people who were a little conscious, like when I spent all my nights of the last war over Paris so that nothing should happen — not integrally, but a part of me. I floated in the air ... Later on, it has become known that some people had seen something: there had been a great white Force, as it were, indeterminate as to its form, hovering over Paris to prevent the city from being destroyed.'[55]

Even that did not dispel the threat by the *Asura*. For it is especially in defeat that he gives free rein to his nature of unconditional egoism, raging fury and the orgiastic pleasure of destruction. The order of the OKW, the German headquarters, is printed with all references in the best-seller by Larry Collins and Dominique Lapierre *Is Paris Burning?*: 'Paris must not fall into the hands of the enemy, or, if it does he must find there nothing but a field of ruins.' And the authors write that the day of the liberation of the city 'every Parisian looking out of his window on that night could gaze at one of the wonders of the war: Paris was unharmed. The Notre-Dame, the Sainte-Chapelle, the Louvre, the Sacré-Coeur, the Arc de Triomphe, all those peerless monuments which had made the city into a beacon of civilized man, had up to that day stood undamaged through five years of the most destructive war in history.'

On 15 August 1945, the Japanese emperor Hirohito, for the first time in history addressing the nation directly, broadcast a message declaring the unconditional capitulation of his country, thus bringing the Second World War to an end. The reader will remember that 15 August is the birthday of Sri Aurobindo – the day on which in 1940 Hitler intended to speak to the world from Buckingham Palace and on which India will become independent in 1947.

Chapter Seventeen

THE FIVE 'DREAMS' OF SRI AUROBINDO

It is not for personal greatness that I am seeking to bring down the Supermind. I care nothing for greatness or littleness in the human sense ... If human reason regards me as a fool for trying to do what Krishna did not try, I do not in the least care ... It is a question between the Divine and myself — whether it is the Divine Will or not, whether I am sent to bring that down or open the way for its descent or at least make it more possible or not. Let all men jeer at me if they will or all Hell fall upon me if it will for my presumption, — I go on till I conquer or perish.[1]

— Sri Aurobindo

INDIA BECAME free and independent on 15 August 1947 without a shot having been fired. On that occasion All India Radio, station Trichinopoly, asked Sri Aurobindo — he who had inculcated the idea of an absolute and unconditional independence upon the minds and the hearts of the Indian people — for a message. Sri Aurobindo rarely complied with such requests, but this time he wrote one of the most important documents in his life. His text, read by a news reader, was broadcast on 14 August.

'August 15th, 1947 is the birthday of free India. It marks for her the end of an old era, the beginning of a new age. But we can also make it by our life and acts as a free nation an important date in the new age opening for the whole world, for the political, social and spiritual future of humanity.

'August 15th is my own birthday and it is naturally gratifying to me that it should have assumed this vast significance. I take this coincidence not as a fortuitous accident, but as the sanction and seal of the Divine Force that guides my steps in the work with which I began life, as the beginning of its full fruition. Indeed, on this day I can watch almost all the world-movements which I hoped to see fulfilled in my lifetime, though then they looked like impracticable dreams, arriving at fruition or on their way to achievement.'[2] Sri Aurobindo then sums up those five 'dreams' one after the other. Let us have a closer look at them.

1. India

'The first of these dreams was a revolutionary movement which would create a free and united India. India today is free but she has not achieved unity.'

To Sri Aurobindo and the Mother, India was not a mass of land but a being, a goddess, 'just like Shiva is a god', called *Bharat Mata*, Mother India. The visible land mass is the material body of this very real being, venerated as the soul of the nation. In the same way other nations too have at their centre a living Being always striving for their integrality, their natural completeness and perfection; it is this Being that inspires the 'cells' of its body, i.e., the beings born from its substance, to the passionate love and defence of their motherland called patriotism. It is indispensable for the realization of the goal of terrestrial evolution that every true nation acquires its material completeness at a culminating point in history. Whatever may be the external, political motives, this is the true impetus of most historical emotion and commotion.

In the view of Sri Aurobindo and the Mother, India occupied a special place in the world. This country has always been the cradle of the most important spiritual discoveries and the highest spiritual realizations, which have spread out in the world from there. It is also the place where the essential gains of humanity were made imperishable and can therefore be integrated in its future evolution to make them into its foundations. Sri Aurobindo wrote: '[India is] a country apart in which as in a fortress the highest spiritual ideal could maintain itself in its most absolute purity.'[3] 'India is the Guru of the world. The future structure of the world depends on India,'[4] wrote the Mother, and also: 'India must be saved for the good of the world since India alone can lead the world to peace and a new world order.'[5] Statements of this kind — and there are many more — will strike some as exaggerated, to put it mildly. But one should not forget that Sri Aurobindo and the Mother advocated a 'spiritual realism' and that they never spoke out of emotional idealism. They based themselves on what they experienced and perceived with their highly evolved inner faculties. The fact that some of their followers have published one-sided selections from their talks and writings about India — as about other subjects — cannot be blamed on them. Sri Aurobindo has more than once castigated the 'cherished torpor and weakness' in his country[6] and its omnipresent *tamas,* i.e., the inertia, the corporeal and mental immovability, lack of effort, etc. So did the Mother too, and she said that, had she been born in India, she would have shattered all its calcified and no longer meaningful habits and traditions, but that, being a French subject, she had to watch her step. A couple of representative quotations in this context may suffice.

K.D. Sethna wrote somewhere in 1978: 'Two generations ago Tagore said that although India was lying in the dust, the very dust in which she lay was holy. Obviously it was in his mind that this dust had been trod by the feet of Rishis and Saints and Avatars. Sri Aurobindo's comment is reported to have been that whatever might be the case the dust could not be the proper thing for a man to lie in and that man had not been created to adopt a prone posture.'[7]

A.B. Purani has noted down Sri Aurobindo's words in one of the evening talks of 1926: 'Present-day Indians have got nothing to boast of from their past. Indian culture today is in the most abject condition, like the fort of Gingee — one pillar standing here, and another ceiling there and some hall out of recognition somewhere else.'[8]

Sri Aurobindo wrote in the *Arya*: 'If an ancient Indian of the time of the Upanishads, of the Buddha or of the later classical age were to be set down in modern India and note that larger part of its life which belongs to the age of decline, it would be to experience a much more depressing sensation, the sense of a national, a cultural debacle, a fall from the highest summits to discouragingly low levels. He might well ask himself what this degenerate posterity had done with the mighty civilisation of the past ... He would compare the spiritual light and energy of the heroic ages of the Upanishads and the philosophies with the later inertia or small and broken fragmentarily derivative activity; after the intellectual curiosity, the scientific development, the creative literary and artistic greatness, the noble fecundity of the classical age, he would be amazed by the extent of later degeneracy, the mental poverty, the immobility, the static repetition, the cessation of science, the long sterility of art, the comparative feebleness of the creative intuition. He would see a prone descent to ignorance, a failing of the old powerful will and tapasya [disciplined effort], almost a volitional impotence.' (*Arya*, vol. V, pp. 423-24)

No, it would not be very difficult to compile from the available literature a selection of texts in which Sri Aurobindo and the Mother draw the attention to the depth of India's fall in modern times, when compared to its past spiritual and cultural heights, still for the most part unknown in the West. (They blame the degeneration on the general spreading of the illusionism of the Buddha and Mahavir during a period of several centuries.) But this detracts nothing from the essential importance of the presence of India in the world, of the message it has to share with humanity, and of the future role it will play on the unified Earth. 'The future of India is luminous in spite of its present gloom,'[9] wrote the Mother. And Sri Aurobindo said as early as 1926: 'I am sure that India is not destined to be destroyed.'[10] He has repeated this as late as in 1950 in a conversation with K.M. Munshi, the last visitor of note before his passing away: 'Rest assured that our culture cannot be undermined. This is only a passing phase.'[11]

We have seen how the ardent nationalist Aurobindo Ghose worked for the freedom of Mother India with a total dedication, the effectiveness of which was multiplied after the acquisition of his spiritual powers as Sri Aurobindo. A.B. Purani, himself a courageous freedom fighter, relates in his *Evening Talks* how he went to see Sri Aurobindo in Pondicherry for the first time in 1918, and how he at that time confided to Sri Aurobindo that the concentration of his whole being was directed at India's liberation. 'It is difficult for me to sleep till that is secured,' Purani said. 'Sri Aurobindo remained silent for two or three minutes. It was a long pause. Then he said: "Suppose an assurance is given to you that India will be free?" "Who can give me such an assurance?" I could feel the echo of doubt and challenge in my own question. Again he remained silent for three or four minutes. Then he looked at me and added: "Suppose I give you the assurance?" I paused for a moment, considered the question with myself and said: "If you give the assurance, I can accept it." "Then I give you the assurance that India will be free," he said in a serious tone.'[12] How could Sri Aurobindo in 1918 be certain that India would be free somewhere in the future and express that certainty, knowing full well that his words would give a new direction to the life of Purani, who would turn away from his involvement in the freedom struggle and become a member of the Ashram?

Once again, the Mother lets us have a look in the occult repository. In the *Entretiens* of 1956, she tells: 'After having gone to a certain place, I said to Sri Aurobindo: "India is free." I did not say: "India *will be* free", I said: "India *is* free." Now, how many years has it taken between that moment, when that was an accomplished fact, and the moment it became translated in the material world on earth? [The occult experience] took place in 1915 and the liberation in 1947 — thirty-two years.' In this case it took thirty-two years for an occult *fact* in a subtle world to become material reality on Earth. Next, Sri Aurobindo asked her *how* the liberation would be accomplished, and the Mother answered 'from the same place': 'There will be no violence. It will come about without a revolution. The British will decide to leave of their own accord because the place will have become untenable as a consequence of certain terrestrial circumstances.' And she said to her audience, the Ashram youth: 'I did neither guess nor prophesy: it was a fact.'[13] A fact that in all particulars has come about exactly like she had seen it that many years earlier on another plane of reality.

In this way they have undoubtedly known a lot of historical events in advance. Concerning the same topic and corroborating for that matter the assurance given to Purani, there is also a passage in Nirodbaran's correspondence bearing witness to the same knowledge. On 16 September 1935, Nirodbaran writes to Sri Aurobindo: 'You have stated that for the spreading of spirituality in the world India must be free. I suppose you must be working for it.' And Sri Aurobindo answers: 'That is all settled. It is a question of working out only. The question is what is India going to do with her independence? ... Things look ominous.'[14]

In his message for the day of India's independence, Sri Aurobindo wrote about the division of the body of Mother India into India and Pakistan: 'The old communal division into Hindus and Muslims seems now to have hardened into a permanent political division of the country. It is to be hoped that this settled fact will not be accepted for ever or as anything more than a temporary expedient. For if it lasts, India may be seriously weakened, even crippled; civil strife may remain always possible, possible even a new invasion and foreign conquest. India's internal development and prosperity may be impeded, her position among the nations weakened, her destiny impaired or even frustrated. This must not be; the partition must go. Let us hope that that may come about naturally ... But by whatever means, in whatever way, the division must go; unity must and will be achieved, for it is necessary for the greatness of India's future.'[15]

If the leaders of the Congress had listened to Sri Aurobindo in 1942, the division of India would most probably never have happened. In March of that year, Sir Stafford Cripps, the British Lord Privy Seal and as such a member of Churchill's war cabinet, came to India to offer the country 'dominion status' in what is known as the Cripps-offer. This meant 'the creation of a new Indian union which shall constitute a dominion, associated with the United Kingdom and other dominions by a common allegiance to the Crown, but equal to them in every respect, and in no way subordinate in any aspect of its domestic or external affairs, and free to remain in or to separate itself from the equal partnership of the British Commonwealth of nations.'[16] This was a huge concession as well from Churchill as from the British Crown and should have led to the full independence of the country within a foreseeable time. The British, involved in a war of life and death with Hitler and the nations supporting him, needed the wholehearted assistance of the Indian subcontinent urgently, notwithstanding the fact that already a million Indian troops were fighting on the side of the Allies and that each month 50,000 more were enlisting. (It was from the prisoners of war that S.C. Bose recruited the volunteers for the Springing Tigers and the Indian National Army.)

Sri Aurobindo perceived that India should not let go of the one-time chance of the Cripps-offer; if it did so, the consequences might be disastrous. He sent Doraiswamy, a prominent Madras lawyer who was also a devotee, to Delhi with a message for M.K. Gandhi, Nehru, Rajagopalachari and the other members of the Congress leadership. 'The scene is still fresh in our memory,' remembers Nirodbaran. 'It was the evening hour. Sri Aurobindo was sitting on the edge of his bed just before his daily walking exercise ... Doraiswamy, the distinguished Madras lawyer and disciple, was selected as the envoy ... He was to start for Delhi that very night. He came for Sri Aurobindo's blessings, lay prostrate before him, got up and stood looking at the Master with folded hands and then departed.'[17] Sri Aurobindo also sent a message to Stafford Cripps personally: 'I have heard your broadcast. As one who has been a nationalist leader and worker for India's independence, though now my activity is no longer in the political but in the spiritual field, I wish to express my appreciation of all you have done to bring about this offer. I welcome it as an opportunity given to India to determine for herself, and organise in all liberty and choice her freedom and unity, and take an effective place among the world's free nations. I hope it will be accepted ...

In this light, I offer my public adhesion, in case it can be of any help in your work.'[18]

Sri Aurobindo's intervention with the leaders of the Congress would be of no avail. They had never understood and perhaps never forgiven his withdrawal from political life. He said that he had known of the failure beforehand and that he had acted only in a spirit of *nishkama karma* — the disinterested or desireless action which is the basis of the authentic *karmayoga*. But historical events, like everything else in the universe, are always complex. In a well-documented article about the Cripps-offer by Divakar and Sucharu in *Mother India*, from which some material is borrowed here, we read: 'It was generally believed that if Cripps brought off the settlement, he would replace Churchill.'[19] We know, however, that Churchill was an irreplaceable instrument of Sri Aurobindo and the Mother — while, on the other hand, India's independence was a matter of great urgency, as well in the then prevailing world situation as for India's future unity. Sri Aurobindo has stressed several times that he did not use the omnipotent supramental force for his work, for the simple reason that the world would not be able to stand it. He said he used the overmental force — which allows a struggle of the cosmic ideas and powers, each pursuing its own expression in the highest possible degree. The events concerning the Cripps-offer are an example thereof in a situation which allowed of nothing but a detached act of *nishkama karma*.

'India has become the symbolic representation of all the difficulties of modern mankind. India will be the land of its resurrection — the resurrection to a higher and truer life,'[20] the Mother wrote in 1968. Three years before, during the second war between India and Pakistan, she had declared: 'It is for the sake and the triumph of Truth that India fights and must fight, till India and Pakistan have become one again, because that is the truth of their being.'[21] The conflict between India and Pakistan is still far from resolved. In what measure the situation on the Indian subcontinent is symbolic of the difficulties of the whole world can be read in the book *Critical Mass*, written by two American journalists, William E. Burrows and Robert Windrem (1994). The authors call the continent 'the most dangerous place in the world' because no less than three times it has been on the verge of a nuclear war and at the present time tensions are once more being raised. They quote Richard Kerr, deputy director of the CIA during the last Indo-Pakistan crisis. 'It was the most dangerous nuclear situation we have faced since I have been in the US government. It may be as close as we have come to a nuclear war. This was far more frightening than the Cuban missile crisis.'

On a wall of the playground of the Sri Aurobindo Ashram still hangs the map of what, according to the Mother, is the true material body of India — inclusive of Pakistan, Bangladesh, Sri Lanka and part of Burma. It was in front of that map that she stood when she took the salute of the Ashram youth marching past her on certain festive days, and she sat in front of it when teaching her 'evening classes'. 'The map was made after the partition [of India]. It is the map of the true India', she wrote, 'in spite of all passing appearances, and it will always remain the map of the true India, whatever people may think about it.'*22 The parties involved would do better to heed Sri Aurobindo's words: 'By whatever means, in whatever way, the division must go.' He also repeated this elsewhere: 'India will be reunited. I see it clearly.'23 The Mother has even predicted how that would come to pass: Pakistan, divided into provinces on the lines of its ethnic populations, will fall apart and the separate regions will seek a confederation with India, which itself, as a solution to its internal problems, will become a still more confederate state than it is at the moment.

India had a grand past. Those who know the country better must be moved by the intelligence, the psychological depth and plasticity, and the physical harmony of the races inhabiting it. The light of which it is the bearer shines in the eyes and the smiles of its children. But because of illusionism, it has temporarily withdrawn its attention

---

* When Pondicherry became a 'Union territory' of India — by a process which thanks to Sri Aurobindo and the Mother had passed off without a hitch — the Mother applied for dual citizenship. Her body had for some reasons been born in France but her soul felt itself as Indian, she said. The Indian government did not comply with her request.

from material reality, thus being weighed down by habits and traditions which have lost their meaning and are devoid of vigour. The
problems are many and colossal: population explosion, poverty,
corruption, political chaos, the caste system, religious division, blind
solipsism of the individual and the group, etc. Despite the country's
apparently unpromising present situation, Sri Aurobindo and the
Mother — they who saw — have predicted a golden future for it.
If they were right, this will be one of the wonders of the future.

2. Asia

'Another dream was for the resurgence and liberation of the peoples
of Asia and her return to her great role in the progress of human
civilisation. Asia has arisen; large parts are now quite free or are at
this moment being liberated; its other still subject or partly subject
parts are moving through whatever struggles towards freedom. Only
a little has to be done and that will be done today or tomorrow.'[24]

Thirty years before, he had written in *The Human Cycle*: 'It is
in Europe that the age of individualism has taken birth and exercised
its full sway.' This individualistic period which started with the
Renaissance was the necessary reaction against the preceding era of
conventions, as we soon will see. 'The East has entered into it only
by contact and influence, not from an organical impulse. And it is
to its passion for the discovery of the actual truth of things and for
the governing of human life by whatever law of the truth it has found
that the West owes its centuries of strength, vigour, light, progress,
irresistible expansion. Equally, it is due not to any original falsehood
in the ideals on which its life was founded, but to the loss of the
living sense of the Truth it once held and its long contented slumber
in the cramping bonds of a mechanical conventionalism that the East
has found itself helpless in the hour of its awakening, a giant empty
of strength, inert masses of men who had forgotten how to deal freely
with facts and forces because they had learned only how to live in
a world of stereotyped thought and customary action.'[25] The reader
of these words sees passing before his inner eye the world of Chinese
emperors and warlords, the traditional Japan of shoguns and samurai,

the India of maharajas, sultans and nizams: the whole colourful but burned-out East of the traditions. When an Indian at the time asked the Mother the question: 'How is India likely to get freedom?' she put him straight: 'Listen! The British did not conquer India. You yourselves handed over the country to the British' — a truth applicable to practically all colonial conquests in the East. (And she then reiterated what she had seen as early as 1915: 'In the same manner the British will themselves hand over the country to you. And they will do it in a hurry as if a ship were waiting to take them away.'[26] In history few enterprises of an importance equal to Indian independence have been dealt with as rashly.)

The East has not always been so powerless. In the *Arya*, Sri Aurobindo had already pointed out the occasions on which its energy had been spilling over into the West. But each time Europe, as a whole or in part, rejected the spiritual substance of the Eastern inspiration and utilized it only as an impulse towards a revivifying intellectual and material effort of progress.

'The first attempt [towards a spiritualization of the West by the East] was the filtering of Egyptian, Chaldean and Indian wisdom through the thought of the Greek philosophers from Pythagoras to Plato and the Neo-Platonists; the result was the brilliantly intellectual and unspiritual civilisation of Greece and Rome. But it prepared the way for the second attempt when Buddhism and Vaishnavism, filtered through the Semitic temperament, entered Europe in the form of Christianity. Christianity came within an ace of spiritualising and even of asceticising the mind of Europe; it was baffled by its own theological deformation in the minds of the Greek fathers of the Church and by the sudden flooding of Europe with a German barbarism whose temperament in its merits no less than in its defects was the very anti-type of the Christian spirit and the Graeco-Roman intellect.

'The Islamic invasion of Spain and the southern coast of the Mediterranean — curious as the sole noteworthy example of Asiatic culture using the European method of material and political irruption as opposed to a peaceful invasion by ideas — may be regarded as a third attempt. The result of its meeting with Graecised Christianity was the awakening of the European mind in feudal and Catholic

Europe and the obscure beginnings of modern thought and science,'[27] which would lead up to the Renaissance.

The fourth attempt at spiritualization of the West by the East is happening at present. As the year of its beginning we could consider 1893, when Swami Vivekananda addressed the Congress of Religions in Chicago. 'The influence of the East is likely to be rather in the direction of subjectivism and practical spirituality, a greater opening of our physical existence to the realisation of ideals other than the strong but limited aims suggested by the life and the body in their own gross nature.'[28] 'Rationalistic and physical Science has overpassed itself and must before long be overtaken by a mounting flood of psychological and psychic knowledge which cannot fail to compel quite a new view of the human being and open a new vista before mankind.'[29] 'The safety of Europe* has to be sought in the recognition of the spiritual aim of human existence, otherwise she will be crushed by the weight of her own unillumined knowledge and soulless organisation'[30] — words which have gained significance in the computer age.

All human beings in East and West have a divine soul, therefore knowledge and wisdom are potentially present everywhere. 'There is no law of Nature by which spiritual knowledge is confined to the East or must bear the stamp of an Indian manufacture before it can receive the imprimatur of the All-Wise,'[31] said Sri Aurobindo crisply. But also, as we have seen, every true nation has its own character and nature, which are the reasons of its existence and place within the spectrum of humanity. Anyone who is in some measure knowledgeable about the past of India cannot deny that this country — 'the Asia of Asia, the heart of the world's spiritual life'[32] (Sri Aurobindo) — has been the carrier and treasurer of the authentic spiritual riches since Vedic times. 'The message of the East to the West is a true message: "Only by finding himself can man be saved," and "what shall it profit a man though he gain the whole world, if he lose his own soul," '[33] wrote Sri Aurobindo. And he also wrote: 'The two

---

*   As usual at the time, Sri Aurobindo often wrote 'Europe' where we now would say 'the West'.

continents [Asia and Europe, and what they stand for] are two sides of the integral orb of humanity and until they meet and fuse, each must move to whatever progress or culmination the spirit in humanity seeks, by the law of its being ... A one-sided world would have been the poorer for its uniformity and the monotone of a single culture; there is a need of divergent lines of advance until we can raise our head into that infinity of the spirit in which there is a light broad enough to draw together and reconcile all highest ways of thinking, feeling and living. That is a truth which the violent Indian assailant of a materialistic Europe or the contemptuous enemy or cold disparager of Asiatic or Indian culture agree to ignore.'[34]

3. World-unity

'The third dream was a world-union forming the outer basis of a fairer, brighter and nobler life for all mankind. That unification of the human world is under way; there is an imperfect initiation organised but struggling against tremendous difficulties. But the momentum is there and it must inevitably increase and conquer ... A catastrophe may intervene and interrupt or destroy what is being done, but even then the final result is sure.'[35] The One World is one of Sri Aurobindo's great prophecies. 'A new spirit of oneness will take hold of the human race.'[36] We who now in the Nineties feel that wind of unity over our face can barely imagine how the world looked in 1947, at the time these words were written by Sri Aurobindo, when everywhere in the world the ruins of the Second World War were still smouldering, the two big ideological blocks were jockeying for position, and the deadly mushrooms of the atomic explosions rose threateningly above humanity.

In 1915 he had written in a letter to Mirra Alfassa: 'The whole earth is now under one law and answers to the same vibrations.'[37] In our consciousness at present is stored the world map and the picture of the earth globe, and since recently the glorious photos taken from space capsules and satellites of that slightly misty blue ball: the material body of our Mother the Earth. Things have not always been like that, however. During the whole of humankind's history as known to us there were many worlds in the world, totally distinct worlds, materially as well as psychologically, which had nothing to do with each other. There was the world of the Mayas, of the Aztecs, of European medieval man, of the Roman and his *mare nostrum*, of the Chinese in his Middle Kingdom, of the Mongol in his steppes·... For all of them the other, that strange being from a strange *other* world, was a barbarian, a psychologically incomprehensible, linguistically gibbering and socially valueless non-human. This is why in the language of so many races the word signifying themselves is the same as 'human being.'

In all those different worlds the curtains have now been drawn on one Planet which always was the womb of their origin and the scene of their existence; and slowly, with much friction, strife and complications, they arrive at the recognition of the others on equal terms, as co-humans, and still more slowly at the acceptance of the right of all of them to co-exist. But deep inside, the selfish instincts of the races are still alive, reacting to differences of the colour of the skin, of the build of the body, of behaviour, common habits, culture and religion. The process of the unification of humanity, consisting of countless painful but also hopeful episodes, is still going on. In actual fact humanity has always been one, despite its colourful diversity, but it is now becoming aware of that fundamental unity. This awareness is indispensable, said Sri Aurobindo, to realize the following step in its evolution.

The idea of 'a soundly organised world-union or World-State no longer on the principle of strife and competition, but on a principle of co-operation or mutual adjustment or at least of competition regulated by law and equity and just interchange'[38] was extensively treated by Sri Aurobindo in his book *The Ideal of Human Unity*. This would be a good manual for all who want to contribute to the unification of mankind. It first appeared in the *Arya* from September 1915 to July 1918 and is an astonishing document from the pen of a yogi who was apparently living in withdrawal, in out-of-the-way Pondicherry, but to whom the past, present and future of humanity were the constant object of care and attention. The book has gained in importance in the meantime and the language reads as masterly and fresh as when it was first put down on paper.

In 1950 Sri Aurobindo added 'a postscript chapter' to it in which he applauded the foundation of the United Nations, although he was very much conscious of the shortcomings of the organization just like he had been of those of its predecessor, the League of Nations. 'The League of Nations disappeared but was replaced by the United Nations Organisation which now stands in the forefront of the world and struggles towards some kind of secure permanence and success in the great and far-reaching endeavour on which depends the world's future. This is the capital event, the crucial and decisive outcome of the world-wide tendencies which Nature* has set in motion for her destined purpose.'[39]

A no less important work is *The Human Cycle*, insufficiently valued by most of Sri Aurobindo's commentators. The reason may be that Sri Aurobindo is generally supposed to have been a Master-Yogi and that therefore his reflections on world events and humanity could be of no more than secondary importance. But another reason in many cases is that the commentators themselves are inadequately familiar with their subject. Sri Aurobindo and the Mother are the Avatar of this era; besides their personal development and the development of the group around them, their interest and constant concern encompassed the whole of humanity in all its elements, races and cultures. *The Human Cycle*, originally written along with *The Ideal of Human Unity*, presents, as few other works do, a norm for the appreciation of the historical, modern and contemporary evolution of humankind and merits a prominent place amongst the writings of sociology and historical philosophy.

Taking the theory of the German historian Karl Lamprecht (1856-1915) as his point of departure, Sri Aurobindo divides the curve of human evolution in a symbolical, a typal,** a conventional and an

---

* Be it understood that Sri Aurobindo normally uses the word 'Nature', with a capital letter, for the conscious creative Power which is the manifesting executrix of the Divine Will.

** Not to be confused with the same word used when describing the non-evolving worlds of the divine manifestation.

individualistic age, and to this he adds a future subjective age. The symbolical age is the one at the very origin of man as a social being at the time of 'the thickly veiled secret of our historic evolution' when the social structures, culture and all human behaviour were still impregnated by the sense of their extraterrestrial origin.

(Here it should be pointed out that, according to Sri Aurobindo and the Mother, the history of humankind, as commonly accepted and taught at present, constitutes only a fraction of the long and winding path of pilgrimage it has been in actuality, 'for not one hundred-thousandth part of what has been has still a name preserved by human Time.'[40] Sri Aurobindo indicates that the time-period of known history is much too short to allow for the mental evolvement of *homo sapiens* to the level it has now reached. He suggests more than once that the primitive peoples, in his time still called savages, are actually degenerated elements of former civilizations — a fact which can be concluded from their mental capacities which equal those of the 'civilized' cultures once they get access to the same environment.)

In the 'typal' age the original all-impregnating symbolism is partially lost; there is a formation of 'types' in a society mainly based on moral norms. The following stage of society, the conventional, comes about 'when the external supports, the outward expressions of the spirit or the ideal, become more important than the ideal, the body or even the clothes more important than the person.'[41] This kind of social system is so suffocating that the individual cannot but revolt against it, thereby initiating the age of individualism and reason. 'It is then that men in spite of the natural conservatism of the social mind are compelled at last to perceive that the Truth is dead in them and that they are living by a lie. The individualism of the new age,' commenced in the West at the time of the Renaissance, ' is an attempt to get back from the conventionalism of belief and practice to some solid bed-rock, no matter what, or real and tangible Truth ... It is the individual who has to become a discoverer, a pioneer.'[42] The renovating truth-impulse of Nature in this individual is then so strong that, like Martin Luther, 'he stands there and can no other.' In Sri Aurobindo's view, the revolution of the individual will ultimately lead up to the subjective period — not of egocentrism in the psychological sense as the term may easily be misunderstood, but of discovery of the subjective truths and realities which will result in the advent of a new world in which authenticity, reality and Truth will again be the bases of experience.

Sri Aurobindo had formulated the principle of world-unity; he now formulated the norm of individual freedom in the ideal future world: 'The principle of individualism is the liberty of the human being regarded as a separate existence to develop himself and fulfill his life, satisfy his mental tendencies, emotional and vital needs and physical being according to his own desire, governed by his reason; it admits no other limit to this right and this liberty except the obligation to respect the same individual liberty and right in others.'[43]

4. The Gift of India to the World

'Another dream, the spiritual gift of India to the world, has already begun. India's spirituality is entering Europe and America in an ever increasing measure. That movement will grow; amid the disasters of the time more and more eyes are turning towards her with hope and there is even an increasing resort not only to her teachings, but to her psychic and spiritual practice.'[44] We have already paid attention to this to some extent when considering Sri Aurobindo's 'dream' concerning Asia.

5. A New Step in Evolution

'The final dream was a step in evolution which would raise man to a higher and larger consciousness and begin the solution of the problems which have perplexed and vexed him since he began first to think and to dream of individual perfection and a perfect society. This is still a personal hope and an idea, an ideal which has begun to take hold both in India and in the West on forward-looking minds. The difficulties in the way are more formidable than in any other field of endeavour, but difficulties were made to overcome and if the Supreme Will is there, they will be overcome. Here too, if this evolution is to take place, since it must proceed through a growth of the spirit and the inner consciousness, the initiative can come from India and, although the scope must be universal, the central movement may be hers.'[45]

Sri Aurobindo concluded his message for *All India Radio* as follows: 'Such is the content which I put into this date of India's liberation; whether or how far this hope will be justified depends upon the new and free India.' When his message was spreading as radio-waves through the ether, nobody knew that they were listening to Sri Aurobindo's testament.

With the termination of the Second World War — 'Where is Hitler now and where is his rule?' said Sri Aurobindo — and the independence of India, the problems of the world were not solved. On the contrary, Sri Aurobindo kept repeating that the world situation was very grave, graver than ever. Stalin was still there, and there were the many little Stalins, and even after Hitler's and Stalin's death the forces who had used them would choose others as their instruments. 'To them, it is as if you change your shirt,' the Mother said. The Lord of the Nations did everything possible to redeem his fearful promise given to her.

In June 1950, Sri Aurobindo therefore wrote about the Korean War to K.D. Sethna, chief editor of *Mother India*, the periodical regarded by Sri Aurobindo as the vehicle for his thought: 'The whole affair is as plain as a pike-staff. It is the first move in the Communist plan of campaign to dominate and take possession first of these northern parts and then of South East Asia as a preliminary to their manoeuvres with regard to the rest of the continent — in passing, Tibet as a gate opening to India. If they succeed, there is no reason why domination of the whole world should not follow by steps until they are ready to deal with America. That is, provided the war can be staved off with America until Stalin can choose his time.

'Truman seems to have understood the situation if we can judge from his moves in Korea, but it is to be seen whether he is strong enough and determined enough to carry the matter through. The measures he has taken are likely to be incomplete and unsuccessful, since they do not include any actual military intervention [at that time] except on sea and in the air.

'That seems to be the situation; we have to see how it develops. One thing is certain that if there is too much shilly-shallying and if America gives up now her defence of Korea, she may be driven to yield position after position until it is too late; at one point or another she will have to stand and face the necessity of drastic action even if it leads to war. Stalin also seems not to be ready to face at once the risk of a world war and, if so, Truman can turn the tables on him by constantly facing him with the onus of either taking that risk or yielding position after position to America. I think that is all I can say at present.'[46]

Sri Aurobindo expounded here summarily but in unmistakable terms what afterwards in world-politics would become known as the 'domino theory'. And he concluded his survey with the words: 'The situation is as grave as it can be.' So it was indeed, on the political front as well as on other, inner battlefields imperceptible to human eyes.

Sri Aurobindo at Amravati, January 1908, after the Surat Congress.

Sri Aurobindo in Pondicherry, c.1918-1920

At the time of the Surat Congress, December 1907.
Front row left to right: G.S. Khaparde, Aswini Kumar Dutta
Middle row: Sirdar Ajit Singh, Sri Aurobindo, B.G. Tilak, Saiyad Haider Reza
Back row: Dr B.S. Munje, Ramaswamy, K. Kuverji Desai

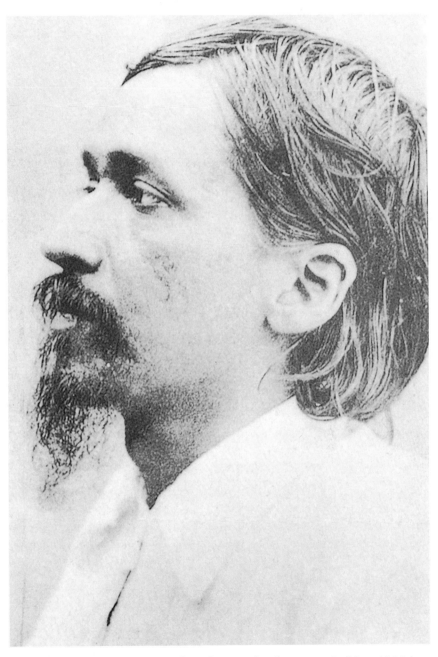

Sri Aurobindo at Alipore Jail, Calcutta after his arrest in May 1908 in the Alipore Bomb Case (photo c. 1909). Photograph from police records

Sri Aurobindo at Amravati, January 1908, after the Surat Congress.

Sri Aurobindo in Pondicherry, c.1918-1920

*Sri Aurobindo in Pondicherry,
c.1918-1920*

*The Mother in Tokyo, Japan,
1916*

The Mother in Japan, 1916

Sri Aurobindo and The Mother giving Darshan on 24 April 1950

Sri Aurobindo in his room, April 1950

Sri Aurobindo in his room, April 1950

Sri Aurobindo Mahasamadhi, 5 December 1950

The Mother at the occasion of 'Kali Puja' in the Sri Aurobindo Ashram, Pondicherry on 21 October 1954

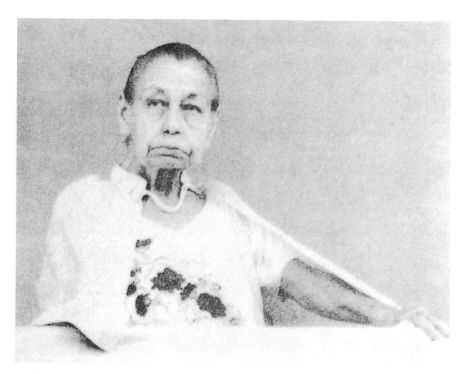

The Mother giving Darshan from her balcony. Photo late 1960's

*Mother with Prime Minister Nehru, Shri Kamraj Nadar,
Mrs. Indira Gandhi and lal Bahadur Shastri. (1955)*

Mother in front of the Spiritual Map of India in the Playground of the Sri Aurobindo Ashram, Pondicherry, 1952

Chapter Eighteen

THE CONFRONTATION
WITH DEATH

*To conquer death, one must be ready
to go through death.*
— The Mother[1]

ABOUT A year before, there already had been signs of trouble with the prostate gland, but Sri Aurobindo had cured that with his spiritual power. In November 1950, the symptoms appeared again. To the astonishment of his entourage, he who always had behaved as if he had eternity in front of him suddenly made them understand that he wanted to make haste with certain things, including the finishing of his epic poem *Savitri*.

Raymond F. Piper, professor of Syracuse University in the USA, has given the following appraisal of *Savitri*: 'During a period of nearly fifty years ... [Sri Aurobindo] created what is probably the greatest epic in the English language ... I venture the judgment that it is the most comprehensive, integrated, beautiful and perfect cosmic poem ever composed. It ranges symbolically from a primordial cosmic void, through earth's darkness and struggles, to the highest realms of Supramental spiritual existence, and illumines every important concern of man, through verse of unparalleled massiveness, magnificence, and metaphorical brilliance. *Savitri* is perhaps the most powerful artistic work in the world for expanding man's mind towards the Absolute.'[2]

With its 23,813 lines, *Savitri* is the longest poem in the English language. Its first version dates back as far as Sri Aurobindo's Baroda period. No less than eleven and maybe twelve versions and revisions have been found. Originally a rather short narrative poem based on a story from Vyasa's *Mahabharata* (one of the greatest literary works in the world qua content as well as extent) it gradually expanded by way of experiment into a poetic epic which reaches far ahead in the future. 'I used *Savitri* as a means of ascension. I began with it on a certain mental level; each time I could reach a higher level I rewrote from that level. Moreover I was particular — if part seemed to me to come from any lower levels, I was not satisfied to leave it because it was good poetry. All had to be as far as possible of the same mint. *Savitri* has not been regarded by me as a poem to be written and finished, but as a field of experimentation to see how far poetry could be written from one's own Yogic consciousness and how that could be made creative.'[3]

Sri Aurobindo has called *Savitri* 'a legend and a symbol'. The legend goes as follows: Savitri, daughter of King Aswapathy, undertakes in her magnificent 'carved car' a journey through the neighbouring kingdoms to choose for herself a husband from among the princes, as was the custom of the time. At the edge of a forest, she unexpectedly meets Satyavan and they fall in love. Satyvan is the son of the blind king Dyumatsena who has lost his throne to an usurper and been banished to the forest. Savitri returns home to tell her parents that she has found the man of her choice and that she wants to marry him and nobody else. However, she hears from the heavenly singer and seer Narad that a curse rests on Satyavan: he must die in exactly a year's time. In her love for Satyavan, Savitri refuses to go back on her decision. The marriage takes place and she goes to live with her husband and his parents in their hermitage in the forest, where she shares the hermits' way of life and performs assiduously all the duties of an Indian wife.

On the appointed day of Satyavan's death, Savitri accompanies her unsuspecting husband who goes to cut wood in the forest. There Yama, the God of Death, awaits him with the noose with which he leads the souls in the realms beyond. Savitri refuses to let go of Satyavan and keeps closely following the two in the hereafter, something she is able to do because of her occult and spiritual powers, acquired through severe ascetic discipline. Death can neither deter her nor get rid of her whatever be his threats or promises. So great is Savitri's strength that Yama at long last lets Satyavan return to life on earth. When Savitri and Satyavan return to their hermitage in the forest, a messenger arrives to inform Dyumatsena, who has miraculously regained his eyesight, that the usurper has died and that the people want him back as their king. In this happy ending, Savitri alone knows of the drama that has taken place in regions inaccessible to human eyes and thought.

So far the legend, used by Sri Aurobindo as a symbol. Satyavan represents the embodied soul of humanity and Savitri an incarnation of the Great Mother, descended upon Earth to save that soul from the night of suffering and death. In other words, Sri Aurobindo has transposed the popular story from the *Mahabharata* into a symbol of the Work of the Mother and himself. By which character in the poem is he then represented? The commentators are unanimous: by Aswapathy, Savitri's father and Lord of the Horse Sacrifice. This is only partially true, and it is at this point that their interpretations go off the rails.

Like all poetry from Sri Aurobindo's maturity, *Savitri* too is a description of real facts and experiences from his yoga, and as such his message, formulated in words of mantric power. The Mother somewhere even calls *Savitri* the message: '*Savitri, c'est le Message.*'[4] She also says that Sri Aurobindo has revealed the most in *Savitri*: 'He has crammed the whole universe in a single book* ... Each verse of *Savitri* is like a revealed Mantra which surpasses all that man possessed by way of knowledge, and I repeat this: the words are expressed and arranged in such a way that the sonority of the rhythm leads you to the origin of the sound, which is OM ... These are

---

* Both the following quotations are extracts from a conversation the Mother had with Mona Sarkar, then a young *sadhak*. The Mother spoke in French and her words were afterwards translated into English.

experiences lived by him, realities, supracosmic truths ... He walked in the darkness of inconscience, even in the neighbourhood of death, endured the sufferings of perdition ... He crossed all these realms, went through the consequences, suffered and endured physically what one cannot imagine ... He accepted suffering to transform suffering into the joy of union with the Supreme.' Each of these words applies to her too, for their Work was that of the one Consciousness in two bodies. Time and again, she heard in astonishment — for Sri Aurobindo often read out to her what he had just written — that in many passages her own experiences were described, sometimes in the smallest detail. 'All this is his own experience, but what is most astonishing is that it is my experience also. It is my *sadhana* which he has worked out. Each object, each event, each realisation, all the descriptions, even the colours are exactly what I saw, and the words, the phrases are exactly what I heard.'[5]

If Sri Aurobindo was Aswapathy, then he certainly was a very different Aswapathy from the character in the *Mahabharata* story, whoever and however great the latter may have been. 'His name was Aswapathy. Performer of Yajnas [ceremonial offerings], presiding over charities, skilful in work, one who had conquered the senses, he was loved by the people of his kingdom and he himself loved them.'[6] Thus read the verses about Aswapathy in the *Mahabharata*. Let us now read Sri Aurobindo's description of Aswapathy in *Savitri*:

> One in the front of the immemorial quest,
> Protagonist of the mysterious play
> In which the Unknown pursues himself through forms
> And limits his eternity by the hours
> And the blind Void struggles to live and see,
> A thinker and toiler in the ideal's air ...
> His was a spirit that stooped from larger spheres
> Into our province of ephemeral sight,
> A colonist from immortality ...
> His birth held up a symbol and a sign;
> His human self like a translucent cloak
> Covered the All-Wise who leads the unseeing world.[7]

This, of course, is not the yogi-king from the *Mahabharata* but the Avatar who was Sri Aurobindo. 'The yoga of the king' as described in *Savitri* is not the yoga of the legendary Aswapathy but the king-yoga of Sri Aurobindo who here, like in his other poetry, lifts a part of the veil covering his personality and its development. For instance, in 'The Book* of the Traveller of the Worlds' he describes his occult-spiritual journeys of discovery through the subtle universes constituting the whole range of the stair, the 'world-stair', of manifested existence, and thus gives us 'his most detailed account of the geography of the inner worlds,' according to P. Heehs. 'It is an exact description ... amazingly realistic,' said the Mother. If all this is not convincing enough, it may be pointed out that Aswapathy's name first appears on page 341 of an epic consisting of 741 pages in the Centenary Edition of Sri Aurobindo's Collected Works. Had this not been intentional, it would indeed have been an incomprehensible oversight of an author who had the same comma deleted and reinstated five times. This key to the reading of *Savitri* is important because without it, it is impossible to evaluate the proper significance of the epic, which in turn would cause us to overlook some of the most relevant data in the life of Sri Aurobindo and the Mother.

This epic is like a very old city of which layer upon layer has been built on the foundations of the original composition. First there was a rather short narrative poem; then, in the various versions discovered after Sri Aurobindo's demise, he went on building and expanding, making the narrative poem into an epic and deepening, widening and heightening its content, extent and spiritual intensity, till finally the poem became the matchless epic as it is now known to us. Sri Aurobindo has worded for posterity his own Work and that of the Mother in order to allow all prepared souls who read those words to breathe the same atmosphere and to contact the same realities behind the surface perceptible by the senses. According to the Mother, *Savitri* even contains the whole supramental yoga. Some parts, however, are less, much less elaborated or elevated, namely the

---

* *Savitri* consists of twelve books, subdivided into cantos.

fragments which have remained nearest to the original legend of which it is the function to prop up or frame the construction of the epic as a whole and to establish the lines of its continuity. Only in such passages is Aswapathy still the character from the *Mahabharata*; in the 'high' spiritual and overmental parts of the epic 'the thinker and toiler', the one 'in front of the immemorial quest', 'the traveller of the worlds' is Sri Aurobindo himself, 'the first of time-born men who had the knowledge' which will lead to a new world-order. '*Savitri* is the record of a seeing, of an experience which is not of the common kind and is often very far from what the general human mind sees and experiences. You must not expect appreciation or understanding from the general public or even from many at the first touch: as I have pointed out, there must be a new extension of consciousness and aesthesis to appreciate a new kind of mystic poetry,'[8] Sri Aurobindo wrote to K.D. Sethna. As we know, Sri Aurobindo held Sethna in high esteem as a poet, and it was with him that he conducted an extensive correspondence about *Savitri* and to whom he sent, in a letter in 1936, the first passage (the opening lines) ever read by eyes other than his own. 'It took the world something like a hundred years to discover Blake; it would not be improbable that there might be a greater time-lag here, though naturally we hope for better things.'[9]

Somewhere in 1945, Sri Aurobindo's eyesight got bad. He probably had cataract, one of the scourges of India. Nirodbaran now became his amanuensis. 'He would dictate line after line, and ask me to add selected lines and passages in their proper places, but which were not always kept in their old order,' writes Nirodbaran. 'I wonder how he could go on dictating lines of poetry in this way, as if a tap had been turned on and the water flowed, not in a jet of course, but slowly, very slowly indeed. Passages sometimes had to be re-read in order to get the link or sequence, but when the turn came of the Book of Yoga and the Book of Everlasting Day, line after line began to flow from his lips like a smooth and gentle stream and it was on the next day that a revision was done to get the link for further continuation. In the morning he himself would write out new lines on small note books called 'bloc notes' [notepads] which were incorporated in the text.... Sometimes there were two or even three versions of a passage. As his sight began to fail, the letters also became gradually indistinct, and I had to decipher and read them all before him. I had a good sight and, more than that, the gift of deciphering his hieroglyphics, thanks to the preparatory training I had received during my voluminous correspondence with him before the accident. At times when I got stuck he would help me out, but there were occasions where both of us failed. Then he would say, "Give it to me, let me try." Taking a big magnifying glass, he would focus his eyes but only to exclaim, "No, can't make out." '10

As mentioned in the beginning of this chapter, somewhere at the end of October or in the first days of November 1950 Sri Aurobindo suddenly seemed to be pressed for time to finish *Savitri*. In the previous years he had worked on all unfinished parts and given them 'an almost new birth, with the exception of the Book of Death and the Epilogue, which for some inscrutable reason he left practically unrevised',11 writes Nirodbaran. 'When the last revision was made and the Cantos were wound up, I said, "It is finished now." An impersonal smile of satisfaction greeted me and he said, "Ah, is it finished?" How well I remember that flicker of a smile which all of us craved for so long! "What is left now?" was his next query. "The Book of Death and the Epilogue." "Oh, that? We shall see about that later on." That "later on" never came and was not meant to come. Having taken the decision to leave the body, he must have been waiting for the right moment to go and for reasons known to himself he left the two last-mentioned Books almost as they were. Thus on *Savitri* was put the seal of incomplete completion about two weeks before the *Darshan* of November 24th. Other literary works also came to an end.'12

Some ten days before the darshan of 24 November, the symptoms of Sri Aurobindo's illness had worsened again. The prostate gland was swollen and traces of albumin and acetone were found in his urine. After the exhausting *darshan*-day, the symptoms became alarming. Dr. Satyavrata Sen found it necessary to apply a catheter, and Dr. Prabhat Sanyal, a devotee and surgeon of repute in Calcutta, was telegraphically summoned to come to Pondicherry straightaway. He has left us his recollection of those days in an article entitled *A Call from Pondicherry*. On his arrival at the Ashram, he was at once informed by Sen and Nirodbaran about Sri Aurobindo's condition and accompanied by them up to his apartment. 'I asked him what the trouble was and whether I could give him any relief. I put to him the regular professional questions, perhaps then forgetting that my patient was the Divine housed in a mortal frame, and he answered: "Trouble? Nothing troubles me — and suffering? one can be above it." I mentioned the urinary difficulties. "Well, yes," he answered, "I had some difficulties but they have been relieved, and now I do not feel anything" ... I explained to [the Mother] that he was suffering from a mild kidney infection — otherwise there was nothing very serious as far as could be judged from the urine report.'[13]

On 1 December, there was some amelioration; the temperature was normal. 'He was in a more cheerful mood and even joked with Sanyal.'[14] December 2 was (and is) the day of the annual sports feast of the Ashram youth, which needed a lot of attention and energy from the Mother. 'As soon as the activities were over, the Mother came to Sri Aurobindo's room, placed the garland from her neck at his feet and stood there quietly. Her countenance was very grave. He was indrawn with his eyes closed.' His temperature had gone up again rapidly. On 3 December, the temperature again dropped to normal, so much so that Sanyal thought of leaving for Calcutta, but the Mother made him change his mind. In the afternoon the temperature shot up again. 'Then for the first time, the Mother said, "He is losing interest in himself ..." The long night passed in distress alternating with an indrawn condition. He would wake up, however, only when we wanted to give him a drink. Sometimes, he even expressed a choice in the matter.'

On 4 December Sri Aurobindo all at once strongly insisted that he wanted to sit up, something the doctors only reluctantly allowed. 'We noticed after a while that all the distressing breathing symptoms had magically vanished and he looked his normal self ... We boldly asked him now, "Are you not using your force to cure yourself?" "No!" came the stunning reply. We could not believe our ears; to be quite sure, we repeated the question. No mistake! Then we asked,

"Why not? How is the disease going to be cured otherwise?" "Can't explain; you won't understand," was the curt reply. We were dumb-founded.'[15]

By midday the symptoms again increased, particularly the breath-ing. Around one o'clock, the Mother said to Sanyal: 'He is withdraw-ing.' A blood analysis showed all the signs of imminent kidney failure. 'He was now always withdrawn, and only woke up whenever he was called for a drink. That confirmed the Mother's observation that he was fully conscious within and disproved the idea that he was in an uraemic coma. Throughout the entire course of the illness he was never unconscious,' writes Nirodbaran; Dr. Sanyal concurs with him in every respect.

In the early evening, the respiratory distress returned with re-doubled force. He went to his bed and plunged within. 'It was during this period that he often came out of the trance, and each time leaned forward, hugged and kissed Champaklal on the cheek, who was sitting by the side of his bed. Champaklal also hugged him in return. A wonderful sight it was, though so strangely unlike Sri Aurobindo who had rarely called us even by our names in these twelve years.'[16] Nirodbaran and others have remained puzzled about this unusual behaviour of Sri Aurobindo. Is it not obvious that the Avatar, in his love for humanity, is here taking leave of that humanity in the person of Champaklal? It was 'the embrace that takes to itself the body of God in man,' as Sri Aurobindo had written in the *Synthesis*.[17]

In the Ashram only a handful of people, taken into the confidence of a doctor or assistant, were aware of what was going on in Sri Aurobindo's rooms on the first floor; the Mother did not disquiet the others and continued following her daily routine. After she returned from the playground, she put her garland at the feet of Sri Aurobindo just like any other evening. Again she said to Sanyal: 'He has no interest in himself, he is withdrawing.' And Sanyal writes: 'A strange phenomenon — a body which for the moment is in agony, unresponsive, labouring hard for breath, suddenly becomes quiet; a consciousness enters the body, he is awake and normal. He finishes the drink, then, as the consciousness withdraws, the body lapses back into the grip of agony.'

At midnight the Mother came again into the room. 'This time he opened his eyes and the two looked at each other in a steady gaze. We were the silent spectators of that crucial scene. What passed between them was beyond our mortal ken.' One hour later, the Mother was back in the room once more. 'Her face was calm, there was no trace of emotion. Sri Aurobindo was indrawn. The Mother asked Sanyal in a quiet tone, "What do you think? Can I retire for an hour?... Call me when the time comes." ' And Nirodbaran comments: 'It may appear strange to our human mind that the Mother should leave Sri Aurobindo at this critical moment. We must remember that we are not dealing with human consciousness ... Besides, we know that at this particular hour she had very important occult work to do.' But the Mother herself has told what actually happened at that moment: 'As long as I remained in the room he could not leave his body.'[18] With a slight movement of the head, he then gave her to understand that she should leave the room.

About ten minutes later, Sri Aurobindo asked Nirodbaran by name for something to drink: ' "Nirod, give me some drink." This was his deliberate last gesture. The quantity he drank was very small and there was no apparent need of calling me by name. Those last words still ring in my ears and remain inscribed in my soul,' writes Nirodbaran. 'I perceived a light quiver in his body, almost imperceptible,' remembers Sanyal. 'He drew up his arms and put them on his chest, one overlapping the other — then all stopped ... I told Nirod to go and fetch the Mother. It was 1.20 a.m. Almost immediately the Mother entered the room. She stood there, near the feet of Sri Aurobindo: her hair had been undressed and was flowing about her shoulders. Her look was so fierce that I could not face those eyes. With a piercing gaze she stood there. Champaklal could not bear it and sobbingly he implored, "Mother, tell me Dr. Sanyal is not right, he is alive." The Mother looked at him and he became quiet and composed as if touched by a magic wand. She stood there for more than half an hour. My hands were still on his forehead.'

One of the Ashram visitors in those days was the American philosopher Rhoda P. Le Cocq, who has related the events in her book *The Radical Thinkers — Heidegger and Sri Aurobindo*. She writes:

'Unexpectedly, in the afternoon [of 6 December, some forty hours after Sri Aurobindo's demise], there was another *darshan*. Sri Aurobindo's face still did not look deathlike. The skin was golden in colour, the white hair blowing on the pillow in a breeze from a fan. The acquiline profile continued to have a prophetic look.' The Mother named *Power* one of the photographs of Sri Aurobindo taken by an Ashram photographer on his deathbed. 'There was no odour of death and little incense was burning. To my astonishment, the repeated viewings of his body had a comforting effect. Previously I had always resented the idea of viewing dead bodies.'[19]

The legal maximum time for a body to remain unburied in the tropics was 48 hours, and therefore everybody expected the burial to take place on 7 December under the big-tree in the Ashram courtyard, where the grave had already been dug. But the Mother had a notice posted on that very same day: 'The funeral of Sri Aurobindo has not taken place today. His body is charged with such a concentration of supramental light that there is no sign of decomposition and the body will be kept lying on his bed so long as it remains intact.'[20]

Rhoda Le Cocq writes: 'From the French colony, already exploding with disapproval and its officials much disturbed by the burial plans, came the rumor that the body *must* have been "shot with formaldehyde" secretly, to preserve it. Moreover, said the officials, the *ashram* was not only breaking the law in burying anyone in the garden, it was worse to keep it so long unburied ... On the morning of December 7th, therefore, a French doctor representing the government, a Dr. Barbet, arrived to inspect the body of Sri Aurobindo. At the end, he reported that it was a "miracle"; there was no deterioration, no *rigor mortis*. It was an unheard of occurrence; the weather had continued to be hot during the entire time. After this official and scientific approval, nothing further could be done to prevent another *darshan*. Visitors were flocking from all over India; and the Indian newspapers now proposed that Sri Aurobindo be suggested, posthumously, for the Nobel Peace Prize.'[21]

On 8 December 'tension grew among the *ashramites*, and incredible speculations became the order of the day.' A phenomenon like this had never occurred in India, where not even yogis whose speciality it was to have themselves buried alive had never performed such a feat. 'No Indian "living saint" in history had preserved his body after death in this fashion.'

'On the afternoon of December 9th, at 5:00 p.m., the burial service finally took place after another final *darshan*. A feeling of force and energy remained in the atmosphere around Sri Aurobindo's vicinity, but that force had now weakened ... There was no orthodox religious service at the burial. The coffin, of rosewood with metal-gold rings, much like an old and beautiful sea-chest, was borne from the *ashram* and lowered into the earth. French officials, all dressed in white, made a line to the left, their faces stern, a bit superior in expression and definitely disapproving of the entire affair. Over the coffin concrete slabs were laid. Then everyone lined up and, one by one, we scattered earth from wicker baskets. It was dark under the spreading tree when each of us had made his last farewell.'

Why has Sri Aurobindo left his body? For the Mother had said to K.D. Sethna, as to others: 'There was nothing "mortal" about Sri Aurobindo,' and also: 'Sri Aurobindo did not die of physical causes. He had complete control over his body.'[22] And Sri Aurobindo himself had written about the results of his yoga in *Savitri*:

> The old adamantine vetoes stood no more:
> Overpowered were earth and Nature's obsolete rule;
> The python coils of the restricting Law
> Could not restrain the swift arisen God:
> Abolished were the scripts of destiny.
> There was no small death-hunted creature more... [23]

We find the same in his sonnet *Transformation*:

> I am no longer a vassal of the flesh,
> A slave to Nature and her leaden rule... [24]

Actually, Sri Aurobindo had advanced much farther in his yoga than his commentators, including the ultrapositive-minded devotees among them, generally assume. Either the latter go to extremes of hyperbolic devotion and praise interlarded with traditional metaphors, or the whole of Sri Aurobindo's personality and work is left by the others in the shadow of his passing on. This does not mean that true devotion or veneration necessarily has to be based on reason, but one does Sri Aurobindo and the Mother great injustice by overlooking the documents of what has been the greatest, because decisive, intervention in the history of humankind. True, their work has been performed on a plane surpassing the ordinary consciousness of human beings, but the insight into it that the documents allow us can only clarify and increase our appreciation of it.

Sri Aurobindo had entered death voluntarily. The Mother said in the same month of December 1950: 'He was not compelled to leave his body, he chose to do so for reasons so sublime that they are beyond the reach of human mentality.'[25] No doubt, the fact is so complex and our knowledge of its real factors and background so limited that our 'understanding' of them is limited too. The Mother herself has never given a complete explanation and told even years later that she remained puzzled by the event. 'Why? Why? How often have I not asked that question!' She had 5,000 copies of an essay by K.D. Sethna printed and distributed among the disciples and devotees to put their anguished mind at rest. Sethna formulated his thesis as follows: 'Nothing except a colossal strategic sacrifice of this kind in order that the physical transformation of the Mother may be immeasurably hastened and rendered absolutely secure and, through it, a divine life on earth for humanity may get rooted and be set aflower — nothing less can explain the passing of Sri Aurobindo.'[26]

Let us examine certain facts. The Mother had said several times that Sri Aurobindo had confided to her at one time: 'We cannot both remain on earth, one of us must go.' To which she had replied: 'I am ready, I'll go.' But Sri Aurobindo had forbidden that. 'No, you can't go, your body is better than mine, you can undergo the transformation better than I can do.'[27] She will refer to this vital conversation later: 'He told me that his body was not capable of enduring the transformation, that mine was more suitable — and he has repeated this.' When did that vital conversation take place? One time the Mother says that it was something 'that he had said in 1949,' another time that it was 'before he broke his leg,' which means in 1938 — that early.

It is indisputable that the Mother did not know that he would depart. In *The Mother — Sweetness and Light*, Nirodbaran recounts in detail his conversation with her on his birthday in 1953. He recalls her saying: 'At any rate, I did not believe till the last moment that Sri Aurobindo was going to leave his body.' And he gives Sethna's comment in a footnote: 'This is correct. On Dec. 3 she told me that Sri Aurobindo would soon read my articles. Later, when I asked her why she had let me go to Bombay on Dec. 3 she said that Sri Aurobindo's going had not been decided yet.'[28] Two days beforehand!

From what precedes we can conclude, firstly, that Sri Aurobindo was fully knowledgeable of the ordeal the supramental physical transformation would mean for a body and that he had unmistakably seen that the Mother's body was better able than his to undergo that transformation — 'unmistakably' because otherwise he surely would have taken on the ordeal himself. In later years, the Mother would wholeheartedly agree with the correctness of his decision.

Secondly, he must have seen that, for practical reasons connected with the Work, it was required that a manifested half of the double Avatar, of the Two-in-One, had to go and work 'behind the veil' — probably to hasten the result of the Work, certainly because Death and everything related to it could only be transformed by confronting it with the full avataric consciousness, in other words: by consciously experiencing and transforming death. The Mother too must have seen this necessity, which was the reason why she spontaneously declared herself prepared for the occult master act.

Thirdly — and there is no circumventing this — Sri Aurobindo had worked out the preparation of his voluntary passage through death in such a way that it remained veiled for part of the active consciousness of the Mother and that his intention remained hidden from her — she who could read the worlds and all they contain like an open book. He had done this for the reason the Mother herself had told us, namely that otherwise she could not have let him go or that she would have left together with him. We will shortly see what an enormous shock Sri Aurobindo's sudden corporeal absence was for her physical consciousness.

As she told Nirodbaran, indications of Sri Aurobindo's departure had not been lacking. To begin with, there had been the conversation between her and Sri Aurobindo which we have literally reproduced above. There also was the exceptional fact that Sri Aurobindo had allowed himself to be photographed, for the first time since his withdrawal in 1926, by the now world-famous Henri Cartier-Bresson,* during the *darshan* days of April 1950.

A very important indication, in retrospect, of Sri Aurobindo's impending departure was finally the fact that he had declared *Savitri* terminated without having worked out the Book of Death and the Epilogue. The Book of Death, barely revised from a very early draft, comprises no more than five pages while occupying a central place in the epic. We have already been reminded several times of the fact that Sri Aurobindo and the Mother never spoke speculatively or theoretically but always from their own practical experience, and that *Savitri* and the poetry of the later years too were based on that experience. Death, however, had *not* been experienced by Sri Aurobindo, though he must have been aware that the confrontation with death was of essential and indispensable importance to enable the immortality of the new species. This explains the fact that, in *Savitri*, he has not gone into or formulated what he had not experienced. Seen in the same way, it should be clear why the epilogue

---

* Henri Cartier-Bresson, held to be 'the father of modern photo-journalism', was at the time travelling through India with his Indonesian wife. He had read French translations of some of Sri Aurobindo's books and requested in writing permission to photograph Sri Aurobindo and the Mother for the Photo Agency *Magnum*, which he had founded with war photographer Robert Capra and others. After the Mother, herself not photographed since her stay in Japan, had seen an album with work of Cartier-Bresson, he got permission to shoot freely during a couple of days in the Ashram. At his instance, the Mother asked Sri Aurobindo's permission for him to be photographed in his room and even during the darshan proper. Thus came about the by now famous photographs of Sri Aurobindo in his big armchair, and the only photo of him together with the Mother, taken during the darshan of 24 April 1950, without special lighting and fairly hazy.

of the poem was not written and only follows sketchily the legend as told in the *Mahabharata*; for the Work is still in progress and its crowning epilogue, the Kingdom of God upon Earth, will be visible, livable and describable only much later.

Sri Aurobindo has not gone 'the way of all flesh' like human beings before him have and still do; he did not die because of a law of nature deemed unbreakable. In the aforementioned words of the Mother: 'He was not forced to leave his body, he has chosen to do so.' When Satprem was writing his *Sri Aurobindo, ou l'Aventure de la conscience*, he read twice or three times a week the last passages he had written to the Mother. Having arrived at Sri Aurobindo's passing, he wrote that Sri Aurobindo on 5 December 1950 had 'succumbed', using the French word '*succombé*'. The Mother corrected him at once: 'He has not "succumbed". It is not so that he was not able of doing otherwise. It is not the difficulty of his work which has made him depart. It is something else ... You must use another word than "succumb." Really, it was his *decision* that things would be done in another way, because he was of the opinion that the result in this way would come about much faster ... But this is a complex explanation which for the time being regards nobody. But one cannot say that he has "succumbed". "Succumbed" evokes the thought that he did not want to [die], that it happened all by itself, that it was an accident. It cannot be "succumbed." '29

When a disciple wrote in 1969 to the Mother: 'May I not be unfaithful to the sacrifice Sri Aurobindo has made for the earth!' the Mother replied: 'For his consciousness it was not a sacrifice.'30 It was a technical, practical, occult exigency to hasten the manifestation of the Supermind and the supramental transformation on Earth. It might not be unreasonable to postulate that this acceleration was seen as imperative by Sri Aurobindo to make it possible that the foundations of the divine future of humankind — the task for which the double Avatar had incarnated — might be built while the Avatar, now physically embodied only in the Mother, would still be on Earth. Otherwise, a new incarnation would have been required somewhere in the future, which means that the manifestation of the Supermind would have been postponed.

Sri Aurobindo, totally free of ego, had no personal desires, pride or purposes; the success of the work of the Avatar was to him the only object of importance. His 'strategic withdrawal' was possible because the Mother remained behind. Had this not been so, their avataric embodiment and effort would indeed have been a fiasco as far as their main objective, the establishment of the Supermind in the Earth-atmosphere, was concerned. The physical half of the body of the Avatar that was better constituted to undergo the transformation remained upon Earth. As the Consciousness was one but the division of tasks different, Sri Aurobindo had to transmit his yogic acquirements to the Mother to allow her to continue the Work at once and in its total extent. This amazing transmission has taken place immediately after Sri Aurobindo had been declared 'dead' by Dr. Sanyal. 'When [Sri Aurobindo] had left, there was an entire part — the most material part of the descent into the material body down to the mental — which visibly left his body and entered into mine,' said the Mother, 'and that was so concrete that I felt the *friction* of the forces going through the pores of my skin ... It was as concrete as if it had been material.'[31] This phenomenon demands some clarification. We will consider it in the following chapter.

And so, the Mother could say, looking back in 1970 on the past twenty years: 'And I see now, I see how much his departure and his work — so ... so enormous, you know, and persistent in the subtle physical — how much, how much it has helped! How much he has helped to prepare everything, to change the structure of the physical.'[32] In 1972 she said: 'There is a difference in the *power* of action. He himself — he himself! — has more action, more power of action now than in his body. Besides, it was therefore that he left, because it was necessary to do so.'[33] And when Satprem once asked her: 'But why that standstill?' (caused by Sri Aurobindo's passing, he meant), the Mother exclaimed: 'But nothing has come to a standstill! ... He had come for that, and he had arranged everything to ... to secure a maximum of chances ... "chances" by way of speaking: possibilities — to put all the trumps in our hand.'[34] And she also said: 'Sri Aurobindo once told me that he had arranged everything in a way that nothing would be able to disrupt the continuation of his work.'

It can hardly be denied that several commentators have underestimated the degree of Sri Aurobindo's personal transformation — in so far as the word 'personal' is appropriate in his case — being deceived as they were by his so-called 'death.' We know now that he went voluntarily into death. We also remember that he was fully supramentalized except for the material part of his *adhara,* and that personal supramental descents in his body were frequent already in 1938. In the following twelve years his personal transformation, in spite of the upheaval caused by the war, must still have progressed considerably. It so happens that his sonnet *Transformation* is not dated, but it already has the lines:

> Now are my illumined cells joy's flaming scheme
> And changed my thrilled and branching nerves to fine
> Channels of rapture opal and hyaline
> For the influx of the Unknown and the Supreme.[35]

In other words, the transformation of his body at the time had progressed very far. This is why after he had left it, it remained unaffected during 111 hours in the tropics, in an aura of light. And it was the supramental force the cells contained which was transmitted to the body of the Mother.

He had arranged everything so that the continuation of his work would not be disrupted. 'He cast his deeds in bronze to front the years.' *Aere perennius* ... In no article, essay or book can one find what he actually meant by that, what actually was the base of the Work he had come to build and on which the Mother would continue building. Nowhere are mentioned those crucial passages in *Savitri,* from the Book of the Traveller of the Worlds, where the Traveller, who was none else than Sri Aurobindo, descends into the night of the Subconscient and Inconscient. 'The ordeal he suffered of evil's absolute reign' in 'the black inertia of our base':

> Into the abysmal secrecy he came
> Where darkness peers from her mattress, grey and nude,
> And stood on the last locked subconscient's floor

Where Being slept unconscious of its thoughts
And built the world not knowing what it built.
There waiting its hour the future lay unknown,
There is the record of the vanished stars.
There in the slumber of the cosmic Will
He saw the secret key of Nature's change ...

He saw in Night the Eternal's shadowy veil,
Knew death for a cellar in the house of life,
In destruction felt creation's hasty pace
Knew loss as the price of a celestial gain
And hell as a short cut to heaven's gates.
Then in Illusion's occult factory
And in the Inconscient's magic printing house
Torn were the formats of the primal Night
And shattered the stereotypes of Ignorance.
Alive, breathing a deep spiritual breath,
Nature expunged her stiff mechanical code
And the articles of the bound soul's contract,
Falsehood gave back to Truth her tortured shape.
Annulled were the tables of the law of pain ...

He imposed upon dark atom and dumb mass
The diamond script of the Imperishable
Inscribed on the dim heart of fallen things
A paean-song of the free Infinite
And the Name, foundation of eternity,
And traced on the awake exultant cells
In the ideographs of the Ineffable
The lyric of the love that waits through Time
And the mystic volume of the Book of Bliss
And the message of the superconscient Fire ...

Hell split across its huge abrupt façade
As if a magic building were undone,
Night opened and vanished like a gulf of dream ...

Healed were all things that Time's torn heart had made
And sorrow could live no more in Nature's breast:
Division ceased to be, for God was there.
The soul lit the conscious body with its ray.
Matter and spirit mingled and were one.[36]

That is what Sri Aurobindo has done. He has descended into the
lower reaches of existence — 'delve deeper, deeper still' — and there
has changed the programme which produces life as we still know it
at present. At the roots of life, he has made possible the supramental
transformation; its realization is on the way and will manifest materially in the future. Since December 1950 he has kept working
behind the veil of gross matter 'to change the structure of matter'
in order that his reprogramming of the foundations of existence
should be worked out more rapidly. He has 'given all trumps' in the
Mother's hand to bring the Work for which both of them had come
to a successful end.

In a sonnet from 1940, *The Inconscient Foundation*, we find a
confirmation of Sri Aurobindo's work of world re-creation:

My mind beholds its veiled subconscient base,
All the dead obstinate symbols of the past,
The hereditary moulds, the stamps of race
Are upheld to sight, the old imprints effaced.

In a downpour of supernal light it reads
The black Inconscient's enigmatic script
Recorded in a hundred shadowy screeds
An inert world's obscure enormous drift;

All flames, is torn and burned and cast away.
There slept the tables of the Ignorance,
There the dumb dragon edicts of her sway,
The scriptures of Necessity and Chance.

Pure is the huge foundation left and nude,
A boundless mirror of God's infinitude.[37]

To conclude the story of Sri Aurobindo's life in this book, we accompany Rhoda Le Cocq on that last *darshan* of 24 November 1950.

'As a Westerner, the idea of merely passing by these two [Sri Aurobindo and the Mother] with nothing being said, had struck me as a bit ridiculous. I was still unfamiliar with the Hindu idea that such a silent meeting could afford an intensely spiritual impetus. I watched as I came up in line, and I noted that the procedure was to stand quietly before the two of them for a few silent moments, then to move on at a gesture from Sri Aurobindo. What happened next was completely unexpected.

'As I stepped into a radius of about four feet, there was the sensation of moving into some kind of a force field. Intuitively, I knew it was the force of Love, but not what ordinary humans usually mean by the term ...

'Then, all thought ceased, I was perfectly aware of where I was; it was not "hypnotism" as one Stanford friend later suggested. It was simply that during those few minutes, my mind became utterly still. It seemed that I stood there a very long, an uncounted time, for there *was* no time. Only many years later did I describe this experience as my having experienced the Timeless *in* Time. When there at the *darshan*, there was not the least doubt in my mind that I had met two people who had experienced what they claimed. They *were* Gnostic Beings. They had realized this new consciousness which Sri Aurobindo called the Supramental.'[38]

Part Three

The Mother Alone

Chapter Nineteen

TWELVE QUIET DAYS

*I do not believe in the limit that cannot
be exceeded.*[1]

— The Mother

*Since the beginning of the earth,
wherever and whenever there was the
possibility of manifesting a ray of the
Consciousness, I was there.*[2]

— The Mother

SRI AUROBINDO'S sudden corporeal absence meant an
enormous blow to the Mother, 'a sledgehammer blow,' as she said
afterwards, 'an annihilation'. 'The very idea that Sri Aurobindo might
leave his body, that that particular way of being might no longer exist
for the body, was absolutely unthinkable. They had to put him in a
box and put the box in the Samadhi* for the body to be convinced
that it had really happened ... Nothing, nothing, no words can
describe what a collapse it was for the body when Sri Aurobindo left.'[3]
By 'the body' she meant her body: that the blow had been so crushing

---

* 'Samadhi' actually means the yogic exteriorization of the consciousness from the
body. Therefore, the word is also used for the grave or tomb of a yogi, when
his consciousness has left his body definitively.

for her body — for in the higher parts of her being such a reaction was impossible. So intimate was the presence of the One Consciousness in the two bodies that the departure of the one had almost made the other follow automatically; this gives us a deep insight in their true relation of divine Unity and Love.

'You see, he had decided to go. But he didn't want me to know that he was doing it deliberately; he knew that if for a single moment I knew he was doing it deliberately, I would have reacted with such violence that he would not have been able to leave! And he did this ... he bore it all as if it were some unconsciousness, an ordinary illness, simply to keep me from knowing — and he left at the very moment he had to leave ... And I couldn't even imagine he was gone once he had gone, just there, in front of me — it seemed so far away ... And then afterwards, when he came out of his body and entered into mine, I understood it all ... It's fantastic. Fantastic. It's ... it's absolutely superhuman. There's not one human being capable of doing such a thing. And what ... what a mastery of his body — absolute, absolute!'⁴ As long as she stayed in the room, he could not leave his body 'and that was very painful to him.' She then had left the room saying: 'Call me when it is time.'

'I had already had all my experiences, but with Sri Aurobindo, during the thirty years I lived with him (a little more than thirty years), I lived in an absoluteness, an absoluteness of security — a sense of total security, even physical, even the most material security. A sense of absolute security because Sri Aurobindo was there ... Not for *one minute* in those thirty years did it leave me. That was why I could do my work with a Base, really, a Base of absoluteness — of eternity and absoluteness. I realized it when he left: *that* suddenly collapsed ... The whole time Sri Aurobindo was here ... individual progress was automatic: all the progress Sri Aurobindo made, I made. But I was in a state of eternity, of absoluteness, with a feeling of such security in every circumstance. Nothing, nothing unfortunate could happen, for he was there. So when he left, all at once ... a fall into an abyss.'⁵

She then had applied her occult powers and closed an inner door, the door of her psychic being which was the seat of the Love that otherwise would have pulled her away. 'When he went out of his body and entered into mine (the most material part of him, the part involved with external things) and I understood that I had the entire responsibility for all the work *and* for the sadhana — well, then I locked a part of me away, a deep psychic part that was living, beyond all responsibility, in the ecstasy of the realisation: the Supreme. I took it and locked it away, I sealed it off and said: "You're not moving until all the rest is ready"... That in itself was a miracle. If I hadn't done it I would have followed him — and there would have been no one to do the Work. I would have followed him automatically, without even thinking about it. But when he entered into me, he said: "You will do the work. One of us had to go and I am going, but you will do the work." '⁶ She opened that door only ten years later, and even then with great caution.

All activities in the Ashram were stopped for a period of twelve days. What went on inside the Mother in the first days of that period is not documented anywhere. She will probably have been in a continuous state of inner concentration and consultation, for the question was whether the Work should be continued by her alone and whether the Ashram as an institution should remain in existence. 'After Sri Aurobindo's passing, it was feared in some quarters that the Ashram would collapse, at least decline,'⁷ writes Nirodbaran. The Mother, 'in some quarters', apparently was still a French lady whose relation with the Divine and the Supramental never could be as authentic as that of an Indian ... But be that as it may, one can only scrutinize oneself and ask how one would have reacted in such unforeseen and dramatic circumstances.

Although the Mother let the period of twelve days run its full course, for herself everything was decided and determined in the first three days. Sri Aurobindo had physically entered into her with all the supramental force he had accumulated in his cells. She now was MOTHERSRIAUROBINDO* and in the coming years she would often tell how intimately both their personalities had melted into each other

* Thus written in her own handwriting.

and how concretely Sri Aurobindo was present in her. She had undoubtedly seen the full scope of Sri Aurobindo's masterly spiritual manoeuvre as well as of the task which rested now completely on her shoulders in so far as the physical *sadhana* on Earth was concerned. She must also have seen that his voluntary confrontation with death, however unexpected in the development of the Work, had been the right action to accelerate that Work in order to make it achievable within the time of the bodily terrestrial presence of the Avatar. And it must have been clear to her that her body, already prepared for its superhuman task in her mother's womb, was better suited than Sri Aurobindo's to endure the first and critical phases of the supramental transformation.

All developments and experiences in Sri Aurobindo's *sadhana* preceding the *Arya* can be regarded as a preparation for the great Work, without in the least disparaging their importance. The same goes for the *sadhana* of the Mother which, as confirmed by Sri Aurobindo himself, had followed of necessity an identical line and goal as his, as both were one and the same Avatar of the Supermind. From the *Arya* onwards, their Work, which received its definitive seal at the time of their second meeting in 1920, was like a mighty river in the landscape of Matter — a river that would branch out into a broadening delta of increasing supramental Force in the earth-atmosphere, and that finally would flow into the ocean of the supramental Presence in the living mother-body of our symbolical planet. Sri Aurobindo and the Mother, being the double-poled supramental Avatar, have 'seen' this river and its destination from the beginning of their integral yoga; they have all along had a profound knowledge of it, but its bed had to be scoured, delved and hewn in the stony terrain of Matter (this was their *sadhana*) — an effort doomed to failure according to all who had thought of it or tried it in former times.

Their elaboration of this effort was at the same time an arduous and heroic journey of discovery. We, who have now been observing this journey for quite some time, have been able to ascertain how right Sri Aurobindo's foresight has been on most points of importance, even in his first major writings. But we also have met with new discoveries on the way, with some surprises and difficulties which put everything that went before in a new light.

Several learned commentators have concocted a fixed system from Sri Aurobindo's philosophy and yoga, and such systems have been expounded in a number of books. It is seldom admitted that Sri Aurobindo has nowhere proposed a yogic system or a fixed framework of his philosophy. The *Arya* was not intended to divulge a system but to explicate mentally his spiritual discoveries — discoveries which Sri Aurobindo considered important, fertile and even revolutionary enough to share with humanity. Sri Aurobindo's first works contain errors, one of them being that, at that stage in his evolution, he still mistook the Overmind for the Supermind — one of the causes of some misconceptions about the significance of the *Siddhi*-day of 24 November 1926. They inevitably contain lacunae too, simply because his *sadhana* had not achieved in 1914 what it would in 1938 or 1950. Another noteworthy difference between the *Arya* and his later writings is that in the *Arya* he usually recommended to follow the yogic techniques of the Sankhya school, while later on he directs his disciples to anchor their yoga unconditionally in the presence, the force and the help of the Mother. (Question: 'Is thinking of the Mother yoga?' Sri Aurobindo: 'Yes'.)

One might argue that, all the same, it should be possible to systematize Sri Aurobindo's' latest, most advanced realizations, but where are these to be found? About his yoga in the last years, he has written only one text, which moreover he left incomplete, namely 'The Supramental and the Yoga of Works,' inserted in *The Synthesis of Yoga*. The editor of this book writes the following in a biographical note: '*The Synthesis of Yoga* as a whole was never completed. Not only was the "Yoga of Self-Perfection" left unfinished, a proposed additional section was not begun. It also should be remembered that only the first part, "The Yoga of Divine Works," was issued during Sri Aurobindo's lifetime in a thoroughly revised form. The second and more especially the third and fourth parts must be considered as belonging to an earlier period.'

We have already drawn attention to the fact that among the most important documents in connection with Sri Aurobindo's own yoga are his poems and *Savitri,* the epic in which he has said the most, according to the Mother. But how does one systematize that? Stronger still, has not Sri Aurobindo explicitly said that his disciples could not understand what he was doing — just like the Mother would say time and again in later years? Those who want to take up the supramental yoga, he said, must first have reached its threshold, situated beyond the complete psychic and spiritual realizations, beyond the highest realizations of the traditional yogas. Once the aspirant has reached that far — and that is very far indeed — the process of the Supramental Yoga would as it were unfold itself automatically to the predestined soul under the direct guidance of the always present but now no longer veiled Most-Highest or Most-Intimate.

Suffice to say that the *sadhana* of Sri Aurobindo and the Mother has been something completely different from the neatly outlined, watered-down system one finds in most of the treatises. Sri Aurobindo has, on rare ocassions, spoken in a most reticent way about his avataric effort, but the Mother has left us more frequent and intimate glimpses of hers, especially in her conversations with Satprem now published in the thirteen volumes (more than six thousand pages) of *L'Agenda de Mère.* Her experiences also provided essential information about the 'virgin forest' of the unknown in which Sri Aurobindo had ventured and put his scarce statements about himself against a background with some more relief and shades of colour. Let us also not forget that, though the course of the great river of their development had been mapped out from the beginning, the evolution of the *sadhana* of the double Avatar has to be seen as a genuine journey of discovery, maybe the riskiest and most adventurous of all time, full of the unexpected, the grandiose and the quasi-insignificant, of the dangerous, venomous and stubbornly malicious, of the agonizingly torturous and the unutterably ecstatic. One of their discoveries was 'the Mind of Light.'

In his book *The Vision and Work of Sri Aurobindo,* K.D. Sethna has included an early essay of his on the Mind of Light in which he quotes the following words the Mother spoke to him: 'As soon as Sri Aurobindo withdrew from his body, what he has called the Mind

of Light got realised in me. The Supermind had descended long ago
— very long ago — into the mind and even into the vital: it was
working in the physical also but indirectly through those intermediaries. The question was about the direct action of the Supermind
in the physical. Sri Aurobindo said it could be possible only if the
physical mind received the supramental light: the physical mind was
the instrument for direct action upon the most material. This physical
mind receiving the supramental light Sri Aurobindo called the Mind
of Light."[8] This needs some elucidation.

The Supermind is the divine Unity-Consciousness or Truth-Consciousness. ('Supermind' and 'supramental' are technical terms denoting a reality far surpassing our consciousness. Sri Aurobindo has
defined them accurately in his writings.) In the view of Sri Aurobindo
and the Mother, the Earth is an evolutionary field in which the mental
being we call human must be succeeded by a supramental being just
as man has been preceded by a whole series of inframental beings.
Man is a transitional creature. For every material, terrestrial embodiment of a new evolutionary gradation, a direct intervention of the
Divine in his creation is required. Such an embodiment — this time
a complete, double-poled Avatar — were the Mother and Sri
Aurobindo. To bring about the new evolutionary gradation, they had
to go down all previous spiritual paths to the end and then advance
into the unknown. This was their Yoga, their *sadhana*: building the
bridge between the present and the future.

In order to bring the supramental Unity-Consciousness upon
Earth, in matter, they first had to realize it in their inner selves and
afterwards gradually bring down what they had realized into the
degrees of existence between the Supermind and Matter. We have
seen that Sri Aurobindo had brought down the Supramental into his
mental consciousness by 1920 (it might be a useful exercise to try
and imagine what these words mean) and how he stopped the
publication of the *Arya* in January 1921 because the Supramental was
descending in his vital being. The Mother, inwardly one with him,
participated in his progress: 'All progress Sri Aurobindo made, I made
too.' When the world of the cosmic forces in the person of the god
Krishna gave its assent for the new creation by agreeing to descend

into terrestrial matter (the matter of Sri Aurobindo's body), Sri Aurobindo withdrew into his apartment. His only aim from then onwards was to bring the Supramental into the lowest gradation of existence, into terrestrial matter that is, and to establish it permanently on the Earth. The result of such an establishment would be a new world-order, the Kingdom of God on Earth.

We have got some idea of the 'Herculean labour' (Sri Aurobindo's words) which this demanded. To make the decisive step forward, he literally had to go through the whole evolution, also in the Subconscient and Inconscient. For in the inseparable Unity of things, every gradation and every unit of existence contains all other gradations and all other units in itself. The atom contains all other gradations of existence, which otherwise could not have evolved from it, while in its turn it is an already advanced evolutionary form emerged from the somber depths of the Subconscient and Inconscient.

The most obstinate resistance to the descent of the Supramental was shown by the mental gradation of matter, called the 'mental physical' in Sri Aurobindo's terminology. How far the transformation of the mental-physical in his own body had progressed was demonstrated by the transmission of the supramental force it contained into the Mother's body each time she came into the presence of Sri Aurobindo's body after his 'death', and also by the 'miraculous' conservation of his body in a climate that is conducive to disintegration.

The supramental transformation of the mind of the body cells, of the matter of which the body consists, was called 'the Mind of Light' by Sri Aurobindo — of the supramental Light that is the supramental Vibration. About this completely new phenomenon on Earth, he has first written in a series of articles requested by the Mother for the *Bulletin of Physical Education*, the quarterly of the section of physical education in the school she had started. These articles, Sri Aurobindo's last prose writings, have appeared in the quarterly during 1949 and 1950 and were later published as a book with the title *The Supramental Manifestation Upon Earth*.

'What we have called specifically the Mind of Light', Sri

Aurobindo writes there, 'is indeed the last of a series of descending planes of consciousness in which the Supermind veils itself by a self-chosen limitation or modification of its self-manifesting activities, but its essential character remains the same: there is in it [in the Mind of Light] an action of light, of truth, of knowledge in which inconscience, ignorance and error claim no place.'⁹ The Mind of Light is the undiminished, authentic golden Unity-Consciousness, secretly present in the lower levels of the body: those of the mental consciousness of matter.* *That far* Sri Aurobindo had actualized the transformation of his body. But his still was an individual realization, which was clearly illustrated by the fact that it had to be transmitted to the Mother in order that she might carry on with the Work from the point reached by him.

K.D. Sethna rightly calls *The Supramental Manifestation* a sequel to *The Life Divine*. Though this short series of articles leaves many questions unanswered, it is not only important for its presentation and definition of the Mind of Light, but also because there the transitory beings between man and superman are for the first time identified and discussed. For, as we know, at the end of the grand perspective Sri Aurobindo and the Mother had seen 'superman' standing, the being with the supramental Unity-Consciousness, the divine Man, the new species on the Earth. It was to make the transition from man to 'superman' possible that they had come. But in the course of their exploration, they found that here too a number of transitory beings would materially give shape to the transition just as happened in the previous transitions of evolution. Sri Aurobindo and the Mother have always stressed that the new evolution was not a divine caprice but a development based on and in the line of already established processes, although this time on a much wider and more elevated scale.

The Mother therefore said in 1958: 'It can with certainty be affirmed that there will be an intermediary being [she used the word

---

* If one might find it strange that matter has consciousness, one should consider its interrelated and purposeful complexity as discovered by the physicists in the present century.

specimen] between the mental and the supramental being, a kind of superman who still has the qualities and partially the nature of man, which means that he will still belong to the human species of animal origin by his most external form, but who will transform his consciousness in a sufficient manner to belong, in his realization and in his activity, to a new race, a race of supermen. One may consider this species as transitory because it may be foreseen that it will discover the way in which to produce new beings without using the old animal method. And it will be these beings — who will be born in a really spiritual way — who will constitute the elements of the new race,* the supramental race.'[10] This means that henceforth we will have to use the word 'superman' for the being which has been procreated and born in the normal human way but which has acquired a supramental consciousness; the 'supramental being' is then the future, truly new species which has as yet no name and of which the procreation will no longer happen in the animal-human way. 'From the new race [of intermediary beings] would be recruited the race of supramental beings who would appear as the leaders of the evolution in earth-nature.'[11] (Sri Aurobindo)

All of which means that on this Earth we may expect the presence of the following species contemporaneously:

1. the *animal-human*, which will prolong the species we all belong to: the half rational mental being possessing an individualized soul; although the term may sound pejorative, the animal-human is *not* the 'naked ape' of the scientific positivists: he is a forward, inward and upward looking transitory being;

2. the *human-human*, who will embody one or more spiritual gradations between the mental and the supramental consciousness; the human-human is a future being that will originate from the animal-human through the influence of the presence of the Supermind on Earth and that will be fully satisfied with its higher, complete humanness;

---

* Sri Aurobindo and the Mother frequently use the words 'race' and 'species' in the same sense.

3. the *superman*, who will still be born from the sexual union of his progenitors, but who will be in possession of the Mind of Light which is a supramental consciousness, even when for the most part veiled; the superman is an intermediary being and will probably appear in many variants;

4. the *supramental being*, who will embody in the refined form of matter of a being from the supramental typal worlds, material-ized in a hitherto unknown way according to an occult proce-dure.

We may conclude that the word 'superman' (in French *surhomme*), as used in all texts of Sri Aurobindo and the Mother previous to *The Supramental Manifestation*, has from the time of the writing of this series of articles obtained a new meaning because of the discoveries in their Yoga. It is of course important to keep this in mind if one wants to understand correctly what the Mother has said, written and realized after 1950. In October 1956, for instance, she said: 'One should not confound supramental transformation with the appear-ance of a new race,'[12] and two years later: 'There will surely be an innumerable quantity of *partial* realizations,'[13] just like in *homo afarensis, habilis, erectus* and all along in the *australopitheci* has been worked out *homo sapiens.*

The task taken on in 1950 by the Mother, then seventy-two years of age, with her enormous occult and spiritual capacities and now with the Mind of Light in her corporeal substance, was *not* the realization of material supramentality but of corporeal supermanhood as identified in this chapter. This is evident from statements like the one spoken by her on 10 May 1958, when she had accomplished that task. 'I have told my body [in December 1950]: "You are going to realize that supermanhood intermediary between man and the supramental being," this means what I call "superman" (*le surhomme*). And this is what I have been doing for the last eight years,'[14] — from the moment she had decided after Sri Aurobindo's passing that she would continue the Work to keep her promise to him.

Chapter Twenty

THE GOLDEN DAY

*The world unknowing for the world
she stood.*[1]
— Sri Aurobindo

THE PERIOD from December 1950 to December 1958 has no doubt been the most 'visible' in the life of the Mother. From before daybreak till after midnight she was up and about in the Ashram, resting not more than a couple of hours — a rest which could hardly be called sleep. 'The Ashram had become a rather gigantic enterprise,' remembers Satprem in his trilogy *Mère*. 'She looked after everything in the smallest detail, from the quality of the paper for a book in the Ashram Press to the way of sticking a stamp on a post parcel and the shifting of a disciple to another room with a bit of a garden and a little better aerated on the east-side ... And letters without end. And quarrels without end. And the finances — unimaginable and miraculous. And the criticisms — so petty, so absurd! One could make an inquiry even into the Archives of the Quay d'Orsay [the French Ministry of Foreign Affairs in Paris] and find out how generations of industrious bureaucrats have secreted their acid reports. It is hard to imagine: not one of them had understood what the Mother meant to France, to their own country!'[2]

In 1950 there were 750 disciples, not including the children. When the Japanese invaded India and threatened Calcutta, the Mother had given shelter to relatives of the disciples and to their children in the Ashram, 'the safest place on earth because of Sri Aurobindo's presence.' The presence of the children had profoundly disturbed the normal state of affairs in the Ashram and had been a shock and a cause of annoyance to the Ashramites of long standing. Children are brimming with life; children never remain quiet for a long time and are noisy; children have no idea of yoga and but little reverence for its practitioners. An Ashram where men and women lived and moved freely among each other and were treated on equal terms had already caused a lot of raised eyebrows in India. And now those children! One can deduce from many sources that most Ashramites needed time to adapt to such an upsetting change. But the inclusion of the children in the community was very typical of the way Sri Aurobindo and the Mother worked things out. Like with most of their actions, be they literary or organizational, the occasion of the coming of the children was something which had come about of itself and which was then inserted in the growing structure of their Yoga. In this case, it had been the war threatening Bengali families related to Ashramites. And behind all that, we see how the Work, guided by Providence, unfolded more and more after first having been securely implanted in the Earth.

Let us briefly follow this unfolding from the beginning. When Aurobindo Ghose and Mirra Alfassa had reached a certain stage in their individual yoga, they had met and started spreading their message by founding the *Arya*. The apparently fortuitous presence of a handful of young political companions around Sri Aurobindo became the initial core of a spiritual community, called 'Ashram' for the lack of a better word, at first organized and then led by the Mother. The early life in the Ashram was very strict, this inner strictness being necessary for the laying of the foundations of the outward Work. As the number of disciples increased, the community expanded physically and the disciples progressed spiritually, the Mother could slacken the reins and rely more and more on the effect of her inner powers. In what had become a multifaceted miniature of the world, necessary for a Yoga which was intended to embrace 'all life', the youth too were taken in — an indication that the Force, the *Shakti* of the Mother was now able to cope with this unusual and very demanding expansion of the outward Work. In later years, the Ashram, cramped within the town of Pondicherry, would reach something like a physical limit, and in 1968 the Mother will found Auroville, the 'City of Dawn'. Auroville once more implied an augmentation of the life forms and forces to be taken up into this Yoga of world-transformation; it was or should become as it were the first fruit of a Tree cultivated by Sri Aurobindo and the Mother and symbolically representing the effectuation of the Great Work of the Avatar on Earth.

A School with a Difference

> *Make of us the hero warriors we aspire to become. May we fight successfully the great battle of the future that is to be born, against the past that seeks to endure, so that the new things may manifest and we may be ready to receive them.*[3]
> (Prayer written by the Mother and printed in the notebooks of the Ashram school)

The children had to be kept busy and educated, and therefore the Mother founded a school. Of course no school like the other schools in India, where even today subdued children sit on the ground with arms and legs crossed, chanting the lines of a lesson they have to learn by heart at the ticking of the rod of a feared schoolmaster. India has outstanding educational institutions too, but relatively few — far too few for that mass of intelligent youth, eager to learn but crushed under the weight of a standardized or rather calcified educational tradition. Sri Aurobindo had denounced that system already during his years as an educator and a politician. The principles of a renewed education he had proposed against the lifeless traditional ones are still worthy of consideration, in India as well as in the so-called advanced countries.

The child has in itself a soul, which has reached a certain phase of its evolutionary growth. This soul *is* the Divine and therefore contains all knowledge. 'Nothing can be taught to the mind which is not already

concealed as potential knowledge in the unfolding soul of the creature.'⁴ This knowledge is provided from inside by the 'universal In-
structor' to enable the human being, in this as in other incarnations,
to have all necessary experiences for its inner growth, which will ultimately lead to the full maturity of its soul. In the course of the adventure of its incarnations, the human being is guided through all
indispensable experiences and protected by its soul. (This is the explanation of the fact that such vulnerable and ignorant beings as humans
can reach an advanced age despite the ever present threats to life in the
world — as it is a justification for an early death as well.)

From this, two conclusions can be drawn. First: all children have
their very own evolution behind them which has built up into their
very own personality with its particular rhythm of development; this
means that no single educational method can be generally applicable
and that each child has to be approached and assisted individually.
The second conclusion: the true educator is not a 'master' in the sense
of a quasi-omniscient authority, formerly and even now still empowered by society to impose his will and inevitably restricted knowledge
by pressure and even physical violence. He has to be a Master in the
spiritual sense of the word, in order to be able to fathom the inner
personality of his pupils or students and to assist them in their true
needs. Much more than a bossy authority, he has to be an understanding and patient companion, himself aware of his own possibilities and limitations, to help in the progress of the children — his
younger brothers and sisters — on their path of life. 'Education is
a ministry,'⁵ said the Mother. And Sri Aurobindo wrote: 'The greatest
Master is much less a Teacher than a Presence.'⁶

This, quite briefly, was the spirit in which the Mother founded
the Ashram school and made it prosper. 'What is important here is
that the principle of the education is a principle of liberty,'⁷ she said
to the students themselves. 'The progress you will make because you
feel in yourselves the need to make it, because it is an impulse which
pushes you forward spontaneously, and not because it is something
which has been imposed upon you as a rule: this progress, from the
spiritual standpoint, is infinitely superior [to ordinary education].'⁸
'If there are among you who do not want to learn and who do not

like to learn, they have the right not to learn,'⁹ but in such cases it is the duty of the educator or 'companion' to point out to the child the potential consequences of his decision. She wanted them mainly 'to learn to see oneself, to understand oneself and to will oneself.' And to the teachers of her school, she said: 'Actually, *the only thing you have to pursue with assiduity is to teach them to know themselves and to choose their own destiny, the road they want to go.*'¹⁰ 'One has to be a saint and a hero to be a good teacher. One must be a great yogi to be a good teacher. One must be oneself in the perfect attitude to demand that the students be in a perfect attitude. You cannot demand from anybody what you yourselves are not doing.'¹¹

Where are such teachers to be found? Those requirements inherently belonged to the ideal of all teachers in the Ashram school, for they had chosen to dedicate their life in this Ashram to the Yoga of Sri Aurobindo and the Mother. But all of them had been inculcated with the prejudices of their own defective education, which in most cases were the prejudices of the obsolete Indian educational system. This is why the Ashram school provided a training at least as much for the teachers as for the students.

'If we have a school here, it is because we want it to be different from the million schools in the world, it is to give the children a chance of discerning between ordinary life and the life divine, the life of truth, of seeing things differently,'¹² the Mother impressed upon them. 'We are not here to do only a little better what others do, we are here to do what others *cannot* do, because they do not have even the idea that it can be done. We are here to open the way of the Future to children who belong to the Future.' No, the Ashram school was not a kind of monastic school, not an other-worldly breeding ground for aspirant-yogis. Most children had been chosen by the clairvoyant sight of the Mother, no doubt, and if there were others, they also must have had some reason for being there. But the fundamental principle of their education and choice of destiny was freedom; though few have broken the tie with the place of their youth and education after leaving it, only a minority have become members of the Ashram after finishing their studies. And did not the Mother say that only a minority of the Ashram members themselves practised the Yoga? But what about all those others, then? 'They are my children,' she said. They were the 'samples' who brought the whole of human existence within her atmosphere for her to work upon. They were a prolongation of her physical self.

To show the teachers how it could be done, she herself started teaching the little ones and the adolescents, and if the adults found it interesting they too were welcome to join the class, for instance in the evening at the Playground. There the Mother gave French language lessons which soon turned into the *Entretiens*, a kind of didactic conversations; these conversations were recorded and written out afterwards, and would become her most widely read texts. 'The genesis of these conversations deserves to be taken note of,' writes the editor in an introduction to the first of the six volumes. 'They did not originate from an arbitrary decision but from a material necessity, like most of the activities of the Ashram, where matters spiritual are always grafted on matters material. The Ashram "school" had been founded in 1943. The children had grown up; they had learned French; new generations had arrived; and there were not enough teachers. The Mother therefore decided that she herself would take classes of French three times a week for the most advanced students. She read a French text from among her own writings, or translations of Sri Aurobindo's, and the children together with their teachers asked questions. Then, little by little, the disciples also joined the classes and started asking questions.'[14]

She sat behind a small table with a reading lamp, before the map of the true India, under the tropical starry sky; on the dirt-ground around her sat the young ones, still in their sports dress, and behind them the adults. In the background, as ever, the roaring breakers of the sea and the hooting of car horns in dusky Pondicherry. And over the top of the highest walls at regular intervals the sweeping ray of the light-house.

Satprem, also present there, writes in his evocative style: 'In the evening, after her game of tennis, one saw her enter the Playground,*

---

* The Playground was a sand-covered courtyard, enclosed on three sides by buildings and on the fourth by a wall with a big permanent filmscreen.

very small, tranquil, white, with Japanese getas on her feet, in long pyjama-trousers tied around the ankles and a *kamiz** of which the colour changed along with the days — for colours too have their specific power and centre of consciousness — and a head cloth of white muslin because of the wind. But her long hair she had cut. And in "winter" a short cape over her already stooping shoulders ... This Playground was actually the centre of her particular laboratory. They did gymnastics there — quite a lot — exercises on the bars, judo, *hathayoga asanas*, and what not, boxing and horse-vaulting, and so on and so forth. There were the girls in white head-cloths and shorts (shorts in India, in 1950! scandalous! indecent!) together with the boys, in age-groups each with its own colour: the blue group, the khaki group, and green for the little ones, and white once they had become eighteen, gray, etcetera. It was all bright, joyful, it had a kind of transparent atmosphere.'[15]

There the Mother took her French translation classes which became the *Entretiens* (conversations or talks). Splendid texts these are, in a French of great simplicity. But then, she could draw from special sources of inspiration. The children could ask anything they wanted, and she answered clearly, patiently, with a touch of humour or with a force that turned her explanations into revelations. She made them see or experience what she spoke. From those talks alone one could distill a complete spiritual or occult system. Satprem has called those evenings 'the greatest de-occultization' ever undertaken. Had not Sri Aurobindo written: 'To know these things and to bring their truths and forces into the life of humanity is a necessary part of its evolution'? And the Mother possessed the rich experience by which she was able to explain to her audience — or to her readers — the most esoteric subjects in a crystal-clear manner. She taught life to those children — 'People do not know how to live!' — with its causes, backgrounds, mechanisms and purposes. And with its difficulties. For those who were present there were destined to tackle those difficulties and conquer them. She taught them the complexity

---

*   A *kamiz* is a kind of loose shirt worn by the women in North-India. *Salwar-kamiz* is trousers and shirt.

of things, from the smallest to the biggest, with the few that is visible and the much that remains hidden. She had such an enormous cultural, occult and spiritual knowledge, the Mother, and she spoke out of the conscious experience of so many lives. Those present were steeped into a purifying Force which caused all that was best in them to blossom; and she enclosed them under the imperceptible glass of her love and protection — an enclosure in which they could breathe much more freely because she assured them an unpolluted supply of oxygen.

The Ashram school with its section of physical education, its playground and later a well-equipped sports ground, its gymnasium, and its physical ideals far ahead of their time, certainly belongs to the important exemplary realizations of the Mother, since then spread and brought into practice everywhere in the world.

The Transformation of the Cells

The 'public life' of the Mother could be watched by one and all throughout the day. She talked often, not only in the *Entretiens*, but also personally with all who went up to her, helping, consoling, encouraging and guiding. Yet, so little is known about her inner work of supramental transformation, her foremost occupation of which all the rest was only a consequence or application. Looking that period up in the writings of the commentators and biographers, one gets an impression as if the years between Sri Aurobindo's departure and the Supramental Manifestation in 1956 are a kind of void in which nothing important has happened as far as the transformation is concerned. It has even been written that the Mother had started the yoga of the cells, which meant the work of her bodily transformation, only at the end of 1958, the year when she in her turn withdrew. Considering the facts and the nature of the Mother, this cannot but be a misjudgment.

On the one hand, the supramental Force realized in the physical by Sri Aurobindo, the Mind of Light, had during his confrontation with death been transmitted to the Mother, so concretely that she had felt it as a friction every time that Force had entered her body through the pores of its skin. The Mind of Light is the supramental Presence in the cells and it would indeed be a bizarre supramental phenomenon that would be present in the Mother's cells, though in a veiled manner, without being active there in one way or another. Maybe it is because Sri Aurobindo wrote little and rather cryptically about the Mind of Light, and because the Mother in the first years after his passing rarely talked about her own *sadhana*, that the physical presence of the Mind of Light on Earth, in her body, has not been included in the Aurobindonian 'system of yoga' by the commentators, and that they do not seem to know very well what to do with it. But supramental is supramental, which means the whole and undivided Divine; a realization of this kind, now effective in the body cells of the Mother, must be considered as an enormous step forward in the Work of transformation, and she surely must have continued building upon it.

One should consider, on the other hand, that the Mother was a cyclone of Force in absolute surrender. 'Mother's pressure for a change is always strong — even when she doesn't put it as a force it is there by the very nature of the Divine Energy in her,'[16] Sri Aurobindo had written. The Mother was the incarnated *Shakti*, the executive, manifesting Energy of the Divine, there present in that 'small, tranquil, white' figure in Japanese *getas* and wearing an Indian *salwar-kamiz*. How often has she not said with a smile that she was doing the *sadhana* 'at a gallop', like 'a hurricane' or 'a jet plane,' without ever halting at an experience. She was a Force, a Will that goes forward step by step and that cannot halt to tell its experiences, to take pleasure in what has been done. 'I have not lost any time,'[17] she said simply. Now she had taken the Work fully upon her, she had promised Sri Aurobindo that she would do it; and the supramental fire was burning in her cells. Would she, then, have remained inactive during those eight years? ... Already in a conversation on 6 January 1951, one month after Sri Aurobindo's departure and hardly a few weeks after the twelve-day-interlude, she said: 'What remains to be changed is the consciousness of the cells.'[18]

What was the situation? Sri Aurobindo, after his great realizations which had led him to the inner discovery of the Supermind, had brought it down gradually in the mental, the vital and finally, as the Mind of Light, in the matter of his body. This had become possible only by his work in the Subconscient and Inconscient, as explained in a previous chapter. We find a confirmation of this explanation in a conversation of the Mother in which she talks about the inveterate habits present in all elements of the human body, about the atavistic formation which determines its functioning. And she says: 'By going down into the subconscient, into the inconscient, one can trace the origin of this formation and undo what has been done, change the movements and reactions of the ordinary nature by a conscious and deliberate action ... This is not a common achievement, but it has been done. So one may assert not only that it can be done, but that it has been done. It is the first step towards the integral transformation, but after that there remains the transformation of the cells.'[19]

Why are we now hearing time and again about the transformation of the cells and not, let us say, of the atoms? For the problem is the transformation of Matter, is it not? And isn't the Divine present in the atoms as well, a presence which constituted the precondition of the whole material cosmos evolving out of those atoms? 'In the centre of *each atom* of Matter, the supreme divine Reality is secretly present.'[20] (the Mother) 'Every particle of what we call Matter contains all [the other principles] implicit in itself ... Where one principle is present in the Cosmos, there all the rest must be not merely present and passively latent, but secretly at work ... In fact life, mind and Supermind are present in the atom.'[21] (Sri Aurobindo)

The instrument of the supramental transformation is the *adhara*, the complex whole of sheaths or 'bodies' forming the housing of the soul of which we with our external senses can see only the most external, gross material sheath. In the *adhara*, the contact with Matter occurs via the cells, which of course consist of matter but which contain vital and mental elements too. Cells live and have their own consciousness formed in the course of millions of years of evolution. Each cell is a micro-universe with multiple dimensions and within the Great Unity it is in contact with the whole cosmos (as will be demonstrated to the Mother later). 'You think that you are separated from each other, but all that is the same and unique Substance in you

310 • *Beyond Man*

despite differences in appearance, and a vibration in one centre automatically awakes a vibration in another.'[22] The microcosm of the cell is the field, the means of the supramental transformation of Matter, where Matter can be touched and ennobled — the indispensable precondition for the supramental body to be realized in this material Creation.

The mental consciousness of the human being encompasses several 'steps', several functional gradations. Its most apparent functions are the intellect and reason, although both are considerably influenced by the desires of the vital and by sensory perceptions. Above the ordinary intellect and reason, there is pure, abstract reason, *die reine Vernunft*, and then the mental means of receptivity to the higher and illumined mind, the intuition and the overmental — spiritual planes above our mind from where it sometimes receives inspirations, intuitions and insights.

The life forces (the vital) in us too have a consciousness, the 'vital mind', which they use to realize their desires and intentions. (We know for instance how some persons who are not very bright, mentally speaking, are endowed with an instinctive cleverness which renders their possession of the world much more direct and self-assured than that of the 'clever dogs'.) And the body as such too has a consciousness, by which its fabulous complexity is coordinated and which is strongly influenced by heredity, environment and education, as it is by elements from former lives. Character is partially determined by this body-consciousness (the truth behind the saying that 'physiology is destiny'). And the organs have their own consciousness, very important for the way in which they function in illness and health. And the molecules and cells have their consciousness, which is a crucial factor in the process of transformation, as we will find out further on. The stuff atoms and particles are made of has a consciousness — a fact formerly held to be alchemistic gibberish by the physicists but now, since the discovery of quantum mechanics, almost a normal way of looking at matter. The exactitude and power of this consciousness is demonstrated by the mind-boggling complexity of the atoms and their potential force, only explicable by the Unity and its Force within which they are formed and exist. A Unity with such enormous power in such tiny units can only be 'God' — or whatever name one chooses to give to That. It has been found that Matter equals Energy, and it will be found that Energy is Consciousness:

$$MATTER = ENERGY = CONSCIOUSNESS$$

This was the basic formula of the genuine alchemists. 'Matter is a form of Spirit, a habitation of Spirit, and here in Matter itself there can be a realisation of Spirit.'[23] (Sri Aurobindo)

All this is necessary information for the explanation of terms which we will still have to use and which, it must be said, have sometimes been mixed up by the Mother herself. The reason of this confusion was that *physique* in French may mean 'corporeal' as well as 'material' and that the French word *corporel* may indicate the body as well as its elements, including the cells. Let us therefore define unambiguously the following terms needed to describe the process of the supramental transformation of the body:

1. *The mind of the body*: the mental consciousness of the body as a whole; the mastery over the mind of the body is an elementary condition in most yogas and had been realized by the Mother long before she went to Pondicherry;

2. *The mind of the cells*: the very own, age-old consciousness of the cell, the transformation of which is indispensable in order to reach out to Matter-as-such and transform it; and

3. *The mind of matter*: the consciousness in the atoms and elementary particles of so-called gross matter as experienced by our senses, but which seems already to escape the grip of the physicists. 'Matter itself is found to be the result of something that is not Matter,'[24] Sri Aurobindo had already written in *The Life Divine*.

Let us now follow some of the phenomena of the process of transformation in the Mother during the period between Sri Aurobindo's departure and the Supramental Manifestation in 1956.

* On 26 February 1951 she ends her *Entretien* (about the Gnostic consciousness) with the words: 'I am telling you this to-night because what has been done, what has been realized by one can

also be realized by the others. It suffices that one body has realized it, a human body, to have the assurance that it *can* be done. You may put that still very far ahead of you, but you may say: "Yes, the Gnostic life is a certainty, for its realization has begun." '[25] The Gnostic life is the supramental life, and that 'one body' cannot have been another than hers.

* In her *Entretien* of 19 April 1951 she talks about the surrender to the Divine, the fundamental attitude in the Integral Yoga. 'This now has become the very movement of the consciousness of the cells.' And she mentions 'the aspiration in the consciousness of the cells for the perfect sincerity of the consecration.'[26]

* 21 April 1954: 'There are still a number of years ahead of us before we will be able to talk knowledgeably about how it [the transformation of the body] will come about, but I can tell you that it has begun. If you read attentively the next issue of the *Bulletin,* which you will get on 24 April, you will see that it has begun.'[27] In that issue appeared her 'Experiences of the Consciousness of the Body' (actually the consciousness of the cells), followed by 'New Experiences of the Consciousness of the Body.' The last series ended as follows: 'In this intensity the aspiration grows formidable, and in answer to it Thy presence becomes evident in the cells themselves, giving to the body the appearance of a multicoloured kaleidoscope in which innumerable luminous particles in constant motion are sovereignly reorganised by an invisible and all-powerful Hand.'[28]

In that year — 1954 — the work of the Mother on the cells of her body clearly had reached a sort of climax, given the possibilities at that moment:

5 May. The power to act on the circumstances can be brought down 'in Matter, in the substance itself, in the cells of the body,'[29] she says. 'This is not a belief, it is a certitude resulting from an experience.'[30]

One week later: 'It is as if the cells themselves burst into an aspiration, in a call. In the body, there are inestimable and unknown treasures. In all those cells there is an intensity of life, of aspiration, of will-to-progress of which habitually one is not conscious.'[30]

9 July. 'Drop all fear, all strife, all quarrels, open your eyes and your hearts — the Supramental Force is there.'[31]

3 November. 'Every part of the being has its own aspiration, which has the character of the part that is aspiring. There even is a physical aspiration ... The cells of the body understand what the transformation will be, and with all their strength, with all the consciousness they contain they aspire to that transformation. The cells of the body themselves — not the central will, not the thinking or emotions — the cells of the body open themselves to receive the Force.'[32]

11-12 November. 'The serene and immobile consciousness watches at the boundaries of the world as a Sphinx of eternity and yet to some it gives its secret. We have, therefore, the certitude that what has to be done will be done, and that our present individual being is really called upon to collaborate in this glorious victory, in this new manifestation.'[33]

How, in the face of all these unmistakable quotations, could one possibly keep asserting that the Mother commenced her work of transformation in the cells only years later? Besides, when following her evolution in this period one understands that precisely this kind of work was necessary to enable the Supramental to manifest. The cell consists not only of a mental, vital and material but also of a subconscious and an inconscient element; for the Inconscient is the womb from which Matter has originated and Matter still remains wholly impregnated by that dark substance, also in the cell. The Mother was now working out what the fundamental preparatory work of Sri Aurobindo during his life, by his confrontation with death and now behind the veil had made a possibility. It was a task taking up each moment of her time, a concentration night and day besides and above the enormous general labour she was performing, and that constant occult effort was only very partially visible to human eyes. Sri Aurobindo once wrote: 'It is only divine Love which can bear the burden I have to bear, that all have to bear who have sacrificed everything else to the one aim of uplifting earth out of its darkness towards the Divine.'[34] One who realizes what Sri Aurobindo and the Mother have done for the Earth and for us, the sons and daughters of the Earth, may well remember this.

A Prediction

Then came the announcement of 31 December 1954, New Year's Eve. As every year, the Mother had a New Year's message printed which was now distributed to all those present at the Playground. Generally, those messages are revealing of what is going to happen in the coming year.[35] The message read: 'No human will can finally prevail against the Divine's Will. Let us put ourselves deliberately and exclusively on the side of the Divine, and the Victory is ultimately certain.'[36]

Her astonishing commentary: 'This message has been written because one foresees that next year will be a difficult year and that there will be many interior struggles — maybe even exterior ones. I therefore tell you what is the attitude you have to adopt in such circumstances. Those difficulties perhaps will not last for twelve months but for fourteen months.'[37] The Supramental Manifestation took place *exactly* fourteen months later, on 29 February 1956!

One of the youngsters asked: 'Will it [1955] be a difficult year for the Ashram or also for India and for the whole Earth?' She answered: 'General: Earth, India, Ashram and individuals ... It is the last hope of the adverse forces to triumph against the present Realization. If we can stand firm during these months, they won't be able to do much afterwards, their resistance will crumble. This is what it is about: it is the essential conflict of the adverse forces, of the antidivine forces, who are trying to push back the divine Realization as much as possible — thousands of years, they hope. And it is this conflict that has reached its paroxysm. It is their last chance. And as the beings who are behind their exterior action are totally conscious, they are fully aware that it is their last chance and they will do everything they can. And what they can is quite a lot. These are no small, ordinary forms of human consciousness; they are not at all forms of human consciousness. These are forms of consciousness who, in proportion to the human capacities, seem divine in their power, their might, and even in their knowledge. Consequently, this is an enormous conflict which is totally focused on the Earth, for they know that it is on the Earth that the first victory must be won — the decisive victory, the victory which will decide the course of the future of the earth.'[38]

We might briefly call to mind the 'external', historical events of that year. The year 1955 was the culmination of the Cold War. It was the year the Warsaw Pact was signed, the first Russian H-bomb was exploded, and the first American nuclear submarine was launched. It was the year of the Conference of Bandung, 'a revolt of Asia and Africa against the white race' by the Nassers, Sukarnos and Nehrus. West Germany became a sovereign state. The struggle for power after Stalin's death raged on in the Kremlin creating an unstable situation with great dangers for the country and the world. China and the Soviet-Union still acted in unison. The nuclear race was in full swing.

We read in K.D. Sethna: 'When she concluded her talk on 5 January 1955, a few questions were put to her by one of the brightest students of our Education Centre: Manoj Dasgupta. He asked: "You have said that in 1955 the hostile forces will try to give a tremendous blow. If we prove incapable of getting the victory, will the transformation at which our Yoga aims be considerably retarded?" The Mother replied with a grave face: "It will be retarded by many centuries. It is just this retardation that the hostile forces are attempting to bring about. And in spiritual matters up to the present they have always succeeded in their delaying tactics. Always the result has been: "It will be done some other time." And the other time may be hundreds of years later or even thousands of years. Now again the same trick is being tried." '[39] She added: 'Maybe all that is ordained somewhere. It is possible. But it is also possible that, whatever has been ordained, it is not good to reveal what has been decided, so that it may come about in the way it has to.'[40] The Great Mother, out of whose hand flows all that is created, all events and all forces, always knows in the three time-modes (*trikaldrishti*): past, present and future. Incarnated as the Mother of the Sri Aurobindo Ashram, however, she had to work out what had been ordained in her difficult *sadhana* for the Earth.

It must have been a terrible battle that she fought, without anybody being aware of it. 'The world unknowing for the world she stood.' Satprem writes somewhere that Sri Aurobindo's yoga is 'the invisible yoga *par excellence*,' and it was most invisible in Sri Aurobindo and the Mother. It is one of the seals of authenticity on their Work.

The Supramental Manifestation

And then it happened. The Sun broke through the mists that had enshrouded the Earth since its beginning and a New Day began, the Day of the concrete Presence of the Divine in his creation. We are still blind like new-born babes and therefore do not see that new Light, but some begin to feel its warmth over their face and in their heart.

It was the evening of 29 February in the leap year 1956. At the Playground, the Mother had read a passage from the *Synthesis*; the young ones had asked questions and she had answered them. And when there were no questions anymore, somebody switched off the light as usual for the meditation. It happened during that meditation.

'This evening the Divine Presence, concrete and material, was there present amongst you. I had a form of living gold,' wrote the Mother, 'bigger than the universe, and I was facing a huge and massive golden door which separated the world from the Divine. As I looked at the door, I knew and willed, in a single movement of consciousness, that *"the time has come"*, and lifting with both hands a mighty golden hammer I struck one blow, one single blow on the door and the door was shattered to pieces. Then the supramental Light and Force and Consciousness rushed down upon earth in an uninterrupted flow.'[41]

The aim for which the supramental Avatar had incarnated on Earth was accomplished. A new evolution, the evolution of a divine species, could begin.

'My Lord, what Thou hast wanted me to do I have done. The gates of the Supramental have been thrown open and the Supramental Consciousness, Light and Force are flooding the earth. But as yet those who are around me are little aware of it — no radical change has taken place in their consciousness and it is only because they trust my word that they do not say that nothing has truly happened. In addition the exterior circumstances are still harder than they were and the difficulties seem to be cropping up more insurmountable than ever. Now that the Supramental is there — for of that I am *absolutely certain* even if I am the only one upon earth to be aware of it — is it that the mission of this form is ended and that another form is to take up the work in its place? I am putting the question to Thee and ask for an answer — a sign by which I shall know for certain that it is still my work and I must continue in spite of all the contradictions, all the denials. Whatever is the sign, I do not care, but it must be *obvious*.'[42]

So strong had been the Force, on that evening of 29 February, that the Mother thought all those present at the Playground would be flattened out on the ground. But when the light came on again, all stood up from their sitting position and simply walked through the gate into the street, probably hungry and looking forward to their supper. 'If all of you who have heard about it, not one time but probably hundreds of times, who have talked about it yourselves, who have thought of it, hoped for it, wanted it ... There are people who have come here for that, with the intention of receiving the Supramental Force and to transform themselves into supermen. But then, how come that all of you were so foreign to that Force that, when it has come, you have not even felt it?'[43] Because only like can know or recognize like. As early as in 1950 she herself had said: 'It is very well possible that at a certain moment the Supramental Force manifests itself, that it will consciously be present here, that it will act on matter, but that consciousnesses which do not share in its vibration be incapable of perceiving it.'[44]

There were some who had felt the new Force, she hastened to add. Not many — a handful. All in all, five. One of them was K.D. Sethna, who has related his experience to students and teachers of the Ashram school. In the evening of that 29 February, he had seen the Mother in his compartment of the night train from Madras to Bombay, with his eyes wide open. 'On my return to the Ashram she explained what had occurred ... She said: "There were only five people who knew about the Supramental Manifestation — two in the Ashram and three outside." She said: "I don't mean that anybody actually knew the Supermind had manifested, but something extraordinary happened to some people. Among those three who were outside, I count you." Puzzled, I asked: "How's that?" She answered: "Didn't you write to me that on February 29 at night you had seen me in the railway compartment?" I said: "Yes, but what did happen?" She replied: "Do you remember I promised in 1938 to inform you? I came now to fulfill my promise." ' Eighteen years later.

The Mother has often emphasized that one should allow an inner experience to work itself out as quietly and undisturbed as possible, without wanting to intervene, to understand or to interpret it mentally. An immediate mental interpretation can but deform the experience — worse, it mostly interrupts it. It is clear that the Mother, as after all her great experiences, wanted to be fully certain of the scope of her Cosmic Act on 29 February; she therefore published the announcement of the new Dawn in the *Bulletin of Physical Education* of 24 April, two months afterwards. There one reads:

Lord, Thou hast willed and I execute:
A new light breaks upon the earth,
A new world is born.
The things that were promised are fulfilled.

These were exactly the same vibrating words which she had written many years earlier in her *Prayers and Meditations*, but what was at the time still a promise for the future, and therefore grammatically written in the future tense, had now become reality and all the verbs were put in the present tense.

And below those words was printed: 'The manifestation of the Supramental upon earth is no more a promise but a living fact, a reality. It is at work here, and one day will come when the most blind, the most unconscious, even the most unwilling shall be obliged to recognise it.'[46]

A new world was born; a new era in the evolution of Mother Earth, the symbolical centre of the cosmos, began. Since that leap day no earthling can escape the effects of the Supramental. In other words, the Divine is since then concretely active in our matter and in all Matter, to transform it and build his Kingdom on Earth. The time this will require may seem long to our human way of experiencing things; for in our childlike naïveté we always expect miracles to happen in a jiffy. But the Miracle is now becoming reality. Who is there who does not feel that we are being carried through the gates of the new millennium in an acceleration, a vortex of time?

'To celebrate the birth of a transitory body can satisfy some faithful feelings.

'To celebrate the manifestation of the eternal Consciousness can be done at every moment of the universal history.

'But to celebrate the advent of a new world, the supramental world, is a marvellous and exceptional privilege.'[47]

Since then, we have to read Sri Aurobindo in a completely different light. For everything he did and wrote was focused on the great future Event which he knew to be 'inevitable', which he also knew to be ordained somewhere, but which had to be executed by him and by the Mother in a merciless battle. Because of his superhuman decision to enter consciously into death and thanks to his work 'behind the veil,' his fifth 'dream' became reality hardly six years after his departure. It is of the essence of his heart as Avatar, of his divine Love, to keep helping humanity on the road forward just as he has always done, 'carrying on the evolution' till he will be visible for everybody in a transformed world. As the Mother said, he has confided to her shortly after his passing that he would come back in the first truly supramental body. 'When I asked him (December 8, 1950) to resuscitate his body, He clearly answered: "I have left this body purposely. I will not take it back. I shall manifest again in the first supramental body built in the supramental way." '[48]

We also draw attention to the question of the Mother to the Supreme: 'Now that the Supramental is there ... is it that the mission of this form is ended?' The answer for us now seems to be self-evident, as everybody knows that she has continued working on Earth till 1973. In 1956, however, the answer was not evident at all, and the question itself shows that she might have left her material body at that time. The following chapters will clarify this important point.

It shows, firstly, that the Work of the Avatar as probably conceived by the Mother up to 1956 was to bring the Supramental upon Earth, in other words, to establish the unshakable base of the Kingdom of God on Earth — and that the working out of the supramental Presence into a new world and a new species was to be left to future elaborations perhaps of very long duration. This is completely in accord with everything Sri Aurobindo has told about this matter: that the Avatar comes to do the pioneering work, to prepare the terrain and to plant the magic seed from which the new tree will grow, however much time that may take. 'What we are doing, if and when we succeed, will be a beginning, not a completion.'⁴⁹

The Mother will repeat more than once in the following years that she was still upon Earth solely because she had promised Sri Aurobindo to do the Work: '*Je fais le travail*' (I am doing the work). In 1956, she asked for an obvious sign; such a sign must have been given to her. We may reasonably suppose that the result of her work between 1956 and 1973 has accelerated the formation of the supramental species by thousands of years. For at first she predicted that the being beyond man would appear thousands of years later, but towards the end she generally spoke about a period of not more than three hundred years. She has made a sacrifice of seventeen years of often pure hell, as we will see further on, so that our hell in this and future lives might be changed into 'a joyful pilgrimage' towards That which is worth being experienced like nothing else. It cannot have been the explicit or even the implicit goal of Sri Aurobindo and the Mother to work out the complete transformation in their own body. It is good to keep this in mind.

From K.D. Sethna is the reflection: 'I wonder when the world will realise that in 1956 the greatest event in its history took place.'⁵⁰

The Mother called 29 February 'the Golden Day.'

Chapter Twenty-one

THE SHIP FROM THE NEW WORLD

One must first of all fight an enormous mass of foolish prejudices which put material and spiritual life irreconcilably against each other ... One must be able to take up all, to combine all, to synthesize all.[1]

— The Mother

THE QUALITY of the atmosphere had changed, the Mother said. 'The development has been much accelerated. The stages of the march forward follow each other much faster ... Things are changing quickly.'[2] She felt that very concretely during the projection of a film at the Playground. (She always had found film a powerful means of expression for better or worse. And why is it so difficult to show a deeply stirring beautiful story with an encouraging, positive ending, she asked.)

It was a Bengali film, *Rani Rasmani*, about the rich widow of that name and Ramakrishna Paramhamsa. In 1847, this lady had the Kali temple built where Ramakrishna passed his later years in adoration of Kali, the Mother. The temple is still a much visited place of pilgrimage.

The Mother saw all films at the Playground together with the young and the adult Ashramites. 'Then I have really understood — for it was not an understanding with the head, not with the intellect, but with the body, you know what I mean: it was an understanding in the cells of the body — that a new world *is born* and that it is beginning to grow ... I have announced to all of you that that new world was *born*. But it has so much been swallowed up, so to speak, in the old world that up to now the difference has not been very perceptible for a lot of people. Yet, the activity of the new forces has been going on in a very regular way, very persistently, very assiduously and, in a certain measure, very efficaciously,' she said in July 1957.[3]

The film gave a vivid picture of the religious life, perhaps as lived by Ramakrishna Paramhamsa at the highest and purest level. But even to him, one of the precursors of the New Age, religion, even in its most unselfish and ecstatic devotion, could not but be directed towards a world hereafter — just like all religion, all spirituality, all yoga up to then. The Mother, now permeated by the manifested Supermind and opening herself totally for its action even 'in the cells of the body', experienced a New World in which the Promise to humankind world be fulfilled here, on the Earth, and not in a hereafter. She experienced this New World as such a contrast with the former one that the difference appeared to her as big as the difference between the new human being and the animals. To realize the importance of the birth of the New World, one had 'to find a comparison, to go back to the time of the transition between the creation of the animal and the creation of the human being.'[4]

This is why she said with such emphasis to her audience, the young sitting there in the sand in front of her, in one of her most lyrical, at times hymnic talks: 'It is a new world that is *born, born, born*. It is not the old one that is transforming itself, it is a *new* world that is *born*. And we are now fully in the transitional period in which both are overlapping: in which the old one still persists in an all-powerful way and entirely dominates the ordinary consciousness, while the new one is penetrating still very modestly, unnoticed — so much unnoticed that on the surface it does not upset much for the time being, and that even to the consciousness of most people it remains as yet altogether imperceptible. But it is active all the same, it is growing, till the moment that it will be strong enough to impose itself visibly.'[5]

And she went on: 'All those former things [the religions] are now looking so old, so outdated, so fortuitous, such a travesty of the true truth. In the supramental creation there will be *no religions* anymore. All life will be the expression, the unfolding in forms of the divine Unity manifesting itself in the world. And there will not be what men now call "gods" any longer. Those great beings will be able to participate in the new creation themselves, but to this end they will have to embody in what one might call "the supramental substance" on earth. And if among them there are some who prefer to remain in their own world as they are, who decide not to manifest physically, then their relation with the beings of the [future] terrestrial supramental world will be a relation of friends, of co-workers, of equals; for the highest divine essence will have manifested in the beings of the new supramental world on earth.

'When the physical substance will be supramentalized, to incarnate on earth will no longer be a condition of inferiority; on the contrary, one will acquire a fullness which otherwise is unobtainable. But all this is in the future. It is a future that has *begun*, but that will take a certain time to realize itself integrally. In the meantime, we find ourselves in a very special situation, extremely special, which never had a precedent. We are present at the birth of a new world, so young, so feeble (not in its essence but in its exterior manifestation), not yet recognized, not even sensed but denied by most. But it is there! It is there, exerting itself to grow and completely *sure* of the result. But the way to arrive at it is totally new and has never been cleared before: nobody has ever gone there, nobody has done this! This is a beginning, *a universal beginning*. Consequently, it is an absolutely unexpected and unforeseeable adventure.'

Through that youth there in front of her she summoned the whole world to the adventure, the present world which in the vortex of accelerated time does not very well know anymore what things are all about or in what direction it is going. Things are about nothing from the past; it is going in the direction of Something completely new.

'There are people who like adventure. They are the ones I am calling up, and I say to them: "I invite you to the great adventure."

'It is not about spiritually doing once again what others have done before us, for our adventure starts beyond. It is about a new creation, entirely new, with everything it brings that is unforeseen, with risks and insecurities — a *true adventure* of which the aim is a sure victory but of which the road is unknown and has to be cleared in unexplored terrain. It is something that *never* has existed in the present universe and that never will present itself in the same way. If you are interested, good, come aboard. What will happen tomorrow, I do not know.

'You have to leave behind everything you had been expecting, everything you had planned, everything you had built, and then go forward into the unknown. What will happen, will happen! And that is that.'[6]

On regarde là où on veut aller.[7]
(One keeps one's sight on the aim one wants to attain.)
The Mother

The victory is assured, she said. The years 1957 and 1958 were years of assurances, with many emphatic affirmations. There is no doubt that the Mother in those months has physically realized the supermanhood of which the general Consciousness will establish itself in the Earth-atmosphere on 1 January 1969. The following passages from the *Entretiens* leave no doubt about this.

* On 29 May 1957 she talked about the transitional being between the present animal-human and the future supramental being, and she said: 'Now, at this moment, that state [of the transitional superman] can be realized on earth by those who are ready to receive the supramental Force that is manifesting.'[8] And she repeats this. Such an unconditional confirmation could only stem from her own experience. ('The only thing I can speak of is my own experience.'[9])

* On 25 September of the same year, she comments on a passage from *The Supramental Manifestation* in which Sri Aurobindo writes about the 'superman' according to his novel definition.

The Mother tells her audience at the Playground: 'That was surely what he was expecting of us: what he saw as the superman (*le surhomme*) who has to be the intermediary being between humankind as it is and the supramental being *created* in a supramental way, which means that it will not at all belong to the animality anymore and that it is free of all animal needs.' And another affirmation: 'I think ... I *know* that it is now certain that we will realize what he expects from us. It has become no longer a hope, but a certitude.' And what she adds is also interesting at the point we have arrived: 'There is a moment that the body itself finds that *nothing in the world* is worth to be lived as much as that: the transformation ... It is as if all cells of the body were thirsting for that Light that wants to manifest. They cry for it, they find such an intense joy in it, and they are *sure* of the Victory.'[10]

* *Durgapuja* is the festival of goddess Durga with her trident and lion, one of the belligerent forms of the Universal Mother. It is a big religious feast in India, especially in Bengal, and lasts ten days of which the last three are the most important. On the tenth day, Durga with her trident kills a demon, a *rakshasa* — a killing which is symbolical for the victory of the Mother over the hostile forces. On 2 October 1957, *vijaya dashami*, the 'day of Victory,' the Mother gave the following message: 'For those who use nothing but their physical eyes, the victory will be apparent only when it is total, that is to say, physical.' And she added the same day: 'But this does not mean that it is not already won in principle.'[11]

* On 16 April 1958, the Mother begins her commentary on a long passage from *The Life Divine*, in which Sri Aurobindo gives one of the earliest indications about the indispensability of a super-human intermediary being, with the words: 'We have now reached a certitude since there is already a beginning of realization.' In whom but in herself ? 'We have now proof that in certain conditions the ordinary state of humanity can be surpassed and that a new state of consciousness can work itself out which at least renders possible a conscious relation between mental man and

higher man [i.e. *le surhomme*]'.[12] And once again she describes in unmistakable terms what that intermediary being will be.

All this is very plain and very positive. In the post-1973 comments on her work, these important realizations, these milestones on the road of the transformation seem to be forgotten, eclipsed in the minds of commentators by 'the fact of the death' of the Mother. But it is no exaggeration to posit that every year of her avataric *sadhana,* of her work on Earth after 1956, when she had voluntarily consented in staying with us, has expedited the supramental transformation of the Earth by thousands of years. A postulate of this kind cannot be rendered in exact numbers, of course, but its general truth is unquestionable.

She concludes that *Entretien* as follows: 'This new realization keeps evolving with what one may call "lightning speed". For if we consider time in the common fashion, only two years have gone by (a little more than two years) between the moment that the supramental substance penetrated into the Earth-atmosphere and the moment that this change in the quality of the Earth-atmosphere has taken place.' And a change in the Earth-atmosphere, just like the manifestation of the Supramental in it, cannot be cancelled, cannot be effaced. The transformational process was and remains irreversible.

On 8 October, the Mother again talks about the superman, 'what we call the superman [*le surhomme*], namely the being born in the human way and which tries to transform its physical being which it has got by its common human birth.' Will there be such intermediary forms? 'There will certainly be an innumerable quantity of *partial* realizations ... There will be a considerable number of essays, more or less fruitful or more or less unfruitful, before arriving at something that will resemble the superman, who himself will be a more or less successful attempt.

'All those who make an effort to surpass ordinary nature, all those who try to realize materially the profound experience that has put them into contact with the divine Truth, all those who, instead of turning their attention to the Hereafter or the Above, try to realize physically, externally, the change of consciousness which they have realized inside themselves: all those are apprentice-supermen ... They have more or less advanced on the way, but before reaching the end of it nobody will be able to tell which degree of his development he has reached. It is the last degree that will matter.' Who or where were those apprentice-supermen then? Who or where are they now? 'How far we have come is of no concern to us.' Defining the position, getting the bearings is for later, for the suprahistory of the future, when the whole of the process of transformation will be surveyable. And she formulated one of those unforgettable dicta of hers: '*On regarde là où on veut aller.*'

Mother Nature

We do not want to obey the orders of Nature, even when enforced by habits having lasted for billions of years.[14]

— The Mother

The New Year's message for 1958 read: 'O Nature, material Mother, Thou hast said that thou wilt collaborate and there is no limit to the splendour of this collaboration.'[15] We know that every message of the Mother was the precipitation of an experience, of something she had perceived or gone through. 'It is an experience, something that has happened.' On what experience could this mysterious message have been based?

Mother Nature is one of the emanations of the Great Mother herself, more precisely the emanation which is in charge of the Earth, of the material evolution of the Earth, and of the beings born from her womb. Which means that she is fairly familiar to us, for example from Greek mythology.

Along a path of aeons serpentine ...
The Earth-Goddess toils across the sands of Time.[16]

— *Savitri*

It is comical, in a sense, that the Mother fell foul with Mother Nature, which meant that she had a quarrel with a part of her own self! We have already seen that emanations lead independent lives. (This is the reason, for instance, that whole 'cascades' — emanations in stepwise gradations — of two of the four great *Asuras* are still active, while the one *Asura* has converted himself and the other has been dissolved into his Origin.)

Mother Nature, though being an emanation of the Creatrix, has her own character and will. What vexed the embodied Mother, she who was the incarnated *Shakti* with always that strong 'pressure for change' and progress, was the fact that Nature executed her task much too slowly and in a roundabout way. 'She throws herself into action with an abundance and a total lack of economical sense.' We can see this for ourselves: the trillions of blades of grass, the trillions of seeds, the trillions of insects' eggs. 'She tries out everything possible in every way possible and with all possible kinds of invention which naturally are quite remarkable, but ... it is like a road without end ... She projects her creative spirit with an abundance that does not calculate, and when a combination is not very successful, she simply eliminates it without any bother. To her, you see, that abundance has no limits. I think that there is no kind of experiment she is not eager to perform. It is only when something has a chance of leading up to a line of development ending in a result that she keeps going on with it ... It is evident that she enjoys it and that she is not in a hurry. If one asks her to work faster and to finish some part or the other of her work, her reply is always the same: "But why? Why? Don't you find this amusing?" '[17] No, the Mother did not find it amusing. The laying of the foundations of the supramental manifestation had to be done now, within a given period of time.

Some months before, the Mother had already talked about the 'macabre whimsy of Nature'. 'She sees the whole, she sees the connections. She sees that nothing is lost, that the quantities, the innumerable minuscule elements without any importance, are only recombined, thrown once more into the cauldron, to be well stirred and produce something new again. But this game is not funny for everybody.' It was time to change the rules of the game. 'It is evident that the biggest obstacle [to the transformation] is the attachment to things as they are. But Nature as a whole finds that those who have a profound knowledge want to go too fast. She likes her meanders, she likes her successive attempts, her failures, her new starts, her new inventions. She likes the whimsicality of a way, the unexpected result of an experiment. One could almost say that for her the more time it takes the more pleasant it is.'[18]

However, Mother Nature had now agreed to collaborate on the New Creation. 'The evening I have told you those things' — when the Mother had expressed her annoyance at the meanderings of Nature — 'I have identified myself with Nature, completely, I have entered into her game. And that act of identification has resulted in a response, a sort of new intimacy between Nature and myself, a long movement of approachment that has culminated in an experience which produced itself on 8 November [1957].

'All of a sudden, Nature has understood. She has understood that this new Consciousness which is born does not intend to reject her but to embrace her fully. She has understood that this new spirituality does not distance itself from life, does not recoil in fear before the amplitude of its movements but that, on the contrary, it wants to integrate all its elements. She has understood that the supramental Consciousness is not there to diminish her but to complete her.

'Then, from the supreme Reality has come the following order: "Wake up, o Nature, to the joy of collaboration!" And the whole of Nature, in an immense impulse of joy, has rushed up to answer: "I agree, I collaborate" ... She accepted. She saw, with all eternity in front of her, that this supramental Consciousness was going to accomplish her more perfectly, that it would add more force to her movements, more amplitude, more possibilities to her game.

'And suddenly I heard, as if coming from the four corners of the Earth, the great musical sounds which one sometimes hears in the subtle physical, somewhat alike to those of Beethoven's [violin] concerto in D minor, as if fifty orchestras burst out together without one single note out of key, to tell the joy of this new communion of Nature and Spirit — the encounter of two old friends who meet again after a long separation.'[19] This was how her message for the New Year had come about.

And so, once more, the veils lifted over the daily existence of the

Mother. She never spoke just like that; her words were always actions — in her environment, in the whole of this world and in all worlds. For what may a message of this kind mean to somebody who sees it printed on paper without any background information? What notion do we have of the echoes vibrating in her words? What notion did her still so young audience have of her multidimensional presence, of the complex play of forces they were involved in, focused on that apparently frail, white, small but so powerful figure sitting there in front of them? 'For instance, in whatever happens, there is at the same time its explanation ("explanation" is not the right word, but anyhow) its explanation by the ordinary human consciousness (by "ordinary" I do not mean banal, I mean the human consciousness as it is), the explanation as given by Sri Aurobindo in an illumined mind, and the divine perception. All three are simultaneous for the same happening. How to express this with words?'[20]

The end of those years of *Entretiens* is now fast approaching; soon this kind of voice will no longer be heard. Let us therefore listen to a very important experience — but what experience was *not* important? — which she has dictated herself (probably to Pavitra) and which she even found worthwhile to read out at the Playground.

'Formerly, I had an individual subjective contact with the supramental world, whereas on 3 February [1958] I walked in it concretely — as concretely as I once walked in Paris — in a world that *exists in itself*, outside all subjectivity. It is as if a bridge is being built between the two worlds. This is the experience as I have dictated it immediately afterwards. [The Mother reads:]

'The supramental world exists permanently and I am there permanently in a supramental body. I got proof of it this very day, because my terrestrial consciousness has gone and remained there consciously between two and three o'clock in the afternoon. I know now that what is lacking for the two worlds to join in a constant and conscious relation is an intermediate zone between the physical world as it is and the supramental world as it is. It is this zone which remains to be built, both in the individual consciousness and in the objective world, and which is being built. When formerly I used to talk of the new world that is being created, it was this intermediary zone that I meant. And similarly, when I am on this side (in the domain of the physical consciousness, that is) and when I see the supramental power, light and substance constantly penetrating into matter, it is the construction of this zone I see and in which I participate.

'I was on a huge ship, which is a symbolical representation of the place where the work is being done. This ship, as large as a city, is fully organized and surely must already have been functioning for some time, for its organization was completely established. It is the place where the people are being trained who are destined for the supramental life. These people (or at least a part of their being) had already undergone a supramental transformation, for the substance of the ship itself and of everything on board was neither material nor subtle-physical, vital or mental: it was a supramental substance.

'This substance consisted of the most material supramental, the supramental substance nearest to the physical world and the first that will manifest. The light was a mixture of gold and red, resulting in a uniform substance of a luminous orange. Everything was like that — the light was like that, the people were like that — everything had that colour, although in various tones so that things could be distinguished. The general impression was that of a world without shadows; there were colour variations but no shadows. The atmosphere was full of joy, calm and orderliness; everything went on harmoniously and in silence. And at the same time, one could discern all the details of an education, of a training in all fields, by which the people on board were being prepared.

'That gigantic ship had just reached the shore of the supramental world* and a first group of people who were destined to become the future inhabitants of this [new] supramental world [on Earth] were to go ashore. Everything had been arranged for this first

---

* It is obvious from the context that the Mother here means the outer border of the supramental world, which seems to be associated with a sea or an ocean (cf. the ship), and that therefore the ship in fact reaches the shore of our material world. One should remember that this text was first dictated and then written down from a tape-recording — which may be an explanation of this error.

disembarkation. Several very tall beings were posted on the jetty. They were not human beings, they had never been human before, nor were they permanent inhabitants of the supramental world. They had been sent down from above and posted there to control and supervise the disembarkation. I was in charge of the whole enterprise from the beginning and throughout the proceedings. I had prepared all the groups myself. I stood on the ship at the head of the gangway, calling the groups one by one and sending them ashore. The tall beings posted there inspected as it were those who were disembarking, letting pass the ones who were ready and sending back the ones who were not and who had to continue their training on board the ship.

'While I was there watching everybody, the part of my consciousness coming from here got extremely interested; it wanted to see and recognize all those people, to see how they had changed and check who were taken at once and who had to remain to continue their training. After a while, as I stood there observing all that, I began to feel that I was being pulled back to make my body wake up — by a consciousness or a person here — and in my consciousness I protested: "No, no! Not yet! Not yet, I want to see the people!" I was seeing and noticing everything with intense interest. Things continued that way till suddenly the clock here struck three, which brought me back violently. I had the sensation of a sudden fall into my body. I came back with a shock but with the full remembrance because I had been called back very abruptly. I remained tranquil, without making a movement, until I could recollect the whole experience and keep it.

'On that ship, the nature of the objects was not as we know on earth; for instance, the clothes were not made of fabric, and what looked like fabric was not manufactured: it was part of the body, it was made of the same substance which took different forms. It had a kind of plasticity. When a change was required, it took place not by any artificial and external means but by an inner movement, a movement of consciousness which gave the substance its shape or appearance. Life created its own forms. There was *one single substance* in everything and it changed the quality of its vibration according to need and usage.

'Those who were sent back for additional training were not of a uniform colour: it was as if their body showed patches of a greyish opacity consisting of a substance which resembled the terrestrial one. They were dull as if not entirely permeated by the Light, as if they had not been transformed. They were not like that everywhere, only in spots.

'The tall beings on the shore were not of the same colour, which means that they did not have that orange tint: they were paler, more transparent. Except for part of their body, one could only see the outline of their figure. They were very tall, seemed to have no bone-structure and could take any shape they wanted. Only from the waist down did they have a permanent density, which one did not suppose in the rest of their body. Their colour was much lighter, with very little red; it rather tended towards gold or even white. The parts of whitish light were translucent; they were not positively transparent but less dense, more subtle than the orange substance.

'When I was called back and saying "not yet", I had each time a fleeting glimpse of myself — of my figure in the supramental world, that is. I was a kind of combination of the tall beings and of the beings aboard the ship. My upper part, particularly the head, was not much more than a silhouette of which the contents were white with an orange fringe. The more down towards the feet, the more the colour looked like that of the people on the boat, that is to say orange; the more upwards, the more it was translucent and white, with less red. The head was only a contour with a brilliant sun in it; rays of light radiated from it, which was the action of the will.

'As for the people I saw on board the ship, I recognized all of them. Some were here, in the Ashram, others were from elsewhere, but I know them too. I saw everybody, but as I knew that I would not remember them all when coming back, I decided not to mention any names. Anyhow, it is not necessary. Three or four faces stood out very distinctly, and when I saw them I understood the feeling I had here on earth when looking into their eyes: such an extraordinary joy. Most people were young. There were very few children and their age was something around fourteen and fifteen, certainly not below ten or twelve. (I did not stay long enough to see all the details.) There were no very old people, apart from a few exceptions. Most of the people who went ashore were in middle age, except a few. Before this experience, certain individual cases had already been examined several times at a place where people capable of being supramentalized were examined. There were a few surprises and I took note of them. I even talked to some of them about it. But the ones I made disembark today I saw very distinctly; they were middle-aged, neither young children nor old people, apart from some rare exceptions, and this agreed very well with my expectations. I decided not to tell anything, not to give any names. As I did not remain till the very end, it was not possible for me to get the exact picture; the picture was not absolutely clear or complete. I do not want to say things to some and not to others.

'What I can say is that the formation of the appraisal, of the assessment [about their readiness to go ashore], rested *exclusively* on the substance of which the people were made, that is on their belonging completely to the supramental world, on their being made of that so particular substance. The adopted view is neither moral nor psychological. It is probable that the substance their bodies were made of resulted from an inner law or an inner movement which at that time did not come into question. It is quite clear, at least, that the values differ.

'When I came back, I knew, simultaneously with the recollection of the experience, that the supramental world is permanent, that my presence there is permanent, and that only a missing link is necessary for enabling the connection in the consciousness and in the substance, and it is this link which is now being established. There, I had the impression ... of an extreme relativity — no, more exactly the impression that the relation of this world with the other one completely changed the standpoint from which things must be evaluated or appraised. This standpoint was not at all mental and it gave the strange inner feeling that lots of things we consider good or bad are not really so. It was very clear that everything depended on the capacity of things, on their aptitude in expressing the supramental world or being in relation with it.

'It was so completely different, sometimes even so much contrary to our ordinary way of appreciating things ... What is very obvious is that our opinion of what is divine or undivine is not right ... Our usual feeling of what is antidivine seems artificial, seems based on something that is not true, not alive. At any rate, what we call life here did not seem alive to me when compared with that world ... In the people too, I saw that what helps them to become supramental or prevents them from it, is very different from what we with our habitual moral notions imagine. I felt how ... ridiculous we are.'[21]

At that time, the supramental world existed already 'somewhere' in the subtle-physical.

There too the Mother was present as the Executrix.

By then many persons were ready to participate in the supramental creation.

A certain number of them were present on Earth in 1958.

The link, the connection, the intermediary world, the bridge between our world and the supramental world had to be built. For this the Mother had remained upon Earth and she worked on it with all her might, with all her Power.

It turned out that her work, especially because it increasingly concerned her physical being — her body and its cells — now demanded her withdrawal too from the active outward life she had been leading all these years. She gave her last talk at the Playground on 26 November 1958; on 7 December, she was present there for the last time to watch the gymnastics. On 9 December, she fell gravely ill. The situation was very serious. 'I have stopped everything, the attack on my body was too severe,' she wrote to Satprem.

That attack came from a mighty Titan, chosen by the Lord of Falsehood; this Titan, 'whose aim is this body,' had been born together with her — her shadow, as it were — to make life difficult for her and if possible to terminate it. (One will remember how Sri Aurobindo was constantly concerned about her protection.) This time, the Titan used black magic. It is worth noting that from now onwards every serious crisis, signifying an important step forward in the Yoga of the Mother, will coincide with an attack of black magic, sometimes through living persons, sometimes through deceased ones or through unearthly beings. The Titan's preference went to persons in the Mother's entourage after he had first taken possession of them. This time, he used a woman who had served the Mother well initially but who had, little by little, become a real devil. When Udar asked the Mother why she had not discarded that person from her entourage, she answered that this would not have solved the problem as the Titan then would have picked out somebody else close to her. We find here one of the reasons of the Mother's extensive occult training in the beginning of the century: she had to be able to confront her opponents at least on an equal footing on this plane too. Life and work of the Avatar form a whole, preordained in time(s) and space(s), connected by a web of invisible threads spun by Providence or by the Unity-Consciousness, without which the execution of his or her Work would be impossible.

The withdrawal of the Mother on 9 December 1958 — exactly eight years after Sri Aurobindo's body had been lowered into the *Samadhi* — was not so abrupt as Sri Aurobindo's. On 15 January, she would again step out on the balcony at sunrise. Yet, she changed her daily schedule drastically. (We will see, though, that her outward activity, parallel to the inward action, was not restricted but only redirected.) In her total surrender, the Mother has never left even a minute of her life unused, in order to accomplish the Work she had accepted. 'The true reason why I am still here is that my physical presence helps humanity to progress,' she said to Mona Sarkar. 'My presence hastens the terrestrial evolution ... I made the descent of the Supramental possible. Otherwise I wouldn't be here. It is not worth spending my time uselessly upon earth if my presence doesn't help humanity to make a decisive progress. I can't spend my time uselessly, I have many important things to do in other worlds. But because my presence helps, I am still here, otherwise I would have left already.'[22]

Her presence at the Playground was of course badly missed. Her 'evening classes' had been the occasion of that admirable collection of *Entretiens*. All the same, her audience could have asked so many more questions. They probably lacked the poignant side of the life-experience which causes questions to arise. 'You never have any questions to ask me.' Was it because they were timid, or because they were afraid to get entangled in their French sentences? 'To all of you who have come here many things have been told. You have been put into contact with a world of truth, you live in it, the air you breathe is full of it.'[23] She let them write out their questions on a piece of paper to be' handed to her before the beginning of the classes. Still nothing was asked. What on earth might be the cause of this 'terrible sleepiness,' of this intellectual drowsiness, this lack of interest?

During the meditation after one of the classes, in November 1958, she asked the question to herself. But for her asking a question meant identifying with the very concreteness of the problem itself. Only knowledge by identity is true knowledge, she said, time and again. Afterwards she has described how she was sucked down into that unconsciousness there in front of her, deeper, and deeper yet, 'looking for the spark of light that answers.' The force pulling her down in that black abyss, in a sort of black volcanic shaft of razor sharp basalt, was so strong that it made her body literally bend forward, her head touching her knees. What was to be found there below in that pit?

At the bottom of the stagnant night of the Inconscient she found the divine Presence, the supramental Golden Light in which she was unexpectedly projected as in a vast of 'dark, warm gold'. And a total surprise it was! She formulated the experience in her New Year's message for 1959 — this being our last look at that Playground where part of the Play of the New World had taken place. 'At the very bottom of the inconscience most hard and rigid and narrow and stifling I struck upon an almighty spring that cast me up forthwith into a formless limitless Vast vibrating with the seeds of a new world.'[24]

'And this almighty spring was a perfect image of what happens, is bound to happen and will happen *for everybody*: all at once one is projected into the Vast.'[25] A miracle, for everybody.

Chapter Twenty-two

MAKING POSSIBLE THE IMPOSSIBLE

By what alchemy shall this lead of immortality be turned into that gold of divine Being?[1]

— Sri Aurobindo

THE MOTHER played her last game of tennis only a few days before she withdrew. She had started playing tennis — 'my passion' — at the age of eight; she was now eighty. 'Being young means never to accept something as irrevocable.' These are her words.

Where had she come by now? As we have seen, the bridge between the already existing supramental world and this, our world, had to be built. The ship from the New World played an important role in the construction. 'This was the significance of the experience of 3 February 1958: the establishing of a link between the two worlds. For both worlds are there all right, not one above the other but one inside the other, in two different dimensions. But there is no connection between them: they overlap each other, by way of speaking, without being connected. In the experience of 3 February, I have seen certain persons from here and from elsewhere who belong already to that supramental world in part of their being, but there is no connection, no junction. The time has come at this very moment in universal history in which the link must be established.'[2]

That happened in her. It was the reason why the Avatar had taken up a material body: to be able to come into contact with Matter, '*pour toucher la matière*', to touch Matter, for this was an indispensable prerequisite for its transformation. This contact occurred on the plane where her embodied being had a direct connection with Matter as such: in the cells of her body.

During the following fifteen years, the transformation of the Mother's body cells is an enormously rich, varied, multifaceted, spellbinding and sometimes also baffling process — for the understanding of beings like us, that is, to whom spiritual experiences are for the most part abstract imaginings, not to talk about experiences of the frequency and range of those taking place in the Mother. To her awareness, things happened at every moment, far too many for her to store in her active memory and talk about it afterwards, although she has been so kind as to share some of her experiences in order that we might construe some idea of that fantastic process of transformation. It is something totally new, never tried out or even thought out before, formulated in words inadequate to express the experiences, which therefore to us at first sight seem unthinkable, unimaginable, and maybe weird or outlandish. We know that Sri Aurobindo was a master of the English language; the Mother, in her way, was a master of French, if only to express such completely new, complex and transmental experiences in simple and clear words.

In this process of transformation some lines of experience can be made out which in the course of years are coming to the fore time and again, but each time further elaborated, more fully developed, larger in scope. We know that the Mother has never had the same experience twice, that she never stopped after an exhausting effort to congratulate herself or to enjoy the fruit of her labour, and that she kept up her progress 'with the speed of a jet plane.' She had remained on Earth to do a specific job in her great love for humanity, the love of Savitri for Satyavan. She had already prepared her body for its task in her mother's womb; she had trained it so that it might fully and exclusively be at the service of this task without any consideration for herself. She never looked forward to a limit, to a crowning of her effort, but always did the maximum possible 'here and now.' Hers was a life of an unimaginable concentration, every hour, every minute, every second. Indeed, so enormous was the effort, so much was at stake and so great the danger that a lack of concentration, even for a moment, could have had disastrous consequences. One remembers Sri Aurobindo's stumbling on the tiger skin.

Typical in the evolution of the Mother were the ups and downs in its curving, broadening course. She noticed it herself: each time she felt strong and energetic, enough for her body to tackle another obstacle, the blow fell — the blow which activated the crisis by which the process of transformation would be further elaborated. In most cases this was a so-called illness, sometimes accompanied by an attack of black magic: a new part of the vicious Subconscient together with its representatives had to be faced, fought and transformed. She waged the battle, strenuously gained the upper hand, conquered the resistance, formulated the experience for herself and sometimes for others — and got ready for the next crisis. What she has suffered none can imagine, because none would be able to endure the same ordeals.

What was it all about again? A new species had to appear on the Earth, this time a divine species of supramental beings, as Sri Aurobindo called them. Somewhere this had been decreed. After the many cycles of the human presence and evolution on Earth, the time had come for the arrival of this new species without humankind even being aware of it. Sri Aurobindo and the Mother, the Avatar, the Two-in-One, had come to make this possible. Therefore, they had to take the past of the evolution upon and into them, and they had to work in order to make the earthly embodiment of the new species realizable. To be able to descend deeper than ever into Matter and its foundations, the Subconscient and Inconscient, they first had to climb higher than ever in the Spirit by means of a new Yoga beyond the existing yogas. Only after discovering there the divine Unity-Consciousness and acquiring it, could they descend more deeply into the caves of existence, guided by the Light of which they had become the bearers.

The supramental world had approached very near to the Earth. Its Light and Power were definitively established on Earth by the Manifestation in 1956. For the beings of the supramental world to embody on the magic planet which is our Earth, it was necessary that her gross matter should be refined or transmuted by the supramental Substance. Thus would come an end to her long agony, for she would literally become the Kingdom of God. Now the last phase of the preparatory work was being done by the Mother, her own body serving as testing material, as the instrument and intermediary by which earthly matter could be 'touched' and transformed. 'I am the guinea pig,' she said with a smile. An indispensable condition and the only means of all this was the transformation of the cells.

To understand what follows, two points should be kept in mind. The first is that the *sadhana* of the Mother now took place *in her body*. All the amazing things we are going to hear are about *her body*, which is not the same as her gross body which people thought they were perceiving. The perceptions of the human being are limited and deformed by the instruments of his perceptions called senses. They are, moreover, limited by the mental processing of the sense perceptions, in its turn influenced by the deformations of the senses and *a priori* limited by our mental consciousness, by the mechanisms of division to which this consciousness automatically subjects the One Existence.

The Mother in that room on the second floor of the central building of the Sri Aurobindo Ashram, Rue de la Marine in Pondicherry, was something completely different from and *more* than that old, frail, stooped body all have kept focusing on. She was the Universal Mother, 'the divine Mahashakti, original Power, supreme Nature, holding in herself infinite existence and creating the wonders of the cosmos,'[3] as Sri Aurobindo wrote. Of herself, she said: 'The central Consciousness, here, in the material world, is the Mahashakti.'[4] And Sri Aurobindo again: 'All powers of all the planes must be seen and known as self-formulations of the one spiritual Shakti, infinite in being, consciousness and Ananda.'[5] He also wrote about 'the supramental personality' of the Mother 'which from behind the veil presides over the aim of the present manifestation.'[6] This was the source of her existence, of her knowledge, of her action. 'There is nothing that is impossible to her who is the conscious Power and universal Goddess all-creative from eternity and armed with the

Spirit's omnipotence.'[7] What happens in the core of the atom and the quasar, in each heartbeat of a body and in the fire of God's Love is her work, intended and executed by her, borne and brought to fulfilment. From this we may conclude that nothing happened to or in the body of the Mother that she herself had not willed and for which she was not responsible, totally, unconditionally. This conclusion is inevitable if she was really *that* — 'either she is that, or she is not' — not only in theory and feelings of devotion, but in most concrete reality.

But: 'There is the Mother who is carrying on the Sadhana and the Divine Mother, both being one but in different poises.'[8] (Sri Aurobindo) The Mother has explained this: how some wanted to see her exclusively in her almighty divine glory, and how they expected from her that also in a body, in an evolutionary world with a pre-ordained process, she would perform what is possible or allowed only in a divine world; others, on the contrary, saw her rather as the human albeit divinely inspired incarnation, as the avant-gardiste of the Integral Yoga and as their guru. With all possible combinations and variations in between. The Divine Mother had taken the burden of the world upon her in a human body and she had accepted all consequences of this commitment.

To do this, it was necessary for her to limit voluntarily her instrumental knowledge and power. This was her sacrifice at the origin of her incarnation, before all the suffering she would be subjected to: the sacrifice of the divine accepting to become human in order that humanity might be divinized. 'All knowledge is available in her universal self, but she brings forward only what is needed to be brought forward so that the working is done,'[9] wrote Sri Aurobindo. (All this had been applicable to himself too.) In *Savitri* we read about 'her deep designs which from herself she had veiled.'[10]

Satprem, for instance, writes in his trilogy about the Mother: 'Mother has never known. This seems unbelievable, but it is true,'[11] and also: 'Mother herself did not know what she was doing.'[12] This is an opinion which at least should be qualified: the Mother as body in transformation did not know what was awaiting her the next moment or at the end of her adventure, the consciousness of her body did not know that; but her soul (as we will see), her higher consciousness (supramentalized and therefore essentially divine) and her inner being as the Great Mother of course knew every bit of it. For anything whatsoever, including her incarnated existence and her own Yoga of physical transformation, could only have been willed, planned and executed by her higher aspects of being. There is no doubt that the Mother knew that the development of her transformation was pre-ordained, but that the knowledge of it was (mostly) denied to her body because such knowledge would have had unfavourable repercussions on her yogic effort. 'It is absolutely certain that it would be wrong if one knew what is going to happen, for then one wouldn't do what is required.'[13] She herself found it so ironical: 'To be sure that one knows' — somewhere — 'and to ask oneself how it is coming about.'[14] 'It is indeed known, somewhere in the back of the consciousness.' Sometimes when she tried to know something, she was bluntly told from Above: 'This does not concern you,' or: 'This is none of your business.' At times she said: 'I know perfectly well how it will be, but I do not know when.'[15] Once, this was in connection with the course of the process of transformation and another time in connection with its outcome.

But it was always *her body* that did not know, the not yet transformed consciousness of the cells of her body, because such knowledge would have influenced its attitude and yogic striving. And this is the second point we should keep in mind: the body of the Mother was something quite different from what was 'naturally' visible. In their interpretations of the *sadhana* and the passing away of the Mother, the commentators always keep their eyes fixed on her external figure, on her visible 'human-like' presence, and it is mainly that external figure they call 'the Mother'. If they express themselves differently every now and then, it is because they cannot but quote statements from her which tell something quite other — but in their conclusions they again fall back into their first attitude concentrating on that apparently deteriorating body, however much respect or devotion they may profess for 'the divine Mother' or for 'sweet Mother'. Still, the Mother had impressed it so strongly on them: 'I am talking about cellular realizations, don't forget it!' or: 'I am talking about something completely material' — in the period of her life we have now reached in our story, when her *sadhana* was the *sadhana* of her body, of the cells of her body, of the matter of those cells. That is why she called her yoga 'the yoga of the body', 'the yoga of the cells', 'the physical yoga', 'the yoga of the physical vibrations.' 'It is the experience of the body, you understand, physical, material — the experience of the body.'[16] In the levels of being above matter, everything was ready, worked out; that work was finished and even the mental and vital were completely supramentalized. This now was about the transformation of Matter, 'don't forget it'. But this *sadhana* was so new that it was still forgotten, wrongly interpreted or simply not understood.

When she said 'I', whom did she mean? Who was that 'I'? In most cases, the 'I' was no more than a personal pronoun as grammatical subject, 'because otherwise one cannot talk.' Or it referred to the body which was narrating its experience. Or it was the psychic consciousness in the heart. ('There [the heart], it is like a sun, all the time. It is like a radiant sun. It is there that I work — it is from there that I work ... This and that [gesture towards her supraphysical forms of being in her heart and above her head] is so natural that I do not pay attention to it anymore: it is my way of being.'[17]) Or 'I' was 'the high Lady Above,' or it was the central Supreme Consciousness, or simply a consciousness enabling her to converse with other people. One could fill pages with definitions of that personal pronoun 'I' as used by the Mother in later years. It is therefore essential to take this into account when reading her conversations so that one does not commit the error of identifying the Mother with the instrument which was her body — a body of which she soon will say that it is not even her own.

The Pillars of the Mother's Yoga

For this sadhana which I am doing, there are certain guiding indications which are being followed. I have some sentences from Sri Aurobindo.[18]

—The Mother

If this yoga of the cells was so new that the Mother even used new names for it, was this still the yoga of Sri Aurobindo, called by him the Integral Yoga? Or was it a continuation, a development of his yoga of which he had had no notion? It goes without saying that Sri Aurobindo could not have experienced everything which awaited the Mother after his departure in the task he had transferred to her, for it was the intention that she would continue the risky journey of discovery in the 'virgin forest.' At first, the Mother more than once let it be understood that she was involved in something completely new, something for which she could find no explanation in her past exchanges with Sri Aurobindo or in his writings. But little by little, and one may say to her own astonishment, she time and again found in his texts indications foreshadowing, as it were, her experience, and this is probably the greatest testimony to Sri Aurobindo's spiritual genius. On the one hand, he must have progressed much farther in his *sadhana* than commonly supposed; on the other hand, this is a striking illustration of the exactness with which he had viewed the whole of the supramental process of transformation, of the course of the great River. Who can tell what he had discovered in his spiritual and occult explorations, what had been revealed to him by the Gods and the Godhead, what he knew without revealing it, not even to the Mother in her *sadhana* because for her the time proper for such knowledge had not yet come?

Looking back over the Mother's experiences in the last fifteen years and trying to consider them as a whole, one finds there clearly the foundations of the Yoga as expounded by Sri Aurobindo in the *Synthesis* and in his letters.

The central pillar of the Integral Yoga is the total SURRENDER of oneself to the Divine. One finds the surrender on each and every page of the *Agenda*: '*Ce que Tu veux, ce que Tu veux*' (what You want, what You want — 'You' again being here the confidential form of addressing the Divine as the most intimate part of ourselves). 'Day and night without interruption: "As You want it, Lord, as You want it." '[19] This, in all her difficulties and suffering, was 'the sole refuge,' 'the sole means,' 'the sole solution.' She said it with words or she only turned the palms of her hands upwards in a gesture of surrender.

346 • *Beyond Man*

It was her central attitude of unconditional openness, acquiescence, availability for the new creation. And in our thoughts we go back as far as 1914, when Sri Aurobindo said that never before had he seen a surrender like that of Mirra at her very first meeting with him. The surrender of the unknowing instrument to the Divine Will is the cornerstone of Sri Aurobindo's yoga, the theme with variations of his *Synthesis* — and the fundamental yogic act of the Mother in the long years of her glorious ordeal. When the sound of her voice ebbed away in the last months of which we have the recordings, these were almost the only words she still spoke: '*Ce que Tu veux.*' It was her central *mantra*.

Of SINCERITY she had said: 'This is why I have told you that it is not easy to take up the yoga. If you are not sincere, don't start.'[20] 'Whatever the way one follows' — and everybody has his own way — 'there is only one means, one only, I know only one: a perfect sincerity — but then a sincerity that is *perfect*.'[21] This kind of sincerity, however, is something completely different from not telling untruth. Essentially, it means that all parts of the embodied being are gathered and in direct contact with the core of the embodiment: the psychic being. At first sight this is a somewhat strange definition perhaps, but on further examination the basic process of the yoga. For the psychic being is the representative of Truth. The parts which stay apart from the psychic being decline the contact with the Light that is Truth and remain the subordinates of their dark origin. 'Sincerity is the safeguard, it is the protection, it is the guide, and finally it is the transforming power.'[22]

Did the Mother then, after all those years of a superhuman *sadhana,* still have 'grey spots' of insincerity, or were there parts of her being still separated from her psychic being — she who was so exalted in the eyes of so many? Yes, she had. Very tiny ones, but innumerable. In fact as many as there were cells in her body. 'Psychologically' (psychically, mentally and vitally) the Mother was the purest, most truthful, most sincere being that has ever walked on this Earth, but her body consisted of the same matter all our bodies are made of — and the base of that matter is the Night of the Subconscient and Inconscient, that is to say of the NO, the Negation at the Origin, of the Falsehood which resulted in the division and separation within the Unity.

'The very first necessity for spiritual perfection is a perfect EQUALITY,'[23] wrote Sri Aurobindo in *The Synthesis of Yoga*. (The yoga of self-perfection was the limit up to which he went in the explanation of his yoga.) Equality is not the same as indifference; it is an active attitude based on the acceptance of the world, of all things manifested, all events, all experiences, for they can only come from the One, there being nothing else. An imperturbable equality was named by the Mother as one of the two characteristics that might allow an outward recognition of the supramental being. (The second was an absolute certainty, 'a cubic certainty,' of the knowledge.) It is the clarity which nothing can render turbid, by which things can happen according to their truth-content, to their divine purity and reality, without being subject to any kind of deformation and darkening caused by the Shadow. Time and again, the Mother, in that explosive process of transformation of hers, felt the absolute necessity of equality in the cells of her body — of a state of equality in which the Unity-Consciousness could express itself in all its purity. Not only was equality precious during the invasions in her body of the Golden Light or the red-golden Fire, but also it was indispensable in the midst of the incessant swarms of vibrations surrounding her and rushing through her, the smallest pulse of which she was fully conscious of.

The fourth fundamental feature of this yoga was the underlying principle of everything was UNITY. All is one, all is one single Being, 'don't forget it.' 'Being', to us, is one of the most abstract words, but in the spiritual experience there are no abstractions. For abstraction is a fictitious projection of the impotently grasping mental consciousness. Unity is the basis; Unity is the stuff of experience; Unity is the aim of the supramental transformation; Unity is the medium in which the supramental being exists. Unity is the Divine. From that we come, in that we live, to that we go. 'There is nothing but That.'

The Mother was familiar with the Unity-experience in her mental and vital being, for in these parts she had realized Unity. But the cells, in their materiality, represented extreme division. Her *sadhana* — it should be stressed again and again — was happening exactly on that level. *That* was where the ultimate Victory had to be won, where the supramental Unity-Consciousness had to replace the infinite inframental division. Let this not be misunderstood: the consciousness of the cells had to be transformed into the divine Unity-Consciousness. In other words: the cells had to be divinized! It was on this level that she underwent also the terrors of the Subconscient, and it was here that, more poignantly than anywhere else, the question was put of the wherefore of our world of darkness, ignorance, suffering and death.

Wherefore?

The question of the wherefore of a world like ours — her so often repeated '*pourquoi?*' — which is supposed to exist in the divinity of Being, Consciousness and Bliss, the question as to the cause of 'that plunge of Light into its own shadow,'[24] sounds like a gloomy litany, like a heart-rending lament through the ages. Suffering is 'so great a stumbling-block to our understanding of the universe,' wrote Sri Aurobindo, 'for we cannot suppose that the only Being is compelled by something outside itself, as no such thing exists.'[25] The question as to the wherefore of things had to be stated 'trenchantly,' he said, and the Mother endorsed this: 'Why would there be a manifestation, then? What would be the use of it? It would mean that there is an absurdity at the beginning of the creation. If it had not been done on purpose, it would mean that things are not done on purpose, or that He had made a mistake, or that He had no understanding of what He intended to do — that he thought he was doing one thing but in fact did another!'[26] Such a God one can only call a blunderer or a monster and his creation a hell. Yet the Divine is assumed to be a Being of Love and Bliss ... Each time she was plunged once more into the fire of her suffering, she again asked the question as to the wherefore of existence. She sometimes cried it out aloud.

There is no mental answer, no answer on our level of comprehension to this problem. 'The mystery of the universe is suprarational ... We have to go beyond the intellect in order to bridge the gulf and penetrate the mystery; to leave an unsolved contradiction cannot be the final solution,'[27] writes Sri Aurobindo in *The Life Divine*. Sometimes the Mother shoved the problem aside: 'Things are what they are because they are what they are ... One has to start from what is and go on from there.'[28] Which reminds us of one of Sri Aurobindo's aphorisms: 'I believe with you, my friends, that God, if he exists, is a demon and an ogre. But after all what are you going to do about it?'[29]

But after every ordeal, the Mother, in her body that had become the body of the world, came out of the crucible more transformed, more divinized. After every cry of existential desperation, which was the cry of humanity in her, the design, the aim and the cause of the divine manifestation became more clearly discernible, not mentally, not abstractly, not theoretically or theologically, but concretely, ec-statically concrete. She found out, literally in the body, that omnipotence remains omnipotent even when apparently impotent, that the Light of Omniscience keeps glowing in the darkness of the ignorance, and that no suffering can exist without Bliss. The universe is without flaws; however, we are involved in processes of evolutionary growth, so much so that the meaning of the whole and of its parts is temporarily hidden from us, as is the meaning of our suffering. 'It is Joy that has created and it is Joy that will accomplish.'[30] (the Mother) Our suffering is necessary in order that our Joy may become complete and that unnamable, unending suffering by which man has permeated matter with his sweat and blood will find its justification in the Joy at the time of man's completion. We have known that at the beginning, no doubt. For it was our-Self, the real Self in us, that has chosen the adventure of discovery and the growth in Matter; we have chosen to forget our Self for the future joy of rediscovering It. This joy must at least be equivalent to all the suffering throughout the ages — which is the mystical equation behind the universe. Somewhere we are remembering this in the depths behind the mists of our consciousness, otherwise we would not be so strongly attached to life. Suffering is 'the hammer of the gods,'[31] the purification and strengthening which enables the divinization.

The multidimensional personality of the Mother, who to the

human eye was only visible in that fragile body, her *sadhana* which by now had completely descended in the body, had become 'the yoga of matter', and her journey into the unknown, a clear continuation of what Sri Aurobindo had begun and partially worked out — all this provides us with the perspective in which we should place the experiences of the Mother's last years in order to be able to understand them to some extent. A complete understanding of matters spiritual, and *a fortiori* of matters supramental, is only possible by identification. Those who want to experience the transformation have to follow behind the Mother on the path she has trodden. She has invited everybody to this adventure.

The Universalization of the Body

The Mother felt that the prerequisite of the process of supramental transformation at this point was the 'universalization' of her body. Is this possible? Can this small, limited and vulnerable body in which we are enclosed be universalized? In *The Life Divine*, Sri Aurobindo wrote that the individual must be the first instrument of the transformation, but that an isolated individual transformation is not sufficient and cannot even be completely attainable. 'It is sure, for I know it by experience, that there is a degree of individual perfection and transformation which cannot be realized without the whole of humanity having made a certain progress ... There are things in matter that cannot be transformed as long as the whole of matter has not undergone a particular degree of transformation. One cannot isolate oneself completely, it is not possible,'[32] said the Mother. Sri Aurobindo stated his own experience: '[The sadhak of the Integral Yoga] often finds that even after he has won persistently his own personal battle, he has still to win it over and over again in a seemingly interminable war, because his inner existence has already been so much enlarged that not only it contains his own being with its well-defined needs and experiences, but is in solidarity with the being of others, because in himself he contains the universe.'[33]

The only real, conscious *sadhaks* of the Integral Yoga in their time were the initiators of it, Sri Aurobindo and the Mother, and after

Sri Aurobindo's passing the Mother alone. Many followed in their footsteps, but then by an inner orientation based more on surrender and intuition than on knowledge or a consciously directed yogic effort; their integral yoga was more a yoga of intention than of knowledge, insight or purpose. Yet, it is clear that the *adhara*, even of the Avatar, is a limited instrument because it is individualized. It was possible to enlarge this limitation on the mental and vital level almost boundlessly, so much so that Sri Aurobindo and the Mother had been able to supramentalize first their mental and then their vital; but the matter of their body cells, however much impregnated by the psychic and supramental presence, remained bound within a given shape of the body. 'An individual transformation would not be the creation of a new type of beings or a new collective life.'[34]

The evolutionary gain to be won by this Yoga, by this new development in the life of planet Earth, was clearly delineated. All previous Avatars had universalized themselves in their mental and vital to turn their evolutionary effort into a terrestrial acquisition. The mental consciousness, for instance, had been turned into an established element of life upon Earth thanks to the work of the Avatar Rama. But now the Avatar had to universalize *his body* as the new evolution of consciousness could no longer take place in the 'subtle' ranges of the mental and vital; it had to happen in matter itself, in the matter out of which the body of the Avatar, just like all other bodies, was made. MATTER had to become conscious with a higher, nay, a divine consciousness, a Unity-Consciousness. What in Sri Aurobindo and the Mother had become possible in the Spirit had now to be realized in Matter. A tremendous revolutionary-evolutionary step, indeed an *Umwertung aller Werte*. Small wonder that those who in former times had seen the future possibility of a step of this order, great beings everywhere on the Earth, never had dared to try out this transmutation in their flesh.

The means, the instruments, the testing material of this transmutation were the tiny but extremely complex little building bricks of the body: the cells. The cells are a product of evolution. They contain matter, they contain life-force, and they have their own consciousness — which irrefutably appears from their wonderful organization in which molecular biology daily discovers new and amazing secrets. The cells too, like everything in the universe, have the divine Presence within them, for otherwise they could not be. Nothing can be without That.

Once, when the Mother was fully involved in the yoga of the cells, their composition and *modus operandi* were shown to her. 'The cells,' she said afterwards, 'have a composition and a structure which agree with that of the universe.'[35] This is not surprising to one who has read, for instance, the books of Fritjof Capra and Gary Zukav. Science is being forced to recognize that in the universe everything exists in relation with everything else, the atoms and the elementary particles* too. The cosmos looks more and more like a living organism, like an individual — as the Seers have always said. 'The cell, in her internal composition, receives the vibration of the corresponding state in the composition of the whole,' said the Mother. 'Every cell was a miniature world corresponding to the whole.' 'Every vibration in one centre awakes automatically a vibration in another centre,'[36] she had said years ago. Behind and in everything is the Unity.

In our body's cells there sits a hidden Power
That sees the unseen and plans eternity.[37]

— *Savitri*

---

* Take for instance the following quotation from Gary Zukav's *The Dancing Wu Li Masters*: 'The astounding discovery awaiting newcomers to physics is that the evidence gathered in the development of quantum mechanics indicates that subatomic "particles" constantly appear to be making decisions! More than that, the decisions they seem to make are based on decisions made elsewhere. Subatomic particles seem to know *instantaneously* what decisions are made elsewhere, and elsewhere can be as far as another galaxy! The key word is *instantaneously*. How can a subatomic particle over here know what decision another particle over there has made *at the same time the particle over there makes it*? All the evidence belies that quantum particles are actually particles ... The philosophical implication of quantum mechanics is that all of the things in our universe (including us) that appear to exist independently are actually parts of one all-encompassing organic pattern, and that no parts of that pattern are ever really separate from it or from each other.' (pp. 72-73)

The cell contains the Unity-Consciousness in itself, but this Consciousness, of course, is not manifest, otherwise the cell — and we too as a consequence — would now already in its appearance as well as in its essence be divine. The cell is a product of evolution and therefore carries in itself its evolutionary past. 'Every cell has its own consciousness,' said the Mother, but this consciousness too is already composite. Deep within, there is the Unity-Consciousness, the reason why the cell is able to vibrate on the rhythms and movements of the whole. Its surface-consciousness, on the contrary, is its evolutionary consciousness, gradually increased by each evolutionary saltus, which each time is experienced as a calamity. (The supramental turn about will perhaps also appear like a catastrophe to us.) The cells carry the remembrance or imprint of those 'calamities' in them.

> Inflicting still its habit on the cells
> The phantom of a dark and evil start
> Ghostlike pursues all that we dream and do.[38]
>
> — *Savitri*

According to Sri Aurobindo and the Mother, the remembrance of Life, therefore of man and therefore of his parts, goes much farther back than one normally imagines, and contains elements of its whole evolution — even of experiences in prehistoric cycles, even of lives on other planets, and all the way back to before the *pralayas*, the cosmic contractions that have followed the cosmic expansions.*

The result of all this is, firstly, that the cell obstinately clings to its evolutionary acquisitions, structure and way of functioning. Thanks to them it has been able to survive, and it knows from

---

* The Mother has said more than once that our universe is the seventh expansion, the one of Equilibrium and Harmony. According to her, this expansion will no more be followed by a contraction, but continue growing richer and fanning out in the Infinity of the One. In this unfoldment, the supramentalization of Matter would be the decisive step. This movement of expansion and contraction will strike a chord with anyone who is in some way familiar with modern cosmology.

experience that every structural genetic alteration (or mutation) may imperil its existence, for mutations are pernicious almost without exception. To a higher form of consciousness, the cell's surface way of functioning therefore looks mechanical, stubborn and dull, not to say irrational or stupid. Secondly, the cell always fears the worst, its attitude is spontaneously catastrophic. Life, of which it is the bearer, has always existed in the shadow and under the threat of death. One look at animal life in nature gives us instant illustrations of this. For all forms Life has created up to now, survival ever remains precarious and is constantly accompanied by hunger, pain, mutilation, illness and finally death, which is their only certainty. It has to be a strong *Ananda* indeed which keeps manifesting life with so much enthusiasm, in such abundance, notwithstanding all these negative factors.

Therefore the supramental yoga had to take up the confrontation with the 'laws' of life, with habits millions of years old, to change the structures built by them or to make these structures susceptible to change. 'We *do not want* to obey the orders of Nature, even if those orders are supported by billions of years of habits,'[39] said the Mother. Good, but once more: is this possible? All sensible people up to then had answered this question in the negative. Who might be so demented to cross swords with a law of nature? Is not even God bound by what He once has ordained? 'Across each road stands armed a stone-eyed law ...'[40]

But Sri Aurobindo and the Mother had come to change the Law. Every Avatar incarnates to establish a new Order which of necessity has to come into conflict with the existing Order. It is precisely through the person of the Avatar that the Divine changes the structure of things established in a previous stage of the evolution against the former Order, etc., all the way back to the Beginning. The laws of Matter do not allow for the laws of Life, they are incompatible with them, and yet Life has colonized Matter and united intimately with it. Likewise Mind has worked out a harmonious coexistence with Life and Matter. This proves that in the course of the evolution of our magic planet the impossible has proved to be possible on more than one occasion. 'The impossible is the certainty of to-morrow,' wrote Sri Aurobindo. We have the extraordinary privilege to assist at the event of those great

Impossibilities becoming possible this very moment.

'No Law is absolute,'[41] Sri Aurobindo wrote in *The Life Divine*. 'What Nature does, is really done by the Spirit.'[42] And the Mother said: 'Down here, there are no fixed laws ... Not two cases are the same.'[43] 'If there are not two combinations in the universe who are the same, how can one establish laws and what is the absolute verity of those laws?'[44] She even said that the universe is re-created at each moment, which means that in principle everything is possible.

But then only in principle. 'All is possible, but all is not licit — except by a recognisable process; the Divine Power itself imposes on its action limits, processes, obstacles, vicissitudes,'[45] Sri Aurobindo wrote in a letter. 'The Law! The Law! It is the Law! Don't you understand that it is the LAW? You cannot change the Law. — But I have come to change the Law. In that case: pay the price.'[46] These are the Mother's words. And she has paid the price.

The domain of the cells in her was the interface where the Old and the New World met. There the transmutation had to take place. There the Unity-Consciousness had to be infused into Matter, from above or from outside, to connect and unite with the Unity-Consciousness that always was and is present in Matter. If this operation was successful, the cells and the Matter of the cells would effectively possess the Unity-Consciousness. The cell, divinized, would be prepared to become part of a divine body, the body of the new species on Earth. That is where the battle was fought. '*Le corps, c'est le champ de bataille*' — the body of the Mother was the battlefield where the battle for the world of tomorrow would be waged and decided.

Mantra

It was while watching another Indian film, *Dhruva*, shown at the Playground on 29 April 1958, that the Mother heard a *mantra* being recited for quite some time and marked that those sounds had a profound and favourable influence on her body, on the cells of her body.

A *mantra* is a formula of words. 'The Word has power,' wrote

Sri Aurobindo, 'even the ordinary written word has a power. If it is an inspired word it has still more power.'[47] 'The mantra is the pronounced word that has a creative power ... It is not only the idea, it is the sound that has the creative power ... Sound always has a power. It has a lot more power than people imagine.'[48] (the Mother)

The poets have always known this. There are those inspired formulations which remain vibrating in the mind or in the heart of the auditor or of the reader listening with his inner ear. It is then as if the reader himself becomes the poet, or rather, both become one in the vibration of the words. This power has also been discovered by the advertising world which exploits it for its commercial purposes. In religions, the mantric power is evoked by constant repetition of certain formulas, an exercise called *japa* in India. An example is the constant repetition of the Lord's Prayer or of the Hail Mary. The essential elements of all religions are closely related. And of course there are also the spells of black and white magic.

K.D. Sethna gave in a talk the following description of the *mantra*: 'The Mantra is the highest spiritual poetry: it is the Divine, as it were, expressing Himself directly, not through any other medium of consciousness. The Divine Being, getting embodied in words on the very plane of the Divine Himself: that is the Mantra. It is the Word from the Overmind, the Supermind's delegate that has been the governing Power of the universe so far.'[49]

The supreme and generally known *mantra* is OM, rendered in Sanskrit by a single graceful glyph. The Mother called OM 'the Lord's signature.'[50] 'With the help of OM one can realise the Divine. OM has a transforming power. OM represents the Divine,'[51] she said. For a long time, actually since her Parisian years, she had had 'a whole stock of mantras,' some of which have been published by Satprem in the first volume of the *Agenda* as 'Prayers of the consciousness of the cells.' In a footnote accompanying the conversation of 11 May 1963, we even read the intriguing words: 'When I say that my mantra has the power of immortality, I mean the other one, the one I do not talk about. I have never given the words of it.'[52]

The basic *mantra* of the Mother was '*Ce que Tu veux*' ('what You want'). This *mantra*, sometimes in a slightly varying form depending on the need of the circumstances, welled up from her heart every second of her existence. It formed the ground of her mission on the Earth. It was her 'sole refuge', 'the only means' of the supramental transformation. These simple words were the expression of her surrender, of the total giving of herself which was the stuff of her whole earthly existence, as it is the stuff of the whole Integral Yoga. When her voice will slowly die away, these are the words we will still hear, and when these words grow too faint it is still their expression in a fervent gesture, both palms turned upwards, we will see. Her *sadhana* was one of surrender; the *mantra* of her soul could be no other but an utterance of that surrender.

But in 1958 *her body* was in need of a *mantra*, the cells of her body needed it. And the reason is understandable. The attitude of the cells, as we have seen, is almost exclusively negative, catastrophic; and as they also have the character of relentless repetition, they keep incessantly repeating their negative, catastrophic obsessions and formations. Normally we do not hear it, this whispering under our skin, under the surface of our personality, because it is drowned by the noise of our thinking, for the most part automatic, and by our feelings, tense from fearfulness and desire. From this alone we can deduce how much our instrumental personality is affected by the mumbling and *angst* at its base, at the level of the cells. The deepest existential *angst* is corporeal. Examining this in ourselves, we discover the measure in which the human being is a wavering, fearful and negatively motivated being. In us, there is still very much alive the fear of the elements, the animals and the co-humans, of the precariousness of existence, of pain, hunger, sorrow and the torments from countless lives. All that remains gnawing at our insides; it embitters our life and poisons our love. It drains and erodes us.

The number of cells in our body is astronomical. The background noise in our life, in our own body, is a cacophony preventing by its incoherent vibrations every direct contact with the Pure, the Harmonious, the Divine. The soul remains forever unstained; our thinking can be quieted or tuned harmoniously; feelings can be purified — but the body in its fundamental elements is the Great Barrier Reef in the tide of the divinization. That is why the Mother felt such a strong need of a *mantra* for her body: the power of the sound of the word would harmonize the cells' vibrations and tune them to the power contained in the *mantra*. OM, I invoke or contact You, NAMO, I bow to You in total surrender, BHAGAVATE, make me as You are, divine. As the atoms in a laser crystal are tuned to the same frequency, so she used the age-old *mantra* 'OM Namo Bhagavate'* to tune the vibration of her cells to the divine supramental Power in order to assist them in their transformation.

'OM Namo Bhagavate' was *her mantra*. For a *mantra* springs spontaneously from the soul, or the soul spontaneously begins vibrating to it when hearing it; the *mantra* is therefore personal, the soul's very own. Moreover, at the time no human body had reached the same yogic stage of evolution as that of the Mother. It was precisely because of its advanced development that the need of the *mantra* had arisen in it, the *mantra* in that stage was the required yogic tool. Sri Aurobindo probably had not known the role and the importance of the *mantra* in the transformation of the cells at the point he had reached; anyhow, he has never written or said anything about it, and it is far from certain that the Einsteinian formula he talked about in his correspondence with Nirodbaran was a *mantra*, as supposed by some. And so the Mother said: 'I have become aware that for this *sadhana* of the body the mantra is essential[53] ... Sri Aurobindo has not given one ... Had he arrived where we are now, he would have seen that the purely psychological method is insufficient and that a japa is necessary, because only a japa has a direct effect on the body. So I had to find the method all alone, I had to find my mantra all alone. But now that everything is worked out, I have done ten years of work in a few months.'

It is true that the Mother, as a guru, has given the *mantra* 'OM Namo Bhagavate' to one or two of her disciples for reasons known only to her, but she has never declared it to be a general instrument of the supramental yoga. One may conclude this from the following quotations, some of them dating from years after she had discovered the *mantra* and started using it.

---

* Pronounced as: ohm naMOH bhagaVAtay (all a's short like in 'vandal').

* '[The *mantra*] wells up in you. It may be different for everybody ... But it has to be a spontaneous movement of the being.' (5 May 1951)

* 'It is not exclusively the words [which contain the power] but everything they are going to represent and carry in their vibration ... It is evident that another centre of consciousness, another concretizaton, another amalgam [the Mother meant 'another *adhara*'] would have a different vibration — that it would of course have another vibration ... What counts, is not the mantra *as such*: it is the relation established between a mantra and the body ... It is purely a personal phenomenon ... A mantra which would lead one straight to the divine realization might leave another cold and unaffected.' (31 May 1962)

* 'Nobody can give you your true mantra. It is not something one gives: it is something that wells up in you ... It is your very own cry ... My mantra has the power of immortality ... My mantra makes no sense for somebody else, but for me it is full, chockfull of sense.' (11 May 1963)

* 'It must be *your own* mantra, not something you have received from whomever — the mantra that has spontaneously risen up from the depth of your being, that has come from your inner guide.' (23 September 1964)

* 'It is good for the mantra to rise up spontaneously with the simplicity of the call of a child — two or three words which repeat themselves rhythmically. If it does not come by itself, then your body can repeat the mantra which your mental consciousness has chosen.' (21 May 1969)

* 'Outwardly — *outwardly* — I say the mantra: OM Namo Bhagavate. To me, it is an external being which says that. But inwardly, I am like this [Mother opens her hands with the palm upwards in a total immobility].' (23 December 1972)

The Conditions of the Supramental Yoga

The conditions to start the supramental yoga have been formulated by Sri Aurobindo and the Mother in clearly defined terms. Let us quote some of their statements about this important subject.

* In 1935, Sri Aurobindo wrote to Nirodbaran: 'There are different statuses of transformation. First is the psychic transformation, in which all is in contact with the Divine through the psychic consciousness. Next is the spiritual transformation in which all is merged in the Divine in the cosmic consciousness. Third is the supramental transformation in which all becomes supramentalised in the divine gnostic consciousness.

'Nobody can have the supramental realisation who has not had the spiritual.

'The psychic is the first of two transformations necessary — if you have the psychic transformation it facilitates immensely the other, i.e., the transformation of the ordinary human into the higher spiritual consciousness.'[54]

* 'One first has to find one's soul,' said the Mother in 1955, 'this is wholly indispensable, and you have to identify with it. Then you can go on towards the transformation ... You cannot skip this link, it is not possible.'[55] In these words, we hear an echo of what Sri Aurobindo had written in *The Life Divine*: 'This is the first step of self-realisation, to enthrone the soul, the divine psychic individual in the place of the ego.'[56]

* The following year, the Mother said again: 'The true spiritual life begins when one is in communion with the Divine in the psychic, when one is conscious of the divine Presence in the psychic and in constant communion with the psychic. *Then* spiritual life begins, not before — the *true* spiritual life.'[57] The true spiritual life is the prologue to the supramental transformation.

* In 1957, she stressed emphatically: 'Now that we are talking about this, I will remind you of what Sri Aurobindo has said, repeated, written, confirmed, and said again and again: that his yoga, the Integral Yoga, can begin only *after* that experience [the realisation of the soul], not before. Accordingly, one should not have any illusions and imagine that one can know what the Supramental is, and that one can make any judgments about it in whatever way, before having had *that experience*.'[58]

These statements are as clear as they can be. They touch the fundamental principle of the Integral Yoga. All the same, one could object that they date from before the Mother's discovery of the importance of the *mantra* for her body. We therefore also add the following:

* In July 1970, she detected: 'But it is the psychic being that will materialize itself and become the supramental being! ... And this gives a continuity to the evolution.'[59] We will return later to this very important discovery.

* 'It is the psychic being, the representative of the Divine in man, that will remain, that will pass on into the new species,' she said in April 1972. 'Therefore one has to learn to centre one's whole being around the psychic. Those who want to pass into supermanhood must get rid of the ego and concentrate themselves around the psychic being.'[60]

* We have from her the following message written in her handwriting on 24 June 1972: 'It is indispensable that each one finds his psychic and unites with it definitively. It is through the psychic that the supramental will manifest itself.'[61]

Now that we are acquainted with the main elements of the process of transformation in the Mother, we can go on with our story.

Chapter Twenty-three

TWO ROOMS

The Mother was so vast and so perfectly immobile in the great battle that was raging. One entered into her as into an infinity of soft snow, although she was so intensely burning in her immobility. One went far, far, and for ever, although there was always here. One felt at home there as in the deepest, most intimate sanctuary, although the heart of the world was felt beating there.[1]

— Satprem

'A FEW months after I had withdrawn [in 1958], I had the experience from the position of the vital,' we read in a conversation of the Mother with Satprem from January 1962. She meant the supramentalization of the vital. The supramentalization of the mental consciousness had taken place a long time ago; so had the supramentalization of the vital, as we have seen. What she was now talking about, however, was the complete supramentalization of the vital under the conditions of the presence of the Supramental on Earth, a presence necessary for the transformation of the cells of the body. 'That was really interesting, so much so that for a few weeks I had to resist the temptation to remain there.' For the supramentalization of the vital meant no less than that the Mother had realized unity with all the life-forces in and outside the cosmos, that she was able to go everywhere in those forces and to use them at will. (Be it noted that in this case there can no longer exist an egoistic arbitrariness, for the obliteration of the ego is the prime condition of supramentalization.) It must have been a realization of unimaginable power and splendour, a realization so great that the Mother had been tempted to abide in it — a very exceptional degree of interest of hers.

'I renounced all that voluntarily to continue to go on, and it is by doing so that I understood what they mean when they say: "He surrendered his experience" ... I said: "No, I do not want to stop here. I give all this as a present to You so that I may go to the very end" ... If I had kept that, oh... I would have become one of those world phenomena who revolutionize the history of the Earth. An enormous power! Enormous, unheard of! But then, you had to stop there, you had to take that as the end. I have gone on.'[2] This must have happened somewhere in 1959 and is related by her in no more than a couple of paragraphs of a conversation, in passing so to say. But it might have become the most brilliant and irresistible world religion of all times as this supramental realization was much more powerful than the overmental realization of 1927-28. We might call this the Mother's second renunciation.

In the night of 24 July 1959, the full supramental power entered for the first time *into the body* of the Mother. It was an experience of a formidable intensity, accompanied by high fever and a feeling as if her body was literally going to burst. All at once she found herself in another world, 'nearly as substantial as the physical world,' where Sri Aurobindo had a permanent dwelling.

One should not misunderstand this: the Mother had access to the supramental world or worlds in many ways through her mental and vital. We have seen an example of this in her story of the supramental ship. This, however, was an experience *of the body*; the supramental Power had taken possession of her body, the result of which was that the Mother got access to the supramental world by means of the body consciousness. There she found Sri Aurobindo present in a supramental body — in the body that during his lifetime he had built up with his supramentalized consciousness. She was surprised to discover that the supramental world was not far from the physical world and that it was waiting, fully developed, to manifest in earthly matter.

Certainly, since his departure Sri Aurobindo had always been together with her, within her. They were 'Mothersriaurobindo', with the Mother's name first because she was still present in front on the Earth, in a visible body. '[He] has not left me, not for a moment,' she wrote in a letter. 'For He is still with me, day and night, thinking through my brain, writing through my pen, speaking through my mouth and acting through my organising power.'[3] She only had to remain quiet for a moment and Sri Aurobindo was there, 'very much present.' They spent practically every night together 'to carry out things.' And as he no longer had to work in a physical body, he could move freely everywhere in the world and in all worlds, in many subtle bodies simultaneously. 'He is as it were multiplied.'

But this encounter was special, completely new. It happened because the supramental Power had entered her body. The supramental world where Sri Aurobindo had his home was very near to the material world, and like the latter it also existed in the physical plane, as it were, (but still hidden behind an invisible screen) and completely worked out. The Mother stayed there two days, two full days of absolute bliss. Sri Aurobindo was together with her all the time: 'When I walked, he walked with me; when I sat down, he sat near me.' It must have been at that time, or shortly afterwards, that she unlocked the door of her psychic being, 'very cautiously,' for Sri Aurobindo was now corporeally present again, not completely there and not all the time, it is true, but enough to prevent her psychic being from rushing away to be reunited with its counterpart.

From then onwards, the Mother mentions both worlds time and again, saying that the one exists, as it were, inside the other, *en doublure*. She often compares them with two rooms or two states of consciousness. For the transition from the one to the other is a phenomenon of consciousness. The transition happens because the consciousness — the consciousness of *the cells of the body* — is at one time in this position and then again in the other: at one time in the position of gross matter on our side and then again in the position of supramental matter on the other side. It is as if consciousness could magically traverse the wall between the two 'rooms' or worlds. ('Magically' is a word we use for a phenomenon of which we do not know how it actually comes about.)

The Mother has said from her very first bodily meeting with the supramental world that she found herself to be in the 'subtle physical'. The more she became familiar with that world, the more she described it as concrete — 'that subtle physical is very concrete' — till she would find the subtle physical more concrete and more material than our world of gross matter and call it 'a world much more concrete than the physical world', 'a physical which seems to me more complete.' Once again, we must beware of mixing up our terms and keep the following definitions in mind:

1. The term 'subtle physical', as commonly used before the last mentioned experience in 1959, is the intermediary level of existence between gross matter and the vital which has to be traversed by everything that appears and happens in matter and where it is prepared. We read in *The Life Divine*: 'In the physical plane or close to it there are believed to be layers of greater and greater subtlety which may be regarded as sub-planes of the physical with a vital and a mental character; these are at once surrounding and penetrating strata through which the interchange between the higher worlds and the physical world takes place.'[4]

2. The term 'subtle physical' is also sometimes used in connection with the substance of the vital and mental worlds because it so strongly evokes everything that is too 'subtle' to be perceived by our senses — in connection, that is to say, with everything that is not gross matter.

3. From 1959 onwards, the Mother uses the term, besides the two above definitions, for the supramental world on the verge of manifesting on the Earth. This is of course a 'subtle' world to the gross physical perception, but it differs radically from the levels of existence referred to by definitions 1 and 2. As we will

see further on, in the supramental world, which is a Truth-world, matter is indeed more concrete, of a higher density and at the same time more plastic than the gross matter of our world. The Mother has used the term 'subtle physical' for this supramental world too because this imperceptible world was so near to the, for us, perceptible one that she only had to make 'a step backwards,' in a movement of the consciousness of the cells, to pass from the one into the other, just as she had always done with her higher consciousness, and in a most habitual way for her, cross from our world into the subtle physical ones.

The Mother had not had an ego for a long time. The ego is one of the least palpable but nonetheless the most real things existing. It is the distorting lens through which we see and experience the world; it is the axis by which all relations in connection with ourselves are defined; it is the magnet which attracts everything to us, the ever present searchlight of which the beam reveals everything within its scope as correlated with ourselves. The ego is a psychological construction which in evolution has been indispensable for human individualization. However, if one wants to exceed ordinary humanity, the ego becomes the greatest obstacle and may be our greatest enemy — which would mean that our greatest enemy is ourselves. For it is tenacious, it doggedly holds on to its evolutionary right of existence, and it is secretly present in the smallest of our inner movements. 'We want a race without ego,' the Mother had said.

But, naturally, the body too has an ego. The bodily ego is what keeps the body together as a definite entity, what unconsciously coordinates its functions and actions, what physically defines its location and position in the world. The ego is the axis around which our world turns, psychologically and physically. Therefore the idea of wanting to universalize the body is directly in opposition to the habitual, physically egocentric manner of living. At this point too the *sadhana* of the Mother clashed with age-old habits, age-old 'laws'. But the supramental does not care about the rationality and the habits of homo sapiens, and the Mother advanced undaunted into the unknown.

Undaunted but not unshaken. By an exercise of the mind we may *imagine* that the body no longer has an ego or a central axis and that it has become one with all things, even with the universe. Many mystics have had this ecstatic experience mentally, and it has been found that drugs create similar experiences vitally. But bodily? For we should not forget that this was the yoga of the body cells.

The Mother never *wanted* to do or try out anything — the experiences of her *sadhana* were imposed on her. In a yoga with surrender as its mainstay, one does not want anything for oneself: one lets the Divine decide in one's stead, for he knows so much better at every step, at every moment. Moreover, what to us is an act of the will, is an act of the mental consciousness; as the mental consciousness within the global Unity is terribly limited and actually ignorant, a self-centered act of the mental will can only lead us astray. Sri Aurobindo had said that he had been progressing step by step in his yoga, instructed in total surrender by the all-wise inner Guide. So too did the Mother. Behind her, within her, was present the guiding hand of the Great Mother, of her Self, and each of her movements in this world of ignorance was supported by the Flame of a total surrender — for that really is a Flame, which knows, which can do things and which grants the needed force.

The first few times she crossed over in the body consciousness from one room into the other, from one world into the other, the experience was so utterly new that it had traumatic effects. (Is not every evolutionary mutation traumatic for the evolving being?) To her body here, in this world, the crossing over meant a sort of momentary death. For what is death but a transition from one world (of gross matter, ours) into another? The consciousness of her body had to learn the movement of the transition; it had to acquire the mastery of that movement; it had to become accustomed to it. At first it got frightened, each time, it panicked. And the Mother fainted, to the consternation of those present, who naturally did not know what was happening. She found it therefore preferable to go and faint in her bathroom.

'Fear must not enter in Yoga,'[5] Sri Aurobindo had written repeatedly. The Mother had impressed the necessity of fearlessness on her youthful audience at the Playground: 'Yoga and fear do not go together.'[6] 'If you have fear, it is as if that fear attracts what you are afraid of ... [Fear] is like a dissolvent, like an acid.'[7] Fear was not in her dictionary. Her former occult training had already taught her how dangerous and even deadly fear and apprehension might be. And was she not, as Kali and Durga, the intrepid warrior of the worlds? 'Intrepid' is indeed the word that is most applicable to her. She said somewhat ironically that for an adventure of discovery of this kind one should not easily be scared, *il ne faut pas avoir froid aux yeux*. She has described several times the vital aspect of her being: a fearless warrior, white, of magnificent stature, neither man nor woman, leaning on his halberd when at rest. This, among the numerous aspects of her being, was the vital personality she had chosen for this life, it was her vital force. An intrepid warrior.

She was building the bridge between our world and the supramental world — and she was universalizing herself. Both processes of transformation went hand in hand. She found that the axis of the physical I, the referential axis in her body, was dissolving. Her body consciousness grew less and less restricted to her physical body; it was expanding, it was present in other things and in other persons. This was possible only by a transformation of the cells, which in their consciousness began to vibrate in attunement with everything. Sri Aurobindo and she herself had always said that each part of their body, a microcosm, symbolically represented a part of the macrocosm. (One day, the Mother would even indicate where the Ashram as an entity was representatively located in her physical body: between the navel and the appendix.)

In this Yoga, we really get directly acquainted with the arcana, the hidden processes of the world, that incredible miracle. Everything is a miracle: a grain of sand and a fishing eagle, a lily-of-the-valley and a galaxy, a red corpuscle and an embrace of love. This is one of the threads Sri Aurobindo has woven through *Savitri*: the amazing magic, the stupendous miracle in everything that has come forth and is coming forth from the hand of the Creatrix, at each moment in time, before time, after time. Together with the seeing attention, the gift of wonder is the indispensable quality of the actually conscious human being, the one Rimbaud had in mind when he wrote: *Il faut être absolument moderne* (one must be absolutely modern) — modern not by way of fashion but as an instrument of experience and knowledge, as an 'attitude in time', with the gaze constantly attached to the Presence.

Like every part of the body and like every organ, the cell too is representative of the vibrations in the cosmos constituting the related cosmic elements, big or small, microscopic or astronomical. Through the vibrations in her cells the Mother entered into direct contact with all related vibrations elsewhere. Being here, she was also there and there and everywhere, corporeally. Her cells, an ever greater number of them, were growing into the Unity-Consciousness, one of whose characteristics is omnipresence. They were developing a supramental body, which is an omnipresent body consisting of a supramental substance. We cannot fully understand this, we are not built and do not exist like that. But the Mother was becoming like that by her *sadhana*. Part of her body was still like ours, part of it was becoming supramentalized. She had one foot here and the other there, as she said herself. This must have been maddening, and that she also said sometimes. But she had known beforehand that the unexpected and impossible would become the everyday reality for her. All the same, it was a strange way of living, making the evolutionary saltus in full awareness.

The Agenda

Every sentence in the preceding chapters and paragraphs, and every one in the following chapters could be illustrated or supported with numerous quotations from the thirteen volumes of *L'Agenda de Mère*. These are the conversations the Mother had with Satprem from somewhere in 1960 till May 1973. The *Agenda* is a document of more than 6000 pages. We can only mention its existence and importance, and briefly refer to it in these last chapters. At the insistence of Satprem, extracts of those conversations have also been published, from the end of 1964 till the end of 1973, in the *Bulletin* under the title *Notes on the Way*, after having been read out to the Mother and approved by her.

The *Agenda* is one of the great documents about the Yoga of Sri Aurobindo and the Mother. What Sri Aurobindo had seen and partially worked out is here being worked out further by the Mother. The *Agenda* is the sequel to *The Synthesis of Yoga* and *The Supramental Manifestation*; it is the development of what had been outlined in Sri Aurobindo's writings and in the *Entretiens*. This document also provides us with an extremely interesting and often revealing light on the lives of Sri Aurobindo and the Mother. No life sketch of them, no biography can be complete without this source.

Satprem, formerly named Bernard Enginger, is a Frenchman who was born in Paris in 1923, but who has always nostalgically remembered his youth on the coast of Brittany. In the Second World War he became a member of the Resistance. He had just turned twenty when the Gestapo arrested him; he spent one and a half years in German concentration camps. After the war, and deeply branded by those experiences, he became an exponent of the problematics and the life-view of Existentialism, although not Sartre and Camus but Gide and Malraux were the main sources of his inspiration.

In 1946, he wrote in a letter to André Gide: 'I loved you, and certain passages from your books have helped me to survive in the concentration camps. From you I got the force to break away from a bourgeois and material comfort. Together with you, I have been seeking "not so much for possession as for love." I have made a clean sweep to stand completely new before the new law. I have made myself free ... Finally, I have broken away from you, but I have found no new masters and life keeps suffocating me. The terrible absurdity of the likes of Sartre and Camus has solved nothing and only opens the gates to suicide.' (André Gide, *Journal 1942-1949*).* Satprem

---

* From Gide's answering letter: 'The world will only be saved, supposing it can be saved, by the unsubmitted. Without them, our civilization, our culture would be finished together with everything we love and which renders to our presence on earth a hidden justification. They are, those *unsubmitted*, 'the salt of the earth' and those responsible before God. For I have got the conviction that God does not yet exist and that we have to deserve him. Can one think of a more noble, admirable and worthy task for our endeavours?'

worked briefly as a functionary in the colonial administration of Pondicherry, but he felt dissatisfied and unfulfilled everywhere and went in search of adventure in French Guyana, Brazil and Africa.

However, when in Pondicherry he had had the *darshan* of Sri Aurobindo and the Mother, and he carried *The Life Divine* with him even in the rain forests of the Amazon. In 1953, after those wanderings, he returned to Pondicherry to meet the Mother and settle in the Ashram against his individualistic and rebellious nature. '[I was] a good rebellious Westerner and all ways of changing the world looked *a priori* excellent to me,' he writes.[8] He was at times teaching in the Ashram school, and with his remarkable literary talent he looked after the French copy for the *Bulletin* of the Department of Physical Education which, in fact, was the Mother's publication. This periodical was (and still is) a quarterly and has all texts printed in English and in French.

Satprem's first years in the Ashram were a period of dissatisfaction, restlessness, doubts, and sometimes loudly voiced revolt. He has included part of his correspondence with the Mother in the first volume of the *Agenda*; these letters present us a moving picture of the patience, understanding and love with which the Mother treated her rebellious children. She has never accepted somebody for the Yoga without a reason, and when she accepted somebody, it was unconditionally and for ever. Time and again Satprem imagined he had to find his inner fulfilment in adventure. There is not an exotic place on Earth he did not feel impelled to go to; the Congo, Brazil (again), Afghanistan, the Himalayas, New Zealand, the Gobi desert, a journey around the globe in a sailing boat — all that and more is dreamt of in his letters. But the Mother knew what was really prompting him and she let him become, in 1959, the disciple of a very able tantric yogi who was also the head priest of the big temple in Rameshwaram. Then, guided by another yogi, Satprem wandered during six months as a *sanyasi* (mendicant monk) through India and received the initiation of the sanyasis. His novel *Par le corps de la terre, ou le Sanyasin* (By the Body of the Earth, or The Sanyasi) is based on these experiences.

But 'the bird always returned to the nest,' to the Ashram in

Pondicherry, to the Mother. She started inviting him from time to time to her room, at first apparently for some literary chores in connection with the *Bulletin*. He became more and more spellbound by her. He asked questions (or she instilled the questions into him) and she answered. 'At first, she had me called, and there was that big chair in which she was sitting, and I sat down on the carpet on the floor and listened to her. Truly, she knew so much. It was wonderful to listen to her. But most important, little by little she began telling her experience.'9

However violently Satprem might express himself emotionally, he was a cultured man and possessed a very keen intellect, widely varied interests, and as a writer a passionate, colourful style. We have already seen that the Mother complained about the lack of intellectual eagerness and cultural as well as general interest in the people around her. She had so much to communicate, to share, her knowledge and experience were so broad in all essential domains where the human being is confronted with 'the great questions,' but so little was asked of her. 'I am a little bell that is not sounded,' she said. Here now was a man with an analytical mind, a poignant life-experience and a thirst for knowledge — the ideal instrument to communicate to others a glimpse of her unbelievable adventure. At the same time she worked on him, in him; she did his yoga as she did the yoga of all those she had accepted and taken into herself.

Satprem started realizing the importance of those conversations with the Mother and took a tape-recorder to her room. Thus the *Agenda* came about. One part of it concerned the literary work he was doing for the Mother; another part concerned his own yogic evolution, his yogic education; and the third part of the conversations was intended by the Mother as the registration, in broad outlines, of the process of her transformation. Everything the Mother said was interesting, everything was informative and instructive, though she herself most probably would never have allowed some confidential passages about persons in her entourage to be published.

After the passing of the Mother, a gap has come about between the Ashram and Satprem, with regrettable consequences. Under the Mother's direction he had written *Sri Aurobindo, ou l'Aventure de la conscience* (Sri Aurobindo, or the Adventure of Consciousness), a book that has led so many to Sri Aurobindo and the Mother. He had also read out to her *La Genèse du surhomme* (The Genesis of Superman), an essay highly lauded by her. Then after her departure, he wrote the trilogy *Mère* (Mother), in which for the first time he analyses and comments upon the invaluable material of the *Agenda* of which he was the only possessor at that time. *Le mental des cellules* (The Mind of the Cells) is a kind of crystallization of the trilogy, and in *Gringo* and recently in *Evolution II* he reports about his own evolution. One gets the impression that he considers himself the only true successor of Sri Aurobindo and the Mother. In a letter from 1983 one reads: 'I had to take the decision to withdraw because I was no longer progressing in my [inner] work, I kept turning around in a circle. There must be at least one human being to prove, to show to the world that the way of the new species is practicable for humans. Otherwise, what is the use of what Mother and Sri Aurobindo have done for humankind?'[10]

'I am no Longer in my Body'[11]

> ... *the harmonically manifest being of God in certain great rhythms ...*
>
> —Sri Aurobindo

A great crisis in the *sadhana* of the Mother started on 16 March 1962. She had felt it coming, as we can read with hindsight in the conversations of 11 and 13 March. 'I was very serious: I laughed. It is precisely when I laugh that I am serious ... When I am like that and seem to laugh at each and everything, it is because there are moments that it is really dangerous, really dangerous. I abhor dramas. I do not want to strike a tragic note. I much rather laugh at everything than strike a tragic note ... I do not want to be a victim, nor a hero, nor a martyr — nothing of all that! ... The God who is crucified — no, no way! If it costs him his life, it costs him his life, that is all ... and it does not matter.' It was really dangerous indeed; her helpers even thought they had to take all necessary steps because she had died.

What had happened?

Her own words, spoken in English on 3 April, after the storm had calmed down somewhat, and noted down by Pavitra, tell the story. 'Exactly between 11:00 and 12:00 last night, I had an experience by which I discovered that there is a group of people — purposely their identity was not revealed to me — who want to create a kind of religion based on the revelation of Sri Aurobindo. But they have taken only the side of power and force, a certain kind of knowledge and all that could be utilised by Asuric forces. There is a big Asuric being that has succeeded in taking the appearance of Sri Aurobindo. There is only an appearance. This appearance of Sri Aurobindo has declared to me that the work I am doing is not his [Sri Aurobindo's]. It has declared that I have been a traitor to him [Sri Aurobindo] and to his work and has refused to have anything to do with me.'

She did not find it necessary to go into all details. 'But I must say that I was fully conscious, aware of everything, knowing that an Asuric force was there — but not rejecting it because of the infinity of Sri Aurobindo. I knew that everything is part of him and I do not want to reject anything. I met this being last night three times.' She remembered everything with perfect accuracy, even the time. 'Between 12:15 and 2:00 I was with the true Sri Aurobindo in the fullest and sweetest relation — there also in perfect consciousness, awareness, calm and equanimity ... I woke up at 2:00 and noticed that the heart had been affected by the attack of this group that wants to take my life away from this body, because they know that so long as I am in a body upon earth their purpose cannot succeed. Their first attack was many years ago ... They would have liked me dead years ago. It is they who are responsible for these attacks on my life. Up till now I am alive because the Lord wanted me to be alive, otherwise I would have gone long ago.' We find here a confirmation of the attacks of black magic that accompanied every important crisis in the Mother's *sadhana*, to impede or weaken as much as possible the result of the crisis, which each time was a step forward in the process of her transformation.

If all of this is astonishing, the further words of the Mother, still spoken in English while her life hung in balance, are not less so. 'I am no more in my body. I have left it to the Lord to take care of it, to decide if it is to have the Supramental or not. I know and I have said also that now is the last fight. If the purpose for which this body is alive is to be fulfilled, that is to say the first steps taken towards the Supramental transformation, then it will continue today. It is the Lord's decision. I am not even asking what he has decided. If the body is incapable of bearing the fight, if it has to be dissolved, then humanity will pass through a critical time. What the Asuric force that has succeeded in taking the appearance of Sri Aurobindo will create, is a new religion or thought, perhaps cruel and merciless, in the name of the Supramental Realisation. But everybody must know that it is not true, that it is not Sri Aurobindo's teaching, not the truth of his teaching. The truth of Sri Aurobindo is a truth of love and light and mercy. He is good and great and compassionate and Divine. And it is He who will have the final victory.'

When these words were noted down and afterwards read out to the Mother for verification, she gave the following comment: 'The fight is within the body. This cannot go on. They must be defeated or this body will be defeated. All depends on what the Lord will decide. It [her body] is the battlefield. How far it can resist, I do not know. After all, it depends on Him. He knows if the time has come or not, the time for the beginning of the Victory. Then the body will survive. If not, in any case, my love and consciousness will be there.'[12]

These are simple words, originally spoken in simple English, but their meaning is so dramatic. There was so much at stake: again thousands of years of evolution or not, again thousands of years of all that madness and suffering — or not? The Supramental was present in the Earth's atmosphere and active in it; it made this battle of the Mother possible. She could have departed earlier, but her presence rendered possible 'the first steps of the supramental transformation,' of the realization of the first supramental body. If this essay did not succeed, then what she could work out in years, days, hours by her corporeal presence would have to be worked out by Nature in thousands or millions of years, and humanity would have to pass through a 'critical time' under a kind of fascist, pseudo-supramental regime. We are reminded of the Hitlerian ideal, known to very few but the true motive behind the 'cruel and merciless' regime of Nazism.

The battle waged by her in her body continued. Those in her proximity, the members of the Ashram and all who knew of her critical health held their breath, though not many realized what it all was about, what was at stake for them then and for us now.

On 13 April came the proclamation of the victory bulletin, again spoken in English by the Mother and this time recorded on tape. She even gave the bulletin a title: 'Experience in the night of 12 April 1962' and it went as follows: 'Suddenly in the night I woke with the full awareness of what we could call the Yoga of the World. The Supreme Love was manifesting through big pulsations, and each pulsation was bringing the world further in its manifestation. It was the formidable pulsations of the eternal stupendous Love, only Love. Each pulsation of the Love was carrying the universe further in its manifestation.

'And there was the certitude that what is to be done is done and that the Supramental Manifestation is realised.

'Everything was personal [experienced by her divine Personality], nothing was individual.

'This was going on and on and on and on.

'The certitude that what is to be done is *done*.

'All the results of the falsehood had disappeared: death was an illusion, sickness was an illusion, ignorance was an illusion — something that had no reality, no existence. Only Love and Love and Love and Love — immense, formidable, stupendous, carrying everything.

'And how to express it in the world? It was like an impossibility because of the contradiction. But then it came: "You have accepted that the world should know the Supramental Truth ... and it will be expressed totally, integrally." Yes, yes ...

'And the thing is *done*.'

Then, after a long silence: 'The individual consciousness came back: just the sense of a limitation, a limitation of pain; without that, no individual.'

And all of a sudden she switched to French: 'And we set out again on the way, sure of Victory. The skies are full of the songs of Victory.

The Truth alone exists; it alone shall be manifested. Forward! Glory to Thee, Lord, Supreme Triumphant! (*Gloire à Toi, Seigneur, Triomphateur suprême!*)

'Now, on with the work! Patience, endurance, perfect equality, and an absolute faith.

'What I àm saying is nothing, nothing, nothing, nothing but words if I compare it to the experience.

'And our consciousness is the same, absolutely the same as the Lord's. There was no difference, no difference.

'We are That, we are That, we are That.'[13]

Chapter Twenty-four

THE TRANSFER OF POWER

Her single greatness in that last dire scene
Must cross alone a perilous bridge in Time
And reach an apex of world-destiny
Where all is won or all is lost for man.[1]
— Sri Aurobindo

An Agglomerate

There was the certitude that what had to be done had been done
and that the Supramental Realization on Earth had *essentially* been
accomplished — six years (only six years) after 1956. We remember
that at the time the Mother had asked the Supreme whether she
should continue her task in her earthly body; she had asked for an
unmistakable sign and she must have received one. This time the
decision to remain upon Earth had been taken in the midst of the
crisis. Those who had taken care of her ('They have done that
splendidly,' she said) had not been mistaken: it had indeed been a
matter of life and death, even more so than they had thought.

The Mother had left her body on the night of 12 April 1962, which
in ordinary parlance means that she had died. There is no doubt about
it. Which means that she had resurrected, for everybody has seen her
alive till 1973. We have encountered a lot of extraordinary facts in
this story: how the god Krishna took Sri Aurobindo's body as his own;

how the Mother twice renounced the occasion to found the greatest world religion of all times; how the divine Unity-Consciousness manifested on the Earth. Now we hear that the Mother left her body and took it up again in 1962! But it is recorded in the written documents, for instance in the following statements of the Mother, a few selected out of many, which have been put in chronological order.

* ' ... when I was that Pulsation of Love [in the night of 12 April 1962] and it was decided that I take up my body again, that I return into my body ...' (7 August 1963)

* 'You must have come back [into your body]. You cannot have the authority over your body without having left it. When your body is no longer yourself, not at all — it is something that has been added and stuck onto yourself — when that is like that and you look at it from above (from a psychological 'above'), then you can again descend into it as the almighty master.' (20 November 1963)

* 'Yesterday or the day before, the whole day long, from morning till evening, there was something [in the Mother] that said: "I am ... I am or I have the consciousness of somebody who is dead and who is on earth." I am translating that into words, but it was as if it was said: "It is like this that is the consciousness of somebody who is dead in relation to the earth and to physical things ... I am somebody who is dead and who lives on earth."' (9 March 1966)

* The Mother talks about herself: 'During two days the impression of not knowing whether one is alive or whether one is dead ... of not being very sure of the difference that makes ...' (14 June 1967)

* 'If you asked it the question, the body [hers] would say: "I don't know if I am alive, I don't know if I am dead." For, indeed, it is so. For some minutes it has completely the impression of being dead; at other moments it has the impression of being alive.' (31 May 1969)

What Satprem writes in his trilogy about the Mother is therefore very true: 'We probably do not understand literally enough that, at the same time, she was really alive on one side and really dead on the other side (ours) — this, while she apparently went on living the old ordinary life.'[2] He also writes: 'Mother will make that reflection [dead or not dead] dozens of times, and more and more often, one might say with ever greater urgency, in the course of the years that were to follow.'[3]

In April 1962, the second stage of the Work of the Avatar was accomplished: six years of intense Integral Yoga representing six hundred or six thousand years of unassisted supramental evolution. The pillars of the bridge connecting the supramental world and our gross material world had been put in place. Normally at this point, the Work of the Avatar would have come to an end. But it was decided that the Mother would remain on Earth to accelerate the process of transformation in the greatest possible measure. Who took that decision? She herself would probably have said: the Lord. But those cosmic Pulsations of Love represented the great rhythms of the Manifestation. Is the Manifestation, ordained by 'the Lord,' not the work of the divine Creatrix? He and She are one, inseparably; but it is good and just to remember that the Great Lady has co-decided that her own presence as the Mother-in-the-sadhana on Earth would be continued.

The fact that to that end a 'mystery' of death and resurrection was necessary may give us some idea about the magnitude of the sacrifice undertaken in this case; for the continuation of the process of transformation in a body, with the total universalization of the consciousness of the cells, the transfer of power and the other elements of the transformation of the body, could only be brought about in a corporeal suffering so intense that the Mother at one time would say: 'I was all the suffering of the world, all felt at the same time.' And it was not in her nature to use hyperbole unnecessarily. She took up that body again — because of its death no longer hers, but because of its yoga by far the most advanced physical form on Earth — and this meant a voluntary, conscious descent into hell. Such was her Love for humanity.

She found that the vital and mental components or sheaths had been taken away from that body; only the physical sheath remained, the physical interface with Matter. 'The whole body has been emptied of its habits and forces, and slowly, slowly, slowly the cells have then woken up to a new receptivity and have opened themselves to the divine Influence, directly ... The mental has withdrawn, the vital has withdrawn, everything has withdrawn. At the time I was apparently ill, the mental had disappeared, the vital had disappeared and the body was, purposely, left to itself. And it is precisely because the vital and mental had disappeared that people got the impression of a very serious illness.'[4]

Who can live without the vital, without the life force? Who can live without a mental consciousness? 'One cannot move a finger, speak a word, make a step without the mental being involved.'[5] We know that the mental is present even in the cells and atoms. And without the life force one is dead. It was a miracle how that body remained alive, how it started talking again with a voice seemingly coming from another world (the voice is an instrument of the life force) and how little by little it again began doing more work than a normal human being might be able to tackle. But something supported it from behind, something that was so much her own self that it took quite a while before she became aware of it, as we will see.

Only the Supreme kept her body still alive, she said. It really was being kept together by a higher Will with a certain purpose. She did not even call it a body anymore but an 'aggregate' or 'agglomerate' of cells, of vibrations which one way or another went on existing in a mutual relationship. And that so very special and strange body was the battlefield where the struggle for the world was being fought.

That body, as we know, had no longer an ego, it had no longer a central axis of reference in the world of the mortals. It had become nothing but an enormous field of experience and was no longer an individuality. It was present everywhere (*le corps est partout*), in the people, in the objects, in the events, around her and everywhere on Earth. If even for a moment she withdrew from her everyday occupations, the consciousness of her body became fully identified with the material substance of the Earth, she said — and not only with the material substance but also with that from which matter originated and in which it still has its roots: the subconscious with its caves and pools, with its vermin and obscurity. 'It is as if the whole Earth is the body'[6] — her body that was no longer her body.

More and more she had in the cells, in matter, 'the same experiences one can have on the heights of the consciousness.' For us it is difficult to imagine what this means, and this causes the Work of Sri Aurobindo and the Mother to be misunderstood so often. Rather naïvely, most people looked forward to the transformation of the body. According to their expectations, Sri Aurobindo, and after his passing the Mother and the disciples, should suddenly have started radiating like a Sun! Sri Aurobindo and the Mother have written and spoken volumes to explain the conditions of the supramental transformation and that the transformation of the body, the appearance of a perceptible, immortal supramental body on Earth, would only be the last, the ultimate result of the process of transformation. They were right when they said that they were understood only by very few who could generate the necessary attention and insight to read and comprehend them. The cells first had to become conscious. The golden supramental Light, after having been first realized in the mental and vital, had to be brought into the cells, where it would awaken the ever present but hidden Unity-Consciousness. The cells had to be as much, in the same measure, to the same extent filled with the supramental Consciousness as the higher 'psychological' levels. In one word, the cells had to be *divinized*.

In the body of the Mother, in that agglomerate of cells, the process of the divinization of the cells was under way. Some cells were transformed or being transformed — a part of the billions, an ever growing part of the billions. It was a chore without end, for each cell was connected with near or distantly related elements in the visible or invisible cosmos, on all planes of existence, in the Supramental as well as in the Subconscious and Inconscient where the merciless battle to bring the light had to be waged. The agglomerate of cells in the body of the Mother was a similitude, a representation, a miniature of the Earth which, as we know, is in its turn a condensation and symbol of the universe. The supramental transformation is a cosmic transformation, naturally, for the Supermind is the matrix of the universe — of this and of all other universes.

The Mother's body became 'large as the Earth.' That was how she experienced it; it was the way she lived while sitting there in that simple chair with her arms loosely on the armrests and her feet on a footstool. 'The person is as it were an image on which to focus the attention,' she said smilingly ... 'In actual fact, I am nothing but a deceptive appearance.'[7] She looked like a human being, but she was something completely different from a human being, now also corporeally. She continued to resemble a human being in order to be able to do her work among human beings, so that human beings might still relate to her. But: 'They have very little contact with what my body really is.'[8]

The Change of Master

'The transformation starts with the opening of the consciousness to the action of the new forces'[9] — the opening of the consciousness of the cells by the surrender to the divine Forces, now directly active on Earth, without the consciousness of the cells knowing what changes will occur because of the surrender. It is an act of absolute confidence in the Higher Presence (*ce que Tu veux*); it is a step into the absolute unknown, 'whatever may happen.' The great adventure, never dared before. The base of the consciousness of all cells had to be altered; the base of the dark, conservative, fearful, age-long tortured consciousness of the cells had to be changed into the divine, joyful, all-encompassing and luminous Unity-consciousness. A stupendous change. Up to then all had sought their salvation in a Hereafter; Sri Aurobindo and the Mother wanted the salvation of mankind here, on the Earth, in the cells, in Matter. '*Le salut est physique*,' said the Mother, 'the salvation is physical.' If this is not true, then this creation of a distressing absurdity as it presents itself to us now can only be the work of a deranged Spirit. If the Divine is what he is supposed to be — Being, Consciousness, Bliss — then he cannot have lured his creatures, having come forth from him and existing in him, into this monstrous farce without a divine intention of Love and Supreme Joy being hidden in it or present behind it. The burning question as to the suffering of the ages ran like lava through the *sadhana* of the Mother, as we have seen. The promise given to mankind since its origin was being redeemed in her, in Mothersriaurobindo. If the Manifestation has a purpose, if Matter has a reason, then the salvation cannot but be physical, *also* physical, because that purpose and that reason of the whole Manifestation cannot but be divine and therefore Matter too must be divine.

To that end, the prevailing laws had to be confronted and dealt with. In the cells, the Mother said, the automatism of the habits of thousands, not to say millions of years had to be changed into a conscious activity under the direct guidance of the divine Consciousness. The transition of one way of functioning (the habitual) into another (the supramental) she called the 'transfer of power' or the 'change of master.' The way the cells were functioning before the transition was ruled by laws which were thousands and even millions of years old; the Master of the new way of functioning was the Divine himself, without any intermediary. It was the passage 'of the ordinary automatical way of functioning to a conscious functioning under the direct guidance and the direct influence of the Supreme ... The whole automatic habit of thousands of years must be changed into a conscious action directly guided of the Supreme Consciousness.'[10]

Words, yes, abstract words. She could communicate her experiences only with words, and this was going to become a big problem for her. But what happens when one experiences such a transition bodily, when in one's body, one's organs, one's cells the ordinary manner of functioning stops, in one's heart and brain and nerves and stomach and intestine, to switch to a new, never experienced functioning, directly caused by a Force the body is unacquainted with and exceedingly strong?

What happens when an organ no longer works as it used to? One becomes ill. When it is not at all working as usual? One becomes very ill. And when the organs and the whole system of their relations gets disorganized? ... The body of the Mother, each of its parts and the relation between the parts were in a permanent state of crisis, an uninterrupted, apparently catastrophic state of emergency which, according to the norms of medical science, was a deadly state of illness. This was not all the time outwardly noticeable. The graph of the Mother's health went up and down — usually a brief 'up' and a long, dreadful 'down' — and at one time it was this organ and then again that other one that was affected. But, fundamentally, it was one continual crisis her body was experiencing, all those years. She really must have decided from beyond death and in divine Love to take this kind of ordeal upon her.

'It's not a joke,' she said in English in the middle of a French conversation, but she had often noticed that it was Sri Aurobindo who spoke in English through her mouth or made her think and write in English. (When he let his presence be felt, even her handwriting started resembling his.) 'It is difficult, it is tough, it is painful,' she said, and she was not a plaintive character nor squeamish about pain. 'It is a grim tapasya,' an arduous yogic effort — and none of the persons around her noticed it. But when it became too much, she sometimes had to interrupt her work for a few days perforce, on doctor's orders. How gruesome it could be can be read in the conversation Satprem has named *L'Agenda terrible*, 'the terrible agenda,' or in the conversation at the time her leg was paralyzed.

'I have a leg that has been dead for a long time (it is just beginning to revive), paralysed ... But it was not an innocent paralysis! For three weeks — at least — for three weeks a constant pain, night and day, twenty-four hours out of twenty-four, and without any relief, none whatsoever. It was as if everything was torn out of me ... One might say that all that time I was nothing but one cry. It lasted a long time. It lasted several weeks. I have not counted them ... You know, it was so ... it was the problem of the whole world, a world that was nothing but pain and suffering, and with a big question mark: "Wherefore?" ... It was really interesting. I believe something will have been done from the general point of view. That was not merely the difficulty of one single body or one single person: I believe something has been done to prepare Matter so that it may receive as it should.'[11]

She found it interesting, also when it was the turn of her heart and her nervous system to be transformed. She has suffered one heart attack after the other, sudden variations of her heartbeat, a jolting, jarring rhythm of the pulse. *'Le pouls est plus que fantaisiste,'* she said then, the pulse is more than fanciful. The transfer of the sensitive nervous system, branched out everywhere in the body, was a scream-ing torture for days on end, without respite.

The Caves and the Pools of Life

There was also the work in the subconscious with all its terrors. We have already mentioned the grottoes and caves of the subconscious. One could also call that the swamps, or the cesspits, or the mud pools of life. It is the first world which originated from the immobile Inconscient; there things started moving, crawling, hungering, scratching, biting, strangling, devouring. Everything there is lowly, elementary, blind, slimy, sticky. It is a world partially discovered by psychoanalysis which has taken it to be the complete hidden side of the human being; therefore psychoanalysis discards *a priori* the subliminal higher vital and mental levels through which we remain in contact with the higher worlds — not to mention the soul. It is difficult to call this kind of analysis of man 'psychology' or knowledge of the soul if one has a real idea of what the psyche or soul actually is. Psychoanalysis has halted at its partial, unsavoury discovery and refused to go beyond; it has drawn its inspiration from that dark level and based its authority on it; it reduces all who confide themselves into the hands of its priests to the lowest, most distasteful and bestial aspect in them, shutting out in disdain the smallest ray of light from higher worlds. When Sigmund Freud aboard an ocean liner was for the first time approaching the coast of the United States, he said: 'They do not know that we are bringing them the plague.' He knew it all right.

We have seen more than once that the Inconscient and Subconscient form the basis of Matter and consequently of the cells, of everything our material body consists of. We *are* those foul worlds under the waterline of our waking consciousness. There is nothing we experience that does not sink down in those twilight zones, peopled by the puny and the big monsters of our deep sea. Everything we have forgotten, everything we have lived through rises up from there again, unexpectedly and irrationally, in our dreams and unquelled emotions. There, we still are the animal, sometimes scared to death, sometimes a stalking beast of prey. Experiences from long ago, from before the ice ages, remain alive in the animal's memory in us; in a trice they can break up our world, constructed with so much difficulty. 'Earthquakes of the soul,' Sri Aurobindo called them.

It was an elementary requirement that that was a place where the Mother had to do the work for the world. It was one of the reasons why she had taken up the physical body which she now no longer considered hers. There she worked 'in the lowest layers of senselessness.' 'I think that not one human being would be able to stand the sight of what has been shown to me,' she said. No, in that kind of exploration and transformation one should not be easily frightened. It was worse than the worst horror films; but these were living experiences, gruesome nightmares that did not end when waking up. One can only transform what one has experienced, what one has suffered. She underwent all the terrors of creation, including physical suffering, torture, deliberately and maliciously thought-out torments. In the torture chambers of history, also those of present-day history, nothing was or is invented by men that does not have an origin in those hellish worlds. There resides the source of inspiration and the impulse to bestiality; the torturers have only to follow their instinct in order to regress, voluptuously, to an order lower than that of the beast.

Suffering and Ecstasy

The Mother had to descend deeper and deeper to bring the Light there also. The cross the Avatar Jesus Christ had been dragging through the streets of Jerusalem up to Golgotha was a symbolic one. His real cross consisted of the fact that he, like all Avatars, had taken the past of humanity on his shoulders, otherwise he would not have been able to help it one step forwards. From the little we know of what Sri Aurobindo and the Mother have gone through, we get some idea of what an Avatar has to suffer. And this time the step forward was an enormous one: it was the quantum jump from animal man to a Divine Being, skipping the intermediary stage of the god. The bitter cup had to be emptied once and for all. Nobody ever saw a sign of the suffering Sri Aurobindo went through. He hid it even from the Mother, out of Love. She became aware of it only when she had to experience it herself and, Satprem writes, her voice got smothered by tears while talking about it. 'I got the awareness of everything he has suffered physically.' She too gave nothing away of 'the dirty job' she was doing, not if it was at all possible. She continued receiving people, smiling at them, listening to their inflated problems, and granting their souls the grace for this and all future lives, which is the privilege of a direct encounter with the incarnated Godhead.

For that she was, the incarnated Godhead, the Great Mother behind the Mother-in-the-sadhana. But that Great Mother could only live in *Ananda*, in the highest Joy, Ecstasy or Bliss. The Mother-in-the-sadhana had been supramentalized mentally and vitally many years ago and therefore had the golden Sun in her mental and vital *chakras*; she was now bringing the Supermind with its *Ananda* into her cells, into her matter. Nonetheless, the suffering was so excruciating that for weeks she had been 'nothing but a cry' — a cry which, in the last years, one sometimes could even hear downstairs, in the courtyard of the central Ashram building. Where was then that *Ananda*?

Strange to say, that *Ananda* seemed to be always present, also *during* the suffering and *during* the terror. In *The Life Divine* Sri Aurobindo has made clear that without *Ananda* nothing can exist, anywhere, not even for a fraction of a second, because the *Ananda* or Joy (Bliss) is an essential part of the Divine. The *Ananda* 'is the sole cause, motive and object of cosmic existence.'[12] And in *The Mother* he wrote about 'the Ananda that alone can heal the gulf between the highest heights of the supramental spirit and the lowest abysses of Matter.'[13] Given this background, we may understand the startling statements of the Mother when she came out of her ordeals, even of the most terrible ones: 'Always, all the time, in all circumstances, whatever happens, even when this body suffers excruciating pain, there is the soul that laughs joyfully within. That is always there, always ... All at once there is a horrendous pain, you say "ah!" — and at the same time I am laughing!'[14] 'At that time, there was an effort to make [me] comprehend the consciousness of the whole at the same time, simultaneously, everything — to put it simply in order to make myself understood: of the suffering, of the most acute disorder, and of the Harmony, of the most perfect Ananda — both at the same time, perceived together. This changes the nature of the suffering, of course.'[15] But it did not diminish it, for all that. 'A few seconds of paradise for hours of hell' ... 'Three minutes of splendour for twelve hours of misery' ... 'There are moments that the body might cry out for pain, and ... a very small, very small change, almost impossible to express with words, and that becomes beatitude. It becomes ... something else. It becomes that extraordinary something of the Divine everywhere.'[16] And even after the paralysis of her leg she would say: 'Even at the moment that outwardly I was suffering so much and people thought that I belonged wholly to my suffering, even then it did not keep me occupied.'[17]

Health, Illness and Transformation

'The most acute disorder,' she said, and with disorder she meant what we call a malfunctioning of the body, an illness. Let this be clearly understood: she was not ill, she underwent the process of transformation. An illness is a powerless regression into a malfunctioning of the *adhara* by which the harmony of its functions is disrupted, and by which the physical body becomes restricted in its life-powers and even, in case of death, deprived of them. As far as the Mother was concerned, however, the 'malfunctioning' was a voluntary and always totally conscious submission to the demands of the transformation (even when at first she lost the surface consciousness). In her case, the disorganization of the organs and body functions did not result in a diminution of the possibilities of the *adhara* but in an augmentation and expansion of them. She once said that her body was 'being disintegrated forwards,' into a greater state of being — not backwards into a state of decomposition. It is the difference between a block of marble eroded by wind, rain and changes in temperature, and a block of marble transformed into a work of art by a sculptor's chisel; the chisel acts faster and sharper than the climatic elements, but its result is that the marble becomes transposed into a higher dimension.

'One is surrounded by persons who think that you are ill and who treat you as somebody who is ill, and you know that you are not ill.'[18] Her so-called illness was in fact indicative of the degree of resistance against the transformation in her body, of the degree of the yet unillumined subconsciousness in the cells, of the proportion between the already physically transformed and the not-yet-transformed. When somebody asked her how she was doing, she answered: 'But Mother is always doing well!' Indeed, who could have been doing better than she did! And she added that it had been *as if* she had been ill. It always was *as if* she was ill — though sometimes as if she was very, very ill. When somebody else asked her how she was going ('*Comment va Mère?*') she retorted: 'Mother is not going ('*Mère ne va pas*'). There is nobody to go anymore. Mother goes where the Divine wants her to go ... It is always going well. I am convinced that everything that happens is willed by the Divine.'[19] The 'I' talking here was the one of the cells, this was the conviction of the cells. Again we encounter the first premise: there is nothing but That. Therefore, logically speaking: if there is only That, all that exists and happens can be willed or executed only by That.

'There is no disease from which I have not suffered. I have taken all the diseases upon my body to see their course.'[20] 'I have in myself the possibility of five or six fatal illnesses.' 'I have no illnesses.'[21] 'These are not illnesses, they are functional disturbances.'[22] 'It is not a matter of health, it is a matter of transformation.'[23] One could continue quoting statements of hers in the same vein, but this may suffice to give an idea of the living, up to then unknown and mostly misunderstood wonder she was. Let us not forget that the Mother at that time was eighty-five, ninety years of age. Her miraculous body, by its consciousness of the cells present in the whole Earth, was so frail and light that it looked like the shadow or the elementary form of the human body. And on top and in the middle of all that, she was doing an incredible amount of 'normal' work.

'My Blessings are Dangerous'

In the meantime, she was still the head of the Sri Aurobindo Ashram with its thirteen hundred members and with the seven hundred students of the Ashram school, now including a kindergarten, sections of elementary and secondary education, and the first two years of higher studies (equivalent to the level of B.A. and B.Sc.). This alone was a task which would keep anyone occupied full-time. She was consulted about everything, took all decisions (and corrected the misunderstood decisions or the deliberately twisted ones with her invisibly acting Power), kept an eye on the finances, signed all documents and cheques (and India is a difficult country where documents and cheques are concerned), took upon her all legal responsibilities, and so on. People are often troublesome. People who want to follow the spiritual path most often are a very troublesome lot, because their effort brings to the fore difficulties which otherwise would have remained untackled and because the aspirants in their struggle with the ego often, also unconsciously, behave under the influence of a magnified egoism. And because thousands of big and little devils find pleasure in the difficulties they can create for the aspirants to make a mess or worse of their spiritual effort.

In the Ashram there was the core of the serious candidate-yogis and in some cases of really great yogis. If there were some of them present in 1936 already, according to the written testimony of Sri Aurobindo himself, then logically speaking there must have been more thirty years later. But it was not easy, in this most invisible of all yogas, to pick them out, and the ones with the most impressive appearances were not necessarily the most advanced. Around them moved the candidate-yogis who at one time had been very serious in their endeavour but who had got stuck somewhere on the path — and the Ashram was, according to Indian norms, not a bad place to spend one's days in a sinecure. Once accepted by the Mother, she never left you in the lurch, materially or otherwise — and it happened that their yoga unexpectedly got restarted. Around these moved the circle of relatives, acquaintances and friends whom the Mother also had admitted to the Ashram because the whole world had to be represented there, and of those who had found an occupation in one of the groups or associations in the periphery of the Ashram. And around those moved, like free electrons around the nucleus, the ones who felt attracted to the Mother, the Ashram or Sri Aurobindo's Yoga for some reason or other, visitors from every corner of India and from

392 • *Beyond Man*

the whole world, and in some cases profiteers and preying vultures. Most of this population wrote to her, sometimes letters that were interminable and in several installments a day; most of then wanted to be received by her, as long and as often as possible. All were moving in her invisible body.

'Careful,' she said with a smile, 'my blessings are dangerous!' For her blessings were charged with the grace of the Power to lead the soul in the shortest way to its divine destination, something which seldom agreed with the conscious and unconscious desires of their receiver. To enable people to keep her blessings within their aura, within their atmosphere, she gave them two or three rose petals charged with her Force, as she had learned from Alma Théon many years ago. And she said: 'In truth, I hold myself responsible for everyone, even for those I have met only for one second in my life.'[24]

To Mona Sarkar she also said: 'You will be surprised to see the work I have done for you all. For each one his own path, well shaped, well chiseled, with all the obstacles, all the impediments removed, all that was blocking the way demolished, so that you may be able to walk freely in the full light of the new consciousness towards·the Truth.'[25] All were her children, probably the vultures too — as long as there was somewhere a spark of sincerity, a spark of a living soul in them. As far as the Mother is concerned, one can never say that somebody has wasted a chance of inner development; one can only say that by the contact with her a seed was planted out of which spontaneously a beautiful tree would grow, in this or in a following life.

And there were the·birthdays. She received all *sadhaks* and many visitors on their birthday. The Mother considered that day as very special in the life-rhythm of everyone. 'It is a very special day, for it is the day of decision, the day one can unite with the Supreme Consciousness. For the Lord lifts us on this day to the highest possible region so that our soul which is a portion of that Eternal Flame, may be united and identified with the Origin. This day is truly an opportunity in life. One is so open and so receptive that one can assimilate all that is given. I can then do many things, that is why it is important.'[26] Each one got a beautiful birthday card, made or chosen by Champaklal, with the name of the person, a few words in her handwriting and her signature (representing a bird of Peace). Each one received that smile and that look. Her body was everywhere, therefore surely in each person in front of her too. ('You are there and I am there.' 'I know all of you much better than you know yourselves,' in past, present and future.) Few would have been able to tell what she had done inside them, but it was always the necessary divine Help, the Grace, the very Best.

She also received so many who, for one reason or another, asked for the grace of a few moments in her presence: newcomers, Ashramites or visitors who were going to leave the Ashram temporarily or for good, personnel plagued with problems, young couples who considered the visit as their marriage ceremony (surely the most effective they could have had), of course the secretaries and heads of departments who represented her in the Ashram organization, ministers and high-ranked functionaries of the diverse Indian states and the central government, heads of state and religious leaders ... The whole world passed by her there in that room on the second floor, where her chair was always turned towards Sri Aurobindo's Samadhi — in that room 'like the bridge of a ship' surrounded by the yellow flamboyant and rustling palm leaves.

To whomever could stand it, she gave *un bain de Seigneur*. How to translate this — a bath in the Lord? An immersion in the Lord? She saw the persons in front of her as her very own self and she put the soul in them directly into contact with their true, their divine Being, with the One she called the Lord, present in everything, but thickly veiled. She took away as many of those veils as the inner being of the person in front of her could stand, for even the angels protect their eyes with their wings for the naked flaming Presence, 'brighter than a thousand suns.' (Of herself, she said: 'I always have to cover myself with veils — one veil, another one, and another one — otherwise people could not stand it.' And: 'The best veil of them all is the body,' her body for which so many thought they had to have compassion.) Therefore, in the person in front of her she heightened the spiritual voltage somewhat, she 'moved the needle a bit' of his spiritual potentiometer to see how receptive he or she was. For the person himself that was a sort of an initiation. But there were those who could not bear that Power, even in a small dose, and some of them even ran out of the room without further ado! There were others who did not feel anything at all and kept politely smiling, souls still in the bud.

She got piles of letters, more than Sri Aurobindo at the time, for she had become known much more to the outside world. Whomever they thought she was, God or a lady with occult talents, it was always worthwhile (and it cost nothing) to ask her opinion about a purchase, an investment, a planned or childless marriage, a long journey, a risky undertaking, a health problem, and what not. 'I am not a soothsayer!' she protested, 'I don't read tea leaves!' And there was the *sadhak* who narrated his past in every detail because he found it so interesting, and that other one who wrote page after page about the 'spiritual' furnishing of the new room he was going to shift into. And there was the man who extensively set forth his revolutionary theories by which Sri Aurobindo and the Mother would become known world-wide, and the pedagogue and the physicist with their latest findings, and the writer with his brand-new manuscript ...

All correspondence was not innocent. A *sadhak* narrates in his memoirs how he had brought a letter of an acquaintance and handed it to the Mother. She supposed the *sadhak* himself had written that letter and opened it without first protecting herself as she used to do. All at once, tells the *sadhak*, the Mother doubled up for pain as if she had received a blow on her stomach. For there were the hostile elements who tried literally to hit out at the Mother, also by means of the written word. Words are forces. We are so much used to the written and printed word that we no longer realize that it is an occult device carrying the spirit of the writer and communicating it to the reader to the degree of his intelligence and receptivity. What we experience by reading *Paradise Lost*, *Of Mice and Men* or *Ulysses* is not caused by the printed configurations we call characters, but by the vibrations communicated by means of those configurations which enable us to enter into contact with the mind of the writer.

There were *sadhaks* and *sadhikas* in difficulty, angry, revolted or spiteful, who projected their own errors upon her and threw their inner dirt at her, sometimes even in an extremely vulgar or nasty way.

They could permit themselves to do so because the Mother reacted exclusively with love, patience and understanding. She never took something personally, for in the lies and distortions, as in the poisonous and aggressive abuse directed at her, the problems of the world were present. The inner horrors with which she had to struggle in the Subconscious cropped up in the persons around her who were open to them. These things should not amaze us, for we shelter them in ourselves; it is they which turn our world into the pitiful place it is — and she wanted to work on all that because she wanted to change it.

The Work in the World

All that was part of her work, the most external part. But for her the external and internal were never separated; everything was one single movement, one single event, and that global reality proceeded in her universalized being. She was here and at the same time in many other worlds; she was present now and at the same time in the past and in the future. (She once even said that certain events or clusters of events from the past came to her to be rectified.) There were the beings of the world of the gods, familiar to her like close relatives and many of whom were direct emanations of herself. 'Krishna walked together with me ... Shiva was present in this room ...' The hostile beings too were fascinated by her earthly incarnation and approached her to find out, in their eternal hunger for egoistic aggrandizement, whether they too might profit and grab some nourishing spiritual morsel.

She worked in the philosophical, religious and political structures of the world to integrate them into the process of transformation. This she mostly did during the night. 'I do not sleep in the common manner. It looks as if I am asleep, but I am not sleeping and I do not "dream": *I am doing things*. I am doing things and I am fully conscious, with the same sort of consciousness as when awake ... I go to America, I go to Europe, I go ... all the time. I go to places in India. And all that — so much work, work, work — during the night.'[27]

She did not want the world to perish or to break down because of the pressure of the golden supramental Power which was covering it and exerting its weight on it. She wanted the existing structures to change from within. This is what has started happening: political edifices are being changed because of the inner intenability of certain systems; religions are being changed from within — for instance Christianity by the charismatic movements and Islam by its confrontation with the Western democratic spirit. 'In the night, I am always given a state of the human consciousness which has to be put straight, one after the other. There are millions of them.'[28]

A *sadhak* asked her the question: 'I think that always, at every moment, someone or other is calling You and You answer. Doesn't this disturb Your sleep or Your rest?' She answered: 'Day and night hundreds of calls are coming — but the consciousness is always alert and it answers. One is limited by time and space only materially.'[29] 'I am constantly seeing some beings, consciousnesses, concentrated parts [of beings], subtle bodies around me, all kinds of elements and movements — aspirations, desires, complaints, and all sorts of things ... But I am not always hearing miserable or unpleasant stories. No, there are beautiful things too, and fair meetings of souls, pure thoughts, noble aspirations which are directly coming to me and all sorts of interesting things happening around me. It is a real game that is taking place before me, with such diversity ... I am blessing them, one after another, relieving them, protecting them, pouring a little bit of peace and love on each one according to his need, his capacity, his receptivity, so that each one may be touched by the Grace and go away happy and satisfied. That is what I am constantly doing in spite of my usual work. And it is difficult to meet every one physically. But in this plane everything happens very quickly and simultaneously. I am not limited by what people call time and space. You understand, I am doing many things at the same time without anybody seeing it or being aware of it.'[30]

Her body consciousness, the consciousness of the cells of her body, was present everywhere, not by way of speaking, not abstractly, but concretely, in physical reality. This does not mean that she registered in her mind, in her active consciousness everything that happened in the world (how many fish the fishermen in Pondicherry had caught or what Lloyd George had had for breakfast, as Sri Aurobindo wrote in jest). She had not been 'thinking' for a long time; she did not utilize a mental consciousness for it had been 'sent packing' in 1962. What she spoke was said by 'something' in her; what she formulated was phrased by 'something' in her, only when necessary and not at other times, by a specially delegated 'I' to enable her to keep functioning among human beings. Using the mental consciousness, which is ours, would for her have been equal to falling back into the old species, which is ours. When something like that happened against her will, (through 'illness', or because of an attack of black magic, or a moment of reduced consciousness in her 'sleep'), the effect was like that of a suffocation, a strangulation, like being grabbed by the coils of the Subconscious and of Death. For to the supramental Unity-Consciousness, larger than the cosmos, infinite like the Godhead himself, our narrow mental cage is a form of death. Death is like thickenings, membranous thickenings in the subtle flow of omnipresent Life, but it is of such thickenings that the stuff of our consciousness consists; our mental consciousness is made up of evolutionary callosities. When these hardenings will be burned away by rays of the supramental Radiation, Life will become fully alive in us, we will possess eternal life.

The Mother was present in the happenings of the world, in the world movement, also at that exceptional moment in history when John Kennedy, Nikita Khrushchev and John XXIII instilled new hope into mankind after years of Cold War and the tense opposition of the two big world blocks. It was the end of the colonial era and the Mother had great hope that the two imperialistic superpowers would look for 'approachment'. But the Lord of the Nations would not let himself be dethroned that easily. The Mother called the murder of President Kennedy an occult assassination. 'The murder of Kennedy has disturbed a lot of things from the standpoint of the general Work ... It is a victory of that [black] Force over the Force that tries to follow more harmonious ways.'[31] It is a fact that, in spite of all official clarifications, statements and 'so-called irrefutable proofs, this assassination remains shrouded in mystery. A year later, Khrushchev was sidelined by the Stalinists. And after the open attitude and the reformations of the 'transitional pope' John XXIII, the conservative Roman Curia took hold of the helm of the Catholic Church again.

But the Sixties were in full swing. 'The whole world is being subjected to an action which at the moment is upsetting', said the Mother. 'It seems that the number of "apparent madmen" is increasing considerably. In America, for instance, the whole youth seems seized by a sort of strange euphoria, possibly disquieting for reasonable people, but certainly the indication that an unusual force is at work. It means a break with all customs and all rules. It is good. It looks somewhat "strange" at the moment, but it is necessary.'[32] In Prague, the 'Velvet Revolution' was about to happen.

The world was in ferment. The old order started coming apart at the seams. This was the beginning of the great Turning Point, of the 'supramental catastrophe' as the Mother called the momentous transition necessary for the birth of a New Era, a New Order, a New World. The readers of this book are knowledgeable about the true cause of the two World Wars and know where the elements of the new fermentation have to be looked for, namely in the Power operating behind the supramental transformation, having then as its centre the transformed physical body of the Mother that had become one with the world. The transformation, the supramental mutation in her cells, vibrated also in everything in the world that was attuned to it.

There were new wars. There was the Indo-Chinese War in 1962, so disenchanting and humiliating for the credulous and totally unprepared Indians who thought they were living in friendship with the Chinese: *Hindi-Chini bhai bhai!* 'The Indians and the Chinese are brothers.' The Mother never underestimated the Chinese. Had Sri Aurobindo not written that they would invade Tibet — as happened in 1959 — to use it as a gateway to India?

The Indian Army was helpless against the hordes of the People's Army descending from the 'roof of the world.' India lay wide-open before them. The tantric yogi who had been Satprem's guru, Panditji, wrote to the Mother to announce that a new world war and a global catastrophe had been revealed to him. The Mother knew that the *Asura* of Falsehood, alias the Lord of the Nations, was doing his utmost to bring about an apocalyptic destruction. According to that yogi, the Indo-Chinese War would be the occasion that would initiate the catastrophe. The Mother applied all her power. And Satprem writes in a footnote to one of the conversations at that time: 'On 20 November [1962], without anything justifying this kind of expectation, the Chinese announced unilaterally a cease-fire and the withdrawal of their troops at a time they were making spectacular gains without encountering any resistance. Nobody has ever known why.'[33]

There was also the Indo-Pakistan War in 1965. The strong viewpoint of Sri Aurobindo that India and Pakistan have to be reunited, and the prophecy of the Mother that Pakistan will fall apart and that its regional sub-states will at their own initiative ask for a federal reunification with India, have already been mentioned in this book.

These are only a few of the known circumstances in those years in which the Mother intervened directly. The intention here is not to emphasize the spectacular aspects of her Work. She herself has never vaunted them. She obstinately kept performing *'la besogne obscure,'* the dark, unseen, unknown labour, in its hidden minutest details as important as in its visible historical consequences — more important perhaps, because more fundamental.

For the transformed cell emits its supramental vibrations to which all correspondent elements in the world are automatically tuned. This has always been the clandestine influence of the yogi, also before the supramental Yoga. 'Thou thinkest the ascetic in his cave or on his mountain-top a stone and a do-nothing. What doest thou know? He may be filling the world with the mighty currents of his will and changing it by the pressure of his soul-state. — That which the liberated sees in his soul on its mountain-tops, heroes and prophets spring up in the material world to proclaim and accomplish.'[34] In the case of the Mother it was no longer a by yoga liberated soul but a liberated body which was directly working from its matter onto Matter everywhere.

A World under Construction

Alexander Dubcek and the Velvet Revolution in Czechoslovakia, Jan Palach immolating himself, the students of Nanterre, the war in

Vietnam and its repercussions in the USA, Kent University, the foundation of Auroville ... We have arrived in 1968. 'I am certain that the [supramental] revolution has begun ... A terrestrial reorganisation and a new creation ... We have not arrived at the end but ... we are on the opposite side.'[35]

Again she had gone through a crisis, one of the severer ones. It had been so bad that her helpers had had to take care of her body, just like in 1962. There are more parallels between the two crises. This time too she said that her mental and vital had been taken away from her, 'sent packing.' 'Do you understand what this means?' she asked Satprem. No ordinary human being could survive such an operation. Now everything was happening in the materiality of that magical body, apparently old, ravaged and very ill (her heart had been heavily battered), but at the same time the eye of the cyclone, the battlefield where all forces were fighting each other in the struggle for the new world against the masters of the old one. No, this could not possibly have been a repetition of 1962, as has been written, not after six years of that Yoga, not in the Yoga of the Mother. 'I never hold on to an experience. I am all the time, all the time going forward, all the time underway. You know, the work of the transformation of the consciousness is going so fast, has to be done so fast, that one does not have time to enjoy or to halt at an experience, or savour the satisfaction of it for a long time. It is impossible.'[36]

For hours on end, while the people around her thought she was on the verge of death, she was present in magnificent landscapes and cities of the future. (The supramental world is waiting close nearby to manifest in Matter.) 'During several hours the landscapes were marvelous, of a perfect harmony. Also for a long time visions of the interior of immense temples, of living godheads. Everything had a reason, a definite goal, to express non-mentalized states of consciousness. Constant visions. Landscapes. Constructions. Cities. Everything immense and of a great variety, occupying the whole field of vision and rendering states of the consciousness of the body. Many, many constructions, immense cities under construction ...'[37] It was a world under construction, she said. She had noted it all down. And she had not only seen that: she had *been* that — those landscapes, those temples with living godheads, those cities. 'It is not "seen" as when one sees a painting: it is *being in it* ... And thinking had nothing to do with it. I could not even describe it. How could one describe it? One can only begin to describe when one begins thinking.'[38] She was *in* everything with her body consciousness, which must have been more and more supramentalized as otherwise it would not have been able to participate in a supramental world.

She had also noted: 'Mighty and long-lasting penetration of the supramental forces into the body, everywhere simultaneously.'[39] And she explained that: 'Penetration into the body, yes. Penetrations by [supramental] currents I have had several times, but that night that came as if there was nothing else but a supramental atmosphere. There was nothing else but that. And my body was in it. And that was *pushing* to enter into it, from everywhere, everywhere, from everywhere at the same time ... from everywhere. You see, it was not a current that entered into me: it was an atmosphere which was penetrating from everywhere. It lasted more than four or five hours.'[40] If one finds 'atmosphere' a little vague, one should not forget that there are no abstractions in the Supermind. 'The head down to the neck was the least receptive part,' because it is the most mentalized part, she explained. Wonderfully beautiful, unique those experiences had been, although at the same time she had looked critically ill. '*J'étais dans une bouillie, mon petit!*' (I was in such a mess, my boy) she said to Satprem, meaning that her body had been in a state of endless agony.

'And therefore, you see, one cannot say that it [her body] was suffering, one cannot say that it was ill, that is not possible. It is not possible.'[41] At times she cried aloud for pain, and at the same time she was in a state of supreme ecstasy, not vaguely, not abstrusely, not somewhere in an unreal world, but in the intensified concreteness of the Supermind of which one drop to us would be like liquid fire, of which one spark would cause us to explode. For that is a world of the free energies which are present here in the bound state of the atom: it is the world of divine Energy.

The story of the vital and mental which had been sent packing is provided with a footnote: 'Some days afterwards, Mother has added: "The vital and the mental have left but the psychic being has not left at all. It is the intermediaries that have left. For instance, the contact with the people (the contact with those present and even with those who are not present), the relation has remained the same, completely the same. It is even more stable." [42] This perception of the presence and the role of the psychic being, mentioned in passing, will prove to be of crucial importance

Chapter Twenty-five

THE NEW UTOPIA: AUROVILLE

You say that Auroville is a dream. Yes,
it is a "dream" of the Lord and
generally these "dreams" turn out to be
true — much more true than the so-
called human realities![1]

—The Mother

IMAGINE THE surrealistic scene: on a plain of red laterite, baked by the sun, a crowd brought there in buses has gathered. They seek shelter under a wide circle of canvas put up for the occasion. In the middle of the circle, a small conical hill has been covered with masonry; at the top, it carries a ceramic urn in the shape of a stylized lotus. Representatives, most of them young ones, from countries around the globe drop a handful of the soil of their country in that urn, after having repeated in their respective languages a kind of formula read out via loudspeakers ... This took place on 28 February 1968 some ten kilometers to the north of Pondicherry. The representatives had come from 124 nations and 23 Indian states. The voice from the loudspeakers was that of the Mother. The formula was the charter of a new city being founded there by her at that very moment: Auroville, the City of Dawn — the new Utopia.

'We still see her [the Mother], half standing half sitting on a stool, writing the "Charter of Auroville" on that window-sill, equipped with a big piece of parchment and a too thick felt-tip pen which made her handwriting look like cuneiform characters,' remembers Satprem. '"I don't write pompous solemnities," she said turning in our direction (and there was always that witty glimmer in her eyes).' And she wrote in the original French:

CHARTER OF AUROVILLE

1.   Auroville belongs to nobody in particular. Auroville belongs to humanity as a whole. But to live in Auroville one must be the willing servitor of the Divine Consciousness.
2.   Auroville will be the place of an unending education, of constant progress, and a youth that never ages.
3.   Auroville wants to be the bridge between the past and the future. Taking advantage of all discoveries from without and from within, Auroville will boldly spring towards future realizations.
4.   Auroville will be a site of spiritual and material researches for a living embodiment of an actual Human Unity.

These were the words that resounded on 28 February 1968 in her voice, in French and English, over that blazing plain where in the distance some slim solitary palmyra trees seemed to dance in the hot air. The charter was being broadcast via all antennae of *Akashvani*, the Indian national radio. And it was preceded by a salutation: 'Greetings from Auroville to all men of good will. Are being invited to Auroville all those who thirst for progress and aspire to a higher and truer life.'

When she had finished writing the charter, the Mother had also said, descending from the stool: '*Voilà*. It is not I who wrote all this. I have marked something very interesting: when it comes, it is imperative, no discussion is possible. I write it down — I am FORCED to write it down, whatever I may try to do ... It is therefore evident that it does not come from here: it comes from somewhere above.'[2]

The City That Wants to Descend Upon the Earth

This did not mean that Auroville came out of the blue on that day and at that moment. The idea of it (or shall we say its hidden presence?) had cropped up several times in the Mother's life, even in her early youth and afterwards during the occult explorations with Max Théon. It was probably in the Thirties that she had the vision of a city with the living Sri Aurobindo at its centre, for Antonin Raymond, the architect of Golconde, had drawn a plan for it. This plan must have remained a distinct possibility for some years as Franticêk Sammer too got involved, but this was already during the war, when Sammer was a Squadron Leader with the Royal Air Force. The plan almost got realized when Sir Hyder Ali, chief minister of the Nizam of Hyderabad, offered the Mother a plot of land before the independence of India (1947) in what was at that time the state of Hyderabad. Who can fancy how the Aurobindonian world, now centered around Pondicherry and Auroville, might have looked if this plan had materialized?

And who knows what events from times long past kept vibrating in the Mother every time the intention to found the city of the future rose again to the surface in her. She has said that she had been the mother of Amenhotep IV, the remarkable queen Tiy. This Amenhotep left Thebes in order to found in the desert a brand-new city, Akhetaton, i.e. dedicated to Aton, the god of the disk of the Sun, and he called himself Akhenaton, He Who Serves the Aton. His wife was Nefertiti, famous for the beauty of her conserved bust, and his son-in-law and successor was the equally famous Tutankhamen. Akhenaton's new religion became 'the closest approach to monotheism that the world had ever seen,' writes an Egyptologist. It created a new life-style and a much more realistic form of art — the reason why Nefertiti's bust is still admired by so many.

The profound influence of queen Tiy on her son is a historical fact, but not much is known of the rationale of the whole enterprise. Could it have been that the sun disk, Aton, never depicted as a personified god, represented the golden sun of the Unity-Consciousness, the 'monotheistic' One that is Everything, and that Akhenaton, the servant of Aton, deemed himself the instrument of the One? To undertake the adventure of the foundation of Akhetaton against the established religious order, his convictions (or inner knowledge?) must have been exceptionally strong and his surrender unconditional.

Those who are familiar with the story of the budding of Auroville feel spontaneously stirred when they read about Akhenaton and his new city in the sands of the desert. But the conservative priests of the traditional religions of Amon and Re finally carried the day against the revolutionary innovator — which was the reason why Tutankhaton changed his name into Tutankhamen. Akhetaton has been sleeping for centuries under the desert sands of a hill near Amarna, Tell-el-Amarna.

After the departure of Sri Aurobindo, the city that wanted to descend upon the Earth disappeared for some time from the immediate interests of the Mother, but not for long. In the beginning of the Fifties, the city again started forcing itself on her attention. In 1952 she wrote: 'The unity of the human race can be achieved neither through uniformity nor through domination and subjection. A synthetic organization of all nations, each one occupying its own place in accordance with its own genius and the role it has to play in the whole, can alone effect a comprehensive and progressive unification which may have some chance of enduring. And if the synthesis is to be a living thing, the grouping should be done around a central idea as high and wide as possible, and in which all tendencies, even the most contradictory, would find their respective places. That idea is to give man the conditions of life necessary for preparing him to manifest the new force that will create the race of tomorrow.'[3] In these words, one finds Sri Aurobindo's vision of world unity as the indispensable condition for world transformation and the divinization of the Earth.

In August 1954, the Mother published her well-known text 'A Dream'. 'There should be somewhere upon earth a place that no nation could claim as its sole property, a place where all human beings of goodwill, sincere in their aspiration, could live freely as citizens of the world, obeying one single authority, that of the supreme Truth; a place of peace, concord, harmony, where all the fighting instincts of man would be used exclusively to conquer the causes of his suffering and misery, to surmount his weakness and ignorance, to triumph over his limitations and incapacities; a place where the needs of the spirit and the care for progress would get precedence over the satisfaction of desires and passions, the seeking for pleasure and material enjoyments ...' She then briefly passes in review the principles on which such a place should be erected, educationally, organizationaly, financially and economically, 'for in this ideal place money would no more be the sovereign lord.' And she continues: 'The earth is certainly not yet ready to realise such an ideal, for mankind does not yet possess the necessary knowledge to understand and accept it or the indispensable conscious force to execute it. That is why I call it a dream.'[4]

But the supramental transformation was advancing with giant strides. In the previous chapters, we have followed its principal phases up to 1968. The circumstances quickly improved to render the realization of the dream possible. The main requirement for such a place on Earth was that it be protected in an occult way. Everything new always meets with strong adversities till in course of time it becomes, if sufficiently viable, the familiar way of viewing things and in its name the next new and unusual something is being attacked. Such are the petty ways of humanity. But *this* new something contained a deadly danger for the established order. It did not want to push it aside to take its place. No, what it wanted was much worse: it wanted to *transform* the established order, so that consequently this order would no longer remain itself or could no longer remain in existence. The new city had to become the ferment of a new Evolution, of a New Order in which there would no longer be a place for the old laws and their Masters. Not only would humanity, arch-conservative in its ignorance (and malicious selfishness), refuse to allow this, the *Asura* of Falsehood, the Lord of the existing Order, would not stand it and launch his legions to hold on to his empire. Without a powerful occult protection the 'cradle of the New World' would never be able to exist; very soon it would become another Tell-el-Amarna, a hill of sand in the desert. How many hills of this kind dot the road of the long march of humanity?

From 1965, the plan of the new city gradually began to take shape. When the Mother was asked how Auroville was going, she answered: 'Auroville is going well and is becoming more and more real, but its realisation does not proceed in the usual human way and it is more visible to the inner consciousness than to the outer eye.'[5] 'Auroville wants to be a universal town where men and women of all countries are able to live in peace and progressive harmony, above all creeds, all politics and all nationalities. The purpose of Auroville is to realise human unity,'[6] she wrote in September of that year. In May 1966 she wrote to a person who probably had read 'A Dream': 'You say that Auroville is a dream. Yes, it is a "dream" of the Lord and generally those "dreams" turn out to be *true* — much more true than the human so-called realities!'[7] About the origin of the future city, she never left place for the least doubt: 'The conception of Auroville is purely divine and has preceded its execution by many years.'[8] Asked who had taken the initiative of building the city, she answered: 'The supreme Lord.'

In between her other external and internal work, the Mother gave a lot of attention to Auroville. The occult task consisted in bringing the city, which existed in the subtle physical, down into terrestrial materiality. When asked where the city should be located, she asked for a map, closed her eyes and planted her finger on a spot some fifteen kilometers to the north of Pondicherry, near the coastline of the state of Tamil Nadu (Land of the Tamils), where at places there are some scattered bits of Pondicherrian territory. Plots of land had to be bought. The establishment of the international city had to be discussed with the government of Tamil Nadu and the central government in New Delhi. UNESCO was asked to recognize the project, and it did so. The first constructions arose on the barren soil, candidates for becoming the first Aurovillians wrote letters to the Mother or came reconnoitering, architects started designing their dream city.

A Centre of Transformation

The Mother laid down that the maximum number of inhabitants should never exceed 50,000, because a city is no longer livable with a population beyond this number. As master plan she chose the grand model of a spiral galaxy, one of the designs by the Builder of the universe himself. She divided the future city in four zones: international, residential, cultural and industrial. It is difficult to find out when exactly the name of Auroville was coined, but she made clear that it meant 'City of Dawn' (*auro*ra), not City of Sri *Auro*bindo, as is often supposed, although the association with his golden name will always resonate in the name of Auroville.

What was the aim of the city and who were expected to become its inhabitants? As is clear from many of the aforementioned quotations, the Mother often stressed the realization of human unity. (Once she called the city 'the Tower of Babel in reverse ... Then they came together but separated during the construction; now they are coming again to unite during the construction.'[9] She even made the reflection whether the Tower of Babel — just like Akhetaton — had not been an early essay to build something like Auroville.) In 1967, she therefore laid down the 'conditions to live in Auroville' as follows: '1. To be convinced of the essential unity of mankind and to have the will to collaborate for the material realisation of that unity; 2. To have the will to collaborate in all that furthers future realisations.'[10] These were the 'psychological conditions,' 'the goodwill to make a collective experiment for the progress of mankind'.[11]

From the spiritual standpoint, however, Auroville was a new step forward in the realization of the supramental transformation process on Earth and in the material accomplishment of the task of the Avatar. The unification of humanity was a necessary condition thereof, but by itself, as an independent 'worldly' attempt, it would have been a rather limited motive. This is why the Mother wrote: 'Auroville wants to be the first realisation of human unity *based on the teaching of Sri Aurobindo*.'[12]* She declared: 'The task of giving a concrete form to Sri Aurobindo's vision was entrusted to the Mother. The creation of a new world, a new humanity, a new society expressing and embodying the new consciousness is the work she has undertaken. By the very nature of things, it is a collective ideal that calls for a collective effort so that it may be realised in the terms of an integral human perfection.'[13] An integral human perfection can be no other than a supramental perfection; all perfections inferior to it remain

---

* Author's emphasis.

under the spell of the Subconscient and Inconscient, and consequently can never be integral. The Mother therefore wrote in a message for UNESCO: 'Auroville is meant to hasten the advent of the supramental Reality upon earth.'[14] Auroville was meant to be 'the cradle of the superman', according to the new definition of the word superman as a transitional being. 'Auroville has been created for a superhumanity, for those who want to surmount their ego and renounce all desire, to prepare themselves for receiving the supermind. They alone are true Aurovillians.'[15] '[Auroville] is a centre of transformation, a small nucleus of men who are transforming themselves and setting an example to the world. That is what Auroville hopes to be.'[16]

From this we may conclude that there was a minimal condition to become an Aurovillian, namely a willingness to turn towards the future and to collaborate in the realization of the essential oneness of humanity, and a maximal condition, the pursuit of supermanhood — with all possible positions and variations in between. One of the causes of this apparent ambivalence, afterwards to be encountered in the attitude of many Aurovillians, was the danger that Sri Aurobindo, the Mother and their teaching might be hardened into a new religion. For it is in the nature of the human being to slide, without noticing it himself, from a living experience (e.g., a spiritual one) into a mental fixation of the experience (e.g., dogmatic religiosity).

'No New Religion'

All religions have grown out of a living revelation, communicated in its purest form by an Avatar, who is the active incorporation of his or her message, or in a lesser form by a human instrument, a prophet. The aim of the revelation is that it should become in the experience of those who accept it as real and living as in the experience of the Initiator. This happens sometimes, in exceptional cases. But up to now it has generally been the mass which has appropriated the revelation for itself, and the general level of mankind is still so low ('humanity is still very little,' as the Mother said) that it always simplifies the message of the revelation, which it is unable to comprehend mentally, and that it degrades its spiritual content. Moreover, the ego is present in humanity, and in spiritual matters, with its usually masked inclination towards selfishness, possession and power.

The living revelation becomes encased in formulated articles of faith, in a creed. This creed appropriates the revelation for itself and strives to impose its skeletal remains on all other professed creeds, on penalty of eternal damnation and even of physical death for the recalcitrant. It proclaims its formulas as the only ones leading to salvation and starts mentalizing and complicating them until they have become a caricature of the original source. Spirituality is based on the direct experience of a supra-mental reality; as such, it is felt to be irrational by the mental consciousness of the human being. Religion is always suspicious of true mysticism and of the true spiritual experience, for it knows itself to move on a much less elevated plane. Once religion has the worldly powers behind it, it will hush up the (irrational) mystics, expel them (even physically from life) or try to bring them back 'within the womb of the community,' within the ranks of a predominantly worldly organization in which all spiritual flowers are artificial.

The teaching of Sri Aurobindo and the Mother, together with their abundantly documented biographies, contain more than sufficient elements to turn it all into a new religion. One will remember how the Mother experienced this in April 1962 as a distinct possibility. In December 1972, *Newsweek* published an article about the Mother under the title: *The Next Great Religion?* And the first sectarian tendencies, fungi on the humus of their vision, are already perceptible.

Those who draw their inspiration from Sri Aurobindo and the Mother have to defend themselves time and again against allegations by religious and worldly organizations that they belong to a sect. At a time when sects are rife (a significant phenomenon caused by the turbulence of a world in transition), most of them with their roots in Eastern soil, it is not easy to show convincingly that this is not a sect. Anyone who has read this book up to here knows how any kind of sectarian mentality is incompatible with the vision (in this

context it even feels incorrect to use the word 'teaching') of Sri
Aurobindo and the Mother. The rich and voluminous literature they
have left was intended as a communication of their own experience*
and for the expansion of the understanding and the knowledge of
the reader; they have always stressed the absolute individuality of the
way; they have made it clear that the path of the transformation, the
road towards tomorrow, is a prospect for the mature souls who, in
surrender, want to respond to the call which cannot be defined by
words or formulas. We know all that. But names like 'Sri Aurobindo'
and 'Mother' are automatically associated with sectarianism by the
prejudiced and unknowledgeable, and it is hard to deny that a lot
of followers of Sri Aurobindo and the Mother take on sectarian
attitudes. The Mother herself said, looking down from her room into
the courtyard of the central Ashram building where Ashramites and
visitors were thronging around Sri Aurobindo's tomb: 'They are
already making a religion of it.' And she wrote by way of admonition:
'Do not take my words for a teaching. Always they are a force in
action, uttered with a definite purpose, and they lose their power
when separated from that purpose.'[17]

This may therefore be an appropriate place to quote the following
words of the Mother in connection with Auroville and religion: 'We
want the Truth ... Auroville is for those who want to live a life
essentially divine but who renounce all religions whether they be
ancient, modern, new or future. It is only in experience that there
can be knowledge of the Truth. No one ought to speak of the Divine
unless he has had experience of the Divine. Get experience of the
Divine, then alone will you have the right to speak of it. The objective
study of religions will be a part of the historical study of the development of human consciousness. Religions make up part of the
history of mankind and it is in this guise that they will be studied
in Auroville — not as beliefs to which one ought or ought not adhere,
but as part of a process in the development of human consciousness

---

* Cf. Sri Aurobindo: 'I was never satisfied till experience came and it was on this
experience that later on I founded my philosophy, not on ideas by themselves.'
(*Sri Aurobindo Archives and Research*, 1983, no. 2, p. 164)

which should lead man towards his superior realisation.'[18]

On 23 November 1968 she said: '*No new religions,* no dogmas, no fixed teachings. It has to be avoided at any price that this should become a new religion. For as soon as it would be formulated in some elegant and impressive way, *that would be the end.*'[19]* But history shows that the sectarian-minded most readily quote the antisectarian statements of their masters or gurus.

The First Aurovillians

In what way would the Aurovillians** interpret the words of Sri Aurobindo and the Mother? And who were the first Aurovillians? A motley crowd. One should keep in mind that everything new or fashionable in spirituality and occultism attracts two categories of persons: on the one hand those who have the call and the sincere seekers who want to get more from life than it can give them in the normal circumstances of their world, on the other hand the adventurers and the confused, who are looking for trips here, there and elsewhere, as long as they can get a kick out of it or simply because things happen to occur, without a conscious, intentional or necessary motivation. And there are those who cross over from one category to the other. One should also take into account that we are now talking about the Sixties. In those years, many had travelled to India before The Beatles, Mia Farrow and Donovan, and still more followed them. Most were flower children, hippies, dressed in their own shabby uniform, sexually liberated, drug users. It would not take long before Auroville became integrated into the hippie-circuit, almost at par with places like Goa and Kathmandu.

The Mother, as always, wanted 'no rules, no laws, no committees': 'Every person has full freedom.' As to the social organization, she foresaw a 'divine anarchy.' This, again, is a concept we find in Sri Aurobindo; he saw it as the final aim of the social evolution, when

---

* The Mother's emphasis.
** The Mother spelled 'Aurovillian' with one l, saying this is an example of the Aurovillian language in the making!

all individuals in the Unity-Consciousness will no longer be governed by a social authority but directly by the Godhead himself, in a concrete relation of unity with all others in divine Love. Any deviation from or resistance against this Order founded on divine Unity will then no longer be thinkable, it will be impossible. The Mother formulated it as follows: 'The [ultimate and real] anarchistic state is the self-government of each individual, and this will only be the perfect government when everybody becomes conscious of the inner Divine and obeys Him, and Him alone.'

They came to South India, alone or in small groups, with Auroville as the destination of their trip, or they were travelling in India and got intrigued by rumours they heard about Auroville, enough to go there and see for themselves. Most of them left, a few stayed on. The climate there is harsh; it is a climate of extremes, with monsoon rains which make everything clammy because of the humidity of the air, and summers when everything gets clammy because of perspiration. The soil was not much better than arid country, with here and there a village now being awakened from a lethargy that had lasted for centuries. '[The Aurovillians] who are in contact with the villagers should not forget that these people are worth as much as they are, that they know as much, that they think and feel as well as they do. They should therefore never have an attitude of ridiculous superiority. [The villagers] are at home and [the Aurovillians] are the visitors.'[20] But it was such a terrible world for the Westerners. India itself was so totally different; and even the elementary western conveniences were still lacking at that time — good razor-blades, a cake of soap that did not melt in your hand, a ball-point that did not leak, cheese, a loaf of bread, a glass of beer ... Being there on a visit was in most cases an interesting, adventurous and colourful experience, as long as you had enough traveller cheques and a return ticket in your pocket. But staying on to spend the rest of your life there?

Everybody had his or her own idea of Auroville, of course. The charter was very inspiring, and to build the city of the future — hey, if you could tell your relatives and friends that *that* was why you went to India, and that you wanted to dedicate your life to the progress of humanity, not to speak about an eventual transformation into a, ahem, superman! But once there, you sweated buckets on that red, sun-baked laterite, and you had to drag *pakamaram* stems about, braided palm leaves, stones and bricks, and many, many buckets of water. You had to get accustomed to live with flies, mosquitoes, ants of a hundred varieties, cockroaches, geckos, rats, scorpions, venomous snakes. You had to learn Tamil and try to get along with the idiosyncrasies of those Frenchmen, Dutchmen, Americans, Australians, Belgians, Argentineans and Koreans.

The fundamental problem was that very few knew what it was all about essentially and that they did not understand very much of the little that they read and heard. All problems were put to the test again — religious, political, racial, sexual, interpersonal, financial — with endless discussions, friction and quarrels about trifles. The Mother listened, gave advice, counsel and encouragement. Really, the certainty in the subtle worlds concerning Auroville must have been very firm and the invisible protection indeed very powerful to allow the Mother to proceed with the foundation of the most utopian of all utopias: 'the cradle of the superman.'

All non-Aurovillians involved in the foundation of the city were unanimous about the fact that those newcomers, for a part idealists but also for a part not so cleanly dressed hippies and even wandering and uncaring good-for-nothings, were totally unsuited and unable to build Auroville. One saw them riding sputtering motorbikes, with smudgy bandannas around their long, entangled hair, the girls half naked (according to the Indian standards of decency), talking in funny, incomprehensible languages, and their legs invariably covered with orange-red Aurovillian dust; thus did they their shopping in the streets of Pondicherry, drank tea or coffee — and what was it again that they were smoking? One saw them also in the Ashram, even in the room of the Mother, who made special appointments for them.

The professional yogis of the Ashram kept their distance — not all of them, but many. So did the Indians of the Sri Aurobindo Society, a body independent of the Ashram that the Mother had put in charge of the organization and the finances of Auroville. And then there were the stories one heard from the first Aurovillian settlements!

The future city would cover a circle, approximately, with a diameter of ten kilometers, from the coast up to the main road to Madras inland. But all the plots could not be bought immediately, of course. Besides, it was an absolute principle never to exert any pressure on the local population. And when the big landowners got air of the situation, they drove up their prices threefold, fivefold, tenfold.

Then in 1973 the Guide, the Lodestar departed. It was an unbelievable shock, especially for the still so young and helpless Auroville. She had understood the man with his music of The Rolling Stones and The Doors, the hippie with his joint or the girl in an unwanted pregnancy. Whatever picture one may construe of the Mother, she was no moralist with a raised eyebrow, no mother superior even when she had to give advice on so many occasions; the advice was asked of her, and together with the advice she always gave something else, more profound, more powerful than her often misinterpreted words. She was, lest we forget, the divine Mother who by her Yoga had become the body of the Earth, who was literally present in the rock, the tree and the yogi, in the swindler and in the secretary-general, in the just and in the sinner, in the somewhat clarified human being and in the distorted, crooked, suffering one. How could she, who said of the *Asura* of Falsehood: 'After all, he is my son', ever have been able to turn her back on a temporarily errant or stultified youth? Every soul is her child. And she spoke those unforgettable words: 'Do not try to be virtuous. See in what measure you are unified, ONE with everything that is antidivine. Take up your share of the burden, accept to be yourself impure and mendacious. Thus you will be able to take the Shadow and offer it. And in the measure that you are able to take it and offer it, things will then change. Do not try to be among the pure. Accept to be with those who are in the darkness and, in a total love, offer all that.'[21]

That voice, that support disappeared, externally anyway — but who was able to see behind the facade of things? For Auroville, the period of the troublesome years started. On the one side there were the real Aurovillians, still for the most part non-Indians with a residence permit, deemed incapable but all the same the ones who were digging, building and planting; on the other side there were the management and the members of the Sri Aurobindo Society, exclusively Indian and some of them with mighty relations in the country, who mostly lived and worked in Pondicherry although some were 'technically' considered to be Aurovillians. The Sri Aurobindo Society owned the land, the money, the prestige, and acted as the direct deputy of the Mother. The Aurovillians had nothing, for the Society cut off their funding; most of them were foreigners in the country and of dubious repute in Indian eyes.

It is such a human, much too human story. An irreconciliable feud arose between the two mightiest administrators of the Society; Auroville itself become internally separated into a French faction, who were able to read the inciting writings of Satprem, and those who did not know French and were mainly of Anglo-Saxon origin. Aurovillians were attacked by paid miscreants from the villages; some Aurovillians were even put in jail. Sensational articles appeared in the press about smuggling, drugs and sex orgies in Auroville. The controversy went all the way up to the Supreme Court in New Delhi. It is worth mentioning that Indira Gandhi and later her son Rajiv kept supporting the Auroville of the Aurovillians through thick and thin, as did people of the stature of J.R.D. Tata, the aviation pioneer and great industrialist-with-a-heart.

All that is now history. Auroville lives, despite everything. In 1993 it has celebrated its twenty-fifth birthday. Its population is slowly increasing. There are now (in 1995) slightly over one thousand permanent residents in forty-five settlements or 'communities', big and small, named Aspiration, Hope, Certitude, Vérité, Ami, Abri, Far Beach, Sri Ma, Two Banyans, Nine Palms, Djaima, Fraternity, Dana, Auro Orchard, and so forth. There are schools, guest houses, a bakery, many handicraft workshops (also for export), libraries, a press, organizations for cooperation with the villages, an information centre for visitors. Auroville is chockfull with life and talent. The basic principle has remained that of liberty, which means lots of meetings and discussions. But where else on Earth would something like this be possible: the rudiments of a city being built by people of many nationalities, with scanty means, in a harsh climate, based on the principle of freedom, in the state of a country with its own laws and administrative structures?

The problems are legion. So many figureheads have been liberal with wise advice but without risking to commit themselves in any personal or durable way. Looking down their nose on those amateurs, still deemed incapable and spiritually underdeveloped, they have in their greatness turned away form such a bungling undertaking.

It is true that for the price of a fighter jet or a space rocket half of the planned Auroville of the 50,000 souls could be built. However, suppose that financially it suddenly becomes possible to build the city, would that, in this early stage of its growth, be the Auroville the Mother envisaged? It might resemble a resort of the *Club Méditéranée*, but what about the spiritual content which is the real rationale of Auroville's existence? Auroville lives in the hearts of the simple Aurovillians, the quiet and patient ones who in surrender keep working in good times and bad times. Buildings have to be constructed; creations have to come about in beauty and harmony; but most important of all is the work on oneself, the inner unfolding, starting from very little (the ordinary human being all of us are) to go towards very much (beyond man). All else has been done before, it is this that is new. And it will automatically externalize itself into a visible city.

At the heart of the city, there will not be a boisterous, chaotic centre, but a place of quietude, harmony and beauty. The lotus bud with soil of the whole planet is still standing there, now in the middle of an amphitheatre with a circle of twelve gardens surrounding it. A stone's throw away, the big banyan tree, the geographical centre of the city, continues spreading out its aerial roots. And both stand in the shadow of the Matrimandir.

Matrimandir

'Matrimandir' is a Sanskrit word which means 'house, or temple, of the Mother'. From outside, it will resemble a golden, slightly flattened globe breaking out of the Earth — the golden world of Supermind breaking out of Matter. The globe, with a diameter of about thirty meters, rests on four gigantic supports representing the four active powers of the Mother in the universe: Maheshwari, Mahakali, Mahalakshmi and Mahasaraswati. The most important feature inside the globe is a 'chamber' with a diameter of about twenty meters and near the wall twelve round columns seemingly supporting the ceiling but not touching it. The chamber is completely white and its marble floor is covered with a white carpet. In the middle of the chamber a crystal ball of seventy centimeters* rests on a pedestal consisting of four gold symbols of Sri Aurobindo, which in turn is placed in the centre of the symbol of the Mother on the floor. Night and day a ray of light falls through a central opening in the ceiling of the chamber straight on to the crystal. During the day, the ray consists of sunlight deflected by a mechanism that follows the movement of the sun; at night, the ray is produced by conserved solar energy. There is nothing else in the chamber and all noise is avoided.

A crystal that projects a ray of light directly into the core of your being, in a harmonious room of material purity — one can give all kinds of interpretations to it or simply undergo the unworldly beauty of the place. The Matrimandir cannot be explained. The Mother has 'seen' it and wanted it to be erected in the centre of Auroville as soon as possible. It represents 'the consciousness of the Divine,' it is 'the soul of Auroville' she said, and 'the sooner it will be finished the better' for the young city.

The Matrimandir only makes sense when it represents something on the level of the forces which have to contribute towards the coming of the New World. It must be a kind of power plant effecting a field with a transforming power which acts upon all who enter into it, upon those who live in its vicinity, and upon the Earth out of whose body it seems to emerge. The transformation of the Earth was the object of the Mother's Work. Auroville is another step in that direction which had become possible in the general process of transformation, a step 'outwards' in the divulgence of the new Force. If the Mother had wanted the occult power source which is Matrimandir

---

* Made especially for Auroville by the Carl Zeiss Werke in Oberkochen, near Stuttgart (Germany).

to be built, then it can only have been, in a vision without religion, with the intention of speeding up the transformation of the Earth.

The Mother has said several times that Auroville exerts an occult influence in the world. That what vibrates in the cell, vibrates in the universe. That what has life in one place of goodwill, spreads in the whole body of the Earth. At first she said that the attempt at world unity which is Auroville contributed in preventing a third world war. Later on, in the beginning of February 1968, Sri Aurobindo gave her the complete rationale for the existence of the city and she had noted down his words: 'India has become the symbolic representation of all the difficulties of present-day humanity. India will be the site of its resurrection, the resurrection of a higher and truer life.' And she explained that: 'The same thing which in the history of the universe has made the Earth the symbolic representation of the universe so as to be able to concentrate the work at one point, that same phenomenon is occurring now: India is the representation of all human difficulties on earth, and it is in India that there will be the cure. And it is THEREFORE that one has made me create Auroville.'[22]

The sea port she had envisioned, the airport, the hotels, the yachting club, the hydroplanes, the film studio, the press and publishing house for publication in all world languages, the grand organ in the auditorium — all that is not there yet. As we have seen, Auroville's material growth can only be the outcome of its spiritual growth, and at the moment it is not yet ripe for a material development of such dimensions. But the real Auroville exists — in the hearts of the Aurovillians; it is there that it has to develop fully before a complete outward shape makes any sense. At present, there is little more than the embryo of a city. But the fact that Auroville still exists after twenty-five years is by itself, considering its purpose and the circumstances of its beginnings, a miracle.

'Auroville is a great adventure,' the Mother said. She had seen the city in that world where is being prepared what has to be realized on the Earth; she also knew that the city already exists in the hankering hearts of so many, not only on that spot on the Coromandel Coast but in the whole world — in all places where women and men can no longer stand the deadening meaninglessness of existence and long with all the intensity of their heart for Meaning, Beauty, Truth, Authenticity, for a totally satisfying, twenty-four carat fulfilment of life, at last.

'The city will be built by what is invisible to you,' said the Mother. 'Those who have to act as instruments will do so despite themselves. They are nothing but puppets in the hands of larger Forces. Nothing depends on human beings, neither the planning nor the execution: nothing! That is why one can laugh.'[23]

Chapter Twenty-six

IN THE CRUCIBLE

The Soul is the Key

The liberation of the individual soul is the keynote of the definite divine action.[1]

—Sri Aurobindo

The previous chapters have given us some idea of the supramental process of transformation the body of the Mother was undergoing. This process is new and unusual for anyone who learns about it for the first time. So it was for her who experienced it in her body. But what had happened to the soul? What about the soul in all of this? We are hearing a lot about body, matter, cells, consciousness of the cells, universalization, and what not, but isn't it the soul that is supposed to play a central role in the existence of man as well as in the cosmic evolution, in which it was said to be the fundamental, active element? One of the last times the Mother talked about her soul had been on 19 May 1959. '[This body] is full of the psychic in each of its cells,' she had then said. Mighty experiences she had gone through since, but the soul she had not mentioned anymore. If the soul held such a central position in the evolution throughout, it should surely play a role, and an important one at that, in the evolutionary process of transformation? But one reads volume after volume of the *Agenda* and the soul is not mentioned anywhere except in passages quoted from former years and comments on such passages.

Till one comes to the conversation of 11 September 1968. Suddenly the Mother had discovered: 'The soul has not left at all,' as her mental and vital had done. She was of course talking about her own psychic being, which means that during all this time she had not been aware of it; perhaps she had even thought that it had been 'sent packing' together with her mental and vital, leaving nothing but the 'agglomerate' of body cells directly exposed to the influence of the radiating, transforming power of the supramental Sun. 'The vital and the mental have left, but the psychic has not left', she stated.

The occasion of this experience had been the presence of a woman with a very developed, matured psychic being, and the Mother's own psychic being had reacted so strongly to that presence that she had again become aware of it. And how! She had now marked that: 'When I say "I", I do not mean the body: I mean the psychic consciousness.' This reduced a lot of her 'I's' to one 'I'. And also this: 'It is possible (I don't pronounce myself because there is nothing as yet ... nothing definitive, that is), it is possible that a new relation or a new intermediary form is developing between the psychic being and the material, the physical. It looks as if this is something that is being done.' A new body? The new body? However that be, her psychic being was 'completely transparent,' which had been the reason why she had not noticed it during all this time. For she *was* that psychic being; she existed and acted from that core and had thus perceived the sheaths around it (the mental, the vital — in so far as these were still present — and the physical), but not what was at the centre of her perception because this was the perceiving element itself. We may also suppose that the perception of her psychic being had temporarily remained veiled for her in order to make her concentrate fully on the physical and its transformation.

It may be appropriate here to remind one briefly what the psychic being is. After the fall of the four original *Asuras*, the Supreme, at the intervention of the Universal Mother, has poured out his Love into the Night of the Manifestation in order that that Night should no longer remain an eternal, coagulated darkness but that it might evolve back towards its Origin. That Divine Love is the essence of the psyche. If that Love is divine, then the psyche must be divine, exist in the Divine, have come forth from Him and carry Him most intimately in its being in the course of its evolutionary journey back towards the full integration into Him. Being divine, the psyche cannot but have willed and itself chosen its journey, its adventure through the Night of the Ignorance, to experience the joy of rediscovering itself as divine in the Divine. (Of course, 'joy' in this case is a rather colourless, insignificant word. One should realize that this 'joy' should counterbalance the horrific amount of suffering during the return journey.)

The psyche, the soul, is simple as a manifesting part of the Divine but complex as a concept. It exists eternally in the Divine (as *jivatman*), is present in all parts of creation in the Love that has been poured out into the creation (as *antaratman*), and regains, individualized, in the human being the potential to build up its own materialization (as the evolving *psychic being*). The reincarnation of the soul, by which it descends time after time into the material manifestation, is necessary because gross matter is not sufficiently plastic to adapt itself to the growth of the soul. In life after life, the soul gains the necessary experiences by which, blow by blow, its divine shape is being sculpted. It comes into each life with 'a very precise programme of experiences it will have to go through in order to be able to make the progress it wants to make'.[2] After death, it assimilates the experiences from the previous life and prepares itself for the following episode of the adventure — which, superficial appearances notwithstanding, it enjoys intensely, as everything in its essence is *Ananda* and cannot be anything else but *Ananda*. We were the Divine, we are the Divine (essentially), and we are again becoming the Divine (in the manifestation). *Tat tvam asi*: you are That.

Considering all this, the psychic being must of necessity be involved in the supramental process of transformation. It must even form the nucleus of this process; it must be its key, for this process determines the higher phases of the divinization of the material manifestation of the psychic being. Even in its mature state — the maturity of the soul is, as we have seen, the primordial condition of supramentalization — the psychic being cannot halt at the point in the evolution now reached by humanity. For its redivinization it has also to experience and integrate into itself the higher levels of existence between mental consciousness and the absolute Divine if its presence in creation has to make any sense at all.

This was exactly what the Mother observed on 1 July 1970, thanks to the presence of the same woman mentioned earlier, an American disciple called Rijuta. 'I had an experience which was interesting for me because it was the first time. It was yesterday or the day before, I don't remember. Rijuta was here, there in front of me, and I saw her psychic being that dominated her by this much [gesture: about 20 centimeters]. It was the first time. Her physical being was small and her psychic being was that tall. And it was an asexual being, neither man nor woman. I then said to myself ... "But it is the psychic being, it is *this* that will materialize and become the supramental being!" '3

She had so often asked herself how the supramental being could possibly arise from an animal humanity. Sri Aurobindo and she herself had seen the prerequisite of transitional beings, of supermen (*surhommes*), but these would still have an animal-human origin and body despite their supramentalized consciousness. It was the leap from animal man to the supramental being that seemed to her so enormous, not to say impossible. 'It is the leap, you understand, which looks so formidable to me.'4 For the divine being really had to be divine, for instance simultaneously present here, there and elsewhere, and not subject to illness, gravity and death. It had to be, physically, a cosmic being and even more than a cosmic being. This meant, proportionally speaking, a much greater difference with our present human condition than the difference between the body of animal man and the primates, who for the most part have the same physical morphology.

Rijuta's psychic being had the same colour as the hibiscus the Mother had chosen as the symbol of Auroville, orange. (Those who from the supramental ship went on land to help found the New World also had this colour. Everything there, the one substance, had this colour.) 'Then you understand that. You understand it: the psychic

426 • *Beyond Man*

being materializes and this gives a continuity to the evolution. This creation then gives completely the impression that it is not something arbitrary, that there is a kind of divine logic behind it which is not like our human logic but very superior to it. But there is a logic and it was plainly satisfied when I saw that. It is really interesting. I was fully interested. It was present there [Rijuta's psychic being], very quietly, and it said to me: "You are trying to find out how it will be? Well, look, this is it." '5

In *The Supramental Manifestation*, Sri Aurobindo had written about the evolutionary continuity: 'The necessary forms and instrumentations of Matter must remain since it is in a world of Matter that the divine life has to manifest, but their materiality must be refined, uplifted, ennobled, illumined, since Matter and the world of Matter have increasingly to manifest the indwelling Spirit.'6

This important passage was now as it were being illustrated by the psychic being of that American woman there in front of the Mother. The process, the mechanism of the supramental transformation at once became clear to her. If one realizes what the psychic being really is, and if one takes into consideration the crescendo of the evolution, which is an evolution of the Spirit, then this cannot but be the logical course of progression. Its key is the soul. 'In this Yoga the psychic is that which opens the rest of the nature to the Supramental Light and finally to the Supreme Ananda. If the inmost soul is awakened, if there is a new birth out of the mere mental, vital and physical into the psychic, then this Yoga can be done; otherwise it is impossible,'7 writes Sri Aurobindo.

The Mother goes on in that same conversation mentioned above: 'I have then understood why the mental and the vital were taken away from this body and why the psychic being was left in place. It was, of course, the psychic being that always guided all movements ... All the complications caused by the vital and mental, who superimpose their impressions, their tendencies — all that was gone. And I have understood: so, this is it, it is the psychic being that must become the supramental being.

'But I had never taken any time to find out how [the supramental being] would look like. And when I saw Rijuta, I understood. And

I see it, I still see it, I have kept the remembrance. It was as if its hair was almost red (but it was not like that). And its expression! An expression that was so refined and so sweetly ironical. Oh, extraordinary. Extraordinary!

'And, you know, my eyes were open, it was a vision that was almost material.

'Then one understands. All at once all questions are gone. It has become very clear, very simple.

'And the psychic is precisely that which survives. So if it materializes, that will mean the suppression of death. But "suppression"... Suppressed is only what is not consistent with the Truth. That disappears — everything that is not capable of transforming itself according to the image of the psychic and to become an integral part of the psychic. It is really interesting.'[8]

Afterwards, she confirmed this important, crucial revelation, as on 13 April 1972: 'It is the psychic being, the representative of the Divine in the human being, that will remain, that will cross over into the new species.' And a couple of days later, on 15 April, she said in passing to Satprem: '[The psychic consciousness] has been governing the being [hers] for a very long time. This is why one has been able to take away the mental and the vital: because the psychic being had taken over the direction very long ago.'[9] In the same conversation, she also says: 'It is possible that there are some supermen (*surhommes*) — THERE ARE SOME* — who execute the changeover ...' And also in passing: 'The heart has switched over from the old dominance by Nature to the divine dominance.' (The heart! The transfer of power of the heart!) On 24 June of the same year, she wrote the words already known to us: 'It is indispensable that each one finds his psychic and unites with it definitively. It is through the psychic that the supramental will manifest itself.'[10]

The psyche, the presence of the Divine in his creation, is not a gradation of existence like the others in the great scale of Being. The psyche is 'behind' the other gradations and uses them for its growth,

---

* Author's emphasis.

just as the psychic world is 'behind' the other worlds. The psyche uses the substance of the various levels of existence as its sheaths or coatings in the material manifestation in order to climb the World Stair from the lowest Inconscience, into which it was sent as pure Love, up to the highest *Ananda*, which is its origin.

Sri Aurobindo writes in *The Life Divine*: 'The material Energy that aggregates, forms and disaggregates,' as for instance in the perpetual transformations of the elementary particles, 'is the same Power in another grade of itself as that Life-Energy which expresses itself in birth, growth and death.' And here he inserts a footnote: 'Birth, growth and death of life are in their outward aspect the same process of aggregation, formation and disaggregation, though more than that in their inner process and significance.' For Life is a higher gradation than Matter. And he continues: 'Even the ensoulment of the body by the psychic being follows, if the occult view of things is correct, a similar outward process, for the soul as nucleus draws to itself and aggregates the elements of its mental, vital and physical sheaths and their contents, increases their formations in life, and in its departing drops and disaggreagates again these aggregates, drawing back into itself its inner powers, till in rebirth it repeats the original process.'[11]

In other words, the psychic being forms an *adhara*, a complex body consisting of several sheaths of mental, vital and physical substance and energy, from what the evolution (as a result of the presence and the work of the Psyche in all its individualities) has realized on Earth. The psychic being utilizes the available substances and energies to help continue the evolution. If the supramental substance becomes available on Earth, then the psychic being that is ready for it can also take up the new, supramental substance into its *adhara*. This means that it would build for itself a supramental body. It is a logical evolutionary development with the psychic being as its essence: the fully grown psychic being will supramentalize itself in the manifestation when the manifestation allows it, i.e., when gross matter will be transformed. We now must have a look at the way the transformation of gross matter was coming about according to the Mother's testimony.

The Sun-vibration

Million d'oiseaux d'or, ô future Vigueur.
(A million golden birds, O Force of the future)
　　　　　　　　—Arthur Rimbaud, in *Le bateau ivre*

Sri Aurobindo's disciples have asked him in writing, and sometimes orally too, countless questions about the Supramental, tomorrow's Wonder. This was only natural. Had we ourselves steered our life on the course of his ideals and had we had the privilege of his company, we too would have asked questions and tried to get an answer from the very source itself. What the Supermind was in itself, in the supramental world, Sri Aurobindo knew without any doubt. For it was the revelation of the Supermind which had made his avataric task clear to him. As 'traveller of the worlds,' who has written down a few of his experiences in the grandiose second 'book' of *Savitri*, he had been up to the ultimate limit of the manifestation, even beyond the supramental worlds, that is.

Nevertheless, he almost systematically brushed aside all such questions for the simple reason that they were impossible to answer for human beings, in human language. The human is a mental being — *the* mental being — which cannot form an idea with its mental consciousness of that which surpasses such a kind of consciousness, not analogically but ontologically. The primates are very intelligent beings, but a jet engine, a recipe for *bisque de homard* or a piano concerto are simply not within the order of their consciousness. We should not forget that the Supermind is a *divine* world, which means a world unimaginably different from ours, which is one of limited mental beings.

Sri Aurobindo therefore gave answers like: 'The supermind alone can discern the method of its own workings,'[12] or: 'Supermind cannot be described in terms that the mind will understand, because the terms will be mental and mind will understand them in a mental way and mental sense and miss their true import.'[13] 'Have you any idea how the Supermind will proceed?' asked Satyendra. 'No idea,' replied Sri Aurobindo. 'If one has an idea the result will be what has been in the past. We must leave the Supermind to work everything out.'[14] He did not want to define the Undefinable because such definitions would inevitably become caricatures of the divine Reality in the mind of his mental audience, perhaps even with negative consequences for them. And in spite of all their ideas and occult experiences, Sri Aurobindo and the Mother have always considered those ideas and experiences as hypothetical as they had to go on marching forward into the unknown. For the supramental world as a typal world is very different from a supramental world being inserted by a process of transformation in an evolutionary manifestation located on a lower level of existence.

Yet, the Pioneers have given some indications of what may be expected in the future. We have just seen that the process of transformation follows a logical evolutionary development with the psychic being as its central agent. When the Mother, sometime in 1966, discussed the characteristics of the supramental body, she said: 'It therefore would be an infinitely greater transformation than that of the animal into the human being. It would be a passage of the human being into a being that no longer would be built in the same manner, that no longer would function in the same manner, that would be a kind of densification or concretization of "something" '. (Two years later she will find out that that 'something' is the psychic being.) 'Up to now, this corresponds with nothing that we have seen physically, unless the scientists have found something that I do not know.'[15] One thing is certain: the true reality of the Supramental 'will be much more marvellous than we are able to imagine, because what we imagine is always a transformation or a glorification of what we see.'[16] Here the Superman of the comic strips and the cinema comes to mind, who is formidably strong, who can fly, see through a wall or burn through a steel plate with his look, who is invulnerable and immune to illness. Or there is the hypothetical hyperintelligent, extraterrestrial being with a brain like a balloon or a supercomputer.

The main quality of the supramental being is its consciousness, its divine consciousness, its Unity-Consciousness. 'Supramental nature sees everything from the standpoint of oneness,'[17] wrote Sri Aurobindo, and: 'The law of the Supermind is unity fulfilled in diversity.'[18] 'Therefore all is in each and each is in all and all is in God and God in all.'[19] The brain is the radio, the consciousness produces the music made audible by means of the radio. The brain is the television set, the consciousness produces the show one can enjoy by means of the television set. The Unity-Consciousness needs a unity-body in order to express itself on Earth.

The Mother once described the characteristics of the unity-body, of the future supramental body, to a young Ashramite: 'You know, if there is something on that window-sill and if I [in a supramental body] want to take it, I stretch out my hand and it becomes — wow! — long, and I have the thing in my hand without even having to get up from my chair ... Physically, I shall be able to be here and there at the same time. I shall be able to communicate with many people at the same time. To have something in my hand, I'll just have to wish for it. I think about something and I want it and it is already in my hand. With this transformed body, I shall be free of the fetters of ignorance, pain, of mortality and of unconsciousness. I shall be able to do many things at the same time. The transparent, luminous, strong, light, elastic body won't need any material things to subsist on ... The body can even be lengthened if one wants it to become tall, or shrunk when one wants it to be small, in any circumstances ... There will be all kinds of changes and there will be powers without limit. And it won't be something funny. Of course, I am giving you somewhat childish examples to tease you and to show the difference.

'It will be a true being, perfect in proportion, very, very beautiful and strong, light, luminous or else transparent. It will have a supple and malleable body endowed with extraordinary capacities and able to do everything; a body without age, a creation of the New Consciousness or else a transformed body such as none has ever imagined ... All that is above man will be within its reach. It will be guided by the Truth alone and nothing less. That is what it is and more even than has ever been conceived.'[20] This is what the Mother told in French to Mona Sarkar, who has noted it down as faithfully as possible and had it read out to her for verification.

The supramental body will not only be omnipotent and omniscient, but also omnipresent. And immortal. Not condemned to a never ending monotonous immortality — which, again, is one of our human interpretations of immortality — but for ever existing in an ecstasy of inexhaustible delight in 'the Joy that surpasses all understanding.' Moment after moment, eternity after eternity. For in that state each moment is an eternity and eternity an ever present moment.

If gross matter is not capable of being used as a permanent coating of the soul in its present evolution, then it certainly is not capable of being the covering of the supramental consciousness, to form the body that has, to some extent, been described above. This means that the crux of the process of supramental transformation lies in matter; the supramental world has to become possible in matter, which at present still is gross matter. Sri Aurobindo and the Mother were supramentalized in their mental and vital, but their enormous problem was the supramentalization of the physical body, consisting of the gross matter of the Earth. As the Mother said: 'It is matter itself that must change so that the Supramental may manifest.'[21] A new kind of matter no longer corresponding with Mendeleyev's periodic table of the elements? Is that possible?

In the One, all substance is one substance. 'All substance is one single substance, completely the same, everywhere.'[22] (the Mother) In order to perceive substance in its unity, the perception has to be actuated from the Unity-Consciousness. In the infinite division of reality by the mental consciousness, conditioned in ignorance, we perceive substance as infinitely divided in apparently separate agglomerates of atoms and elementary particles. But the Mother has clearly said, for instance in her narrative about the supramental ship, that everything is one single substance out of which all things and beings are made; and as she once told her youthful audience at the Playground: 'It is one and the same single substance which is in all of you.'[23]

Considering the various levels of existence, however, it is clear that within the Unity there are gradations or distinct densities of that one Substance, otherwise transformation would not be necessary nor even possible. Sri Aurobindo writes in *The Life Divine*: 'Being, consciousness, force, substance descend and ascend a many-runged ladder on each step of which being has a vaster self-extension, consciousness a wider sense of its own range and largeness and joy, force a greater intensity and a more rapid and blissful capacity, substance gives a more subtle, plastic, buoyant and flexible rendering of its primal reality.' And it is here that he says: 'For the more subtle is also the more powerful, — one might say, the more truly concrete; it is less bound than the gross, it has a greater permanence in its being along with a greater potentiality, plasticity and range in its becoming. Each plateau of the hill of being gives to our widening experience a higher plane of our consciousness and a richer world of our existence.'[24] The supramental body therefore requires 'a substance other than ours, a subtle substance tangible only to subtle sense, a supraphysical form-matter.'[25]

The Mother had perceived this new substance as early as 1954, for in that year she wrote her 'New Experiences of the Body Consciousness,' and one of these experiences was: 'In this intensity the aspiration grows formidable, and in answer to it Thy Presence becomes evident in the cells themselves, giving to the body the appearance of a multicoloured kaleidoscope in which innumerable luminous particles in constant motion are sovereignly reorganized by an invisible and all-powerful Hand.'[26]

In 1957 she said at the Playground, as ever speaking from her own experience: 'It seems — it is even sure — that the very substance of that intermediary world which is being elaborated will consist of, will be a substance that is richer, more powerful, more luminous, more resistant, with certain new qualities of a greater subtlety, a greater power of penetration, and a sort of inborn capacity of universality, as if its degree of subtlety and refinement allowed for a larger, not to say total perception of the vibrations; and it eliminates the impression of division one has within the old substance, the ordinary mental substance. There is a subtlety of vibration which makes that the global, universal perception is something spontaneous and natural. Within this substance, the sense of division, of separation disappears in a wholly natural and spontaneous way. And this substance is at present almost universally spread in the terrestrial atmosphere.'[27] As early as 1957.

In 1967, the Mother said to Satprem: 'There is a continuous

perception, rendered by a vision, of a multicoloured light, consisting of all colours — of all colours not in layers, but as if it were [gesture: dots everywhere] an association by dots of all colours. Two years ago (somewhat more than two years, I don't remember anymore) when I met with the Tantrics and got in relation with them, I started seeing this light and I thought that it was a "tantric light," the tantric way of perceiving the material world. But now I see it constantly, in connection with everything, and it seems to be something that one might call "a perception of real Matter." All possible colours are mutually associated without being mixed, [same gesture] associated in luminous dots. Everything consists of it. And it seems to be the true way of being. I am not yet sure, but it is anyway a much more conscious manner [of being].'[28]

This is another striking example of the Mother's attitude, just like Sri Aurobindo's, *vis-à-vis* her experiences: meticulous, exact, detailed, scientific. 'I am not yet sure,' she said, and she waited for a confirmation, and another one, and yet another one, to be certain of not being the victim of a misconception or an illusion. The supramental yoga is an undertaking with the broadest perspectives, but at the same time exacting attention for the smallest detail. The Truth-Consciousness is the opposite of Illusion, which is a falsehood. If one imagines the Mother as a kind of occultist juggling with pseudo-realities, one cannot get a proper insight into the Work she has done. She had to descend into ever more profound layers of reality in the body, in Matter, where there is no place for fancy or imaginings, neither occult nor spiritual, nor of any other kind.

As her *sadhana* was progressing, she perceived that the presence of the supramental substance in her body became more frequent. At first, she described that substance as dots in all colours of the rainbow, every dot being of one single colour; that substance was a sort of powder consisting of atoms or dots, apparently immobile but with an incredible intensity of vibration, 'that moves and does not move.' (This is now one of the accepted paradoxes of modern physics.) Or it was a diamond with the brilliance of trillions of dots; or it was pure gold, 'a Light that is golden and absolutely immobile, with such an inner intensity of vibration that it cannot be perceived, it escapes all perception.'[29] In a letter, Sri Aurobindo quoted the *Isha* Upanishad: 'The One unmoving is swifter than thought, the gods cannot overtake It, for It travels ever in front; It moves and It moves not, It is far away from us and It is very close.'[30] That motionless dance of the new, pure substance took place *within* gross matter, which seemed to be 'porous.' The supramental substance penetrated effortlessly in matter as we know it and which was being transformed from within. It was a penetration which 'changed the composition'. Sri Aurobindo, in this context, had used the word 'permeation.'

The presence of this supramental substance was not neutral or inactive. Supramental substance is charged with supramental consciousness. Reading about the wonders of gross matter as discovered by physics in this century, one can to some degree imagine how much more wonderful the 'physics' of supramental matter must be. For it is a substance that must allow a presence on several places at the same time; it is a substance that concretely expresses the divine attributes. The Mother did not live in a world like ours anymore since Tlemcen, there were no boundaries to her inner experience. But she now found that supramental substance in her body which had become the body of the Earth; she saw that marvellous substance illuminating her body, sparkling like gold and diamonds. *Million d'oiseaux d'or ...*

That substance proved to be totally different from the material substance we are accustomed to. Its power over gross matter was much greater than the power of physical things. It was a substance 'with a greater density than the physical', 'more concrete than matter'. 'Solid' and 'massive' were the adjectives she used for it. And at the same time it was subtle, supple, fine like gold dust, but with an enormous Power. Subtle, but anything other than fuzzy or indeterminate. 'There is nothing nebulous about the supramental; its action depends on the utmost precision possible.'[31] (Sri Aurobindo) Greater than the precision in physics, which astonishes us no end.

Already in 1926 Sri Aurobindo had said in one of the evening talks that the supramental substance was 'harder than diamond and more more fluid than gas.' It cannot be otherwise if it is to possess all those wondrous qualities. The Mother called the immobile vibration that is quick as lightning a 'sun vibration.' It was something glorious, as if the world of gross matter which it penetrated 'suddenly became a sun world.' 'The sun is sallow and pale and cold and almost black compared with it,'[32] she said. She observed how much Sri Aurobindo had been working in the 'subtle physical' since his departure to change the structure of gross matter. Would this mean that Mendeleyev's table of the elements yet would not remain the table of the law? 'It is indeed possible that at present things are happening which one is not in the habit of experiencing,' said the Mother. 'The only fact of which I am sure is ... that the quality, the quantity and the nature of the possible universal combinations is suddenly going to change so considerably that it will probably be baffling for all those who are doing research in life. Now, we are going to see.'[33]

The Yoga of the Earth

> *By the fact that you are now living on earth ... you absorb with the air you are breathing that new supramental substance that is spreading in the earth's atmosphere.*[34]
>
> —The Mother

Because of its universalization, the body of the Avatar became identified with the Earth in the consciousness of its cells. As the cells grew more and more supramentalized, their universalization too increased, the Supramental being the Unity-Consciousness. How many among those who met her realized that that apparently shrivelling body in front of which they sat was the conscious centre of the Earth, of the solar system, of the physical cosmos? Most of them kneeled out of respect, in the belief that they were in the presence of the divine All-Mother, or because her presence was so overwhelming that one took an attitude of devotion even without reflecting about it, or because some happenings in their life were not explainable without her direct although invisible intervention. Some had seen her in another shape, in one of her other shapes; some fostered the burning Flame of Love for her in their breast. But who had an idea of the process of transformation the Mother was going through? Who saw, behind or beyond the theory of what Sri Aurobindo's yoga was supposed to be, the fantastic event of the unfolding of a New World, through her, in her?

She talked about 'the general yoga' (*le yoga général*), the Yoga of the Earth. 'It is the miracle of the whole Earth.'[35] This too was a line of development which had been discernible years ago. The Mother had already said in 1957 about the supramental Force: 'It is active in the whole world, and at all places where a receptivity is present that Force is at work.'[36] A year later, she had talked about 'the new substance that is spreading and active in the world,' a substance with 'a warmth, a power, such an intense joy that in comparison all mental activity seems cold and dry.'[37] In that same year she said to her usual audience at the Playground: 'I can tell you that, by the fact that you are now living on earth — whether you are aware of it or not, even whether you want it or not — you absorb with the air you are breathing the new supramental substance that is spreading in the earth's atmosphere. And it prepares in you things which *quite suddenly* will manifest once you have made the decisive step.'[38]

Sri Aurobindo had already mentioned the future general spreading of the Supramental, for instance in a letter from 1936: 'Your idea that [the supramental Force] may spread and happen elsewhere is not without foundation; for, when once something is there in the earth-atmosphere that was not there before, it begins to work on many sides in an unforeseen way. Thus, since the Yoga has been in action, its particular opening movements have come to a number of people who were at a distance and not connected with us and who understood nothing of what was happening to them.'[39] He wrote in a letter from 1939: 'As the Conscious Force descends in matter and radiates, it seeks for fit instruments to express and manifest it.'[40]

'I know that there are people in the whole world,' the Mother said in 1972, and she meant people who, at least in a part of their being, were receptive to the supramental Force and influenced by its workings. Moreover, had not Sri Aurobindo written: 'A number of souls have been sent to see to it that it is for now,' and: 'Some psychic beings have come here who are ready to join with the great lines of consciousness above'?[41] And hadn't the Mother told in her story about the supramental ship: 'I have seen some persons from here — and from elsewhere — who already belong to the supramental world in a part of their being'?

While she was sitting there like that, the world was present in her and she was working in the world, meanwhile listening to the forty, fifty or more persons who daily passed by her, making an effort to swallow a morsel of food, or dozing, as her assistants thought, which after all is normal of little old ladies. She was never unconscious, not for a moment. For unconsciousness meant tumbling back into the old mode of being, into the so very narrow housing within which we move and live our life and which actually is a construction of the consciousness proper to our species, the mental consciousness. If we can break out of our consciousness, then we step out to other, more spacious rooms, or into the supramental consciousness outside all rooms. For one who possesses the Unity-Consciousness, falling back into our mental prison is the same as plunging into suffocation, darkness, death, hell. These metaphors are not merely poetic ones but stem from the experience of the Mother; she suffered them as painful reality when, for some reason or other, she yet happened to fall back into the conscious unconsciousness of our humanity, pulled down into its narrowness by some negative presence far or nearby, by an attack of black magic, or by a part of the as yet untransformed cells of the body that formed the terrain of her yogic activity. While sitting there, she was being the world. While sitting there, she was working in the world. While sitting there, she was making the world more and more transparent to the divine Sunlight.

'What expresses this best, I think, is: in the ordinary human consciousness, one is in a point and all things exist in their relation to this point of consciousness. And now such a point does not exist anymore, and as a result the things exist by themselves.' The axis of reference of the corporeal ego had disappeared. 'You see, my consciousness is *in* the things, it is not "something" that receives. It is much better than that, but I don't know how to say it. It is better than that because it is not only "in the things," it is in "something" that is in the things and that makes them move. I could express this in a literary way. I could say: "It is no longer a being among others.

It is," I could say, "the Divine in everything." But I don't feel it like that. "That what makes things move," or "that what is conscient in things." It is evidently a matter of consciousness, but not of a consciousness like the human beings normally have. It is the quality of the consciousness that has changed.'[42] The whole process of transformation is a phenomenon of consciousness, a switching over from the mental consciousness to the supramental.

Her own body functioned only as 'a means to contact the Earth' (*pour toucher la terre*). With this purpose she had taken it up again in 1962: in order that the supramental Force might enter, via her body, into contact with the Earth, with Matter, and penetrate into Matter to transform it. She was 'the centre of descent' of that Force, liquid-like sun-fire, and she tried to be an obstacle as little as possible, she said. She tried to be 'a pure passer-on,' a channel, a connecting pipe (her own similes). Her Work consisted in connecting the Supramental with the Earth, to be a mediating presence without whom the two worlds would have had no interface, and to purify her cells in the highest possible degree so that the action of the Supramental would not be hindered or deformed by them. '*Ce que Tu veux*' — what You want — was the formulation of her active-passive attitude by which she put herself unconditionally at the disposal of the divine Will in the smallest elements of her being, in order that her physical presence on Earth might have the greatest possible supramental output.

Be it noted that what is being talked about here is *the body* of the Mother. In the other parts of her being she was divine purity itself. But physically she consisted of the terrestrial stuff all of us are made of. The Avatar incarnates in Matter in order that the evolution of Matter may continue. The cells of her body were a hindrance to the transformation and they were its means. In every cell, we have seen, the whole universe is present, but every cell represents a specific differentiation too, a specific function of the universe. The whole universe being present in it, the cell can if necessary and in certain circumstances take over the function of other cells, as biology has found out; but representing a specific aspect of the universe, the cells enable the building of a body with specific parts and functions. This is an illustration of 'unity in diversity,' the basic principle of the Unity-Consciousness. Another application of this principle: 'If one sincerely wants to help the others and the world, the best thing one can do is to be oneself what one wants the others to be, not only as an example, but because one becomes a centre of a radiating power which, by the very fact of its existence, compels the rest of the world to transform themselves.'[43] (the Mother)

'Everything that happens is interconnected; all things are closely connected consciously; there cannot be a vibration at one place without consequences at another,'[44] the Mother said. 'You think that you are separated from each other, but it is the same unique Substance which is in you in spite of all differences of appearance, and a vibration in one centre automatically awakens a vibration in another one.'[45]

The Contagion

The phenomenon by which everything reacts to everything in the universe was called the 'contagion' by the Mother (*la contagion*). 'Everything is nearly reduced to a capacity of spreading the experience, of including [the rest] in the experience (this means the same). One must forget, you see, that there is this person and that person, this object and that object. If you cannot visualize this concretely, imagine that there is only ONE Thing, excessively complex, and that an experience which happens on one point spreads like an oil stain, or expands, or englobes everything else, according to the case. This [words are] only an approximation, but it is only like this that one can understand. And it is the only explanation of the 'contagion': Unity.'[46] The vibration of the elementary particle has a repercussion in the whole universe, and vice versa; to the vibrations of one cell answer the vibrations of all cells, and the life of all cells has an effect on the life of the single one. The spiritual vibrations, and certainly the supramental ones with their immense power, are 'contagious.'

'The only thing that is really effective is the possibility to transfer to others a state of consciousness in which one lives oneself. But this is a power that cannot be the result of the imagination. It cannot be imitated, it cannot be possessed only in appearance.'[47] Because it is not a mental but a physical power, and in the physical something is or is not. 'What the body [her body] now accomplishes is contagious, and in the measure of the receptivity of the others it passes them on its experience,'[48] she wrote to a disciple. With a smile she warned everybody that her presence was dangerous, for that she was the carrier of a contagion, of the supramental contagion. Indeed, those who wanted to march on in their habitual tracks, who did not want to be sucked into the vortex of the unexpected, would do better to stay away from her. And neither should they think of her, for thinking too established a contact and consequently the danger of contagion. But how to keep her at a distance? For her body was everywhere. Where, then, could one find shelter from the contagion? At the Time of the Great Turn no being on Earth will be able to find shelter from the Light that may, to him, reveal himself in his naked Truth. Nobody can escape the Choice between the future and the past: the entering into the Kingdom of God on Earth the possibility of which is borne by all in themselves, or the fall back into the animality of a past which also is borne by all in themselves. If there is some truth in the Last Judgment, it is now being passed by ourselves on ourselves.

Rounded and Square Vibrations

Practically speaking, it was all a matter of vibrations. The Mother said that she had become an incredibly sensitive apparatus for the registration of vibrations. 'To my consciousness, the whole life upon earth, including the human life and all its mentality, is a mass of vibrations.'[49] 'It's a rather curious development. For some time, but ever more and more accurately, when one reads something to me, when I listen to music or when I am told a fact, I feel immediately the origin of the activity of the plane on which that is located, or the origin of the inspiration is automatically rendered by a vibration in one of the centres [*chakras*]. And that is then, in accordance with the quality of the vibration, something constructive or negative. And when at a certain moment that touches even in the least a domain of Truth, there is ... — how to say this — like a spark of a vibration of Ananda ... And that is of such a precision — oh, infinitesimal — in its details ... I am an infinitely delicate machine for the reception of vibrations.'[50]

Depending on her experiences, she described the vibrations as rounded or square, constructive or destructive, true or false, and so on. There were vibrations of suffering — or, as she said, 'vibrations that suffered' — and 'a state of vibration in which *exclusively* the Divine Vibration possesses some truth,'[51] namely the state of surrender. Once she called the Divine 'that Sun-Vibration.' Science has now arrived at a point where mass is energy, which means vibration (a particle is no longer a thing or object, but a vibratory 'event'); but it is clear that in the experience of the Mother the vibrations were something very dissimilar from supposedly neutral, purely quantitative configurations, mathematically represented as graphic alternations along a given axis. To her, vibrations were not only quantitatively but also qualitatively definable, they had qualitative characteristics. To her, vibrations were not only material entities, but also vital, mental, overmental, supramental and essentially divine entities.

The fundamental cosmic reality of one Being incorporated in one Substance — the world of the Unity-Event and Unity-Consciousness — became for the Mother an ever more concrete reality as her cells were more and more supramentalized. We, ordinary humans, see everything as separately existing objects and beings. She, on the other hand, saw everything as states of consciousness which are the expression of the One in its infinite diversity, and as vibrations of the Truth-Consciousness much more tangible than the concretion of gross matter and therefore dangerous to the concretion of gross matter. When the supramental vibrations permeated her body, especially in the beginning, she sometimes thought that it would break up, that it would burst — although that body of hers was suited and prepared for the transformation like no other.

Therefore, one of the wonders that kept amazing her was the way in which, in the process of transformation, everything was dosed from Above so that nothing catastrophic happened. For supramental matter, 'harder than diamond and yet more fluid than gas,' is not a bound but a free nuclear force. 'Almighty powers are shut in Nature's cells,' Sri Aurobindo had written in *Savitri*. This will be the physics and the microbiology of tomorrow, but before the world reaches there we may expect a lot of sensational discoveries and shifts in the paradigms of science. The near future will be an interesting time.

The world does not consist of matter alone. Physical science at present looks at reality from below, from the lowest level of existence where the laws of gross matter are most applicable (though not exclusively) — material laws for material processes. Of Life and the life forces hardly anything is understood, and everybody, including the psychologist, knows that psychology is little more than a caricature of a reality which remains unformulable — sometimes even a sinister caricature. The mental consciousness is still being confused with the soul, and the soul is ... well, some kind of epiphenomenon, in other words a functional illusion.* Everything that is most ourself (love, creativity, the sense of harmony and beauty, the aspiration to aggrandize and elevate ourself, the divination of the soul and the Divine), all of that is declared to be functional illusions or an equally mysterious sublimation of our animality — all of that, except the functional illusion of materialistic science itself, which always as it were instinctively takes the lower to be more real than the higher..

Let us listen once more to the French biologist and Nobel laureate Jacques Monod, a contemporary militant exponent of materialistic positivism. At the end of his book *Le Hasard et la Nécessité* (chance and necessity), he writes: 'If he accepts this message [of positivistic materialism] in its entire significance, then Man cannot but finally awake from his eternal dream to discover his total loneliness, his radical foreignness [*étrangeté*]. He knows now that, like a gypsy, he moves in the margin of the universe where he has to live — a universe

---

* 'We ourselves experience what we call our 'psyche' as something very intangible, something very immaterial. But this cannot prevent it from being an effect of our nervous system, of our brain, and that this effect therefore is completely defined by the molecular construction of the brain.' Dr. W. F. Kruit, biologist, in *Elsevier Magazine* of 21 May 1988.

that is deaf to his music and indifferent as well to his hope as to his sufferings and his misdeeds.'[52] 'Living beings are chemical machines' to Monod. His lyricism of despair is the lyricism of a chemical machine.

The sober answer of the Mother to the materialist was the following: 'It so happened that I had some philosophical interest and that I have studied all problems in a certain measure. And I have discovered the teaching of Sri Aurobindo. And what he has taught — I would say 'revealed', but not to a materialist — is of all revealed human systems by far the most satisfactory *to me*. It is the most complete [system] and it answers in the most satisfying manner all questions that can be asked. It is what helps me most in life to have the feeling that it has some purpose ... I do not give a whit whether others believe in it or not.' She concluded her conversation on this subject with the words: 'Even if everything I think is nothing but imagination, I prefer this imagination to that of yours.'[53]

'The Cells are Conscious'

One can hardly call imagination what she has gained for humanity with so much suffering. 'Once *one* body has done it, it has the power of passing it on to others ... It is contagious,'[54] she said. But who believed her? For a body is a body, that body there, talking, smiling, giving you your birthday card with a friendly *'Bonne Fête!'* And it eats and rests, and sometimes it even improvises on an electronic organ. Everybody kept seeing that ... functional illusion. They understood that the mental consciousness could go anywhere, for the mind could be compared to something like radio waves. They also could accept that the vital could go anywhere, for one experiences this in one's dreams. But matter? The cells? How could they be present here and somewhere else at the same time? A cell is a thing; therefore when it is here it cannot be there and when it is there it cannot be here.

She had stressed it time after time, she had explained it and illustrated it with examples from her experiences: supramentalization was a phenomenon of consciousness and the *consciousness of the cells* was supramentalized. The part of the supramentalized cell that remained discernible to *our eyes*, to the perception of the mental consciousness, was a kind of thin external covering, a membrane composed of the *residue* of the animal origin and existence of the cell. What human eyes still saw of the Mother consisted thereof, of that dark covering of the cells of her animal-human body, while the 'essence' of the cells, with their supramentalized consciousness and substance, was literally divinized and therefore, as 'all in one and one in all,' present everywhere. Not yet the essence of all cells however, which is why her *sadhana* still had to go on, but of a sufficient number to consider the supramentalization of her body as a fact. The transfer of power of all body parts and functions was in progress; more and more cells of those parts and functions were being transformed, which required that, as illustrated in the *Agenda*, those parts repeatedly became the focus of the process of transformation. The importance of the 'residue' will soon become clear.

'The consciousness [of the cells] is more and more being awakened. The cells live consciously, aspire consciously. I have been trying to explain this — good grief! — for months! For months I have been trying to explain this!' And she tried to explain it again: 'The same consciousness which was the monopoly of the vital and the mental has become corporeal: the consciousness is active in the cells of the body. The cells of the body are becoming something that is conscious, totally conscious. A consciousness that is independent, that not in the least depends on the vital or the mental consciousness: it is a corporeal consciousness ...

'But because this happens in one body, it can happen in all bodies! I am not made of something different from the others.' (Matter is one.) 'What is different is the consciousness, that is all. [My body] is made of exactly the same substance, with the same parts. I eat the same things, and it has been made in the same way, completely. And it was as foolish, as dark, as inconscient, as stubborn as all the other bodies in the world.

'And it has started when the doctors declared that I was very ill, that was the beginning [in April 1962]. For the whole body has been emptied of its habits and its forces; and then slowly, slowly, slowly the cells have woken up to a new receptivity and they have opened to the divine Influence, directly ...

'This is the denial of all spiritual confirmations of the past: "If you want to live fully conscious of the divine life, leave your body, for the body cannot follow." But Sri Aurobindo has come and he has said that the body can not only follow: it can be the base manifesting the Divine. The work still has to be done.

'But there is now a certainty. The result is still very far off ... very far off. A lot has to be done in order that the crust, the experience of the most external surface as it is at present, should manifest what is going on inwardly — not "inwardly" in the spiritual depths but inwardly in the body ... That will come last, and this is very good, for if it came first, one would neglect the work to be done. One would be so content that one would forget to finish one's work. It must be completely finished inside, it must be thoroughly, thoroughly changed, and then the outside will express that.

'But everything is one single substance, totally the same everywhere and which was everywhere inconscient. And what is remarkable is that things are *automatically* taking place [gesture showing multiple points in the world], completely unexpected, here and there, with people who do not even know anything.'[55]

This is what the Mother said in 1967 to Satprem. In 1970, he asked again — and he was all the same somebody who followed the process of transformation with utmost attention and from very nearby — how the permeation of the Supramental into gross matter was taking place. 'But like this! *This is it*, this is the work: permeation,' answered the Mother. Because of her *sadhana*, the supramental Force penetrated via her body into the gross matter of the Earth. She found that so natural and she had been explaining it so often that words failed her yet to answer this kind of question so late in the process. 'But is this happening over the whole earth?' — 'Yes.' — 'In everybody?' — 'Yes.'[56]

One reads a lot about the intrinsic unity of everything; it sounds beautiful, mystic, and if one is susceptible to such emotions, they provide you with a vaster, profounder way of experiencing things. But who is *living* in that way? Who moves with a clear awareness in the one Consciousness, in the one Substance, in the one Body? Who experiences that? Whatever she had said — whatever one had been able to read in the *Notes on the Way*, which after all was little more than a few pages every three months — practically nobody understood it. Her statements were always mentally interpreted according to 'Sri Aurobindo's system of the Integral Yoga.' It is true that the contact with the Mother and the surrender to her sufficed to bring you all the way to the end of the road. All the same, who showed some understanding for the stupendous Work of Love she was performing for the world? Or was it not necessary that humans should understand? 'The work is being accomplished in spite of the mental lack of understanding and even in spite of the mental understanding,'[57] she said not without irony. When somebody asked her in writing: 'From Your long experience of over sixty years, have You found that Your expectation from us and from humanity has been sufficiently fulfilled?' she answered: 'As I am expecting nothing I cannot answer the question.'[58]

No doubt, the supramental Force is active in the whole world. She has repeated it so often. 'All bodies are learning their lesson.' Or: 'It is not for one body that it is happening, it is for the whole Earth.'[59] 'I feel that there are people over the whole Earth,' who were touched by the Force. 'There are exceptional responses' — though most of those who had those responses did not realize what was actually happening to them. 'Whatever it be, everything that is ready to receive even a spark or a particular aspect of the supramental Consciousness and Light must *automatically* receive it. And the effects of this Consciousness and Light will be innumerable because they certainly will adapt themselves to the possibility, to the capacity of everybody in accordance with the sincerity of his aspiration.'[60] The being which vibrates on the supramental frequency, even partially, is transformed by it, everywhere, ineluctably. The iridescent dots radiate in the whole world with 'effects which according to their dimension are insignificant but enormous because of their quality.'[61] But there remained the crust, the residue on the surface which is the result as well of the terrestrial past as of our mental way of perception.

'To calm down all personal ambitions, I must declare the following: "If for some reason or other this body becomes unusable, the universal Mother will recommence manifesting herself in hundreds of individualities according to their capacity and receptivity, every one being a partial manifestation of the Universal Consciousness." '[62]

'Mother is Getting Old'

I am the only one who is young.[63]

—The Mother

The battle in her body between the new and the old world was leaving its traces. After all, she was now ninety years old, more than ninety. She was a living contradiction: on the one hand she was the Great Mother whose terrestrial body was partially supramentalized, on the other hand she was 'a poor piece of cloth,' but 'a piece of cloth that suffers.' These are her words. The crucifixion of this Avatar has lasted for years, and she too had voluntarily accepted the bitter chalice when in 1962 she had taken up her body again to hasten the coming of the Kingdom of God on Earth. But her suffering for the Earth was not spectacular. 'I have a dislike for dramas.'

As far as the others were concerned, that little woman there was simply becoming very old. That she did not hear well anymore and found it difficult even to take a sip of fruit juice, that she had serious heart problems and a lot more symptoms here and there in her body, well yes, that is how things are when somebody reaches a very old age, isn't it?

'I think — I don't know, but this seems to be the very first time — that the instrument [she herself in her incarnation], instead of having been made to bring the "Good News," the "Revelation," to cause the illumination, has been made to try out the realization: to do the work, the hidden labour.'[64] According to her, the advanced phases of the transformation were happening at such an old age to make her physical perils look normal to the others. 'The people are therefore convinced that I am always dozing, that I can't hear any

longer, and so on, and of course I can hardly speak anymore —
[smiling] all of which means that I have become a little old woman
... I hardly still belong to the old world; therefore the old world says:
"She is finished." It leaves me completely cold.'[65]

We know that all organs and functions of her body were subject
to the transfer of power, which is another way of saying that they
were being transformed from an animal-human state into a
supramental state. From the millennia-old way in which those organs
and functions were used to work, they had to be transferred to a
working under the direct governance of the divine Unity-Consciousness. The body had to be divinized, and if one remembers more or
less how a divine body is supposed to work, one can hardly find
words for the awesomeness of the undertaking. The most perceptible,
external side of the process of transformation was that all organs and
functions were being disorganized, which each time required a transitional period of crisis in which the Mother seemed to be terribly
'ill.' She therefore had to repeat time and again: 'These are not
illnesses, these are disruptions of the functionings,' and: 'I have
nothing doing with an illness of which one can be cured: I can't be
cured! What this is all about is a labour of transformation!'[66]

This meant, practically speaking, that all at once she did not know
anymore how to walk or how to bring a spoon to her mouth. We
do not realize how much our simplest movements are learned and
practiced, how much everything is mentalized even in the 'instinctive'
aspects of the mental beings we are. In the womb of the mother the
human baby already practices the use and the mastery of its body.
But here now an end was made to the dominance of the mental
consciousness; here the body was no longer governed by means of
the subconsciously mentalized nervous system: it was being tuned to
the direction from a supramental centre. This could not be effected
all at once, for it would have caused instant death. Organ after organ
and function after function were being 'processed,' repeatedly, and
again the miracle was the dosing of the transforming Power by which
each focus of the transformation — the apparent 'illness' — was
treated up to the utmost limit bearable, after which followed a period
of recuperation and assimilation of the newly heightened capacities.

During the periods of recuperation, the Mother felt all right and had the most brilliant experiences; the phases of intense transformation were pure hell — 'twenty-four hours of hell for ten minutes of paradise.' Who else would have been willing to bear that, for years in succession, not for oneself but for others? Again we hear Sri Aurobindo's words, which might have been hers too: 'It is only divine Love which can bear the burden I have to bear.' Who else would have been *capable* of bearing that? Which other body would have been capable of being taken apart, as it were, and then reconnected to another power source, to another Force, in each of its cells? Sri Aurobindo, 'he who knew,' had said to her: 'Only your body is capable of undergoing the transformation.' She said that in order to undergo the transformation one had to be prepared to become apparently totally senile: 'You have to accept the helplessness and even the feeble-mindedness.' Who else would have been willing to become like that? 'Sri Aurobindo has told me that I was the only one who had the courage for it.'[67] The consequence was that, as to appearances, she looked rather like 'a negation of the Truth' than like its incarnation. What occurred in the Mother is without precedent.

She could hardly see anymore, but she saw very well with her eyes closed. She was almost deaf, but if necessary she could hear a pin drop. She had trouble swallowing a bite, except when she placed her consciousness into the One that was the bite and her mouth and her throat, and then there was no trouble at all. Hunger is an expression of the corporeal life force, a need to uphold life; but the life force, the vital, had in several operations been taken away from the Mother's body and it was only by an act of the will, in order to keep the body going, that she could eat, with great difficulty. And food always contains a certain amount of unconsciousness which she had to swallow too. The person who is healthy does not realize how much life force speaking demands; it was only by an act of the will that the Mother still spoke, with a voice that seemed to come from afar or from deep in the body, artificial as it were, sometimes shrill and often breaking. It looked as if she were dozing (the poor dear!) while she was working everywhere in the world. 'When I remain silent and quiet for hours, there is *so much* work that is being done, but everywhere at the same time.' 'What are you seeing?' she was once asked when she had been staring in front of her for a long time. She answered: 'Nothing. I see nothing. There is no longer "something that sees." But I *am*. I am a countless number of things. I *live* a countless number of things. And so there is so much, so much, so much, that there is nothing anymore. I don't know how to say this.'[68]

From the *Agenda*, we can get some idea of that extraordinary process of body-transformation and of the experiences the Mother had. Otherwise we would know as little of what she has gone through as we know of Sri Aurobindo. 'You would not understand,' he had said. The Mother too sometimes complained, more and more frequently, about 'the general and total incomprehension' even by those who were nearest to her — physically, that is. It would nevertheless be a misconception to suppose that the *Agenda* contains the full picture of her *sadhana* in the last years. The Mother has been so kind as to share some of her experiences by means of those conversations, in order that those really interested might get an idea of how the human being has been transformed into the being beyond man. The *Agenda* contains some communiqués but not the full report of the battle for the Future that was being waged in her.

She was involved in it every hour of the day, living in an unfailing concentration. To narrate one minute of what was happening in her Consciousness, a whole book would have been necessary, she said. 'One might compose a whole teaching with a single one of those experiences, and I have at least several a day.'[69] During the time she was discussing one of those experiences again so much more had happened. 'I am not limited by what people call time or space. You understand, I am doing many things at the same time without anybody seeing it or being aware of it. You see,' she said to Mona Sarkar, 'what is happening [while he was sitting in front of her], you are not conscious of it, not even of what happened within yourself.'[70] She did narrate an experience of hers every now and then, but the experiences came in droves, even the one through the other, 'a world unfurling at each moment.' And they thought that she was dozing, that she drowsed her time away. 'Look, Mother is falling asleep again!'

Or they thought she was 'in trance.' A yogic trance is most often an exteriorization into one of the worlds above the mental; the trance of the mediums is mostly an exteriorization into a vital world. But the Mother did not exteriorize, she did not leave reality behind. During a certain period, it was even forbidden for her to leave the material reality, something she had been so skillful at. She was forced to stay where her job of transformation needed her, in the crucible of the transformation, by a merciless Mercy. The pain, the suffering were closely related with the old Matter. The only way in which she still felt a separate personality was because of the pain. It was the old Matter that suffered, and at one time she even spoke the mysterious words: 'It is the pain that suffers.' In *Savitri*, Sri Aurobindo had called pain 'the hammer of the gods,' and the Mother said that pain was the goad which had awakened the Inconscient and made the evolution possible.

The Mother analyzed all that, even when for days she was nothing but a cry of pain and had to endure all the suffering of the world, all of it simultaneously. She was always present as a witness at everything that happened, and everything happened *in* herself, the vibrations suffering pain in a cell of her own body as well as the agony of a person at the other side of the Earth. 'It is obvious that things would never change if they were not unbearable.'[71] She had to go all the way to the utmost limit possible in order that the Turn-about might happen all at once.

It is a principle of the evolution: a new possibility can manifest itself only when the old order has reached the point of the impossible. Were it otherwise — and it is important to comprehend this — the divine Action would be little more than a kind of divine comedy. This applies also to the world as a whole: it has to reach the impossible point if the transition to the New World must become possible. But such a transition then happens all of a sudden — just like a child after a long, hidden growth in the womb of its mother reaches the point of impossible further gestation and is suddenly born in a kind of cataclysmic happening. All signs point to the fact that the old world has arrived at the impossible point. 'And at the end there will be a miracle': a New Birth.

Every day, if in the least feasible, she also continued performing her enormous task as the head and heart of the Ashram and as the Avatar who proffers the grace and blessings of her earthly presence to all who cross her path. Representatives of the whole world came crossing her path on those few square meters of her room on the second floor in the Rue de la Marine. Some insisted that she should stop that daily labour that lasted for hours, or that she should at least drastically curtail it, but she put them right. Her reasoning was simplicity itself, based on the first premise: everything is That, consequently nothing happens without the Will of That, for reasons absolutely valid within That. 'I know that everything that comes to me is necessary, otherwise it would not come ... There is nothing that is not willed and that does not come with a well-defined reason.'[72] 'I am convinced that everything that happens is willed by the Lord.'[73] She lived in the absoluteness of the perception and concrete experience of the Unity, in the absoluteness of the surrender to That — which, after all, is the only sensible attitude if one has some notion of what That is.

And That, mostly called by her the Lord (*le Seigneur*), talked to her: 'Each time I am complaining or grumbling a bit, he says: "But it is for me ... I am the one, I, who brings all those people to you. I am the one who is arranging everything. I am the one who makes them ask. It is me! ..."[74] What happened at each and every moment was the best that could happen in the present general circumstances. 'It is evident — it is evident — that one is placed in the best possible circumstances and with the maximum of possibilities for the action, if one sincerely wills it.'[75]

All the same, it was rather much: forty, fifty, sixty letters per day, fifty to one hundred or more visitors per day, plus the secretaries and heads of departments for the organization of the Ashram. And no, everything was not innocent. Using that person there in front of her, the Enemy slashed out with his stiletto, or petty humanity secreted its acids. 'Do not be ill-humoured, you make me ill,' she said, for she felt that within herself, like poison. She had it printed and distributed in the Ashram: know that every lie strikes my body like a blow! And there was the covert hatred towards her: 'Go away, disappear from here.' 'A considerable number of persons desires that it [her body] would die.' For so many were sure that that stooping, shrivelled, ill, suffering body would not last much longer. When on their birthday or on another occasion they sat in front of her, they thought: 'This may be the last time I see her,' and the Mother read their thoughts like an open book without their being aware of it. There were even some who spread stories that the Mother during their last visit had made them understand with a look that she would depart soon!

The important thing was to hold out, *'il faut durer.'* 'The victory is for those who are the most enduring.' Twenty times she has said something like this. And she talked less and less. No doubt, talking was an enormous physical effort for her — 'It has become very difficult to talk, I mean the material fact of speaking' — but this was not the main reason, for she has never avoided a physical effort.

In the first place, talking about an experience meant fixing that experience, as it were, and thereby limiting it. 'It is very, very inexpressible; this means that, as soon as you try to express it, it becomes mentalized and is no longer that. This is the reason why it is so difficult to express. I cannot talk about it.'[76] One sees time and again how the Mother gradually gives an ever more accurate account of her important experiences — and there are so many we know nothing of — encircling them as it were with intense concentration to be sure not to distort them, and that she only defines an experience definitively when it has run its full course and thus has become completely clear. 'It is not good to talk when one is still underway,' she said, and this regarded as well her separate experiences as her *sadhana* as a whole. 'As soon as you begin to see, to understand and to formulate [the experience], it is already something that belongs to the past.'[77]

Secondly, her experiences occurred outside and above the mental domain, which meant that the fact of expressing them in (mental) words pulled the whole experience down unto a level that no longer corresponded with it. What is supramental cannot be put into mental words.* 'The consciousness is lowered as soon as I begin to talk,' the Mother said. 'Words, languages are inappropriate to express something that surpasses the [human] consciousness. As soon as one formulates it, it descends on a lower level ... As soon as one expresses it in words, it looks like a caricature.'[78] 'The spiritual truth is a truth of the spirit and not of the intellect,'[79] Sri Aurobindo had said.

Thirdly, to express an experience in words means concretizing it in a plane where undesirable and hostile forces may get a grip on it and can thereby thwart the results of the experience. This is the rationale of the age-old yogic principle that one should talk about one's experiences to nobody except to the guru.

Fourthly, to really understand an experience, one has to have had the experience oneself, or one should at least have access to the spiritual level on which it has occurred. The Pioneers were too far ahead. This was the reason for Sri Aurobindo's refusal to answer certain questions or to explain certain matters; it was also the reason for the Mother's relativizing everything she had said or written. 'If one has not had the experience oneself, reading about it is of no use. We do publish the *Bulletin*, but what I have just said is true.'[80] And this truth is applicable to everything Sri Aurobindo, she herself and others have published or are publishing about them. The Supramental on the Earth is a fact of realization by the Avatar. If this fact is a reality, it works itself out despite all human opinions and actions or reactions. But, of course, all inspired writings have an intrinsic force and may have an effect on the readers because their soul may understand what their intelligence cannot, and because an intellectual approach may be of great importance in certain phases of the soul's development.

Sometimes she still formulated and wrote things when they were (inwardly) dictated to her, and then the wording occurred spontaneously together with the imperative compulsion to pronounce them or write them down (as in the case of the charter of Auroville). But she hardly spoke on her own initiative in the last year. 'I can do so

---

* 'The problem is not *in* the language, the problem is the language.' (Gary Zukav)

much more without words.' Besides, what visitors had to say or to ask was usually so petty in comparison with the panorama of their soul which was spread out before the Mother, including the soul's past and future, and on which she could work directly. Even to Satprem she said as early as in 1970: 'If you want to make me talk, you have to come with questions, otherwise it is impossible.'[81] She needed a receptivity, a questioning presence to make answer a body that never acted on its own initiative anymore. Bertolt Brecht has written a poem about the unknown person who must have begged Lao-tzu for his wisdom and to whom we therefore owe the *Tao-te Ching*. Without Satprem's questioning presence, cultural baggage and analytical intellect, the conversations which constitute the *Agenda* would never have taken place. That afterwards he put himself so much to the fore will prove to be of minor importance.

It is touching how the conversations in the last part of the *Agenda* are as it were ebbing out. '*Je finirai par me taire,*' a day will come that I will remain silent, the Mother had said already in 1969. And this is indeed what has happened. '*Rien à dire,*' nothing to say, were her words towards the end of her life practically time after time. 'Mother manages to say nothing,' Satprem notes about the meeting of 30 May 1970. 'The [body] likes speaking less and less ... I would prefer to say nothing anymore ... I cannot speak. Besides, I have nothing to tell.'

Although the documents may give the impression to the reader that the Mother was slowly slipping into a sort of lethargic state, on the one hand because her health became apparently more and more miserable and on the other hand because she hardly spoke anymore, it would be a mistake to conclude, as most have done, that she was deteriorating, with death as the inevitable consequence. 'It is impossible to put into words because it is so multifaceted, so complex,' she said about her experiences. Then too there was the worldwide dynamic action of the Mother-in-the-*sadhana*, whose physical visible body (that functional fiction) as the interface with the Earth, as the means to 'touch the Earth,' was transforming Matter with the utmost intensity. The whole of her 'yogic' act was her surrender, expressed in word or attitude in 'what You want,' in order to allow the supramental Force, which she saw as a golden mass above the Earth, to penetrate into Matter as purely as possible. There was the paradox of apparent deterioration and an ever greater Glory. 'Outwardly I am nothing anymore, but inwardly there is such an enormous power.' And because she saw her outward deterioration reflected in the consciousness of the persons present, she reminded them from time to time, with sweet irony, that her consciousness had not deteriorated: 'This old age is purely physical ... but from the standpoint of the perception, of the consciousness, there is no diminution; on the contrary, it is becoming ever more clear and ever more accurate.'[82]

And finally she kept silent.

What has happened in those last six months?

Six months, at the speed with which her action, her transformation and her experiences took place, is a long time.

And she had then a supramental body.

Chapter Twenty-seven

THE NEW BODY

'Happy New Year!'

1 January 1969. 'That has been gradually increasing during the night, and at the time of waking up this morning there was as it were a golden Sunrise and the atmosphere was very lightsome. The body felt: "Indeed, this is really, really new. A golden light, delicate and benevolent. "Benevolent" in the sense of a certitude, a harmonious certitude. It was something new ... And when I say "Happy New Year" to the people, it is that that I am passing them on. And this morning I have spent my ·time like that, spontaneously, saying: "Happy New Year! Happy New Year!" '[1]

4 January 1969. 'On the 1st something really strange has happened. And I was not the only one to feel it, several persons have felt it. It was just after midnight, but I felt it at two o'clock and others at four o'clock in the morning ... It was something very material, by which I mean that it was very external · – very external. And it was luminous, with a golden light. It was very strong, very powerful, but its character, nevertheless, was of a smiling benevolence, a peaceful joy, and a kind of unfolding in joy and light. And it was like a "Happy New Year", like a wish. It has taken me completely by surprise. It has lasted ... I have been feeling it for three hours at least. Afterwards, I no longer gave any attention to it, I don't know what has happened to it. But I have told it to you [Satprem] in passing, and I have also spoken about it to two or three other persons: all of them had felt it. This means that it was *very* material. All of them had felt it, just like that, like a kind of joy, but a joy that was congenial, powerful and, yes, very, very sweet, very much smiling, *very benevolent*. I don't know what it is, but it is a kind of benevolence and therefore very close to humanity. And it was so concrete, so concrete! As if one could taste it, so concrete was it ... It has not left. One does not have the impression that it came to leave again ...

'My own impression was that of an immense personality. Immense. By which I mean that the Earth was tiny to it. The Earth was like this [gesture: like a tiny ball in the palm of the hand], like a ball. An immense personality, very, very benevolent, coming in order to ... coming to help. And so very strong and at the same time so sweet, so understanding. And that was very external: the body felt it everywhere, everywhere [the Mother touches her face, her hands], it was everywhere ...

'It was luminous, smiling, and so benevolent *because of its power*. By which I mean that benevolence, ordinarily in the human being, is something that is somewhat feeble, in the sense that it does not like struggling, that it does not like fighting. But this is not at all like that: it is a benevolence which imposes itself [the Mother plants both fists on the armrests of her chair] ...

'It is perhaps the superman [*le surhomme*], I don't know, the intermediary between the two [the human and the supramental being]. Perhaps the superman. It was very human, but of a humanity with divine proportions, you see. A humanity without weaknesses and without darknesses: it was nothing but light. It was all light and smiling and ... sweetness at the same time.

'Yes, perhaps the superman.'

8 January 1969. 'Have I told you that I have identified that consciousness? ... It is the descent of the consciousness of the superman. I got the confirmation afterwards.

'It happened on the 1st of January, after midnight. I woke up at two o'clock in the morning, surrounded by a consciousness that was so very concrete, and *new*, in the sense that I have never experienced something like it. And that lasted, in all its concreteness and forcefulness, for two or three hours, and afterwards it spread out and went to find all those who were able to receive it. And I came to know that it was the consciousness of the superman, which means the intermediary between the human and the supramental being.'

18 *January 1969.* 'That [consciousness of the superman] is very consciously active. It is like a projection of power and it has now become habitual.

'It contains a consciousness — something *very* precious — that teaches lessons to the body [of the Mother], that teaches it what it has to do, the attitude it has to take, that is, the reaction it has to have. I had already told you several times that it is very difficult to find the procedure of the transformation when one has nobody to give one the necessary indications. Well, this seems to be the answer. It comes and says to the body: "Take this attitude, do this, do that, like that." And the body is very glad, it is completely reassured: it can no longer make mistakes. It's very interesting.

'It has come as a mentor, practical, completely practical: "This you must refuse, this you must accept, this you must generalize ..." — all the interior movements. And this becomes even very material, in the sense that for certain vibrations, it says: "This should be encouraged", and for others: "This has to be guided into channels," and for others: "This must be dispensed with." A lot of small indications like that.

'In one of the former *Entretiens,* I have said, when I still was speaking there at the Playground: "No doubt, the superman will be in the first place a being of power so that he may be able to defend himself." This is it, it is that experience. It has come back as an experience.'[2]

The New Man is among us.[3]

—Nolini Kanta Gupta

Sri Aurobindo had written in *The Synthesis of Yoga*: 'It is impossible to rise into [the gnostic or supramental consciousness] at once; if that could be done, it would mean a sudden and violent overshooting, a breaking or slipping through the gates of the Sun ... without near possibility of return. We have to form as a link or a bridge an intuitive or illuminated mind, which is not the direct gnosis, but in which a derivative body of the gnosis can form.'⁴ Shortly before he departed, he wrote in the series of articles for the *Bulletin*: 'It might be that a psychological change, a mastery of the nature of the soul, a transformation of the mind into a principle of light [the Mind of Light], of the life-force into power and purity would be the first approach, the first attempt to solve the problem, to escape beyond the merely human formula and establish something that could be called a divine life upon earth, a first sketch of supermanhood, of a supramental being in the circumstances of the earth-nature.'⁵

In 1959 the Mother said, looking back on her *sadhana* since 1950: 'I have told [to my body]: "... You are going to realize that intermediary superhumanity between the human and the supramental being, which is what I call *le surhomme*. And it is that what I have been doing in the last eight years.'⁶

In May 1957 she said: 'One can go beyond this state [of the ordinary humanity], open oneself to the supramental Force which is now active upon the Earth, and enter into a zone of transition where both influences meet and penetrate each other, where the consciousness is still mental and intellectual in its functionings but sufficiently penetrated by the supramental Power and Force to be able of being the instrument of a higher truth. At the present moment, this state can be realized upon earth by those who are ready to receive the supramental Force that is manifesting.'⁷

September 1957: 'It is evident that intermediary beings are needed, that it is these intermediary beings who have to find the means to create the beings of the Supramental. And without any doubt, when Sri Aurobindo wrote this [the series of articles for the *Bulletin*] he was convinced that it was what we had to do. I think ... I *know* that it is now certain that we will realize what he expects of us. It is no longer a hope, it has become a certitude.'⁸ As the Mother was always talking from her own experience, a confirmation like this could only be based on her experience.

April 1958: 'One can with certainty assert that there will be an intermediary specimen between the mental and the supramental being ... It looks like ... it is even certain that the substance which will constitute this intermediary world which is in course of being elaborated will be a substance that is richer, more powerful, more luminous, more resilient, with certain new qualities, more subtle, more penetrating. That substance will have a sort of inherent capacity of universality, as if its degree of subtlety and refinement allowed for the perception of vibrations in a much larger if not completely total way; and it eliminates the sensation of division which one has with the former kind of substance, with the ordinary mental substance ... This [new] substance is at present almost universally spread in the terrestrial atmosphere.'⁹

March 1969: 'It is as if that new Consciousness has brought with it a whole new field of experiences in the very material domain, with the abolishment of a number of things declared by people to be impossible ... This consciousness has a great power of attraction. There are now people coming from everywhere, from everywhere [to the Ashram and Auroville].'¹⁰ The instrument in many cases used by that power of attraction was *Sri Aurobindo, ou l'Aventure de la conscience* (Sri Aurobindo, or the Adventure of Consciousness), the book written by Satprem under the guidance of the Mother and (behind the veil) of Sri Aurobindo.

April 1972: 'The change of the human into the supramental being occurs, or doesn't occur, through the superman. It is possible that there are some supermen — there are some — who are carrying out the transition.'¹¹

1987: 'Although we may not know it, the New Man, the divine race of humanity, is already among us. It may be in our next neighbour, in our nearest brother, even in myself. Only a thin veil covers it. It marches just behind the line [between the visible and invisible]. It waits for an occasion to throw off the veil and place itself in the forefront.' This is a note by Nolini Kanta Gupta, who died in 1984, published above his signature in the *Sri Aurobindo Mandir Annual* of 1987.

Sri Aurobindo had foreseen the necessity of the transitional being; he had begun to work it out in himself and had transferred the result of his material realization to the Mother at the time of his departure in 1950.

The Mother *immediately* continued to build on Sri Aurobindo's realization. She wrote as early as 1954: 'For the last few days when I wake up in the morning I have the strange sensation of entering a body that is not mine — my body is strong and healthy, full of energy and life, supple and harmonious and this one fulfills none of these qualities; the contact with it becomes painful; there is a great difficulty in adapting myself to it and it takes a long time before I can overcome this uneasiness.'[12] These words cannot be interpreted in any other way than that the Mother already had a new subtle-physical body in 1954 besides and apart from her visible, gross material body. It was in this subtle-physical body that many saw her in their dreams and visions. 'They see me like I really am,' she said.

The above quoted statements of May and September 1957 leave no doubt about the fact that she had then reached the superhuman state for her bodily self.

On 1 January 1969, the superhuman consciousness manifested in the atmosphere of our Earth to establish itself here. Since then, it is a new element in the evolutionary process and seeks out the human instruments capable of embodying it.

The Mother and also Nolini Kanta Gupta have expressed in unmistakable terms that in the mass of the human species now populating the Earth potential supermen are already present — a fact that moreover could be deduced from her narrative about the supramental ship.

But the Mother herself was far ahead again.

The New Body

The Avatar had come to establish permanently upon the Earth the foundations of a new evolution — one might say to bring into the earth-atmosphere the 'archetype' of the possibilities and forms of the new evolution. The Supramental Consciousness, the main goal of the Work of Sri Aurobindo and the Mother, had come into the earth-atmosphere in 1956. The Mother had been forming the archetype of the 'superman' (*surhomme*) and the superhuman consciousness had manifested upon the Earth on 1 January 1969, with the inevitable consequence that this consciousness would embody itself in suitable instruments, in supermen. Though for the Mother this consciousness acted as a mentor, helping her in her avataric *sadhana*, she had not been waiting for it to go forward as fast as possible and with all means at her disposal. Ahead now lay the formation of the prototype, of the archetype of the supramental body. Once those embryos were formed in the womb of Mother Nature, all the elements for the elaboration of the New World would be present and the Avatar would have realized more than the full purpose of her incarnation.*

This too the Mother has brought to a good end, she has formed the archetype of the supramental body. To understand the course of matters as described in the *Agenda* and the *Notes sur le chemin*, it is necessary to keep three points in mind.

The first point concerns the 'subtle physical,' also called the 'true physical' (*le vrai physique*) by the Mother, and which has been defined already. The Mother in many instances still calls the true physical 'subtle' because normally it cannot be perceived by human beings, the field and medium of perception of the human senses being gross physical matter. (Physics has gradually advanced so far behind the wall of perceptible reality that it does not realize it is dealing with an occult world, where it is meeting and will continue to meet with one astounding surprise after the other.) The 'true physical' is supramental; were it not so, Sri Aurobindo would not be able to dwell in it in his supramental body, for instance. It was also in the 'true physical' that the Mother saw some of the living and the dead meet in a most natural way; this was only possible because part of their body was supramentalized and because to the Supermind death is no existential boundary. Time and again the Mother has described the 'true physical' as more material, more concrete, more real, more complete and much more powerful than the physical we are familiar with. She also said that the two worlds existed separately and inside

---

* It might not be superfluous to remind the reader once more of the fact that the Mother's *sadhana* concerned her *body*. As the Great, Eternal Mother, she did not need a mentor to help her with the execution of what she herself had ordained and now fulfiled, for there is nothing in the Manifestation that has not been decreed and supported by her as the Mediatrix and Creatrix.

one another. 'I think that [the true physical], now that the Supramental has descended, will become more and more active on earth. For it is in the subtle physical [which in this case in the true physical] that the new creation will be formed before it descends, before it can become fully visible and concrete.'[13]

The second important point, also already known to us, is that it is the psychic being that takes on the supramental body. We remember the words of the Mother: 'It is the psychic being that will materialize and become the supramental being ... The psychic being materializes and this gives a continuity to the evolution ... The psychic being is immortal and it is by the psychic being that immortality will be established upon the Earth ... It is the psychic being, the representative of the Divine in man, that will remain, that will cross over into the new species.' These statements need no comment. It is understandable that only the souls matured in and by the evolution (Sri Aurobindo somewhere speaks about 'the cosmic training' of the soul) can be ready for this important step, for the great evolutionary saltus.

The third point is not the least important although it is the least evident. The universalization of the body of the Avatar, the precondition of her Work in Matter, was the result of the universalization of the consciousness of the cells. The Supramental is by definition a Unity-Consciousness. If all elementary particles are constantly in a cosmic relation, then it stands to reason that the cells too must be in this kind of relation, for they consist of elementary particles. The relationships within the cosmic unity are a fundamental capacity of the cells though not in their surface consciousness, otherwise all of us would be conscious cosmic beings, which we are not. (Consisting of cells, elementary particles, a subliminal mind and vital, and a soul, we are indeed cosmic beings *unconsciously*, and even more than cosmic beings.) To put it graphically, we could say that the cell shows the respective gradations of the evolution going from the outside towards the inside — from the gross materiality, supported by the Inconscient, of its surface to the supramental Unity-Consciousness in its inmost core. Because the cells of the Mother's body were being supramentalized ever more and in ever greater numbers, the Unity-Consciousness was also increasing in her material substance: she became ever more bodily, or rather cellularly, conscious of the One Existence, which she experienced as her own physical existence. This did not happen in an egoistic way, in which one feels oneself the centre and relates everything to oneself, but in a 'unity way,' in a supramental, divine way by being present in everything, by being everything. She *was* the others, therefore feeling their inwardness with all their weal and woe as her own (so much so that once, in a critically ill person far away, she received the last sacraments!) *Le corps est partout* — the body is everywhere.

Good, but what if those cells died? Did they become dust again and had all her trouble been in vain? This was a question she had asked herself and others more than once till on 19 March 1969 she got a clear and indubitable answer. 'The question had been asked: "All that transformative work of the cells, of the consciousness in the cells — it seems that in the usual way all that is wasted as it is going to be dissolved?" And then came in a very precise, almost concrete way: "There is a way, namely before dying to prepare in oneself a body with all the cells that are transformed, illumined, conscious — to gather them and to form a body with the maximum number of conscious cells. Then, when this work is finished, the full consciousness enters in it [in the new body] and the other one [the gross physical] can be dissolved, for it is of no importance anymore.' And she concluded: 'This possibility exists.' This possibility existed in her body, she knew that. Her mentor showed her how the formation of the new body had to be done 'for hours and hours, and that insisted and did not want to go away. It insisted till the body had thoroughly understood. And there is no need of a material intervention ... The material intervention was replaced by an intervention in the subtle physical, which was sufficient.' In the true physical. 'It was really unexpected. I had never thought of something like it ... And all objections were solved.'

The supramentalized consciousness of the cell supramentalizes the inner substance of the cell and makes the Unity-Consciousness in the cell concrete and active. The psychic being covers itself with the supramentalized substance, in other words it forms a supramental body which exists in the supramental world of the true physical, just like it earlier formed a material-vital-mental body (*adhara*) in the material-vital-mental world. This is not something we can 'understand'*, but we can conceive that it fits into the line of evolution with the soul as the central element of the evolutionary development. One hesitates to put the label 'important' on a specific experience of Sri Aurobindo and the Mother's for all their experiences were important links in the chain of the whole; all the same, without the experience of the Mother just mentioned in her own words, the transformation of her body, and therefore the work of the last years of her life, could not be envisioned. The supramental transformation of the body was of course the continuation and the provisional culmination of all the preceding avataric labour of Sri Aurobindo and the Mother. (The definitive pinnacle will be the visible supramental body on Earth.) We have seen time and again that the expansion of their realization, however surprising and overwhelming in some of the separate stages, with hindsight was usually discernible here and there in their previous reports, till the concretization of a certain line of development became inevitable, as it were, like a subterranean vein of ore suddenly appears on the surface because of a rift in the terrain. The same kind of consideration is applicable to the Mother's realization of the supramental body. It is very instructive to follow this growth-process in the *Agenda* and the *Notes on the Way*, and to give a broad outline of its chronological sequence.

* As early as 24 January 1961, the Mother said to Satprem: 'In the night of the day before yesterday, during the night, in the middle of the night, I woke up — or rather I was woken up — with the impression that I had in my body a much greater being — with 'greater' I mean bigger, more voluminous — than usual. It was as if it could hardly fit into it: it exceeded its limits. And it had such a *compact power* that it was almost annoying.' She also said that this big body caused reactions which were in no

---

* We 'understand' as little how we ourselves have come forth from the unification of a male and female reproductive cell although the outward process of cell-division and cell-specification has been described by science and is supposedly known by us.

proportion to a human body, and that this was accompanied by a storm of compact power in order that things might change. This statement dates from *before* the dramatic experience of 1962. Should we suppose that the perception in this case was that of her fully built superhuman body?

* 23 June 1962, i.e. after her death and resurrection in April of that year: 'Last night, I have noticed that I was very tall. I am generally tall [during the night], tall and strong.' Her earthly body at that time was eighty-four years old, very much stooped, and suffered crisis after crisis.

* On 27 June, Satprem says to the Mother: 'I wanted to tell you something strange. Sujata [then his companion, later his wife] told me that every time she sees you at night since you have withdrawn into your room in March, she sees you *much taller* than you were before.' The Mother: 'But everybody [has this experience]! Everybody! And I myself, when I see myself, I am very tall. What has happened? ... It is the new being ... When is this going to express itself physically? I don't know. It is a being from the subtle physical. It is not a vital being, it is a being from the subtle physical. And I am tall and strong ... It has no age, it is neither young nor old ... it is completely different. And tall, strong ... A day will come that it will be visible concretely, one will see it ... Of course, logically speaking I should remain invisible until I appear in my new form. But this does not seem to come about very quickly.'

* 3 November 1962: 'Now that I think of it, I have noticed last night that I was very young physically! It was the subtle physical, of course, but I was very young.'

* 22 December 1962: 'These last days, I have marked that I remembered having gone downstairs, having met people and seen certain things, having talked, having organized certain things — a lot of different scenes from the *physical* memory. Not at all things which I have seen with the internal sight in a state of exteriorization: the *material* memory of having done certain things ... I have asked myself: "But have I gone downstairs materially then?" All present here can testify that I have not gone

downstairs, that I have not left this room. All the same, I have the material memory of having done that, and of having done some other things also, even of having gone outside. You see, I am faced with a problem. This memory is not only material through and through, but the consequences of what I have done *exist*.'

* 22 June 1963: 'Sri Aurobindo came with the notion, or the Order, or the conviction that it was for now. But in how far is the transformation for now? And what does that mean, "now"? How much time does it mean? ... There is such a certitude, such a certitude that at present it *is* already like that, but seen from the other side.'

24 August 1963: 'The ferment which makes everything rise is *at least* as important [as the personal realization]. After all, this is perhaps the main reason of the continuation of this body ...

'All those problems I am talking about are problems posed by the body, for the body. Within everything is perfect, everything is exactly as it should be ...

'It will not at all happen in the way people think or expect ...

'I have *seen* myself like I am ...

'But if one says so, people think that it is a psychic or mental seeing. It is not that, I am not talking about that! I am talking about a *physical* seeing, with these eyes [the Mother touches her eyes]. But it is a *true* physical seeing instead of the deformed seeing as it is now [in ordinary human beings].

'I mean that the true reality is in fact much more marvellous than we can imagine, because what we imagine is always a transformation or a glorification of what we see. But it is not that! It is not that!

'I am not very sure that I do not already physically exist in a true body. I say "I am not very sure" because the outward senses have no proof of it, but ... I am not trying and I have never tried to see or to know. I am not trying, but from time to time there is something that imposes itself: for a moment I see myself, feel myself, objectivize myself like I am. But this lasts a few seconds and, phhht, it is gone, again replaced by the old habit.

'You see, we can only think of things that are changing from one into the other — one becomes young again, all signs of old age disappear, and so on. That is old hat, it is not like that. It is not like that!'*

* 11 August 1964: 'During two hours the experience of the Omnipotence, the Omnipotence of the Lord — during two hours, with all decisions taken in the meantime, by which I mean the expression of what is going to be transposed into the terrestrial consciousness ...

'And what is strange (I was conscious, fully conscious; the "Witness"-consciousness is never annulled, but it is not disturbing): I knew, I saw (although my eyes were closed, I was lying on my bed), I saw my body move ... Every gesture, every finger, every attitude was something that was being realized ...

'I have the impression that Action is not at all limited to the moment that the here active consciousness participates in it: it is all the time like that. One second [of interiorization] is enough — that I don't talk, that I don't do anything — and I feel that golden Glory behind everything. "Behind?" It is not "behind," it is not "in," it is ... that what supports everything, what is always present. But in the course of the experience, I have been given two hours of *total* participation in it: there was nothing but That, nothing existed anymore but That. And an unforgettable joy has been given to all cells: they had become That ...

'In any case, the work is progressing very fast. This is really what Sri Aurobindo has called "The Hour of God." It is going very fast.'

* 7 November 1964: 'I was resting — after lunch I rest half an hour — and at the end of my rest I suddenly see myself: I see myself standing beside the bed, very tall, in a magnificent robe, and with somebody dressed in white next to me. And I saw that just at the moment that it was as if I was going to faint: I was

---

* 'All those who expected to see Mother suddenly young again, without wrinkles, no longer stooping and glorious in the *same* old bodily substance, had a wrong view of the phenomenon.' Satprem, *Mère II*, p. 250.

at the same time the person standing there and the person seeing all that from the bed. And at the same time I felt what sinks, what sinks down from the head: the head is being completely emptied. And the standing person smiled, and the person in the bed asked herself: "What is this? I am fainting but I am in my bed!" That is how it was. And as it was time for me to "wake up," which means returning into the external consciousness, I have come back. And I remained stuck with that problem: who was the one standing there?'

* 2 August 1967: 'The subtle physical seems to be transformed more and more. There is still a mystery between the two [between the physical and the subtle physical body]. A mystery. They are coexistent and yet ... [gesture as of a link which is missing] the subtle physical seems to have no influence on this [the physical body]. There is still something that has to be found ...'

* 9 April 1969: 'During the night, the body is tall and active, it does things. It is the subtle body that is doing things, that is active, that has an existence that is fully conscious. And it is different from this [the Mother touches the skin of her hands]. But it is a body that is *physical* in the subtle physical and it is already something permanent, in the sense that one *remains* like that, one finds things like one has left them. They exist in a permanent way but they are not visible to the ordinary vision. But their existence is logical and continuous. Well, there the form is the true expression of the consciousness, while here the form is the result of ... one could say: the lies disseminated in the consciousness.

'Those who see me during the night, those who have that vision in the subtle world, do not see me like this [the Mother points at her body]. They see me like I am and they say: "Oh, but you are like this, you are like that." But for the one to take the place of the other ...?'

* 19 July 1969: 'The physical seems to be less imperative. Before, one had the impression, well yes, that [the subtle physical] was not a "dream" like people say, but that it was a more subtle and less precise consciousness, and that the physical consciousness

was fully concrete and precise. But now this distinction [is no longer valid]. The other one [the subtle, true physical consciousness] has become almost more concrete and real than the physical consciousness. The purely material consciousness is more vague than [the true physical consciousness]. It gives the impression of being something that is not very ... secure, yes, not very secure. Isn't that strange.'

* 28 February 1970: 'My body is now bent materially, but during the night it was completely normal again! And I do not sleep! What may this be? I don't know ... And I do not leave my body ... Or is this body replaced by another one? I do not know.'

* On 9 May 1970, the Mother had an experience in which she saw her new body. 'Well, I have seen it, my body — how it will be. It is quite good,' she said with a smile. The form was not that different from the present human form, but 'so refined.' It was sexless, 'neither man nor woman,' and its colour was 'somewhat like the colour of Auroville' (orange). With her was 'the physical Mother' whom we would call Mother Nature, and who accepted the formation of the new body with a symbolic gesture. 'This means that material Nature has accepted the new creation.'

24 March 1972. 'For the first time, early in the morning, I have seen myself, my body. I do not know whether it is the supramental body or — how to say — a transitional body. But I had a completely new body, in the sense that it was asexual, it was neither woman nor man. It was very white, but I think that this is because my skin is white, I don't know. It was very slender — it was beautiful. Really a harmonious form. So, this is the first time. I did not know at all, I had no idea of how it would be or anything, and I have seen ... I *was* like that, I had become like that.'

The next day, Satprem asked for some explanation. The Mother said: 'I *was* like that. That was me. I did not see myself in a mirror, I saw myself like this [the Mother bows her head in order. to look down at her body]. I *was* like that.

'It was the first time. It was around four o'clock in the morning, I think. It was something completely natural. You see, I was not seeing myself in a mirror, I was completely natural. I remember only what

I have seen [gesture: from the chest down to the hips]. I was not wearing any veils, so I have seen only ... What was very different was the trunk, from the chest down to the waist: neither man nor woman.

'And it was beautiful. I had a very, very slender form, very thin — very thin but not emaciated. And the skin was very white. The skin was like my skin. But a very beautiful form. But no sex, one could not tell ... neither man nor woman. The sex was gone.

'Here too [the Mother points to her chest], nothing of all that anymore. I don't know how to say. It was like a remnant, but it had no forms anymore, not even as much as men have. A very white skin, very even. Practically no belly. The stomach ... no stomach. All that was very svelte.

'You see, I haven't paid special attention to it because I was like that, it was completely natural.'

'But was it like that in the subtle physical?' asked Satprem. 'It must be like that in the subtle physical,' the Mother answered. Satprem again: 'But how will that come down into the physical?' 'That is what I do not know,' the Mother answered. 'It was also evident that there was no longer a complicated digestive system like now nor the elimination as it is now ... But how will the [physical] body itself change? I don't know.'

Considering all this, it is evident that the Mother had a supramental body in the supramental world which was ready to be manifested upon Earth.

The problem was how the supramental 'archetype' she had formed would manifest in gross matter. It was indispensable that the gross matter would in an ever greater degree have to be transformed by the process of 'permeation,' the more and more omnipresent penetration. The supramental body, with its divine qualities, can logically speaking only take shape in a refined, supramentalized matter. Seen from the human side, this requires a pure miracle — the miracle of a new creation in evolution, accomplishing the greatest saltus, the greatest change ever brought about in the history of the Earth. One should not forget, however, that the appearance of Life in matter has also been a stupendous miracle, as was the capacity of the reflective consciousness of evolutionary beings. 'At the end, there will be a miracle,' the Mother said.

How much time would it take, that miracle of the visible presence of the supramental species upon the Earth? In 1956, the Mother's estimation was still in the range of millions of years. 'I have told you that before the results of the supramental manifestation will be visible and tangible, able to be perceived by one and all, millions of years may go by.'[14] Later on, her guess was in the range of thousands of years, and still later of something like three hundred years — the period foreseen by Sri Aurobindo which now probably looked acceptable to her because of her own progress. That she had remained working on Earth in 1956 and 1962 has no doubt shortened the process by thousands of years. 'The world unknowing for the world she stood.'

But the time of the presence of her earthly body among humankind was nearly over.

1972 was the centenary year of Sri Aurobindo's birth. The Mother wanted it to be celebrated in a way worthy of him. In the whole of India commemorative functions were held, with committees of dignitaries, long winding speeches and glossy memorial volumes. One talked about the Supermind here and the Supermind there, and about Sri Aurobindo's philosophic and yogic system — but it was all so theoretical, abstract, academic and uninspired. Of all the speechmakers, those with real insight into the significance of Sri Aurobindo's Work as Avatar and into the intense effort of his 'successor and collaborator' could perhaps be counted on the fingers of both hands.

At midnight, the hour the centenary day began, the disciples and many visitors sat around Sri Aurobindo's tomb, so beautiful in its bareness under that large tree. Then Sunil's soul-stirring music, specially composed for the occasion, resounded, with a crystal-clear woman's voice chanting the *mantra* of Sri Aurobindo's name in Sanskrit. And straight above the tomb, which was covered with a wealth of flowers and curling clouds of incense, shone the Full Moon.

The next morning everybody received the Mother's message for the day, summing up the meaning of Sri Aurobindo's action in utmost simplicity: 'One more step towards eternity.'

Chapter Twenty-eight

THE CATERPILLAR AND
THE BUTTERFLY

'Dying to death,' in other words no
longer being able to die because death
has become unreal.[1]

—The Mother

And death shall have no dominion.
— Dylan Thomas

THE MOTHER laid down her material body on
17 November 1973.

A European *sadhak* remembers: 'On 18 November, at about seven
o'clock in the morning, my downstairs neighbour, a Tamil who had
served in the French army and who had become like a brother to
me, pounded nervously on my door and on my window. He shouted:
"The Mother is dead! They say that the Mother is dead!" As I woke
up, I slowly realized the significance of his words; I got out of my
bed and simply knelt on the floor, a gesture of surrender with the
words reminiscent of her fundamental surrender: "Your will be
done." I cycled through the park to the Ashram. It was a gloriously
sunny day. I met other ashramites who were already coming back

from the Ashram on foot or on cycle, and who looked at me with very serious faces to see if I was already aware of the shocking news. A long queue was already winding around the central Ashram building consisting of Ashramites and people from town of all kinds and standings. The first ones had been allowed into the building a little after four. There was whispering and crying, and the atmosphere was one of deep dejection. Order was maintained by boys and girls of the Ashram led by 'captains' of the physical education. It did not take long before I too could enter the building and then the meditation hall. There she lay under humming electric fans, the Mother, whom I last had seen six months ago. She appeared to be sitting rather than laying down. If I had not known that this was the Mother, I would not have recognized her, so much her face had changed.'

How had it happened? The best source of information about the last days and the departure of the Mother is the improvised talk Pranab Kumar Bhattacharya held for the ashramites at the Playground on 4 December 1973. For years, night and day, he had been living in the company of the Mother, which means that he had not only seen what had happened from nearby, he had also been personally involved in it. He was the head of the department of physical education and some called him the 'bodyguard' of the Mother. When in the last years she could not walk that well anymore, she leaned on his arm to give darshan. He had a difficult character and Narayan Prasad calls him in one of his books 'the most loved and the most hated man in the Ashram.' There are many indications that the relation between the Mother and him was a very special one, important for her Work as a whole. In one of his birthday cards, she wrote: 'To thee whom my love selected when the time had come to start my work on the most material level.'[2]

The serious troubles with the Mother's health, Pranab told, had started in the month of April 1973. Nonetheless she did not want to stop her daily task and went on receiving about a dozen persons per day, mainly the secretaries and heads of departments. On 20 May, the problems suddenly became very serious. 'She said she didn't have any control over her body. From then onwards, she completely stopped seeing people and almost all the time remained in bed with her eyes closed.' Eating had been a problem for a long time; now it became worse. 'All those who were in the courtyard below must have heard how we had to fight with her to make her eat a little.'

On 10 November, she had her daily medical examination by doctor Prabhat Sanyal; he found that her blood pressure was very low and that her heart was very weak and missed several beats. 'In fact, the heart started failing from that time.' She now stayed in bed all the time. On the night of the 13th, she asked Pranab to lift her shoulders from the bed, then her legs, then her whole body. It seemed to give her some relief. Her suffering, once again, must have been terrible. 'I am nothing but a speck of dust, but a speck of dust that is suffering,' she once had said. Her body started showing bedsores. That night, she asked every ten or fifteen minutes to be lifted from the bed, and Pranab and Champaklal did so till she fell asleep around four o'clock in the morning.

On 14 November, she wanted to walk: 'Make me walk' 'We were hesitant,' says Pranab, 'but as she insisted, we lifted her up from the bed. She could not walk, staggered a little, almost collapsed. Seeing this, we put her back in bed. We saw that her face had become absolutely white and the lips blue. Then we decided that whatever she might say, we must not take her out from the bed again to walk. She took about twenty minutes to recover. She started saying: "Lift me up again, I shall walk." We refused ... Then we gave her Siquil as the doctor had prescribed. It took her about 45 minutes to become quiet and she slept from 2 to 4 o'clock, but after waking up she started saying: "Pranab, lift me up and make me walk. My legs are getting paralyzed; if you help me to walk again, they will become all right." But we did not listen.'

15 November was a slightly better day. The Mother also ate a little more than on previous days. Then she asked again to be lifted from the bed and to walk. When her assistants refused, she did not insist any longer. 'From that day she became absolutely obedient,' says Pranab. Her whole life long she had drilled her body to go to the limit: '*Va, continue, marche*,' come on, continue, keep walking! 'There is one thing that is always necessary, and it is: never to give up the game,'[3] was one of her mottoes. But now somewhere a limit had been reached.

André, her son, like on every other day, came to briefly meet her on the evening of the 17th. But Kumuda, her assistant, noticed that all at once the behaviour of the Mother was very unusual and had doctor Sanyal called. 'Slowly everything stopped. The doctor gave an external heart massage to her. It had no effect. Then he declared that the Mother had left her body. This was at 7:25 p.m. ... I was holding her when she left her body. It looked to me as if a candle was slowly extinguishing. She was very peaceful, extremely peaceful ...' Pranab says. Before, 'her suffering had to be seen to be believed.'

The body was left untouched till 11 o'clock. Except for those present in the room nobody knew what had happened there on the second floor. At 11 o'clock her body was washed and dressed up. At 2 o'clock it was carried down the staircase and laid out in the meditation hall. Those responsible for maintaining the order, photographers and some prominent Ashramites were woken up. A message for *All India Radio* was drafted. At a quarter past four the doors of the central Ashram building swung open for a last darshan. During two days thousands passed by her from early morning till late in the evening.

'And then, on 20 November, at a quarter past eight in the morning, they have put her in a coffin,' Satprem writes. 'We were standing to the right of the coffin. She was sitting more than she was laying down on those white cushions, with her hands on her knees. A ray of light touched her neck. Then the lid was closed — no ray any more, nothing any more.'⁴ The central Ashram building was full of people up to the rooftops. The body of the Mother was let down into the Samadhi, where it still is in a vault above the material remains of Sri Aurobindo — a vault which in accordance with the Mother's will had been kept for her since 1950.

A Canadian Question

And so, what remained of the grandiose dream of a 'life divine' upon Earth, of the immortal superman who would create a new world order? Sri Aurobindo was dead, and now the Mother was dead too.

aspirant? Or has discipleship on the material level in the path of the Integral Yoga come to an end?' Put in whatever way, it was certainly a problem that bothered many.

Nolini's answer: 'Obviously, the immediate programme of a physical transformation is postponed — not cancelled. But what we have been given is not less of a miracle. Mother has prepared for us her new body in the inner world, in the subtle physical which is as living and tangible as her physical body even though not as concrete. In one of her last Notes [*Notes on the Way*] she refers to this new transformed body and she describes it as presented in her vision. That body she has built up in her long arduous labours, built up in a complete form and left with us and with humanity.

'This new body of hers, prepared behind the material curtain, she sought to infuse into the material form, even press into it or force into it this new element; but Matter and man's physical nature were not ready: Earth still considered it as an intrusion, as something foreign. The material casing broke down in consequence — perhaps not broke down, rather broke through; but that must be another story.

'But it is there living and glorious in its beauty and power and is still at work within us, and around us in the world, incessantly, towards the final consummation of its material embodiment.'

From this text the following points can be filtered: 1. the Mother had a new body in the subtle physical; as Nolini refers to the *Notes on the Way* which have been quoted in the previous chapter, he can only mean her supramental body, and when he writes 'not as concrete,' he intends to say: *to us* not as concrete as gross matter; 2. the Mother has tried to 'infuse' her supramental body 'into the material form;' because gross matter was not yet ready, it has rejected the supramental body and the 'material casing' has broken down; what Nolini means with 'perhaps broke through' is not clear; 3. because the material, gross physical casing broke down 'the immediate programme of a physical transformation is postponed — not cancelled.'

We find the opinion that the transformation process might have been postponed already in the talk of Pranab: 'For the moment

Their bodies were there in that tomb, under colourful layers of d
renewed flowers. The disciples sat around the tomb or leaned aga
it like ants around a drop of honey. What would become of
Ashram? What would become of them? It was normal that everybo
turned for explanation and solace towards the most highly esteem
disciples, those who were supposed to know — especially to l
reassured that there was a profound meaning to it all, that everythin
fitted into the right outline of things, and that despite all appearance
the very best would be their part.

In the Indian family the eldest brother holds the highest position,
he is the head of the family and takes all important decisions. The
role of Eldest Brother in the Ashram was held by Nolini Kanta Gupta,
whose life had been closely associated with that of Sri Aurobindo
since their time in the prison of Alipore and who as a *sadhak* was
considered a paragon of the Integral Yoga. Therefore it was to him
that the disciples looked up for a message of hope and an explanation
of the inexplicable with which they were confronted. In the very first
days after the departure of the Mother, Nolini already had had a
message posted: 'The Mother's body belonged to the old creation.
It was meant to be the pedestal of the New Body. It served its purpose
well. The New Body will come. This is a test, how far we are faithful
to Her, true to Her consciousness. The revival of the body would
have meant revival of the old troubles in the body. The body troubles
were eliminated so far as could be done by Her while in the body
— farther was not possible. For a new mutation, a new procedure
was needed. "Death" was the first stage in this process.'[5]

In the issue of March 1974 of *Mother India* and simultaneously
in the April issue of *The Advent*, also an Ashram publication, another
text of Nolini appeared which would have far-reaching consequences.
Somebody from Canada had sent him the following quotation from
Sri Aurobindo: 'The physical nearness to the Mother is indispensable
for the fullness of the sadhana on the physical plane. Transformation
of the physical and external being is not possible otherwise.' Therefore the 'Canadian question' was formulated: 'How are we to interpret these words in the light of the Mother's recent passing? Does
this mean that a full transformation is no longer possible to the

perhaps what has happened is just a postponement of the work that she was doing on her own body.'⁶ One gets the impression that 'postponement' had become, in those dramatic and traumatic days, the magical consoling word in the conversations among the prominent disciples. For those involved in the effort of Sri Aurobindo and the Mother, it was taboo to talk about failure. 'Postponement' was a word which still allowed for some hope — especially after one had lived to see the passing of Sri Aurobindo and to what a miserable, pitiable shadow of her former self the Mother had been reduced, 'a pitiful picture of helplessness, if not even of absurdity.'⁷ (K.D. Sethna) As the hearts and the faith had been severely shaken, 'postponement' was a toffee on which the mind could suck and be appeased.

K.D. Sethna, as the editor of *Mother India* an important presence in the intellectual landscape of the Ashram, has accepted the postponement-thesis unconditionally and kept defending it through thick and thin. 'Wide-eyed amazement, dim-eyed despondence, cold-eyed scepticism, sharp-eyed opposition as well as calm-eyed acceptance have met our reasoned presentations of Nolini's brief pronouncement that the physical transformation, though not cancelled, has been postponed because of the Mother's giving up of her body ... The physical transformation can be considered either as a process or as an end-product. The end-product, the accomplishment of the body's supramentalization, may legitimately be taken as delayed in the sense of being put off for a future time or being deferred. The process cannot be so regarded: the Mother, whether physically present or not is constantly at work on her followers as well as, in a lesser degree, on the rest of mankind, and the new power that has become a factor in evolution is also pressing on to produce an effect in the world's surface-life. The process is postponed only in the sense of being retarded, slowed down.'⁸

And he writes: 'I am afraid the logic of their revelations [of Sri Aurobindo and the Mother] can conduct us only to one conclusion: the Mother has first to come back in whatever manner and stand before us physically transformed before we can reach the last stage of Sri Aurobindo's Yoga of Supramental Descent and Transformation ...'⁹ The physical absence of the Gurus is bound to postpone

482 • *Beyond Man*

the success of the disciples in this particular part of the Integral Yoga [i.e. the physical transformation]. The postponement will end not before one of the Gurus reappears in some fashion or the manifested Supermind and the Superman Consciousness start operating directly in the forefront of universal evolution.'[10] In the last part of the sentence, Sethna seems to leave a door ajar.

A Unanimous Conviction

From all this we may conclude that, according to those who were supposed to know, the Work of Sri Aurobindo and the Mother, because of the departure first of the one and then of the other, was not a failure although it looked like it; the last phase of the Work, the material supramentalization of the body of the Gurus, followed by that of the disciples, was only postponed ... for reasons nobody knew. Especially on this point K.D. Sethna reverts to shrill rhetoric, using expressions like 'the paradox of a victorious retreat,' 'her heroic fall,' 'conquering all while appearing to perish utterly,' 'a *reculer pour mieux sauter,*' 'a supreme strategic sacrifice,' and so on. He even compares the passing of the Mother to the passing of Sri Aurobindo, as if in the twenty-three intermediate years of the avataric *sadhana* nothing worthwhile had happened.

We could put this way of seeing to the test with a simple question: who has ever heard of an Avatar who had to come back to finish his work? Sethna is so hopeful to write that we may expect the return of the Mother 'perhaps even in one hundred years,' without giving any ground for this period of time, while in all known cases a lot more time has passed between the incarnations of the Avatars.

The basis of this way of seeing is the conviction that if not the body of Sri Aurobindo then surely the body of the Mother *should have been visibly transformed*, now, as the end-result of the on-going process of transformation in them. The documents leave not the slightest doubt about this ingrained conviction of the disciples.

For instance, consider Pranab again, in his talk of 4 December 1973: 'I am absolutely sure that if she [the Mother] had not the conviction that she would bring the Supramental Transformation to her present body, she would not have been able to do all the Great Work that she has done.'[11]

Then Sethna, in an article from November 1974: 'It is extremely improbable, if not absolutely impossible, that those who lived in close contact with the Mother from 24 November 1926 onward should have hopefully but erroneously waited to see the Mother's body completely transformed and that yet the Mother, knowing their minds, should not have unequivocally corrected their error but left it to them to discover it by studying her talks after she had left her body on 17 November 1973! There is not the slightest doubt that she allowed those [e.g., he himself] in close contact with her for forty-seven years to believe that she was striving with all her spiritual might to achieve complete transformation of her body.'[12]

Dyuman too expressed the same opinion. Dyuman had come to Pondicherry from Gujarat in 1923; since then, he had been serving Sri Aurobindo and the Mother personally, while at the same time managing the kitchen and the dining-room, thus having in fact the whole food-provision of the Ashram in his care. He was one of the six official trustees of the Ashram and was generally considered the example of 'the worker,' of the model practitioner of the karmayoga as an aspect of the Integral Yoga.

In February 1988, Dyuman had a conversation with a group of students of the Ashram school in front of his room, located in the central Ashram building a few steps away from the *Samadhi*. He talked to the youngsters about the history of the buildings they saw around them, about the cats the Mother had kept as a kind of experiment in evolution, and so on. Talking about the tomb itself, he said: 'Why the place was kept here from 1930, that she [the Mother] knew, though she was telling us, though Sri Aurobindo was telling us from 1920 that he would remain for ever and 24 November 1926 was declared the Day of Victory, and two days later was the Day of Immortality. The Mother brought down the Force of Immortality. But the Divine Grace has other ways. He left his body and the Mother decided to keep him in this Ashram at the centre ...'[13]

These statements by prominent and sincere disciples, who at the time of the passing of the Mother had been living for thirty-five,

forty-five or more than fifty years in the Ashram, unanimously proclaim the same, namely that Sri Aurobindo and the Mother had said
or let it be understood all along that they would not die, and that
the body in which they had incarnated also would be the body of
their supramental transformation. It is a unanimous conviction difficult to doubt at first sight by an outsider. What have Sri Aurobindo
and the Mother themselves said or written about the *immediate* aim
of their Yoga?

In an undated letter of Sri Aurobindo's from the *Letters on Yoga*,
we read: 'What we are doing, if and when we succeed, will be a
beginning, not a completion. It is the foundation of a new consciousness on earth ...' [14] In a letter from 31 July 1935, he writes: 'I am
not trying to change the world all at once but only to bring down
centrally something into it that it has not yet, a new consciousness
and power.' [15] He had already written in *The Synthesis of Yoga*: 'It
must be kept in mind that the supramental change is difficult, distant,
an ultimate change; it must be regarded as the end of a far-off vista;
it cannot be and must not be turned into a first aim, a constantly
envisaged goal or an immediate objective.' [16]

Had Sri Aurobindo perhaps spoken differently in the early
conversations preceding his seclusion? We can look this up in
A.B. Purani's *Evening Talks* which cover the period from 1920 to
1926. On this subject, we find for instance:

* 'Even I do not know the result [of my *sadhana*]. An indication
  I have received from within saying that it is going to be. Yet I
  myself do not know the end of my adventure. Very few in the
  past have followed this yoga and none has conquered the
  material plane. That is why it is an adventure into the Unknown.'
  (13 February 1923)
* 'We can make a beginning, afterwards it can be perfected.'
  (2 July 1926)
* 'It is perfectly possible that we may be able to make a beginning
  and that it will go on gradually developing in man.' (2 July 1926)
* 'This yoga is not a cut-out system. It is a growth by experience.'
  (21 August 1926)
* Question: 'Do you promise that the world of the Gods will

descend?' Sri Aurobindo's answer: 'I don't promise anything. "If the Supermind comes down," that is what I say.' (9 November 1926)

All this is in the line of what we have seen before, of the Vision and the Assurance which were given to Sri Aurobindo and then the working out of his *sadhana*, step after step in the Unknown, in the 'virgin forest' with all its insecurities and perils. Peter Heehs, at present probably the greatest expert on the life and works of Sri Aurobindo, therefore writes: '[Sri Aurobindo] did not look forward to full success in his lifetime. But he believed that whatever he accomplished would help in the eventual establishment of a divine life on earth, in a body, and not only in an insubstantial heaven or nirvana.'[17]

We must conclude that Sri Aurobindo cannot have been the source of the belief or conviction that he and the Mother would transform their material body supramentally. Might it be that the Mother had given cause for this opinion to be rife? Some of her statements in this context are as follows:

* 'Of course, if suddenly there were luminous apparitions and if the physical forms changed completely, I think that then even a cat or whatever would see it. But this will take time, it is not for all at once. It is not for all at once, it is for further on, for much later. Before that, many great things will happen which, note, are much more important than that [the visible transformation of the body]. For [the visible transformation of the body] is only the flower that opens. But before it opens, the principle of its existence must be present in the root of the plant.' (4 January 1956)

* 'If one follows the line of what Sri Aurobindo has written at the end, one sees very clearly that after what he has strewn ... (yes, that is like the rich seed of light) and after having said: "It is now that it will be realized," even while going on with his work, working precisely on the realization, he saw more and more all stages one had to go through. And the more he saw that, the more the portent of his words was: "Do not believe that you will arrive at the end all at once. Do not think that the way is an immediate miracle."

'And after having talked of the descent of the Supramental, he said that one had to prepare an *intermediary* between our present mental condition (even in the highest levels of the higher mind) and the supramental region. For he said that if one entered directly into the Gnosis, it would be such an abrupt change that the constitution of our physical state would not be able to stand it. An intermediary is necessary. Of this I am absolutely convinced by the experiences I have had. Two times it was a veritable seizure by the supramental world [of her physical body], and both times it was as if the body — truly the physical body — was going to be completely torn apart by what one could almost call the opposite of the condition.' (15 October 1961)

Be it noted that Sri Aurobindo has told explicitly and repeatedly: "My will is for now," but that every time he was talking about the descent, the establishment of the Supramental Consciousness on Earth, which would indeed take place in 1956. As we have seen elsewhere, he refused pertinently to be drawn into utterances about the working of the Supermind, consequently also about the how or when of the supramental transformation of the body. Another point is that nowhere, in not a single analysis by the disciples of the subject under consideration, the necessity of the apparition of intermediary beings is taken into account.

* '... the aim for which this body is alive, namely the first steps towards the supramental transformation ...' (3 April 1962, during the prelude of the great experience at that time.)

* 'It is evident that something is happening, but it is not something that has been seen and foreseen and that will be the accomplishment: it is *one* of the stages that is going to be realized, it is not the final result.' (31 December 1966)

* Satprem: 'One has the impression that if nothing miraculous happens in the sense people understand this, well, that it will take centuries.' — The Mother: 'But you have never hoped that it wouldn't take time?' Satprem: 'Well yes, of course.' — The Mother: 'But I have never believed that it could come quickly! ... If the divine Consciousness, the divine Power, the divine Love, if the Truth would manifest too quickly upon the Earth, the Earth would be dissolved!' (15 November 1967)

* 'We think that this, this appearance [the Mother points to her body] ... for the ordinary consciousness this seems to be the most important, but it is evidently the last that will change. And to the ordinary consciousness this is the last that will change because it seems to be the most important: it will be the surest sign [to the ordinary consciousness]. But it is not like that at all! It is not like that at all. It is the change *in the consciousness* — which has been effected — that is important. All the rest are side-effects ... When the body will be able to be visibly something different from what it is, one will say: "Aha, now the thing is done." This is not right: *the thing is done*. This [the change of the gross material body] is a side-effect.' (29 April 1970)

It would be difficult to keep asserting, taking into consideration quotations of this kind, that the Mother saw the transformation of her physical body as the goal of her *sadhana*. Besides, Sethna himself mentions the words of 'a co-disciple' who had written to him: 'I have searched everywhere in all the available writings but nowhere the Mother seems to have promised or given us even a remote hint that in the immediate present, at the present stage of evolution, in Her present body She was going to achieve the transformation of the entire physical being, including that of the external structure.'[18]

The inevitable conclusion from all this is that the conviction that the Mother had to or would transform her physical body was one of the 'Ashram legends,' as Sri Aurobindo called some of the opinions which had attached themselves like parasites to the stem of his teaching, even in the mind of some who were looked up to as the intellectual beacons. 'There are hundreds of wrong notions current in the Ashram,'[19] he wrote to Nirodbaran.

Legends and Myths

Nirodbaran himself, for instance, in his exceptionally confidential relation with Sri Aurobindo, formulates candidly one of the myths common in the Ashram in 1935. It has to do with the descent of Krishna in Sri Aurobindo's body on 24 November 1926. 'Datta seems to have declared that day that you had conquered sleep, food, disease and death. On what authority did she proclaim it then?' (The various versions of what Datta is supposed to have said on that occasion are mentioned elsewhere in this book.) Sri Aurobindo answers him: 'I am not aware of this gorgeous proclamation ... If all that was achieved on the 24th November 1926, what on earth remained to work out, and if the Supermind was there, what blazing purpose did I need to retire? Besides, are these things achieved in a single day?'[20]

A more recent instance is the still widely spread legend that Pondicherry was called Vedapuri (town of the Vedas) in olden times and that the central building of the Sri Aurobindo Ashram stands exactly on the spot where thousands of years ago the hermitage of rishi Agastya stood. In an article in *Sri Aurobindo Archives and Research* of April 1989, Peter Heehs has decisively proved that both assertions are based on the wrong interpretation of some findings by the French archeologist Gabriel Jouveau-Dubreuil. A pity, but it was too good not to be true.

One of the most wide-spread legends — closely connected with the expectation about the physical transformation of the body of Sri Aurobindo and afterwards of the body of the Mother — was, however, that the *sadhaks* and *sadhikas* by the fact of their acceptance as members of the Ashram had become immortal, just like their Gurus! As K.D. Sethna recollects: 'Psychologically, one of the most central facts of the early days [of the Ashram] was the conviction that complete divinisation of the physical being was not only an aim of Sri Aurobindo's Yoga but also a practical goal. "Supramentalisation" was clearly understood to include a complete change in the body itself. What is most significant is that by "body" was meant the physical instrument of even the sadhaks and not simply of the Master and the Mother ... In this context I remember some words of Amrita, one of the earliest sadhaks. He used to be often in my room. Once when he was there we heard the sound of a funeral passing in the street. In a whisper as if conveying a secret, he said: "I have the feeling that this will not happen to me." I did not raise my eyebrows in the least, for most of us who understood the originality of Sri Aurobindo's spiritual vision and his reading of the Supermind's implications could not help the expectation of a radical bodily change.'[21] (Amrita had been among the first followers of Sri Aurobindo; later on, he would become one of the secretaries of the Ashram. He was loved by everybody and had an ever ready sense of humour.)

In March 1935, Nirodbaran wrote to Sri Aurobindo: 'I firmly believed that death was impossible here ... You said, I hear, that you have conquered Death, not only personally, but for others as well.' Sri Aurobindo: 'I am unaware of having made any such statement. To whom did I make it? I have not said even that personally I have conquered it. All these are the usual Ashram legends ... The sadhaks have a habit of turning spiritual truths into crude downright statements of a miraculous kind which lead to many misunderstandings.'[22] The next day, Nirodbaran wrote: 'Amal* and myself firmly believe that those whom you have accepted [as disciples] are absolutely immune to death.'[23]

On 9 October 1936, Nirodbaran again brings up the subject: 'In [your] letter to me, there was a very high optimistic, almost a certain tone about the conquest of death. Now it appears that you no longer hold that view and say that death is possible because of the lack of a solid mass of faith [in the *sadhaks*] ...' Sri Aurobindo: 'In what does this change of views consist? Did I say that nobody could die in the Ashram? If so, I must have been intoxicated or passing through a temporary aberration ... Surely I never wrote that death and illness could not happen in the Ashram ... Conquest of death is something minor and, as I have always said, the last physical result of it [i.e. of the supramental change of consciousness], not the first result of all or the most important ... To put it first is to reverse all spiritual values.'[24]

It is important to illustrate the existence of certain legends among the Ashram population[25] because the legend of the physical transformation is related to the passing of the Mother in 1973. This was the last perceptible event in the epic of the Work of the double-poled Avatar Mothersriaurobindo; being the perceptible outward event, it places the interpretation of everything that preceded in a certain light.

---

* Amal Kiran was (and is) the Ashram name of K.D. Sethna.

To put it simply: the positive or negative interpretation of the passing of the Mother creates a positive or negative evaluation of the Work of the Avatar, a confidence that the Work either has been successful or has failed. If the 'postponement' is a fact, then practically speaking it means their work was a failure, whatever clamouring metaphors and other figures of speech one may use to cover up the fact. There is no known example of an Avatar who had to come back to finish his job. Asserting that the result of the physical transformation has been postponed is equal to wiping out all important intermediary stages like the establishment of the Supramental Consciousness in the Earth-atmosphere in 1956 and that of the instrumental Overmental Consciousness in 1969 — a fact that, just like the necessity of the appearance on Earth of transitory beings, never crops up in the reasonings of K.D. Sethna and like-minded commentators. Neither do they ever mention that Nolini Kanta Gupta must have revised his opinion about the postponement, as can be deduced from the fact that he testifies to the presence of the superman among us. It is worthwhile here to repeat the words of the great yogi Nolini was: 'Although we may not know it, the New Man, the divine race of humanity, is already among us ... It waits for an occasion to throw off the veil and place itself in the forefront.' If this is so, then nothing has been postponed and the supramental change-over is in full swing.

'The Radiance of a Thousand Suns ...'

The expectation that the very aged, ravaged body of the Mother would one day, as it were in the blink of an eye, be turned into a radiant divine body was an example of what Sri Aurobindo had called 'crude downright statements of a miraculous kind.' Surely, the coming about of the supramental world as a whole can be considered a miracle, but then a miracle of the kind by which the terrestrial substance of gravel and rock has become alive and started running about in the armadillo, flying in the crow and writing a letter in the bipedal human being. In most of the preceding parts of this book, we have been following the process of the new worldwide miracle, the greatest of them all, and we remember that Sri Aurobindo and the Mother have always stressed that the supramental manifestation, however miraculous, follows certain lines of development which are the continuation of the general evolutionary process.

The belief that the Mother suddenly would be supramentalized physically was the expectation of an 'unreasonable' miracle, totally contradictory to the many years of struggle and suffering spent by Sri Aurobindo and the Mother on the transformation of the evolutionary process. Sri Aurobindo had to remind his correspondents so often that the Avatar comes to work out processes which he himself, as the essential Divine, has built into the Creation. Were it not so, then the Creation would be a divine caprice, a *Lila* without rhyme or reason, and, considering the terrible suffering caused by it, a cruel joke.

How could the Mother all at once become a supramental Sun without gross matter being transformed to a sufficient degree in order to allow the functioning and even the presence of a supramental body? Every time she questioned the invisible but always present Sri Aurobindo about this, he answered: 'Not ready,' that terrestrial matter was not ready, even though he himself was working behind the veil to hasten its transformation.

The Mother has built the 'archetype' of the supramental body in the 'true physical' with her supramentalized cells. When the terrestrial substance will be sufficiently transformed to enable the functioning of a supramental body in it, that archetypal supramental body of hers can take shape in all those on Earth who are adequately prepared — in the ones from the supramental ship who set foot ashore, in the candidates of supermanhood, the mature souls present on Earth (*il y en a*, there are some), in the new men among us referred to by Nolini. And the first essays to work out supermanhood in the sufficiently transformed terrestrial substance will result in the formation of intermediary links between the human and the supramental beings, the *surhommes*. As the Mother said to Satprem in this connection: 'I would be very glad if it is somebody else, whoever it may be. I have not the least desire that it should be myself,' and: 'There is nothing in this body that even "aspires" to be that, which means that it is not its work.'[26]

Still nearer the end, the Mother said: 'We are — at best, at best — transitional beings ... The use of this body now is therefore simply: the Order of the Will of the Lord so that I may do as much preparatory work as possible. But [the transformation of this body] is not at all the goal ... The problem that keeps me occupied is to build that supramental Consciousness in a way that *that* may be the being. It is that Consciousness that must become the being ... Therefore all the consciousness that is in the cells must become grouped, organized, and form an independent conscious being. The consciousness that is in the cells must be gathered and organized, and form a conscious being that can be conscious of Matter and at the same time of the Supermind. This is what it is about. This is what is happening.'[27] These words date from April 1972. The Mother was constantly perfecting her 'archetypal' supramental body, which she had already repeatedly seen and which she would describe shortly afterwards.

Another fact never taken into account by the naïve belief in a visible supramental miracle in the Mother is that the Supermind is a Truth-Consciousness. To us this is merely a word; in reality it is an energy of which only nuclear power can give us some idea and 'compared to which the sun is a black spot.'[28] It was not for nothing that the physicist J.R. Oppenheimer, when witnessing the first nuclear explosion in the desert of Alamogordo, was reminded of the words of the *Bhagavad Gita*: 'If the radiance of a thousand suns were to burst into the sky, that would be like the splendour of the Mighty One.' One of the capacities of the Truth-Consciousness is that it automatically dissolves the Falsehood in all its forms. The Falsehood is the fundamental Ignorance, the Inconscient with its daughter the Subconscious, of whom all of us in our cells and the Earth in its matter are the children. (This is why by means of the supramental 'permeation' gross matter must be changed into refined, supramentalized matter.) Which means that the world as it is and the beings of the world as they are would be dissolved by a sudden contact with the unveiled supramental Force — for instance by the appearance of a supramental body; they would be dissolved as if by magic, they would simply vanish! 'The supramental Power is dangerous ... It is so powerful and so formidable, even in an infinitesimal quantity, that it may disrupt the whole established order,'[29] the Mother said. 'They don't even understand that this Vibration of Truth, if it would impose itself, would mean the destruction of all that — which means of themselves, of what they think is themselves.'[30] She was familiar with the supramental Force from experience and had feared more than once that it would destroy her body. And each time she then uttered her astonishment at the way everything was regulated with such a great accuracy.

A World for Crawling, a World for Flying

One can only conquer death when death makes no sense any more.[31]

—The Mother

So, what had actually happened on that 17 November? The answer can be found in the information we have discovered up to now. And it is a logical answer, or let us say an answer that stands to reason. It is not 'a cause for heartfelt pain' (Nirodbaran), but — and how could it be otherwise? — as grand and hopeful as everything that preceded and everything that inescapably must follow.

We could make the whole event of the departure of the Mother clear with a comparison she has used herself: the pupation of the caterpillar into the butterfly. When its time comes, the caterpillar withdraws into a cocoon which it builds around itself. In this cocoon the pupation takes place, a wonderful transformation resulting into a wholly different being: a butterfly. The process of pupation is one of the numerous inexplicable miracles invented by Nature millions of years ago. Can one say that the caterpillar dies in the cocoon? Can one say that the caterpillar has died when becoming a butterfly? The butterfly has originated in the body of the caterpillar, from the body of the caterpillar. The body of the butterfly is an (invisible and scientifically inexplicable) transformation of the body of the caterpillar. The caterpillar exists in the dimension of the crawling-world of the caterpillars; the butterfly exists in the dimension of the flying-world of the butterflies.

The human body of the Mother existed in the world of the humans, who are mental beings. Unseen by human eyes, the pupation, the transformation has taken place in the cells of that material body into a supramental body existing in a supramental world. The world of mental man is a world of darkness and ignorance, comparable to the crawling-world of the caterpillar; the supramental world is the flying-world of the colourful, light and winged butterfly, imperceptible to beings of the crawling-world and beyond the horizon of their interests.

The human being is seldom aware of the fact that his world is the result of his consciousness, of the manner in which he perceives and knows things. 'We exist within a formation,' the Mother said, a consciousness-formation which we might call 'the mental projection,' 'the veil of falsehood upon Truth.'[32] We are living in the one Unity, yes, because there is nothing else. But we have seen how, within the Unity, an evolutionary world has come into being having as its base the Ignorance, which is unconsciousness, blindness, endless division. We are on our way back towards the Unity-Consciousness which is the Supramental Consciousness. We are actually very near to it as it has been actively present in our world since 1956. But we are still being born as mental beings, as children of the Ignorance living under a magic spell, under the curse of the Ignorance, blind and so very vulnerable in our magic but to us quite realistic crawling-world. 'We are living in a consciousness of falsehood,' said the Mother. 'All substance of being in Space is a flowing sea not divided in itself, but only divided in the observing consciousness,' wrote Sri Aurobindo in *The Life Divine*. And the Mother said: 'There is a *constant* Reality, a *constant* Divine Order, and it is only the incapability to perceiving it which constitutes Disorder, the actual Falsehood.'[33] We do not experience the world as it is, we experience a distorted reproduction of the world, distorted by the way our mental consciousness functions. All is One, all is connected and coherent, all exists in Unity, but thereupon we project our pettiness, our impotence to comprehend the Unity, and we see everything as separate entities. We live in a pseudo-world, a false world — which outside of our consciousness nonetheless is the true world of the divine Unity.

'They forget that, if they stood face to face with the Divine himself when he is present on earth, with their gross physical mental they would fatally see nothing but what is gross,'[34] the Mother said. The human beings saw, of the complex being that was the Mother, only the human aspect — the human body and the apparently human way of behaving. Sure, the Mother was considered to be divine and by many also experienced as such in their heart, but who dared to contradict radically in their mind what their eyes were seeing? It was expected that the eye would see that the supramental transformation had succeeded, there, in that rosewood chair on the second floor in the Rue de la Marine in Pondicherry. All else, the theories and experiences the books and periodicals were full of, was excellent to meditate on and fantasize about, but, all the same, nobody could deny that that body there in that chair was deteriorating, that the Mother was continuously in dire difficulty, and that the end might be expected before long! She could not eat, was often dozing, forgot everything, sometimes lost consciousness, had one illness after the other or several at the same time, her heart was beating faintly and irregularly ... Those were facts, weren't they?

The caterpillar in the *sadhaks* was unable to see anything but the caterpillarhood of its own world. It remained not only limited but also mesmerized by its own manner of existence. The black magic of the habit of centuries had everybody believe that what was happening to the Mother was exactly what should happen, deterioration and death being the laws of Nature. Nobody can be prevented from imagining great things like the cancellation of death, a divine life upon Earth, an end to suffering, and what not — but, you see, Sri Aurobindo too had succumbed, even Sri Aurobindo. Therefore one could be practically certain that this lady, called the Mother, would also fail to succeed.

And the Mother was sitting there, fully supramentalized except for the outward appearance, with a Power which compelled her to cover herself with veil upon occult veil not to harm those who approached her. 'They are totally inconscient,' she said. 'It is all the time as if I am putting up a screen not to be really unbearable ... When that luminous Power comes, it is so compact, so compact; it gives the impression to be much heavier than Matter. It is being screened off, screened off, screened off [by herself], otherwise *unbearable.'*[35]

'This body is no longer a body within a skin,' she had said years ago. She talked about her 'apparent' body, the visible one, and about the other, the real one. The two bodies were existing at the same time, she said, in two still separate worlds. 'It is as if the physical had become double,' and we know that she experienced the subtle physical as much more real than the gross physical. Her visible body was like an empty shell, she said, with that enormous Power inside. 'It is as if a superhuman Power wants to manifest through millennia of powerlessness.'[36] 'These hands are not hands, my boy,' she once said to Satprem. What were they, then? One could say: instrumental fictions for her to be able to contact matter and human beings. So was her whole visible body. A kind of hologram by which the butterfly could still be present in the world of the caterpillars till the Work was completed.

The Residue

The material body of the Mother had been conceived and borne like the body of all of us. It was a child of Mother Earth, grown according to the procedure she had developed up to now. Therefore it carried, like all of us, the past of the whole evolution in itself 'like a residue of everything that had come before: of the mineral, the plant, the animal — of all that'. The base of all that, the substance from which it had developed and of which it consisted, was the Inconscient. 'Infrarational life still bears some stamp of the Inconscient in an underlying insensitiveness, a dullness of fibre, a weakness of vibratory response,'[37] Sri Aurobindo wrote. It had become clear to him, as we have seen, that a being with a body of this sort could effectively

---

* In English in the text.

acquire the supramental consciousness but that it was impossible to supramentalize the material substance of its body through and through. Although Sri Aurobindo had changed the 'programming' of the Inconscient at its base, by which it had become accessible to the Light, the evolutionary machine still kept turning; the complete supramental transformation was a realization still in the making for something like another three hundred years, according to his estimation. It was in the body of the Mother, the occult battlefield of the world, the interface between the Supermind and gross matter, that the process of transformation was taking place. She was supramentalized in all her layers of existence except in the lowest, the most external, the visible, the one consisting of gross matter: in the 'residue.'

Could this residue, this sediment of the Inconscient, also be transformed? 'What I don't know yet, what is not yet completely clear, is what will be the fate of this residue,'[38] the Mother said. Sri Aurobindo had said that it could *not* be transformed, 'he had said that nothing could be done with it,' the Mother said. She herself, on the contrary, thought from 1965 onwards that it could be transformed and she described on several occasions how the mental physical, the housing of the residue, got more and more involved in the process of transformation. But later she was again confronted with the untransformability of the mental physical:

* '[There is] a residue that remains unconscious ... What will be the fate of this residue? ... One has the impression that there is a waste product.' (15 June 1968)

* 'The substance of which we are built is not sufficiently purified, illumined, transformed — whatever, the words don't matter — to express the Supreme Consciousness without deforming it.' (25 September 1968)

* 'Only is rejected what does not exist according to Truth — everything that is not capable of transforming itself in the image of the psychic being and to become a part of the psychic being.' (1 July 1970)

'This body belongs to this, to the earth,'[39] the Mother said of her gross material body. 'There is what we might call the "inner" consciousness of the cells and which is fully, fully conscious, but there is something that remains like this,'[40] like a crust on the surface, untransformable. 'It will only be the untransformable residue that ... that really will be death.'[41]

The presence of this residue and the metaphor of the pupation of the caterpillar into the butterfly let us understand what happened on 17 November 1973. On the one hand, there was the Mother who had accomplished her avataric mission: 'The change has been accomplished. It will perhaps take centuries [before the supramental body becomes visible physically], but it has been accomplished.'[42] The butterfly had resulted from the pupation and existed as such. On the other hand, there was the gross material body that she had taken up again in 1962 to go all the way to the destined end; this human body was the most external, atavistic aspect of her being, the remainder from the past that would not be able to cross over into the refined substance of the future. This was the body of the caterpillar, visible to our caterpillar-eyes, which had undergone the terrible process of the pupation; this was what stayed behind — a thin, dry, but extremely resistant covering 'not thicker than an onion peel,' representing the untransformable element of the cells.

Did the Mother die on 17 November 1973?

Can one say that the caterpillar dies? It lives on in the butterfly. Nothing has died there except an old manner of existing. What to the comprehension of the caterpillar-world is death is in fact a transmutation of life into another manner of existence. The corpse was the residue, a kind of dry membrane consisting of the elements which were untransformable and belonged to the caterpillar-world. It was because of the 'caterpillar-body' that the Mother still remained visible and addressable for the 'caterpillar world,' that she could work upon that world to transmute as much as possible of its substance into the substance of the 'butterfly-world.'

To die means to leave one's material body. The Mother existed simultaneously in two material bodies, one in gross matter, one in the true physical, supramental matter. The supramental body is by definition immortal, for it is divine. Conclusion: it is impossible to say that the Mother has died. She has laid down the untransformable residue, the pupa that was her gross material body, but she goes on living as concretely as before in her much more real and much more material supramental body. What was death to caterpillar-eyes was in fact the final phase in the Work of the humanly embodied Avatar, the Work of the Mother and Sri Aurobindo.

On 5 December 1950, Sri Aurobindo entered willingly and consciously into death, but in the process he transferred the part his already supramentalized substance materially into the body of the Mother.

On the night of 12 April 1962, the Mother died but took up her body again.

On 17 November 1973, the Mother laid down the untransformable remainder of her gross material body but went on living materially, for ever, in her archetypal supramental body built up by her with the supramentalized true physical substance.

The same kind of substance is now constantly being formed in gross matter on Earth by the process of 'permeation.' Once the substance of the Earth is changed to a sufficient degree, the prepared souls descending on the planet will build for themselves a body with the changed substance after the example of the archetypal supramental body worked out by the Mother, and the first being(s) of the new species will be visibly present on planet Earth (and in the cosmos). 'The transformation may up to a point even take place without one being conscious of it. It is said, isn't it, that now there is a great difference, that when the human being arrived the animal did not even have the means to be aware of it. Well, I say that it is exactly the same, that in spite of all the human being has realized, it does not have the means [to be aware of the arrival of the new being]. Certain things may happen, but it will know about them only much later, when "something" in it will be sufficiently developed to become aware of it.'[43]

Possible Solutions

The Mother has said several times that it was her task to make possible the transition from the one world into the other, to build the bridge, to carry out the transfer of power, to be the transparent link in order that the supramental Power may penetrate into matter and make matter suitable as building stuff for the body of the supramental beings. The Mother has not been the cause of a postponement or a delay of the process of supramentalization; on the contrary, in her love for humanity she has probably gone much farther than was originally foreseen in the Plan, or at least as far as possible. Everything Sri Aurobindo had intended to obtain was realized in 1956. At that time, the Mother asked for an unmistakable sign that she had to go on with her task in her earthly body. The fact that she has gone on with it lets us assume that the sign was indeed given to her. In 1962, she confirmed that the Work was done: 'What had to be done is done!' Nonetheless, she took her body again to continue working on the Earth. The result of this third phase was the establishment of the Consciousness of the Superman on Earth and shortly afterwards the realization of her supramental body, in a 'true physical substance,' as the mould of all future supramental bodies in what will then have become the true physical substance of the Earth. These are the facts found in the documents.

That an end could come to the existence of the gross material body of the Avatar has always been a possibility as far as the Mother was concerned. (This is a strong argument against the expectation of the visible supramental transformation of her body.) We remember what she wrote to her son André in the first years of the Ashram about the rights of succession. Dyuman told that the place of the tomb in the courtyard of the central Ashram building had been reserved since 1930. In December 1950, the Mother had a space built for herself in Sri Aurobindo's *Samadhi*. After the manifestation of the Supermind in 1956, the Mother thought that she might perhaps leave her body. Already in 1961, she had taken all necessary precautions in case she would depart and the persons concerned had received relevant instructions ...

The Avatar had come to establish the Supramental Consciousness upon the Earth. He has gone as far as possible and maybe farther than possible to hasten the first result of that manifestation: the formation of the visible supramental being upon the Earth. That at a certain moment his own terrestrial instrument, exhausted and worn out by the Work, would have to be discarded has always been held to be the normal way of things by the Avatar himself.

Many disciples, not to say all, have been painfully moved by the deterioration that the Mother's body was subject to towards the end of her life. Courageous in their convictions and faith, they were severely put to the test by the sight of that stooped and tortured body, apparently ever more suffering of the pitiful symptoms of very old age. This was the fundamental mistake. We have seen how the Mother underwent even the harshest suffering with a cry of pain and simultaneously of ecstasy. 'This is no longer a body in a skin,' she said to Satprem. 'Each cell is totally conscious.' To caterpillar-eyes the caterpillar-appearance, however, was completely different and all have remained mesmerized by that appearance despite their faith: the Mother was mortally ill; she went downhill fast; death was — alas, alas — inevitable. What the Mother published in the passages of her conversations in the *Bulletin* was of little use. She tried to make herself understood by coining expressions like 'dying without dying,' 'a necessity to stay but without staying,' 'not dying, but the body may be dissolved' ... 'The body deteriorates in a forward direction,' she said in a statement at first sight bizarre but so very significant: her material body was being dissolved not backwards towards a death in the night of the Inconscient but, as a result of its transformation, forwards into the supramental world. Death, supposedly the ever present companion of man, had ceased to exist for her, for she had a permanent, immortal body consisting of permanent supramental matter.

The negative opinion of the disciples in 1973 is understandable. The published passages in the *Bulletin* were neither frequent nor extensive, and difficult to place in the right context because their tone and even their terminology were so different from 'Sri Aurobindo's system of yoga,' not to speak about their content. The *Agenda* as a whole would be published only years later (the first part in 1978), in the original French and with introductions, annotations and foot-notes by a Satprem violently inimical to the Ashram. Who, in the presence of the harrowing tangibility of the signs of deterioration in the body of the Mother, had the faith and especially the insight to dare and look behind what his eyes were seeing? And the Mother herself had said some of those things ...

She spoke about the oppressing terror which suddenly took hold of her body without any apparent reason. It was the existential anguish of a personal, self-centered, humanly egoistic way of existing, of the body's fighting to stay alive, to remain itself; it was a way of existence in a death-struggle. 'Suddenly such a horror of death.' One should not hurry to put her body in a coffin and into the tomb, she said. 'It will know that. It is conscious. The cells are conscious.' She asked 'the Lord' to be warned when the time had come. And then again: 'Isn't it strange, I ask myself: "Does the Lord want that I go?" And I am completely in agreement, *quite willing** ... But does He want that I stay on? ... No answer. There is no other answer than: "Transformation." '[44] She was the Handmaid of the Lord, unto her it would be according to his word — from the beginning right through to the end. '*Ce que Tu veux.*'

As Mother-in-the-sadhana she did not know whether and eventually how it would end. 'To tell the truth, it does not keep me occupied very much.' Several possibilities presented themselves to her, some of them probably reminiscences from previous lives. One of those possibilities she dictated: 'It is possible that this body, because of the demands of the transformation, enters into a state of trance that has the appearance of being cataleptic. No doctors, by all means! This body must be left in peace. And do not be in a hurry neither to announce my death or to give the government the right to intervene. Keep me carefully protected from all kinds of deterioration that may come from outside — infection, poisoning, and so on — and have an unflagging patience. It may last days, perhaps weeks and even more, and you will have to wait patiently for me to come naturally out of that state when the work of the transformation will be accomplished.'[45] (14 January 1967)

Afterwards, a lot of noise has been made because of this statement. For the body of the Mother was brought downstairs and laid out in

---

* In English in the text.

the meditation hall no more than seven hours after her official passing away — a body that, indeed, still seemed to be in intense concentration. Two days afterwards, it was put into the *Samadhi*. Had those responsible thrown her instructions to the winds? Had they in their haste broken off the cataleptic trance and therefore spoiled the definitive transformation of the Mother's body?

That the Mother has dictated those words and that later on she has referred to them a couple of times is, of course, a matter of fact. One should however consider that she herself had said that there were 'all kinds of possibilities' to achieve the transformation of the body, and also: 'The highest part of the consciousness [hers] is clearly in favour of the fact that this trance be not necessary.' (18 January 1967) One should not forget either that the Mother has afterwards seen several other possibilities to form the supramental body.

In October 1967, for instance, she said, in connection with a woman who had died in the Ashram, that it was *normal* that the material consciousness of the body cells of that woman had left her body together with the inner being, 'and this means that everything the cells have gained is not lost.' It was the answer to her question of some time earlier whether, at the time of death, nothing but dust remains of the cells and all the sadhanic work has therefore been in vain. Once she had said: 'Suppose I leave my body tomorrow; this body will revert to dust — not immediately but after some time — and everything I have done for these cells will be of no use at all.'[46] This did not seem to be true any longer.

For in March 1969, she also said: 'That consciousness [of the superman which had manifested on 1 January of the same year] has a fantastic imagination! It makes me see all kinds of fantastic possibilities of what will happen in the future.' One of these possibilities was that the transformed cells of her body 'would gather *within* to form a new body with a higher matter than the usual one.' 'It was so interesting that I have been considering that this morning in every detail.'

Some days before, she had said: 'The body-consciousness has become at once individualized and independent, which means that it can enter into other bodies and there feel absolutely at ease ... This changes altogether the attitude of the body towards the solutions; you see, there is no longer any attachment [to life] or sense of disappearance [because of death], for the corporeal consciousness has become independent. And this is very interesting. It means that in any physical substance which is sufficiently developed to receive it, it can manifest itself.'[47] The supramentalized consciousness of the Mother's cells was able to pass into all sufficiently prepared bodies!

But the question about the dissolution of the cells and their return to dust kept coming back: 'All this work of transformation of the cells, of the consciousness in the cells, seems to have been wasted since the body will disintegrate.' This time, the (inner) answer was not to be misunderstood, doubted or forgotten: 'There is a way, which is to prepare within oneself before death a body with all the trans- formed, illumined, conscious cells — to assemble and form them into a body with the maximum number of conscious cells. Once this is completed, the consciousness enters this body and the other one [the gross material body] can dissolve, it doesn't matter any more.'[48] Considering everything we have seen, this is indeed what has hap- pened: the supramental body has been formed within — the Mother has seen and described it — and the gross material body, which had served as the cocoon, was put off, it did not matter any more.

One is reminded of the fact that the central process of the trans- mutation is the growth of the supramental consciousness in and of the cells, by which the transmuted cells are divinized in the fullest sense of the word. For the equation Matter = Energy = Conscious- ness can as well be turned around: Consciousness = Energy = Matter. In the case of a supramental transmutation, the adjective 'supramental' is added to each term of the equation. The supramentalized Consciousness in the cells of the Mother became supramental Energy and supramental Matter; the micro-universe of every cell became universalized and a part of the whole supramental body, the cell itself containing the whole. In the infinity of what is divine, each part is equal to the whole and the whole is equal to each part. The difficulty to understand the transformation of the body of the Mother and therefore the Integral Yoga has two reasons. The first is that we cannot conceive that a cell may really acquire the divine

Unity-Consciousness, that it can be divinized and become the Divine, and the second reason is that the Unity-Consciousness exists concretely in its own substance, which is a supramental substance.

Kireet Joshi writes in his book *Sri Aurobindo and the Mother*: 'When Sri Aurobindo left his body, the accumulated result of all his physical consciousness was transmitted to Mother's body, and thus there was no waste. But now, apart from Mother's body, there was no other body which was so developed that it could receive, if Mother left her body, the accumulated result of her physical consciousness. This was a formidable problem. But as we see from what she said, this problem was now solved. Even if she left her body, the work would not be spoilt, there would be no waste. The work would continue.'[49]

The Entourage

The Mother's entourage has been blamed in several quarters for the way her body was treated after her heart stopped beating. As mentioned above, there are some who have blamed those who assisted her day and night in the most difficult years of having spoilt the process of transformation. This is not an imputation to be passed over lightly. It goes without saying that what is at stake here is not the agreeable or less agreeable character of the persons involved, but something of much greater importance.

After the crisis of 1962, the Mother said of her assistants: 'This body has been delegated to three persons, who have taken care of it marvellously, with ... — really, I was constantly full of admiration — with an abnegation and a care, oh, admirable! And all the time I was saying to the Lord: "Lord, really, You have arranged all the conditions in an absolutely marvellous way, unimaginable, all the material conditions so that everything necessary was brought together, and You have put near me people above all praise." They have had a very difficult time during at least a fortnight, very difficult. [This body] was a sort of rag, you know. They had to think of everything, to make all decisions, to take care of everything. And they have kept it very well, very well indeed.'[50] Her assistants in 1973 were, with the exception of Vasudha who had been replaced by Kumud, the same.

Time and again she expressed her admiration about the way everything was being arranged up to the smallest details, in the world generally and in connection with her body and *sadhana* in particular. 'How wonderfully everything is being arranged,' she said, and: 'The life of this body is a miracle.' On 28 June 1972 she said: 'Those near me must have a certain attitude towards me, they must take some precautions. You see, they must think, they must believe certain things to act as they have to, otherwise they would not act [as they have to] ... Everything is arranged up to the smallest detail. It is not foreseen as we foresee things in our ordinary consciousness: it is the Force that EXERTS PRESSURE and that produces the desired result — I would almost say: by whatever means, by whatever means necessary.'[51]

How, then, can one still talk about errors and mistakes where the Mother was concerned? We have seen that in the Unity-Consciousness, in which we are burrowing our tunnels like blind moles, there are no errors or mistakes possible, as there are none in all that concerns the Avatar, his Work and the consequences of his Work. If we ourselves have a psychic being that guards us through all so-called good and all so-called evil, how much more the Great Mother must have protected that so vulnerable and so often attacked material body of hers. How could the Yoga of the Evolution, accelerated by the dynamic presence and the labour of the Avatar, have been ruined by a mistake or an idiosyncrasy of a human being?

And there are those last six months about which we know nothing except what some human eyes have seen. 'The Mother remained practically the whole time with her eyes closed,' Pranab said. It is absolutely essential that we wipe out in our mind the picture of a little old lady who was suffering terribly and was fast nearing the end. Then as before she was the Avatar in his *sadhana* in which every moment was a kaleidoscope of experiences in space and time, and in many spaces and times, but particularly focused on the body of the Earth. To Mona Sarkar the Mother told how she had prepared the lives of all her children, of all those who were tuned to her, for their whole future. In an identical way she has prepared the body of the Earth as a whole for the future. In the seed planted by the supramental Avatar, the fully grown tree of the Kingdom of God on Earth is present.

All have made the same all too human error and, despite their belief in the divine presence of the Mother, have gone on considering that battered body of hers as a human reality. Even on 31 March 1973, after all those years of conversations, Satprem still asks her: 'Are you active, or are you simply in — [in trance, withdrawn]?' And the Mother answers quite trenchantly: 'Yes, I'm active. But what do you actually mean? ... I'm active!' — 'For instance, when you are within, when you are in an inner state ...' — 'But I act then much better than ... It looks as if I am within, but it is not so. Everybody is making the same mistake ... When I am in concentration like that, it is not because I am within, it is because I am in another consciousness ... No, you are trying to translate this mentally, but it is impossible, impossible. One must enter into this consciousness and ... and then one knows how it is. But there is no "active" and "passive," "within" and "without." All that has been replaced by something else that I cannot express ... I don't have the words for it.' And she stopped trying to talk.

All of us would probably have committed the same mistake seeing that apparent impotence, the twitching of that body, that apparent decay. But that was the Great Mother and the supramentalized Mother nonetheless — except for the body of the caterpillar with that kind of membranous residue that was not nice to look at.

'Mother made an effort at a complete transformation of the body, although she had no assurance whether this goal could be reached or not. The effort went up to the extreme point of acuteness; that effort had long ago become the effort of the body of the earth; that effort continues. Mother had said that it would require three hundred years to bring about the transformed body. She had also spoken of the need to follow the rule of several intermediate bodies as in the case of the evolution of man in succession of the chimpanzee. That work is on, and there is no obstacle. There is continuity; in that continuity all the bodies are involved; the body of each one of us is in the cauldron of transformation. This is the cosmic yoga which none can escape and in which salvation and realisation are at once physical and collective.'[52] Thus Kireet Joshi concludes his book on Sri Aurobindo and the Mother. In the light of what we have seen ourselves, we cannot but endorse his conclusion.

The Certitude

> *... like a sword of Light, intangible, the Certitude ...*[53]
> —The Mother

In one's mind's eye one stands again before the laid out body of the Mother in the meditation hall of the Ashram. One stands again near the *Samadhi*, now opened to receive her body too. And one hears that voice again.

A new world is born, is born ...

Nature has accorded her collaboration ...

There are some who have gone ashore and who are already supramentalized in parts of their body ...

This new substance is now generally spread in the atmosphere of the Earth ...

What is won remains won ...

The certitude that what had to be done IS DONE *...*

There is such a certitude that it is already like that, but seen from the other side ...

The foundations of the new world are being established ...

It is impossible that a change somewhere, a change towards perfection, would not have its repercussions on the whole Earth ...

As if something has been established that is unshakable ...

As far as the Earth is concerned, we have turned the corner ...

It is the miracle of the whole Earth ...

The fact is certain — it is not a possibility but a fact ...

I am certain that it is happening now; we have not reached the end, but we are on the other side ...

The consciousness of this new race is active on the Earth ...

The change has taken place, the physical is able to manifest the Truth ...

Some supermen are needed — there are some ...
I have seen my new body; it is a supramental body ...
This really is a new world ...

When the Mother's material body was lowered into that tomb in the inner courtyard of the central Ashram building, there was sobbing, and crying, and lamenting. Twenty-three years earlier she had said that crying because of Sri Aurobindo's departure was an insult to him and to his Work. Now the same petty human behaviour was being repeated, caused by a small-minded understanding, while the laying down of that body was the symbol of the success of her Work. Nothing has gone wrong and nothing has been postponed — or nothing is true of what the Mother and Sri Aurobindo have said. What they have accomplished is totally new on Earth; it has to be judged according to new norms and requires a new kind of insight. It is worthwhile to make the effort and to open oneself for this new vision because — if it is true — it is about the world of tomorrow and the meaning of the dawning millennium, and, far beyond that millennium, about the Great Meaning which lets us look ahead with confidence. *On regarde là où on veut aller* — one keeps the eye fixed on the aim.

'When an Avatar comes, he comes to fulfill a certain purpose,'[54] Sri Aurobindo said.

The Mother talked about the descent of those 'polarized forms of consciousness,' meaning the Avatars, and she said: 'They always come on earth with a well-defined purpose and for a special realization, with a mission decided, determined before their incarnation.'[55]

Sri Aurobindo has said so many years ago: 'I know with absolute certitude that the supramental is a truth and that its advent is in the very nature of things inevitable. The question is as to the when and the how. That also is decided and predestined from somewhere above; but it is here being fought out amid a rather grim clash of conflicting forces. For in the terrestrial world the predetermined result is hidden and what we see is a whirl of possibilities and forces attempting to achieve something with the destiny of it all concealed from human eyes. This is, however, certain that a number of souls have been sent to see that it shall be now ... My faith and will are for the now.'[56]

The Supermind has manifested and is present and active in the Earth-atmosphere; the supramental body has been formed in the true physical substance and is ready to appear in terrestrial matter when this matter will be sufficiently refined; in the meantime, the Supramental Consciousness is directing the great Turn-about and forming the first transitional beings between animal man and the supramental new species.

The Great Change in evolution is happening around us and within us, whether we want it or not.

Epilogue

THE SUN FOR EVER

> *At present mankind is undergoing an*
> *evolutionary crisis in which is*
> *concealed a choice of its destiny.*[1]
> — Sri Aurobindo

BEGINNING WITH the Renaissance, a period of new awakening started which has accelerated history and is unifying the Earth. From that time onwards, the New Era was growing unperceived, like a child in the womb; the twentieth century has been the century of the birth, of the fruition of the seed that, so many centuries earlier, had been implanted by the representatives of the 'New Knowledge.' Like every birth, the coming to light of what was before a hidden potentiality has been a miracle, happening all of a sudden (a century is but an instant in the long march of evolution) and in great pain. Eighty years ago, Sri Aurobindo commenced his *Synthesis* with the words: 'We are in an age, full of the throes of travail, when all forms of thought and activity that have in themselves any strong power of utility or any secret virtue of persistence are being subjected to the supreme test and given their opportunity of rebirth. The world to-day presents the aspect of a huge cauldron of Medea in which all things are being cast, shredded into pieces, experimented on, combined and recombined either to perish and provide the scattered material of new forms or to emerge rejuvenated and changed for a fresh term of existence.' (*The Synthesis of Yoga*, p. 1)

We, humans, experience a linear time, measured out by our mental consciousness in a global Time, which in the Unity-Consciousness is a harmonious coexistence of the various time-experiences of the various forms of consciousness. The spectacular twentieth century with the dawning awareness of the unity of the one Earth was foreseen long before Leonardo da Vinci,* as long before Giordano Bruno, Johannes Kepler, Erasmus, Mercator, Vesalius, Christiaan Huygens and Galileo Galilei the coming had been foreseen of the being that would be the fulfillment and at the same time the surpassing of man. None can tell why this had to happen now, as our notions of the development of humanity and of her true past are much too limited.

We situate the origin of civilization 12,000 years ago while most probably civilizations were already there 120,000 years ago, now buried under the sands of Sahara and Gobi or sunk in the waters of the oceans, but still alive in the collective memory of humankind. According to Sri Aurobindo 'not a one hundred thousandth part' of what has happened in human history, and at what we ourselves have been present so often, has been conserved in the memory of humanity. The Mother told the children of the Ashram that the civilization of Atlantis had been much more advanced than our own, not only on the occult but also on the technical level.

Edgar Cayce, 'the sleeping prophet,' said in the beginning of the Forties that almost all prominent figures at that time were reborn Atlants. This might be an explanation of the revival of the theory of the master race and the inferior races — as it might be of the spirit of technical inventiveness producing at an amazing pace what was perhaps being remembered from times long past: telecommunication, independently functioning fast vehicles, flying machines, television, radar, rockets, death rays and bombs for mass destruction, space vehicles, machines imitating the functioning of the brain ... All this machinery is still in its first stages, which is the reason why it is so immensely complicated and in its complexity easily vulnerable and

---

* 'What Leonardo da Vinci held in himself was all the new age of Europe on its many sides.' (Sri Aurobindo)

often unreliable. 'The Earth is more and more charged with forces originating from ever higher regions (to our consciousness), which means that their action is faster and faster and that they give more and more the feeling of instantaneity,'[2] the Mother said.

'Humanity has been waiting for centuries and centuries for this moment. It has come,'[3] she said. 'It is a step for which the whole of evolution has been a preparation,'[4] wrote Sri Aurobindo. We have the privilege of being present at it, but few are aware of this privilege and still fewer appreciate it or profit from being alive during this unprecedented moment in full awareness, although their number is increasing throughout the world. Deep down, most people are very confused. No philosophy offers them an outlook or intellectual support any more; the great religions are for the most part nothing but backward mammoth organizations; matter itself keeps escaping the grasp of science and technology suffers from the syndrome of gigantism, its machines being no longer in proportion with the psychological and even economical means of human kind. Astronauts and cosmonauts? Fearful explorers in the garden of planet Earth. A Unified Theory that will explain it all, matter, the cosmos, the human being and God? But what is the psychological wisdom we have gained from Einstein's famous formula? And how do we arrive at a unified theory when it does not take into account all the essential factors of Existence except matter, and this too only quantitatively described?

The first articles and books have already been published and thousands more will appear about all these subjects and, fundamentally, about the consternation of man on the threshold of the Unknown. Not only 1 January of the year 2000 is such a threshold: man has always stood on the threshold of the Unknown because it is a feature of his own mental consciousness which he cannot escape, except by a transformation of that consciousness which would take him beyond himself.

In this book, we have seen that such a transformation of consciousness has taken place in Those who were sent for it and that it is transpiring in humanity as a whole. 'We are at one of those moments Sri Aurobindo called "the hour of God," ' the Mother wrote, 'and the evolution has acquired an accelerated and intensified movement.'[5]

The Hour of God

'The Hour of God' is one of the many texts by Sri Aurobindo that was found somewhere in a notebook after his death. It dates from 1918 or thereabouts and must be quoted here, at the end of the curve of the work of the modern Avatar and at the beginning of its manifest elaboration in the imminent millennium.

'There are moments when the Spirit moves among men and the breath of the Lord is abroad upon the waters of our being, there are others when it retires and men are left to act in the strength or the weakness of their own egoism. The first are periods when even a little effort produces great results and changes destiny, the second are spaces of time when much labour goes to the making of a little result. It is true that the latter may prepare the former, may be the little smoke of sacrifice going up to heaven which calls down the rain of God's bounty.

'Unhappy is the man or nation which, when the divine moment arrives, is found sleeping or unprepared to use it, because the lamp has not been kept trimmed for the welcome and the ears are sealed to the call. But thrice woe to them who are strong and ready, yet waste the force or misuse the moment; for them is irreparable loss or a great destruction.

'In the hour of God cleanse they soul of all self-deceit and hypocrisy and vain self-flattering that thou mayst look straight into thy spirit and hear that which summons it. All insincerity of nature, once the defence against the eye of the Master and the light of the ideal, becomes now a gap in thy armour and invites the blow. Even if thou conquer for the moment, it is the worse for thee, for the blow shall come afterwards and cast thee down in the midst of thy triumph. But being pure cast away all fear; for the hour is often terrible, a fire and a whirlwind and a tempest, a treading of the winepress of the wrath of God; but he who can stand up in it on the truth of his purpose is he who shall stand; even though he fall, he shall rise again; even though he seen to pass on the wings of the wind, he shall return. Nor let wordly prudence whisper too closely in thy ear; for it is the hour of the unexpected, the incalculable, the immeasurable. Mete not the power of the Breath by thy petty instruments, but trust and go forward.

'But most keep thy soul clear, even if for a while, of the clamour of the ego. Then shall a fire march before thee in the night and the storm be thy helper and thy flag shall wave on the highest height of the greatness that was to be conquered.'[6]

We are All Amateurs Again

Birth is a moment of crisis. The twentieth century has been a single crisis from beginning to end. The Mother even said that all wars in the twentieth century have been a single war. They were part of the process of mutation by which the Earth is growing more and more conscious of itself. Humanity is essentially one, in origin and destination; what matters is that it again becomes conscious of this unity and succeeds in living up to it effectively.

Not many are aware of the forces which have been at work in the past one hundred years or so. At the very beginning of this book, the question was asked if the history of humanity, for instance in the twentieth century, could happen in interaction with one or two Beings. This question was answered in the affirmative if the Being(s) involved is an Avatar, this time a complete, double-poled one. The whole twentieth century can be read as the dialectical process of the action of, and the counteraction against, the Force this double Avatar embodied and which he introduced into the earth-atmosphere. 'Night itself carries in it the burden of the Light that has to be,'[7] (Sri Aurobindo) — and to a New Era the old one is always the night.

The Old Order is an established world, worked out in the greatest measure possible and — when the New Order presents itself — exhausted. Western Man realizes too little the degree to which the world is a complex structure, a balanced whole of forces, invisible but therefore not less real; Eastern Man still knows that, but he has let this authentic feeling be stultified by worn-out forms of thought and superstition. We have seen the important role the hostile forces play in the world people consider their own. The hostile forces dominate and govern this world of Ignorance in which the human beings are as blind and powerless as marionettes. They have been permitted to do so by the Supreme Authority, for whom everything exists and moves within the Unity-Consciousness, this evolutionary world included. Our world is a materialized, elaborated gradation of evolution, and in the present stage the hostile forces, all of them offspring of the Four *Asuras*, still play their indispensable and irreplaceable role.

Seen from a distance, all this is a sort of dismal fairy tale, 'The Lord of the Rings' but on a cosmic scale. To our experience, however, it is a raw, painful reality of which all our limitations and miseries are the outcome. Through it all, we carry the Divine in us, whom we are in essence; but our consciousness is veiled and our forces totally inadequate. Yesterday was unsatisfactory, today is a problem, tomorrow is an intimidating uncertainty. The presence of the lower vital forces, those of the diabolical kind, has become much more widespread because of the wars. War is hell for us but it is an amusement park for those beings, and who will chase them away once they have, in their insatiable selfishness, taken possession of something? Their actions are obvious in all newspapers, they grin, dance and romp on all television screens: manslaughter and murder, shameless and on a large scale, prostitution and pornography, bestial treatment of women and children, corruption, lying, undisguised and aggressive egoism, the hypocrisy of greatness and holiness ... Yes, surely, all that was there formerly too, but rarely so widespread, on so large a scale and so openly as at present. And now there is something in man that knows better, but because of this profounder awareness the enjoyment of evil seems to be amplified. Exponents of evil are being exalted as heroes. Yesterday is long ago, today is a spasm of self-gratification, tomorrow is for afterwards.

The *Asura* of Falsehood, alias the Lord of Nations, knows that his hour has struck. 'The Asura is unleashing all his fury, just like somebody who expects that he will disappear.'[8] He has prepared an ideal terrain for himself: colossal problems caused by a colossal population increase and combined with a colossal shortage of food, energy and living space, together with a colossal pollution, intensified by a colossal insecurity taking refuge in a colossal inflation of the ego of the individual, the race, the nation, the religious conviction. The world is on the boil; the problems are insoluble; everything creaks and swirls, foams and roars, everywhere. One has to climb very high to be able to look over it and to see the sense of the whole. The vision of Sri Aurobindo and the Mother is probably the only platform that is high enough.

History shows that the birth of something new always creates a period of confusion and bewilderment. Krishna was on Earth at the time of the war of the *Mahabharata*; before him, the Avatar Rama had to do battle with the asuric Ravana of Lanka and his legions; around the Mediterranean and especially in the Middle East the time of Christ was a whirlpool of races, cultures, religions and sects. Every Avatar had a worldwide influence, for his embodiment was intended as a progress for the entire humanity even when this humanity knew little or nothing of it; for the world in former times consisted of many separate worlds, and it could take a long time before an event of global importance penetrated from the one into the other.

This time, and from the very start, the intention of the avataric incarnation was humanity and the world as a whole. Nobody yet lives outside the ongoing process of transformation, there is no escape from it. The Earth has grown ripe for it. Sri Aurobindo and the Mother represented, even through the cultures they had been born in, the one Earth. To them, the tension, the fermentation, the confusion, the complexity of the historical scene of the twentieth century were an unmistakable sign of an all-encompassing Change in progress. 'I am coming to the conclusion that there must be a great power, probably a transforming power, in the extreme tension of the circumstances,' the Mother said. 'This always reaches a point, a point of such tension and complexity that, if one did not have this inner certitude, it would quite simply indicate the catastrophe, the sudden reversal. And it is always when things have reached such a point that everything changes — not before, not one minute before.'[9]

She therefore wrote: 'The hours before the dawn are always the darkest. The servitude just before freedom comes is the most painful of all.'[10] The events have to develop all the way up to the ultimate point if the sudden reversal, the sudden breakthrough of the ray of light in the night, has to become possible. This is a little known law of nature. Pregnancy reaches the point of impossibility for the body of the mother just before birth. The seed reaches the point of impossibility just before it bursts and makes new life grow. The caterpillar reaches the point of impossibility as a caterpillar just before it spins itself into a cocoon and becomes a butterfly. Everywhere we find that at the point of impossibility a crisis erupts, often resembling death or close to death, to make the new life possible. Thus it becomes clear that every life-process, every process of mutation or transformation has to progress to the point of impossibility if the mutation or transformation really is to have a Sense in the whole of processes designed by the Divine for the elaboration of evolution. A partial effort, a góing of the way up to somewhere halfway, would be a sort of a sham event, a caricature of the profound meaning of things whereby the Creation would be turned into a farce. 'Often the decisive turn is preceded by an apparent emphasising and raising to their extreme of things which seem the very denial, the most uncompromising opposite of the new principle and the new creation.'[11] (Sri Aurobindo)

It is through the confusion that the Truth-Consciousness develops, the Mother said. We remember her words that even those who think they are acting against the Great Work are in fact collaborating. In the intensified action of the hostile forces she saw the acceleration of the process of transformation whose duration had been reduced to the minimum by her and by Sri Aurobindo, in order that humanity would have to suffer as little as possible in this terrestrial hell and that it might share as soon as possible in a higher life on the Earth itself.

Everything indicates not only that we are entering the decisive time-period but also that we are already fully in it. We may expect that totally unforeseen changes will take place which will lead to the unity of humankind, to the abrasion of human egoism, to the transformation of gross matter and to the presence of superhuman and later on supramental beings. The superhuman Consciousness, delegated by the Supermind, has been working to this end since 1 January 1969. Pointers to its action are the sudden surprise of the supposedly impossible event, the radicality of the event, the dosage, all else notwithstanding, of the event to avert any irreparable disaster, and the 'benevolence' of its interventions, its intimate understanding of all things involved in the process of transformation and its divine Love for them, be they people, objects or structures.

Considering this, the events of 1989 will probably come to the reader's mind. The East European communist bloc collapsed like a house of cards, suddenly and unexpectedly. This is only one example, albeit the most spectacular, of a whole series of political, economical and financial events in recent history which were as 'miraculous,' even if afterwards they were placed within a 'reasonable' context of causes and effects by the linear functioning mental consciousness. When in 1973 the oil tap in the Middle East was closed for the first time, everybody thought the world economy was going to break down; but a year later, Kermit Lansner wrote in *Newsweek*: 'We are all amateurs again,' for the very pessimistic predictions of the economic and other experts had proved false for unexplainable reasons. Yes, rape and murder are still rife on such an enormous scale that it blunts the mind. The dark forces will not do without this fun and their derision of the new creation as long as they can. But the miracles, facets of the diamond of The Miracle, are happening, and they are far more numerous than we are able to see.

'The advance [of the transformation], however it comes about, will be indeed of the nature of a miracle, as are all such profound changes and immense developments; for they have the appearance of a kind of realised impossibility. But God works all his miracles by an evolution of secret possibilities which have been long prepared, at least in their elements, and in the end by a rapid bringing of all to a head, a throwing together of the elements so that in their fusion they produce a new form and name of things and reveal a new spirit.'[12] Thus writes Sri Aurobindo in *The Human Cycle*, where we also find: 'The principle of such changes in Nature seems to be a long obscure preparation followed by a swift gathering up and precipitation of the elements into the new birth, a rapid conversion, a transformation that in its luminous moment figures like a miracle.'[13]

The Earth is undergoing the perceptible miracle now, in our time.

This miracle has been prepared in all its elements by the Avatar and it is happening now, everywhere on Earth. In 1968, the Mother said: 'There are long, long, long periods in which things are being prepared. Then afterwards, there is a long, very long period in which things develop, are being organized, established, and have consequences. But in between [the preparation and the consequences] there is a moment when it happens, when things happen. This is not always very long — it is sometimes long, sometimes very short, but this is when it happens. And it is this "it" that will give a new development to the world. Well, we are at the right moment — it so happened that we are exactly at such a moment. This means that, if we are not blind (people are blind most of the time), if our eyes are open, that we will *see*, we will see things happen.'[14] She invited everyone to heighten their capacity of attention and not let it weaken. The most important and perhaps the only instrument of the outer and the inner act of consciousness is the presence to what happens, the directed concentration, the attention — in the beautiful formulation of Louis Pauwels in *Ce que je crois* (What I do believe): *une attention priante*, an attention as an attitude of prayer, an attention attuned to the Living Presence in everything.

'A Child Shall Destroy Them'

It has been the constant concern of Sri Aurobindo and the Mother that the breaking through of the new world into the old one would happen without irreparable damage. The phasing out of a world is always a catastrophe, a loss of everything built up by it. The present Change is not without danger, for the sudden presence of the Supramental Power in whatever quantity, even the most minute, might have a destructive effect on that what is and those who are unprepared. We know the reasoning: Truth automatically effaces Falsehood as light effaces darkness; the world and man, as they still are at the present moment, consist for the greatest part of Falsehood, for they are constructed with subconscious and inconscient substance; therefore, if the Supermind, which is the Truth-Consciousness, would come into direct contact with man and with the world, they would literally be dissolved and disappear.

The process of transformation of the world is going on, thanks to the work of the Mother and of Sri Aurobindo behind the veil, with an incredible speed, but according to the notions of time of the human beings miracles have to happen instantly, by a touch of the magic wand. A miracle that takes some ten weeks or ten years is no longer a miracle to them, probably because they confound the external with the internal procedure. If a person would be transferred from the Earth to the Moon in an instant, it would be a miracle according to everyday reasoning; if he flies to the Moon in a space capsule, then it is no longer a miracle but the result of man's scientific and technical acquisitions. How come then that each and every important scientific discovery has been deemed by experts to be impossible *before* its realization, including space travel and the visit of man to the Moon? An impossibility can only become possible by a 'miracle.' We forget that our technological progress based on science is a concatenation of big and small miracles that have resulted in the atom bomb, the visits to the Moon and the personal computer. The question is how long humankind will be able to keep mastering all these miracles — if it is mastering them at all.

It is in science that the mental, dividing consciousness has its greatest expansion. Of this, the computer is the striking example and symbol; it is increasingly influencing life on Earth and there is already a lot of talk about electronic 'super highways' which will cause a revolution in human society and perhaps in the human being. All the same, one should not lose view of at least three things: the computer gets its instructions from somewhere, which means that its programmers or those who obtain command of the supernet acquire a formidable and for the most part invisible power over their fellow human beings; secondly, the computer is a very vulnerable apparatus, a compound of numerous vulnerable parts, which is a dubious omen for the society that bases its organization on it; thirdly, the mental consciousness has a great admiration, not to say veneration, for the computer which surpasses it by far in its quantitative, analytic functions, and which it therefore considers the divinization, as it were, of itself. For the materialist considers quality to be a kind of quantum leap of quantity, and holds it perfectly possible for the computer to acquire human characteristics or even a human personality. It cannot be denied that materialistic science as practised now has a dark side which likes to denigrate all human and spiritual values and if possible to eliminate them from every consideration.

One of Sri Aurobindo's aphorisms says: 'Europe [i.e. the West] prides herself on her practical and scientific organisation and efficiency. I am waiting till her organisation is perfect; then a child shall destroy her.'[15] The Mother, who at one time gave regular comments on these aphorisms, refused on several occasions to say something about this one because it was a prediction of the bankruptcy and the collapse of the techno-scientific world as we know it at present and because she did not want to frighten people unnecessarily or prematurely. Science and the world it has created represent the high tide of the mental consciousness. Its greatest merit is its contribution to the unification of the world. This is why it is of use for the time being and why in its present form it may continue to exist for some time, for as long as it is indispensable within the global process. Once the Supermind takes over the helm, however, the mental consciousness under all its aspects will become the surpassed cosmic element. The 'child' in Sri Aurobindo's aphorism, who must be a very powerful child, is the soul in its supramental body which will effortlessly bring the artificial techno-scientific world to an end. Sri Aurobindo wrote already in the first pages of *The Life Divine* that the technical hardware is in fact a demonstration of the impotence of the mental consciousness, and that in the change-over to the Unity-Consciousness the technical machinery will be replaced by the awakened, activated inner senses and capacities of the being beyond man.

Satprem writes: 'It is strange, our imaginings of the future or our comic strips invent all the time a world equipped more and more with miraculous super machines. Nobody ever looks in the direction of a simplification of the means, of a direct power. And the more marvellous the machines, the more distorted are the faces of those operating them.'[16] We should heed Sri Aurobindo's warning in the *Arya*: 'The one safety for man lies in learning to live from within outward, not depending on institutions and machinery to perfect him, but out of his growing inner perfection availing to shape a more perfect form and frame of life.'[17] 'The next century will be spiritual or it will not be,' is a well-known statement by André Malraux. And one century earlier, the seer-poet who was the young Arthur Rimbaud had concluded *Une saison en enfer* (a season in hell) with the words: 'We are going towards the spirit! It is very certain, it is oracular what I say!' Many, since, feel likewise and look in the same direction.

No Catastrophe

The Mother said in 1968 that the result of the supramental transformation was a certainty and that it would come about with a minimum of destruction 'although this minimum is still considerable.' For it is impossible that things change without changing! And change is probably what human beings fear most of all. They are so insecure, so defenseless in their world that the assurance of their expectations is like the firm support under their feet. The falling away of the security of those expectations in all their forms (by death, divorce, accident, imprisonment, serious incapacitation, and so on) tops the list of the causes of illness and death.

The Mother was Love incarnate. She has made the greatest sacrifices so that this Earth, this 'place of desolation,' may become in the shortest possible term a paradise, and she has done everything for the change to cause as little suffering as possible. When Satprem insisted time after time that she use her Kali-power on the world, she tried every time as kindly and prudently as possible to make him see that such violent interventions by her were no longer in order, that her method of acting was not the same any more. 'There is the method of Kali which consists in administering a thorough spanking, but this means a lot of damage for meager results.'[18] Kali is the goddess who destroys to bring the world faster to its divine goal by a new creation. There is however a whole hierarchy of Kalis, from those in the lower vital up to Mahakali, the Great Kali, who is one of the four aspects or direct emanations of the Mother. The lower Kalis are as depicted in the Indian iconography: naked, black, with bulging eyes, the tongue hanging out, a garland of skulls around the neck, terrible weapons or powers in their eight hands, and blood-thirsty. The lower Kalis are goddesses of murderers and thieves, of power-hungry magicians and tantrikas, and they can give a lot of trouble to those adoring them. Mahakali, on the contrary, is as described by Sri Aurobindo in his booklet *The Mother* and is a magnificent, noble being with an enormous militant energy for a better world, but always in the first place motivated by her motherly love for all her children: objects, plants, animals and men, saints and sinners, gods, *asuras*, *rakshasas* and *pishachas*.

The Mother has strongly condemned violence: 'Violence is an asuric deformation. True power acts in peace.'[19] 'The divine manifestation takes place in calm and harmony, not by catastrophic upheavals.'* [20] 'It is always preferable to save, to illumine, to transform, instead of having to destroy brutally.'[21] 'We do not want any catastrophes,' she emphasized, and she called catastrophes 'a terrible waste'. 'Up there [in her higher consciousness] one is not in favour of breaking things, for that is a waste of time.' She once said in a certain context: 'To kill is not on my programme.'

When somebody wrote to him about the terrible catastrophes and upheavals that would happen when the Supermind appeared on the scene, Sri Aurobindo answered: 'There need not be. There will necessarily be great changes but they are not bound to be catastrophic. When there is a strong pressure from overmind forces for change, then there are likely to be catastrophes because of the resistance and clash of forces. The supramental has a greater — in its fullness a complete — mastery of things and power of harmonisation which can overcome resistance by other means than dramatic struggle and violence.'[22]

'The force which is at work at this moment is a Force of harmony that makes for unity,'[23] the Mother wrote. In 1972 she said: 'There is like a golden Force which presses [on the material world], which has no material consistency but nevertheless seems terribly heavy and which presses on Matter. And the apparent result is as if catastrophes

---

* This is actually a sentence of Sri Aurobindo's, from *Bases of Yoga*, on which she commented.

were inevitable. And together which this perception of inevitable catastrophes there are solutions to the situation, events which seem to be utterly miraculous. It is as if the two extremes were becoming still more extreme, as if what is good became better and what is bad worse. This is how it is. With a formidable Power *pressing* on the world.' And she continued: 'It is no longer like it was ... This really is a new world. We may call it "supramental" to avoid misunderstandings' — the Mother has never liked this technical term very much — 'for as soon as one speaks of "Divine" people think of a God and that spoils everything ... It is the descent of the supramental world, which is not something purely imaginary: it is an absolutely material Power but which has no need of material means. A world which wants to incarnate into the [material] world.'[24]

Sri Aurobindo and the Mother have protected the world with all their divine power at moments when elements of humanity were not only able but also inclined to destroy their own planet. The moment had come for the supramental Transmutation to be possible and such crucial moments are extremely rare in history. A nuclear catastrophe could have turned the continents into radioactive deserts and wiped out civilization, the fruit of centuries. And everything would have had to be rebuilt from out of that primitivity — for the umpteenth time? How many civilizations like Atlantis have, in humanity's past, disappeared in the water or under the sand? All indications are that we owe the continuation of our world to Sri Aurobindo and the Mother, the only Power able to counteract the human and material instruments of the destructive designs of the *Asura*.

The miracle is not for tomorrow: it is happening NOW. Those who have eyes can see it, those who have ears can hear it. Those who have a living soul can feel it. We have already witnessed the first surprises; the following ones may happen tonight or tomorrow. This is the Hour of God, the time of the unexpected. 'What is happening now is something that never happened before, and therefore *nobody* can understand it.'[25] (the Mother) In this book we have got some idea of the Work of Sri Aurobindo and the Mother, and we may use this insight to try and prolong the lines of their Work into tomorrow as a not totally unfounded thought-experiment. It is already worthwhile to know that something indeed is happening and to watch out with intensified attention for other signs of the birth of the New World and of its first embodied representatives.

Five Indications

On 15 August 1925, more than seventy years ago, Sri Aurobindo in his evening talks gave a few indications by which to recognize the dawning of the New Era. The first indication was that the knowledge of the physical world would increase to a degree that it would break its own bounds. In this book it has already been pointed out that physical science has been moving for decades in occult territory without being aware of the fact or willing to recognize it. The present moment is especially interesting, as physical science now says it has discovered the sixth quark and its system of the composition of matter therefore should be complete. For the Mother has said that the transformation takes place quite materially in the mutual relations of the elementary particles and also that new particles will be discovered of which the scientists have no idea yet.

'Secondly,' Sri Aurobindo said, 'there is an attempt all over the world towards breaking the veil between the outer and the inner mental, the outer and the inner vital and even the outer and the inner physical.' People are becoming more 'psychic' he said, using the word in the ordinary sense (according to A.B. Purani's notes). A visit to any bookshop can only confirm Sri Aurobindo's assertion.

Sri Aurobindo's third indication: 'The vital is trying to lay hold on the physical as it never did before. It is always the sign that whenever the higher Truth is coming down, it throws up the hostile vital world on the surface, and you see all sorts of abnormal vital manifestations, such as an increase in the number of persons who go mad, earth-quakes, etc.' We have already been reflecting on this. The vital beings perform their frenetic dance in an orgy of violence and stupefaction, in a hellish roar from batteries of loudspeakers of thousands of watts, under flashing, blinding lights and on pounding rhythms, with hair-dos, face paintings and clothing from domains of vital beings or dwellings of vicious clowns. (Grinning evil is perhaps the most repulsive of all.)

Fourthly: 'The world is becoming more united on account of the discoveries of modern science ... Such a union is the condition for the highest Truth coming down.' We know that technology is indispensable in the present stage of planetary development. If technology in this world would fall away, the realization of the necessary human unity would become a practical impossibility, for the different parts of the planet would lose their intense exchange with one another and be enclosed in their separate existences again. We may therefore conclude that humanity will retain its command of the necessary means of communication till something will be available to replace them. As the problems related to planetary communication are urgent, because of the dwindling energy resources and all kinds of widespread pollution, their solution may not be that far off. This would mean that the unexpected is of the order of the day. The formerly mentioned colossality of all worldwide problems, moreover, points in the same direction of a solution in the (relatively) short term.

'I have a sort of certainty that, when the Work will be finished, the result will come almost like a bolt of lightning,' the Mother said. Was the Work finished? 'The change has been accomplished. The physical *is able* to receive the higher Light, the Truth, the true Consciousness.' (14 March 1970) 'It is in the year 2000 that it will take a clear turn,' she said too. But in the meantime 'it' is active everywhere.

Sri Aurobindo's fifth indication was 'the rise of persons who wield tremendous vital influence over large numbers of people,' the emissaries, directly or indirectly of the *Asura* of Falsehood. When Sri Aurobindo said this, the world had not yet seen the hordes of khaki-shirts and black-shirts parading before their Leader (Führer, Duce, Caudillo, Netaji), with symbols of death as their emblems. Neither had it seen that the number of those attending ideological or religious mass-manifestations was used to corroborate the truth of a religion or an ideology.

Taking all this into consideration, what is the future that humanity can expect? 'It must be conceded at once that there is not the least probability or possibility of the whole human race rising in a block to the supramental level,'[26] Sri Aurobindo wrote in *The Life Divine*.

He foresaw 'an achievement by the few initiating a new order of beings, while humanity will have passed sentence of unfitness on itself and may fall back into an evolutionary decline or a stationary immobility.'[27] The Mother said the same: 'Three quarters of humanity is passed by.'[28]

'The few' are the mature souls who, at the end of their adventure through the lower evolution, have reached the end of their series of incarnations. Sri Aurobindo called them 'the great dynamic souls,' 'the handful of pioneers,' 'the born-free,' 'the predestined.' 'Throughout the course of history a small minority has been carrying the torch to save humanity in spite of itself,'[29] he said. Having arrived at this point, the soul is free to choose what it prefers to do. These souls of 'the few,' in their great love for their brothers and sisters who are still struggling in the evolution towards maturity, have chosen to incarnate again upon the Earth to help the others and quicken the advent of the new era. They have chosen the moment of their return on Earth and the task they want to accomplish. They have chosen either to help prepare the coming of the Avatar, or to work together with him at the time of his presence on Earth, or to continue the work when he has left the material scene, in the trying period between his bodily presence and the concrete realization of his Work. This is a period which only can be traversed leaning on the staff of Faith — the Faith that always is a form of precognition.

These fully matured souls are the first supermen (*surhommes*), a certain number of whom are already present among the enormous mass of humanity. In the near future (in 'three hundred years'), when gross matter will be sufficiently transformed, they or others of their kind will receive into themselves the descending great beings from the supramental world and thus become the first incorporated supramental beings on planet Earth and in the cosmos; for then the Earth has no bounds for them any more, they being by definition cosmic and divine. These few ones 'can still be counted,' the Mother said.

He who chooses the Infinite has been chosen by the Infinite.[30]

— Sri Aurobindo

If there is some truth in all this, humanity will very probably develop into the following species:

1. *Animal-man.* By far the greatest part of present animal-humanity, which has not kept the pace in the ongoing evolution and to which the fact of a possible evolutionary change is not even a concrete notion, animal-man will drop back to the level on which the greatest part of its being still moves: the animal level. Animal-man as a species, the kind of being we ourselves are, has to remain in existence, however, to keep occupying its evolutionary niche and enable the continuation of evolution from the existing lower to the future higher species;

2. *Man-man.* This future species will have assimilated into itself the capacities of the higher mental, the illumined mental and the intuition (according to the significance given to these terms by Sri Aurobindo). Because of this, it will be able to lead a totally satisfying life and have no higher ambitions. Sri Aurobindo called this species 'a higher order of mental human beings' and the Mother saw them as 'a very happy humanity.' One will remember that gross matter can become supramental only when the Augean stables of the Subconscious and the Inconscient will be cleaned. This fact alone will completely change the way of existence of animal-man and man-man from the endless road of suffering which is our lot into 'a happy pilgrimage.' The presence of the supramental beings too will inevitably have a beneficial reflection on the environment in which both these species live and therefore on all lower species of the animal and semi-human kind;

3. *Superman.* The superhuman consciousness established itself on Earth on 1 January 1969 and has been active ever since. The Mother probably would have accredited all 'miraculous' events after that date to this Consciousness. The big scale events, however, are always prepared by small scale transformations caused by this Consciousness; the latter are much more important than the big events because they are the seed that makes the changes on the surface possible. The superhuman Consciousness has its instruments in the supermen already present on

Earth. One is here reminded of the Mother's words '*il y en a*' (there are some) and Nolini's declaration that the new man is present among us. Much more important than the external is the internal work — of openness to the new Consciousness and surrender to it, of faith in the transformation which is an inner certitude, and of a total and no longer egoistic preparedness to do everything the guiding Consciousness demands. ('We want a race without an ego.') Seen spiritually, the supermen are the radioactive element in humanity effecting the (trans)mutation;

4. The *supramental species*. The supramental being is the divine being of the future; it will no longer be embodied in the manner of the present animal-human procreation. The process by which it will acquire a body of supramentalized substance is not yet known. The fact that the Subconscious will no longer hold the Earth in its grip will surely result in new evolutionary processes and mechanisms. The supramental being, as the incorporation of the Unity-Consciousness which in essence is divine Love, will transpose the world into a higher mode of happiness and well-being.

What is to happen? The unexpected, the unimagined, the unparalleled — tomorrow, today, now. The possibility of all impossibilities, the bankruptcy of the theories of the experts, the dream of the soulful amateurs raised to its highest power. A Sun is breaking out of the Earth. 'If mankind only caught a glimpse of what infinite enjoyments, what perfect forces, what luminous reaches of spontaneous knowledge, what wide calms of our being lie waiting for us in the tract which our animal evolution has not yet conquered, they would leave all and never rest till they had gained these treasures,'[31] Sri Aurobindo wrote.

But it would have been a long wait if mankind had to take the initiative. It has shut itself up within its own enclosures (to protect itself from the world that it is!), and it has given plenipotentiary powers to its self-created higher instances to terrorize itself with the scourges of sin, death, and hell, to formulate its credos and encase its mysteries, and to make a past of slavery into the norm of an ever unsatisfactory future on the planet from whose womb it has been

born. This spell is now broken by an act of God, at this moment of
moments in the history of the Earth. For this Act the collaboration
of man was not required; neither is it required for its execution. The
fact exists and this fact is imposing itself.

'It is a Force that exerts pressure on the Earth and that makes
people do the most improbable things,'[32] the Mother said. 'Just do
what you feel like, it is of no importance any more,'[33] she said. 'The
Work is being done in spite of the mental incomprehension and even
of the mental "comprehension" '[34] 'The motive why people do things
must no longer be taken seriously. What matters is that they do
them.'[35] 'All our common sense, all our logic, all our practical sense:
useless! finished! ... All that does not correspond to what *is*.'[36] 'Anyway, all the former notions, all the former ways of understanding,
all that is good and well finished, it belongs to the past,'[37] she also
said.

When she tried to give the Ashram youth an idea of what the
Divine is, she suggested they aggrandize to the highest degree in their
imagination everything they could conceive of as the most valuable
or desirable; in this way they could begin forming some idea of the
ecstatic experience which is the contact with the Divine. Is he or she
who has only caught a glimpse of it not described in many mystical
texts as love-drunk? We normally do not know this from experience.
Yet our values and desires are reflections in us of the Divine, they
are inspired into us by the Divine. It makes no sense, Sri Aurobindo
said, to impose on the Supermind and its future world the norms and
expectations of our mental manner of thinking and seeing. But as
an experiment of the imagination, as a thought-experiment, we can
project our values and our truly desirable desires on to the horizon
of the improbable — and there begins Tomorrow.

> I saw the Omnipotent's flaming pioneers
> Over the heavenly verge which turns towards life
> Come crowding down the amber stairs of birth;
> Forerunners of a divine multitude,
> Out of the paths of the morning star they came
> Into the little room of mortal life.

I saw them cross the twilight of an age,
The sun-eyed children of a marvellous dawn,
The great creators with wide brows of calm,
The massive barrier-breakers of the world
And wrestlers with destiny in her lists of will,
The labourers in the quarries of the gods,
The messengers of the incommunicable,
The architects of immortality.[38]

Once, sometime in 1956, Nirodbaran went within himself during his daily morning meditation and talked there with somebody for almost an hour. Back in his everyday consciousness, he asked himself who that might have been and wrote about it to the Mother. She answered: 'Last night we (you and myself and some others) were together for quite a long time in the permanent dwellling of Sri Aurobindo which exists in the subtle physical (what Sri Aurobindo used to call the true physical). All that happened there (much too long and complicated to be told) was, so to say, organised in order to express concretely the rapid movement with which the present transformation is going on; and Sri Aurobindo told you with a smile something like this: "Do you believe now?" It is as if he was evoking these three lines from *Savitri*:

God shall grow up while the wise men talk and sleep;
For man shall not know of the coming till its hour
And belief shall be not till the work is done.'[39]

The need of the True, the New, the Real, of Something Different, lives in the breasts of so many. The seed of the New World has been strewn out and the attentive eye sees the signs of its germination everywhere. Jacques Lacarrière, for instance, ends his remarkable book on *Les Gnostiques* (the Gnostics) as follows: 'The Gnostic of today can no longer be a preacher of salvation, a magus in seclusion on his mountain, or some illuminatus in the big city with his nose glued to old texts. He must be a sentient man, turned towards the present and the future, with the intuitive certitude that above all else he holds within himself the keys of the future. This certitude he has to oppose to all reassuring myths, so-called religions of salvation, and alienating ideologies, which do nothing but screen off his true presence to reality. For what is important today is not so much to discover new stars as to break down the new barriers which unceasingly rise up around us or within ourselves, in order to go through them, like through death, with the eyes wide open.'[40]

'The coming of a spiritual age must be preceded by the appearance of an increasing number of individuals who are no longer satisfied with the normal intellectual, vital and physical existence of man,'[41] Sri Aurobindo wrote eight decades ago. These individuals are the ones who can no longer stand the lies and the almost unrealistic improbability of the whole mess of life because something inside them knows that it can be otherwise and that the moment of the other way has arrived. They have inside them a lacuna which the Mother called a 'Need' — the pressing need of Reality which is a hunger for sustenance of the soul. This Need is the sign of the mature psychic being. It is inevitably guided towards its very own place and contribution in the construction of the New World, often by an improbable coincidence — a word, an encounter, a book, an article in a newspaper wrapped around a pair of shoes. For it is for this specific contribution that it has come into the world again, and it will find the like-minded psychic beings, even though most of them are still moving incognito among the mass or within a religious or spiritual community. For it belongs to the planetary group of those who have been sent. And in the ear-shattering din of a world in travail it will discern the pure call which fills the eyes with tears of Joy because the call will tell that That is present in this world and that life will no longer be a crawling act but a boundless flight with wide and light and colourful wings.

The world is coming apart at the seams 'till the day that it will be the Sun for ever, the total Victory,'[42] as the Mother put it. Those who feel the unquenchable thirst for Something Different will be protected in a cocoon of light, she said, to traverse all perils of the convulsions of the old and dying world, for in part of their being they already belong to that light, to the New World. And 'all one has dreamed to be the most beautiful, the most marvellous, the most fantastic is nothing compared with what will be realized.'[43]

'The absoluteness of the Victory is in-dis-put-able,' she stressed staccato — she who possessed the certitude 'like a sword of Light, intangible.' And like Joan of Arc to her standard which had been with her in so many battles, she said to those then and now who dedicate themselves to the advent of Tomorrow: 'You have shared in the hardship, you will share in the honour.'

For: 'It is not a crucified but a glorified body that will save the world.'[44]

Auroville, 6 January 1996

REFERENCES

A   : *L'Agenda de Mère*
AR   : *Sri Aurobindo Archives and Research*
CP   : *Collected Poems* (Sri Aurobindo)
CSA   : *Correspondence With Sri Aurobindo* (Nirodbaran)
E   : *Entretiens* (the Mother)
EG   : *Essays on the Gita* (Sri Aurobindo)
ET   : *Evening Talks* (recorded by A.B. Purani)
FIC   : *The Foundation of Indian Culture* (Sri Aurobindo)
Glimpses   : *Glimpses of the Mother* (compilation)
HC   : *The Human Cycle* (Sri Aurobindo)
IHU   : *The Ideal of Human Unity* (Sri Aurobindo)
LD   : *The Life Divine* (Sri Aurobindo)
LY   : *Letters on Yoga* (Sri Aurobindo)
M   : *The Mother* (Sri Aurobindo)
MI   : *Mother India* (periodical)
NC   : *Notes sur le chemin* (the Mother)
OH   : *On Himself* (Sri Aurobindo)
P&M   : *Prières et Méditations* (the Mother)
SM   : *The Supramental Manifestation* (Sri Aurobindo)
SY   : *The Synthesis of Yoga* (Sri Aurobindo)
T&A   : *Thoughts and Aphorisms* (Sri Aurobindo, revised ed. 1977)
TSA   : *Talks With Sri Aurobindo* (recorded by Nirodbaran)
12 Years   : *Twelve Years With Sri Aurobindo* (Nirodbaran 1972)
WM   : *Words of the Mother* (the Mother)

Prologue — 1. OH, 49 — 2. E54, 80 — 3. John Toland, *Adolf Hitler*, 833 — 4. Op. cit., 835 — 5. TSA IV, 4 — 6. Op. cit., 117 — 7. OH, 38-39 — 8. Letter of 5 June 1958, in *Sri Aurobindo Circle no. 42*, 66 — 9. MI January 1989, 26 — 10. LY, 402 — 11. EG, 148 footnote — 12. OH, 202 — 13. LY, 411 — 14. OH, 463 — 15. *Savitri*, 537 — 16. CSA, 166 — 17. CSA, 172 — 18. OH, 153 — 19. *Savitri*, 537.

1. A Perfect Gentleman — 1. OH, 378 — 2. Peter Heehs, *Sri Aurobindo: A Brief Biography*, 9 — 3. Op. cit., 2 — 4. Op. cit. 14 — 5. TSA II, 240 — 6. 12 Years, 236.

2. The Most Dangerous Man in India — 1. OH, 153 — 2. AR, December 1977, 85 — 3. OH, 430 — 4. OH, 21 — 5. OH, 400 — 6. Manoj Das, *Sri Aurobindo in the First Decade of the Century*, 1 — 7. TSA I, 172 — 8. OH, 25˚— 9. P. Heehs, op. cit., 47 — 10. OH, 49 — 11. P. Heehs, op. cit., 57 — 12. Manoj Das, op. cit., 64 — 13. P. Heehs, op. cit., 66 — 14. T&A, 49 — 15. OH, 27

3. A Backdoor to Spirituality — 1. TSA IV, 277 — 2. Ibidem — 3. Centenary Edition of Sri Aurobindo's Collected Works, volume 2, *Karmayogin*, 4-5 — 4. P. Heehs, op. cit., 70 — 5. OH, 53 — 6. OH, 64 — 7. TSA I, 212 — 8. P. Heehs, op. cit., 99.

4. Of Painters and Occultists — 1. A III, 299 — 2. Jean Jacques Crespelle, *Le vie quotidienne des Impressionnistes*, preface — 3. E 50-51, 331 — 4. LD, 652 — 5. Francis King and Isabel Sutherland, *The Rebirth of Magic*, 185 — 6. A I, 458 — 7. A II, 71 — 8. A II, 72 — 9. Glimpses I, 78 — 10. LD, 876 — 11. A XIII, 268.

5. Twelve Pearls — 1. *Savitri*, 327 — 2. A VII, 41 — 3. *Savitri*, 355 — 4. P&M, 106 — 5. WM 13, 39 — 6. A IV, 143 — 7. *Savitri*, 284 — 8. *Sri Aurobindo Circle* no. 36, 93 — 9. *Savitri*, 683 — 10. AR 1988, 200 — 11. Glimpses I, 144 — 12. WM 13, 39 — 13. P&M, 113 — 14. MI 1975, 95 — 15. *Savitri*, 21 — 16. P&M, 242.

6. The *Arya* — 1. AR 1987, 114 — 2. AR 1985, 215 — 3. Nolini Kanta Gupta, *Reminiscences*, 52 — 4. ET, 20 — 5. AR 1989, 103 — 6. *Arya*, volume 1 no. 2, 63 — 7. OH, 374 — 8. AR 1983, 165 — 9. P. Heehs, op. cit., 108 — 10. *Arya*, volume 2 no. 1, 1 — 11. *Arya*, volume 4, 763 — 12. A X, 131 — 13. P&M, 291 — 14. *Savitri*, 399 — 15. *Sri Aurobindo Circle* no. 34, 122.

7. Sri Aurobindo's Vision — 1. A II, 440 — 2. OH, 456 — 3. LD, 33 — 4. E 53, 256 — 5. E 53, 185 — 6. A II, 220 — 7. LD, 31 — 8. *Savitri*, 61 — 9. CSA, 991 — 10. T&A, 30 — 11. LD, 3 — 12. M, 40 — 13. SM, 235 — 14. LD, 42 — 15. LD, 185 — 16. LD, 612 — 17. Fritjof Capra, *Uncommon Wisdom*, 228 — 18. LD, 124 — 19. LD, 126 — 20. A II, 140, footnote — 21. HC, 59 — 22. LY, 385.

8. *Homo Sum* ... — 1. *Arya*, volume I, 575 — 2. LD, 17 — 3. LD, 846 — 4. A II, 321 — 5. E 53, 112 — 6. SY, 4 — 7. WM 13, 376 — 8. E 57, 364 — 9. M, 373 — 10. E 50-51, 269 — 11. A I, 412 — 12. T&A, 18 — 13. LD, 780 footnote — 14. AR 1982, 113 — 15. AR 1979, 182 — 16. AR 1983, 3 — 17. E 29, 34 — 18. LD, 139 — 19. LD, 710 — 20. LD,

714 — 21. E 56, 145 — 22. E 57, 247 — 23. AR, April 1985, 2 — 24. LD, 844 — 25. LY, 212 — 26. Paul Davies, *God and the New Physics*, 166 — 27. Jacques Monod, *Le hasard et la nécessité*, 178 — 28. Francis Hitching, *The Neck of the Giraffe, or Where Darwin Went Wrong*, 103 — 29. Idem, 22 — 30. LD, 708 — 31. LD, 29 — 32. LD, 468 — 33. *Savitri*, 686.

9. From Man to Superman — 1. *Troisième millénaire*, no. 5 — 2. OH, 376 — 3. A VIII, 84 — 4. A II, 211 — 5. A IX, 336 — 6. OH, 125 — 7. E 56, 279 — 8. WM 13, 54 — 9. SY, 604 — 10. E 55, 387 — 11. WM 15, 338 — 12. LD, 939 — 13. LD, 257 — 14. LY, 236 — 15. LY, 234 — 16. CSA, 1063 — 17. OH, 469 — 18. LY, 168 — 19. SM, 384 — 20. T&A, 3 — 21. *Savitri*, 691 — 22. T&A, 19 — 23. LD, 845 — 24. LY, 267 — 25. E 57, 486 — 26. E 50-51, 270 — 27. A VI, 18 — 28. A VI, 19 — 29. E 54, 446 — 30. Idries Shah, *The Way of the Sufi*, 113 — 31. Joe Fisher, *The Case for Reincarnation*, 66 — 32. *The Illustrated Weekly of India*, 1 December 1985, 13 — 33. J. Fisher, op. cit., 4 — 34. *Arya*, vol. II 240 — 35. LY, 434 — 36 LY, 455 — 37. LY, 451 — 38. *Arya*, vol. V, 574 — 39. TSA IV, 204 — 40. CSA, 277 — 41. *Savitri*, 454 — 42. J. Fisher, op. cit., 95 — 43. AR 1982, 64.

10. The Two-in-One — I. *Savitri*, 295 — 2. SY, 145 — 3. *Savitri*, 411 — 4. Glimpses *I*, 160 — 5. *Supplement* to the Centenary Edition of Sri Aurobindo's Collected Works, 426 and 427 — 6. Nolini Kanta Gupta, *Reminiscences*, 59 — 7. Idem, 63 — 8. ET, 21 — 9. K.D. Sethna, *Our Light and Delight*, 161 — 10. AR, April 1980, 11 — 11. *Advent*, August 1981 — 12. P. Heehs, op. cit., 71 — 13. *Savitri*, 16 — 14. LY, 417 — 15. M, 19 — 16. M, 48, 49, 50 — 17. E 54, 136-38 — 18. OH, 456 — 19. OH, 457 — 20. Ibidem — 21. A I, 121 — 22. E 56, 69 — 23. *Savitri*, 314-15 — 24. SY, 40 — 25. A X, 460 — 26. M, 234 — 27. N.K. Gupta, op. cit., 81 — 28. K.D. Sethna, op. cit., 7 — 29. *Savitri*, 315 — 30. K.D. Sethna, op. cit., 2 — 31. Idem, 57 — 32. Idem, 3 — 33. *Savitri*, 15 — 34. 12 Years,107 — 35. MI, November 1988 — 36. Satprem, *Mère II*, 177 — 37. M, 317 — 38. OH, 154 — 39. Glimpses II, 23 — 40. Idem, 61 — 41. M, 179 — 42. *Savitri*, 356 — 43. E 29, 221 — 44. WM 13, 83 — 45. WM 13, 103 — 46. E 29, 104 — 47. K.D. Sethna, op. cit., 48 — 48. OH, 175 — 49. ET, 10 and 11 — 50. Dilip Kumar Roy, *Sri Aurobindo Came to Me*, 64 — 51. Idem, 515.

11. 'All Life is Yoga' — 1. SY, 2 — 2. ET, 20 — 3. E 53, 402 — 4. A III, 299 — 5. TSA I, 6 — 6. SY, 51 — 7. LY, 188 — 8. E 53, 81 — 9. LY, 161 — 10. LY, 162 — 11. SM, 291 — 12. E 56, 268 — 13. E 53, 322 — 14. SY, 521 — 15. LY, 73 — 16. OH, 464 — 17. LY, 229 — 18. SY, 14

— 19. AR 1982, 196 — 20. OH, 80 — 21. ET, 303 — 22. TSA II, 199 — 23. SY, 47 — 24. SY, 180 — 25. SY, 49 — 26. SY, 192 — 27. SY, 260 — 28. OH, 78 — 29. SY, 87 — 30. *Savitri*, 315 — 31. SY, 50 — 32. OH, 144 — 33. E 57, 41 — 34 . OH. 122 — 35. SY, 17 — 36. CSA, 139 — 37. LY, 101 — 38. SY, 268 — 39. *Savitri*, 45 — 40. CSA, 673 — 41. HC, 251 — 42. A II, 168 — 43. *Supplement*, 433 — 44. P. Heehs, op. cit., 44 — 45. MI 1993, 554 — 46. ET, 29 — 47. Both quotations: OH, 144 — 48. A II, 417 — 49. SM, 344 — 50. HC, 35 — 51. HC, 219 — 52. M, 130 — 53. ET, 139.

12. Krishna and the World of the Gods — 1. ET, 481 — 2. *Savitri*, 261 — 3. LY, 385 — 4. CSA, 299 — 5. A III, 377 — 6. LY, 257 — 7. *Savitri*, 660 — 8. LY, 257 — 9. LD, 280 — 10. K.R. Srinivasa Iyengar, *Sri Aurobindo*, 529 — 11. MI, August 1979, 474 — 12. A II, 329 — 13. A II, 320 — 14. A II, 331 — 15. OH, 446 — 16. *Champaklal Speaks*, 12 — 17. OH, 137 — 18. OH, 191 — 19. A II, 331 — 20. ET, 12 — 21 M, 317 — 22. K.R. Srinivasa Iyengar, *On the Mother*, 246 — 23. OH, 455 — 24. CSA, 850 — 25. E 57, 168 — 26. A II, 330 — 27. MI, November 1986, 673 — 28. MI, February 1958, 9 — 29. Narayan Prasad, *Life in Sri Aurobindo Ashram*, 64 — 30. E 57, 168 — 31. A III, 486 — 32. TSA I, 179 — 33. MI, February 1958, 9 — 34. MI, November 1986, 673.

13. Sri Aurobindo and the 'Laboratory' — 1. CSA, 175 — 2. LD, 665 — 3. OH, 474 — 4. E 56, 57 — 5. Glimpses II, 46 — 6. A III, 459 — 7. CSA, 247-8 — 8. CP, 101 — 9. LD, 603 — 10. CSA, 314 — 11. LY, 393 — 12. CSA, 154 — 13. *Savitri*, 153 — 14. E 50-51, 209 — 15. WM 15, 366 — 16. ET, 364 — 17. CSA, 914 — 18. OH, 472 — 19. *Savitri*, 44 — 20. CSA, 242 — 21. OH, 490 — 22. Ibidem — 23. CSA, 525 — 24. Idem, 549 — 25. Idem, 553 — 26. Idem, 127 — 27. Idem, 689 — 28. Idem, 79 — 29. P. Heehs, op. cit., 139 — 30. OH, 465 — 31. CSA, 176 — 32. OH, 467 — 33. HC, 5 — 34. CP, 120 — 35. ET, 455 — 36. ET, 539 — 37. OH, 169 — 38. WM 13, 3 — 39. A IX, 149 — 40. CSA, 1024-25.

14. The Mother and the 'Laboratory' — 1. TSA I, 4 — 2. P&M, 520 — 3. AI, 429 — 4. *Sri Aurobindo Circle* no. 34, 11 — 5. M, 79 — 6. SY, 544 — 7. OH, 482 — 8. M, 20 — 9. WM 13, 113 — 10. A I, 429 — 11. E 57, 42 — 12. E 50-51, 287 — 13. A XIII, 153 — 14. E 29, 5 — 15. E 53, 2 — 16. E 50-51, 347 — 17. *Savitri*, 343 — 18. E 50-51, 164 — 19. M, 168 — 20. A VIII, 232 — 21. E 55, 425 — 22. E 50-51, 360 — 23. E 56, 319 — 24. WM 13, 96 — 25. CSA, 409 — 26. M, 270 — 27. TSA I, 85 — 28. CSA, 1047 — 29. M, 233-34 — 30. E 54, 338 — 31. ET, 164 — 32. SY, 268-69 — 33. HC, 156 — 34. WM 15, 197 — 35. WM

14, 259 — 36. M, 71 — 37. Glimpses II, 59 — 38. Idem, 61 — 39. Idem, 58-59 — 40. CSA, 55-56 — 41. Idem, 820-21 — 42. Amal Kiran and Nirodbaran, *Light and Laughter*, 63 — 43. K.D. Sethna, *Our Light and Delight*, 95-96 — 44. M, 315 — 45. M, 316 — 46. M, 317 — 47. CSA, 275 — 48. HC, 160 — 49. M, 106 — 50. K.R. Srinivasa Iyengar, *On the Mother*, 349-50 — 51. M, 227 — 52. CSA, 108 — 53. OH, 489 — 54. TSA II, 232 — 55. OH, 175 — 56. MI, April 1984, 237 and 242 — 57. CSA, 593 — 58. CSA, 987 — 59. *Champaklal Speaks*, 135 — 60. M, 371 — 61. E 54, 65 — 62. OH, 502 — 63. M, 230 — 64. MI, January 1989, 27 — 65. MI, January 1990, 13 — 66. MI, January 1989, 26 — 67. MI, February 1989, 116.

15. A Night in November — 1. Louis Pauwels and Jaques Bergier, *Le Matin des magiciens*, 253 — 2. CSA 36 — 3. Idem, 55 — 4. *Collaboration*, 15th year, no. 2 — 5. A.B. Purani, *Life of Sri Aurobindo*, 227 — 6. 12 Years, 4 — 7. TSA I, 44 — 8. ET, 209 — 9. A III, 23 — 10. TSA I, 52 — 11. K.D. Sethna, *The Mother: Past, Present, Future*, 21 — 12. 12 Years, 277 — 13. A II, 410-11 — 14. *Bulletin of Sri Aurobindo International Centre of Education*, vol. XXXI, August 1979, 104 — 15. TSA I, 44 — 16. L. Pauwels and J. Bergier, op. cit., 366 — 17. TSA I, introduction — 18. 12 Years, 53 — 19. TSA III, 178 — 20. 12 Years, 47 — 21. CP, 146 — 22. 12 Years, 51 — 23. Idem, 55 — 24. Idem, 36.

16. The Lord of the Nations — 1. L. Pauwels and J. Bergier, op. cit., 280 — 2. Dusty Sklar, *The Nazis and the Occult*, 125 — 3. L. Pauwels and J. Bergier, op. cit., 357 — 4. Idem, 284 — 5. TSA I, 298 — 6. A I, 410 — 7. E 53, 30 — 8. E 53, 429-30 — 9. D. Sklar, op. cit., 50 — 10. E 50-51, 206 — 11. J. Toland, op. cit. 86-87 — 12. André Brissaud, *Hitler et l'Ordre noir*, 53 — 13. Ibidem — 14. Ibidem — 15. D. Sklar, op. cit., 62 — 16. Idem, 72 — 17. L. Pauwels and J. Bergier, op. cit., 282 — 18. Idem, 323 — 19. Idem, 284 — 20. D. Sklar, op. cit., 54 — 21. J. Toland, op. cit., 885 — 22. Idem, 970 — 23. Idem, 383 — 24. A. Brissaud, op. cit., 175 — 25. L. Pauwels and J. Bergier, op. cit., 286 — 26. TSA IV, 143 — 27. TSA IV, 121 — 28. Hugh Toye, *The Springing Tiger Subhash Chandra Bose*, 85 — 29. Idem, 39 — 30. TSA III, 216 — 31. TSA III, 236 — 32. OH, 393 — 33. OH, 394 — 34. J. Toland, op. cit., 891 — 35. Idem, 977 — 36. Idem, 990 — 37. TSA III, 237 — 38. TSA IV, 206 — 39. TSA IV, 206 and 321 — 40. TSA IV, 244 — 41. TSA IV, 51 and 85 — 42. Maggi Lidchi-Grassi, *The Light that Shone in the Dark Abyss*, 77 — 43. Idem, 72 — 44. Idem, 73 — 45. TSA IV, 143 — 46. K.D. Sethna, *Our Light and Delight*, 194 — 47. J. Toland, op. cit., 743 — 48. AII, 410 — 49. J. Toland, op. cit.,

854 — 50. Ibidem — 51. A II, 410 — 52. A VI, 17 — 53. J. Toland, op. cit., 935 — 54. TSA IV, 36 and 39 — 55. A II, 410.

17. The Five 'Dreams' of Sri Aurobindo — 1. OH, 143 — 2. OH, 404 — 3. SY, 23 — 4. WM 13, 361 — 5. Ibidem — 6. *Arya*, vol. V, 424 — 7. K.D. Sethna, *Our Light and Delight*, 174 — 8. ET, 285 — 9. WM 13, 363 — 10. *Sri Aurobindo Circle* no. 33, 8 — 11. 12 Years, 241 — 12. ET, 17-18 — 13. E 56, 34-35 — 14. CSA, 323 — 15. OH, 405 — 16. MI, March 1992 — 17. 12 Years, 153 — 18. OH, 399 — 19. MI, March 1992, 189 — 20. WM 13, 376 — 21. A VI, 257-58 — 22. WM 13, 368 — 23. 12 Years, 242 — 24. OH, 405 — 25. HC, 12 — 26. 12 Years, 156 — 27. SM, 309 — 28. HC, 19 — 29. HC, 18 — 30. SM, 311 — 31. *Sri Aurobindo Mandir Annual*, 1970 — 32. *Arya*, vol. II, 4 — 33. SM, 312 — 34. FIC, 81 — 35. OH, 405 — 36. OH, 406 — 37. OH, 424 — 38. IHU, 406 — 39. IHU, 556 — 40. LY, 456 — 41. HC, 7 — 42. HC, 11 — 43. HC, 48 — 44. OH, 406 — 45. Ibidem — 46. OH, 417.

18. The Confrontation With Death — 1. A XIII, 253 — 2. K.R. Srinivasa Iyengar, *Sri Aurobindo*, 636 — 3. CSA, 543-44 — 4. A IV, 86 — 5. Mona Sarkar, *Sweet Mother*, 26 — 6. R.Y. Deshpande, *The Ancient Tale of Savitri*, 3 — 7. *Savitri*, 22 — 8. Idem, 794 — 9. Idem, 799 — 10. 12 Years, 179 — 11. Idem, 166 — 12. Idem, 255-56 — 13. MI, December 1991, 778 — 14. 12 Years, 262 — 15. Idem, 264 — 16. Idem, 266 — 17. SY, 722 — 18. A III, 24 — 19. Rhoda P. Le Cocq, *The Radical Thinkers — Heidegger and Sri Aurobindo*, 200 — 20. K.D. Sethna, *The Passing of Sri Aurobindo*, 5 — 21. R.P. Le Cocq, op. cit., 201 — 22. K.D. Sethna, *The Mother — Past, Present, Future*, 13-14 — 23. *Savitri*, 83 — 24. CP, 161 — 25. 12 Years, 247 — 26. K.D. Sethna, *The Passing of Sri Aurobindo*, 16 — 27. A X, 277 — 28. Nirodbaran, *The Mother — Sweetness and Light*, 69 — 29. A III, 491 — 30. *En route — Correspondance avec Shyam Sundar* — 31. A VIII, 311 — 32. A XI, 106 — 33. NC, 364 — 34. A II, 288 — 35. CP, 161 — 36. *Savitri*, 231-32 — 37. CP, 153 — 38. R.P. Le Cocq, op. cit., 199.

19. Twelve Quiet Days — 1. E 56, 354 — 2. WM 13, 37 — 3. Kireet Joshi, *Sri Aurobindo and the Mother*, 112 — 4. Idem, 113 — 5. Idem, 110 — 6. Idem, 118 — 7. 12 Years, 69 — 8. K.D. Sethna, *The Vision and Work of Sri Aurobindo*, 105 — 9. SM, 71 — 10. E 57-58, 356 — 11. SM, 67 — 12. E 56, 368 — 13. E 57-58, 466 — 14. A I, 160.

20. The Golden Day — 1. *Savitri*, 13 — 2. Satprem, *Mère II*, 147 — 3. WM 15, 197 — 4. SY, 48 — 5. E 50-51, 103 — 6. SY, 61 — 7. E 54, 489 — 8. Idem, 490 — 9. E 56, 205 — 10. Idem, 207 — 11. Idem, 404 — 12. E 50-51, 4 — 13. A II, 367 — 14. E 50-51, *Note de l'Éditeur* —

15. Satprem, *Mère II*, 10 — 16. CSA, 850 — 17. A III, 41 — 18. WM 15, 315 — 19. Idem, 316-17 — 20. E 57, 239 — 21. LD 258, 269 and 271 — 22. E 56, 89 — 23. LD, 664 — 24. Ibidem — 25. E 50-51, 177 — 26. Idem, 377 — 27. E 54, 128 — 28. WM 15, 303 — 29. E 54, 144 — 30. Idem, 162 — 31. WM 15, 100 — 32. E 54, 446 — 33. WM 15, 101 — 34. OH, 152 — 35. E 57-58, 3 — 36. E 54, 516 — 37. Ibidem — 38. E 54, 523 — 39. K.D. Sethna, *Our Light and Delight*, 134 — 40. E 55, 3 — 41. WM 15, 102 — 42. *Champaklal's Treasures*, 96 — 43. E 56, 150 — 44. E 50-51, 248 — 45. Amal Kiran and Nirodbaran, *Light and Laughter*, 80 — 46. E 56, 145 — 47. WM 15, 106 — 48. WM 13, 9 — 49. LY, 10 — 50. K.D. Sethna, *The Mother — Past, Present, Future*, 83.

21. The Ship From the New World — 1. E 57-58, 99 and 107 — 2. E 56, 301 — 3. E 57-58, 168-69 — 4. Idem, 166 — 5. Idem, 170 — 6. Idem, 172 — 7. M, 71 — 8. E 57-58, 126 — 9. WM, 351 — 10. E 57-58, 217-18 — 11. WM 15, 207-08 — 12. E 57-58, 355 — 13. Idem, 466-67 — 14. E 56, 277 — 15. E 57-58, 279 — 16. *Savitri*, 50 — 17. E 57-58, 247-48 — 18. Idem, 40 — 19. Idem, 281 — 20. NC, 266 — 21. E 57-58, 308 — 22. Mona Sarkar, *Sweet Mother*, 22 — 23. E 57-58, 82 — 24. WM 15, 381 — 25. Idem, 385.

22. Making Possible the Impossible — 1. LD, 49 — 2. A I, 244 — 3. SY, 731 — 4. E 54, 331 — 5. SY, 737 — 6. M, 51 — 7. M, 71 — 8. M, 383 — 9. M, 106 — 10. *Savitri*, 270 — 11. Satprem, *Mère II*, 158 — 12. Idem, 237 — 13. A III, 437 — 14. E 54, 482 — 15. A III, 111 — 16. NC, 151 — 17. A XI, 279 — 18. NC, 13 — 19. NC, 194 — 20. E 50, 88 — 21. E 54, 153 — 22. E 56, 456 — 23. SY, 671 — 24. LD, 162 — 25. LD, 404 — 26. E 50, 365 — 27. LD, 463 — 28. E 55, 16 — 29. T&A, 95 — 30. E 55, 454 — 31. *Savitri*, 443 — 32. E 53, 346 — 33. SY, 71 — 34. LD, 1061 — 35. A IX, 202 ff. — 36. E 56, 89 — 37. *Savitri*, 169 — 38. Idem, 140 — 39. E 56, 277 — 40. *Savitri*, 18 — 41. LD, 267 — 42. LD, 355 — 43. E 30-31, 225-26, — 44. E 56, 360. — 45. OH, 202 — 46. AI, 495 — 47. OH, 277 — 48. E 55, 396 — 49. Amal Kiran and Nirodbaran, *Light and Laughter*, 36 — 50. WM 15, 37 — 51. Mona Sarkar, *Sweet Mother I*, 2 — 52. A IV, 136 — 53. A I, 315 — 54. CSA, 218, 216 and 327 — 55. E 55, 403 — 56. LD, 631 — 57. E 56, 155 — 58. E 57, 381 — 59. A XI, 263 — 60. A XIII, 152 — 61. WM 15, 117.

23. Two Rooms — 1. Satprem, *Mère III*, 284 — 2. A III, 36 — 3. Champaklal Speaks, 251 — 4. LD, 798 — 5. CSA, 737 — 6. WM 14, 259 — 7. E 53, 361 — 8. Satprem, *Mère II*, 142 — 9. Frédéric de Towarnicki, *Sept Jours en Inda avec Satprem*, 91 — 10. Yolande Lemoine, *La Fête en*

profondeur, 315 — 11. LD, 372 — 12. WM 15, 408 ff. — 13. WM 15, 411-12.

24. The Transfer of Power — 1. *Savitri*, rev. ed. 1993, 461 — 2. Satprem, *Mère II*, 416 — 3. Satprem, *Mère II*, 338 — 4. NC 108-9 — 5. E 57, 20 — 6. A V, 226 — 7. A XIII, 304 and 359 — 8. WM 13, 84 — 9. A XII, 306 — 10. NC, 37 and 38 — 11. NC, conversation dated 16.1.1971 — 12. LD, 142 — 13. M, 36 — 14. AIII, 164 — 15. NC, 160 — 16. NC, 264 — 17. NC, 278 — 18. A XI, 207 — 19. A XIII, 311 — 20. WM 13, 60 — 21. A X, 450 — 22. A II, 109 — 23. *Sri Aurobindo Circle* n° 34, 8 — 24. WM 13, 77 — 25. Mona Sarkar, *Sweet Mother II*, 7 — 26. Mona Sarkar, *Sweet Mother I*, 17 — 27. A X, 46 and 246 — 28. A V, 182 — 29. WM 13, 74 — 30. Mona Sarkar, *Sweet Mother II*, 29 — 31. A IV, 431 — 32. NC, 1 — 33. A III, 436 — 34. T&A, 50 — 35. NC, 134-35 — 36. NC, 37 — 37. NC, 135 — 38. NC, 144 — 39. NC, 140 — 40. NC, 140 — 41. NC, 145 — 42. NC, 136.

25. The New Utopia: Auroville — 1. *The Mother on Auroville*, 7 — 2. A IX, 54 — 3. *The Mother on Auroville*, 10 — 4. Idem, 6 — 5. Idem, 12 — 6. WM 13, 194 — 7. *The Mother on Auroville*, 7 — 8. WM 13, 207 — 9. *Auroville References in the Mother's Agenda*, 37 — 10. WM 13, 198 — 11. *The Mother on Auroville*, 16 — 12. Idem, 3 — 13. WM 13, 210 — 14. WM 13, 221 — 15. WM 13, 224 — 16. WM 13, 225 — 17. WM 13, 1 — 18. WM 13, 212 — 19. NC, 152 — 20. *The Mother on Auroville*, 56 — 21. A III, 46 — 22. *Auroville References in the Mother's Agenda*, 61 — 23. *The Mother on Auroville*, 13.

26. In the Crucible — 1. LD, 40 — 2. E 50-51, 161 — 3. NC, 267 — 4. NC, 53 — 5. NC, 267 — 6. SM, 39 — 7. MI, March 1975 — 8. NC, 268-69 — 9. A XIII, 154 — 10. WM 14, 358 — 11. LD, 185 — 12. SY, 771 — 13. LY, 12 — 14. TSA I, 277 — 15. NC, 52 — 16. A IV, 300 — 17. LD, 965 — 18. LD, 971 — 19. LD 372 — 20. Mona Sarkar, *Sweet Mother II*, 18 ff. — 21. A XIII, 367 — 22. A VIII, 400 — 23. E 56, 89 — 24. LD, 257-58 — 25. LD, 775 — 26. WM 15, 302 — 27. E 57-58, 356 — 28. NC, 64-5 — 29. A IV, 236 — 30. *Savitri*, 816 — 31. OH, 162 — 32. A VI, 283 — 33. E 56, 359 — 34. E 57-58, 382 — 35. A V, 602 — 36. E 57-58, 45 — 37. Cf. E 57-58, 359 — 38. E 57-58, 382 — 39. OH, 475 — 40. M, 227 — 41. M, 168 — 42. NC, 312-13 — 43. E 57-58, 473 — 44. E 50-51, 456 — 45. E 56, 89 — 46. A III, 215 — 47. NC, 472 — 48. Shyam Sundar, *En route*, 36 — 49. WM 13, 95 — 50. NC, 10-11 — 51. A X, 413 — 52. Jacques Monod, *Le Hasard et la Nécessité*, 216 — 53. A IV, 321 and 325 — 54. NC, 115 — 55. NC, 107 ff. — 56. A XI, 164

— 57. A X, 133 — 58. WM 13, 103 — 59. A V, 108 — 60. E 56, 203
— 61. A IV, 397 — 62. A XI, 371 — 63. A XII, 57 — 64. NC, 100 —
65. A XIII, 249 — 66. A III, 224 — 67. A VI, 271 — 68. A XIII, 251 and
275 — 69. NC, 101 — 70. Mona Sarkar, *Sweet Mother II*, 30 — 71. A IX,
300 — 72. A VI, 316 and VIII, 69 — 73. A XIII, 311 — 74. A II, 232 —
75. NC, 38 — 76. NC, 80 — 77. E 56, 391 — 78. NC, 127 — 79. E 57-
58, 478 — 80. A VI, 317 — 81. A XI, 155 — 82. A XII, 319.

27. **The New Body** — 1. NC, 168 — 2. NC, 169 ff. — 3. *Sri Aurobindo
Mandir Annual*, 1987 — 4. SY, 646 — 5. SM, 21 — 6. A I, 160 — 7. E
57-58, 125-26 — 8. E 57-58, 218 — 9. E 57-58, 356-57 — 10. A X, 97
and 94 — 11. A XIII, 152 — 12. WM 13, 56 — 13. A IV, 36 — 14. E 56,
332.

28. **The Caterpillar and the Butterfly** — 1. A III, 254 — 2. Pranab Kumar
Bhattacharya, *I Remember...*, 336 — 3. E 50-51, 60 — 4. Satprem, *Mère III*,
323 — 5. *The Advent*, vol. XXXI no. 2, 5 and 6 — 6. P.K. Bhattacharya,
op. cit., 323 — 7. K.D. Sethna, *The Mother — Past, Present, Future*, 28 —
8. Idem, 35 ff. — 9. MI, October 1982, 667 — 10. K.D. Sethna, op. cit.,
36 — 11. P.K. Bhattacharya, op. cit., 323 — 12. K.D. Sethna, op. cit., 45
— 13. MI, January 1989, 30 — 14. LY, 10 — 15. OH, 166 — 16. SY, 267
— 17. P. Heehs, *Sri Aurobindo*, 105 — 18. K.D. Sethna, op. cit., 42 — 19.
CSA, 899 — 20. CSA, 294-95 — 21. MI, November 1986, 674-75 — 22.
CSA, 188-89 — 23. CSA, 194 — 24. CSA, 702 ff. — 25. cf. E 50-51, 78
— 26. A X, 223 and 228 — 27. A XIII, 166-67 — 28. E 50-51, 108 — 29.
E 57-58, 275 — 30. A VII, 207 — 31. A III, 469 — 32. WM 15, 403 —
33. A IV, 227 — 34. E 29, 221 — 35. A VIII, 97 — 36. A XIII, 355 —
37. HC, 161 — 38. Satprem, *Mère III*, 171 — 39. A XIII, 355 — 40. A X,
427 — 41. A X, 264 — 42. A XI, 108 — 43. A VI, 106 — 44. Kireet Joshi,
Sri Aurobindo and the Mother, 196 — 45. A VIII, 23 — 46. K. Joshi, op.
cit., 196 — 47. Idem, 199 — 48. Ibidem — 49. Ibidem — 50. A III, 162
— 51. A XIII, 212 — 52. K. Joshi, op. cit., 235 — 53. A VI, 263 — 54.
Sri Aurobindo Circle, no. 35, 19 — 55. A II, 23 — 56. OH, 167.

Epilogue: The Sun For Ever — 1. LD, 1053 — 2. E 50-51, 245 — 3.
A XIII, 121 — 4. LD, 1059 — 5. A VIII, 63 — 6. Sri Aurobindo, *The Hour
of God*, ed. 1991, 3 — 7. OH, 155 — 8. A X, 510 — 9. A IV, 369 and
371 — 10. WM 15, 190 — 11. HC, 172 — 12. Ibidem — 13. HC, 252
— 14. A IX, 141 — 15. T&A, 14 — 16. Satprem, *Mère II*, 411 — 17. *Arya*,
vol. V, 300 — 18. A VI, 108 — 19. A VII, 70 — 20. E 55, 17 — 21. E
55, 349 — 22. LY, 33-34 — 23. WM 15, 112 — 24. Satprem, *Mère III*, 147
— 25. A III, 484 — 26. LD, 842 — 27. LD, 724 — 28. A XIII, 60 — 29.

TSA I, 241 — 30. SY, 47 — 31. T&A, 2 — 32. A XIII, 212 — 33. A III, 346 — 34. A X, 135 — 35. A IV, 199 — 36. NC, 351 — 37. NC, 188 — 38. *Savitri*, 343-44 — 39. TSA I, introduction — 40. Jacques Lacarrière, *Les Gnostiques*, 150 — 41. HC, 248 — 42. A I, 247 — 43. A IV, 384 — 44. E 57-58, 3.